WASHINGTON
HANDBOOK

WASHINGTON HANDBOOK

MOON
PUBLICATIONS INC.

WASHINGTON HANDBOOK

Please send all comments,
corrections, additions,
amendments, and critiques to:

ARCHIE SATTERFIELD
c/o MOON PUBLICATIONS
722 WALL STREET
CHICO, CA 95928 USA

Published by
Moon Publications Inc.
722 Wall Street
Chico, California 95928 USA
tel. (916) 345-5473

Printed by
Colorcraft Ltd., Hong Kong

PRINTING HISTORY

First edition
March 1989
Second edition
June 1990
Third edition
July 1992

Library of Congress Cataloging in Publication Data

Lyons, Dianne J. Boulerice, 1958-
    Washington Handbook / Dianne J. Boulerice Lyons and Archie
Satterfield—3rd edition.
        p.   cm.
    Includes bibliographical references (p. 417) and index.
    ISBN 0-918373-81-6 : $13.95
    1. Washington (State)—Description and travel—Guidebooks. I. Satterfield, Archie.
    II. Title.
    F889.3.L96 1992
    917.9704'43—dc20   92-8723
                                                        CIP

Cover photo: Courtesy of Tom Stilz, State of Washington Tourism Division,

ACKNOWLEDGEMENTS

This is something of a dual acknowledgement page because this third and fourth edition will carry the names of Dianne J. Boulerice Lyons, who wrote the first two editions before moving away from the region, and Archie Satterfield, who took over the book.

Satterfield is very grateful to Ms. Lyons for leaving the book in such excellent condition; he is also impressed with the amount of work a book like this requires. He would also like to thank Tom Stilz, Travel Media Specialist for the state's Tourism Development Division for his assistance. Thanks also go to editors Taran March and Anne-Marie Nicoara, computer specialist Asha Johnson, copy editor Mark Morris, and layout artists Nancy Kennedy and Carey Wilson.

IS THIS BOOK OUT OF DATE?

Every guidebook writer eventually comes to the conclusion that hours, addresses, telephone numbers, prices, and the other facts so diligently pursued are changed only after the newest edition has gone to press. Of course if nothing changed, we'd be out of a job. So although I've made every effort to ensure accuracy, errors, omissions, and oversights inevitably creep in. I'd appreciate it if you'd call these things to my attention, so they can be included in the fourth edition. Make notes right in the margins of your book as you travel. And while you're at it, what do you think of the book? I'd love to know. Send your letters to:

Archie Satterfield
c/o Moon Publications Inc.
722 Wall Street
Chico, CA 959528

TABLE OF CONTENTS

MAPS

CHARTS

MAP SYMBOLS

EXPRESSWAY
MAIN HIGHWAY
SECONDARY ROAD
UNPAVED ROAD
FOOT TRAIL
INTERSTATE HWY.
U.S. HWY.
STATE OR COUNTY HWY.
OTHER ROAD NUMBER

O LARGE CITY
O MEDIUM CITY
o SMALL TOWN
▲ MOUNTAIN
■ POINT OF INTEREST
▲ CAMPGROUND
TUNNEL
BRIDGE
)|(PASS

U.S. BOUNDARY
STATE BOUNDARY
COUNTY LINE
OTHER BOUNDARY
WATER
STATE FERRY
OTHER FERRY
N.P. = NATIONAL PARK
S.P. = STATE PARK
C.P. = COUNTY PARK

ABBREVIATIONS

a/c—air conditioned
B&B—bed and breakfast
C.—century
d—double occupancy
E—east

I—interstate highway
N—north
OW—one way
pp—per person
RR—railroad

RT—roundtrip
s—single occupancy
S—south
t—triple occupancy
W—west

BOB RACE

INTRODUCTION

THE LAND

CLIMATE AND GEOGRAPHY

A few years ago a young Seattle native went away to a university in St. Louis, and when he came home for the first Christmas he regaled his family by repeating the questions fellow students asked him about Washington, after he repeatedly explained that he lived in the state rather than the nation's capital: Do you have wide streets in Seattle? Do Indians still come into town? Do you have touch-tone phones yet? Isn't Seattle a suburb of San Francisco?—that sort of thing.

Many Americans still think of Washington as being half-wild and separated from the rest of the country. In all fairness, Washington is remote. It is tucked away in the far northwest corner of the country with Canada for a neighbor to the north. The Pacific Ocean forms its western boundary, the Columbia

River separates it from Oregon for most of its southern border, and Idaho is its eastern neighbor. Unlike the East Coast, where major cities are only an hour or two apart, the whole state of Washington is a long drive from California, the only West Coast state of any consequence to most Americans who live east of the Rockies.

To the surprise of many first-time visitors, instead of having only evergreen forests, natural lakes, and lots of saltwater with snowcapped mountains towering over it, Washington has almost a dual personality. It is divided into the dramatically different eastern and western halves by the Cascade Range, which extends 600 miles from Canada through Washington and Oregon before flattening out and disappearing in northern California. Those who expect to see only the evergreen land of the state's promotional campaigns are surprised when they travel through the treeless, brown hills of eastern Washington that are covered with wheat and row crops. The Cascade Range has a powerful effect on the state's climate and scenery (see "The Cascades," p. 270, for more information).

Much smaller but with an equally dramatic silhouette, the Olympic Range is quite different from the ancient and volatile Cascades. The Olympics (the backbone of Olympic National Park) are some of the world's youngest mountains, just one or two million years old. Though not exceptionally tall (Mt. Olympus is the highest at 7,965 feet), they produce dramatically varied weather. Storms spawned over the Pacific dump 70-100 inches of annual rainfall on the coastal plains, and 150 inches or more (with a record of 184 inches at Wynoochee Oxbow) in the rainforests on the western and southwestern slopes—the heaviest precipitation in the continental United States. But on the northeast slopes of this range, Port Angeles, Sequim, Port Townsend, Whidbey Island, and the San Juans are in the driest area of western Washington, receiving only 12-20 inches annually. The

most familiar example of this is Sequim, which has become a retirement haven because it sits in the rain shadow of the Olympics and is so dry that farmers must irrigate their crops.

Western Washington
Aside from the Olympic rainforests, most of the "wet side of the mountains" actually isn't all that wet: Seattle's annual rainfall of 32-35 inches is less than that of Chicago or New York. Winter snowfalls are generally light and melt quickly; a real snowstorm paralyzes the city for days due to the lack of snow-removal equipment and snow-driving expertise among natives.

Typical western Washington weather is mild and wet in the winter, warm and dry in the summer. Semipermanent high- and low-pressure systems in the North Pacific create predictable patterns of clouds and light rain beginning in October, with daytime temperatures in the 40s throughout most of the winter; December and January are the region's wettest months. In spring, the clouds give way to partly sunny days, and it's not unusual

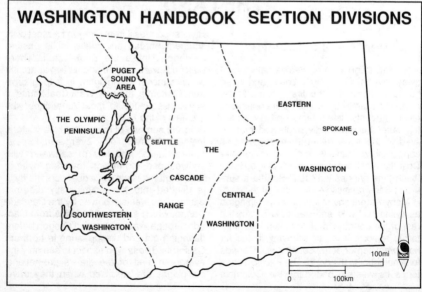

WASHINGTON HANDBOOK SECTION DIVISIONS

PUGET SOUND AREA

EASTERN

THE OLYMPIC PENINSULA

SPOKANE

SEATTLE

THE

WASHINGTON

CASCADE

CENTRAL

RANGE

SOUTHWESTERN WASHINGTON

WASHINGTON

0   100mi

0   100km

© MOON PUBLICATIONS, INC.

ARCHIE SATTERFIELD

Long Beach Peninsula

to have six weeks of cloudless skies in July and August. Summer daytime temperatures are usually in the 70s and 80s, with perhaps half a dozen 90° days each year. Thunderstorms are rare, and humidity is low.

Seattle averages about an inch of snow per month in winter, though many winters are snow-free; the record snow depth is 29 inches. Mt. Rainier is the place to go for snow—in the winter of 1955-56, the Paradise ranger station (elev. 5,500 feet) received 1,000 inches—83 feet of snow. Cascade ski areas usually open in November and remain open through early spring, beginning and ending with Mt. Baker's eight-month ski season.

Western Washington's skiing may be good, but the swimming is not. Water temperatures along the Pacific Coast and in the Strait of Juan de Fuca average 45° in January, rising to 53° in July, with some secluded coves and bays getting into the 60s. Puget Sound stays around 55° year-round, though again some protected areas warm up to the mid-60s and become swimmable. Most swimming and waterskiing are done in the region's numerous lakes.

Eastern Washington

Compared with western Washington, the "dry side of the mountains" has hotter summers, colder winters, more snow, and less rain. The Ellensburg Valley and Columbia

Basin east to the Palouse River have the hottest, driest weather in eastern Washington, averaging 7-15 inches of annual rainfall and summer daytime temperatures in the 90s, with many days each year over 100°; the state's record high of 118° occurred at Ice Harbor Dam (near Pasco) in 1961. The bonus is that it's not humid. July and August are the driest months, often devoid of any precipitation at all; what rain they do receive generally comes packaged in thunderstorms. Winters bring 10-35 inches of snowfall and daytime temperatures in the 20s and 30s.

The Okanogan and Methow valleys, in the northcentral part of the state, are a cross-country skier's paradise. Annual winter snowfalls range from 30 to 70 inches, beginning in November and staying on the ground through March or April. January maximum temperatures hover around 30°, with some nighttime below-zero temperatures recorded each year. In summer, the Okanogan Valley is another eastern Washington hot spot, with average temperatures from 85 to 90 and several 100s each season, plus occasional thunder- and hailstorms.

Much of central Washington, from the Columbia River east to the Spokane area and the Palouse hills south of Spokane, is technically a desert because the rainfall is less than 12 inches a year; in a few places no more than eight inches are measured. It

Grand Coulee
at Dry Falls

DIANNE BOLL ERICE LYONS

doesn't look like the Sahara or Death Valley because of the vast irrigation systems that have been built there. The largest, of course, is the Columbia Basin Project, created by Grand Coulee Dam, which puts water on nearly one million acres. The remainder of the irrigation water comes from smaller rivers, such as the Yakima, or from deep wells. Most of eastern Oregon, which has almost no rivers and only a limited number of wells, can give an idea of what eastern Washington looked like before irrigation.

As you travel east toward the state's eastern boundary, the elevation gradually rises and the weather moderates. The clouds are forced upward and as they cool they drop some of their precipitation here: rainfall averages 10-20 inches per year, with 20-40 inch-

es of snow. The farms in the Palouse Country, which is in the Clarkston-Colfax-Pullman area, are among the most productive wheat farms in the world, and because the climate is usually so predictable, eastern Washington wheat farmers have never had a complete crop failure in history, a surprising statistic in a business fraught with weather problems. Washington orchardists wish they could make the same claim.

Summer temperatures in central and eastern Washington are in the upper 80s and winter averages in the 30s, with a few extremes of 100° recorded every year. The Blue Mountains in the southeast corner get up to 40 inches of precipitation, while Pend Oreille County in the northeast corner gets 28 inches of rain and 40-80 inches of snow.

FLORA AND FAUNA

Washington has a widely varied assortment of flora and fauna due to its rich diversity of climate and geography. The Pacific Ocean and Puget Sound, the Olympic rainforest, the mountainous regions of the Cascades and Olympics, and the arid land of eastern Washington each support a unique population of birds, animals, and plantlife.

MARINELIFE

Killer Whales

The orca, or killer whale, is the largest member of the family Delphinidae, a classification that includes toothed whales and dolphins. The males are significantly larger than the females of the species: up to 32 feet long, weighing five to six tons, with dorsal fins up to 6½ feet high and four feet wide and tail flukes spanning nine feet. Unencumbered by its size, the orca frequently travels at upwards of 30 mph. Named "killer whales" because they take warm-blooded prey, these cetaceans eat anything from harbor and ringed seals to seabirds, otters, dolphins, fish, and squid, depending on the local food supply. In Puget Sound, they generally eat only fish—mostly salmon, rockfish, and cod —and leave the other species alone.

Reports of killer whale attacks on humans and boats have been recorded as far back as 1911. In that year, H.G. Ponting, a photographer for the Scott expedition to the South Pole, was reportedly standing on ice within six feet of the water when eight whales broke through the ice and threw him into the sea. Reports such as these are so rare that one can only surmise that in those situations the orca mistook men for marine mammals. The fact that whales and dolphins do not attack man is one of the mysteries of nature. The orca is much more famous in this country for kissing women at Sea World.

Orcas are highly social, traveling in packs or "pods" of 2-40 individuals. Families stay together, protecting their young (who, at eight feet long and 400 pounds at birth, would seem to require little protection) and mourning their dead. There are three resident pods in Puget Sound and along the Washington coast, with a total of about 80 members; other transient pods occasionally swim into the area but don't stay long. The most frequent sightings are around the San Juan Islands, especially at Lime Kiln State Park on the west side of San Juan Island— the only park in the U.S. dedicated exclusively to whalewatching.

Gray Whales

Every spring, tour boats leave the docks at Westport and a few other coastal towns for a close-up look at the migrating California gray whales. These enormous whales—ranging up to 42 feet in length and upwards of 30 tons—migrate from the Bering and Chukchi seas to the warm breeding lagoons off Baja California in winter, passing the Washington coast southbound in November and December and northbound from April to June.

Occasionally a group of gray whales comes into Puget Sound and several have beached themselves and died for thus-far unknown reasons. Most, however, follow the outer coastline. The gray is a baleen whale: it feeds by stirring up mud in shallow water, sucking in the water, mud, and organisms, and using its baleen—a fringelike sieve in its mouth—as a filter to trap its prey while forcing the mud and water back out. Gray whales are easily identified by their gray color, absence of a dorsal fin, and bumpy ridges on their backs; their faces are generally covered with patches of barnacles and orange whale lice. Unconcerned with their appearance, gray whales often lift their faces out of the water up to about eye level in a motion referred to as "spyhopping." Although gray whales aren't aggressive and are often even friendly, whalewatchers in small boats should

gray whale

FLORENCE BOULERICE

keep a respectful distance, since the whales may "breach," or jump completely out of the water, creating one heck of a wave as 30 solid tons splash back into the water.

Porpoises

Visitors often think that the black-and-white sea creatures riding the bow waves of their ferry or tour boat are baby killer whales, but these playful characters are Dall's porpoises. Commonly seen in the Strait of Juan de Fuca alongside the ferry *Coho* from Port Angeles to Victoria, B.C., the porpoises frequently travel south through the Admiralty Inlet and, on rare occasions, as far south as Tacoma. Dall's porpoises reach lengths of 6½ feet and weights of up to 330 pounds; they feed primarily on squid and small fish.

The harbor porpoise is Puget Sound's smallest cetacean, ranging to nearly six feet in length and 150 pounds. Although similar in appearance to the Dall's porpoise, the harbor porpoise is much more shy and rarely spotted in the wild. Accurate counts are impossible, but the population around the San Juan Islands has been estimated at fewer than 100; none live in Puget Sound, though resident populations were spotted there in the 1940s.

In summer and early fall, schools of up to 100 Pacific white-sided dolphins enter the Strait of Juan de Fuca, traveling as far inshore as Port Angeles but rarely any farther east. Reaching up to seven feet in length and 200 pounds, these dolphins are common off the shores of Japan, where their numbers are estimated at 30,000-50,000, and along the continental shelf from Baja California to the Gulf of Alaska. These dolphins have black backs, white shoulders and bellies, and hourglass-shaped streaks that run from their foreheads to their tails; the rear half of their dorsal fins are light gray. Like the Dall's porpoise, white-sided dolphins enjoy riding bow waves and often leap full-length out of the water alongside a boat.

Seals And Sea Lions

Harbor seals are numerous throughout Puget Sound and the Strait of Juan de Fuca, with their statewide population estimated at 7,000. They can be seen at low tide in isolated areas sunning themselves on rocks, but they will quickly return to the water if approached by humans. Though they appear clumsy on land, these 100- to 200-pound seals are poetry in motion underwater; they flip, turn, and glide with little apparent effort, staying underwater for as long as 20 minutes. (You can see harbor seals up close at the underwater viewing tank at Point Defiance Zoo in Tacoma.) Harbor seals have a bad reputation with area salmon fishermen, although studies of the seals' stomach contents and fecal material indicate that they feed primarily on flounder, herring, pollock, cod, and rockfish, as well as some mollusks and crustaceans.

The California sea lion is a seasonal visitor to the Strait of Juan de Fuca and northern Puget Sound, though on some mornings in winter and early spring their barking can be heard in shoreline communities as far south as Tacoma. These dark brown sea lions breed off the coast of California and Mexico in the early summer, then some adventurous males migrate as far north as British Columbia for the winter. A large group of them collects just offshore from Everett, where a commercial tour boat takes visitors out for a closer look. A group of them discovered how easy it is to capture salmon and steelhead trout as they mill around in front of the fish ladder at Hiram Chittenden Locks in Seattle's Ballard District. Given a group nickname of Herschel, the sea lions have thus far evaded every attempt by wildlife biologists to keep them from the easy pickings, including being shipped back to California; in only a matter of days the sea lions made the swim from the San Francisco area and were back at the locks. While the situation is humorous, still the group devoured almost an entire salmon run one year.

The lighter-colored northern sea lions are more numerous in the Puget Sound area, numbering up to several hundred in winter, primarily around Sucia Island in the northern Sound. The males of the species are much larger than the females, growing to almost 10 feet in length and weighing over a ton, while the females are a dainty six feet long and 600 pounds. Both are almost white when wet; the male has a yellow mane.

Other Marine Creatures
Puget Sound is home to the largest species of octopus in the world. Though it grows to 12 feet across the arms and weighs 25-30 or more pounds, it's not dangerous, and, in fact, often plays with divers. These octopi can make themselves incredibly flat to get where they have to go: according to a local octopus legend, one of these giants slid out of its tank and under a door into its owner's bedroom.

Another peculiar Puget Sound inhabitant is the geoduck (pronounced gooey-duck, from the Indian *gweduck* meaning "dig deep"). These large, obscene-looking clams can dig as deep as five feet, weighing in at four or five pounds with reports of some clams exceed-

ing 15 pounds. The fleshy part of the body is so large that neither the entire body nor the siphon can be completely withdrawn into the shell. (Stop by Pike Place Market in Seattle to see what these creatures look like.) Geoducks are generally cut up and used in chowder, but some quality restaurants serve them as regular menu items or specials.

The horse clam is the second-largest Pacific Northwest clam, weighing up to five pounds; they can't completely withdraw their siphons, but at least their bodies fit inside their shells. Horse clams only dig about two feet deep, so they're much easier to gather, and can be found in Cultus and Useless bays at the south end of Whidbey Island. Both geoducks and horse clams prefer sandy or sand-gravel beaches. For information on clamming, contact the Washington State Department of Fisheries, tel. (206) 753-6600.

geoduck, the Pacific Northwest's most revolting clam

DIANNE BOULERICE LYONS

LAND ANIMALS

Washington is home for a wide variety of land mammals, some of which have been brought back from the edge of extinction. Federal and state wildlife agencies alike have worked to preserve habitat for all forms of wildlife, and the state has become a richer place to live as a result.

Mule deer, the rare Columbia white-tailed deer, Rocky Mountain and Roosevelt elk, bighorn sheep, mountain goats, black and grizzly bears, and a wide variety of smaller mammals, such as marmots, beaver, badgers, muskrat, nutrias, rabbits, and squirrels are some of the animals you can expect to see, especially in the numerous wildlife refuges scattered across the state. Present but less likely to be seen are woodland caribou and moose, occasional visitors in the far northeast corner of the state.

Columbia White-tailed Deer
Lewis and Clark were the first explorers to comment on this subspecies of mule deer that evolved along the lower Columbia River between the Willamette River and the Pacific Ocean. By the time a 5,200-acre refuge was set aside for them in the 1960s, their numbers had dwindled into the dozens. Now they are thriving and number in the hundreds.

They look very much like their larger cousins, but they are smaller, have a slightly longer tail, and have a white underside. The refuge is just west of Cathlamet on Hwy. 4. Part of it is farmland still in use on the mainland, and the remainder is a group of islands in the Columbia River, where they often swim to browse on the willows and other low-growing plants.

Roosevelt Elk
Another subspecies, the Roosevelt elk live on the Olympic Peninsula, mostly inside the boundaries of Olympic National Park, and are thus given adequate protection to prevent them from being hunted to extinction. They are a subspecies of their Rocky Mountain relatives, which were almost killed off in the Cascades. They look similar to their relatives, but their antlers aren't as spectacular as those coveted by trophy hunters.

Bears
Black bears are fairly widespread in Washington, with large populations on the Olympic Peninsula and in Pend Oreille County. All of the black bears on the Olympic Peninsula are black; in other areas, they may be black, brown, or honey-colored. They'll eat anything, from carpenter ants to berries to dead elk to salmon, plus anything you pack in from Safeway. Black bears are so numerous that 400 of them are "harvested" each year in northeastern Washington.

Grizzly bears are rare in Washington, but there may be a few in the North Cascades and in the northeast corner of the state, spilling over from Idaho's Selkirk Mountains. Grizzlies once roamed throughout the western states, but now fewer than 1,000 bears live in remote areas of Washington, Idaho, Montana, and Wyoming, and they are considered a threatened species. A female grizzly must be five to eight years old before reproducing, and she cares for her cubs for two to three years before having any more offspring, so her reproductive capacity is low. The best way to protect both the grizzly bear population and yourself is to avoid encounters with them.

When hiking in bear country, make noise: sing, talk, or wear bear bells so they'll hear you coming, and don't hike after dark. If you see bear tracks or droppings, don't be a hero; hike somewhere else. Don't let your dog run free—it may sniff out a bear and lead it back to you. When camping in the backcountry, store all food, soaps, garbage, and clothes worn while cooking in a sack hung from a tree branch at least 10 feet up and four feet out from the tree trunk. In an established campground, keep those items in your car's trunk. Don't sleep where you cooked dinner, and keep sleeping bags and gear away from cooking odors. Stories are sometimes heard about grizzlies attacking women during their menstrual period; though nobody knows for sure if the scent actually causes an attack.

Cautious women may choose to hike in grizzly country at another time.

If you do encounter a bear, here's how to identify it: a grizzly is generally lighter in color than black bears, though color alone can't be used for identification. Look for the grizzly's shoulder hump (behind its head) and a "dish face" profile, with a distinct snout. (Black bears have no hump and a straight profile.) While you're looking for identifying marks, slowly detour out of the bear's path and stay upwind so the bear will know you're there; don't make abrupt noises or movements. While retreating, look for a tree to climb—one in which you can get at least 12 feet up. Don't try to outrun the bear—grizzlies can hit 40 mph in short bursts, and you can't beat that, no matter how scared you are. If the bear comes after you, drop your pack or jacket to distract him, get up that tree, or roll up into a ball with your face and stomach protected, and play dead.

Slugs

If western Washington had an official creature, it could easily be the common slug: the region is famous for them. The damp climate is just what slugs need to thrive: not too wet, because slugs aren't waterproof (they will absorb water through their outer membranes until their bodily fluids are too diluted to support them), and not too dry, because insufficient humidity makes them dry up and die. Optimum humidity for slugs is near 100%, which is why you'll see them crossing the sidewalk very early in the morning, at dusk, or on misty days.

During the dry parts of the day, they'll seek refuge under the pool cover you casually tossed onto the lawn, or under the scrap lumber piled in the back of your lot.

banana slug

FLORENCE BOULERICE

Slugs look like snails that have lost their shells, or little green or brown squirts of slime about three to five inches long. Though more than 300 species of slugs exist worldwide, the Northwest is home to little more than a dozen. The native **banana slug**, light green or yellowish with dark spots, has been rapidly outnumbered by the imported European **black slug**, which is now far more common in area gardens than the native variety. Slugs can curl up into a ball to protect themselves, or flatten and elongate themselves to squeeze into tight places. They move on one long foot by secreting mucus that gets firm where the foot must grab hold and stays slimy under the part that must slide. They see (probably just patterns of light and dark) with eyes at the ends of a pair of tentacles; they have a mouth, and eat primarily plants and mushrooms.

Getting rid of slugs is no easy matter. Traditional home remedies include saltshakers and beer traps; both require a strong stomach. Most residents just try to avoid stepping on them.

BIRDS

Bald Eagles

Approximately 300 pairs of bald eagles make their year-round home in Washington, primarily west of the Cascades. In winter that number swells to over 1,600 birds, drawn to rivers throughout the state by the abundant carcasses of spawned-out salmon. Several whitewater rafting companies operating in the North Cascades offer midwinter Skagit float trips just for the thrill of seeing these majestic birds (see p. 291 for more information).

The bald eagle often gets bad press, being blamed for the deaths of sheep and other domestic animals. Actually, eagles much prefer dead and dying fish to anything running around on hooves; their common fare, aside from dead salmon, is sick or injured waterfowl or rabbits that don't make it across the road. An aggressive bird, the eagle will often purloin the catch of an osprey or other bird in favor of finding its own. Occasionally a pair of eagles will team up to catch a gull or diving

DIANNE BOULERICE LYONS

bald eagle wintering on the Skagit River

bird, with each eagle taking a turn at striking the bird when it surfaces from its dive and following above it as it attempts to escape underwater. When the prey eventually becomes exhausted from the diving and dodging, it is snatched from the water and carried off.

The adult bald eagle's distinctive white head and tail make it easy to spot. But it takes four years for it to acquire distinctive markings, making the immature eagle confusing to identify, as it may show whitish markings anywhere on its body. In contrast, the somewhat similar golden eagle has distinct white patches on its tail and underwings.

Bald eagles are sensitive to disturbances in their environment; the Department of Fish and Game recommends that an undisturbed circle 660 feet in diameter surround a nest during the breeding season to preserve the nest site. Their large nests, sometimes measuring over eight feet wide and 12 feet high, are often found in old-growth spruce and fir; snags are popular for sunning, resting, and watching for their next meal.

The state's heaviest concentration of breeding bald eagles can be seen on the San Juan Islands, enjoying the warm updrafts around Mt. Constitution on Orcas Island and Mounts Findlayson and Dallas on San Juan Island, and along the Strait of Juan de Fuca. The annual "salmon festival" brings the resident and migrating birds to the inland reaches of the Skagit, Sauk, Nooksack, and Stillaguamish rivers, with some enterprising pairs seen along southern Puget Sound and the lower Columbia River.

Owls

The bird of the hour in western Washington is the **northern spotted owl**, which nests in old-growth forests along the Pacific Coast—forests that are more than 150 years old, filled with snags and broken trees that provide ideal nesting spots, and smaller, sheltered trees for young owls who can't yet fly properly and must use their feet to climb from tree to tree. These forests are full of spotted owl food: snowshoe hares, flying squirrels, and wood rats. They are big eaters and quite territorial: 1,000 acres of old-growth forest will support but a single pair of owls. Because suitable forest is being greatly reduced by logging, the spotted owls' numbers are diminishing—only an estimated 2,500 pairs remain in the Pacific Northwest's old-growth forests, and researchers believe they'll all be gone in 30 years if logging continues at its present rate.

Other Birds

Other noteworthy birds in western Washington include the **great blue heron,** frequently seen along harbors or suburban lakes. The **belted kingfisher** is a common year-round resident of Puget Sound and the Strait of Juan de Fuca. **Red-tailed hawks** are often perched along I-5 and other highways, waiting for a meal. Noisy **Stellar's jays,** blue with a black head, are common in picnic areas and neighborhoods.

In the Cascades and east of the mountains, the beautiful **mountain bluebird** is sometimes spotted in snags in open areas, and the town of Bickleton in the Horse

Heaven Hills of southern Washington maintains several dozen houses for bluebirds that stand on fence posts, in trees, and in front of the church. East of the mountains, striking black-and-white **magpies** are frequently seen flitting over the highway.

Birders will find Eugene S. Hunn's *Birding in Seattle and King County* an invaluable guide to birding sites from Seattle to Snoqualmie Pass. Included are maps, charts, bird lists, and additional information on mammals and plantlife. The *Pacific Coast Bird Finder,* by Roger J. Lederer, is geared more toward the beginning or backyard birdwatcher; it describes 61 common Pacific Coast birds (with illustrations) and their habitats.

IN THE SHADOW OF MAN

Washington's forests, coastlines, and waterways host literally thousands of wildlife species. For millennia wolves slipped through forest undergrowth, deer grazed in the eastern Palouse, and otters dove for oysters among the San Juans. But they're disappearing now.

European trappers took out beaver and otter pelts, ranchers grazed wild species out of existence, and a host of other animals couldn't compete against farmers and developers with plows, pesticides, and shotguns.

Endangered Species
Today, at least 21 species are listed as **endangered** (being eliminated from portions or all of its former range) in the state of Washington, and seven as **threatened** (not now endangered, but could become so in the foreseeable future). Among them are the following:

White Pelican: The last time these birds nested in Washington, Calvin Coolidge was president and the Great Crash was still three wild years away. Land reclamation and irrigation projects steadily eroded their habitat. Although nearly 2,000 white pelicans were counted in the Columbia Basin during September 1990, and they were spotted all across eastern Washington, white pelicans still don't nest here.

Brown Pelican: A record 4,980 brown pelicans were counted along the Washington coast during 1990 with the greatest numbers in Gray's Harbor, and Pacific, Clallam, and Jefferson counties. The bird is on the federal endangered list because chemical pollutants drastically reduced the population in the 1970s. They do not breed in Washington but

have always migrated to the state. As their numbers increase, the Fish and Wildlife Service is considering reclassifying brown pelicans from endangered to threatened.

Aleutian Canada Goose: These geese originally nested on several small islands in the Sound, but after the introduction of foxes, immature goslings, unable to escape, were decimated. During a 20-year recovery program the wild population has increased from a known 800 in 1975 to more than 6,300 in 1990.

Today Aleutians primarily use Washington habitats during migration and are found mostly in Willapa Bay and along the lower Columbia River.

Peregrine Falcon: By 1975 pesticides and hunters left only one pair of these falcons in Washington, but in 1990 15 pairs were known. Nine of the nesting sites were along the coast, four in the San Juan Islands and two in the Columbia River Gorge. Few bird species have been the subject of such intensive recolonization programs; they have partially adapted to urban living, with some spotted in Seattle and Tacoma.

Sandhill Crane: Both the lesser and the greater sandhill cranes occur in Washington, although the latter's numbers are dismally small. Breeding cranes were virtually absent in Washington by 1941 but more than 5,500 lesser cranes were seen in October 1990 in the Columbia National Wildlife Refuge area in the Columbia Basin.

Snowy Plover: This small, darting creature is in trouble. Plovers nest only on sandy or gravelly beaches and spits; for developers, this is prime beachfront property. Drastically

IN THE SHADOW OF MAN (CONTINUED)

reduced habitat has sent plover populations spiralling.

In 1987 nesting areas were closed to off-road vehicles, but the closure resulted in more camping and fishing in the area. The garbage left behind by campers and fishermen attracted more seagulls and crows, which prey on plover eggs. By 1990, with only two known breeding areas in the state and an "estimated" adult population of 17, the Fish and Wildlife Service finally listed the snowy plover as *threatened*—not endangered.

Upland Sandpiper: Washington is on the western edge of this bird's breeding range; the only known nest is in eastern Spokane County. Sandpipers once flourished in several places in eastern Washington. Their decline has been attributed to habitat loss due to farming, overgrazing, and land development.

BOB RACE

Spotted Owl: This is the bird of the 1990s. More hoopla surrounded the listing—and management proposals—of this species than any other in recent history. Logging interests called it the beginning of the end for the Pacific Northwest's timber industry; environmental interests saw it as a long-overdue plan to save the last islands of old-growth forest (to date, less than five percent of Pacific Northwest *hasn't* been cut at least once already). Tempers flared. Battle lines were drawn.

In July 1991 the Fish and Wildlife Service listed the northern spotted owl as a threatened species throughout all three West Coast states, and set forth guidelines recommending that habitat within at least a 1.8-mile radius of nests in the Cascade Range, and a 2.2-mile radius on the Olympic Peninsula, be maintained. Under tremendous political pressure, the plan is now under review.

The Endangered Species Act was specifically written to prevent economic considerations from derailing its intent. If the spotted owl controversy succumbs to logging, it will be the first time since the Act's passage that neither the letter—nor the intent—of the law was followed.

Gray Wolf: Early in this century trappers had virtually wiped out wolf populations in the Western U.S. But in 1990, breeding gray wolves were back in Washington. Wolf pups and adults have been seen and heard in North Cascades National Park and in the Okanogan and Wenatchee national forests.

Grizzly Bear: Six ecosystems have been identified by the Fish and Wildlife Service in the Selkirk Mountains and the North Cascades as recovery areas for bringing grizzlies into the forests. The state's population is estimated at about 30.

Sea Otter: These amazing creatures, whose scruffy faces originally inspired sailors to spin "mermaid" tales, once ranged the breadth of Washington's coastline. By the early 1900s trapping had almost completely depopulated the western North American coast.

In 1990, biologists counted 212 sea otters off the Olympic coast, where a group was transferred from Alaska in 1969 and 1970. Most live in the area protected by both the Olympic National Park and the Washington Islands National Wildlife Refuge.

Mountain Caribou: The Selkirk Mountain caribou herd had dwindled to only 29 animals at

IN THE SHADOW OF MAN (CONTINUED)

one point, but the herd had grown to about 90 by 1990. All but this small herd had disappeared from the continental U.S., and the mountain caribou was listed as endangered by the state in 1982 and in 1984 was placed on the federal list. To increase the herd, 12 mountain caribou were trapped in British Columbia and brought to the Selkirk herd.

Threatened Species
Oregon Silverspot Butterfly: The first silverspot butterfly seen in Washington since 1986 was spotted on the Long Beach Peninsula in 1990. The site where it was found is under consideration for purchase or management agreement by the state Department of Wildlife. The butterfly is wholly dependent on blue western violets—it is the only plant on which the larvae feed and develop.

Western Pond Turtle: These methodical fellows once roamed, however slowly, throughout the southern Puget Sound around lowland lakes and ponds. Development has

BOB RACE

since swallowed almost all their habitat whole, and nonnative predators—bullfrogs and bass—finished off the rest. Currently they are found only in three locations within Klickitat and Skamania counties.

It is believed that only about 40 remain after a 1990 outbreak of pneumonia caused by a pathogen killed 36. Twenty more were treated at Woodland Park and Point Defiance zoos, and survived. They were moved to the South Puget Wildlife Area. A "head start" program at the Woodland Park Zoo is getting populations moving, ahem, a little more quickly.

Ferruginous Hawk: Wildlife officials believe that the population of these hawks is holding steady, and most of the management problems involve protecting nest sites from human disturbance. An extensive survey in 1987 found 62 nesting pairs. Nesting poles and tree platforms have been built for them in the Juniper Forest of eastern Washington.

Pygmy Rabbit: This species is found in only five locations in an eastern Washington county, with a population estimated at about 300. Two of the five known sites are on state land and the other three on private land. A land exchange was arranged to allow game biologists three years to study the site and develop a plan to protect it. Habitat loss was the major factor in the pygmy rabbit's decline: pygmys prefer dense sage where the soil is soft enough to dig burrows. These were the first lands to come under agricultural use when eastern Washington was settled.

FLORA

The Forests
In 1946, an Oregon newspaper teased Washington, "The Evergreen State," for not having a state tree. Oregon had already chosen the Douglas fir, so Washington State Representative George Adams suggested the western hemlock, which he claimed would become the backbone of the forest

industry. Now the state tree, the **western hemlock** is widely used in the forest industry as a pulpwood species, and it and **Douglas fir** are two of the most abundant low-elevation trees in the state; above 3,000 feet elevation, **silver fir** and **mountain hemlock** take over. **Big-leaf maples** are distinguished by—you got it—their big leaves, often as much as a foot across. The **Pacific madrone,** or madrona, is characterized by

STATE OF WASHINGTON, TOURISM DIVISION

*Hoh Rain Forest in
Olympic National Park*

waxy, evergreen leaves and peeling reddish bark that exposes a smooth underskin. Other common trees are the **western red cedar, black cottonwood, red alder,** and **vine maple.**

Olympic Rainforest

At Olympic National Park, the Hoh, Queets, and Quinault valleys comprise the better part of the Olympic rainforest, an area unique in the world. Purists would say that 150 or more inches of annual rainfall don't qualify this region as a rainforest, a term usually reserved for the steamy jungle tropics. Whatever it's called, this area produces some of the world's largest trees. The largest known

western hemlock is growing in the Quinault Valley, the largest Douglas fir is in Queets, and the largest red alder is in the Hoh. The four major species here—the Sitka spruce, western red cedar, Douglas fir, and western hemlock—all grow very tall: trees average 200 feet, with many topping 300.

The height of the trees isn't the only fascinating aspect of the rainforest: the visitor is immediately struck by how green everything is, and how pristine. These areas have never been logged; what you see is nature, pure and simple. Enormous trees spring out of the long-since-decayed "nurse logs" that gave them life, with club moss eerily draping the branches; ferns and mosses cover nearly every inch of available ground in a thick carpet. Though most rainfall occurs from fall to spring, even summer days feel damp from high humidity and ocean fog.

Rhododendron

In 1892, Washington needed a flower to represent the state at the Chicago World's Fair. Many flowers were nominated, but the contest came down to two: the coast rhododendron and the common clover. While it doesn't seem that clover would offer much competition, it was a close call—the rhody won with just 53% of the vote. The region from British Columbia south to northern California and east to the foothills of the Cascades is prime rhody-growing territory. There are about 500 pure species hardy to the climate, and several hundred more greenhouse varieties, that are combined and cross-pollinated to produce thousands of hybrids.

Rhodies are standard equipment in western Washington gardens, relatively easy to grow and beautiful to behold, in colors from yellows to pinks to bright reds and whites. The well-known rhododendron gardens on Whidbey Island and smaller gardens in area parks have impressive displays in spring and early summer.

TACOMA PUBLIC LIBRARY

HISTORY

PREHISTORY

Although Washington is one of the more recent additions to the U.S., archaeological evidence suggests that the Pacific Northwest was one of the first populated areas in North America. In recent years, animal and human remains as much as 13,000 years old have been found throughout the state.

Throughout the late 1950s and early 1960s, archaeologists uncovered numerous artifacts and partial skeletons of 10 people known as "Marmes Man" in a cave overlooking the Palouse River near its confluence with the Snake River.

In the state's northwest corner, archaeological work has been underway since 1970 on the Hoko and Ozette sites near Neah Bay, once inhabited by ancestors of the Makah Indians. Thumbnail-sized quartz knife blades have been found at the Hoko River site, and radiocarbon dated it at 2,500 years old; some artifacts from the Ozette site date back 2,000 years.

At Ozette, an entire village was covered by a mudflow, perhaps triggered by an earthquake some 500 years ago. More than 50,000 well-preserved artifacts have been found and cataloged, many of which are now on display at the Makah Museum in Neah Bay.

One of the most fascinating discoveries occurred in 1977, when Emanuel Manis, retired on a farm outside of Sequim, was digging a pond on a back corner of his land and found two enormous tusks. A Washington State University archaeological team, led by zoologist Carl Gustafson, concluded that these were mastodon tusks, between 12,000 and 14,000 years old. The group discovered other mastodon bones, including a rib that contained the bone point of some prehistoric weapon used to kill the animal. These bones are now on display at the Sequim-Dungeness Museum in Sequim (see p. 204 for details).

Native Americans

According to one theory, Native Americans originally crossed over to Alaska from Asia at the end of the last ice age, when the sea was 300 or more feet below present levels and the strait was a walkable passage. As these Native Americans spread throughout the Pacific Northwest, they adopted significantly different life-styles on each side of the Cascades.

West of the mountains, salmon, shellfish, whales, and other seafood made up a large part of the Indian diet; western red cedars provided ample wood for canoes, houses, and medicinal teas and ointments. A mild climate and plentiful food allowed these coastal tribes to stay in one place for most of the year, and in fact the North Coast Indians were among the wealthiest in America. They often built "longhouses," wooden structures up to 100 feet long and 40 feet wide that housed several families. They kept many slaves and engaged in the potlatch ceremonies in which they gave away everything they owned (but later got it back when other tribal members gave away all of their belongings).

Coastal tribes were skilled canoe carvers and could travel up the Columbia as far as The Dalles, where rapids prohibited further progress. Inland tribes would meet them here for an annual fair with trading, dancing, gambling, and general hell-raising.

East of the Cascades and particularly near the Columbia River, salmon was an important part of their diet, though dependence on deer, elk, bear, squirrel, and rabbit led these tribes to live seminomadic lives. The introduction of the horse to eastern Washington in the mid-1700s made hunting, especially for large bison, much easier. Indians in eastern Washington lived in caves or rock shelters while hunting, and in well-insulated pithouses that could hold several families.

The Pacific Northwest tribes were introduced to the by-products of white man's culture, such as knives, guns, and the deadly smallpox virus, before ever laying eyes on a white explorer. The European's arrival was met with reactions ranging from tolerant acceptance to swift murder. Relations between the races are still strained today; the interpretation of peace treaties signed in the 1850s are being hotly debated in the 1990s, with

Totem poles such as this are common throughout Washington.

STATE OF WASHINGTON, TOURISM DIVISION

many lawsuits concerning property, water, and fishing rights pending. Though they make up only 1.3% of the Pacific Northwest's total population, today's Native Americans are a growing force: there were nearly 100,000 Indians in Washington, Idaho, and Oregon in 1980, representing an 88.5% increase since 1970. Most of them do not live on reservations, though there are 22 reservations scattered throughout the state, the largest being the Yakima and Colville.

A NEW WORLD

Apparently the first foreigners to land on Washington's shores were Chinese and Japanese fishermen who arrived weeks or months after they were blown off course. None of the Oriental nations were interested in expanding across the Pacific in those days, and nobody particularly cared about the land to the east. Records, if any, were skimpy and ignored. That was definitely not the case in southern Europe.

In 1592, exactly a century after Columbus made his landfall in the Caribbean, a Greek explorer sailing along Washington's coast under the Spanish name Juan de Fuca, claimed to have discovered the fabled "Northwest Passage," an inland waterway crossing North America from the Pacific to the Atlantic. Later explorers did find a waterway close to where de Fuca indicated, but it led only into today's Puget Sound, not all the way to the Atlantic Ocean.

Spain, hoping to regain some of its diminishing power and wealth, sent an expedition out in the 1700s to explore the Northwest coast. In 1774, Juan Perez explored as far north as the Queen Charlotte Islands off Vancouver Island, and was the first European to describe the Pacific Northwest coastline and Olympic Mountains before being forced to turn back by sickness and storms.

In 1775, a larger Spanish expedition set out, led by Bruno de Heceta and Juan Francisco de la Bodega y Quadra. Heceta went ashore at Point Grenville, just north of Moclips on the Washington coast, and claimed all the Northwest for Spain. Farther south, Quadra sent seven men ashore in a small metal craft for wood and water; they were quickly killed and their boat torn apart in the whites' first encounter with coastal Indians. The two ships sailed away without further incident; Quadra named the island Isla de Dolores ("Isle of Sorrows"), today's Destruction Island. Quadra continued his explorations as far north as Sitka, Alaska, while Heceta sailed north to Nootka Sound. Heceta failed to note the Strait of Juan de Fuca, but he did come across "the mouth of some great river," presumably the Columbia, though the death or illness of much of his crew prevented further exploration and robbed Spain of an important claim.

Russian exploration of the Pacific Northwest began in the mid-1700s, when Vitus Bering led two expeditions to determine whether a land bridge connected Russia with North America. Bering sailed as far south as the Columbia River before turning back. The abundance of sea otters and beavers led Russian fur traders to establish posts from Alaska to northern California, which posed a serious threat to other nations hoping to stake a claim.

Robert Gray sailed out of Boston to explore and trade along the Northwest Coast for the United States in the late 1700s. Stopping first at Nootka Sound, the hot spot to trade on Vancouver Island, Gray worked his way south and spent three days anchored in today's Gray's Harbor. Continuing south, Gray discovered the mouth of the Columbia River and traded there with the Chinook Indians before heading home.

England was the force to be reckoned with in the battle for the Northwest. In 1776, Captain James Cook took two ships, the *Discovery* and the *Resolution,* and 170 men on an expedition that brought him to the Hawaiian Islands, the Oregon coast, and Vancouver Island's Nootka Sound. Though he charted the coastline from Oregon to the Bering Sea, he made no mention of the Columbia River or the Strait of Juan de Fuca. Cook was killed by hostile Hawaiians in a dispute over a boat in 1779, and his crew returned to England.

Other English sailors continued in Cook's footsteps. In 1787, Charles Barkley and his wife Frances explored and named the Strait of Juan de Fuca. In 1788, John Meares named Mount Olympus and other features of the Olympic Peninsula. Best known today, however, is the expedition led by George Vancouver in 1792. His goal was to explore the inland waters and make one last attempt at finding the Northwest Passage. Vancouver's lieutenants and crew members read like a list of Washington place-names: Baker, Rainier, Whidbey, Puget. The expedition carefully charted and thoroughly described all navigable waterways and named every prominent feature. When Vancouver heard of Gray's discovery of the Columbia River, he sent William Broughton upriver to a point east of Portland to strengthen England's claim on the land.

The U.S. answer to Vancouver was Charles Wilkes, a naval captain who sailed up the Columbia and into Puget Sound as part of a worldwide expedition in 1841. Wilkes added details to Vancouver's charts, naming some of the less prominent features such as Anderson Island, Elliott Bay, and McNeil Island.

Overland Expeditions

Until 1792, only the coastal areas of the Pacific Northwest had been explored. The first explorer to cross North America north of Mexico was a British trader, Alexander Mackenzie. In 1788, he traveled as far as the Arctic in search of the fabled Northwest

Passage. In 1792-93, Mackenzie followed the Bella Coola River from the Canadian Rockies to just north of Vancouver Island. His two expeditions proved that there was no Northwest Passage, at least north of the 50th parallel.

The best-known overland expedition began in St. Louis in 1804, led by Meriwether Lewis and William Clark. President Thomas Jefferson sent these men and their party to study the geology, animals, and plantlife of the 827,000 square miles acquired in the Louisiana Purchase, which extended as far west as the Rocky Mountains, and to explore and map the rivers and lands west of the Rockies. The group left St. Louis in canoes, heading north on the Missouri River to present-day North Dakota. After wintering there with the Mandan Indians, the party, numbering 28 now, set out again on the Missouri River, crossed the Rockies on foot, and headed down the Clearwater River in search of the Columbia. In October 1805, the party got their first view of the Columbia, and followed it downriver for many a "cloudy, rainey, disagreeable morning" until they reached the Pacific Ocean.

They built a winter camp, Fort Clatsop, south of the river and spent a cold, wet winter there, plagued by sickness. In spring they headed for home. The two leaders split up, with Lewis returning much the way they had come and Clark exploring the Yellowstone River to the south. They met up again in North Dakota and returned to St. Louis in September 1806.

Wilson Price Hunt, partner in the fur-trading business with John Jacob Astor, led the second American overland expedition in 1811. His party joined others who arrived by ship—first the Tonquin, in 1811, and then the Beaver, arriving a year later—to establish Astoria, a fort on the south side of the Columbia River. Hunt was instructed to follow Lewis and Clark's route through Montana, but aggressive Blackfeet Indians changed his mind. Instead he traveled through present-day Wyoming, taking to canoes—a poor choice for the wild Snake River. One canoe was smashed and its experienced navigator killed, leading to Hunt's decision to divide the expedition into three groups and continue overland.

Donald McKenzie's team reached Astoria in January 1812; Hunt's group arrived a month later. The last third of the expedition straggled in a year after the first, in January 1813.

British overland exploration was accomplished mainly by David Thompson, a fur trader and chief cartographer for the North West Company in the early 1800s. In 1810, under Thompson's direction, Finan McDonald and Jacques Finlay built Spokane House, the first trading post in the state of Washington. Thompson traveled extensively throughout the Canadian Rockies, south into Kettle Falls and downriver to the mouth of the Columbia in 1811, where he found the Americans had already established a fort at Astoria—Astor's men had arrived four months earlier. Though he was disappointed, Thompson's detailed maps and sketches of the Columbia were used for many years by settlers and traders.

The First White Settlers

During the time between the early exploration and the permanent settlement of the Northwest, British and American trading posts emerged to take advantage of the area's abundant supply of beaver and sea otter pelts. Two English companies, the North West Company and Hudson's Bay Company, merged in 1821; American fur-trading outfits included many small, independent companies as well as John Astor's Pacific Fur Company and the Rocky Mountain Fur Company.

The most influential of them, the Hudson's Bay Company, built its temporary headquarters on the north side of the Columbia, 100 miles inland at Fort Vancouver across the river from the confluence with the Willamette.

The settlers planted crops (including the apples and wheat that are so important to Washington's economy today), raised livestock, and made the fort as self-sufficient as possible. At its peak, 500 people lived at or near the fort. Fort Vancouver served as a model for other Hudson's Bay Company posts at Spokane, Okanogan, and Nisqually.

Fort Vancouver, one of the Pacific Northwest's most successful settlements

When settlers began arriving in droves and the beaver population diminished, the Hudson's Bay Company was crowded out and moved its headquarters north to Fort Victoria on Vancouver Island.

Missions were another important method of establishing white settlements in Washington. The first missionary, Jason Lee, was sent by the Methodist Church in 1834 to introduce Christianity to the Native Americans, but instead he spent much of his time and resources ministering to whites at Fort Vancouver.

In the 1840s, "Oregon Country" north of the 42nd parallel was jointly occupied by the U.S. and England. The westward movement gained momentum when a New York editor coined the phrase "Manifest Destiny" to symbolize the idea that all of the land west of the Rockies rightfully belonged to the United States. Between 1840 and 1860, 53,000 settlers moved west to Oregon Country to take advantage of the free land they could acquire through the Organic Act of 1843 and the Donation Land Law of 1850. Under the Organic Act of the Provisional Government, each adult white male could own 640 acres (one square mile) by simply marking its boundaries, filing a claim, and building a cabin on the land. The Donation Land Law put

additional restrictions on land claims: 320 acres were awarded to white or half-white males who were American citizens and had arrived prior to 1851; another 320 acres could be claimed by his wife.

These and other restrictions effectively eliminated claims by blacks, Asians, single women, non-U.S. citizens, and Native Americans, thereby giving pioneers the legal right to take Indian land. These land grants were too large for most families to farm and prevented towns and industries from growing as quickly as they might have; people were simply too far apart. By 1855, all the land in the Willamette Valley had been claimed.

The promise of free land fueled the "Great Migration" of 1843, in which 875 settlers traveled to the Oregon Country, six times the number of the previous year. More pioneers followed: 1,500 in 1844 and 3,000 in 1845. Most settlers came by way of the Oregon Trail from St. Joseph, Missouri, along the North Platte River, through southern Wyoming and southern Idaho into Oregon, then north to the Columbia River. Soon the route looked like a cleared road; traces of it can still be seen. The settlers congregated around five fledgling cities: Seattle, Port Townsend, Oysterville (now a historic community on Wilapa Bay), Centralia, and Walla Walla, and

THE WHITMANS

Dr. Marcus Whitman and his wife Narcissa were sent out in 1836 by a group made up of various New England Protestant churches. The Whitmans established a mission among the Cayuse Indians near Walla Walla, and soon thereafter Narcissa gave birth to a daughter, Alice Clarissa. When she was two years old, Alice wandered off and drowned in the Walla Walla River; though the Whitmans had no more children of their own, they adopted the orphaned Sager children and cared for others whose parents were dead or away.

The Whitmans had the usual attitude toward the Indians—that they were childlike savages of inferior mental capacities, and that they should be punished as schoolchildren were in that era. Whitman often whipped them, and did not credit them with average intellectual capacities. When the Indians sickened from the laxatives and poisons Whitman used to

Dr. Marcus Whitman

keep animals away from his gardens, and contracted measles and other heretofore unknown diseases, the Cayuse became convinced that the Whitmans were trying to kill them to make room for white settlers.

On November 29, 1847, Indians attacked and murdered the Whitmans and 12 others. This only added fuel to the increasing hostilities between Indians and whites, and the ensuing Indian Wars, particularly the 1855-58 Yakima Wars between the Plateau Indians and the settlers and the U.S. Army, halted white settlement in eastern Washington until the Indians agreed to accept reservation lands and the Army declared the lands safe for settlement. The wars weren't as widely publicized as in other parts of the West, and the fighting was confined mostly to 1855-56, just prior to the Civil War. Some of the battles were severe, however, and many lives were lost.

Narcissa Whitman

ARCHIE SATTERFIELD

other smaller communities at Tumwater, Steilacoom, Olympia, and Fairhaven, now part of Bellingham.

Eastern Washington was forming communities, too, in particular Spokane and Walla Walla.

Growth Of A New State

By 1846, only the U.S. and England retained claims to Oregon Country; Spain and Russia had sold or lost their North American possessions. Negotiators brought the U.S. and England to agreement on a division at the 49th parallel from the Rockies to the main channel between Vancouver Island and the mainland, running through the center of the Strait of Juan de Fuca to the Pacific Ocean.

The unspecified "main channel" was viewed to be either the Rosario Strait or the Haro Strait, leaving the San Juan Islands in the middle of the disputed waterway. Both American and British troops set up posts on San Juan Island, and had cordial relations until an American settler shot and killed a British-owned pig that had repeatedly rooted in his garden. The ensuing "Pig War," a 13-year dispute during which no further shots were fired, ended in 1872 when the German kaiser, chosen to conduct arbitration, awarded the islands to the Americans and pronounced the Haro Strait as the dividing channel.

In spite of all this arbitration, one small piece of real estate managed to be overlooked. A peninsula hung down from the Canadian mainland into the Strait of Georgia south of the 49th parallel, making it American land. Rather than settling the matter when it was discovered, the appendix still dangles there and is known as Point Roberts, a bit of America attached to Canada.

In 1848, President Polk created Oregon Territory and appointed Joseph Lane as the first territorial governor a year later. In the early 1840s, most Americans lived south of the Columbia River. By 1849, only 304 people lived north of the river, but in the next year that number tripled as more and more settlers ventured northward. As they moved farther away from the territorial government, the settlers felt left out of governmental matters and decided to separate from Oregon. Delegates met at the Monticello Convention in 1852 to list reasons for the proposed separation, and Congress found little opposition to the bill. Washington Territory, which included much of present-day Idaho, was created in 1853.

In 1863, Idaho Territory was created, followed by Montana Territory in 1864, giving the territories much the same boundaries that the states occupy now.

When Washington became a territory, its population was under 4,000 people; by the 1880s, it had grown to over 125,000 and was considered a serious candidate for statehood. Washington was admitted as the 42nd state in 1889, with Olympia as its capital and a growing population of over 173,000.

The Twentieth Century

The 40 years between 1870 and 1910 marked a period of tremendous growth in Washington. In 1870, the territory's population was just shy of 24,000; in 1910, the new state, created with the same boundaries, had 1,142,000 residents. Much of this growth was a direct result of the arrival of the Northern Pacific and Great Northern railways in the late 1880s, bringing industry and settlers to Puget Sound and creating new towns all along their routes. Spokane saw rapid economic growth during the 1880s outfitting miners for the gold, silver, and lead rush in Idaho.

The 1880s also spelled disaster for Spokane, Ellensburg, and Seattle, when major portions of these cities' thriving downtown areas were destroyed by fire. Though the cities were rebuilt quickly in brick, the state was hit hard by a nationwide depression, the Panic of 1893, when growth slowed on both sides of the mountains and businesses failed. A gold rush in the Yukon and the emergence of hydroelectric power helped get the state back on its feet. At the end of this period of growth, the Alaska-Yukon-Pacific Exposition brought nationwide attention and over 3,700,000 visitors to the University of Washington campus in Seattle in 1909, to

SEATTLE-KING COUNTY CONVENTION AND VISITORS BUREAU

*Seattle's Space Needle, a legacy
from the 1962 World's Fair*

promote the ties between Washington, the far north, and Pacific Rim countries.

The Great Depression slowed Washington's population growth to just 11% between 1930 and 1940. Seattleites were the first to call makeshift "towns" of boxes and crates "Hoovervilles," named in honor of President Herbert Hoover, whom they blamed for the nation's ills. One of the largest covered nine acres about where the Kingdome stands today.

The first and second World Wars changed Washington's economy from one based largely on mining, farming, logging, and fishing to manufacturing, and ship and airplane building, highlighted by Boeing's B-17: over 13,000 of the "Flying Fortresses" were built for WW II. Boeing continues to be one of the state's largest employers and most important industries.

Seattle's 1962 World's Fair was the first such exposition to be an economic success, drawing over 9,600,000 people during its six-month run and creating a permanent addition to the city's culture at Seattle Center. Spokane followed suit 12 years later with Expo '74, emphasizing environmental concerns and cleaning up its own Spokane River in the process.

Perhaps all of this self-imposed media attention was a mistake: Washington, especially west of the Cascades, continues to grow at a rate that many residents find alarming. Cities and suburbs alike are beginning to suffer from overcrowding, pollution, traffic, increased crime, and other big-city problems as more and more visitors are opting to stay for good, putting stress on water, refuse, and highway systems that were designed for smaller populations. The challenge of the '90s and beyond will be to preserve the state's unsurpassed natural resources and beauty while allowing controlled growth.

INDUSTRY AND ECONOMY

Washington's earliest industries—fishing, mining, farming, and logging—depended upon the abundant natural resources that the pioneers found here. Even today, lumber remains one of the Evergreen State's most important industries (though Weyerhauser's multimillion-dollar operation is a far cry from Yesler's turn-of-the-century waterfront mill), farming remains the basis for much of eastern Washington's economy, and hydroelectric power creates jobs and low electric rates from the state's plentiful resources. Over the years, though, manufacturing, shipping, and other industries have become increasingly important to the state's economy.

Mining
Coal was first discovered east of Bellingham in 1849, and mining began in 1855. Later discoveries of coal in the Cascades in the late 1800s gave rise to a number of small mining towns on both sides of the Cascades such as Black Diamond, Carbonado, Wilkeson, Newcastle, Cle Elum, and Roslyn. Though coal was plentiful—geologists today believe there are from six to 65 billion tons in the state—it was soft and therefore limited in its uses; often found in steep ravines or streams, it was difficult to extract and transport. Underground explosions and other accidents gave Washington more mining fatalities per number of miners than any other state for several years in the late 1800s. By the turn of the century, coal from the Rocky Mountains had become a cheaper and more practical fuel source, and by 1930 coal mining had virtually disappeared. Today, coal mining is seeing a minor revival: for the past several years, over five million tons of coal per year have been strip-mined near Centralia for use in a thermal-electric power plant there.

Other minerals begat industries that met with varying degrees of success. Discoveries of gold and silver in the mountains of Washington's northeast corner caused short-lived rushes—and Indian wars, as whites crossed onto reservation lands—but outfitting miners for the gold rushes of Idaho and the Yukon yielded a better return for Seattle and Spokane. Silver, gold, and lead mines in Monte Cristo were to have been the economic basis of Everett, John D. Rockefeller's city on Port Gardner Bay, until the depression of 1893 forced him to withdraw his support. A steel mill in Kirkland, an iron refinery in Port Townsend, and a copper mine in Holden either

Washington led the country in mining disasters for many years. Here, miners at the Carbonado mining disaster of 1930.

TACOMA PUBLIC LIBRARY

never got started or met with limited success. A successful silver, gold, and lead refinery in Tacoma was started in 1890 by William R. Rust; he later sold the plant to the American Smelting and Refining Company (ASARCO) for processing copper.

Recent mining at Wenatchee's Asamera's Cannon gold mine is predicted to yield over a million ounces of gold over the next 10-15 years, and two gold mines are operating now in Republic. However, Washington's most valuable minerals are still the least exotic: 60% of the money made from mineral production is derived from cement, stone, and gravel pits in the western half of the state.

Lumber

The Pacific Northwest states of Washington, Oregon, and Idaho supply about 60% of the total lumber in the United States. Washington is generally the third- or fourth-largest producer of the 50 states, with Oregon taking the lead since 1938. Douglas fir, western hemlock, and western red cedar are some of the commercially important trees native to the area west of the Cascades.

Wood and wood products have been a vital part of Washington's economy ever since the Coastal Indians first began using cedar for longhouses, totem poles, canoes, and even clothing made from cedar bark. The first white settlers and missionaries used wood for construction of their forts, homes, and blockhouses, and British explorer John Meares was the first to ship lumber to the Orient in 1788. Seattle's founding fathers depended on shipments of lumber to San Francisco for much of their income; Yesler's waterfront sawmill was an important part of the city's early economy. The lumber business boomed with the cheaper transportation provided by the arrival of the railroads in Puget Sound in the late 1880s and '90s.

In 1900, Frederick Weyerhaeuser purchased 900,000 acres of prime forest land from the Northern Pacific Railroad for $6 an acre, later increasing his holdings to over two million acres by 1913. With over six million acres today, the Weyerhaeuser Corp. is now the largest lumber company in the country.

Forests cover over 23 million Washington acres, 18 million of which are commercial forests. It's difficult to look at the shaved hillsides of the Cascades and not think it offensive, but the trees are replanted, and the logs and wood products produce $5-7 billion annually and employ a large proportion of Washington's workers.

Farming

Washington's Native Americans relied on hunting and food gathering rather than agriculture to supply their families' needs. It wasn't until Fort Vancouver was established in the 1820s that commercial agriculture took hold in Washington, as Hudson's Bay Company acquired a surplus of cattle to sell to the early settlers. Farming took hold slowly west of the Cascades, as the heavily forested land first had to be cleared, and the acidic soils produced minimal yields. As settlers spread east of the Cascades, the wide-open spaces were perfect for cattle ranching, sheep herding, and grain growing.

Agriculture grew rapidly through the turn of the century due to the arrival of the railroad, irrigation projects, and the free land provided by the Organic Act of 1843 and the Donation Land Law of 1850. Agriculture flourished during the first and second World Wars, and quickly rebounded after the Depression when refrigeration allowed Washington farmers to compete on a national scale.

More recently, the 1952 Columbia Basin Irrigation Project opened up a half-million parched acres for farming around Moses Lake. Today, Washington farmers and ranchers produce more than $3 billion annually, over 80% of which is derived from agriculture east of the Cascades. The biggest money crops are wheat, hay, and potatoes, followed by livestock, apples, pears, cherries, grapes, onions, and other fruits and vegetables.

One of the state's fastest-growing crops is wine grapes. In 1972, Washington had just six wineries; today there are over 60, and visitors come to tour the Columbia and Yakima valleys much as they would California's wine-producing regions. Washington is now recognized as one of the prime wine producers in the country, with many award-winning wines, most notably those produced by Chateau Ste. Michelle, being sold nationwide.

Fishing

Fishing is one of the state's oldest industries, as the original Native Americans on both sides of the Cascades depended on Columbia River salmon and other fish for much of their diet, and Coastal Indians from the Neah Bay area were whalers. Commercial fishing, less important to the early settlers than logging and other industries, wasn't firmly established until the 1860s, when canneries, new salmon fishing techniques, and new markets at home and abroad led to the industry's rapid expansion.

The Pacific Northwest salmon industry now harvests over 250,000 pounds of salmon annually, worth about $100-150 million. To ensure adequate supplies of the commercially valuable chinook, coho, sockeye, chum, and pink salmon, Oregon and Washington have developed state fish hatcheries; Washington alone has 26, producing a total of 150 million salmon and half of the commercial catch every year.

Hydroelectric And Nuclear Power

Washington's first hydroelectric power was generated in the late 1880s in Spokane, when Spokane Falls were used to power a saw to cut wood for a local hotel. Uses multiplied to include street lighting, trolley lines, and more, and in 1899 Spokane's Washington Water Power Company was established as one of the first hydroelectric power companies in the country. Tacoma was the first major city to produce its own power when, in 1898, it took over a local utility company and later built dams on the Nisqually and Skokomish rivers.

Franklin D. Roosevelt's New Deal paved the way for the construction of the first federally built dam on the mighty Columbia River: the Bonneville Dam, completed in 1938. It was quickly followed by the Grand Coulee Dam and others, until 14 Columbia River dams produced electricity to much of the Pacific Northwest and California and provided water to irrigate much of central Washington. By the 1970s, 96% of the state's power was hydroelectric in origin.

Inexpensive hydroelectric power has been taken for granted since its inception; Tacoma City Light has been boasting for years that it offers the cheapest electric rates in the nation. But the state's recent drought has demonstrated that even in the soggy Pacific Northwest, low electric rates are not guaranteed, and other energy alternatives must be considered. Even with the abundance of dams, the Pacific Northwest has to import energy from Canada to supply the growing demand.

Public outrage, way-over-budget construction costs, and safety concerns have made nuclear power a poor second choice. In 1968, the Washington Public Power Supply System (WPPSS) began work on five nuclear generators, three at the Hanford site near Tri-Cities and two at Satsop in Gray's Harbor County. The $6 billion budget stretched to $24 billion, and public outcry over the inevitable rate hikes to pay for the construction resulted in approval of an initiative limiting such groups' spending and the mothballing of all but one reactor at Hanford, which was completed in 1981 and began producing power in 1984. The other two partially constructed reactors at Hanford and Satsop will likely never be completed, though customers are paying for these white elephants through the Bonneville Power Administration's substantial rate hikes.

What's left? Coal-fired plants, such as the Centralia Steam Plant, may become more important if coal reserves can be efficiently and economically mined. Solar energy, geothermal energy, and other alternatives will require years of research and economic sup-port before they can become any more than token energy producers.

Aircraft Manufacturing

Washington's economy is closely tied in with the success of the Boeing Company, the state's largest employer and manufacturer of both commercial and military aircraft. Its founder, William E. Boeing, started his fledgling aircraft business in a hangar on Lake Union, then moved to a shipyard on the Duwamish River in 1916. WW I brought orders for training planes, and the company held on after the war by producing boats, furniture, and other items, plus U.S. Post Office transport planes and Army fighter planes. WW II brought over 13,000 orders for its B-17 bomber, and at the end of the war, B-29 bombers dropped the infamous atomic bombs on Nagasaki and Hiroshima.

After the war, William Allen took over as president of Boeing and the company produced its first jet-powered passenger plane, the 707, in 1958. In the late 1960s, Boeing's 747 plant opened in Everett in the world's largest building, and Boeing was established as the world leader in aircraft manufacturing. The late '60s and early '70s were hard times for Boeing, as government contracts for the SST and other military aircraft fell through; employment fell from 110,000

Grand Coulee is one of 14 dams on the Columbia River.

DIANNE BOLL ERICE LYONS

Seattle and Tacoma economies depend heavily on containerized shipping.

to 38,000 workers. The company had to diversify to survive, so it created subdivisions in commercial aircraft, military aircraft, hydrofoils, and helicopters. In the '80s, Boeing's employment was stabilized at 68,000 to 80,000 workers, and the company is still the world's leader in commercial aircraft production, supplying over 180 airlines worldwide.

Shipping

From the time Seattle's earliest settlers dropped a horseshoe on a clothesline into Elliott Bay to determine its depth, shipping has played an important role in the development of Puget Sound communities. Today, Seattle and Tacoma are among the most important seaports in the world, and other sea- and riverports along the Columbia as far inland as Kennewick helped to establish waterborne trade as one of the state's largest industries.

The first goods shipped from Seattle were logs that would be used as dock pilings in San Francisco. Lumber and wood products still account for a good portion of the area's exports, particularly from smaller ports such as Everett, Port Gamble, Port Angeles, Hoquiam, Olympia, and Bellingham. Seattle and Tacoma are important containerized shipping ports, where bulk and manufactured goods from airplanes to wheat are exported to Japan, China, Taiwan, Canada, and Australia. Telecommunications equipment, cars and trucks, clothing, and petroleum products are the primary imports, arriving from Canada, Japan, Taiwan, and Hong Kong. Oil tankers also arrive in Port Angeles from Alaska to supply the oil refineries in Anacortes and Ferndale. As the port of Tacoma plans a major expansion and Seattle continues to be a national trade leader, the future for containerized shipping in Washington looks very bright.

ACCOMMODATIONS AND FOOD

ACCOMMODATIONS

Hotels And Motels

The largest cities—Seattle, Spokane, Tacoma, Olympia, and others—obviously have the greatest range of accommodations, from Motel 6's $24 rooms to Sheratons, Hyatts, Red Lions, Olympic Four Seasons, and more for $100 and up per night. All of these cities, without exception, have very inexpensive lodging just outside city limits, so you can stay a half-hour away and spend the extra money having fun.

In Seattle or Spokane, you can stay at the budget chains near the airport; in Tacoma, stay up the road in Fife. Call ahead for reservations whenever possible; the least expensive rooms fill up fast.

Finding a room—any room—can be extremely difficult in summer (even on weekdays) at popular resort areas such as Lake Chelan, the San Juan Islands, the national parks, or along the ocean. Staying a half-hour from the action can save you money—try the motels in Wenatchee when Lake Chelan's filled up, or stay in Forks or Port Angeles instead of at Olympic National Park lodges.

Bed And Breakfasts

Some parts of the state, particularly Port Townsend, are filled with restored turn-of-the-century Victorian homes that have been converted to B&Bs. Other B&Bs are old farmhouses, lodges, or modern homes with private entrances. In most cases, a room at a B&B will cost as much as a moderately priced motel room. You may miss the cable, HBO, pool, and room service, but you'll get breakfast (ranging from coffee and cinnamon rolls to a full eggs-bacon-and-toast feast), often complimentary evening wine or tea, and peace and quiet.

Many B&Bs don't allow kids, pets, or smoking; probably half the rooms won't have a private bath. B&Bs are a good way to get acquainted with a new area, and the best choice for people traveling alone, since you'll have opportunities to meet fellow travelers in the library, over tea, or at breakfast.

Camping

Washington's state parks offer excellent camping facilities in clean, scenic parks for next to nothing: $7 for tent sites, up to $9.50 for hookups (see below). A dozen state parks accept advance reservations, but most operate on a first-come first-served basis. See individual national forest and park listings for details on camping there; camping is good but generally more primitive; some are free, but most campgrounds charge a small fee. Private campgrounds are usually combination mobile home/RV parks with a minimum of natural surroundings and a maximum number of vehicles per acre.

FOOD

Lately a lot of restaurants in western Washington, and food writers, have talked endlessly about "Northwest cuisine," which is probably a misnomer because most food experts insist that only two genuine cuisines exist: French and Chinese. But as all parts of the country do, Washington places an emphasis on certain kinds of food. Fresh salmon is popular and can be found on virtually every restaurant's menu, from Ivar's fish bars to Black Angus steakhouses. Red snapper, halibut, and cod are also served fresh almost everywhere in western Washington. Less common are the local Olympia oysters and geoduck.

As you head east, the seafood is generally frozen, though some restaurants pride themselves on their fresh fish and will mention it in their ads. Steaks are often imported from the Midwest and are generally very good. West-

CAMPING IN THE STATE PARKS

• More than 90 Washington state parks have camping facilities. A large proportion of these have trailer hookups, and with a $9.50 maximum charge, the parks are a good value—and generally more aesthetically pleasing than private RV parks. The following information will help you to plan your trip and understand the individual park descriptions.

• Seventy-five percent of the state's campsites are classified as "standard." This means you get a picnic table, campstove, nearby running water, garbage disposal, a flush toilet, and, in most parks (except Horsethief Lake, Wallace Falls, Mt. Spokane, and Spencer Spit), hot showers. Standard sites cost $7.50 per night.

• Many of the parks have "utility sites" with water, sewer, and/or electric hookups. Some of these can be as short as 35 feet in length (that's total length of RV or car plus trailer). So if you're traveling in an extra-long RV, be sure to get a copy of the guide below. Prices for utility sites vary with the type of hookup: add to the $7.50 standard site fee $.50 for water, $.50 for sewer, and $1.50 for electricity. If the utility sites are full or nonexistent, RVers may park in standard sites.

• Some parks also have "primitive" sites; that means no flush toilet, sometimes no running water. If you hike or bike in, the fee is $3; if you're in a motorized vehicle, it's $4.50.

• Camping is limited to 10 consecutive days per park from May through September.

• No chopping or gathering of firewood is allowed. Some parks sell campfire logs, but it's best to bring your own.

• Campsites are available on a first-come, first-served basis in all but 11 parks, where reservations are accepted from the second Monday in January until two weeks before Labor Day for the summer camping season. Reservations must be made at least 14 days in advance.

• Parks that allow reservations are Belfair State Park, Belfair; Fort Flagler State Park, Nordland; Moran State Park, Eastsound; Twin Harbors/ Grayland Beach, Westport; Birch Bay State Park, Blaine; Ike Kinswa State Park, Silver Creek; Pearrygin Lake State Park, Winthrop; Fort Canby State Park, Ilwaco; Lake Chelan State Park, Chelan; Steamboat Rock State Park, Electric City; Lincoln Rock State Park, Wenatchee.

• Fort Worden State Park in Port Townsend has its own reservation system for campsites and other accommodations, year-round; phone (206) 385-4730 for a brochure or details. Call or write the State Parks Commission for a reservation application (address and phone below).

• Most parks are open all year, but some close from Oct. through March; those that remain open often have limited winter camping facilities. Be sure to phone the parks or Parks Commission (number below) if you're traveling in the off-season.

• No more than eight people per campsite.

• Every camper should get a copy of the *Guide to Washington State Parks*. It lists each state park by region and includes information on number, type, and length of campsites, type of hookup, and other facilities. To get this guide, or detailed brochures on the parks you plan to visit, write the Washington State Parks and Recreation Commission, Public Affairs Office, 7150 Cleanwater Lane, KY-11, Olympia, WA 98504, or phone (206) 753-2027. In the summer you can phone (800) 562-0990 Mon. through Fri. during normal working hours for park information.

Turtlebrook Farm Inn,
Orcas Island

ern Washington is also known for its strawberries, blackberries, and various other kinds of berries. The King County Cooperative Extension Service publishes lists of U-Pick vegetable and berry farms, and the tabloid can be found at nearly all public libraries and some tourist-information bureaus.

Eastern Washington is the place to go for fresh fruit and produce. Washington apples are mostly of the Red and Golden Delicious, Rome Beauty, and Granny Smith varieties. Many other kinds of fruit are grown along the central corridor—cherries, peaches, apricots. The Walla Walla sweet onion is reputedly mild enough to bite into, raw, like an apple, and it is sold in gift packs, much like Harry & David holiday packs. Asparagus, pears, and berries of all kinds are also big eastern Washington crops.

Wine grapes are a large part of the Yakima and Columbia River valleys' agriculture. Wineries line the highway between Yakima and the Tri-Cities and into Walla Walla; others are scattered east to Spokane. Washington wines have become world class in just a few years, winning awards and gaining in popularity across the country. Try to visit at least a few wineries (western Washington also has a number of them, though the grapes are usually grown in eastern Washington); or, stop by the local grocery store for a wide selection of Washington and other Northwest wines.

MONEY, MEASUREMENTS, AND COMMUNICATIONS

Money
Prices of all lodging, tours, attractions, and services were current at press time, and will inevitably go up; use them as a basis for comparison, not as absolutes. Lodging prices are the basic prices listed for summer months and do not take into account corporate or special weekend rates, so in many cases you can get better prices by asking for discounts (AARP, AAA, weekend or off-season). Most prices are given before state sales tax has been added, a whopping 7.8% on most purchases and 8% on restaurant meals and lodging. However, grocery-store food is exempt from state taxes.

Measurements
The metric system's major contribution to Washington is the two-liter bottle, although you will see signs in both miles and kilometers as you approach the Canadian border; some banks display the temperature in both centigrade and Fahrenheit. For the most part Washington, like the rest of the U.S., is sticking stubbornly to the old English system.

Fahrenheit   Centigrade

Water Boils

Water Freezes

          1 inch = 2.54 centimeters
          1 foot = 0.31 meter
          1 mile = 1.61 kilometers
     1 sq. mile = 2.59 sq. kilometers
        1 acre = 0.40 hectare
1 pound (lb.) = 0.45 kilogram

Communications
Post offices generally open between 7 a.m. and 9 a.m. and close between 5 p.m. and 6 p.m.; only a few are open on Saturdays. Some drug or card stores also operate a postal substation where you can buy stamps or mail packages within the U.S. (you'll have to go to a real post office for mailing to foreign addresses or other special services). Many grocery stores also sell books of stamps with no markup.

Washington has two telephone area codes; with only an occasional exception, **206** is west of the Cascades and **509** is east of the Cascades. It is confusing only in some mostly rural areas along the crest of the Cascades. For directory assistance, dial 1 (area code) 555-1212.

HEALTH AND HELP

In most of Washington, dial 911 for **medical, police,** or **fire** emergencies. More remote areas have separate numbers for all three, and they're listed under "Services And Information" in each section; as a last resort, dial 0 for the operator. Most hospitals have 24-hour emergency room service; some cities have dial-a-nurse services that offer free medical advice.

OUTDOORS

Dealing with bears is discussed under "Flora And Fauna," p. 8. But by far the greater danger to the outdoors enthusiast in the Northwest is **hypothermia,** often referred to in the past as "exposure," in which the victim's core temperature drops to 95°F or below. It doesn't have to be below freezing for hypothermia to be a threat; exposure to wind and/or water can cause a serious loss of heat at temperatures well above freezing. It is a problem during the Northwest summers more often than winters because people often mistakenly believe that the bright, sunny morning weather is going to last. In the higher elevations of the Cascades and Olympics the weather is unpredictable, and the temperature can drop dramatically in a matter of hours or even minutes.

Prevention is the best bet: wear wool (the best insulator even when wet), and put on rain gear *before* it starts raining; head back or set up camp when the weather looks threatening; eat candy bars, keep active, or snuggle with a friend in a down bag to generate warmth.

If the conditions are right for hypothermia, watch your hiking partner for signs of slurred speech, stumbling, drowsiness, memory lapses, shivering (particularly if shivering stops once it's started), or poor judgment. Once the victim's core temperature falls below 95°, he'll be unable to recover by himself and immediate action must be taken on his behalf, whether or not he thinks he needs help. Get him out of the wind or rain and into dry clothing and a pre-warmed sleeping bag (have another hiker strip to the skin and warm the bag first, or in severe cases, have the victim and warmth donor skin-to-skin in the bag). Be sure the sleeping bag is well insulated from the ground, and build a fire on each side of the bag if possible; warm, wrapped rocks or canteens can also help. If he can eat, feed him candy bars or sweetened snacks; if he's semiconscious, keep him awake.

Frostbite is a less serious but quite painful problem for the cold-weather hiker, caused by direct exposure or by heat loss due to wet socks and boots. Frostbitten areas will look white or gray and feel hard on the surface, softer underneath. The best way to warm the area is with other skin: put your hand under your arm, your feet on your friend's belly. Don't rub it with snow or warm it near a fire. In cases of severe frostbite, in which the skin is white, quite hard, and numb, immerse the frozen area in water warmed to 99 to 104° until it's thawed. Avoid refreezing the frostbitten area. If you're a long way from medical assistance and the frostbite is extensive, it is better to keep the area frozen and get out of the woods for help; thawing is very painful and it would be impossible to walk on a thawed foot.

The most important part of enjoying—and surviving—the backcountry is to be prepared. Know where you're going; get maps, camping information, and weather and trail conditions from a ranger before setting out. Don't hike alone. Two are better than one, and three are better than two; if one gets hurt, one person can stay with the injured party and one can go for help. Bring more than enough food so hunger won't cause you to continue when weather conditions say "stop."

Tell someone where you're going and when you'll be back. Bring a compass, and know how to use it. Carry a water bottle, first-aid kit, flashlight, matches and fire starter, knife, and extra clothing (a full set, in case you fall in a stream), including rain gear. Check your ego at the trailhead; stop for the night when the weather gets bad, even if it's 2 p.m., or head back, and don't press on when you're exhausted—tired hikers are sloppy hikers, and even a small injury can be disastrous in the woods.

INFORMATION

Ranger stations at the national parks and forests can sell you forest and topographical maps, campground and trail information, and other printed material. For a list of books, maps, and pamphlets available by mail, write the Pacific Northwest National Parks and Forests Association, Forest Service/National Park Service, Outdoor Recreation Information, 1018 First Ave., Seattle, WA 98104, or phone (206) 442-0170. Get more specific information on your destination (trail and campground descriptions, maps, sightseeing, wildlife) by writing or phoning one of these offices:

Colville National Forest
Colville Ranger Station
775 S. Main St.
Colville, WA 99114
(509) 684-4557

Gifford Pinchot National Forest
Mt. Adams Ranger Station
Trout Lake, WA 98650
(509) 395-2501

Gifford Pinchot National Forest
Mt. St. Helens National Volcanic
Monument Headquarters
Rt. 1, Box 369
Amboy, WA 98601
(206) 247-5473

Mt. Baker/Snoqualmie National Forest
Supervisor's Office
1022 First Ave.
Seattle, WA 98104
(206) 442-5400

Okanogan National Forest
Supervisor's Office
Box 950
Okanogan, WA 98840
(509) 422-2704

Olympic National Forest
Supervisor's Office
Box 2288
Olympia, WA 98507
(206) 753-9535

Wenatchee National Forest
Supervisor's Office
301 Yakima St.
Wenatchee, WA 98801
(509) 662-4335

For national park information, see the "Services and Information" section under the appropriate chapter.

Every city or town has a chamber of commerce. Most have offices that are filled with free brochures, maps, information on lodging and restaurants, and more. Take advantage of the help they offer. See "Services and Information" in each chapter for the chamber's address and phone.

TRANSPORTATION

TOURS

Your travel agent or hotel concierge can give you numerous choices of bus tours of Washington's highlights; or, phone one of the following tour companies for dates and rates.

Gray Line offers one-day and longer tours of Seattle, Mt. Rainier and Mt. St. Helens, Olympic National Park, the North Cascades, Washington wine country, and Spokane, often including Vancouver and Victoria, B.C., Coeur D'Alene Lake, Portland, or other western national parks. In Washington, phone (800) 426-7532 or (206) 624-5813 for details.

American Sightseeing has one-day tours of Seattle, Mt. Rainier, and Victoria, B.C.; phone (206) 626-5208. **Don and Diane Fun-Tours** operates one-day and longer tours from Seattle to Spokane, Leavenworth, Mt. Rainier, Olympia, and out to Reno, San Francisco, and beyond; phone (206) 282-3508 or write Box 21007, Seattle, WA 98111, for a brochure.

Creative Tours, tel. (206) 771-4721, offers one-day tours to western Washington sights and events from Poulsbo's Midsommer Viking Fest to Port Townsend's Historic Homes Tour; write Box 403, Edmonds, WA 98020, for information.

Continental Crown, tel. (509) 456-5104, offers bus tours through eastern Washington and on to Idaho and Montana or north to British Columbia.

BY AIR

Washington's two major airports are Seattle-Tacoma International (Sea-Tac) and Spokane International, served by most major carriers and a handful of smaller airlines. United, tel. 441-3700; Continental, tel. (800) 525-0280; Delta, tel. (800) 221-1212; American, tel. (800) 433-7300; TWA, tel. 447-9400; USAir, tel. (800) 428-4322; Northwest, tel.

(800) 225-2525, among others, provide national and international service. Alaska Airlines, tel. (800) 426-0333, serves the western states; America West, tel. (800) 763-0737, flies to California, Las Vegas, and the Southwest and Midwest states. Horizon Air, tel. (800) 547-9308, is the big "little" airline, connecting many medium-to-large Washington cities, including Seattle, Spokane, Wenatchee, and the Tri-Cities.

Try for a south-side window seat (on an east-west route) when flying into or out of Sea-Tac for a spectacular close-up view of Mt. Rainier and, in the distance, Mt. St. Helens. On the north-south routes the plane usually flies within a mile or two of Mt. St. Helens.

BY TRAIN

Amtrak serves Washington with two major routes. The north-south route along the west coast is aboard the *Coast Starlight,* which has daily service to Seattle, Tacoma, East Olympia, Centralia, Longview/Kelso, and Vancouver, through Oregon and south to San Francisco and Los Angeles. The *Mount Rainier* runs Thursday through Sunday from Seattle to Portland, stopping at the Washington cities listed above.

Amtrak's east-west route, aboard the *Pioneer,* operates three days a week in winter, daily from spring through late fall. The train departs Seattle, passing through Tacoma, East Olympia, Centralia, Longview/Kelso, and Vancouver as it continues through Portland and Idaho to Salt Lake City and Chicago. Another daily east-west route to Chicago is on the *Empire Builder,* which stops at Spokane, then turns southwest to Portland with stops at Pasco, Wishram, Bingen/White Salmon, and Vancouver, or to Seattle through Ephrata, Wenatchee, Everett, and Edmonds.

For route, schedule, and fare information, phone Amtrak at (206) 464-1930 in Seattle, (509) 747-1069 in Spokane, or (800) 872-

7245 toll-free nationwide. Be forewarned, though: Amtrak requires advance reservations; you can't just go down to the station and climb aboard.

BY CAR

The national parks and other remote areas of the state are not served by any air, rail, or bus lines, and the public transportation within cities is often limited and difficult for the newcomer to use, so having a car of your own is a vital part of getting the most from your visit. Numerous car rental agencies operate at or near Sea-Tac and Spokane International airports, as well as in all large cities.

Washington's major interstates are I-5, running north to south from the Canadian border through Bellingham, Mt. Vernon, Everett, Seattle, Tacoma, Olympia, Centralia, Longview, and Woodland to Vancouver; I-90, running west to east from Seattle over Snoqualmie Pass to Ellensburg, Moses Lake to Spokane; I-82 heads south from Ellensburg almost to the Tri-Cities. These are all multi-lane freeways with speed limits of 55 mph in metropolitan areas and 65 mph in rural areas.

From late fall to early spring, expect snow at I-90's Snoqualmie Pass (between North Bend and Cle Elum in central Washington), Stevens Pass on U.S. Hwy. 2 and White Pass on State Hwy. 12. Cayuse Pass on State Hwy. 410 and Rainy and Washington passes on State Hwy. 20 (the North Cascades Hwy.) are closed each winter.

Snow tires or chains are frequently required, and the passes are sometimes closed during storms because of hazardous road conditions, blocking accidents, or avalanche danger. Skiers and other winter travelers passing through the Casades should always carry a set of chains, emergency equipment (flares, shovel, blankets, and food). Before you set out, be sure to phone 1-976-7623 for the state patrol's **mountain pass report** (there's a $.35 toll); they give road and weather conditions for all of the Cascade passes from Nov. through March or April. AAA Washington also has a free 24-hour recorded message on major highways

within a day's drive of Puget Sound: tel. (206) 448-8611.

Out-of-state visitors may be surprised by the abundance of wide-open spaces, particularly in the mountains and eastern half of the state—and the long distances between gas stations, rest rooms, and other niceties. Worse yet, some little towns close up tight after 5 p.m. and on Sundays. Play it safe and fill the tank whenever you pass through a moderately populous area; stock a cooler with drinks and sandwiches; and be sure your destination motel has a room ready and waiting for you.

BY BUS

Greyhound, tel. 624-3456, serves most major cities in Washington, providing nationwide connections. Their main routes are along I-5 from Canada to Oregon, and along I-90 from Seattle to Spokane, with additional service on the Oregon side of the Columbia Gorge and west to Astoria.

Regional and city bus lines can get you around most western Washington cities and a few large eastern cities as well. Seattle's **Metro,** tel. 447-4800, has extensive service within the city and regular daily routes throughout most of King County. **Pierce Transit,** tel. 581-8000, serves Tacoma and Pierce County. **Intercity Transit,** tel. 786-1881, has daily routes throughout Olympia and Thurston County. **Grays Harbor Transit,** tel. (800) 562-9730, connects Olympia with Hoquiam, Ocean Shores, Westport, and Lake Quinault in Olympic National Park. **Pacific Transit,** tel. 875-9418, has service to the Long Beach Peninsula from Raymond with connections to Astoria, Oregon. **C-Tran,** tel. 695-0123, serves Vancouver and Clark County with connections to Portland. Longview, Kelso, and Cowlitz County are served by Community Urban Bus Service (CUBS), tel. 577-3399. In Chehalis, take **Twin Transit,** tel. 330-2072, to Centralia and parts of Lewis County.

The bus line coverage in eastern Washington isn't as thorough. In Spokane, take **Spo-**

WASHINGTON STATE HIGHWAYS

BRITISH COLUMBIA

ROSS LAKE

NORTH
ROSS LAKE NAT'L. REC. AREA

CASCAD
N.

VANCOUVER ISLAND

SAN JUAN ISLANDS

BELLINGHAM

MT. BAKER WILDERNESS

ANACORTES

SEDRO WOOLLEY

MT. VERNON

VICTORIA

WHIDBEY ISLAND

DARRINGTON

PORT ANGELES

PORT TOWNSEND

SEQUIM

MARYSVILLE

LAKE WENATCHEE

FORKS

OLYMPIC N.P.

EVERETT

EDMONDS

KITSAP PENINSULA

SEATTLE

SKYKOMISH

BREMERTON

BELLEVUE

SNOQUALMIE

NORTH BEND

ISSAQUAH

KACHE LAKE

TAHOLAH

SHELTON

SNOQUALMIE PASS (3,022 ft.)

KEECHELUS LAKE

CLE ELUM

OCEAN SHORES

OLYMPIA

TACOMA

HOQUIAM

WESTPORT

MT. RAINIER N.P.

CENTRALIA

CHEHALIS

MORTON

PACIFIC OCEAN

LONG BEACH

MOUNT ST. HELENS NAT'L. VOLCANIC MONUMENT

MT. ADAMS WILDERNESS

TROUT LAKE

COLUMBIA RIVER

KELSO

LONGVIEW

OREGON

GOLDENDA

WHITE SALMON

0   20 mi

0   20 km

VANCOUVER

COLUMBIA RIVER GORGE

PORTLAND

© MOON PUBLICATIONS, INC.

kane Transit, tel. 328-7433, throughout Spokane and Cheney. **Empire Lines,** tel. 624-4116, serves several communities west from Spokane, and **Borderline Stage,** tel. 684-3950, serves Northeastern Washington.

Valley Transit, tel. 525-9140, serves Walla Walla and College Place. **Yakima Transit,** tel. 575-6175, has nine routes throughout Yakima and the surrounding area. The Tri-Cities have **Ben Franklin Transit,** tel. 735-5100, with service to Kennewick, Pasco, Richland, W. Richland, and the Tri-Cities Airport, and **Northwestern Stage Lines,** tel. 838-4029, serves Clarkston, Colfax, Pullman, and smaller communities along the Idaho border.

BY BOAT

The most scenic way to get around western Washington is by Washington State Ferry; be sure to take a ride, even if it's just "there and back." The best sightseeing is on the Anacortes-San Juan Islands route, which once a day continues to Sidney, B.C. (see "San Juan Islands," p. 173, for details). Ferries also connect Port Townsend with Keystone (Whidbey Island); Clinton (Whidbey Island) with Mukilteo (west of Everett); Edmonds with Kingston (on the Kitsap Peninsula); Seattle with Winslow (Bainbridge Island) and Bremerton; Fauntleroy (Southwest Seattle) with Southworth (southeast of Bremerton) and Vashon Island; and Tacoma (at Point Defiance) with Tahlequah (at the south end of Vashon Island).

Fares range from $2.15 RT for a walk-on passenger (Mukilteo to Clinton) to $26 RT for car and driver (Anacortes to Sidney, B.C.), depending on route and season (some fares are higher in summer). Senior citizens receive a 50% discount with proof of age, applied only to the passenger or driver portion of the fare (not the vehicle). Fares must be paid with cash, traveler's checks, or personal checks (Washington residents only); no credit cards.

The larger ferries have food service, which was improved in 1991, and at a lower price. Beer is sold, and vending machines dispense candy bars and junk food; the smaller boats

soaking up the sun on a Washington state ferry

STATE OF WASHINGTON TOURISM DEPARTMENT

have vending machines only. Pets on leashes are allowed on the car decks or in carrying containers on passenger decks. The ferries operate every day, including holidays. For more information about the ferry system, phone (800) 542-0810, tel. (800) 542-7052, or in Seattle, tel. 464-6400.

Other Washington ferries include the Anderson Island Ferry, tel. 581-6290, which has daily service between Steilacoom, Anderson Island, and Ketron Island. **Ed's Charter,** tel. (800) 562-0107, provides passenger-only ferry service between Westport and Ocean Shores in the summer. **The Horluck Transportation Co.,** tel. 876-2300, has a daily route between Bremerton and Port Orchard for foot traffic only. Various counties operate ferries, including the ferry to Lummi Island near Bellingham (tel. 676-6730), the ferry between Anacortes and Guemes Island (tel. 293-6356), between Puget Island near Cathlamet and the Oregon side of the river (tel. 795-3301), the two free ferries across the upper Columbia River at the Keller crossing just above Grand Coulee Dam (no phone) and between Gifford and Inchelium (tel. 684-4335) on the Colville Indian Reservation.

Take the MV *Coho,* tel. 457-4491, from Port Angeles to Victoria, B.C., across the

Strait of Juan de Fuca; from Seattle, *Victoria Clipper,* tel. 448-5000, sails to Victoria daily in summer from the waterfront Piers 69 and 63. See "Port Angeles," p. 220, and "Seattle," p. 71, for details.

Just as this edition was being updated, **SeaCat,** which operates high-speed car and passenger ferries between England and the Continent, to islands in the Irish Sea, and between Australia and Tasmania, announced it is beginning service between Seattle and Victoria with a vessel that averages 50 mph and carries 450 passengers and 80 automobiles. The cost will be about $80 roundtrip for walk-on passengers, and $30 per car. No address of phone number was available yet.

Independent tour and charter boat companies in Seattle, Tacoma, Everett, San Juan Island, Westport, and other coastal cities offer sightseeing, fishing, whale- and sea lion-watching tours throughout the year.

BY BICYCLE

Washington, and particularly Seattle, is praised by bicycling magazines as being among the most bicycle-friendly places in America. Puget Sound's numerous islands provide great scenery, some of the state's best weather, and little automobile traffic: Whidbey Island, for instance, gets about a third of Seattle's annual rainfall, and offers spectacular vistas from little-traveled back roads, plus plenty of camping at the state parks.

The beauty of the San Juan Islands is best experienced on a bike, and you'll save $10 or more on the ferry toll to Friday Harbor when traveling without the cumbersome automobile. Vashon, Bainbridge, Mercer, and Camano islands are also easy to get to and have little automobile traffic.

The urban areas have ample opportunities for cyclists. Seattle has received the blessings of *Bicycling* magazine as the "Best North American City for Bicycling," crediting the city's friendly atmosphere and the many miles of scenic and safe paths. Seattle adopted a comprehensive policy toward biking that led to more signs, more bike racks, Metro buses with bike racks, special bike lanes, and so forth. An example of this enlightened attitude toward self propulsion is the Burke-Gilman Trail, a 12½-mile paved bike path from Gasworks Park to Kenmore's Log Boom Park at the north end of Lake Washington. Almost but not yet connecting with it is the Sammamish River Trail, which runs 9½ miles from Bothell Landing to Redmond's Marymoor Park, passing just east of Woodinville's Ste. Michelle winery—a great place to stop for lunch with a bottle of wine.

In West Seattle, the road and bike path from Alki Beach to Lincoln Park is a popular 12-mile loop. Five Mile Drive in Tacoma's Point Defiance Park is open to cars as well, but cyclists are given a wide berth; the road passes through an impressive old-growth forest. Most chambers of commerce can supply you with maps of bike routes throughout their city or county for a nominal fee.

BOB RACE

THE PUGET SOUND REGION

SEATTLE

Seattle is consistently ranked as one of the best U.S. cities in which to live, visit, ride bicycles, raise kids, or locate a business by organizations as varied as *Money* magazine, Rand McNally, *USA Today, Bicycling,* and the National Conference of Mayors. The phenomenal growth the Puget Sound region has experienced in recent years attests to the area's increasing popularity—and causes natives to shudder at the "Californication" of their once-pristine state. The obvious charms of Seattle and the Puget Sound region are drawing more tourists each year, many of whom come back to stay.

Throughout its history Seattle has been a gateway: first to Alaska and western Canada during the Klondike Gold Rush, today to the Orient as planes refuel here for their Asian

destinations, and of course to the beauty of the Pacific Northwest. Three of the country's most spectacular national parks and moody Mt. St. Helens National Monument are within two hours' driving time from the city; skiing, hiking, year-round boating, swimming, and fishing are less than an hour away.

Seattle's charm isn't just a function of what it's near, but also what it is—and was. Oddly shaped towers and preserved historical districts stand alongside modern skyscrapers and busy waterfront in a jaunty kind of disharmony. Every major event in the city's short life span, from Yesler's 1850s sawmill to the 1962 World's Fair, has left its legacy; the resulting mishmash of periods gives the city a flavor absent in showpieces of urban renewal.

History doesn't make a city livable. No one event or attraction here can ever take that credit. Rather, it's a thousand incidents, enjoyed daily: dining at the waterfront, watching the sun set behind the Olympics as sailboats head home; reading the *Seattle P.I.* on your early-morning ferry commute, accompanied by a lively porpoise escort service; listening to a free outdoor lunchtime concert at Freeway Park; stopping for fresh vegetables or fish at Pike Place Market; cleansing your lungs with fresh, rain-rinsed air as you dodge slugs and puddles on your morning run; attending a summertime office party on a harbor tour boat; being surprised by a clear view of bashful Mt. Rainier from the highway or the Safeway parking lot.

All these moments that can be enjoyed only in Seattle, as well as the cultural events, shops, and restaurants, make it a delightful, relaxing place.

Climate

Despite the stories you've heard, it doesn't rain in Seattle *all* the time. Seattle actually gets less annual rainfall than New York City—it just falls more slowly here. Gray and drizzly is standard fare from October to May; when it does rain, it's usually a who-needs-an-umbrella sprinkle. The winter weather pattern remains nearly constant; storms off the Pacific coast send swirling clouds over Seattle for months, leading you to believe that the TV weather forecaster uses the same satellite photo all season. Nearly all of the precipitation is rain; less than an inch of snow per month is the average, so plows are few . . . and generally in disrepair. When snowstorms dropped 17 inches on Seattle in November of 1985, only four of the city's seven snowplows worked; commuters, few of whom had much experience driving on snow, relied on chains to traverse the I-5 snowfield and some actually reached their destinations; most simply abandoned their cars and turned the freeway into a disorderly parking lot. Automobile insurance companies hated that storm.

Seattle and other western Washington residents have learned to expect at least three seasonal events: a windstorm on Thanksgiving that knocks out electrical power while the turkey is in the oven; floods on the Snohomish and Skagit rivers around Christmas and New Year's that force evacuation of many farms, and perfect Santa Barbara weather the last weekend of July.

When spring arrives the clouds move more quickly; rain comes in unpredictable spurts. Summer convinces many visitors to move

SEATTLE AND VICINITY

© MOON PUBLICATIONS, INC.

here: low humidity, temperatures in the high 70s to 80s, and cloudless skies; sometimes two entire months pass without a drop of rain. It makes natives restless. Then, as suddenly as it began, summer ends: clouds return, temperatures go down, and residents stockpile firewood, books, hot chocolate, and party invitations for the soggy season ahead.

HISTORY

The city was named after Suquamish Chief Sealth, or Seattle—Indian names didn't translate well into English—and both spellings are used on his tomb. Chief Seattle claimed to have witnessed Capt. George Vancouver's visit in 1792, and 50 years later befriended early settlers, encouraging a policy of peace between Indians and white newcomers.

Most Indians feared the consequences of the utterance of their name after death; historians debate whether the chief was happy that the city was to be named in his honor. Some claim it was against his will; others hold that Seattle was paid handsomely by the city's founders for his name. In any case, the name stuck. Today a bronze sculpture of Chief Seattle stands at the corner of Fifth and Denny Way; his burial site, a peaceful Suquamish cemetery across the Sound, overlooks his namesake's skyscrapers.

Although some white men were in the Duwamish River Valley not far from Puget Sound, David Denny and Lee Terry were the first white men to arrive at what became Seattle. Twenty-two pioneers had left Cherry Grove, Illinois, in wagons bound for Portland, Oregon; they then boarded the schooner *Exact* and sailed to Alki Point in 1851. The settlers ambitiously planned to develop "the New York of the Pacific Coast" at their landing site.

Lumber was the focus of their early economy, beginning with the arrival of the *Leonesa* from San Francisco in 1852. The ship's captain had been wandering northward when he stumbled across the Alki settlement. The settlers sold the skipper 35,000 board feet of logs. Seeing an economic future in

shipping lumber, the pioneers took to the waters in Indian canoes, and with the help of Mrs. Denny's clothesline and Lee Terry's horseshoes, took soundings along the Puget Sound shoreline. Discovering that the deepest waters were in today's Elliott Bay, the group relocated to Pioneer Square.

Logs were rolled down the original "Skid Road," now Yesler Way, to Henry Yesler's steam-powered sawmill. Yesler enjoyed such success that by the 1880s Yesler's Wharf was a town unto itself, with saloons, warehouses, shops, homes, and offices built on pilings extending 900 feet over the mudflats.

Women were scarce in Seattle's early years, so in the 1860s, Asa Mercer made two trips to New England to find refined, educated, single women willing to endure a little hardship to get a husband. The "Mercer Girls" brought culture and class to the rowdy pioneer town.

Until the 1880s, most transport to and from Seattle was by boat. Hopes for alternative methods were dashed when the Northern Pacific Railroad chose Tacoma as its Northwest terminus. Though they received intermittent service via Tacoma by 1883, Seattleites wanted to be part of a regular, mainline route. As James J. Hill began expanding the Great Northern Line westward, rumors of a Seattle terminus resulted in a population boom and rising real estate values; the rumor became fact in 1893.

The intermittent railroad service of the '80s and highly successful lumber and coal export businesses encouraged a phenomenal population boom: from 3,500 in 1880 to 43,000 in 1890. The city's quality of life also improved rapidly, with the grading and planking of streets and sidewalks, the installation of sewer systems, electric lights, telephones, and home mail delivery. Horse-drawn streetcars were quickly replaced by the electric variety.

Chinese workers began arriving in the 1860s; by the mid-1880s they numbered more than 500. Anti-Chinese sentiment rose as whites feared that cheap Chinese labor would cost them their jobs; the ensuing riots convinced most of the Asian laborers to

AN UNLIKELY HERO

One of the most respected pioneer names in Seattle is Mercer, and one of the most famous incidents in early Seattle was engineered by Asa Shinn Mercer.

Asa Mercer graduated from Lafayette College, Pennsylvania, in 1861 and immediately set out for Seattle to join his elder brother, Judge Thomas Mercer, who was busy settling the new city. He became the first president of the University of Washington before it even existed; he helped clear the site on a hillside overlooking the village of Seattle, put up classrooms, and then scouted the region for students. For the first two terms, he not only was president of the university, he was the entire faculty.

As he toured the region, he heard the same complaint repeatedly: not enough women. Inter-racial marriages were common, alcoholism was high, and morale was low. Mercer believed the area could not thrive until it had a firm family footing.

He tried to get the territorial government to subsidize female immigration, but while the men who ran the government were sympathetic, the treasury was empty. The disgruntled would-be marriage broker packed a suitcase and caught a ship back to Boston. The Civil War was creating thousands of young widows, many, many women of marrying age who were willing to go. But when sailing time came, only 11 showed up. Mercer was probably disappointed, but it wasn't bad for a start. They arrived in Seattle on May 16, 1864. Within only a few months all the women were married, and Mercer was a local hero.

Mercer left again in 1865, this time promising to enlist no less than President Lincoln's assistance. But when his ship arrived in New York from Panama, he found almost the entire nation hung in black crepe paper; President Lincoln had been assassinated the night before Asa's arrival.

Mercer was almost crushed by this news, but he made a quick recovery and went down to Washington, D.C., to talk to President Andrew Johnson and his cabinet. Another strikeout.

Asa Shinn Mercer

UNIVERSITY OF WASHINGTON/2209/3392

Feeling more hopeless by the minute, he took a chance and called on General Ulysses Grant, and found an unlikely ally. Grant had been assigned to Fort Vancouver not too long before the war; he remembered the excruciating loneliness men suffered in the settlements that were hardly more than clearings in the dark, damp forests. He promised to do what he could.

Grant persuaded the president to donate a steamboat to Mercer's cause, and ordered the quartermaster of the Army to provide it. Believing the ship was his, Mercer went on a recruiting mission all over the East Coast, speaking at churches in New York, Boston, and Washington, D.C., and in only a short time he had more than 500 women signed on.

When he returned to claim his ship, there was a hitch. He could have it, but would have to buy it at a bargain-basement price: $80,000 in cash, only one-third its value. Mercer, of course, had no money and neither did the territorial treasury. And the women began arriving in New York to sail west to matrimony.

No railroads ran coast to coast yet, but a tycoon named Ben Holladay had a

AN UNLIKELY HERO (CONTINUED)

stagecoach and ship line, and he cut Mercer a deal: Holladay would buy the ship and in return he would haul 500 of Mercer's brides-to-be for a very low price.

Mercer quickly agreed, and the end finally seemed in sight. But no. The *New York Herald* newspaper caught up to the story, and began printing accusations that he was little more than a white slaver. The headlines were imaginative and painful:

HEGIRA OF SPINSTERS
PETTICOAT BRIGADE
CARGO OF HEIFERS
MERCER-NARY ADVENTURE

More than half of the women returned home and Holladay cancelled his offer, but he offered to haul the remainder at the regular fare. Then Mercer saw what had really happened: It was Holladay who had planted the white-slave stories, to get the vessel at the bargain price without having to keep his end of the deal.

Still, on January 6, 1866, the *Continental* cast off from New York with more than 300 women aboard, bound for the frontier. It wasn't a cruise-ship crossing. By the time they reached South America, the first mate was in chains for murdering a seaman. The food was horrible; for a 17-day stretch the menu was boiled beans and tea made of saltwater.

But it wasn't such a terrible crossing that romance was impossible. Mercer fell for one young lady, who promptly rebuffed the luckless hero. So he transferred his intentions to another woman, who accepted his proposal

and they were married as soon as they arrived in Seattle.

When the ship called in San Francisco it almost caused a riot. Hundreds of lonely or curious men rowed boats out for a look at the women—one really anxious fellow climbed up a rope hanging over the side, but Mercer knocked the man back into San Francisco's cold bay. Ministers and do-gooders, believing the newspaper stories that had preceded the ship, tried to talk the women into leaving.

And Ben Holladay wasn't through with his piracy—he refused to take the women on to Puget Sound. Mercer was again on the street without any money; desperately, he wired the territorial government for money, and in return he received a rather long—collect—telegram of congratulations.

Everyone finally booked passage aboard the schooner *Tanner*, and at each stop on the way north rumors of lynch parties awaiting Mercer grew. A minister suggested that he hide in the hold of the ship and stay there until the excitement of their arrival died down.

But Mercer instead stood on the bow of the ship as it docked, and his bluff worked: everyone was too engrossed in the arrival of the brides to bother with Mercer; all except one of the women were married within months.

But the debtors caught up with Mercer, and although they didn't lynch him, they excluded him from the city's social and business community. Feeling old, cold, and very poor, Asa Mercer left Seattle shortly thereafter and showed up at various other cities around the West, his enthusiasm back at full throttle, his belief in the future of the West always strong.

---

leave. Judge Thomas Burke and others tried to maintain control and ultimately some Chinese remained.

The Great Fire
On June 6, 1889, 58 city blocks—the entire downtown area—was destroyed by the Seattle Fire. Starting in a basement carpenter shop at about 2 p.m., the flames spread within minutes to the adjoining wooden liquor

storeroom. Within a half-hour the entire city was threatened. The flames were nearly under control when the hydrants abruptly dried up; firefighters tried to stop the blaze by blasting structures in the fire's path, to no avail. Jacob Levy refused to surrender his house; his 70-man bucket brigade repeatedly doused it, while a man in the street laid 10 to one odds that the house would burn down. Levy won.

turn-of-the-century Seattle

SEATTLE-KING COUNTY CONVENTION AND VISITOR'S BUREAU

Firemen threw burning sidewalks over the cliff, ripped up roadway planking, and fought the flames with bucket brigades; the fire was finally contained at 8:30 that night. The next morning it was decreed unanimously that wooden structures would be forever prohibited in the burnt district. Business was conducted under canvas tents until the rebuilding—in brick—was completed a year later.

Seattle always had problems with drainage: streets were mudflows much of the year; toilets backed up when the tide came in; and a small boy drowned in a puddle. While rebuilding, a clever solution was suggested: raise the sidewalks! First-floor storefronts became basements, creating Seattle's Underground (see p. 50).

The Klondike Gold Rush

On August 16, 1896, George Washington Carmack and two Indian friends, Skookum Jim and Tagish Charley, discovered gold deep in Canada's Yukon on a creek that fed into the Klondike River near its confluence with the Yukon River. Word reached Fortymile, an Alaska settlement on the Yukon River, and the town was almost entirely evacuated as the miners hurried to stake a claim. A year later, when the first 68 wealthy prospectors and their gold arrived in the Lower 48, the "Klondike Gold Rush" began.

The first ship to return, the *Excelsior,* arrived in San Francisco on July 15, 1897, and created some interest, but Californians knew all about gold rushes and weren't enthusiastic; the coastal steamer *Portland* arrived in Seattle two days later. Beriah Brown, a reporter on the *Seattle Post-Intelligencer,* hitched a ride on a tug and met the ship when it cleared customs at Port Townsend. He wrote that the ship was laden with "a ton of gold"; actually more than two tons left the ship in suitcases, crates, and coffee cans. Brown's words were electrifying. The rush was on: fathers left their families, even Seattle's mayor resigned to seek his fortune in the Klondike.

The Klondike trip wasn't an easy one: a 1,000-mile sea voyage to Skagway, Alaska, then an arduous hike over the snowy 33-mile Chilkoot Trail to Lake Bennett, where wouldbe prospectors slapped together all manner of craft for floating down the Yukon to the Klondike. The Northwest Mounted Police required that each prospector carry a year's supply of food plus necessary tools and clothing, leading to the catchphrase, "a ton of gold, a ton of goods."

Erastus Brainerd, a former newspaperman, formed a publicity committee for the chamber of commerce and promoted Seattle as *the* place to get outfitted for the Klondike. Tacoma,

Seattle, Vancouver, and Portland competed for the gold-rushers' dollars, but Brainerd ensured that Seattle received five times as much advertising as the other cities by writing feature articles, sending stacks of special newspaper editions to every postmaster in America, and encouraging citizens to write "letters to the editor" for papers worldwide.

Brainerd was enormously successful—Seattle emerged as the undisputed outfitting leader. The streets became open markets: clothing, condensed milk, evaporated potatoes, and tools were piled high. Anything named "Klondike" was a potential big-seller, giving rise to "Klondike underwear" and "Klondike milk." Shady operators capitalized on their customers' eagerness: the Trans-Atlantic Gopher Company sold gophers allegedly trained to dig for gold. Siberian Huskies and other rugged breeds were enlisted to help pull dogsleds through the Alaskan snowfields. As the supply dwindled, families had to keep a close eye on their pets—dogs of every breed and size were stolen.

Though a handful of prospectors did strike it rich, the best claims had been staked long before most treasure-hunters arrived—leaving thousands of men worse off than when they began. Seattle emerged as the real winner, though: many of those who found gold returned to the city to establish businesses, while Seattle's "gold" was gained from outfitting the prospectors.

Modern Seattle

At the start of WW II the Boeing Airplane Company employed only about 4,000 workers, manufacturing planes on a subcontract basis for the Douglas Company of California. Orders for Boeing's B-17 bomber, developed in the mid-'30s, swelled their employment to 30,000 by 1942. Sales peaked in 1944 at $600 million, while employment figures topped 50,000.

After the war, Boeing's sales fell sharply—to $14 million in 1946, when 11,000 workers were laid off. Business picked up again during the Korean conflict and the U.S./ Russia Cold War with the sale of B-47s and, later, B-52s. William M. Allen, Boeing's post-war

president, sought to end this roller-coaster economy by gambling all of the company's reserves on a commercial jet-powered plane, the 707, that permanently changed civilian air travel. Later successful developments—the short-range 727, 737, and jumbo 747—brought employment figures up to 58,000 in 1959 and established Boeing as a worldwide leader in aviation.

Civic leaders decided to throw a party to celebrate Boeing's—and, synonymously, Seattle's—success. City Councilman Al Rochester was a leading advocate of "Century 21," the 1962 World's Fair. Rochester wanted something very special, "not just another showcase for the state seal done in corn tassels, milk cans, and steers' rears." Senator Warren G. Magnuson somehow maneuvered $9 million out of the Pentagon for the event—which became the first world's fair to show a profit.

Century 21 drew over 9½ million people and left the entire Seattle Center—the Space Needle, monorail, Pacific Science Center, Opera House, Coliseum, and more—as a legacy to the event.

SIGHTS

The Waterfront

Generally a sightseer's first stop, Elliot Bay's Piers 48 to 70 comprise the waterfront: restaurants, gift shops, tourist traps, museums, the Aquarium, and harbor-tour departure points, connected by a sidewalk and the **Waterfront Streetcar.** These three 1927 Australian trolleys run the 1.6 miles between Piers 48 and 70 every 20-30 minutes and continue to Pioneer Square. It's a good way to bypass the empty warehouses and ferry terminals between the two developed ends of the waterfront. Park your car under the Alaskan Way Viaduct and try for a meter; as a last resort, pay the exorbitant fees at the Diamond lots. Get a streetcar ticket for $.75 ($1 peak) at the self-serve ticket machine at any streetcar station.

Pier 59's **Seattle Marine Aquarium,** tel. 386-4320, features an underwater dome for

SEATTLE

SEATTLE

1. Latitude 47
2. Anthony's
3. Liz's
4. Ray's Boathouse
5. Hiram's at the Docks
6. Hiram M. Chittenden Locks
7. Franco's Hidden Harbor
8. Triple's
9. Ivar's Salmon House
10. Lake Union Cafe
11. University Bookstore
12. Burke Memorial Museum
13. Henry Art Gallery
14. Husky Stadium
15. Seattle Museum of History and Industry
16. Japanese Tea House & Garden
17. Volunteer Park/Seattle Art Museum/Conservatory
18. Seattle Center
19. aquarium

viewing life in the Sound. It has a resident population of everyone's favorite marine mammal, the playful and inventive sea otter. Open daily at 10 a.m., admission $4.50 adults, teens and seniors $2.50, kids $1.75.

The Omnidome, also on Pier 59, tel. 622-1868, lets you experience erupting volcanoes, outer space, foreign countries, and ocean excursions on their 180-degree dome screen with six-channel sound. The 45-minute-long programs run continuously from 10 a.m.; admission $4.95 adults, $3.95 students/seniors, and $2.95 kids.

Public fishing is allowed at Waterfront Park on Pier 57; but have a look at the water before you decide to eat what comes out of it. Worth a stop is **Creative Northwest** at Pier 55; everything they carry has been caught, grown, or handcrafted in the Northwest. Pick up Anacortes smoked salmon, Oregon glass and ceramic goblets, Mt. St. Helens ash ornaments and oil lamps, and gift packs with teas, jams, and chocolates. **Ye Olde Curiosity Shop,** a combination museum-gift shop on Pier 54, tel. 682-5844,

specializes in the bizarre: shrunken heads, mummies, "Skinny Stubbs" human skeleton, a two-headed calf, plus souvenirs and curios. Pier 70 has more stores and restaurants, including **Whales World Gift Shop,** with whale-related T-shirts, books, toys, and more. **Myrtle Edwards Park,** at Alaskan Way and Broad St., has a one-mile path along the bay to Grain Terminal. At the other end, Pier 36 hosts the **Puget Sound Vessel Traffic Service,** tel. 286-5650, providing 24-hour weather and marine traffic information for boaters in Puget Sound and the Strait of Juan de Fuca. See a free slide show and take the 15-minute guided tour.

The **Coast Guard Museum,** tel. 286-9609, also on Pier 36, has nautical artifacts, models, and photographs, and a 15-minute slide show. Closed Tues. and Thurs.; free.

Washington State Ferries depart Pier 52 for Winslow and Bremerton across the sound (see "Getting Around By Ferry," p. 72). The *Victoria Clipper* docks at Pier 63 between trips. Elliott Bay tour boats leave from other waterfront points in summer (see "Harbor Tours," p. 72).

Pike Place Market
From Pier 59 follow the signs to the **Pike Street Hillclimb.** This enclosed staircase leads past the open guitar cases of sometimes good, always loud, street musicians, through numerous levels of boutiques and coffee shops to the Pike Place Market, which is eclecticism gone mad.

This is one of Seattle's most cherished spots, one of those things longtime residents want to remain exactly the way it always has been. Like Steinbeck's Cannery Row, it is a sensory and social statement. Here visitors and locals buy the freshest fish and produce in town—one of few places where you can see, and buy, geoducks. The majority of the main level is given over to food, mostly produce from farms within 50 miles of Seattle, and fresh seafood, some of which came in that morning from Alaska.

As the market stretches down Pike Place, merchants are progressively more tuned to tourist dollars—stands sell the usual sweat-

DIANNE BOULERICE LYONS

Pike Place Market

shirts and jewelry, even some unusual laser prints. Charitable organizations such as Goodwill and the Salvation Army have outlets, and a few cafés, such as **The Athenian,** have working-man's lunches with some of Seattle's best views of Elliot Bay.

The markets change constantly, but the following are the old standbys:

Studio Solstone at 93 Pike St. has quality limited-edition prints of Seattle and Pike Place Market scenes, plus calendars and note cards at reasonable prices. The Travel Accessories Store on the market's south side has maps, guidebooks, bags, car games for kids, and other travel-related items. **Design Concern** on Western Ave. (to the side of the hillclimb staircase) has everything from watches to phones to cookware; the emphasis is on innovative design, not just function, of the object.

Market tours are available daily; call 682-7453 for more info. Leave your car in the parking lot below; it's nearly impossible to drive up Pike Place with lunch-hour pedestrians overflowing the sidewalks.

Pioneer Square

If the Pike Place Markets are eclecticism gone mad, then Pioneer Square is eclecticism gone upscale; boutiques, art galleries, Oriental carpet stores, and sidewalk cafés are nestled between corner missions; executives in tailored suits pass Occidental Park's homeless residents. In spite of frequent complaints about the aggressiveness of the panhandlers and the occasional fights that break out among them, the 20-block restored historical district along First Ave., Yesler Way, and S. Main St., south of downtown, is one of Seattle's most varied areas.

From the waterfront take the **Waterfront Streetcar** ($.55-.75), walk up Yesler Way from Pier 52, or drive and pay an arm and/or leg to park in a private lot. **Bill Speidel's Underground Tour** is one of the city's most unusual tours. From Doc Maynard's Public House at First Ave. and James St. you roam the Pioneer Square area above and below; a guide provides humorous anecdotes along with local history. The 1½-hour tours leave several times daily; $4.75 adults, $3.50 kids, $3.50 seniors, reservations recommended; phone 682-1511 for schedule, 682-4646 for reservations.

Smith Tower, 42 stories counting the spire, was the tallest building west of the Mississippi when completed in 1914 and remained Seattle's tallest building for several decades. Now dwarfed by neighboring skyscrapers, you can still view Pioneer Square from its observation deck ($1 fee).

The **Klondike Gold Rush National Historic Park,** 117 S. Main St., is Seattle's portion of a two-part national park commemorating the gold rush; the other part is in Skagway, Alaska, and Chilkoot and White passes. Soon it will be part of the **Klondike Gold Rush International Park,** in conjunction with Parks Canada's work along the Yukon River, Whitehorse, and Dawson City. Housed in the 1901 Union Trust Annex, the Seattle portion of the park traces Seattle's role in the 1897 gold rush with films on the event, including Charlie Chaplin's

Gold Rush, exhibits, and gold-panning demonstrations. Open daily, except Christmas, New Year's Day, and Thanksgiving, 9 a.m.-5 p.m., free; tel. 553-7220.

Get a free brochure, here or at the cash register of almost any area merchant, with a map pointing out the historical buildings in the square. Some intriguing shops here include **Iris Fine Crafts,** handcrafted jewelry, pottery, glassware, and gifts at 317 First Ave. S, and **SoundWinds/AirArts,** a colorful windsock showcase at 206 First Ave. South. Art galleries include **Silver Image Gallery,** 318 Occidental S, devoted to photography by masters and contemporary artists, and **Northwest Gallery of Fine Woodworking,** 202 First Ave. S, exhibiting wood sculpture and furniture produced by Northwest artists.

One of the best ways to enjoy the collection of art galleries in Pioneer Square is to join the art crowd for the **First Thursday Gallery Walk.** All galleries hold their openings on the evening of the first Thursday evening of each month.

Seattle Center
From Pier 59, walk up Pike and take a left on Fourth Ave. to get to the **Monorail Terminal.** Ride the monorail ($.60) from downtown Westlake Center to Seattle Center, between Fifth Ave. N, Denny Way, First Ave. N, and Mercer Street. The **Space Needle,** tel. 447-3100, is Seattle's trademark, with two restaurants, observation deck, banquet facility, and gift shops; the elevator ride costs $4.75 ($2.75 kids) if you're not having dinner. The **Pacific Science Center** has a science museum with over 120 hands-on exhibits, the IMAX (Image Maximum) Theater, and a Laserium. Admission is $5 adults, $4 seniors, $2 kids, and includes the IMAX Theater and Laserium shows; tel. 443-2001. The **Center House,** a tri-level shopping and eating emporium, caters to the tourist: 50 shops and restaurants feature international cuisine and Northwest gifts, plus free entertainment year-round. Some restaurants are open for breakfast.

Seattle Center has a lot of options for kids. The **Seattle Children's Museum,** tel. 441-1767, is on the lower floor of the Center House; their hands-on exhibits cater to the under-10 crowd but grown-ups will enjoy them too. Admission is $3, closed Monday. **World Mother Goose,** next door, tel. 441-SNOW, is a nonprofit professional theater company with performances geared toward kids 2½-8. Their regular season runs from May to Oct., but special carnivals and performances fill out the off-season. **Fun Forest,** the Center's amusement park, is open late spring to early autumn.

Seattle Center also contains the **Coliseum,** home of the NBA's Seattle SuperSonics; the **Bagley Wright Theater** where the Seattle Repertory Theater performs; and the **Opera House,** home of the Seattle Opera, Seattle Symphony, and Pacific Northwest Ballet (see "Entertainment," p. 65).

International District
Often called "Chinatown," many people of Filipino, Cambodian, and Vietnamese ancestry live here as well. Start your exploration of

Policemen dressed in 19th-century costumes patrol Pioneer Square.

SEATTLE-KING COUNTY CONVENTION AND VISITOR'S BUREAU

this area with an **International District Tour,** beginning with a 45-minute multimedia show in Nippon Kan Theater, a national historic site at 628 S. Washington Street. The rest of the tour is self-guiding; all roads lead to Hing Hay Park, a Chinese pavilion donated by the city of Taipei. Individuals are fit into scheduled group tours; admission $2, tel. 624-6342 . **Vi Mar Travel,** 803 S. King St., tel. 623-5124, offers Chinatown Discovery Tours for $18.75 (daytime) and $26 (evening), which include a narrated tour plus lunch or dinner; reservations required. For a do-it-yourself tour, the **Wing Luke Memorial Museum** at 414 Eighth St. S is a good starting point; their changing exhibits of Asian folk art are displayed Tues. through Sun. afternoons; admission $1.50 adults, $.50 kids, tel. 623-5124.

King St. is the heart of the district; Chinese shops line both sides. The second-largest Japanese supermarket on the West Coast, **Uwajimaya,** at King and Sixth streets, sells everything from groceries to furniture.

Shilshole Bay And Marina

Located north of the city along Seaview Ave. NW, Shilshole Bay and nearby Ballard were the Nordic section of Seattle when immigration from Norway and Sweden peaked from 1890-1910. By 1900, Nordic immigrants made up one-fourth of Seattle's wood indus-

try work force, and also significantly contributed to mining, farming, fishing, and shipbuilding.

Sivert Sagstad established his Ballard Boat Works in Shilshole Bay four months after his arrival, and built more than 300 wooden boats there and at his newer (1916) location at 20th Ave. NW. Today Shilshole Bay is home to the Shilshole Marina, Seattle's major pleasure boat moorage.

Along Seaview are quality seafood restaurants (see p. 64) with Sound views and outdoor decks. One, the rebuilt Ray's Boathouse, is the departure point for **Major Marine Tours'** saltwater fishing trips. Their 48-foot *Emerald Star* departs at 6 a.m. for Puget Sound fishing holes. You're "guaranteed" to catch good edible fish, or the next trip is on them. The 5½-hour trip costs $42 pp, tel. 292-0595. At the north end of Seaview, **Golden Gardens** is one of the Sound's best bathing beaches.

South of Seaview, on N.W. 54th St., the **Hiram M. Chittenden Government Locks,** tel. 783-7001, connect saltwater Puget Sound with freshwater Lake Washington. The locks are one of Seattle's most heavily visited attractions. Here you can watch the tugs and pleasure craft make the transition between salt and fresh water, and see the salmon return home to spawn via the fish ladder.

The monorail carries passengers from downtown to Seattle Center.

SEATTLE-KING COUNTY CONVENTION AND VISITORS BUREAU

Sailboats are a common sight year-round in Puget Sound.

Watching sailboats skim by may inspire you to take up the sport. **Wind Works Sailing School,** headquartered at Shilshole Bay Marina, has "Learn to Sail" packages starting at $47.50 for a four-hour introductory sail, or $95 for two four-hour lessons, available daily year-round. For a skippered trip, charter a sailing excursion to Elliott Bay, Poulsbo, or Bainbridge Island; $160 for four hours, $300 for eight hours, six-person maximum; tel. 784-9386. Or, board the research vessel *Snow Goose* for one of **Anchor Excursions'** four-hour marine-science cruises on Puget Sound. A scientific expedition, these cruises depart from Fisherman's Terminal, southeast of Chittenden Locks, as demand requires; $15 adults, $10 under 12; tel. 282-8368.

West Seattle
Take Spokane St. to west Seattle where viewpoints, a scenic drive, a beach, parks, and a bike path await. For photography buffs, **Hamilton Viewpoint** at California Way SW provides a panoramic view of Seattle's skyline, the Cascades, and Elliott Bay, as does Belvedere Viewpoint at SW Admiral Way and 36th Ave. SW.

For a leisurely scenic drive, proceed up Harbor Ave. SW to Duwamish Head, then south on Alki Ave. to Alki Beach Park, a long, narrow, sandy stretch—as close to a real beach (out-side Golden Gardens, above) as you'll find on this part of Puget Sound. In warm weather a whole beach culture emerges here: cruising cars, illegally parked cars, bonfires, suntan goop, the works—even though the water rarely gets above 55° F, so only the hardiest souls actually go in. Keep going on Alki Ave. to the **Alki Point Light Station.** tel. 932-5800. Tours of the station are available Mon. through Fri., day's notice required.

Continue south on Beach Dr. SW to **Lincoln Park's** trails and beach. A bike path follows the same scenic route.

Other Parks
Ranked among the world's best, the **Woodland Park Zoo** features a five-acre "African savanna" where zebra, lions, and giraffes roam freely. Their "Nocturnal House" is home to bats and other creatures of the dark. Also included are a tropical forest and gorilla habitat. The big field in the middle, with convenient hot-dog stand, is a good place for a lunch break.

Situated between Phinney and Aurora, N. 50th and N. 59th, the zoo opens daily at 8:30 a.m.; admission $3 adults, $1.50 teens, seniors, and kids; tel. 789-7919.

A three-mile paved bicycle, jogging, and skating loop—watch out for errant skateboards—encompasses **Green Lake** at

DOWNTOWN SEATTLE

DOWNTOWN SEATTLE

1. Le Tastevin
2. Hansen Baking Co.
3. Jake O'Shaughnessy's
4. Bahn Thai
5. Thai Restaurant
6. Monorail Terminal/Westlake Center
7. Space Needle
8. Best Western Executive Inn
9. AAA Auto Club of Washington
10. Tropics Motor Inn
11. Seattle Times Building
12. Myrtle Edwards Park
13. Old Spaghetti Factory
14. Edgewater Inn
15. Two Bells Tavern
16. Best Western Loyal Inn
17. Days Inn Town Center
18. Regency
19. Jazz Alley
20. Sixth Ave. Inn
21. Warwick Hotel
22. Cutters Bay House
23. Kaleenka Russian Cafe
24. Westin Hotel
25. visitor information
26. Vance Downtown Hotel
27. Greyhound Bus Depot
28. Century Square
29. public fishing pier
30. Victoria Clipper to Victoria, B.C.
31. Seattle Aquarium and Omnidome
32. Rainier Square
33. Four Seasons Olympic Hotel
34. YWCA
35. Hotel Seattle
36. Gray Line Water Sightseeing and public fishing pier
37. Seattle Harbor, Alderbrook Sightseeing, and public fishing pier
38. Creative Northwest
39. Major Marine Tours and Ivar's Acres of clams
40. Washington State Ferry Terminal
41. Ye Olde Curiosity Shop
42. Alexis Hotel
43. public library
44. YMCA
45. Metro
46. Comedy Underground
47. Amtrak
48. Frye Art Museum
49. Egyptian Theatre
50. Intiman Theatre Co.
51. House of Hong
52. Nikko
53. F.X. McRory's

Green Lake Way N, across Aurora Ave. N from Woodland Park Zoo. You can sail and swim, or rent a paddleboat. A "children only" fishing pier is at the east end of the lake. Crocodile hunting was popular here in 1986 when assorted reports of a lake creature took on the proportions of a Loch Ness Monster. When the monster was finally caught, the three-pound, 28-inch **caiman** was shipped to a private breeder in Kansas City and the lake was unofficially declared crocodile-free.

All but hidden from view in a ravine under the 15th Ave. NE bridge, **Ravenna Park** has 52 acres of woodlands and a babbling brook, accessible via a three-quarter-mile loop trail, plus a children's play area and soccer field, all in a most unlikely location. Douglas fir, Pacific madrone, western red cedar, big-leaf maple, and English and Pacific yew line the nature trail (borrow a pamphlet from the box at the trailhead). Take I-5 exit 170 (Ravenna Blvd.); turn right at the light, then left on 20th Ave. NE; the street ends at the bridge over the park, and the park entrance is on the right.

North of Shilshole Bay is **Carkeek Park,** NW 110th St., where you'll find a beautiful picnic area, playground, hiking, and Puget Sound access via a footbridge over the railroad tracks. If the tide's in, chances are the beach will be out.

At 34th Ave. W and W. Government Way, the 535-acre **Discovery Park** is the city's largest, featuring a 2.8-mile loop trail through forest and meadow, with access to two miles of Puget Sound beaches, plus the half-mile interpretive Wolf Tree Nature Trail. Discovery Park's West Point is reputedly Seattle's best birding spot, with frequent sightings of loons, grebes, cormorants, terns, and other marine birds.

Army memorabilia lovers should visit the **Fort Lawton Military Museum,** while a fine collection of American Indian art and an all-Indian dinner theater are part of the park's **Daybreak Star Indian Cultural Education Center.** If you happen to be here for this irregularly scheduled event, don't miss the authentic ethnic experience, which includes Indian fry bread, alder-smoked salmon, and dancers from various Indian clans. Tickets are about $20; call 285-4425 for reservations. Discovery Park's Visitor Center is open Tues. through Sun.; tel. 625-4636.

Magnolia Park, perched upon a high bluff, is a great place for views of Puget Sound and the Olympics from Magnolia Blvd. W, while Mt. Rainier, downtown Seattle, and the harbor can all be seen from **Kerry Park** at W. Highland Dr. and Second Ave. W on the south slope of Queen Anne Hill.

At Sixth Ave. and Seneca *over* I-5, aptly named **Freeway Park** has greenery, waterfalls, fountains, and free summertime lunch concerts, just outside the new Convention Center.

Volunteer Park on Capitol Hill (enter from 14th or 15th Ave. E) has 44 acres of lawn, gardens, and a reservoir, as well as a tropical-plant conservatory, a 75-foot water tower (climb its spiral staircase for a great view), and the old Seattle Art Museum (see "Museums" below).

Built on the site of a former gas plant, **Gas Works Park** at N. Northlake Way and Meridian Ave. N is the world's only industrial site conversion park. Amidst a great deal of controversy, architect Richard Haag incorporated much of the original rusting gas equipment into the park's landscaping, including a play barn kids love. Enjoy the views of Seattle and Lake Union.

The **Burke-Gilman Trail,** a 12½-mile bike and pedestrian path, runs from Gas Works to Kenmore's Log Boom Park, following the route of the former Northern Pacific Railroad.

Trees and shrubs from all over the world thrive at the 267-acre **University of Washington Arboretum** on Lake Washington Boulevard. A half-mile trail leads visitors past lodgepole pine, Oregon crabapple, evergreen huckleberry, Pacific dogwood, madrone, and more. The **Waterfront Trail** is a one-mile roundtrip stroll through wooded islands and Union Bay's shores at the north end of the arboretum, passing through the largest remaining wetland in Seattle (duck sightings guaranteed). The trail is level, with numerous benches for resting; get a nature guide at the west end, at the Museum of History and Industry's parking lot (or inside) or at the arboretum visitor center at the east end. At the south end of the arboretum (near Lake Washington Blvd. E) is the **Japanese Garden**—manicured ornamental trees, a secluded lake, and an authentic teahouse, given to Seattle by its sister city, Kobe. Admission is $2 adults, kids/seniors $1; tel. 684-4725.

Jutting into Lake Washington on a forested peninsula is **Seward Park,** on Lake Washington Blvd. S and S. Juneau St., with trails, picnic areas, fishing, swimming, and Mt. Rainier views. A one-mile loop trail takes you past Douglas firs six feet in diameter, madrones, big-leaf maples, and the shores of Lake Washington.

The Floating Bridges

When the **Lake Washington Floating Bridge,** connecting Seattle and Mercer Island, was completed in 1939, it was the first of its kind in the world. Previously, the only connection between the island and mainland had been via ferry; as the ferries grew more crowded, a bridge seemed the logical solution. However, because of the 200-foot depth of the lake and the soft, mucky bottom, a conventional bridge would have been impossible—at least too expensive!—to build.

Using the concrete cell technology developed for WW I barges, the Washington Toll Bridge Authority designed a floating bridge that could withstand 90-mph winds with six-foot waves, while supporting bumper-to-bumper 20-ton trucks. The bridge was supported by 25 floating concrete sections, each 350 feet long, 59 feet wide, and 14 feet high; each concrete pontoon contains 96 watertight 14-foot-square compartments, or cells. The pontoons are cabled together and connected to stationary fixtures at either end.

When seasonal variations cause the lake level to rise or fall (as much as three feet), the pontoons attached to the stationary approaches are flooded or emptied to ensure that the rest of the pontoons maintain their flotation level. The Lake Washington (it's real name is Lacey V. Murrow Floating Bridge, in honor of a prominent civil engineer who also *the Fine Arts building constructed for the 1909 Alaska-Yukon-Pacific Expo*

TACOMA PUBLIC LIBRARY

was the brother of the famed newscaster, Edward R. Murrow) is now part of I-90 traffic. While being refurbished, the original sank during a winter storm in November 1990, and is being replaced while traffic uses the new one. The span is just over 1¼ miles long; the **Evergreen Point Floating Bridge,** connecting Seattle with Bellevue and Kirkland on Route 520, is the world's longest at 1.4 miles.

Museums

The **Seattle Art Museum** opened its new downtown building, at a cost of $62 million, in December 1991. The new building, at 100 University St., has 155,000 square feet of gallery space, a 299-seat auditorium, a 109-seat lecture hall, a gift shop and a café. The former museum building in Volunteer Park at 14th St. E and Prospect will continue to be used as a home for the outstanding Oriental art collection. Open daily till 5 p.m., Thurs. till 9 p.m.; closed Mondays. Admission is $5 adults, $3 students/seniors; tel. 443-4670. Every Tuesday is free.

The city's best museum for local history is the **Museum of History and Industry** at

2161 E. Hamlin Street. Exhibits include one of Boeing's first planes and films and displays of Seattle in the 1880s. Open daily, tel. 324-1125; admission $3 adults, $1.50 kids/seniors. The entire Pacific Northwest, from Petersberg, Alaska, to Eureka, California, has a large Nordic population. Discover the contributions of Seattle's immigrants at rotating exhibits and a small permanent display at the **Nordic Heritage Museum,** 3014 N.W. 67th St., tel. 789-5707. Open daily till 4 p.m., Thurs. till 9 p.m. (closed Mon.); admission $2.50 adults, $1.50 seniors/students, and $1 kids.

The **Museum of Flight,** 9404 E. Marginal Way S, tel. 764-5720, has displays of the history of aviation in the Pacific Rim, including a B-17 and other smaller historic warbirds suspended from its ceiling. It also has one of the best aviation libraries in America. Open daily till 5 p.m., Thurs. till 9 p.m.; admission $5 adults, $3 teens/seniors, $2 kids.

American and European artists of the 19th and 20th centuries are represented in **Frye Museum** at 704 Terry Ave., tel. 622-9250. Open daily till 5 p.m.; free.

University Of Washington

The turn-of-the-century "Expo"—the Alaska-Yukon-Pacific Exposition of 1909—was held on the UW campus. In exchange for use of the grounds, the fair's promoters constructed several permanent buildings and landscaped the grounds, making UW one of the nation's largest and most beautiful single-campus universities. Park your car ($3) and stroll through the grounds: exquisite architecture, fountains, and views of the Evergreen Point Floating Bridge. The Visitor Center is located at 14th Ave. NE and N.E. Campus Parkway.

Here also, the **Henry Art Gallery** exhibits 19th- and 20th-century American and European prints, paintings, and ceramics daily except Mon.; $2 admission, tel. 543-2280. Another campus attraction is the **Thomas Burke Memorial Washington State Museum** with North American Indian artifacts and natural history displays, at 17th Ave. NE and N.E. 45th Street. Open daily; phone 543-5590 for hours. Donations requested.

Other Tours

The **Seattle Times,** Fairview Ave. N and John St., tel. 464-2285, offers free one-hour tours of its press room and news departments on Mon., Tues., and Thurs. from Sept. to May. Reservations required; no kids under nine. Take a free tour of **Rainier Brewery,** tel. 622-2600, weekdays from 1 p.m.-6 p.m. Kids must be accompanied by an adult. Take Airport Way South (exit from I-5).

ACCOMMODATIONS

See charts on pp. 59, 60, and 61 for inexpensive downtown and airport motels plus moderately priced hotels in the heart of Seattle. The "budget" listings include only those places where you won't be afraid to close your eyes at night, and where a family can feel at ease. If you're on a tight budget, stay near the airport rather than in run-down city center hotels; motels with little more than a bed and shower line Pacific Hwy. S near Sea-Tac and Aurora Ave. N, and generally display their rates—often $30 or less—on reader boards. From either area it is a short $.90 Metro bus ride to the city.

Some of the B&Bs below also offer clean, friendly accommodations at budget prices. For lodging in neighboring areas, see the cities listed under "Vicinity of Seattle," p. 73. For camping info, see Renton, p. 75, and Federal Way, p. 104.

Youth Hostel

As every young traveler knows, youth hostels are by far the cheapest places to stay: They offer clean and safe lodging at flophouse prices. **The Seattle International AYH-Hostel** is at 85 Union St., tel. 622-5443, and lodging is $10 a night.

Bed And Breakfasts

B&Bs are popular in the Northwest, and Seattle has its share. In the heart of Pike Place Market at 1923 First Ave., **Pensione Nichols,** tel. 441-7125, is a European-style B&B with views of Puget Sound and the Market.

Eight antique-furnished guest rooms share three baths for a reasonable $50 s, $70 d, including continental breakfast.

The College Inn, 4000 University St. NE, tel. 633-4441, is a budget-priced European-style B&B, with 27 rooms featuring period furnishings, sinks, shared baths, and a deli, pub, and café on the first floor. Rooms are only $36-45 s, $45-51 d, including continental breakfast; children are welcome.

The Williams House, atop Queen Anne Hill at 1505 Fourth Ave. N, tel. 285-0810, is a family B&B—the owners have two kids of their own to make yours feel welcome! Most of their five rooms command city and mountain views (shared and private baths); rates are $65-75 s, $70-85 d. No pets or smoking in the rooms.

At 1727 15th Ave., the stately **Gaslight Inn,** tel. 325-3654, has two rooms with shared bath at $54-60, five rooms with private bath for $64-74, a library, outdoor pool, and continental breakfast.

The Beech Tree Manor, a turn-of-the-century mansion at 1405 Queen Anne Ave. N, tel. 281-7037, sits atop Queen Anne Hill with convenient access to downtown Seattle via trolley. The four-bedroom, three-bath inn features English decor, a period fireplace, and wicker rockers on the shady porch. Rooms are $60-70 s, $65-75 d. Smoking outdoors only; kids over five are welcome.

Chelsea Station, 4915 N. Linden Ave., tel. 547-6077, is directly across from the rose gardens at the south entrance to Woodland Park Zoo, within walking distance of Green Lake. Enjoy a hot tub, endless supply of cookies, all-day coffee and tea, and a library of books to help with your sightseeing. Three guest rooms, each with private bath, are $79 s or d; two spacious suites, also with private bath, offer uncommon comfort for $94. No pets or smoking; kids 12 and over okay.

Chambered Nautilus, 5005 22nd Ave. NE, tel. 522-2536, offers Cascade views on a hill within walking distance of UW and just 10 minutes from downtown. The Georgian colonial home was built in 1915 by Dr. Herbert Gowen, founder of the university's Department of Oriental Studies. Their six rooms

SEATTLE BUDGET LODGING

Name	Address	Phone	Rates	Comments
Best Western Continental Plaza	2500 Aurora Ave. N	284-1900	$44-64 s $50-66 d	restaurant, pool
Best Western Loyal Inn	2301 8th Ave.	682-0200	$44-62 s $48-68 d	Jacuzzi, sauna
Days Inn Town Center	2205 7th Ave.	448-3434	$49 s or d	coffee shop
Marco Polo Motel	4114 Aurora Ave.	633-4090	$28 s $30-34 d	
Rodeside Lodge	12501 Aurora Ave. N	364-7771	$36-50 s $39-55 d	exit 174 N/175 S, exercise room, pool
TraveLodge	200 6th Ave. N	441-7878	$48-54 s $54-70 d	near Space Needle, pool
TraveLodge	2213 8th Ave.	624-6300	$45-54 s $50-66 d	
Tropics Motor Inn	225 Aurora Ave.	728-7666	$36-58 s $38-60 d	indoor pool, restaurant
Vance Downtown Hotel	620 Stewart St.	441-4200	$41-46 s $47-54 d	restaurant
YMCA	909 4th Ave.	382-5000	$25-39 s $31-50 d	men/women, use of facilities
YWCA	1118 5th Ave.	447-4888	$21-26 s $32-37 d	women and kids only

are $60-89 d; two have private baths. No indoor smoking or pets; kids under 12 by prior arrangement.

The Baker Guest Apartments, 700 E. Mercer, tel. 323-5909, is a cluster of three buildings just off Broadway that is within walking distance of most attractions in the area, and a short bus or taxi ride downtown. Several sizes of apartments are available. Studios are $65, one-bedrooms $75, two-bedrooms $100, and a two-bedroom townhouse in the newest building is $105.

The most unusual B&B in Seattle is the "Bunk & Breakfast" **MV Challenger,** 809 Fairview Pl., tel. 340-1201. This is a retired 96-foot oceangoing tug that has been cleaned

up and only slightly redecorated. Tied up permanently at the west end of Lake Union (no, you don't have to worry about it steaming out to meet a ship while you're asleep), it has seven cabins, including the two-room Captain's Cabin with many amenities—private bath, stereo, refrigerator, desks, and a view of the skyline. The cabins range from $50 s to the Captain's Cabin at $110 s or d.

One of the newest B&Bs is the **Capitol Hill Inn,** 1713 Belmont Ave., tel. 323-1955. The four rooms are decorated in authentic Victorian-era furnishings, including hand-screened wallpaper, European antiques and original woodwork. Rates are $65 for shared bath up to $105 for the suite.

SEATTLE MODERATE LODGING

Name	Address	Phone	Rates	Comments
Best Western Executive Inn	200 Taylor Ave. N	448-9444	$63-94 s $70-100 d	near Space Needle, restaurant, bar, shuttle, some rooms Jacuzzi, wet bar
Edgewater Inn	Pier 67 2411 Alaskan Way	624-7000	$70-90 s $85-105 d	higher-priced rooms overlook bay
Inn at the Market	Pike Place Market 86 Pine St.	443-3600	$75-180 s $85-180 d	French country design, most rooms have view, rooftop deck
Hotel Seattle	315 Seneca St.	623-5110	$48-52 s $54-58 d	restaurant
Mayflower Park	405 Olive Way	623-8700	$66-77 s $74-85 d	near shopping, bar, restaurant
Meany Tower	4507 Brooklyn NE	634-2000	$69-79 s $79-93 d	near UW, all rooms have lake/mountain view, bar, restaurant
Quality Inn City Center	2224 8th Ave.	624-6820	$47-57 s $52-62 d	restaurant
Ramada Inn	2140 N. Northgate Ave.	365-0700	$75-80 s $85-90 d	exit 173, pool
Sixth Avenue Inn	2000 6th Ave.	441-8300	$54-61 s $54-61 d	restaurant
West Coast Camlin	1619 9th Ave.	682-0100	$69-72 s or d	luxury for less, restaurant, lounge

Some of the cities surrounding Seattle have less expensive B&Bs; check them out in "Vicinity of Seattle," p. 73.

For a wider selection contact **Pacific Bed and Breakfast,** 701 60th St. NW, tel. 784-0539, a reservation service for more than 200 B&Bs in the Seattle area.

Luxury Accommodations

Sheraton Hotel & Towers, Sixth and Pike, tel. 621-9000, is one of Seattle's finest and largest hotels. The 840 guest rooms were renovated in 1991, and it proves that quality doesn't always decrease with the number of rooms. Rates begin at $145 s, and go up

from there. It has an extensive art collection, including glass by the Northwest master, Dale Chihuly, and a collection of paintings by Mark Tobey, Ken Calahan, and others is in its top-rated restaurant, **Fullers,** named for Dr. Richard Fuller, the late founder of the Seattle Art Museum.

One of Seattle's most popular hotels—the kind of place locals sometimes go for special occasions—is the **Inn at the Market**, First and Pine, tel. 443-3600. This small (65 rooms) hotel is wrapped around a small courtyard and shops, and overlooks Pike Place Market and the waterfront, yet it is soundproofed well enough to avoid much of

LODGING NEAR SEA-TAC AIRPORT

Name	Address	Phone	Rates	Comments
Airporter Inn Motel	14845 Pac. Hwy. S	248-1061	$23 s, 29 d	shuttle
Allstar Inn	16500 Pac. Hwy. S	246-4101	$25 s, 32 d	shuttle
Best Western Airport Executel	20717 Pac. Hwy. S	878-1814	$69-80 s $75-86 d	pool, hot tub, exercise room, bar, restaurant, shuttle
Comfort Inn	19333 Pac. Hwy. S	878-1100	$52-54 s $58-60 d	shuttle, sauna, Jacuzzi
Hilton	17620 Pac. Hwy. S	244-4800	$89-113 s $104-128 d	pool, hot tub, shuttle, restaurant, bar
Holiday Inn	17338 Pac. Hwy. S	248-1000	$72-88 s $82-98 d	pool, bar, restaurant, shuttle
Imperial Inn	17108 Pac. Hwy. S	244-1230	$34 s $37-40 d	shuttle, pool
La Quinta	2824 S. 188th St.	241-5211	$56-61 s $64-69 d	shuttle
Mini-Rate	20620 Pac. Hwy. S	248-2442	$29 s, 35 d	shuttle, car rentals
Motel 6	18900 47th Ave. S	241-1648	$25 s, 31 d	pool
Nendel's	16838 Pac. Hwy. S	248-0901	$42-48 s $48-54 d	shuttle
Nendel's Value Inn	13910 Pac. Hwy. S	244-0810	$39-49 s $44-56 d	pool, hot tub, shuttle exercise room
Quality Inn	3000 S. 176th St.	246-9110	$51-55 s $59-65 d	pool, bar, restaurant, shuttle
Ramada	18118 Pac. Hwy. S	244-6666	$61-95 s $71-105 d	across from airport, indoor pool, bar, restaurant, exercise room
Red Lion	18740 Pac. Hwy. S	246-8600	$100-115 s $100-125 d	2 restaurants, bar, shuttle, pool
Sandstone Inn	19225 Pac. Hwy. S	824-1350	$42 s $44-52 d	shuttle, bar, restaurant
Sea-Tac Crest	18845 Pac. Hwy. S	433-0999	$32 s, 36-48 d	shuttle
Super 8	3100 S. 192nd St.	433-8188	$39 s, 42-46 d	shuttle, laundry
Tac-Sea	17024 Pac. Hwy. S	241-6511	$24 s, 30 d	
West Coast Sea-Tac Hotel	18220 Pac. Hwy. S	246-5535	$54-64 s $58-65 d	sauna, hot tub, pool, shuttle

the noise from the street, market, and waterfront. Rooms are $85-155 s, $95-155 d; suites begin at $175. Two restaurants are on the premises, **Gravity Bar,** from which you can order room-service breakfast, and **Champagne,** a good place for dinner.

The Warwick, Fourth and Lenora, caters to the well-heeled traveler or expense-account utilizer. Their 230 rooms go for $125-145 s, $150-170 d, with suites—living room, panoramic city views, and personal whirlpool—starting at $325. Even the basic rooms include a marble bath with handy bathside telephone, plus a wet bar, refrigerator, balcony, use of the hotel's indoor pool, sauna, whirlpool, and fitness center, and complimentary transportation within downtown Seattle. Their restaurant, the **Liaison,** serves seafood, steak, and chicken accompanied by a relaxing piano concerto. The Warwick's weekend packages start at $100 d and include such goodies as breakfast in bed, gourmet chocolates, and champagne. For information and reservations (ask about half-off weekend specials) call (800) 426-9280 or 625-6700.

For luxurious accommodations with a European flair, try the **Alexis** at First and Madison; tel. (800) 426-7033 or 624-4844. Take your choice of 18 styles of guest rooms, all decorated in subdued, classic colors, from fireplace suites ($275) to courtyard rooms ($145 s, $160 d) to the cheapies ($95 s or d). Every guest receives a bottle of sherry upon arrival, nighttime turndown service, a shoeshine, continental breakfast, morning paper, and use of the steam room. Their restaurant (same name) is about the only Seattle hotel restaurant that draws customers from outside its confines, particularly for its expensive (over $60 for two) seafood.

The **Four Seasons Olympic Hotel,** 411 University St., tel. (800) 828-1188 or 621-1700, opened as the posh Olympic Hotel in 1924, had been sorely neglected for years. Prior to its 1982 reopening, Four Seasons Hotels from Toronto invested $60 million in the renovation of the Italian Renaissance-style hotel where senators and presidents stayed during its earlier era of elegance. Today the hotel still hosts political celebrities in

its silk-wallcovered, $800-a-night Presidential Suite, as well as the proletariat in its $95-160 s, $111-235 d. All guests receive twice-daily maid service, one-hour pressing, shoeshines, evening turndown service, ribbons on their laundered socks, and chocolates on their pillows. The **Georgian,** the hotel's French restaurant, serves breakfast from $5, lunches from $12, and dinners up to $30 à la carte under the original hotel's crystal chandeliers. For dinner reservations, call (800) 828-1188.

The **Westin Hotel,** twin corncobs at 1900 Fifth Ave., tel. (800) 228-3000 or 728-1000, is another of the city's most luxurious hotels. Standard rates for the 865 rooms start at $110 s, $135 d, escalating to $200 d if you'd like a view. The Westin has all the usual: sauna, pool, exercise center with fitness specialists, piano bar, plus three restaurants, **The Palm Court,** *Travel/Holiday* award winner, and replacing that Seattle institution, Trader Vic's, is **Nikko,** a Japanese restaurant that reflects the Japanese ownership of the chain.

The **Holiday Inn Crowne Plaza,** Sixth and Seneca, tel. 464-1980, is among the best in town, though perhaps less elaborate in appearance. Weekday room rates are $125-155 s, $125-175 d; enjoy their quality surroundings, including sauna, hydrotherapy pool, and exercise room, in the heart of downtown for as little as $76 s or d on weekends.

One of the best views any hotel can offer is from the **Sorrento Hotel,** Ninth and Madison, tel. 622-6400. This copy of a castle in Sorrento, Italy, is a tall but small hotel—only 76 rooms, all recently renovated by the new owners to best display the extensive use of mahogany. Rooms go for $140-160 s and d, and suites are $170-190. The acclaimed restaurant, the Hunt Club, is on the ground floor.

Although the **Stouffer Madison,** Sixth and Madison, tel. 583-0300, is popular with tour groups, it still manages to be both intimate and elegant with a small but well-appointed lobby, quiet bar, and well-lit but not too bright hallways. Its 554 rooms have wooden cabinetry, marble counter tops, and soft colors for the walls and carpets. Rates begin at $134 s, $154 d. Suites begin at $154.

*Washington's bounty
in a Seattle
open-air market*

FOOD AND DRINK

Entire books are available on dining in Seattle; the best restaurant guide to Seattle is *Seattle Best Places* published by Sasquatch, the book-publishing arm of *The Weekly*. The same house also publishes *Northwest Best Places,* which has restaurant and lodging reviews for Washington, Oregon, and British Columbia. Another source is (pardon my self-promotion) *The Seattle GuideBook,* by Archie Satterfield, which describes more than 100 of the most reliable, well-established restaurants. What follows here is only a sampling of what's available.

Dinner With A View

So many cityscapes, plus lakes, mountains, and boats are in and around Seattle that view restaurants are commonplace.

Cutter's Bay House, 2001 Western Ave., tel. 448-4884, just up the street from Pike Place Market, has a lively bar with a long list of hors d'oeuvres; their specialties—mako shark, fresh Northwest fish, and regular pasta and steak dishes—are moderately priced ($10-12 average), accompanied by an extensive wine-by-the-glass list and imported beers served at their proper temperatures. Sunsets over the Olympics are striking.

Schwartz Brothers Restaurant and Delicatessen, 1333 Fifth Ave., is a New York-style deli with a full-service restaurant with some tables overlooking the Rainier Square underground shops and others overlooking a quiet courtyard.

Ivar's Acres of Clams, on the waterfront at Pier 54, was folksinger Ivar Haglund's original restaurant (open since 1938). Prior to his restaurateur days, Haglund sang a ballad called "Acres of Clams" telling of the Sound's then-lonely beaches resting atop a wealth of clams. The restaurant is an unpretentious, cavernous place with a take-out bar on the sidewalk.

Maximilian's French restaurant-café in Pike Place Market offers bay and mountain views, open from breakfast to dinner with moderate prices; tel. 682-7270.

Union Square Grill, 621 Union St., tel. 224-4321, is patterned after a French brasserie with big, high-backed booths and specializes in bouillabaisse, grilled steaks and chops, cassoulet and chicken, all served in lavish proportions. Expensive.

Metropolitan Grill, Second and Marion, tel. 624-3287, is one of the best places in town for steak and has been rated by some critics as one of the top 10 in America. It is owned by Consolidated Restaurants, who also owns Union Square Grill, and the decor is almost identical. Seafoods and pastas are also on the menu. Expensive.

Shilshole Bay And Marina

A number of restaurants on Shilshole Bay are worthy of mention, if not for their seafood then at least for their spectacular sunsets. As you drive from the locks toward the marina and Golden Gardens (see p. 52) restaurants are all on the west, or water, side.

Hiram's at the Locks, 5300 34th Ave. NW, tel. 784-1733, has an industrial look to it and has been, perhaps undeservedly, maligned by some Seattle restaurant critics in the past; it serves steak and seafood that is properly prepared and simply delicious ($15-20), plus a popular Sunday brunch. Besides, it's fun to watch the Chittenden Locks in action.

A few blocks away, **Ray's Boathouse,** 6049 Seaview Ave. W, tel. 789-3770, came back better than ever after a fire destroyed the restaurant in 1987. The large place has a slightly nautical design with wooden floors and beams like an old boat shed, and it is a bit expensive, but the seafood is great, and so is the view—reservations are a must.

Anthony's Homeport, 6135 Seaview Ave. W, tel. 783- 0780, is just up the road with moderately priced fresh fish and a saucy cioppino; Sunday brunch, too.

Lake Union

Ivar's Salmon House, on Lake Union at 401 N.E. Northlake Way, tel. 632-0767, is famous for its alder-smoked salmon but also offers prime rib and barbecued chicken in a cedar facsimile of an Indian longhouse.

Franco's Hidden Harbor, 1500 Westlake Ave. N, tel. 282-0501, has a mellow water-level view of Lake Union through a forest of boat masts and rigging. The Champagne Sunday brunch is outstanding.

Liz's, across the street from Franco's at 1515 Westlake Ave. N, serves homemade soups, sandwiches, chili, and some of the best burgers in town, for lunch or dinner daily.

Lake Union Café, 3119 Eastlake Ave. E., tel. 323-8855, hangs out over Lake Union with walls of glass for views across the urban lake. It has free live comedy with its seafood and pasta dinners Thurs. through Sun. nights.

Triple's, 1200 Westlake N, tel. 284-2535, specializes in seafood with a varying menu ranging from Hawaiian *kiawe*-grilled fish to Norwegian salmon to sushi.

Latitude 47, 1232 Westlake Ave. N, 284-1047, serves fresh salmon and 40 other seafood items on the shores of Lake Union; open for lunch and dinner plus Sunday brunch.

Seattle Center

The Center House, a former armory that was reborn as a shopping and fast-food mall for Century 21, is lined on two levels with fast-food restaurants serving everything from Mexican food to apple strudel, and tables are scattered around the large open area.

The **Space Needle Restaurant,** tel. 443-2100, is a top-of-the-world dining experience at 600 feet, very popular with tourists, visiting relatives, and teens on prom night. As much as it seems a tired cliché, the food is good and the view is unsurpassed, as the revolving restaurant completes a 360-degree turn by the time you get to dessert. Summer Sunday Champagne brunches are a moderately priced way to see the daytime views unfold. The **Emerald Suite,** tel. 443-2150, also on the Space Needle but at a lower level, is a little dressier and more expensive.

Foreign Flavors

As you might guess, the International District is laden with Oriental restaurants. Among the best is **House of Hong,** 409 Eighth Ave. S, with seafood, chicken, and Hong Kong barbecue. For Japanese cuisine, the district has **Mikado,** home of one of the city's best sushi bars at 514 S. Jackson and well-known for fresh fish. **Nikko,** 1306 S. King, tel. 322-4905, is best known for its sushi bar, accompanied by a moderately priced Japanese menu. For Thai cuisine try the **Thai Restaurant** near the Seattle Center at 101 N. John St., tel. 285-9000, or **Bahn Thai,** 409 Roy St., tel. 283-0444; both are inexpensive and popular with the locals.

European taste buds can feel at home in Seattle too. For French cuisine, **Le Tastevin** at 19 W. Harrison St., tel. 283-0991, is considered by many to be the best, though pricey; also noteworthy is **Le Gourmand,** fairly expensive, at 425 N.W. Market St. in

Ballard, tel. 784-3463, and certainly **Crepe de Paris,** Rainier Square, 1333 Fifth Ave., tel. 623-4111, which was one of the first French restaurants in Seattle.

You can have a pricey Italian feast at Pioneer Square at **Umberto's,** 100 S. King St., tel. 621-0575; it's a little on the expensive side, but worth it. Nearby is the equally fine **Boccalino,** One Yesler Way, tel. 622-7688. **Paparazzi,** 2202 45th St. N, tel. 547-7772, has more moderately priced Italian meals. Try **Labuznik** (Czech for "Lover of Good Food") at 1924 First Ave., tel. 441-8899, for a high-priced Czechoslovakian dinner, or **Kaleenka Russian Café,** a homey, lace-curtained change of pace at 1933 First Ave., tel. 728-1278.

Others
Café Sport, 2020 Western Ave. at the north end of Pike Place Market, tel. 443-6000, is one of the most popular spots in town, serving lunch to the exercise nuts next door and dinner to people who love good food, with an emphasis on Northwest specialties; breakfast is a treat of omelettes and waffles; moderate prices.

At 100 Mercer, **Jake O'Shaughnessy's,** tel. 285-1897, has good steak, fresh seafood, and giant stuffed potatoes big enough to share for moderate prices, plus a noisy Irish bar that warrants a visit.

Join the crowds—the very noisy crowds—for oysters, steak, or just a beer at **F.X. McRory's** before and after Kingdome events; it's across the street from the Kingdome's parking lot at 4199 Occidental Ave. S, tel. 623-4800. Open weekdays for lunch, daily for dinner.

Noggins at Westlake Center brews its own beer and serves big burgers and sandwiches, English pub style; pick up your order at the counter.

The two **Thirteen Coins** are Seattle's classiest 24-hour restaurants. Here you will see the famous, infamous, and people like yourself. They offer more than 100 menu items in two locations: 125 Boren Ave. N, tel. 682-2513, in downtown Seattle, or 18000 Pacific Hwy. S, tel. 243-9500, near Sea-Tac Airport.

For those on tight budgets, or simply those who like waitresses to call them "dear," **The Dog House,** 2230 Seventh Ave., is another 24-hour restaurant, and it has probably the best-value eats in town, along with a rowdy bunch at the piano bar.

The Old Spaghetti Factory, across from Pier 70 at 2801 Elliott Ave., tel. 441-7724, is always noisy, good, and inexpensive—a popular family spot—with a pasta-only menu that stays under $10.

For a quick burger or sandwich try the **Two Bells Tavern,** a small, artsy bar at 2313 Fourth Avenue. **Olympia Pizza and Spaghetti House,** 1500 Queen Anne Ave., tel. 285-5550, or 1330 45th Ave. N, tel. 633-3655, serves some of the city's best pizza, plus pasta and subs. When the chains lose their charm, try **Puerco Lloron,** 1501 Western Ave. on the Pike Place Market Hillclimb, tel. 624-0541. "The Crying Pig" is inexpensive, a good place to take the kids, and the food is fresh, genuine Mexican fare. **Toreador,** 47 Fourth Ave. NW, tel. 784-4132, is another popular, inexpensive Mexican spot.

ENTERTAINMENT AND EVENTS

Nightlife
The best guide to Seattle's current goings-on is *The Weekly,* a $.75 weekly news magazine with concert information, club dates, restaurant reviews, movie, lecture, sports, dance, and theater listings—everything a visitor needs. *The Weekly* is available at stores or in paper boxes throughout the city. The *Seattle Times* and *Seattle Post-Intelligencer* also have weekly entertainment sections in their Friday editions, and the old standby that out-of-towners find in their hotel rooms is *Bill Speidel's Seattle Guide,* which has hundreds of inches of listings.

New wave may come and go, but jazz lives on in Seattle, particularly at **Dimitriou's Jazz Alley,** Sixth and Lenora, tel. 441-9729, where big-time national acts and up-and-coming talent can be heard. No cover charge—food and drink prices make up the difference. The **New Orleans Creole Restaurant,** 81 Yesler Way, tel. 622-2563, besides having popular Creole food, serves up Dixieland jazz on Mon. nights with varying performances on weekends. **Chicago's,** 315 First Ave. N., tel. 282-7791, has a variety of jazz groups.

For a taste of salsa music try **La Esquina** at 5000 Rainier South. The **Old Ballard Firehouse,** 5429 Russell Ave., serves up reggae, jazz, blues, and more, often from top-name artists.

Seattle's biggest comedy club is **Comedy Underground,** 222 S. Main St., tel. 628-0303, where local and national talents perform for capacity crowds. **Giggles,** another comedy club at 5220 Roosevelt Way NE, tel. 526-5653, has cheap food and beer with local, smaller-time acts. **Seattle Improv Comedy Club,** 1426 First Ave., tel. 628-5000, has well-known and beginning comics.

For a bar with a view, check out the view restaurants listed above at Shilshole Bay, the waterfront, Lake Union, and of course, the Space Needle (where, if you're not having dinner, you have to pay $4.75 to ride in the elevator). In addition, the **Cloud Room** atop the Camlin Hotel at 1619 Ninth Ave. has great cityscape and Lake Union views. The **Adriatica,** 1107 Dexter Ave. N, offers a view of Lake Union and the Cascades. More casual drinking can be enjoyed on **Red Robin's** outdoor deck overlooking Portage Bay at the corner of Eastlake east and Fuhrman St. E; their extensive list of gourmet hamburgers is a plus. The sunset view draws the crowds to **Ray's Boathouse,** 609 Seaview Ave. NW at Shilshole Bay. The best view of Seattle's skyline is from **Salty's,** 1936 Harbor SW, tel. 937-600, a large seafood restaurant on the water's edge in West Seattle.

The bars at **Jake O'Shaughnessy's,** 100 Mercer, and **F.X. McRory's,** across from the Kingdome at 4199 Occidental Ave. S, are at least as popular as the restaurants themselves. For 24-hour food (diner price and quality) plus a rowdy piano bar, try **The Dog House** at 2230 Seventh Avenue.

Pub Tours

Groups of six or more can enjoy an escorted tour of three or four Seattle pubs and alehouses, complete with van transportation, free beer samples and snacks, and souvenirs. Tours average 3½ hours and can be scheduled for the afternoon or evening; $24 pp. Call Towerbridge Marketing, tel. 547-1186, for schedule and information.

Sports

Major league sports are thoroughly represented in Seattle. The American League's **Mariners,** who didn't have a winning season until 1991, play at the Kingdome under the constant threat of extinction by being moved to a better market. At this writing the team is for sale for something in the neighborhood of $100 million, which helps explain why a plastic cup of beer costs $4 at the concession stand. Call 628-3555 for tickets, the schedule and the team's whereabouts.

The National Football League's **Seahawks,** tel. 827-9766, draw capacity crowds at the Kingdome, as do the National Basketball Association's **Supersonics** at the Seattle Center Coliseum; tel. 281-5850. Seahawks tickets are scarce—most are sold to season-ticket holders—but the Sonics are generally not sold out until the day of the game.

The Seattle **Thunderbirds,** tel. 728-9124, play minor-league hockey at the Seattle Center Arena for the Western Hockey League from Oct. to May. College sports are big here too, particularly the University of Washington's Husky football (tel. 543-2200) and basketball (tel. 543-2200) teams. That also applies to the women's basketball team because they have been edging into national prominence and the University of Washington recently hired a woman sports director.

Another big Seattle-area sporting event nearly year-round is auto and motorcycle racing at **Seattle International Raceway,** 31001 144th in Kent, tel. 631-1550.

The Arts

Nobody is quite sure why—maybe it really is the weather—but live theater has always done well in Seattle. Consequently, if you don't see a good movie, you have a wide choice of plays and musicals to try. **Seattle Repertory Theatre** produces six plays from

The **Seattle Youth Symphony**, tel. 362-2300, which will make you wish you'd practiced more, also plays in the Opera House, and the **Pacific Northwest Ballet**, from Oct. to May, produces the traditional *Nutcracker* for Christmas with sets by Maurice Sendak; tel. 628-0888. **Ladies Musical Club** is a Seattle institution that brings soloists to Meany Hall on the UW campus, and sometimes the Fifth Avenue Theater for four concerts a year.

Movies

Seattle has earned an international reputation among filmmakers as having one of the most discriminating audiences in America. Nobody quite knows why live theater and movies are taken so seriously, but movies are sometimes tested on Seattleites before being released, and Seattle viewers have often made a little-known film a winner.

For rainy-day moviegoing, **Cinerama** at 2100 Fourth Ave., tel. 443-0808, and **UA Cinema 150** at Sixth and Blanchard, tel. 728-1622, offer first-run movies in a standard movie-house atmosphere, as do the cinemas at Northgate and Southcenter malls. The **Egyptian Theatre** at 801 E. Pine, tel. 323-4978, and **Market Theatre** at 1428 Post Alley, tel. 382-1171, are both part of the annual **Seattle International Film Festival** held in May; they show off-the-beaten-track films the remainder of the year.

Festivals And Events

Chinese New Year is celebrated in late January or early February when the International District comes alive with parades and colorful displays; call 623-8171 for info. **Fat Tuesday** is Seattle's week-long Mardi Gras celebration at Pioneer Square in February with jazz and Cajun music, a Spam-carving contest ("works" from the contest are placed in the Spam Museum, or that's what they say), arts and crafts, and a parade.

In May the celebrations get serious and one of the first is the **University Street Fair,** which brings more than 400 artists to display their wares on University Way NE on the third weekend in May. More than 5,000 musicians

Oct. through May in the Bagley Wright Theater at Seattle Center, tel. 443-2222. **ACT** (A Contemporary Theatre) fills out the other half of the year, performing at 100 W. Roy; tel. 285-5110. **Pioneer Square Theater's** Mainstage, a former burlesque joint at 512 Second Ave., and two smaller stages host local and national dramas and comedies, including Seattle's longest-running production, *Angry Housewives,* which ran strong for more than five years; phone 622-2016 for tickets. The **Intiman Theatre Company** brings classic theater to Seattle from June through Nov. at Seattle Center's Intiman Playhouse, tel. 626-0782.

Seattle Center Opera House hosts the **Seattle Opera Association,** whose Sept. to May regular season is almost always a sell-out, even though the special July performance of *Ring of the Nibelungen* in German has been dropped from the regular schedule.

The Opera House is also home to the **Seattle Symphony** from Oct. through April, tel. 443-4747. The symphony has been getting more and more international attention under the leadership of conductor Gerard Schwartz, a leading proponent of modern American composers and promoter of the Mostly Mozart series.

(Nigerian, Chinese, Appalachian, Indonesian, and bluegrass, among others), dancers, and craftspeople display their talents while enormous amounts of food are consumed at the **Northwest Folklife Festival** held at Seattle Center on Memorial Day weekend; tel. 684-7300. Also in May, the **Pike Place Market Festival** has free entertainment on three stages, strolling clowns and musicians and a kids' area; tel. 587-0351.

In June the **Pioneer Square Fire Festival** celebrates Seattle's great fire of 1889 (any excuse for a party, right?) with free activities in the park, a parade of classic fire-fighting equipment, contests, and free entertainment; tel. 682-4648. Also in June, the **Dixieland Jazz Festival** is held at four sites in West Seattle; tel. 932-4044. The Fremont District is one of Seattle's more funky neighborhoods (here you'll see the city's most popular piece of artwork: a life-size group of commuters and a dog "Waiting For The Interurban" by Richard Beyer), and each June the district holds a street fair with booths, live music, ethnic food and drink, and assorted street performers and residents of the lunatic fringe.

July begins with twin fireworks displays, one on Lake Union sponsored by Fratelli Ice Cream, and the other on Elliott Bay, sponsored by Ivar's seafood restaurant chain. Shortly afterward, the **Lake Union Wooden Boat Festival** is held at the south end of the lake, where you'll see some of the most beautiful boats on Puget Sound. In mid-July the **Bite of Seattle** is held in the Seattle Center, which gives restaurants, wineries, micro-breweries, and coffee-makers an opportunity to show their products; tel. 232-2982. Later in the month more than 1,500 runners participate in the **Emerald City Marathon**, tel. 285-4847. **The Chinatown International District Festival** is held in mid-month to celebrate the district's diversity. Pacific island dancers, Thai musicians and dancers, dragon dancers from China, Talko drummers, and others perform in Hing Hay Park, Maynard Ave. S and S. King St.; tel. 725-1842.

Seattle's biggest fair of the year, **Seafair**, tel. 623-7100, is a three-week-long extravaganza of crafts, parades, triathlons, and ethnic festivals, culminating in the unlimited hydroplane races on Lake Washington in early August. New restrictions on alcohol consumption have made the infamous rowdy, beer-guzzling hydroplane crowds a thing of the past. Labor Day weekend arts festival, brings writers, performing artists, and craft people together at Seattle Center, tel. 684-7200. In early August the **Pacific Northwest African-American Festival** celebrates black heritage with a parade, arts and crafts, and music; tel. 224-2511. One of the more unusual events in August is the **Bubble Festival** held in the Pacific Science Center where professional bubble blowers show how to blow square bubbles and how to freeze them; tel. 443-2001. **Bumbershoot,** Seattle's Labor Day weekend extravaganza, brings together writers, poets, musicians, artists, and food booths for the last big party of the summer.

The last festival of the year is the **Christmas Ships Parade,** a lighted flotilla that cruises Lake Washington in mid-Dec.; the Visitors and Convention Bureau, tel. 447-7273, has route and viewing information.

SHOPPING

Unlike most other cities around the Sound, Seattle's downtown shopping district has not died out under the pressure of surrounding suburban malls. In fact, downtown shopping is more alive than ever, with the addition of **Westlake Center** at Fifth Ave. and Pine St. and **Century Square** at Fourth Ave. and Pike Street. Top-shelf jewelry, perfume, art, leather goods, and clothing stores abound in these two small centers.

The giants still do well downtown: **Nordstrom** at Fifth between Pike and Pine, and **Frederick and Nelson** at Fifth and Pine (although its future is uncertain and Seattleites who are accustomed to Frederick's Frango mints are sighing); **The Bon Marché** at Fourth and Pine and **I. Magnin** at Sixth and Pine. Another downtown shopping center, this one underground, is **Rainier Square** be-

Shoppers are drawn to Pike Place Market and stores along the hillclimb.

DIANNE BOULERICE LYONS

tween Fourth and Fifth Ave. and Union St., with small shops, including the **Lynn McAllister Gallery,** with a fine collection of Northwest paintings, prints, art glass, and sculptures. On Fifth near University, **Wild Wings** specializes in wildlife and Western art, with limited edition prints by Bateman, Parker, Maass, and more, plus duck stamp prints and woodcarvings.

The **waterfront** and, up the hillclimb, **Pike Place Market** are loaded with tiny wine shops, boutiques, craft stores, plus the big, obvious produce stands and tourist traps; see pages 47 and 49 for a detailed description of these areas. **Pioneer Square** offers some of the city's finest galleries, antiques, and book and clothing stores; see p. 50. The **Elliott Bay Book Company,** 101 S. Main St., tel. 624-6600, is something of a local legend, with both a good selection and wonderful atmosphere, plus café and monthly readings. **University Bookstore,** across from UW at 4326 University Way NE, is reputedly the nation's largest bookstore, carrying an impressive array of books plus office supplies, clothing, cameras, records, and more. **The Hansen Baking Co.** at the foot of Queen Anne Hill, 100 Mercer St., houses shops and restaurants in a block of renovated early 20th-century buildings.

Shopping malls abound in the Seattle area, the biggest being the **Northgate Shopping Mall** seven miles north of Seattle (exit 173 from I-5), the **Southcenter Mall,** down I-5 into Tukwila, and **Bellevue Square** (see "Vicinity of Seattle" below).

Photographers can stock up on supplies or have their film processed at **Cameras West,** 1908 Fourth Ave., tel. 622-0066. Other services include in-shop camera repairs and quantity film discounts; open daily, free parking.

You'll find one of the widest selections of Northwest wines at, believe it or not, **Safeway** grocery stores. The prices are low and you can pick up your cheese and crackers at the same time. Shop at the one nearest you: 530 Broadway E (closest to downtown), 3020 45th Ave. NE in the University district, 516 First Ave. W in the Queen Anne section, and 3920 Stone Way N in the Wallingford area. If your tastes run closer to Europe, try the tiny brick **Esquin Wine Merchants** shop at 1516 First Ave. S, tel. 682-7374; big on Italian wines, they also carry Northwest varieties and offer tastings, classes, and low prices. **Pike and Western Wine Merchants** at the Pike Place Market has groceries, Northwest wines, a Northwest wine expert, and European selections.

SERVICES

For information on Seattle attractions and events, plus maps or other assistance contact the **Seattle-King County Convention and Visitors Bureau,** 666 Stewart St., Seattle, WA 98101, tel. 461-5840. Statewide information is available toll-free by calling (800) 541-WASH (out-of-state) or (800) 562-4570 (statewide).

If you're a member, the **AAA Travel Store** at 330 Sixth Ave. N is a good source of maps and area information plus travel guidebooks, luggage, and other travel-related accessories. You might find the information you need for free at the main branch of the **Seattle Public Library,** 1000 Fourth Ave.; tel. 625-4952.

For an automobile emergency, call **AAA** (again, if you're a member) at 292-5353. For mountain pass conditions, call the State Department of Transportation at 1-976-7623 (for $.35) from Nov. to March or in the Seattle area, **AAA's** free number, tel. 448-8611.

Exchange foreign currency at **First Interstate Bank,** 1215 Fourth Ave., tel. 292-3111; **Rainier Bank,** 1301 Fifth Ave., tel. 621-4111; **Westin Hotel,** Fifth and Westlake, tel. 624-7400; **Four Seasons Olympic Hotel,** 411 University St., tel. 621-1700.

TRANSPORTATION

Arriving By Air

Flying in, you arrive at **Sea-Tac Airport,** midway between Seattle and Tacoma. If you've got a touch-tone phone handy, call (800) 544-1965 or 431-4444 for updates on airport parking, weather and traffic conditions, ground transportation schedules and rates, and other airport services. **Gray Line Airport Express** has airport pick-up service to and from nine downtown hotels about every half hour; $7 one way adults, $5.50 one way kids, tel. 626-6088. **Shuttle Express,** tel. (800) 942-0711 or 286-4800, has door-to-door limo-van service from Sea-Tac to downtown Seattle ($14 and up), Everett, and Tacoma. **Metro's** buses #174 and #194 run between Sea-Tac and downtown Seattle about every half-hour; one-way fare is $.85 off-peak, $1 peak; tel. 447-4800. **Suburban Airporter,** tel. 455-2353, runs from north to Everett and along the east side (Bellevue, Kirkland, Issaquah, etc.) and Sea-Tac for $15 and up.

To do it the easy way, grab a cab on the airport's second level; they recently went through an image change, cleaned up the cabs (and in some cases, themselves), and

now all are required to charge the same rates—$17.50-24, depending on destination and number of passengers, one way to Seattle.

Arriving By Train

Amtrak serves Seattle at its King St. station (3rd Ave. S and S. King St.); tel. 464-1930 or (800) USA-RAIL. The *Coast Starlight* has daily service connecting Seattle with Tacoma, Portland, and south to San Francisco and L.A.; the *Pioneer* connects Seattle with Salt Lake City (also daily); and the *Mount Rainier* connects Seattle and Portland.

Getting Around By Bus

Metro buses run from 6 a.m. to 1 a.m. every day, about every 30 minutes on the city routes. The Metro customer-assistance office is at Second and Marion; get a handy one- or three-day pass. If you ride outside the "Magic Carpet" area—a free zone extending from the waterfront to Sixth Ave. and from S. Jackson to Battery—fares are $.75 off-peak, $1 peak within the city, $1 off-peak, or $1.50 peak outside city limits. Call 447-4800 (24 hours) or (800) 542-7876 for info.

Trailways, tel. 728-5955, provides daily service to Vancouver, B.C., via Everett and Anacortes, and loop service north through Whidbey Island to Anacortes, Everett, and back three times a week.

Greyhound, the bigger carrier, serves Vancouver, B.C., to the north; Portland, San Francisco, Los Angeles, and San Diego to the south; Port Angeles to the west; and eastern Washington from their terminal at Ninth and Stewart; tel. 624-3456. A new service is offered by **Greyhound Lines of Canada,** between Seattle and Vancouver. Four daily departures from each city provide four-hour service with on-board movies and snack service. Fare is $21.75 each way with children under 11 paying 50% and seniors getting a 10% discount.

Getting Around By Car

Driving around downtown Seattle is much more difficult than walking, and almost as

The newest ferry service between Seattle and Victoria, B.C., includes SeaCat catamarans.

ARCHIE SATTERFIELD

expensive as flying to Portland, because at some point you've got to park the car.

Diamond and U-Park lots are scattered throughout the city; rates rise with the desirability of the area; $4 for up to two hours near the waterfront, but they generally have empty spaces. Be sure and pay because if you don't your car will be chained to 55-gallon barrels filled with concrete until the fee has been paid. (Locals still talk about the time a car was seen roaring down I-405 with a parking-lot barrel lashed to the bumper; or maybe it is an urban folk tale.)

The cheaper metered spaces are taken the moment they're surrendered, but if you're fortunate enough to get one, remember to put in money—the meter readers are fleet of foot and the fines are climbing. By all means avoid the 3-6 p.m. weekday rush hour, when I-5 and the floating bridges are often virtual parking lots. One of the more difficult aspects of Seattle city driving isn't getting there, but getting back: finding an I-5 entrance ramp can be frustrating, especially after you zig-zag over and under the highway a few times. One sure cure: head down Fifth Ave. because signs for both north and south entrances are along it.

Air Tours

To see the city from about 1,500 feet, try one of **Chrysler Air's** 20-minute scenic float-plane rides over Seattle; only $27.50 pp, two-person minimum. Longer flights are available to Mt. St. Helens, Mt. Rainier, or the San Juan Islands for $130 per hour for one to three people and $155 per hour for four to five people. Flights take off and land at Lake Union seven days a week, year-round; reservations are recommended but not required, tel. 329-9638.

Bus Tours

Gray Line, tel. 623-4252 or (800) 426-7532, offers a number of Puget Sound tours. Discover Seattle with a 2½-hour tour highlighted by the Ballard Locks, Kingdome, UW, and waterfront for $17 adults, $9 kids 5-12; operates year-round. A six-hour city tour, offered March through Nov., includes the Space Needle, UW, International District, and Chittenden Locks for $27 adults, $14 kids. A six-hour land and water excursion runs April through Oct. for $34 adults, $17 kids. Gray Line has several other sightseeing trips, including one-day tours to Victoria, B.C., Blake Island, the San

Juans, Mt. Rainier, and Everett's Boeing 747/767 plant, plus three-day tours combining several Puget Sound attractions (see below for harbor and Blake Island tours).

Don and Diane FunTours offers scheduled one-day tours throughout western Washington, including a cruise aboard the *Goodtime III* in December's Christmas Ships Parade on Lake Washington for $42. Write them at Box 21007, Seattle, WA 98111 for a current brochure, or call 282-3508.

Harbor Tours

A number of boat tours and ferry services depart from Seattle's waterfront, providing a relaxing, scenic change of pace for the foot-weary traveler. Probably the most popular is offered by **Seattle Harbor Tours;** their one-hour informative tour of Elliott Bay and the waterfront describes the hows and whys of containerized shipping along with historical background. The tours depart at least three times daily from Pier 55 starting in April (weekends only), with daily service from May through Oct.; $8.50 for adults, $6 kids, tel. 623-1445. No reservations necessary.

Gray Line Water Sightseeing operates from April through Oct., taking you to Elliott Bay from Lake Union via the Lake Washington ship canal and Government Locks. Their three-hour narrated tour costs $17 adults, $9 kids. Reservations are required, tel. 626-5208.

Departing hourly from Pier 54, **Major Marine Tours** offers one-hour narrated tours of Elliott Bay, complete with barbecued chicken at no extra charge. Tours run from June to mid-Sept. on one of Seattle's premier nightclubs, the *Emerald Sea*. Enjoy a fully licensed bar, appetizers, and dancing on this two-hour cruise (mid-June to mid-Sept.); fares are $7.50 (must be over 21). Major Marine Tours also offers 1½-hour dinner cruises, with live music and a grilled chicken dinner. For information, phone 292-0595.

Tillicum Village Tour

For a full-day trip including dinner, try Gray Line's **Tillicum Village Excursion** to Blake Island, a state park accessible only by boat. Enjoy a salmon bake, interpretive Indian dances, craft displays, nature trails, and Indian artifacts. Departing from the Seattle waterfront, the 5½-hour tour is available daily from May through mid-Oct.; fares are $35 adults, $24 kids 2-12. Reservations required, tel. 443-1244.

Victoria Cruises

For a day-long excursion to Canada, take the **Victoria Clipper** from Pier 63 to Ogden Point in Victoria. Reservations are required for the 2½-hour cruise; tel. 448-5000 or (800) 888-2535. The round-trip cruise can be completed in one day (8:30 a.m. departure and 9:30 p.m. return) while allowing a generous stay in Olde English Victoria. Roundtrip fares are $69 mid-May to mid-Sept., $55 off-season.

Hood Canal Cruise

Another day-long adventure is the **Alderbrook Sightseeing Cruise,** departing from Pier 56 at 9 a.m. and arriving at the Alderbrook Inn Resort on the Olympic Peninsula at noon. The cruise takes you into Hood Canal, past the Trident nuclear submarine base, and beneath the Hood Canal floating bridge. Have lunch at the Alderbrook and return to Seattle at 6 p.m., or stay on at the resort. The cruises run from May to Oct. on most Sun., Tues., and Thurs. mornings; roundtrip fares are $30 adults, $25 seniors, and $20 kids under 12; tel. 623-1445.

Getting Around By Ferry

Washington State Ferries depart from Pier 52 for Winslow and Bremerton, giving you an inexpensive harbor tour. To either destination, car-and-driver fares are $6.65 one way; passengers and walk-ons pay only $3.30 roundtrip. The Fauntleroy ferry dock in west Seattle serves Southworth on the Kitsap Peninsula every 30-50 minutes for the same rates as the Seattle runs above; also, a 15-minute Fauntleroy-Vashon Island crossing costs $4.50 one-way car and driver, and runs about every 30-40 minutes.

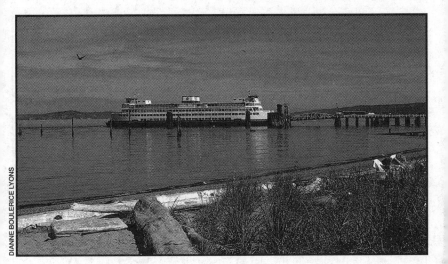

VICINITY OF SEATTLE

MERCER ISLAND

Mercer Island is primarily an upper-middle-class Seattle suburb, connected to the city only at its north end by I-90's floating bridge. It has been a regional leader in preserving its rural environment and accomplished this in part by putting a freeze on new-home construction and severely limiting both the size of its commercial district and the height of buildings.

Luther Burbank Park at 2040 84th Ave. SE is the island's best waterfront park, with a beach, hiking trails, picnic area, and fishing in Lake Washington.

Start here for a 15-mile loop bike tour of the island: first go east on N. Mercer Way, then south on E. Mercer Way to the island's southern tip, then back up north on W. Mercer Way. At S.E. 68th St. and Island Crest Way, **Pioneer Park** has equestrian and hiking trails in a natural, wild setting (no rest rooms), including a three-quarter-mile interpretive nature trail.

A good escape from the noise and fast pace of Seattle is a quiet night at **Mercer Island Hideaway,** 8820 S.E. 63rd, tel. 232-1092, in a wooded area at the south end of the island adjacent to Pioneer Park. Facilities include a music room with two grand pianos, reed organ, and harpsichord, plus a full breakfast. The rates beat most of Seattle's downtown hotels: $40 s, $55-65 d, with a two-night minimum; no smoking.

If you prefer the anonymity of a chain motel, **Mercer Island Travelodge,** 7645 Sunset Hwy., tel. 232-8000, is small (35 rooms) and has a hot tub, fax available and coffee in the rooms; $39 s, $48 d.

Getting There
The only way to drive to Mercer Island is by taking I-90 over the Mercer Island (Lacey V. Murrow) Floating Bridge; see p. 99, for insight into the bridge's history and construction.

Metro has regular service to the island; tel. 447-4800.

BELLEVUE AND MERCER ISLAND

1. Mercer Island Hideaway
2. Bellevue B&B
3. Fountain Court Off Main
4. Marian's
5. TraveLodge
6. Red Lion
7. Hilton
8. Holiday Inn
9. library
10. Bellevue Chamber of Commerce
11. Best Western Greenwood
12. Overlake Memorial Hospital
13. C.I. Shenanigan's
14. Thai Kitchen
15. Days Inn
16. Petersen B&B
17. Residence Inn

© MOON PUBLICATIONS, INC.

RENTON/TUKWILA

The **Renton Historical Museum** at 235 Mill Ave. S, tel. 255-2330, has a number of exhibits, among them pioneer furniture, antique vehicles, and Indian and mining artifacts.

Accommodations

As always, **Motel 6,** 20651 Military Rd. at I-5 exit 51, tel. 824-9902, features the least expensive area lodging: their 124 rooms go for $34 s, $36 d, with pool and Jacuzzi. **Traveler's Inn,** just off I-405 at 44th (7710 Lake Washington Blvd.), tel. 228-2858, also offers convenient budget lodging from $32 s, $34-36 d. Near Longacres at 3700 E. Valley Rd., tel. 251-9591, **Nendel's Valu Inn** has 130 rooms from $42-56 s, $44-61 d, with a hot tub, airport shuttle, and adjacent restaurant and lounge. At 15901 W. Valley Rd., tel. 226-1812 or (800) 547-0106, **Nendel's Inn** has 147 rooms from $78-86 s, $86-92 d, with a heated pool, hot tub, exercise room, airport shuttle, restaurant, and lounge. For about the same money, you can stay at the **Sheraton Renton Inn,** just off I-405 at 800 Rainier Ave. S, tel. 226-7700 or (800) 325-3535. Rooms start at $68-76 s, $70-80 d, and include a heated pool, dining room, lounge with entertainment, and airport shuttle. At the Southcenter Mall, the **Doubletree Inn,** tel. 246-8220, has an indoor pool, playground, shuttle, restaurant, and lounge with entertainment, not to mention 200 rooms starting at $72-84 s, $78-90 d.

Campers and RVers will enjoy the amenities at **Aqua Barn Ranch,** 15227 Renton-Maple Valley Hwy., tel. 255-4618. The 200 RV and tent sites (starting at $13.50) come with an indoor pool, horse rentals, a big-screen TV, and movies. **Riverbend Park,** 17410 Maple Valley, tel. 255-2613, has 42 adults-only tent sites on 12 acres from $15. Both campgrounds are open year-round.

Food, Shopping, And Services

You don't have to kiss off the diet because you're on vacation; **Andy's Tukwila Station** has approved "Diet Center" meals, as well as

steaks, seafood, chicken, sandwiches, and salads, served in restored railroad cars at 2408 W. Valley Hwy.; open for three meals. Stop by **T.C. Colby's Restaurant and Bar,** 200 S.W. 43rd at E. Valley Rd. near Longacres, for a post-race brew.

Rainier Ave. is the city's commercial strip, lined with fast- and slow-food restaurants, shopping centers, a smattering of motels, and some of the most obnoxious new car salesmen this side of the Cascades. For consistently good steak and seafood, visit **Stuart Anderson's Black Angus Restaurant** just off Rainier near the airport at 95 Airport Way, tel. 226-9600. Mexican food fanciers will appreciate this member of the **Mazatlan** chain at 540 Rainier. The major shopping center here is **Renton Center,** with Sears, JCPenney, and other shops; also on Rainier are K mart, Pay Less Drug Store, and grocery stores.

Southcenter, at the Southcenter exit off I-5, is one of the largest shopping malls in the area with major department stores that include the Bon Marché, Nordstrom, and JCPenney. Several smaller shopping plazas and fast-food restaurants surround it, including **The Pavilion,** an off-price mall one mile south of Southcenter.

For medical emergencies, dial 911 or phone **Valley Medical Center,** 400 S. 43rd, tel. 228-3450 for the main switchboard or tel. 251-5185 for 24-hour emergency room service.

Getting There

From Seattle, take I-90 across Mercer Island, or go south on I-5, then take I-405 north to Renton. The city has daily **Metro** service to Seattle and throughout King County; tel. 447-4800.

ISSAQUAH

At the foot of the "Issaquah Alps," Issaquah (pop. 6,000) offers an escape to country-fresh air in a small town loaded with history, without sacrificing modern shopping centers and restaurants. Just two exits east of Renton on I-90, Issaquah's hills are within a half-

LAKE SAMMAMISH S.P.

TO VASA PARK RESORT

NW SAMMAMISH RD.

90

NEWPORT WAY

E. LAKE SAMMAMISH PKWY. SE

ISSAQUAH-PINE LAKE RD.

ISSAQUAH-FALL CITY RD.

TO PINE LAKE

ISSAQUAH

NW GILMAN BLVD.

SE NEWPORT WAY

900

RENTON-ISSAQUAH RD.

RAINIER BLVD.

NE GILMAN BLVD.

TO SNOQUALMIE VALLEY HOSPITAL

90

W. SUNSET WAY

E. SUNSET WAY

WILDWOOD BLVD.

2 AVE SE

FRONT ST.

ISSAQUAH-HOBART RD.

0   0.5mi
0   0.5km

MOON

SQUAK MTN. S.P. NATURAL AREA

© MOON PUBLICATIONS, INC.

1. Waterworks Park
2. Motel 6
3. Holiday Inn
4. Meadow's S.C.
5. Heritage Square
6. Safeway/Pay 'N' Save
7. Harry O's
8. Gilman Station
9. La Costa
10. St. George's Square
11. Gilman Village
12. Originally Ellens
13. chamber of commerce
14. Issaquah Gallery
15. Boehm's Chocolates
16. Village Theatre
17. Odd Fellows Hall
18. Mandarin Garden
19. railroad depot
20. Grand Hotel
21. Issaquah Historical Society Museum
22. Greyhound
23. mine shaft and bulkhead
24. The Wildflower B&B

hour drive of Seattle and Tacoma. These are very old, worn-down mountains; their lower elevation keeps them mostly snow-free—and hikeable—virtually year-round.

Historical Tour

Issaquah was in its glory during its coal-mining and lumbering days around the turn of the century. Several buildings from this period are still in use; remains from the mine are also evident. Go down Newport Way to Park Blvd. and turn right onto Wildwood for a look at the original miners' homes, preserved and still occupied; at the end of the block, a depression in the ground near a grove marks the entrance to the mine's first shaft; to the right is the concrete bulkhead, used to anchor the mine's hauling machinery.

Downtown, a number of historically significant buildings face Front Street. **Odd Fellows Hall** is the oldest, built in 1888; the second-oldest commercial building is the **Grand Central Hotel**, dating from 1903; today it houses offices and apartments. Adjacent to the railroad tracks on Sunset Way, the old **Railroad Depot** was built in 1889 (the year Washington became a state), out of Washington Territory timber—note the "W.T." symbol. The depot is currently undergoing restoration for its 100th birthday. For more information on Issaquah's historical sights, follow the visitor information signs to the chamber of commerce at 160 Gilman Blvd. NW, tel. 392-7024, or stop by the **Issaquah Historical Society Museum** at 165 S.E. Andrews, tel. 392-3500, for a self-guiding tour map.

Museum

Railroad tools, a pioneer kitchen, and grocery store, artifacts, and photographs are on display at the **Issaquah Historical Society Museum** at 165 S.E. Andrews, tel. 392-3500, open weekend afternoons and by appointment.

Parks

A mile and a half northwest of Issaquah, **Lake Sammamish State Park** is one of the more popular Puget Sound area day-use parks. Swimming, waterskiing, and boating

on the enormous lake combined with a large picnic area and concession stand attract summertime crowds—and traffic jams at the boat launch. Though there's no camping at the park, you can stay at one of 16 tent sites and five trailer hookup sites at **Vasa Park Resort,** on the west side of Lake Sammamish at 3560 W. Lake Sammamish Rd., tel. 746-3260; rates start at $10.

Owners of smaller motorboats, canoes, and rafts may prefer **Pine Lake,** a county park off 228th SE with a five-mph speed limit on the lake.

Accommodations

Enjoy a stay in a two-story log home surrounded by evergreens at **The Wildflower Inn,** a B&B at 25237 S.E. Issaquah-Fall City Rd., tel. 392-1196, two miles from I-90. Four large rooms, furnished with antiques and quilts, are $40 s, $45 d (no single rate June through Aug.); some have a private bath. No smoking, pets, or kids under 12.

Standard, inexpensive motel rooms are available at **Motel 6,** 1885 15th Pl. NW at I-90 exit 15, tel. 392-8405, for $24 s, $30 d; pool, small pets OK. More luxurious accommodations are available at the **Issaquah Holiday Inn,** 1801 12th Ave. NW (I-90 exit 15), tel. 392-6421 or 1-800-HOLIDAY. Amenities include a salmon-shaped outdoor pool, sauna, hot tub, and **Annie's Garden Restaurant;** rooms are $59-62 d.

Food

Although Issaquah has numerous restaurants serving everything from fast food to high-class fare, the best known of Issaquah's eating establishments is probably **Originally Ellen's,** 305 N.W. Gilman Blvd., tel. 392-1209. Renowned for gourmet hamburgers, Ellen's serves breakfast on weekends plus lunch and dinner daily; lunch is about $4-6 and dinner is generally under $10. **Cooper's Roost,** 120 N.W. Gilman Blvd., tel. 392-5550, is a new and welcome addition to town. Owned by Mick McHugh (of F.X. McRory and Jake O'Shaughnessey fame), Cooper's Roost has an extensive seafood menu plus open-hearth-roasted chicken, lamb, prime rib, and more, all at moderate prices. Reservations are a good idea. **Harry O's,** one of Issaquah's most elegant, has moderately priced lunches and dinners plus Sunday brunch at 719 N.W. Gilman Blvd., tel. 392-8614. The **Mandarin Garden,** 40 E. Sunset Way, was voted the best Chinese restaurant around Puget Sound by the *Seattle P.I.* in 1984. Closed Mon.; call 392-9476 for takeout. For Mexican food try LaCosta, 240 N.W. Gilman Blvd. at Gilman Station, open daily for lunch and dinner. Gilman Blvd. is also lined on both sides with fast-food restaurants and smaller bakeries, sub, and coffee shops at the numerous shopping centers.

Theater
From September to May the semiprofessional **Village Theatre** stages five musical performances at 120 N. Front St., tel. 392-2202 (or call Ticket Master at 628-0888), in their original building that dates from 1914. Performances are held Wednesday through Sunday and tickets cost $12-14 ($3 discount for seniors and under 18).

Festival
Every fall, salmon return to their birthplace at the state salmon hatchery, and Issaquah doesn't miss the opportunity for a celebration. The two-day **Salmon Days Festival** is held the first weekend in October with a parade, children's carnival, salmon bake, arts and crafts displays, live music, hatchery tours, a Village Theatre performance, and 5- and 10-km runs; tel. 392-0661.

Hiking
The **Issaquah Alps Trails Club,** a local organization, organizes hikes every Sat. and Sun. plus twice during the week, all year, to points of interest along 200 miles of trails in the surrounding "Issaquah Alps"—a range older than the Cascades that includes Tiger, Cougar, and Squak mountains. No membership or previous registration is necessary; just meet the group at the south end of the Issaquah Park and Ride lot on Hwy. 900 and join a carpool to the trailhead. Call 328-0480 for 24-hour information. To receive their quarterly newsletters send $5 to Box 351, Issaquah, WA 98027.

The county's largest park, **Cougar Mountain Regional Park,** encompasses most of this 1,595-foot peak and surrounding forest. Well-marked trails go past an old mining camp and waterfalls. **East Tiger Mountain** is the highest peak in the range (3,004 feet), and the hike up East Side Rd. to the summit provides spectacular views. To get to the trailhead, take I-90 exit 25; go right onto Hwy. 18 and drive three miles to a dirt road on the right; proceed to the powerline and park. Start your 6.9-mile hike on the uphill road under the powerline. For more hikes, described in precise detail, see *Guide to Trails of Tiger Mountain* by William K. Longwell Jr., published by the Issaquah Alps Trails Club.

Horseback Riding
Even with no prior experience, riding a horse along wooded trails can be a relaxing, enjoyable way to view the scenery. **Tiger Mountain Outfitters,** 132nd Ave., tel. 392-5090, offers guided three-hour trips three times a day in Tiger Mountain State Forest; their ride to Poo Poo Point, a departure point for hang gliders, is $35 and is open to anyone over 10, though experienced riders under 10 are welcome. **Kelly Ranch,** 7212 Renton-Issaquah Rd., tel. 392-6979, has guided trips to the top of Cougar Mountain for $25 and other tours around the base of Squak Mountain for $10 an hour.

Water Park
Take exit 15 off I-90 to **Waterworks Park** for over a mile of waterslides on 22 runs including "The Black Hole," a 140-foot run in total darkness; other features include a picnic area, refreshments, gift shop, and video arcade. The park operates from mid-June to early Sept.; admission $11 adults, $8 kids, tel. 392-8127.

Shopping
Boehm's Chocolates at 255 N.E. Gilman Blvd. offers candy factory tours by appointment, tel. 392-6652, but the front counter is all you really need to see; you'll spend more than you planned.

Old Bellevue

EAST KING COUNTY CONVENTION BUREAU

Designed to trap the tourist dollar, **Gilman Village** at exit 17 off I-90 is a collection of early-1900s' Issaquah homes, all moved and restored to form a quaint collection of small shops. Restaurants and fudge shops, clothing and craft stores, gift and kitchenware boutiques, and jewelers abound; open daily. **St. George's Square**, 355 N.W. Gilman Blvd., has a bakery, gift shops, and clothing stores.

In historical downtown Issaquah, the **Issaquah Gallery** has paintings, photography, stained glass, pottery, and prints by Northwest artists at 49 N. Front St., tel. 392-4247.

Services

The Issaquah area code is 206. For maps and information contact the **Issaquah Chamber of Commerce**, 160 N.W. Gilman Blvd., tel. 392-7024. For groceries, drugs, film, and the like, the shopping center at 12th and Gilman Blvd. has a Safeway, Pay 'N' Save, Ernst, and more. Across the street at Heritage Square you'll find a liquor store, pizza place, and **Salvino Sports**, tel. 392-8440, a sporting goods store with camping, fishing, and hunting equipment, bait, ammunition, and hunting and fishing licenses.

Call 911 for medical, fire, or police emergencies. **Snoqualmie Valley Hospital**, 1505 S.E. Meadowbrook Way in Snoqualmie, tel. 888-1438, has 24-hour emergency room service.

Transportation

To get to Issaquah from Seattle or Renton, take I-90 to Lake Sammamish State Park (exit 15) or exits 17 or 18 to get downtown. From Tacoma and points south, take I-5 to I-405 to eastbound Hwy 900. Issaquah has no city transit system, but you can get to and from Seattle, North Bend, Redmond, and other points in King County via **Metro**, tel. 447-4800. To connect to virtually anywhere in the country, take **Greyhound** from 55 Sunset Way, tel. 392-7142.

BELLEVUE

Across Lake Washington, Bellevue has grown from a Seattle suburb to Washington's fourth-largest city and home of expanding high-tech industries. Bellevue is often accused of attracting people concerned about living in the "right" neighborhood, driving the "right" automobile, sending their children to the "right" schools—in other words, Bellevue is considered, by people who don't live there, the Southern California of Puget Sound.

It *is* upscale even though the homes are often no nicer than many other Seattle suburbs. But you can add about $40,000 to the price for the pleasure of saying that you live in Bellevue.

Sights

Paul Thomas Winery, 1717 136th Pl. NE, tel. 747-1008, is open Fri. and Sat., noon-5 p.m. for tours and tastings; open Mon.-Thurs. for sales only. Stop in and taste his award-winning chenin blanc, chardonnay, or

A ROSE BY ANY OTHER NAME . . .

An early visitor to the Washington Territory in 1874 was a journalist named Charles Nordoff. During his travels he found the land beautiful—but the place-names had to go.

On your way to Olympia by rail you cross a river called Skookum-Chuck; your train stops at places named Newaukum, Tumwater, and Toutle; and if you seek further, you will hear of whole counties labeled Wahkiakum, or Snohomish, or Kitsap, or Klikatat; and Cowlitz, Hookium, and Nenolelops greet and offend you. They complain in Olympia that Washington Territory gets but little immigration; but what wonder? What man, having the whole American continent to chose from, would willingly date his letters from the county of Snohomish, or bring up his children in the city of Nenolelops? The village of Tumwater is, as I am ready to bear witness, very pretty indeed; but surely an emigrant would think twice before he established himself either there or at Toutle. Seattle is sufficiently barbarous; Steilacoom is no better; and I suspect that the Northern Pacific Railroad terminus has been fixed at Tacoma—if it is fixed there—because that is one of the few places on Puget Sound whose name does not inspire horror and disgust.

pear and rhubarb wines. **Vernell's Fine Candies,** 11959 Northup Way, tel. 455-8400, offers guided tours of their candy factory for groups of four or more.

The **Bellevue Art Museum,** tel. 454-3322, in the third-floor atrium of Bellevue Square (see "Shopping" below), has ancient and modern art exhibits, including work by Northwest artists; open daily except Mon., admission $2 adults. See celebrity international artwork and openings at **Universal Fine Art,** 2032 148th St., tel. 454-2484.

Parks
Chism Beach off 100th St. SE has swimming, trails, and picnic areas on the shores of Lake Washington. **Bellefields Nature Park,** along the Mercer Slough at 118th St. SE, has 48 acres of marshland and trails in the city's center, outlined by a one-mile loop trail around its perimeter. At 128th St. SE is **Kelsey Creek Park,** Bellevue's largest; a Japanese garden, one-mile loop trail, children's zoo, and 1888 pioneer log cabin add to your picnicking pleasure. Bellevue's newest park, **Lake Hills Greenbelt,** off 156th St. SE, offers a 1½-mile paved trail through wetlands and pines in the heart of the city. Open to joggers, cyclists, wheelchairs, and hikers, the first section of trail was developed in 1986; now the greenbelt trail links Larsen and Phantom lakes.

Accommodations
In spite of its reputation for being upscale, Bellevue has some of the most reasonably priced B&Bs in the Puget Sound region.

Bellevue Bed and Breakfast, 830 100th St. SE, tel. 453-1048, offers a homey atmosphere, kitchen and laundry privileges, gourmet coffee, and city and mountain views for a reasonable $50 s, $55 d. No pets, smoking, or kids under 10.

Petersen Bed and Breakfast, 10228 Eighth St. SE, tel. 454-9334, welcomes kids in their modern home that is five minutes from Bellevue Square. A home-style breakfast and use of the hot tub on the deck are included in their low rates of $40 s, $45 d (eighth night free). No smoking.

Days Inn, 3241 156th St. SE, tel. 643-6644, has 108 rooms complete with marble baths, balconies, and queen-size beds for a budget price: $44-49 s, $49-54 d. The **Bellevue TravelLodge** is another inexpensive motel (with a pool) at 11011 Eighth St. NE, tel. 454-4967; the 55 rooms start at $45 s, $45-60 d.

Prices jump up from there, as the major chains cater more to business travelers than tourists. The **Holiday Inn,** 11211 Main, tel.

455-5240, has 182 rooms from $85 s, $95 d, plus a heated pool, restaurant, and some balconies. The **Best Western Greenwood Hotel,** 625 116th St. NE, tel. 455-9444, has an outdoor pool, two restaurants, and 176 rooms from $76 s, $84 d. The **Bellevue Hilton,** 100 112th St. NE, tel. 455-3330, has an indoor pool, hot tub, sauna, three restaurants and lounges, and 184 rooms for $86 s, $96 d.

For a bit more luxury, stay at either of the two Red Lion hotels. The **Red Lion Hotel Bellevue** at 300 112th St. SE is just off I-405 exit 12 (northbound) or 13 (southbound), tel. 455-1300. The 355 rooms start at a mere $118 s or d, climbing to $109 and up for the executive level; amenities include a heated pool, restaurant, and lounge with entertainment. Just down the street is the **Red Lion Bellevue Center,** 818 112th St. NE, tel. 455-1515, the first of the two, built with 209 recently remodeled rooms, indoor pool, two restaurants, and lower weekend and corporate rates.

Toward the top of the scale is **Hyatt Regency at Bellevue Place,** Eighth St. NE and Bellevue Way, tel. 462-1234. It is one of the tallest (24 stories) buildings in Bellevue and has 382 well-appointed rooms. It is part of the small shopping center, Bellevue Place, and is only a few blocks from the enormous Bel-Square Mall.

Enjoy a home away from home at the **Residence Inn,** 14455 29th Pl. NE (148th Ave. NE exit off Hwy. 520), tel. 882-1222. One- and two-bedroom suites go for $124 and $144 s and d, and $169 for the penthouse suites. This includes a heated pool, whirlpools, sport court, and airport shuttle.

Food And Drink

At 10733 Northup Way, **Bravo Ristorante,** tel. 827-8585, has received "Best Italian" awards from three local media. Enjoy Italian cuisine, fresh seafood, and gourmet pizza, plus piano bar music on weekends; open daily for dinner, weekdays for lunch. The **Atrium,** a multistory open area with lots of skylights and plants in the Red Lion Hotel, 300 112th Ave. SE, tel. 455-1300, is one of the more pleasant lunch places. **The Thai**

Kitchen, 14115 20th St. NE, tel. 641-9166, has Thai vegetarian, chicken, and seafood dishes, prepared from mild to hot according to your specifications. For a more formal dinner, but with moderate prices, try **Eques** in the Hyatt Regency Hotel, Eighth St. NE and Bellevue Way. It is billed as serving Northwest cuisine, meaning seafoods, fresh vegetables and berries, and other dishes, such as duck and veal.

Entertainment And Events

For your listening pleasure, the city boasts the **Bellevue** Philharmonic Orchestra, with classical and pop concerts performed at Westminster Chapel, 13646 24th St. NE, tel. 455-4171. The **Eastside Theater Company** performs at Bellevue Community College, 300 Landerholm Circle, tel. 641-2415.

The Bellevue Art Museum sponsors the annual **Pacific Northwest Arts and Crafts Fair,** held in Bellevue Square the last weekend of July. It is one of the state's largest such fairs, and many artists' careers have been helped along by the juried show and the enormous crowds. As a climatological aside, it is an oddity of history that rain has never fallen on the fair, and it has been going for decades. As a result, some locals always plan picnics for that weekend.

Hear Northwest jazz at three days of outdoor concerts during the **Bellevue Jazz Festival,** held the third weekend in July at Bellevue Central Park, tel. 451-4106.

Shopping And Services

At Eighth St. NE and Bellevue Way NE, **Bellevue Square** is one of the Northwest's largest shopping malls—more than 200 stores (including Nordstrom, The Bon, Frederick & Nelson, and JCPenney) and 16 restaurants, plus the Bellevue Art Museum in the third-floor atrium (one of the few cities of that size to have its art museum in a shopping mall), and glass-enclosed elevators for added panache.

For a glimpse into Bellevue's past, visit the shops and galleries in **Old Bellevue's** restored business district on Main St. between 100th and Bellevue Way.

For additonal information on Bellevue and the surrounding area, contact the East King County Convention and Visitors Bureau, 515 116th Ave. NE, Ste. 111, Bellevue, WA 98004, tel. 455-1926, or stop by the **Bellevue Public Library** at 11501 Main, tel. 455-6889. For a medical emergency, dial 911 or **Overlake Hospital Medical Center**, 1035 116th NE, tel. 454-4011 for the switchboard or 462-5200 for the 24-hour emergency room.

Transportation

To get to Bellevue by car, take either the floating bridge (Hwy. 520 or I-90) from Seattle; from Sea-Tac, take I-5 to I-405 through Renton to Bellevue. **Metro,** tel. 447-4800, has several buses serving Bellevue from Seattle. **Suburban Airporter,** tel. 455-2353, serves the east side from Sea-Tac for $14-20.

REDMOND

Redmond, like neighboring Bothell and Woodinville, began as a boat landing along the Sammamish Slough, the slow-moving stream that links Lake Washington and Lake Sammamish. Foot travel in pioneer days was virtually impossible due to the dense forests and extensive marshland so most inland travel was accomplished via river. Today the city is the self-proclaimed bicycle capital of the world, holding regular bicycle races at its Velodrome in Marymoor Park.

Parks

Marymoor Park on the West Lake Sammamish Pkwy. has 486 acres of open space on Seattle banker James Clise's 1904 estate. The mansion is now **Marymoor Museum,** tel. 882-6401, featuring exhibits of local history; open Tues. through Thurs. and Sun., free. Marymoor Park is better known for its **Velodrome,** a 400-meter bike-racing track that draws competitors from across the United States. Bike races are held Fri. and Sat. evenings from May to Sept.; admission is $3, tel. 882-0706. The park also features a 2¼-mile loop trail through woods and marshes with a Lake Sammamish view.

From Marymoor Park, bike or hike the paved 10-mile **Sammamish River Trail** to Bothell following the route of the Sammamish River. Sixty-eight-acre **Farrel-McWhirter Park,** 10400 192nd Ave. NE, has horse and hiking trails, picnicking, and a barnyard zoo. Charlotte's Trail is a paved path that extends the length of the park, ideal for disabled visitors.

Practicalities

The **Silver Cloud Motel,** 15304 N.E. 21st St., tel. 746-8200, has 59 rooms with queen-size beds, free laundry room, and airport pick-up service for $34-38 s, $38-44 d. The **Redmond Motor Inn** at the intersection of Hwy. 520 and Redmond Way, tel. 883-4900, has 137 rooms starting at $54 s, $56-60 d, plus a seasonal pool, Jacuzzi, and adjacent pancake restaurant.

Lisa's, 8412 164th Ave. NE, tel. 881-3250, features a moderately priced, varied (and variable) menu with a Southern accent. Open weekdays for breakfast and lunch, Wed. through Sat. for dinner.

The **Antique Connection,** 16701 Cleveland St., tel. 882-3122, has 65 antique dealers under one roof. For more antiques, try **Days Gone Bye Antique Mall** on the lower level of the Ethan-Allen Bldg., 2207 N.E. Bel-Red Road.

From Seattle, take Hwy. 520 to Hwy. 920 to Redmond or hop aboard **Metro,** tel. 447-4800.

WOODINVILLE

Woodinville, far enough away from Seattle to have its own identity, is a small (but rapidly growing), self-contained, unincorporated town.

Wineries

Woodinville is home to the state's largest winery, **Chateau Ste. Michelle,** off Hwy. 202 at 14111 N.E. 145th St., tel. 488-1133. Though the wine grapes are grown in eastern Washington (the vineyards here are experimental), the winery is among the nicest to visit: the original 1912 residence (once

NORTHEAST KING COUNTY

SNOHOMISH COUNTY
KING COUNTY

BOTHELL

522

405

KENMORE

LOGBOOM
PARK

BOTHELL WAY

BEAR CREEK INN

FRENCH CREEK CELLARS

WOODINVILLE

NE 170 ST

JUANITA DR

SAINT
EDWARDS
S.P.

100 AVE. NE

140 AVE. NE

SAMMAMISH RIVER

COLUMBIA
WINERY

STE
MICHELLE
WINERY

WOODINVILLE-REDMOND RD.

NE 124 ST.

NE 142 AVE.

JUANITA BEACH
PARK

SHUMWAY
MANSION

JUANITA BAY

KIRKLAND

202

REDMOND

AVONDALE WY.

TO
FARREL-McWHIRTER
PARK

WILLOW RD.

SAMMAMISH RIVER TRAIL

405

LAKE WASHINGTON

908

REDMOND RD.

520

MARYMOOR
PARK

BRIDLE
TRAILS
STATE
PARK

LAKE
SAMMAMISH

0   1 mi

0   1 km

1. Teo's Mia Roma
2. Gerard's Relais de Lyon
3. Bothell Landing
4. Above-it-all
5. Evergreen General
   Hospital
6. Silver Cloud Motel
7. Totem Lake Mall
8. Best Western Arnold's
9. Peter Kirk Building
10. Covey Run/Kirkland
    Roaster & Ale House
11. Old Heritage Place
12. Marina Park
13. TGI Friday's
14. Woodmark Hotel
15. library
16. Anthony's Home Port
17. Marymoor Museum
18. Velodrome
19. Redmond Motor Inn

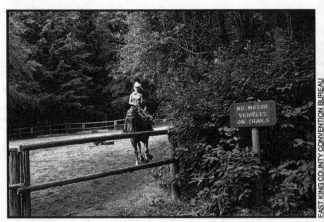

Bridle Trails State Park

owned by Seattle lumber baron Fred Stimson) is surrounded by manicured grounds, an arboretum, trout ponds, and features a full summer season of music and arts events in the amphitheater. Informative cellar tours and tastings are offered daily 10 a.m.-4:30 p.m. Enjoy a basket lunch and a bottle of chardonnay in the picnic area.

Columbia Winery, tel. 488-2776, one of the state's oldest, is across the street from Ste. Michelle—the first castle on the left—on N.E. 145th Street. Columbia has been in the varietal wine business since 1962, producing award-winning chardonnay, riesling, cabernet sauvignon, semillon, and more, now available in 40 states. The tasting room is open daily, 10 a.m.-5 p.m.

French Creek Cellars, 17221 132nd Ave. NE, tel. 623-WINE, is the newest member of the Woodinville wine family, having recently moved here from Redmond. French Creek started as an amateur wine-making group in 1973 and has since achieved international acclaim for its premium wines, which include chardonnay, riesling, cabernet sauvignon, pinot noir, and the less common lemberger and ice wines. The tasting room and gift shop are open daily between noon and 5 p.m.

Outdoor Recreation

For a bit of fresh Woodinville air try the **Tolt Pipeline Trail,** a 10½-mile hiking and horse trail that passes through town just around the corner from Ste. Michelle as it extends from Norway Hill in south Bothell to Snoqualmie Valley near Duvall. The paved **Sammamish River Trail** passes through on the other side of Ste. Michelle on its way north to Bothell and south to Redmond for a 10-mile total.

For *a lot* of fresh air take a balloon trip with **Lighter Than Air Adventures,** 21808 N.E. 175th St., tel. 788-2454. Prices begin at $125 pp for flights that give you great views of the Cascades, Puget Sound, Seattle, and surrounding countryside; includes Champagne brunch.

Accommodations

Bear Creek Inn, 19520 N.E. 144th Pl., tel. 881-2978, features river-rock fireplaces, patios, fluffy comforters, hot tub, and a sunken tiled bathtub (shared by two guest rooms) surrounded by an acre of lawn and firs. Rooms are $58; no smoking, no pets (black lab in residence).

Food

Woodinville has a wide variety of dining experiences. **Le Courtyard** offers nouvelle cuisine in a French country inn atmosphere at 17705 140th Ave. NE, tel. 483-1088. The hunting lodge surroundings will gear you up for **Newman's** (13120 N.E. 177th Pl., tel. 485-9372) menu: wild boar, antelope, bison, elk, quail, caribou, and more; pasta dishes for those who aren't "game." Open for dinner only. The **Creekside Restaurant,** upstairs at the same address, has American food—steak, chicken, seafood—in the $9-12 range; tel. 485-0721. At **Armadillo Barbecue,** 13109 N.E. 175th St., tel. 481-1417, you may not find armadillo, but you will find real Texas-style BBQ ribs, chicken, baked beans, and more, plus wine and beer; open for lunch and dinner daily. Feast on Mexican food at **Las Margaritas,** 13400 N.E. 175th, tel. 483-5656. For diner-style food along with some gourmet surprises, try **Granni's Woodinville Inn** at 175th and 132nd; standard burgers and sandwiches are accompanied by French onion soup, crab quiche, and chocolate amaretto mousse. Breakfast is in the $3-4 range; lunches cost $4-6.

Shopping And Services
Molbak's, a nursery at 13625 N.E. 175th, is much larger than it looks—more than 2,000 varieties of indoor and outdoor plants, garden tools, trees, bulbs, and conservatory/aviary fill for numerous greenhouses—and is as popular with browsers as serious gardeners; an espresso bar and gift shop add to the fun. Open daily.

Visit **Hollywood Schoolhouse,** Hwy. 202 and 120th Pl. NE (head east from Ste. Michelle), for a novel shopping experience. You'll find antiques, arts and crafts shops, and galleries in this old-time country school. At the same intersection (across the street), Emerald City Antiques, tel. 485-5555, features 150 shops with over 12,000 square feet of antiques, collectibles, jewelry, prints, glassware, and more. Open daily 10 a.m.-6 p.m.

Pennsylvania Woodworks, 17601 140th Ave. NE, tel. 486-9541, sells furniture, quilts, woven rugs, wooden toys, and more handmade by Amish craftspeople.

The recently constructed **Towne Center** plaza on 175th has a grocery store, pharmacy, liquor store, fast food, and cleaners; across the street there's another grocery store (Albertson's), Payless Drugstore, and Urgent Care Medical Center for any medical problems (for a real emergency, dial 911).

Transportation
Metro has daily service to Seattle and environs from Woodinville. To drive to Woodinville from Seattle, either cross the lake and head north on I-405, turning east on Hwy. 522; or, take I-5 north from Seattle to Hwy. 522 through Bothell.

BOTHELL

Bothell was founded in 1884 by David Bothell and his family. Apparently without competition, they logged the area, built a hotel, platted the town, and sold lots to pioneers who wanted to get away from the bustle of the city. Northeast of Lake Washington on the Sammamish River, Bothell is a small town about a half hour from Seattle, with one small distinguishing characteristic: **Bothell Landing,** 18120 N.E. Bothell Way, where a park, small shopping complex, and the **Bothell Historical Museum** mark the original steamboat berth. The museum, housed in the 1893 William Hannan house, is open Sun. afternoons from March to mid-December. You can pick up the **Sammamish River Trail** (see "Redmond," p. 82) here by crossing the footbridge behind the museum. **Country Village,** between Bothell Landing and I-405 at 23714 Bothell Hwy. SE, has 30 antique, food, jewelry, clothing, and gift shops open Tues. through Sun. until 4 p.m.

Lodging And Food
Open year-round, **Seattle North RV Park,** 22910 15th Ave. SE, tel. 486-1245, has 227 tent and RV sites on 30 acres. Other than that, there's not much here for accommodations; try Kirkland, Lynnwood, or Edmonds.

One of Bothell's big surprises is **Gerard's Relais de Lyon,** a rather expensive French restaurant in an elegant house at 17121 N.E. Bothell Way, tel. 485-7600; open for dinner only, daily except Monday. Other European tastes can be satisfied at **Teo's Mia Roma,** an Italian restaurant at 7614 N.E. Bothell Way in Kenmore, just west of Bothell. Open for dinner only; tel. 486-6200 or 485-9545.

Transportation

To get to Bothell from Seattle, take Hwy. 520 across Lake Washington to Bellevue, then connect to I-405 north; or, take Hwy. 522 from I-5 north of Seattle. Better still, take **Metro,** tel. 447-4800. Once in Bothell you can travel to Lynnwood, Edmonds, or Everett on **Community Transit,** tel. 353-7433.

KIRKLAND

Surprisingly enough, Peter Kirk wasn't Kirkland's founding father—that honor belongs to Leigh Smith Jones Hunt. Hunt persuaded Kirk to build his steel mill, originally slated for Tacoma, in his town instead and offered to change the name to "Kirkland" as an added incentive. Kirk hoped to build the "Pittsburgh of the West"; fortunately or not, he never succeeded.

Kirkland is becoming more and more gentrified, but it retains much of its original small, lakefront charm in spite of the row of boutiques, condos, and hotels that are lining Lake Washington.

Outdoor Recreation

Moss Bay, on the east side of Lake Washington, hasn't been a bay since the Lake Washington ship canal was completed in 1916, lowering the water level nine feet; and there's never been any moss. The name came from a bay in England, Peter Kirk's home. Nonetheless, Moss Bay features a small beach, marina, and shops.

Bridle Trails State Park, 480 acres off 116th Ave. NE, has 28 miles of horse and hiking trails (more horses than hikers), including their Bridle Crest Trail which reaches to Redmond's Marymoor Park (see p. 82). Horses can be rented at the park for $10 an hour with a day's notice; call Sandene's Horse Trail Rides, tel. 822-1805. Just north of downtown on Lake Washington is **Juanita Beach Park** at 98th Ave. NE and N.E. Juanita Way, with an impressively long pier and one of the area's best beaches. Northwest of Juanita, **O.O. Denny Park,** Holmes Point Dr., has a small beach, picnic area, and a hiking trail

leading to King County's largest Douglas fir, standing 255 feet in height, 8½ feet in diameter, and estimated to be 575 years old. Head farther north to N.E. 145th St. to **St. Edward State Park,** a 316-acre retreat from civilization. This beautiful piece of property was part of a Catholic seminary until 1977; when the seminary closed, the diocese sold the land to the state and the park opened the following summer. St. Edwards boasts three quarters of a mile of forested, undeveloped Lake Washington shoreline and five miles of hiking trails, plus picnic areas, gymnasium, and pool.

Accommodations

Kirkland's newest hotel, **The Woodmark at Carillon Point,** 1200 Carillon Pt., tel. 822-3700 or (800) 822-3700, goes way beyond the comforts of home: fully stocked mini-bar, a second TV *in the bathroom,* panoramic views of Lake Washington in most rooms, plus terry robes, full breakfast, VCRs, and an invitation to "raid the pantry" for late-night snacks. Of course, there's no such thing as a free breakfast: rooms start at $130 s, $145 d, $190-500 for suites.

Those on tighter budgets can enjoy inexpensive lodging at **Motel 6,** 12010 120th Pl. NE at I-405's 124th St. exit, tel. 821-5618. Rooms are $32 s, $36 d, with a pool. The **Kirkland Silver Cloud Motel,** 12202 N.E. 124th St., tel. 821-8300, has 98 rooms for $42 s, $47-52 d, plus free laundry room and airport pick-up service, heated outdoor pool and Jacuzzi. For a little more, stay at **Best Western Arnold's Motor Inn,** 12223 N.E. 116th St., tel. 822-2300. Their 64 units begin at $60 s or d; pool, whirlpool, athletic club access, and airport transportation available. **La Quinta,** 10530 N.E. Northup Way, tel. 828-6585, or (800) 531-5900, has an outdoor pool, adjacent restaurant, and 120 rooms from $61 s, $69 d.

The **Shumway Mansion,** a 23-room B&B and reception center at 11410 100th Ave. NE, tel. 823-2303, is a three-minute walk from Juanita Beach. The antique-furnished inn was built in 1909; it was bought in 1982 by the Harris family and moved down the hill to its present location on 2.4 acres overlooking Juanita Bay. Two floors of the mansion are devoted to receptions and banquets; the seven B&B rooms range in price from $60-95 s or d; all have private baths, five have water views, two have balconies. Please call regarding children; no smoking.

Food And Drink
Stop for a drink at **TGI Friday's,** part of the chain at 505 Park Place (kids are welcome in the restaurant). Then head to Moss Bay Marina for moderately priced, consistently good steak or seafood at **Anthony's Homeport,** tel. 822-0225. Next door to Covey Run Winery, **Kirkland Roaster & Ale House,** 111 Central Way, tel. 827-4400, roasts chicken, lamb, and other meats on a huge spit; moderate prices.

Shopping And Services
The **Old Heritage Place** is a collector's paradise. Located at 151 Third St., this antiques mall has 65 shops filled with collectibles. Open daily 10 a.m.- 5:30 p.m., Sun. 1-5 p.m. The **Totem Lake Mall** (take the 124th St. exit from I-405) has 70 stores, restaurants, theaters, a post office, and a waterslide. At 620 Market St., the **Peter Kirk Building** houses shops and galleries in one of Kirkland's oldest buildings, constructed in 1891.

For maps or other information, visit the **Kirkland Chamber of Commerce,** 301 Kirkland Ave., tel. 822-7066. They will probably ask you to pay for the brochures. Or stop by the **Kirkland Public Library,** 406 Kirkland Ave., tel. 822-2459. Throughout King County, dial 911 for medical, fire, or police emergencies; or, in Kirkland, phone Evergreen Hospital, 12040 N.E. 128th St. near the Totem Lake Shopping Center, tel. 821-1111 for the switchboard or 823-7468 for 24-hour emergency service.

Transportation
From Seattle, take Hwy. 520 across the Evergreen Point Floating Bridge, then follow Hwy. 908 north to Kirkland for a total one-way trip of about 10 miles. **Metro** provides daily service to Kirkland from Seattle and other points in King County; tel. 447-4800.

LYNNWOOD
Lynnwood hasn't yet made its identity known. It just grew along Hwy. 99 before the Interstate era, and remains a strip between Seattle and Everett. The enormous **Alderwood Mall** on the east side of town hosts The Bon, Nordstrom, JCPenney, Sears, Lamonts, and many smaller stores; the mall is surrounded by other, smaller shopping plazas. You can catch a **Community Transit** bus here for Edmonds, Everett, or Bothell; tel. 353-7433.

Lynnwood's **Silver Cloud Inn,** 19332 36th Ave. W, tel. 775-7600, is one of the area's best deals with rooms from $44 s, $52 d.

The **Best Western Landmark Motor Inn,** 4300 200th SW, tel. 775-7447, has a heated indoor pool, hot tub, steam rooms, restaurant, and lounge, plus 102 rooms from $76 s, $84 d. It is also a stop for some airport vans.

The **Heather House,** 1011 B Ave., tel. 778-7233, is a B&B with Scottish influence: Scottish flags fly overhead and breakfast scones are a morning treat. Your king-size bed, private deck overlooking Puget Sound, and bath are only $40 s, $45 d, but breaking tradition, they charge $3 for breakfast. No kids or pets.

EDMONDS
Edmonds, 20 miles north of Seattle on Puget Sound, is a small city (pop. 28,700) surrounded by rolling hills and pine forests that some Californians (older ones, of course) say looks like Sausalito before the deluge of humanity. In spite of its spurt of growth since the mid-1980s, downtown Edmonds has retained its small-town appearance, and if you live there you can walk to everything, including the auto mechanic.

Park your car free along any downtown street and walk around—plenty of shops, galleries, bakeries, and restaurants to explore. When you tire of downtown, take a stroll along Sunset, a street fronting Puget Sound with frequent signs reminding you that it is illegal to play any electronic instrument

EDMONDS
AND
LYNNWOOD

1. Underwater Park
2. Kingston Ferry
3. Arnie's
4. Harbor Square
5. Harbor Inn
6. Brusseau's
7. museum
8. chamber of commerce
9. Old Mill Town
10. library
11. Best Western Landmark Motor Inn

(radios or tape decks to be specific) loud enough to be heard 30 feet away; Edmonds is that civilized. At low tide you can walk along the beach and watch the ferries cross the Sound to the Kitsap Peninsula.

A dozen or more shops and restaurants in a former automobile agency remodeled into old-time atmosphere make up **Old Milltown** at Fifth South and Dayton. For a more modern flavor, try **Harbor Square's** boutiques and galleries near the waterfront on W. Day-

ton. One of the more notable is the **Howard/Mandville Gallery,** with one of the largest inventories of collectible prints in the Northwest, and a large number of Western and nature paintings.

The **Edmonds-South Snohomish Historical Museum,** 118 Fifth Ave., has a working shingle mill model, a marine room, and other displays depicting Edmonds's past; open Tues., Thurs., and Sun. afternoons.

rafting on the Skykomish River (Archie Satterfield)

(top) a Washington State Ferry at sunset (Archie Satterfield)
(bottom) sunset on the Lower Columbia River (Archie Satterfield)

Outdoors And Underwater

Off the shoreline of Brackett's Landing (at the ferry dock) is **Edmonds Underwater Park,** the first such park in the region where divers can explore the marinelife that thrives in the 300-foot DeLion dry dock, sunk there in 1935 to serve as a breakwater and marinelife habitat. Since then, other underwater structures—including old tires, steel shelving, a model of the Evergreen Point Floating Bridge, and two tugboats—have been added for the enjoyment of both fish and diver, resulting in one of the Pacific Northwest's most popular underwater parks. From the shore, you'd never know anything was down there.

The **Edmonds Fishing Pier,** three blocks south of the ferry landing, at the foot of Dayton, was specifically constructed for fishing: the two enormous arms of the pier and parallel underwater structures direct migrating fish along the length of the pier and, with any luck, onto your hook. You can fish year-round, 24 hours; a bait shop, stores, and restaurants are adjacent.

Edmonds's beaches are frequented by "Beach Rangers" (trained naturalists) as part of a nature program cosponsored by the city of Lynnwood. **Sunset Beach** is visited by rangers most afternoons two hours before and after low tide; feel free to ask them any marinelife questions you may have; groups can book an interpretive lecture or tour by calling the Edmonds Parks and Recreation Dept., tel. 775-2525.

Accommodations And Food

Edmonds Harbor Inn, 130 W. Dayton, tel. 771-5021, is close to the waterfront in Harbor Square. Their 60 rooms go for $50 s, $60 d, including continental breakfast.

Enjoy Northwest seafood with a view of the bay for lunch, dinner, or Sunday brunches at **Arnie's,** 300 Admiral Way, tel. 771-6533, two blocks south of the ferry terminal beside the city park. **Brusseau's,** Fifth and Dayton, tel. 774-4166, is Edmonds's trendiest restaurant and serves three moderately priced meals daily. Edmonds has always had at least two good French restaurants and now has **Café de Paris,** 109 Main St., tel. 771-2350, near the ferry landing, and **L'escargot French Restaurant,** 417 Main St., tel. 778-9888, just off the square. **Tasters,** 100 Second Ave. S, tel. 778-7979, is one of the best Chinese restaurants in the area.

Other Practicalities

The **Edmonds Chamber of Commerce,** 120 Fifth Ave. N, tel. 776-6711, will be happy to help you out with maps or other current information; or, try the **Edmonds Public Library** at Seventh and Main, tel. 771-1933.

To get to Edmonds from Seattle, drive north on I-5 and take exit 176 and follow the can't-miss signs that lead to Edmonds-Kingston Ferry. Once you're there, you can get around town and to Bothell, Lynnwood, and Everett via **Community Transit,** tel. 353-7433.

Take the **Washington State Ferry** from Edmonds to Kingston, the Olympic Peninsula's drop-off point. The crossing takes 30 minutes and leaves Edmonds about every 1½ hours off-peak (early mornings and late evenings), every 40 minutes during the day. Fares are $6.65 one way car and driver; tel. (800) 542-7052 or (800) 542-0810 statewide.

Edmonds is one of the few towns its size to still have train service. **Amtrak's** trains stop there in the morning going into Seattle, and in the evening leaving Seattle, but Amtrak insists that you make reservations the previous day, which means you can't board the train on a whim. For information call (800) 872-7245.

TACOMA

Despite being the butt of Seattle jokes for many years, Tacoma is the next logical benefactor of western Washington's phenomenal growth. "The City of Destiny" has several things to be proud of: a world-class zoo system; a vibrant cultural life that includes live theater and dance; the world's largest wooden domed stadium; an AAA baseball team, an indoor-league soccer team, and a Western Hockey League team; top-quality hotels and waterfront restaurants, an excellent university and established community colleges; and new business dollars to provide a healthy base for what will most likely become one of the 1990s' fastest-growing cities.

The new Frank Russell building just off the 11th St. bridge is a good example of the shape of Tacoma to come. The city has been a leader in the containerized shipping business for many years, and also relies on wood products, shipbuilding, primary metal and chemical plants, health care, and a growing high-tech industry. Agriculture is also big business in Pierce County, particularly the Puyallup bulb farms, which produce more tulip and daffodil bulbs than Holland.

Like any city, Tacoma has its problems and has some neighborhoods that are unsafe. But that is true of nearly every city in America today. Tacoma has outgrown its image of that town where the pulp mills perfumed the air, and is a contender for second billing behind Seattle in things to offer visitors.

History

English sea captain George Vancouver and his entourage first stumbled across the Puget Sound area in 1792 when Peter Puget, under Vancouver's orders, sailed by Point Defiance and the Narrows. Members of Hudson's Bay Company came along and built Fort Nisqually in 1833, which has since been reconstructed at Point Defiance State Park. Another sea captain, Charles Wilkes, surveyed the Sound in 1841 and gave his starting point the name it still bears: Commencement Bay.

The first settler, Nicholas Delin, built Tacoma's first sawmill and cabin in 1852 and in 1863, Job Carr, built his cabin on Commencement Bay and voilà . . . Tacoma was born and Carr served as its first mayor. Once the Northern Pacific Railroad reached the city in 1873, Tacoma's industries blossomed. Tacoma wasn't "Tacoma" (from "Tahoma" or "Takhoma," meaning "Mother of Waters," the Indian name for Mt. Rainier) until 1869; General M.M. McCarver had originally named it Commencement City.

SIGHTS

Point Defiance

Tacoma's most famous attraction is **Point Defiance Park,** 500 acres of gardens, virgin forests, footpaths, and shaded picnic areas jutting out into Puget Sound at the tip of a peninsula. It reminds visitors of the best metropolitan parks in America but once you've seen it, the cliff setting with its views and thick forest will make most other similar parks seem modest. In addition to its natural beauty, it has the **Point Defiance Zoo and Aquarium,** home of beluga whales, polar bears, walruses, elephants, and more. In summer, kids can ride an elephant; summer evening Zoosounds concerts are fun for the whole family (Tim Noah has appeared in years past). In December, come in the evening to see the twinkling animal Zoolights. Regular zoo admission is $2.50; kids under four free; tel. 591-5335. Also at Point Defiance, **Never Never Land** has scenes from children's stories—Humpty-Dumpty, Hansel and Gretel, Mother Goose—depicted throughout a 10-acre wooded area.

Visit the reconstructed **Fort Nisqually,** a replica of the mid-1800s' Hudson's Bay trad-

*downtown Tacoma
and the 11th St. Bridge*

ing fort, and **Camp Six,** an old logging camp
with a short steam railroad ride that the kids
will love. A popular jogging route, **Five-Mile
Drive** winds through the park, offering viewpoints and picnic stops along the way. **Owens
Beach** on Commencement Bay offers summer sun or a pleasant shoreline stroll any
time of year. Rent a boat with a small motor
and a tankful of gas for $36 a day at the Point
Defiance Boat House ($5 more gets you a
rod and reel); the water off the point is always
littered with fishermen, particularly during
salmon season. Point Defiance is open every
day, 10 a.m.-7 p.m. in the summer; some
attractions charge a small admission fee. For
more information call 591-5335.

Other Parks
Tucked away where you'd least expect it is
the **Snake Lake Nature Center.** The 54
acres of marshland and evergreens are just
a stone's throw from busy 19th St. (1919 S.
Tyler St., tel. 591-5939), but 25 species of
mammals and over 100 species of birds call
it home. They've got two miles of self-guiding
nature trails for the do-it-yourselfers, and offer guided tours the second Saturday of
every month at 10 a.m. Don't let the name
scare you off—the lake was named for its
shape, not its inhabitants. Open daily from 8
a.m. until dark.

If you're in the downtown area and get the
urge for a quick jog, head to **Wright Park** at

S. Third and G streets. A small, shady park
with gardens and paved paths, it also hosts
the Seymour Conservatory. Built in 1907 and
on the National Register of Historic Places,
the conservatory hosts a stunning array of
flowering plants.

Wapato Lake is a good practice pond for
novice rowboaters. Located at S. 72nd St. and
Sheridan Ave., the park also has picnic tables
and some small flower gardens. House rules:
if your boat fits on top of your car and doesn't
have a motor, you're in; or, if you forgot to pack
yours, you can rent a boat there.

If you've wandered into northeast Tacoma,
Browns Point Lighthouse Park is a sunny
spot for picnicking, ship-watching, or launching your own boat. Here you've got a great
view of downtown Tacoma and Point Defiance, Vashon and Maury islands, the Olympics, and of course, the Sound. The trick is to
find it (see map p. 92).

Narrows Bridge
Connecting Tacoma with the Olympic Peninsula, this bridge is the second bridge to
cross the sound at this location. The first
was the famous "Galloping Gertie," so-
named for its habit of bucking and swaying
with every passing breeze. Finally, in 1940
the winds were too much for it and after
whipping up and down and twisting like taffy,
the bridge crashed into the Sound. The only
life lost was that of a dog who refused to

come out of the car when the owner could no longer drive it on the twisting deck and dashed for safety. The new Narrows Bridge is 500-plus feet above the sea, 6,000 feet long, and quite stable.

Mt. Rainier

If you're in Tacoma on a semi-clear day, there are few places you can be without a view of 14,411-foot Mt. Rainier. It dominates the landscape with its permanent whitecap,

and looks particularly dramatic from the Cliff House parking lot (see "Food," p. 93), the 11th St. bridge, Ruston Way, and Gig Harbor. The first peek of it will quicken your pulse, guaranteed.

For a closer look, visit Mt. Rainier National Park (see p. 312). It is worth noting here that the Native Americans called the mountain Tahoma, and every few years a campaign to return its original name is launched by someone in the Tacoma area, which revives the

TACOMA

1. boat house
2. zoo and aquarium
3. Camp Six
4. Never-Never Land and Fort Nisqually
5. Antique Sandwich Co.
6. Lobster Shop South
7. Hogan's Bay Co.
8. Katie Downs Tavern
9. C.I. Shenanigan's
10. Harbor Lights
11. The Spar
12. Knapp's
13. Grazie Cafe
14. Bavarian Restaurant
15. Tacoma General Hospital
16. Lorenzo's
17. Engine House-9
18. Prosito's
19. Casa Bonita
20. Cloverleaf Tavern
21. Tacoma Community College
22. Cheers West
23. Cheney Stadium
24. Humana Hospital
25. Snake Lake Nature Center
26. Tacoma Salmon House
27. Tacoma Dome
28. Quality Hotel Tacoma Dome
29. Greyhound
30. Johnny's Dock
31. Amtrak Station
32. La Quinta
33. Portage Inn
34. Traveler's Inn
35. La Casa Real
36. Nendel's
37. King's Palace
38. King's Motor Inn
39. Royal Coachman
40. Best Western Executive Inn
41. Motel 6
42. Stanley & Seafort's
43. Java Jive
44. Days Inn
45. Shilo Inn
46. Sherwood Inn
47. Nendel's
48. Best Western Tacoma
49. Days Inn
50. Motel 6
51. Traudel's Haus
52. Black Angus
53. Best Western Lakewood
54. Lakewood Center
55. Sunnyside Beach Park
56. Bair Drug
57. Salter's Point Park
58. museum
59. E.R. Roger's

old quarrel between Tacoma and Seattle, which resists the renaming.

Museums

The Tacoma Art Museum at S. 12th and Pacific Ave., tel. 272-4258, is open daily with displays of American and French paintings, a children's gallery, library, Pilchuck glass, frequent photography shows, and other traveling exhibits. Admission is $2 adults, $1 kids and seniors.

The Washington State Historical Society Museum, 315 N. Stadium Way, tel. 593-2830, has Eskimo, Native American, and Oriental artifacts, a large photo collection, pioneer exhibits, and natural history thrown in. Admission is $2 adults, $1 kids and seniors.

Dome Tour

The **Tacoma Dome,** the giant blue geometric-patterned structure off I-5, offers one-hour tours Mon. through Fri., June through Aug. (except when events are in progress); admission is $2 adults, $1 kids and seniors. The tour of the world's largest wooden dome includes information on the dome's history, construction, and how they convert from soc-

cer to football to concert hall. For more information call 272-DOME (for event schedule, call 591-5318).

ACCOMMODATIONS

See the chart on pages 96-97 for hotels and motels in and around Tacoma.

For a change from the high-rises, spend a night at **Traudel's Haus,** 15313 17th Ave. Ct. E (off 152nd St. E—call for directions), tel. 535-4422. Enjoy Old World hospitality, antiques, and handmade lace along with private bath, fireplace, continental or full gourmet breakfast, all for just $30 s, $40 d, or $60 for the suite.

For information on camping and B&Bs in Gig Harbor, Federal Way, and Vashon Is., see "Vicinity of Tacoma," p. 100.

FOOD

Ruston Way

Several of Tacoma's best restaurants are on the waterfront along Ruston Way and on N. 30th St., one street up from the water. At 2761

Ruston Way, **Harbor Lights** (the one with the tacky sign) is a very popular, moderately priced seafood restaurant. **C. I. Shenanigan's**, up the road at 3017 Ruston Way, is a tad pretentious for some tastes, but the food—moderately priced American—isn't bad and the upstairs bar is a lively place, frequently the site of local radio stations' theme parties. **Katie Downs Tavern**, at 3211 Ruston Way, sits on a pier and offers pizza, a jeans-and-sneakers atmosphere, and a good-sized crowd with outdoor seating in the summer; over 21 only. Next to Katie Downs, **Hogan's Bay Co.** serves moderately priced seafood and steak. Farther north on Ruston, the **Lobster Shop South** is another popular, moderately priced seafood and steak restaurant, open daily for lunch and dinner plus an impressive Sunday brunch. At 2301 N. 30th St., one street away from the water, the **Grazie Café**, tel. 627-0231, offers lunch, dinner, Sunday brunch, and a Sound view. A few doors down, **The Spar** has burgers, sandwiches, and great homemade soups, but it is a bar, so no kids.

An exercise course and bike path run along Ruston Way, good for a breezy post-lunch or dinner walk. There are also two public fishing piers here, complete with a bait shop and refreshment stand; the piers are a better bet for sightseeing than fishing, though, because Commencement Bay is one of Puget Sound's "hot spots," where the bottom fish and even salmon have shown unhealthy levels of toxins.

More Views

Johnny's Dock, on 1900 E. D St. (near the Dome), is in one of Tacoma's less attractive sections, but the view of the city and the boats docked outside is spectacular (particularly at night). The basic steak-and-seafood menu is reasonably priced, and good; the service is friendly, not overbearing. Don't miss it. Overlooking the Dome is **Stanley and Seafort's Saloon and Grill**, at 115 E. 34th, tel. 473-7300, with another view that gets better as the sun goes down. The restaurant has a reputation for being overpriced, but that doesn't deter the crowds; if you're on a budget,

DOWNTOWN TACOMA

© MOON PUBLICATIONS, INC.

just stop in for a beer and watch the sun set behind the Olympics.

If you want a sweeping Sound view plus a look at Mt. Rainier, try the **Cliff House,** 6300 Marine View Dr. at Browns Point, tel. 927-0400. The atmosphere may be stuffy, but the steak and seafood are very good—though not cheap; the downstairs lounge offers the same view and a sandwich menu if you want to keep costs down. Farther north on Marine View Dr. (a.k.a. East Side Dr. and Dash Point Rd.) at Dash Point, you'll see a sign for the **Lobster Shop,** 6912 Soundview Dr. NE, tel. 927-1513, sister to the Lobster Shop South across the bay. This is the original, more rustic version, where the steaks, seafood, and wine list are unequalled; open for dinner only, and reservations are always a good idea.

Downtown
Downtown Tacoma offers a number of lunch spots at Broadway Plaza and Tacoma Market. **The Judicial Annex,** at 311 S. 11th (right at the corner of the Plaza), is a popular soup/sandwich/espresso stop with a full bar. One street up is the **Ark Delicatessen and Restaurant,** a small place tucked into the Market at 1140 Court C. In serve-yourself deli-style, they offer sandwiches, salads, and a nice selection of wines. **Bimbo's,** 1516 Pacific Ave., tel. 383-5800, has been serving Italian specialties at this location for almost 70 years—the food's still great, but a change in locale is in order.

Others
The Old Spaghetti Factory at 1735 S. Jefferson, part of a small national chain, can fill you to capacity with an assortment of low-priced (under $8) pasta dishes and some terrific sourdough bread. This is a good spot to take noisy kids, but be prepared for a wait on the weekends. **Lorenzo's,** 2811 Sixth Ave., tel. 272-3331, is a local favorite with its real Italian food at low to moderate prices.

Just up the street, **Prosito's** serves good, low-priced Italian food and live jazz in a tiny little hole of a joint at Sixth and Proctor. The **Bavarian Restaurant** at 204 N. K St., tel. 627-5010, specializes in "old country-style" German steaks and seafood, beer and wine, with live music on the weekends and a Sunday Champagne brunch. For a bite of the local catch, try the **Tacoma Salmon House,** near the Dome at 2611 Pacific Ave., tel. 627-0141. Though salmon is their specialty, they have other seafood, prime rib, and beef dishes to choose from.

Stuart Anderson's Black Angus restaurants are consistently good; there's one in Tacoma at 9905 Bridgeport Way SW, tel. 582-6900. **The Cloverleaf Tavern** at 6430 Sixth Ave. cooks up—and delivers—some of the best pizza in town (rumor has it actress

Linda Evans gets her pizza here). Stay away from the chains and try a charming, casual, and inexpensive Mexican restaurant, **Casa Bonita,** at 6104 Sixth Ave., tel. 565-1546. Another of the city's best Mexican restaurants is **Moctezuma's,** in a new location at 56th and Tyler.

Over in Proctor, **Knapp's** (2707 N. Proctor) offers casual dining and hearty, better-than-Mom's breakfasts; open 6 a.m. to 11 p.m.

Pacific Hwy. E in Fife is lined with fast-food restaurants and budget motels; a good spot to stay if you're short on cash. Besides Burger King and McDonald's, there are a couple "real" restaurants here: **La Casa Real,** 3410 Pacific Hwy. E, tel. 922-8877, is open daily for Mexican lunch, dinner, and Sunday brunch (with dancing in the lounge); **King's Palace,** 4903 Pacific Hwy. E, tel. 922-0911, has Chinese food to eat in or take out, plus dancing in the lounge on weekends.

ENTERTAINMENT

Nightlife
There's plenty of nightlife in Tacoma: **Christie's** at the Executive Inn (exit 137 off I-5 in Fife) has dancing Mon. through Sat. to Top-40 bands. The lounges at C. I. Shenanigan's and other Ruston Way restaurants (see above) come alive at night. A favorite with some of the locals is the unusual **Java Jive,** a teapot-shaped tavern on S. Tacoma Way; you won't want to come here for dinner, but the jukebox features classics from the '60s and the live organ entertainment is, well, unique.

Engine House No. 9, 611 N. Pine, tel. 272-3435, is right around the corner from Lorenzo's and calls itself the Northwest Microbrew Headquarters because it stocks nearly 20 Northwest beers in addition to an equal number of imported draft beers and perhaps three dozen imported bottled beers. Sandwiches, soups and salads, and pizza are also served. Of course October is a big month for the pub, when several kinds of Bavarian brews are imported for the Octoberfest.

Cheers West, 7102 27th St. W, alleged to be the hangout of the Tacoma Stars and

TACOMA AREA LODGING

Name	Address	Phone	Rates	Comments
Best Western Executel	31611 20th Ave. S, Federal Way	941-5888	$99-109 s $109-129 d	pool, hot tub, shuttle, restaurant, bar
Best Western Executive Inn	5700 Pacific Hwy. E, Fife	922-0080	$53-59 s $57-65 d	pool, hot tub, sauna, exercise room, lounge, restaurant, airport limo
Best Western Lakewood	6125 Motor Ave. SW, Lakewood	584-2212	$44-54 s $50-62 d	pool, lounge, restaurant nearby
Best Western Tacoma Inn	8726 S. Hosmer, Tacoma	535-2880	$54-60 s $58-70 d	pool, hot tub, exercise room, restaurant, bar
Budget Inn	9915 S. Tacoma	588-6615	$28 s, 30 d	laundry
Kings Motor Inn	5115 Pacific Hwy. E, Fife	922-3636	$32 s or d	hot tub, laundry
La Quinta	1425 E. 27th St., Tacoma	383-0146	$52-59 s $60-67 d	pool, hot tub, exercise room, restaurant, bar
Motel 6	5201 20th St. E, Fife	922-1270	$28 s, 32 d	pool
Motel 6	1811 S. 76th St., Tacoma	473-7100	$30 s, 34 d	pool, Jacuzzi
Best Western	31611 20th Ave. S,	941-5888	$99-109 s	pool, hot tub, shuttle,

Tacoma Tigers, is a sports-nuts bar with big weekend crowds plus weeknight trivia contests. The **Antique Sandwich Co.,** 5102 N. Pearl St. (right outside Point Defiance), offers acoustic and folk music (plus health-nut sandwiches) in a family, no-alcohol setting. For an exhaustive list of night spots, plays, concerts, etc., check the Tacoma *Morning News Tribune's* TGIF section on Fridays.

Sports
Tacoma's claim to fame is its Major Indoor Soccer League team, the **Tacoma Stars;** they play at the Tacoma Dome at 2727 East D Street. For information: tel. 572-7827. The Pacific Coast Baseball League is represented by the **Tacoma Tigers,** a AAA team that plays at Cheney Stadium, 2525 Bantz Blvd.

(off Hwy. 16), and sometimes outdraws the Seattle Mariners. Information: tel. 752-7707. The **Tacoma Rockets** are the Western Hockey League franchise opening for business in the 1991-92 season. Their season is from Sept. to March and they play in the Tacoma Dome, tel. 627-4625.

Theater
The **Pantages Centre** at Ninth and Broadway always has something going on—plays, acrobats, concerts—but unfortunately, a lot of their events sell out fast. Give them a call at 591-5894 to see what's on the agenda. The building itself is an ornate, restored vaudeville palace dating back to 1918. The **Tacoma Actors Guild (TAG),** 1323 S. Yakima Ave., tel. 272-2145, features nightly performances (except

TACOMA AREA LODGING (CONTINUED)

Name	Address	Phone	Rates	Comments
Best Western	31611 20th Ave. S,	941-5888	$ 99-109 s	pool, hot tub, shuttle,
Nendel's	8702 S. Hosmer, Tacoma	535-3100	42-45 s 52-60 d	pool, bar, restaurant
Portage Inn	3021 Pacific Hwy. E, Fife	922-3500	30 s, 34-40 d	restaurant adjacent
Quality Hotel Tacoma Dome	2611 East E St., Tacoma	572-7272	66 s 71-76 d	near Dome; sauna, exercise room, restaurant, bar
Royal Coachman	5805 Pacific Hwy. E, Fife	922-2500	52-57 s 57-60 d	hot tub, library
Sheraton	S. 1320 Broadway Plaza, Tacoma	572-3200	95-105 s 105-130 d	hot tub, sauna, restaurant, bar
Sherwood Inn	8402 S. Hosmer, Tacoma	535-2800	39-56 s 41-66 d	pool, lounge, restaurant
Shilo Inn	7414 S. Hosmer, Tacoma	475-4020	54 s 61-67 d	pool, hot tub, steam/sauna, exercise room
Super 8	1688 S. 348th, Federal Way	838-8808	35 s, 38-41 d	
Traveler's Inn	3100 Pacific Hwy. E, Fife	922-9520	26 s, 30 d	pool

Mon.) through the winter season, with matinees on selected days. Every weekend in the summer, **565 Broadway** (guess where it is) offers dinner theater. Dinner and the show go for $15; for $7.50 you can get the show with dessert only. Phone 272-8118 for information and reservations. The **Tacoma Little Theater** claims to be the oldest continuously performing theater west of the Mississippi. Information: tel. 272-2481.

SHOPPING

The **Tacoma Mall** is one of the largest shopping malls in the Northwest with more than 140 stores, including Sears, JCPenney, Bon Marché, Nordstrom, all on one level. From I-5 follow the signs for Tacoma Mall Blvd., at the S. 56th St. exit. Smaller shopping centers line S. 38th St., just north of the mall; closer to the center of town, Sixth Ave. has K mart, Drug Emporium, and numerous other discount stores and small plazas.

Another similar shopping area is **The Lakewood Mall** at 10509 Gravelly Lake Drive SW. Not quite as large as the Tacoma Mall, the Lakewood has a Frederick & Nelson, Mervyn's, and Lamonts as anchor stores.

A small, mostly upscale cluster of shops called the Proctor District runs along the 2700 block area of North Proctor. It has several shops, including the Proctor District Antique Mall with more than 40 dealers and the Pacific Northwest Shop, which stocks only goods produced in the region.

INFORMATION AND SERVICES

The Tacoma area code is 206. If you need more information on Tacoma and the surrounding area while you're here or in advance, stop by or phone the **Tacoma-Pierce County Visitor and Convention Bureau** at 950 Pacific Ave., Ste. 450, tel. 627-2836. The **Tacoma Public Library**, tel. 591-5666, is operating out of temporary quarters at Broadway Plaza (on Broadway between 11th and 13th) until their main building at 1102 Tacoma Ave. S is renovated.

For fire, police, and other emergencies, dial 911. Plenty of hospitals in the area have 24-hour emergency room service: **Humana Hospital**, S. 19th and Union, tel. 383-0011; **Tacoma General**, 315 S. K St., tel. 594-1050; or **St. Joseph Hospital**, 1718 S. I St., tel. 591-6660.

TRANSPORTATION

Getting Around By Car
Tacoma's street numbering system is relatively easy to follow. The system that allegedly provides faster 911 response time would work much better on flat terrain with straight roads; as it is, some streets change names seven or more times as they move in and out of boxes on an imaginary grid. But as a general rule, anything prefixed or suffixed by a "Northeast" is between Browns Point (Marine View Dr.) and Federal Way; "North" is up by Point Defiance; "South" is the tricky one, as it takes up the whole midsection of Tacoma, and sometimes looks more west or north than south; "East" is in the Dome area; and "West" is over by the University Place section, south of the Narrows Bridge. But pay attention: the "Avenue" or "Place" or "Street" appended to the number is critical; for example, there's a 42 St. S, a 42 Pl. S, and a 42 Ave. S, and as a general rule such streets never intersect or even come near each other.

By Bus
Pierce Transit, tel. 593-4500 or (800) 562-8109 statewide, serves Tacoma, Puyallup, Gig Harbor, Lakewood, Steilacoom, Spanaway, Fife, and east to Buckley. **Greyhound,** 1319 Pacific Ave., tel. 383-4621, provides cross-country service.

Arriving By Air
If you're flying into Tacoma, you'll probably arrive at **Seattle-Tacoma International Airport.** As the name suggests it's about halfway between Seattle and Tacoma. Sea-Tac is small enough so you can make all your connections but big enough to be a respectable international airport. The **Travelines Airporter,** tel. 848-8788 or 839-2886, has service to Federal Way, Fife, and downtown Tacoma; fares are $8-10 one way. **Capital Aeroporter,** tel. 572-9544, serves Fife, south Tacoma, and southwest Washington, starting from $6 one way. For up-to-the-minute information on airport parking, ground transportation schedules and rates, and weather and traffic conditions, dial (800) 544-1965 or 431-4444 from a touch-tone phone.

By Train
Amtrak serves Tacoma from its passenger station at 1001 Puyallup Ave., between the tideflat area and I-5 in the eastern part of the city. The Coast Starlight provides daily service to the Puget Sound area from Portland, San Francisco, and Los Angeles; the Pioneer also serves Seattle, Tacoma, and Olympia from Salt Lake City. Phone (800) 872-7245 for info.

By Ferry
The Washington State Ferry System is a heavily used method of everyday transportation around the Puget Sound region. From Tacoma, however, it can only get you to Vashon Island (see p. 101) departing from Point Defiance; fares are $2.15 roundtrip for walk-ons, $7.50 roundtrip for car and driver. For information on the ferry system call 464-6400 from Seattle, (800) 542-0810 or (800) 542-7052 from elsewhere in the state.

Harbor Tours
For a close look at Commencement Bay, Puget Sound, and The Narrows, take a cruise with **Tacoma Harbor Tours.** Evening

DISASTER ACROSS THE SOUND

Tacoma's most famous disaster involved a cocker spaniel, an automobile, and an extremely long and high bridge.

Tacoma needed a bridge across The Narrows to link it with the Kitsap Peninsula and the shipyards at Bremerton only 20 miles north. The ferry service was being overworked and after many attempts, backers finally got the mile-long bridge built; it was then the third-longest suspension bridge in the world.

It was quite an undertaking, and the construction process was exciting for sidewalk superintendents from both shores. The towers stood 500 feet above the swift currents below and more than 19,000 miles of wire were wound into the cables that supported the roadbed.

When it was finished, the workmen reported that the roadbed didn't behave properly; it rippled. A professor of engineering at the University of Washington, F. Bert Farquarson, was commissioned to make wind-tunnel tests, and he urged a much more comprehensive study. his warnings went barely heeded, and the insurance agent who sold the bridge insurance pocketed the premuium—after all, who had ever heard of a new bridge falling?

In the meantime, the bridge earned its nickname of Galloping Gertie from its great rippling effect, and motorists in search of a thrill could pay their toll on a windy day and drive onto the bridge and watch the car ahead completely disappear in the ripples.

It all ended on the morning of Nov. 7, 1940, when a strong wind came up and held steady at about 40 mph. The bridge began a corkscrew twist so severe that it was closed. But Leonard Coatsworth, editor for the Tacoma *News Tribune,* was driving across at the time with his cocker spaniel, Tubby. Coatsworth found that he couldn't drive safely, and he decided to run, or crawl, for his life. He tried to get the dog out but she bit him. Leaving the unwilling dog, he crawled to the Tacoma side.

College student Winfred Brown walked out onto the bridge a short distance, but returned when the bridge twisted so far that he seemed to be looking straight down at the water.

Professor Farquarson had heard of the contortions and drove down from Seattle to film the event. He went out onto the bridge to try and save Tubby, but wasn't able to walk upright so he retreated to the shore.

The twisting became worse and lampposts began snapping off and chunks of concrete were flying. Finally about 100 feet of roadway with Coatsworth's car and Tubby fell into the narrows. Soon most of the roadway was gone. The towers that had been supporting the conrete snapped back toward each shore until the cables stopped them, humming in the wind, and finally the whole twisted mess fell into Puget Sound.

dinner tours, offered from March through Sept., last two hours and feature baked salmon, prime rib, and chicken cordon bleu for $25-27 adults, $23-25 seniors. Sunday brunch tours, scheduled from March through Sept., depart at 10:30 a.m. and 1 p.m. and last 1½ hours; a full buffet is included in the price: $20 adults, $19 seniors, $13 kids 3-12.

Enjoy a 4½-hour cruise to Tillicum Village on Blake Island for an alder-smoked salmon dinner and authentic Indian dance performance. These cruises depart every Sat. from March through Sept. at 10:30 a.m. and cost $30 adults, $28 seniors, $15 kids, and $10 toddlers. Sailing from May through Sept., their one-hour harbor tour departs at 3 p.m. weekdays, 3:30 p.m. weekends; fares are $6.50 adults, $4.50 kids. Reservations are required; phone 572-9858 from Tacoma or 621-1941 from Seattle. The boat leaves from 535 Dock St. (just off Schuster Pkwy.), the barnlike McCormick Steamship Dock with a bar, ice-cream shop, and galleries inside the drive-through building.

VICINITY OF TACOMA

PARKLAND-SPANAWAY AND LAKEWOOD

Technically separate towns, but in reality an extension of the Tacoma metropolitan area, the Parkland-Spanaway area hosts a few good restaurants and a beautiful park, while Fort Lewis and McChord Air Force Base reside in neighboring Lakewood.

Sights
Twice a week **McChord Air Force Base** opens for tours that include boarding their C-130 or C-141 cargo planes. The free two-hour tours are held Tues. mornings and Fri. afternoons; phone 984-1910 for reservations.

Kopachuck State Park

Take exit 119 from I-5 to the **Fort Lewis Military Museum,** one of the Army's largest permanent posts. The museum emphasizes Northwest history, including artifacts from the Lewis and Clark expedition. Open Tues. through Sun., noon-4 p.m.; free.

One of Spanaway's summertime attractions is the **Spanaway Speedway,** with Sat., Sun., and Wed. night racing. The speedway is located at 159th and 22nd Ave. E; call 537-7551 for the week's schedule.

Located off Pacific Ave., **Spanaway County Park** is an ideal place to take a walk, go for a swim, or take out the boat. Back to back with Spanaway Lake Golf Course, the park has a beach, trails, lots of trees, and picnic areas.

Food
Just off I-5's 72nd St. exit, **The Olive Garden,** tel. 475-1772, and **The Red Lobster,** tel. 474-1262, first cousins in the chain, deliver consistently good, moderately priced, Italian and seafood dinners, respectively. The Olive Garden's nonstop breadsticks are legendary.

GIG HARBOR

Just across the Narrows Bridge from Tacoma, Gig Harbor definitely warrants a visit. The harbor is considered one of the best and most scenic on Puget Sound, with colorful boats, towering pines, and seaside houses, all against the picture-perfect backdrop of Mt. Rainier—a photo that graces many a calendar and magazine cover. The town itself is tiny, with a population of only 2,500 (probably 2,498 of them boat owners) and a slightly touristy flavor, but the shops, galleries, good restaurants, and at least one great tavern will keep you busy. To get there, take the Soundview Dr. exit off Hwy. 16.

Kopachuck State Park
You'd never expect so much solitude so close to a major city. Located 12 miles north-

west of Tacoma off Hwy. 16 (just follow the signs), Kopachuck has 41 campsites ($7) shaded by skyscraping pines as well as a beach for swimming or fishing.

Accommodations

Built in 1901 by volunteers for the First Methodist Episcopal Church, **The Parsonage,** 4107 Burnham Dr., tel. 851-8654, is a Victorian B&B within walking distance of Harborview Dr., Gig Harbor's main street. Their two guest rooms with shared bath go for $35 d. Another B&B, **No Cabbages,** 7712 Goodman Dr. NW, tel. 858-7797, has two rooms with harbor views for $30 per room. A newer B&B is the **Davenport,** 7501 Artondale Dr., tel. 851-8527, which has three rooms, one with private bath, which rent for $65 and $75. For something more exotic, book a room (or is that stateroom?) aboard the **Ketch Krestine,** a 100-foot Baltic trading ketch built in 1903 and now moored "a mere monkey fist heave" from Gig Harbor's shops. The "Captain's Stateroom" is $60 s, $70 d, while two cozier crew cabins each go for $40 s, $50 d; full breakfast is included, dinners by special arrangement. Phone 858-9395 for reservations, or write Box 31, Gig Harbor, WA 98335.

Food

The **Tides Tavern,** 2925 Harborview, is alone worth the trip across the bridge. No waitress service—you order your beers and food at the bar, leave your name, and when your burger's ready it'll be delivered to you. You can arrive by car or boat (dock right outside), and they've got a small deck for outdoor drinking and boat-watching. Besides burgers, the Tides offers pizza, sandwiches, soup, nachos, cheap beer, and weekend entertainment.

For a classier meal, these three steak-and-seafood restaurants all operate around the same price range—$10 dinners, on the average. The **Harbor Inn Restaurant,** 3111 Harborview Dr., tel. 851-5454, has chicken and an occasional mako shark in addition to the standard steak and seafood. **W.B. Scott's,** 3108 Harborview Dr., tel. 627-5446, adds lamb stew and rabbit. **Neville's Shoreline Restaurant,** 8827 N. Harborview Dr., tel. 627-1784, is the only one of the three that affords a view of Mt. Rainier.

Entertainment

Gig Harbor's **Performance Circle Theater** has performances in Celebrations Meadow during the summer months and at Burton Park Theater, 6615 38th Ave. NW, on winter weekends. Celebrations Meadow is on the left side of Peacock Hill Ave., about one-half mile up from Harborview; the theater is at the extreme north end of 38th Ave. NW. For information call 851-PLAY or 549-2661.

The **Breakfast-in-Bed Race,** a bizarre Gig Harbor tradition, is held every spring. A team of runners, generally in drag or something otherwise unidentifiable, push an old-fashioned bed frame some 500 feet while the bedridden breakfast-eater must ingest oatmeal, soft-cooked eggs, and juice before the finish. Other annual events include a Fourth of July bash and a summertime "Good Times Boat Cruise" around Vashon Island with a live band and dinner. For information on any of these events call the chamber of commerce at 851-6865.

VASHON ISLAND

Vashon Island is not the place to go if you're expecting a hot time on the ol' town; cows and horses probably outnumber humans. This rural, slow-paced, homey environment is fine for bike tours but not bar-hopping. The island was discovered in 1792 by (who else?) Capt. George Vancouver who, having named enough things after himself, decided to give this one to his Navy buddy, James Vashon. Maury Island, the piece of land east of Vashon, is connected to it by a natural sandbar and lots of manmade fill (and therefore not an island at all). Maury was separately named and identified by a member of the Wilkes survey party in 1841. The Vashon piece is 12½ miles north to south and a maximum four miles wide; Maury is only 5½ miles long and, at most, two miles wide—definitely bikeable, although the rolling hills may poop you out.

VASHON ISLAND

SOUTHWORTH FERRY

SEATTLE FERRY

103 AVE. SW

99 AVE. SW

99

SW 106 AVE. SW

102

104 SW

123 AVE. SW

VASHON ISLAND HWY.

COVE RD.
SW 168 ST.

BANK RD.
SW 176 ST.

VASHON

SWAN INN

VASHON ISLAND

BLUE HERON CENTER FOR THE ARTS

SW 204 ST.

SOUND FOOD

111 AVE. SW

91 AVE. SW

BEALL GREENHOUSE

SW 220 ST.

SW 232 ST.

WAX ORCHARDS

131 AVE. SW

MAURY ISLAND

75 PL. SW

SW 240 ST.

DOCKTON RD.

TAHLEQUAH RD.

131 AVE. SW

TAHLEQUAH

TACOMA FERRY

0   1 mi

0   1 km

© MOON PUBLICATIONS, INC.

Things To Do
Vashon's biggest summertime event is the two-day **Strawberry Festival** in mid-July. Parades, music, and crafts highlight the event, and since ferry traffic will be heavy, it's a good idea to arrive early. Other attractions include the **Beall Greenhouse**, on 91st Ave. SW, with its 1½ acres of orchids under glass, and **Wax Orchards** on S.W. 232nd and 131st Ave. SW, where the cider-making process is explained. **The Blue Heron Center for the Arts,** mid-island at Vashon Island Hwy. and S.W. 196th St., puts on various shows from time to time; call 463-5131 for info.

Accommodations
For a B&B in a quiet farm setting, try **The Swan Inn.** Rooms cost $40-65 s, $50-75 d, including a bacon-eggs-and-the-works breakfast. To get there, take Vashon Island Hwy. from either ferry dock to Vashon center; turn west at the light onto S.W. 176th St.; then watch for the blue mailbox (Box 454) and the swan sign.

The least expensive place to stay on the island is the **Vashon Island Ranch/Hostel,** 12119 SW Cove Rd., tel. 463-2592. It is on 10 acres and has a log lodge, tepees, covered wagons, and 14 bunkrooms in the log lodge. Cost is $8 for hostel members, $11 for nonmembers. A single B&B room is available for $55 a night.

Food
Sound Food, mid-island on the Vashon Island Hwy., has a homey atmosphere and tasty food, not to mention a bakery and neighboring natural-foods store. The dinners are reasonably priced; there's a good lunch selection (try the hot sausage sandwich), lots of beer and wine options, and Sunday brunch (closed Tuesday).

Getting There And Around
Washington State Ferry departs at least hourly from Tacoma's Point Defiance to Tahlequah on Vashon Island. The 15-minute trip costs $7.50 (no credit cards) for car and driver on the Point Defiance side; $2.15 for passengers or walk-ons; the return is free, whether you come back to Tacoma or opt for Southworth on the Kitsap Peninsula or Fauntleroy in West Seattle. Call the ferry system—tel. 464-6400 from Seattle, tel. (800) 542-0810 or (800) 542-7052 statewide—for times, or get a schedule when you buy your ticket; there are chunks of time during midafternoon slow periods when the ferries just sit at the dock. For information on Vashon Island buses call 447-4800, or out of area, (800) 542-7876.

ANDERSON ISLAND

As quiet as it is, Vashon Island seems the thriving metropolis when compared to Anderson Island. Miles of roads and rural bike paths are the only attractions to draw mainlanders, with the possible exception of the **Johnson Farm,** founded by John Johnson in 1881. Tour the restored farmhouse, as well as the pilothouse from the *Tahoma,* the island's ferry from 1943 to 1954. Tours are conducted Sat. and Sun. afternoons from Memorial Day weekend through Labor Day.

Getting There
The **Pierce County Ferry System** is the proud owner of the tiny Anderson Island-Steilacoom ferry, which leaves Steilacoom Dock about every two hours from 6 a.m.-6 p.m. Roundtrip fares are $4.30 for car and driver, $1.25 for a foot passenger, and $1.60 for a bicycle rider for the 20-minute run. Don't miss the last 6:30 p.m. departure; you'll be sleeping in the woods or knocking on doors, since there are no motels on the island.

STEILACOOM

The state's oldest incorporated city had established itself as the busiest port on Puget Sound by 1854. Today Steilacoom still clings to and respects its historic heritage. **Bair Drug and Hardware Living Museum** at 1617 Lafayette is an 1895 drugstore, complete with 1906 soda fountain where you can still get a soda or sundae. The museum also serves weekend breakfasts and lunch daily; open 9 a.m.-6 p.m. daily, tel. 588-9668. The **Steilacoom Historical Museum** focuses on the town's pioneer period. Pick up their "Guide to Historic Steilacoom" for a walking tour. It's open Tues., Thurs., and Sun. afternoons, located in the Town Hall on Main and Lafayette; free. The Historical Society also owns the **Nathaniel Orr Home and Orchard,** 1811 Rainier St., a two-story clapboard home built by its owner, who built wagons, coffins, and cabinets. The orchard includes apple, cherry, and plum trees and is well tended. Admission: $1. For information call 584-4133.

Parks
Sunnyside Beach Park off Lafayette St. and **Salters Point Park** off First St. are both small waterfront parks with picnic facilities. **Fort Steilacoom County Park** on Steilacoom Blvd. has game fields plus good-sized Waughop Lake (drive down Dresdon Lane, then park by the barns and take a walk around the Waughop Loop).

Restaurant
Crystal chandeliers, antiques, and a Victorian home overlooking the Sound—an elegant setting for some of the best food around Puget Sound, at out-of-the-way **E.R. Rogers,** 1702 Commercial in Steilacoom, tel. 582-0280. The steak-and-seafood dinners are moderate to expensive, but well worth the money; service is relaxingly slow. If you can't get reservations, at least have a drink in the cozy, upstairs-bedroom bar. Open daily for dinner only, plus Sunday brunch.

FEDERAL WAY

Just north of Tacoma, over the line into King County, is Federal Way. This newly incorporated city is one of the casualties of King County's uncontrolled growth, as developers race to fell the last tree, neighboring houses are maybe 10 feet apart, and gridlock is a way of life. But aside from the malls, fast food, and traffic, Federal Way does hold a few worthwhile surprises.

Amusements
For a commercial form of entertainment, **Wild Waves** and **Enchanted Village,** sister enterprises at 36201 Kit Corner Rd., will keep the whole family amused. Wild Waves, tel. 838-8828, offers 400 feet of whitewater rapids on their Raging River Ride, waterslides, a "beach" with artificial five-foot waves for bodysurfing, and scaled-down versions of the adult attractions for the kiddies. All this for the somewhat steep admission price of $13 ($11 for the kids). They're open from about Memorial Day through Labor Day. All the water is heated so don't worry about the weather. Neighboring Enchanted Village, tel. 838-1700, has rides, a children's museum, and a petting zoo for $8 a head. Open April through Sept. (hours and days vary by season, so call ahead).

Gardens, Parks, And Camping
The Rhododendron Species Foundation Garden, Weyerhaeuser Way, has over 1,800 varieties of rhododendrons from around the world in a 24-acre garden—*something's* in bloom from March through September. Admission is $5 adults, under 13 free; call 927-6960 for days and hours.

Dash Point State Park is located on Puget Sound, on the Pierce-King County line on Hwy. 509, a.k.a. Dash Point Road. The wooded camping area, on the east side of the road, has 108 tent sites and 28 trailer hook-ups (from $7-9.50). On the west, or Sound, side of the park, are a beach (the water here is warm enough for swimming—or at least wading—in summer), picnic tables, and trails that lead to the water.

Saltwater State Park, two miles south of Des Moines on Hwy. 509, has camping at 52 tent sites, a bigger beach, larger picnic area, and a refreshment stand.

Food
Redondo is just west of Federal Way, on Puget Sound; go west on First Ave. S, where

you'll find a fishing pier, boat launch, and one of the area's best restaurants: **Salty's at Redondo.** Primarily a seafood restaurant (moderate to expensive), Salty's has one of the best sunset views around, and you can drink or dine outdoors on the pier in the summer months.

Federal Way seems to have at least one representative from virtually every restaurant chain in the Northwest. There's a **Black Angus** at 2400 S. 320th, where you'll get a decent steak time after time. The **Sea Galley,** 30333 Pacific Hwy. S, specializes in crab legs, very reasonable prices, and fair-to-good food. **The Keg,** 32724 Pacific Hwy. S, specializes in prime rib dinners, but also features a long list of appetizers and sand-

wiches. **Garcia's,** 31740 23rd S, in back of the McDonald's on S. 320th, has reliable Mexican food and some good combination platters. The **Red Robin** at the east end of the Sea-Tac Mall on S. 320th has gourmet burgers, Sunday brunch, and a bar popular with the football crowd. Across 320th from the Sea-Tac Mall, the yuppified **Red Lobster** is quite good, but far too popular to attempt on a Saturday night without reservations—good choice for midweek.

A good place for a light meal is **Lolli's,** 32925 First Ave. S (in the Quad), a restaurant/tavern that serves huge burgers and good sandwiches, along with an extensive selection of beers on tap; it might feel like a bar, but kids are legal and welcome. For home-style Mexican food in a casual setting, try **Bernal's**, 2325 S.W. 336th (in the Safeway Plaza), tel. 838-0448; the lounge features live entertainment every night.

Shopping And Services

The **Sea-Tac Mall** (on the south side of south 320th St., about two lights into Federal Way from I-5) has a Sears, Mervyn's, Lamonts, and The Bon, plus numerous smaller specialty stores. Other shopping centers, drug, and grocery stores line S. 320th on both sides.

The **Greater Federal Way Chamber of Commerce,** at the corner of S. 320th and First at 32015 First Ave. S, tel. 838-2605, can help you out with maps and other area information. The **Federal Way Public Library** is at 848 S. 320th, tel. 839-0257. St. Francis Community Hospital has 24-hour emergency care at 34515 Ninth Ave. S, tel. 927-9700 or 838-9700; from Pacific Hwy. S, go west on 348th and follow the signs.

Transportation

Since Federal Way is in King County, it's served by **Metro,** tel. (800) 542-7876 or 447-4800.

PUYALLUP VALLEY

Events

Puyallup (pronounced pew-AL-up), southeast of Tacoma, is famous, at least in western Washington, for being the home of the **Puyallup Fair,** officially known as the Western Washington Fair. One of the nation's 10 largest, the fair runs for 17 days in Sept. (starting the Friday after Labor Day) and attracts a crowd of more than one million to its concerts, livestock displays, rides, and refreshments. The fairgrounds are located at the intersection of Meridian St. and Ninth Ave. SW.

The **Daffodil Festival** is another of Puyallup's well-known attractions. Sponsored by the region's bulb farms, it's a two-week series of events throughout Pierce County: the daffodil parade (the third-largest floral parade in the nation), a golf tournament, the "most magnificent mutt" show, a boat parade,

and free daffodils everywhere you look. For information on any of the events call 627-6176. The **Van Lierop Bulb Farm** is one of the festival's sponsors; their spring garden display of over 150 varieties of crocuses, irises, tulips, and, of course, daffodils, is something to see. Van Lierop's is located at 13407 80th St. E in Puyallup.

Yet another fair in the Puyallup Valley is the **Pierce County Fair,** held in Graham at 218th and Meridian (Hwy. 161) during the second weekend in August. Highlighted by the infamous cow-chip-throwing contest, there are also floral and photo exhibits, livestock displays, and a five-km race. For information call 843-1173 before, or 847-4754 during, the fair.

Another big summer event is the outdoor production of *Jesus of Nazareth* in Puyallup's open-air amphitheater at 14422 Meridian S, performed at 8 p.m. every Fri. and Sat. night July and August. One of only seven major passion plays in the country, the cast of more than 200 is assisted by horses, cows, sheep, pigeons, and a donkey. For ticket information call 848-3577; the show is a bargain at less than $10.

Parks

Speaking of animals, one of the region's biggest attractions is **Northwest Trek.** On Hwy. 161 near Eatonville (as you drive toward Mt. Rainier), this 600-acre wildlife park is a refuge for bighorn sheep, great blue herons, wild turkeys, bison, elk, moose, and more. A tramway transports tourists on a 5½-mile, hour-long tour through the park; also available are five miles of nature trails. Share your picnic lunch with the tame deer in the visitor center's meadow, or join in a park-sponsored weekend festival, salmon bake, or photo tour. The park is open daily from Feb. through Oct. at 9 a.m. (closing times vary), weekends the rest of the year. The trams leave hourly beginning at 11 a.m. Admission is $6.50 adults, $4.50 kids, $5.50 seniors; phone 832-6116.

Museums

Also near Eatonville, between Hwys. 7 and 161, is the **Pioneer Farm Museum.** Here

TACOMA PUBLIC LIBRARY

Daffodil Princesses surrounded by Puyallup's bounty

you can experience what pioneer life was really like as you grind grain, churn butter, and milk a cow. Hour-and-a-half guided tours leave every 45 minutes. The museum is open daily in summer, on weekends in spring and fall, for a small admission fee.

The "world's largest" collection of Western artifacts is at the **Western Frontier Museum** at 2301 23rd Ave. SE (Trails End Ranch) in Puyallup, tel. 832-6300. They're the proud owners of the "world's largest" longhorn as well as the "world's biggest" longhorn collection, not to mention carriages, arrowheads, guns, and all that other cowboy stuff. Open 9 a.m.-5 p.m. Wed. through Sun., or by appointment; admission $3.50 adults, $2.50 kids and seniors.

Furnished in 1890s style, the 17-room Victorian **Ezra Meeker Mansion** was built by the city's founder and first mayor. Meeker was a pioneer hops grower and also the only person to arrive in the Northwest over the Oregon Trail who also went back over it twice, once driving a team of oxen. He drove over it in an automobile and flew over it in an airplane. Located at 321 E. Pioneer in Puyallup, the mansion is open for tours Wed. through Sun. afternoons, March through mid-Dec.; admission $2 adults, $1 teens and seniors, tel. 848-1770. The Ezra Meeker Days celebration, a week-plus celebration from the end of June through July 6, features a barbecue and extended mansion tour hours.

Accommodations
Puyallup has some of the least expensive lodging around at the **Northwest Motor Inn,** 1409 S. Meridian, tel. 841-2600. The 50 rooms start at $35 s, $39-43 d; whirlpool too.

ENUMCLAW

Home of the King County Fair, Enumclaw (or "Place of the Evil Spirits") was established in 1885, and named for a nearby mountain where local Indians were once frightened by a severe thunderstorm. The views of Mt. Rainier, from just about anywhere in town, are outstanding.

Parks
Eighteen miles southeast of town on Hwy. 410, **Federation Forest State Park,** tel. 663-2207, has 619 acres of virgin forest, plus interpretive displays, hiking trails, fishing, picnicking, and part of the Naches Trail, a pioneer trail that connected eastern Washington with Puget Sound.

Twelve miles north of Enumclaw on Hwy. 169, **Green River Gorge State Park Conservation Area** is a 12-mile-long protected area of the Green River that includes wildflowers, caves, fossils, and **Flaming Geyser State Park.** Here old coal-mining test holes produce two geysers, one burning an eight-inch flame and the other sending methane gas bubbling up through a stream. Enjoy hiking, picnicking, fishing, and boating, and a playground; no camping.

Mud Mountain Dam, seven miles southeast of Enumclaw off Hwy. 410, tel. 825-3211, is one of the highest earth and rock flood-control dams. The park features a nature trail, wading pool, playground, picnic areas, and overlooks. The dam is open daily at 9 a.m.; free.

Bed And Breakfast

Enjoy English hunt club atmosphere in an elegant 1911 home at **Porter House B&B,** 3155 Porter St., tel. 825-7671. Oriental carpets, European antiques, tapestries, and a blue enamel fireplace in the dining room complement the four upstairs guest rooms (two shared baths with claw-foot tubs and shower). Rooms are $55-65 d (singles $5 less) including buffet-style continental breakfast. No pets, indoor smoking, or kids under 14.

Camping

Green River Gorge Resort, tel. 886-2302, has 60 tent sites and 20 drive-through trailer or motorhome sites (30 feet max. length), plus sewer and electric hookups, piped water, flush toilets, showers, and laundromat. Fees are $8 per night (hookups extra). From

Enumclaw, take Hwy. 169 north to Black Diamond Rd., then head four miles east on Green River Gorge Rd.; reservations accepted. Eleven miles northeast of Enumclaw on Farman Rd., Kanaskat-Palmer Recreation Area, tel. 886-0148, has 31 tent sites and 19 drive-through sites (35 feet max. length) on the Green River. Electricity, flush toilets, showers, and boat rentals are available. Fees are $6 per night, no reservations necessary; open all year (limited facilities in winter).

Food

East Coast-style delis are hard to find in the Northwest, but Enumclaw has a good one at **Baumgartner's,** 1008 E. Roosevelt, tel. 825-1067. Pick up a croissant, sausage sandwich, or some wine and cheese for a picnic at Mt. Rainier. Up in Black Diamond at 32805 Railroad Ave., **Black Diamond Bakery,** tel. 886-2741, bakes over 25 varieties of bread in a wood-fired oven, plus donuts, cookies, and other goodies. Closed Monday.

Events

The oldest county fair in the state, **King County Fair,** is held the third week of July at Enumclaw's fairgrounds. A rodeo, live music, 4-H exhibits, food, crafts, and a logger's show highlight the event.

OLYMPIA

Olympia was settled in 1846 by Edmund Sylvester and Levi Smith, who filed claims of over 300 acres each under the Oregon Land Law. The town was named Smithfield until Smith died, leaving his share to Sylvester; then "Smithster" was born. Probably due to the awkward pronunciation, the city's official name was changed to Olympia, after the majestic mountains to the west.

When Washington became a territory in 1853, Governor Isaac Stevens named Olympia the capital—and for the next 40 years, Olympia fought North Yakima, Vancouver, Ellensburg, Centralia, and other growing cities to retain the title. A bill was actually passed in 1861 moving the capital to Vancouver, but because of a minor flaw in wording and the omission of the date, the bill was ruled unconstitutional. (This faulty document is on display at the Washington State Capital Museum.) It wasn't until 1890 that Olympia was finally officially named Washington's state capital.

Although among the oldest of Washington's cities, Olympia certainly isn't one of the biggest, with a population of fewer than 30,000. Being at the southernmost end of Puget Sound would presumably mean an active shipping industry, but the Port of Olympia doesn't begin to compare to Tacoma or Seattle; Olympia's port is primarily a log-moving convenience, as lumber from the forests of the Olympic Peninsula is shipped to its destination. The Olympia Brewery in nearby Tumwater is among the area's biggest businesses; oysters, berries, and mushrooms round out the county's agricultural business. But it's the Capitol Campus that gives Olympia its distinctive stately flavor.

SIGHTS

Capitol Campus
Clearly the highlight of the city, the landscaped grounds and majestic buildings of Olympia's Capitol Campus make it one of the country's most beautiful state capitals. Located between 11th and 14th avenues off Capitol Way, the campus consists of 55 acres of greenery, including an arboretum, a sunken rose garden, and an abundance of rhododendrons and cherry blossoms; a replica of Denmark's Tivoli fountain; and a number of historical buildings dating back to the early 1900s.

The best place to start is at the **visitor information center;** here you can get maps of the campus, brochures, tour information, plus a metered parking space. All of the on-street parking is leased, so visitors must park in one of the visitor lots; or, follow the signs from I-5 exit 105A to the free shuttle bus. The impressive **Legislative Building** is hard to miss: its 287-foot dome was the fourth-largest in the world when it was completed in 1928. Tours of the capitol are offered hourly most of the year; call 586-TOUR. The **Governor's Mansion,** recently restored, is the oldest building on the campus, dating back to 1908. Tours are given Wed. afternoons by appointment; call 586-TOUR. One of the most popular tourist stops is the **State Greenhouse,** which provides all of the floral arrangements and greenery for the Capitol complex. The **State Library** houses a collection of murals, mosaics, paintings, and sculpture by Northwest artists. All state buildings are open Mon. through Fri., 8 a.m.-5 p.m.

A few blocks off the campus at 211 W. 21st Ave., the **Washington State Capital Museum** has permanent exhibits depicting Washington's movement toward statehood, pioneer settlements, and the early history of Northwest publishing, plus rotating exhibits, lectures, and programs. Closed Mon. in winter; tel. 753-2580.

Also off campus at Legion Way and Franklin St., the **Old State Capitol Building** was constructed in 1891 and served as the state capitol from 1903 until the completion of the current Legislative Building in 1928; prior to 1903 it was the Thurston County Courthouse. Today the building is on both the

DOWNTOWN OLYMPIA

BUDD INLET

CAPITOL LAKE

THURSTON

OLYMPIA

STATE AVE.

4 AVE.

5 AVE.

LEGION WAY

7 AVE.

8 AVE.

9 AVE.

10 AVE.

UNION AVE.

11 AVE.

12 AVE.

13 AVE.

14 AVE.

15 AVE.

MAPLE PARK

16 AVE.

17 AVE.

18 AVE.

19 AVE.

20 AVE.

22 AVE.

CAPITOL CAMPUS

WATER

COLUMBIA

CAPITOL WAY

WASHINGTON

FRANKLIN

ADAMS

JEFFERSON

CHERRY

CHESTNUT

E. BAY DR.

PEAR

QUINCE

PLUM

CHESTNUT

HENDERSON BLVD.

5

0   0.1 mi

0   0.1 km

© MOON PUBLICATIONS, INC.

DOWNTOWN OLYMPIA

1. Capitol Lake Park
2. Olympia Oyster House
3. Percival Landing &
   Budd Bay Cafe
4. Farmer's Market
5. Rainbow Restaurant
6. Golden Gavel Motor Hotel
7. Capitol Theatre
8. Crackers
9. Partlow Gallery
10. Washington Center
    for Performing Arts
11. Urban Onion
12. Execulodge/Governor
    House Hotel
13. Sylvester Park
14. Old Capitol
15. Carnegie's
16. Greyhound
17. Best Western Aladdin
18. Gardner's Seafood & Pasta
19. State Greenhouse
20. Governor's Mansion
21. Legislative Building
22. Insurance Building
23. Public Information Center
24. state library
25. State Capital Museum

State and National Register of Historic Places and houses the State Department of Public Instruction. The Old Capitol is open 8 a.m.-5 p.m. Mon.-Fri. (closed during noon hour); group tours are available by calling 753-6740.

Parks

Located at the north end of Capitol Lake at Fifth Ave. and Water St., **Capitol Lake Park** offers cherry blossoms in April, the "Lakefair" festival in July (see p. 114), and swimming, sailing, hiking, biking, and picnicking the rest of the year. At Seventh Ave. and Capitol Way, **Sylvester Park,** named for city founder Edmund Sylvester, hosts noontime concerts on Fri. from June through August. Six miles north of Olympia on Boston Harbor Rd., **Bur-**

foot County Park has an interpretive trail, hiking trails, saltwater beach, playground, and an open, grassy picnic area. Closer to the city on both sides of E. Bay Dr.,**Priest Point Park** has 253 wooded acres of picnic areas, trails, a wading pool, and playground, plus access to Budd Inlet; no overnight camping. Located on Henderson Blvd., the main attraction of **Olympia Watershed Park** is its two-mile hiking trail through woods, marsh, and streams. A walk along the boardwalk at **Percival Landing** at State Ave. and Water St. provides views of the port's activities. This is also the scene of the Labor Day weekend "Harbor Days" festival (see p. 115).

Zabel's Rhododendrons

Washington's state flower is displayed en masse at this four-acre park, where 1,200 rhodies and azaleas are yours to behold on an hour-long, self-guided tour from early May through Memorial Day. This is private property, so smoking, pets, and picnicking are not allowed. To get there, go east on San Francisco Ave. from E. Bay Dr., then go north on N. Bethel St. and follow the signs to 2432 N. Bethel; call 357-3370 for exact dates and times.

Olympia Oysters

The rare and tiny Olympia oyster lives only in the southernmost reaches of Puget Sound in beds in Big Skookum, Little Skookum, Oyster, and Mud bays. In the mid-1920s the average annual harvest peaked at about 48,000 bushels, but then a Shelton pulp mill released pollutants that sharply decreased their numbers. The oyster population dwindled still further after the 1930s, when the importation of Japanese oysters began. These oysters brought with them two pests: the Japanese oyster drill and the Japanese flatworm, harmful only to smaller oysters like the Olympia.

By 1978 the Olympia oyster harvest amounted to a mere 500 bushels. They're bisexual in the truest sense, performing as males in the spring when they release a large quantity of sperm into the water, then changing into females and producing up to 300,000

the old state capitol

eggs which become fertilized as the oyster takes in the sperm it had previously expelled.

To see how the rare Olympia oysters are raised, opened, and packed, visit the **Taylor United, Inc.**, plant. Tours are by appointment only; tel. 426-6178. To get there take exit 104 from I-5 onto Hwy. 101; take Hwy. 101 to Taylor Farm, S.E. 130 Lynch Rd., about three miles south of Shelton.

ACCOMMODATIONS

Bed And Breakfast

Built in 1910, **Harbinger Inn,** 1136 E. Bay Dr., tel. 754-0389, has three rooms with shared bath from $44-48 s, $48-56 d, plus a two-room suite with marina view and private bath for $73 s, $78 d. Enjoy late afternoon tea and cookies with a book from their library; no pets or kids under 12.

Hotels

Downtown at 909 Capitol Way, the **Golden Gavel Motor Hotel,** tel. 352-8533, has 27 budget rooms from $32 s, $37 d. Just off I-5 at exit 105B, the **Carriage Inn Motel,** 1211 S. Quince, tel. 943-4710, has 63 rooms from $34 s, $43 d. Within walking distance of the capitol, the **Execulodge Governor House Hotel,** 621 S. Capitol Way, tel. 352-7700 or (800) 356-5335, has 120 rooms from $70 s, $76 d, in an eight-story building overlooking Sylvester Park and Capitol Lake. Also on the premises are a restaurant, bar, coffee shop, and heated outdoor pool.

Best Western Aladdin Hotel, 900 Capitol Way, tel. 352-7200, is just three blocks from the Capitol Campus. Their 99 rooms are $42-46 s, $47-56 d, with outdoor pool, restaurant, and lounge; pets okay. Perched atop the hill on Evergreen Park Drive.

The **Westwater Inn** has the city's best viewpoint, taking in the Capitol Dome, Capitol Lake, the Budd Inlet, and the Cascades. Rooms in this top-shelf hotel are surprisingly affordable: $54 s, $62 d and up. For real luxury, Jacuzzi suites ($75-85), and parlor suites ($120) are also available; pets are $10 extra. Standard equipment includes a heated outdoor pool, whirlpool, laundry facilities, and outdoor volleyball court; restaurant, lounge, and coffee shop on premises. Phone (800) 562-5635 statewide or 943-4000 locally to make reservations.

For other hotels and motels in the Olympia area see "Vicinity of Olympia," below.

Camping

Tenters and RVers can stay relatively close to town at **Black Lake RV Park,** 4325 Black Lake-Belmore Rd. SW, tel. 357-6775, on the east shore of Black Lake four miles southwest of downtown Olympia. Open year-round, the resort offers full hookups for $9 per night, non-hookup sites for $7, with weekly and monthly rates. Lake swimming, boat rentals, game room, hot showers, and groceries are also available.

Camping for hundreds of vehicles is available year-round at the **ORV Sports Park** on Hwy. 8, 16 miles west of Olympia. Fees are $5 per night on non-event days, $3 per night on event weekends (the $2 gate makes up the difference); hot pay showers and picnic tables are provided. See "Entertainment," below, for events held.

Open May through Sept., **American Heritage** at 9610 Kimmie St. SW, tel. 943-8778, has over 100 campsites with full hookups, showers, heated pool; other amenities include free evening movies, arcade, kiddie farm, and go-carts. To get there, take exit 99 from I-5 and head east.

FOOD

Waterfront and view restaurants aren't as common in Olympia as in other Puget Sound cities. The **Ebb Tide Inn,** one of few, sits right on the water at the end of N. Washington St., past the none-too-busy Port of Olympia. Their steak-and-seafood menu is highlighted by a seafood bar and outdoor deck, and the lounge offers entertainment nightly; tel. 943-7770. The **Budd Bay Café** at Percival Landing is open for lunch and dinner daily, with outdoor dining in summer featuring a peaceful marina view. **Seven Gables,** 1205 W. Bay Dr., tel. 352-2349, looks across Budd Inlet toward Mt. Rainier, and the view isn't even the best part; the moderately priced menu features a wide variety, including steak, chicken, fettucine, and seafood. Open for dinner Tues. through Sat., Sun. for brunch.

Washington's oldest seafood restaurant, the **Olympia Oyster House,** has been serving the precious delicacies for over 50 years at 320 W. Fourth Ave., tel. 943-8020. Prices for a plate of Olympia oysters haven't changed much in that time; they're still about $20, though at lunchtime you can get a smaller portion for $10. Other dinners include fettucine, steak, chicken, and seafood-and-steak combinations.

Carnegie's, Seventh and Franklin, tel. 357-5550, serves moderately priced Northwest seafood, Cajun food, and prime rib in the old Carnegie Library, a national historic site. **Gardner's Seafood and Pasta,** 111 W. Thurston St., tel. 786-8466, is the place to go for local specialties—Dungeness crab, geoduck, Olympia oysters—at moderate prices; open for dinner daily. **Patrick's,** in the Execulodge Governor House Hotel at 621 S. Capitol Way, tel. 352-7700, features Pacific Northwest seafood, steak, and veal, with a piano bar; closed Sunday. **Ceazans,** the restaurant at the Westwater Inn, has the best views in the area from its hilltop setting at 2300 Evergreen Park Dr., tel. 943-4000, with a fancy steak-and-seafood menu in the moderate range. Dinner is served Mon. through Sat., with a Sunday Champagne brunch.

One of the city's most lively late-night eating spots is **Crackers,** in the Wards Building at 317 E. Fourth Avenue. They're open Sun. through Thurs. till midnight, weekends till 3 a.m., and open daily at 7 a.m. for breakfast. The menu (loaded with puns) includes a number of breakfast omelettes in the $4-5 range, burgers and sandwiches around $5, and dinner entrees, including seafood, chicken, veal, pasta, and steak, from $7-14, in oak-and-hanging-plants decor.

For an all-natural breakfast, lunch, or dinner, try the **Urban Onion** at the corner of Legion and Washington, tel. 943-9242. Their "wholesome cuisine," consisting of salads and sandwiches, pasta, stir-fries, and Mexican meals, is served daily from 7 a.m.-midnight.

The local pizza chain is **Brewery City Pizza,** with free delivery from 1621 Harrison Ave. NW, tel. 754-7800, on the west side. For dinner with a horse show, see below.

ENTERTAINMENT AND EVENTS

Nightlife
The more upscale restaurants and hotels (see above and "Tumwater," below) generally have subdued entertainment nightly (except Sunday) in the lounges. **Patrick's** at the Execulodge Governor House Hotel has live comedy on Sat. nights. The **Columbia St. Pub,** Fourth and Columbia, is known for its Sat. night jazz. **Trails End** at the Tumwater Trails End Arena is fully licensed with Tues. night comedy acts and dancing to Top 40 tunes on Fri. and Sat. nights; to get there, follow Capitol Blvd. South to Trails End Drive.

Equestrian Competitions
Follow Capitol Blvd. south to the **Trails Arena** at 7824 Trails End Dr. SE (technically in Tumwater), where horse shows of various types are held several times a week, as well

DIANNE BOULERICE LYONS

the Legislative Building

as an occasional circus and BMX race. The **Trails Restaurant,** tel. 753-8720, overlooks the arena, offering moderately priced lunch and dinner, including a build-your-own-dinner menu where you can select the side dishes to accompany your entree. Entry to the lower arena is generally free. Restaurant reservations are highly recommended.

ORV Sports Park

Thurston County provides an abundance of opportunities for off-roaders, with the ORV trails in Capitol Forest and 157 acres devoted to ORV usage in the **Thurston and Grays Harbor Counties ORV Sports Park,** located on the south side of Hwy. 8 about 16 miles west of Olympia. The park has a motocross track, hillclimb, trail riding area, kiddy motocross track, and camping (see "Camping" above). Motocross and four-wheel-drive competitions are held nearly every weekend, year-round; admission is $2. Call 495-3243 for recorded information.

The Arts

Masterworks Choral Ensemble performs four concerts a year including Handel's *Messiah,* most of them at the **Washington Center for the Performing Arts,** 512 S. Washington Street. Tickets are $10 or less and are available in advance by writing Box 1091, Olympia, WA 98507. The WCPA also hosts an "Artists Series" featuring such performers as the Seattle Symphony, the Vienna Boys' Choir, ballet, theater, and the Peking Acrobats (from Oct. to April). Tickets are $12-23, depending on the performance and seating; to order ahead, write to the Washington Center for the Performing Arts at Box 202, Olympia, WA 98507. Tickets for all performances are also available at the box office (subject to availability) from 10 a.m.-6 p.m. Mon. through Fri., 10 a.m.-2 p.m. Sat. and two hours prior to the event.

Capitol Playhouse '24, located in the historic Capitol Theatre at 206 E. Fifth Ave., tel. 754-5378, produces four plays from Dec. to May as well as a summer Shakespeare Festival, consisting of three plays from June through August. Tickets may be purchased at the playhouse.

Galleries

Downtown Olympia has a number of art galleries and boutiques on Fourth and Fifth avenues good for browsing. The **Marianne Partlow Gallery** at Fifth and Washington, tel. 943-0055, is probably the most impressive, representing artists from the Northwest and beyond; open Tues. through Saturday.

Festivals And Fairs

The **Wooden Boat Festival,** tel. 357-3370, held in mid-May at Percival Landing, includes a regatta and wooden boats open for public viewing. The first Sat. in June, Evergreen State College's **Super Saturday** features arts and crafts, food, and entertainment for all ages; phone 866-6000, ext. 6192, for information. The city's biggest summer festival is **Capital Lakefair,** held in mid-July, tel. 943-7344. Activities include a bicycle road race, twilight parade, bed races, regatta, fireworks, and crowning of the Lakefair queen. The **Capital City**

Marathon brings runners from across the U.S. to compete the fourth Sat. in July; phone RUN-1-RUN for information.

Summer's end brings the **Harbor Days Festival** to Percival Landing over Labor Day weekend, highlighted by a regatta and tugboat races in the Sound; call 866-1988 for information.

SHOPPING

Olympia's **Farmer's Market** at the corner of N. Capitol and Thurston has fresh fruit and vegies Thurs. through Sun. 10 a.m.-3 p.m. **Capital Mall,** Ninth Ave. SW and Black Lake Blvd., is the area's largest shopping center with nearly 100 shops and restaurants, including Frederick & Nelson, Bon Marché, JCPenney, and Lamonts. Just up Black Lake Blvd. is another shopping plaza, Capital Village, with grocery, drug, and hardware stores plus a sprinkling of fast-food restaurants. See "Lacey" below for South Sound Center.

INFORMATION AND SERVICES

The area code in and around Olympia is 206. For maps and general information stop by the **Greater Olympia Visitors and Convention Bureau,** 316 Schmidt Pl. in Tumwater, tel. 357-3370, or write Box 7249, Olympia, WA 98507; or, try the **Olympia/Thurston County Chamber of Commerce,** 1000 Plum St., Olympia, WA 98501, tel. 357-3362.

Surrounding communities have their own chambers of commerce: **Lacey Chamber of Commerce,** next to Pay 'N' Save at 7 S. Sound Center, Box 3206, Lacey, WA 98503, tel. 491-4141; **Tumwater Area Chamber of Commerce,** 488 Tyee Dr., Tumwater, WA 98502, tel. 357-5153; **Tenino Chamber of Commerce,** 208 Sussex Ave., Box 726, Tenino, WA 98589, tel. 264-5075.

Members of AAA can get guidebooks and area maps from their office at 1000 E. Union, tel. 357-5561.

For medical emergencies, **St. Peter Hospital** has 24-hour emergency room service at 413 N. Lilly Rd., tel. 456-7289. To get there, take exit 107 from I-5 northbound, exit 109 from I-5 southbound. **Black Hills Community Hospital** is near Capital Mall on Olympia's west side, tel. 754-5858. For non-life-threatening emergencies, try **Westcare Clinic,** on the west side at 3000 Limited Lane NW, tel. 357-9392.

TRANSPORTATION

Arriving By Car
Olympia is 60 miles, about an hour's drive, south of Seattle (a half hour south of Tacoma) on I-5, at the south end of Puget Sound.

Arriving By Air
To get to the capital city via a major carrier, you'll have to fly into Sea-Tac Airport (just south of Seattle) and get ground transportation into the city. **Capital Aeroporter,** tel. 754-7113, serves Olympia 12 times a day from Sea-Tac; the one-way fare is $17. Get up-to-the-minute information on ground transportation schedules and rates, weather and traffic conditions by calling the airport at (800) 544-1965 from a touch-tone phone.

Arriving By Train
Amtrak serves Olympia along its north-south *Coast Starlight* route from Seattle to Los Angeles and via its *Pioneer* route from Seattle to Salt Lake City. The Amtrak station is in east Olympia at 83rd and Rich Rd. SE. For schedule and fare information call (800) 872-7245.

Getting Around By Bus
Intercity Transit serves Olympia, Tumwater, and most of Thurston County Mon. through Fri., 7 a.m.-5:30 p.m. The regular adult fare is $.35, kids $.25; day passes are available for $.75 adults, $.50 kids. Take advantage of the free zone covering downtown Olympia and the Capitol Campus area from 11 a.m.-2 p.m. weekdays. For route and schedule information call 786-1881, or stop by the customer-service office at 526 S. Pattison during normal working hours.

Pierce Transit, tel. 581-8000, offers an "Olympia Express" route from the Lakewood

Park and Ride (south of Tacoma at I-5 exit 127) to the Capitol Campus. Geared toward commuters, the bus leaves Lakewood at 6:40 a.m. and 7 a.m., then departs the Capitol for the return to Lakewood at 4:40 p.m. and 5:10 p.m. The one-way fare is $1.25.

Greyhound connects Olympia to Seattle, Tacoma, Portland, and other cities along its north-south I-5 corridor, connecting to virtually anywhere in the country. For specific route and fare information call 357-5541 or visit the bus station at Capitol and Seventh.

BOB RACE

VICINITY OF OLYMPIA

LACEY AREA

A few miles northeast of Olympia right off I-5, Lacey is primarily a suburban shopping area and retirement village. Just east and slightly north of Lacey proper is the Nisqually Delta, preserved wetlands geographically identical to Tacoma's industrial tideflat area.

Parks

Just off I-5 at exit 114, **Nisqually National Wildlife Refuge** is a protected home for 300 species of wildlife, including great blue herons, bald eagles, and red-tailed hawks, as well as a resting area for over 20,000 migrating ducks and geese. A 5.6-mile hiking loop trail, a one-mile loop trail, a half-mile interpretive trail, and photo blinds assist you in your birdwatching; be sure to bring binoculars and a field guide. A boat-launch ramp is available at Luhr Beach; to use the landing you'll need a hunting, fishing, or trapping license, or a conservations decal, available from the State Game Dept., 516 N. Washington, Olympia, tel. 753-5717. Visitors are welcome at the refuge seven days a week during daylight hours; a $2 entry fee covers the permit holder and his spouse, children, and/or parents. No jogging, bicycling, motorbikes, pets, fires, or camping.

The **Audubon Nature Center,** 4949 D'Milluhr Rd. NE at Luhr Beach on Nisqually Reach, tel. 459-0387, has marine animals and birds, a museum, fishing dock, boat launch, picnic area, guided tours, and raft trips. Open Wed., Sat., and Sun. afternoons.

Tolmie State Park, five miles from exit 111, has 1,800 feet of waterfront on Nisqually Reach with swimming, fishing, 3½ miles of hiking trails, and an underwater park with an artificial reef created by the intentional sinking of three wooden barges. Open for day use only, the park also provides an outdoor shower for swimmers and divers near the lower restroom. The park was named for Dr. William Frazer Tolmie, who spent 16 years at Fort Nisqually as physician, surgeon, botanist, and fur trader for Hudson's Bay Company. Tolmie also studied the languages of the Northwest people—his communication skills proved invaluable for negotiations during the Indian Wars of 1855-56.

Accommodations

Just 500 feet from the entrance to Tolmie State Park, **Puget View Guest House,** a B&B at 7924 61st Ave. NE, tel. 459-1676, has two-room waterfront cottage suites for $65 d (they'll hold four) on peaceful Nisqually Reach—a beautiful, natural setting only five minutes from I-5. Breakfast is brought to your cottage door; overnight anchorage is available for boaters. For motel accommodations just 10 minutes from downtown Olympia, the **Super 8** at 4615 Martin Way, tel. 459-8888, is just off I-5 at exit 109. Rooms are $38 s, $42-46 d.

Food

Lacey's **Brewery City Pizza** is at 4354 Martin Way, tel. 491-6630. Next door, **O'Blarney's Pub,** 4411 Martin Way, has hard-to-find Irish music and sing-alongs on Tuesdays. Martin Way and Sleater-Kinney Rd. are lined with fast-food restaurants. **La Palma II** has Mexican food and a lounge at 523 South Sound Center, tel. 459-9805.

Fairs And Festivals

Lacey's **Spring Fun Fair** is held in early May at St. Martin's College and South Sound Center; phone 491-4141 for details. The **Thurston County Fair,** held the first full weekend in August at the County Fairgrounds in Lacey, is a five-day festival with entertainment, food, and booths. Call 786-5453 for hours and information.

VICINITY OF OLYMPIA

PUGET SOUND

OYSTER BAY

STEAMBOAT ISLAND RD. NW

COOPER RD. NW

BUDD INLET

TOLMIE S.P.

17

MARVIN RD. NE

AUDUBON NATURE CENTER

101

SOUTH BAY RD. NE

NISQUALLY NAT'L WILDLIFE REFUGE

8

11

12

3

2

DOWNTOWN OLYMPIA

NE 4 AVE.

13

16

14

15

5

LACEY

OLYMPIA

10

510

4

BLACK LAKE BLVD. SW

TUMWATER

1

DELPHI RD. SW

BLACK LAKE

5

6

YELM HWY. SE

OLYMPIA MUNI AIRPORT

8

LITTLEROCK RD. SW

7

AMTRAK

EAST OLYMPIA

DELPHI

TO CAPITOL PEAK

MILLERSYLVANIA S.P.

OFFUTT LAKE

MIMA MOUNDS

DEEP LAKE

LITTLEROCK

121

9

MAYTOWN

DEEP LAKE RESORT

TILLY RD. SW

TENINO

507

121

SUSSEX ST.

OLD HWY. 99 SE

TENINO CITY PARK DEPOT MUSEUM

5

OLD HWY. 99

507

12

GRAND MOUND

0   3 mi

0   3 km

MOON

© MOON PUBLICATIONS, INC.

VICINITY OF OLYMPIA 119

VICINITY OF OLYMPIA

1. Black Lake RV Park
2. Capitol Village Shipping Center and Capitol Mall
3. Seven Gables Restaurant
4. Olympia Brewery, Tumwater Historical Park, Crosby House, Henderson House, South Pacific, and Falls Terrace Restaurant
5. Tyee Motel
6. Motel 6
7. American Heritage KOA
8. The Trails Arena
9. Wolf Haven
10. Olympia Watershed Park
11. Priest Point Park
12. Zabel's Rhododendrons
13. St. Peter's Hospital
14. Brewery City Pizza and O'Blarney's Pub
15. South Sound Shopping Center
16. Super 8
17. Puget View Guest House

Shopping

Just off I-5 at exit 108 is **South Sound Center,** an enclosed mall with over 100 shops and restaurants, including Sears, Mervyn's, and Nordstrom Place Two. **Olympia Square,** just off I-5 on both sides of Pacific Ave., has a Ross Dress for Less, Food Pavilion, and Sizzler's Restaurant. Enjoy one-stop shopping for warehouse-priced groceries, clothes, jewelry, and more at **Fred Meyer,** just off Sleater-Kinney Rd. across from South Sound Center.

TUMWATER

The home of Olympia beer was Washington's first community—then named New Market—settled in 1845 along the Deschutes River at the end of the Oregon Trail. Starting at Independence, Missouri, the families in the Wagon Train of 1844 endured 19 months of cold, rain, and wearying travel through

what's now Kansas, Nebraska, Wyoming, Idaho, and Oregon, en route to their final destination above Tumwater Falls. Members of Hudson's Bay Co., who had been stationed at Fort Nisqually since 1833, provided the settlers with the makings for the first sawmill north of the Columbia and traded Army supplies for wood shingles.

Brewery

Heading down Deschutes Way toward Tumwater, you can't miss the **Olympia Brewery** immediately adjacent to Tumwater Falls Park (see below) at Custer Way and Schmidt Place. A 40-minute tour of their facilities runs daily from 8 a.m.-4:30 p.m.

Parks

The **Tumwater Historical Park,** 602 Deschutes Way, is the site of the first American settlement in the Puget Sound region, founded in 1845. The neatly landscaped grounds include picnic areas, a boat launch into the Deschutes, an exercise trail, and lots of hungry ducks. Farther south on Deschutes Way, butting up against the brewery, you'll find **Tumwater Falls Park,** where you may see salmon heading upstream in the fish ladders.

Museums

Henderson House Pictorial Museum, 602 Deschutes Way, has photographic exhibits depicting life along the Deschutes River during the late 1800s, and recent photos of Tumwater's people and events; open daily in summer, Tues. through Sat. in winter. The **Crosby House,** adjacent to Tumwater Historical Park at Deschutes Way and Grant St., is Tumwater's oldest home; it was built in 1860 by Bing Crosby's grandfather, Capt. Nathaniel Crosby III, who came around the Horn to the Oregon Territory in 1847 and inspired the whole Crosby clan to follow him out West. Open by appointment only.

Accommodations

The **Tyee Hotel,** 500 Tyee Dr., provides a resort-like atmosphere to its guests with 20 landscaped acres of grounds, outdoor pool, and pickleball and basketball courts, while still offering reasonable rates from $57 s or d. Their restaurant, **Sutter's,** serves seafood, steak, and prime rib. For reservations call (800) 426-0670 or 352-0511.

For a distinctively non-resort atmosphere, **Motel 6,** near the brewery at 400 W. Lee St., tel. 754-7320, has 119 standard motel rooms for $24 s, $30 d with an outdoor pool.

Food
In front of the Olympia Brewery and next to Tumwater Falls Park, **Falls Terrace** has a new peach paint job and some nice surprises inside. Lunches include sandwiches, fish, burgers, steaks, and salads; moderately priced dinners feature chicken dishes, steak, seafood, veal, and traditional meals like pot roast and turkey dinners. A lower-priced early-bird menu is offered before the dinner crowds show up.

Migel's serves Mexican food at the Tumwater Valley Golf Course, 4611 Tumwater Valley Dr. SE. For Chinese and Polynesian food, try **South Pacific,** next to the brewery at 3507 Capitol Blvd., tel. 352-0701. Or have a **Brewery City Pizza** delivered free from 5150 Capitol Blvd., tel. 754-6767.

Festival
The third weekend in May the **Tumwater Bluegrass Festival** brings fiddlers and banjo-pickers to Tumwater High School on Israel Road. Bluegrass concerts run from Fri. through Sun. with contests, booths, and Sun. morning gospel music. Call 357-5153 for information.

Golf
Open to the public, the 18-hole **Tumwater Valley Golf Course,** 4611 Tumwater Valley Dr. SE, tel. 943-9500, has a driving range, pro shop, and lessons.

TENINO

From downtown Olympia, follow Capitol Blvd. S onto Old Hwy. 99 to Tenino, a small, old, quiet town probably best known for its sandstone quarry. The name Tenino has a handful of possible origins, from the Indian name for a fork or junction, to the more colorful Engine Number 1090 (ten-nine-oh) that ran on the Kalama-Tacoma railroad line in the 1870s.

Wolf Haven
This 30-acre wolf refuge is home to 39 wolves (plus coyotes and red foxes) who were taken in for a variety of reasons; some were no longer needed by researchers, some were mistreated or unwanted by zoos and refuges, and others were family "pets" who grew predictably wild. These former misfits are now loved and wanted—even introduced to visitors by name. The sanctuary offers guided tours and "howl-ins," featuring a marshmallow roast, reciting of Eskimo and Indian folk legends, singing, and howling with the wolves, 7-10 p.m. on Fri. and Sat. nights during the summer. Wolf Haven is at 3111 Offut Lake Rd., just off Old Hwy. 99, tel. 264-4695; open daily May to Sept., Wed. to Sat. in winter. Tours $3 adults, $2 kids; howl-ins $4 adults, $2.50 kids.

Park And Museum
One block off Sussex St., **Tenino City Park** has overnight camping and picnic areas plus the **Tenino Depot Museum,** 399 W. Park St., tel. 264-4321, an original sandstone train depot housing a collection of historical Tenino and southern Thurston County artifacts. Open Sunday 1-4 p.m or by appointment, tel. 264-4620.

Festival
The fourth weekend in July brings all kinds of commotion to quiet Tenino with the **Oregon Trail Celebration.** A parade, muzzle-loading camp, and kids' carnival highlight the fair.

LOUISE FOOTE

(top) Riverfront Park, Spokane (Washington State Tourism Division)
(bottom left) downtown Seattle and Elliot Bay (Seattle-King County Convention and Visitors Bureau)
(bottom right) Seattle's Space Needle (Seattle-King County Convention and Visitors Bureau)

(top left) Palouse Falls (Archie Satterfield)
(top right) San Juan Islands (Dianne Boulerice Lyons)
(bottom) sunset at Olympic National Park (Dianne Boulerice Lyons)

DELPHI

Eight miles south of Tumwater is the **Mima Mounds Interpretive Area,** a registered national landmark with nature walks, an interpretive center, and picnic area. These grass-covered mounds, ranging in height up to eight feet, are also scattered throughout southern Thurston County, parts of China, and Alaska. They're often referred to as "mysterious" because no one really knows how they got there; theoretical origins range from glaciers to giant gophers.

From Mima Mounds continue north on Waddell Creek Rd. to Capitol Forest, a multi-use "working" forest (look out for logging trucks) in the Black Hills. Free primitive campsites are available for tents and small trailers at nine locations within the forest; hiking and horseback riding trails are clustered in the south end of the park while trailbikes may use those in the north end. Hunting and fishing are also permitted. To get a panoramic view of the area, follow the marked dirt road from Waddell Creek Rd. to 2,658-foot Capitol Peak, highest point in the Black Hills.

MAYTOWN

Maytown's most notable attraction is **Millersylvania State Park** on Deep Lake. Constructed between 1933 and 1939 by 200 members of the Civilian Conservation Corps, the park has facilities for swimming, boating, trout fishing, hiking, picnicking, and camping within its 840 forested acres on Tilly Road. Just south of the entrance to Millersylvania, **Deep Lake Resort**, 12405 Tilley Rd. S, tel. 352-7388, has lakeside cabin rentals ($210-350 per week, $35-58 per day if available), camping (tents to full hookups) for $10-13 per night, lake swimming, playground, showers, laundry facilities, boating, and bike rentals on Deep Lake. Open late April through September.

EVERETT

Jumping suddenly north of Seattle, Everett is on Puget Sound about 25 miles north of Seattle. It is a largely industrial city (pop. 57,000), with most people employed by the Boeing 747 plant but still economically dependent on lumber and wood products. The city is flanked by mountains, with Mt. Baker to the north, Mt. Rainier to the south, and 5,324-foot Mt. Pilchuck to the east. Coupled with its waterfront location, Everett is surrounded by recreational opportunities, as well as more indoor fun than most cities its size.

HISTORY

Everett is one of the few Puget Sound areas that prompted Capt. George Vancouver to get off his boat. After coming ashore, Vancouver named the area "New Georgia" for King George III, and the English claim to this land lasted for more than 50 years.

The city of Everett was established in 1891 in boomtown fashion when John D. Rockefeller and other big Eastern investors planned to build the "New York City of the West," aided by rumors that the Great Northern Railroad would make Port Gardner its first Puget Sound stop. As much or more influential than Rockefeller in Everett's development was a man named Frederick Weyerhaeuser. Born in Germany in 1834, he immigrated to the U.S. in 1852, where he worked in an Illinois lumber mill and married a German woman, Elizabeth Bloedel. Weyerhaeuser was so hard-working and thrifty that he was able to buy the mill a few years later, and then expanded his operation westward. His main Pacific coast lumber mill was built in Everett in 1903, becoming—and long remaining—the city's most important industry. When he died, Weyerhaeuser's lumber company was the biggest in the country.

SIGHTS

Mansions
In its early years, Everett was home to some of the timber industry's most successful entrepreneurs. Not bashful about their financial success, these lumber barons built elaborate mansions in the north end of town on Grand and Rucker avenues, many of which are still there.

Boeing's 747-767
assembly plant

DIANNE BOULERICE LYONS

Everett's lumber barons lived in exquisite mansions.

DIANNE BOULERICE LYONS

Boeing Tour

For kids over 12, touring Boeing's 747-767 assembly plant is the highlight of a visit to Everett. The plant itself, 115 feet high, has the largest cubic capacity of any building in the world; seeing one of these enormous airplanes indoors is an impressive visual experience. Ninety-minute tours, held weekdays, include a slide show; tel. 342-4801. To get there, take I-5 exit 189 west onto Hwy. 526. For a bus tour from Seattle, see p. 71.

Museums

One of Everett's oldest commercial buildings, constructed in 1906, houses the **Snohomish County Museum,** 2915 Hewitt Ave., tel. 259-8849. See a kitchen and bedroom typical of Everett at the turn of the century, plus photographs and Indian artifacts. Open Wed. through Sun. afternoons; free. At the 13th St. dock, see a collection of fire-fighters' equipment at the **Firefighters Museum** any time; the museum was designed for through-the-window viewing.

PARKS AND RECREATION

Located on Alverson Blvd., **Legion Park** features a par course, tennis courts, and ballfield. **Forest Park** on Mukilteo Blvd. has a children's zoo, heated indoor public pool, and

live music performed by local bands on Sun. afternoons June through August.

Golf

There are three public 18-hole golf courses in the Everett area. In Everett proper, there's **Legion Memorial** at 144 W. Marine View Dr., tel. 259-GOLF, and the **Walter E. Hall Golf Course** at 1226 W. Casino Rd., tel. 353-GOLF. Up north a bit is the **Kayak Point Golf Course,** 13 miles west of Marysville at 15711 Marine Dr., tel. 652-9676 or (800) 562-3094.

ACCOMMODATIONS

Motels And Hotels

Everett has a good selection of clean, cheap lodging: **Motel 6,** 10006 Evergreen Way, tel. 347-2060, has 119 rooms and a pool for $24 s, $30 d; the **Royal Motor Inn** at Hwy. 99 and 10th St., tel. 259-5177, has 35 rooms and a heated pool for $25-29 s, $29-38 d; and the **Everett Mall Inn,** 1602 S.E. Everett Mall Way, tel. 355-1570, has a pool, coffee shop, and 63 budget rooms from $38.50 s, $42.50 d. The **Cherry Motel,** 8421 Evergreen Way, has complimentary continental breakfast and nonsmoking rooms for $29-32 s, $33-41 d; call 347-1100.

At 9602 19th Ave. SE, the **Northwest Motor Inn,** tel. 337-9090, has 120 rooms across from the Everett Mall for $35-45 s, $41-48 d, with a pool, hot tub, and kitchen units available. At the **Cypress Inn-Everett,** 12619 Fourth Ave. W, tel. 347-9099 or (800) 752-9981 statewide, enjoy king Jacuzzi suites, continental breakfast, van service, outdoor pool, and more, starting at $49.

For something significantly nicer, the **WestCoast Everett Pacific Hotel,** 3105 Pine St., has an exercise room, indoor pool, sauna, hot tub, lounge with nightly entertainment, some in-room refrigerators, children's activity center, room and poolside service, free airport, bus station, or railroad shuttle, and 254 rooms from $66 s, $76 d; tel. (800) 833-8001 toll-free statewide or 339-3333 locally for reservations.

Another larger facility is the **Holiday Hotel** off I-5 at 128th St., tel. 745-2555, with an indoor pool, sauna, hot tub, tennis courts, shuttle, valet service, entertainment nightly except Sun., and 210 rooms starting at $50-60 s, $55-65 d. With many of the same features plus access to the local health club, **Nendel's Motor Inn** at 2800 Pacific Ave. has 133 rooms starting from $57 s or $63 d; tel. (800) 547-0106 in Washington or 258-4141 locally.

For exceptional lodging, stay at **Marina Village Inn** at the Everett Marina on W. Marine View Dr., tel. 259-4040. Several of the 28 rooms overlook the water; other amenities include wet bars, bathroom phones, and refrigerator, with Jacuzzis in the higher-priced doubles. Rates are $68-140 s or d.

RV Park

Located at 11621 W. Silver Lake Dr., **Silver Shores RV Park,** tel. 337-8741, has tennis, swimming, and fishing at Silver Lake, and water and electric hookups for $15, tent sites for $10.

FOOD

Everett Marina Village has four waterfront restaurants: **Anthony's Home Port,** tel. 252-3333, has fresh Northwest and imported seafood flown in fresh daily to serve at lunch, dinner, or Sunday brunch, or on their New Orleans-style oyster bar; dinner prices are in

the $9-19 range. **Bacchus By The Bay,** tel. 258-6254, serves three meals (including lunch omelettes) and one of the widest wine selections in the area; take-out deli sandwiches are available for boaters or picnickers. **Pelican Pete's,** tel. 252-3155, is a little more casual, with seafood, steaks, pasta, and a fish-and-chips-and-burger bar, all at moderate prices; you can also dance at this popular singles spot from 10 p.m.-2 a.m. Tues. through Sat. nights, with Tues. night comedy at 9:30 p.m. **Bee-Bee's Fish and Chips** is open daily for three meals, specializing in fresh fish and chips, onion rings, burgers, and more.

Panivino, 6309 Evergreen Way, tel. 353-4635, serves moderately priced, top-quality pasta, sandwiches, and salads in unlikely shopping center surroundings. For more Italian cuisine including fresh pastas, seafoods, imported wines, and pizza-to-go try **Gianni's Piccola Italia,** 5030 Evergreen Way, tel. 252-2435. Open for dinner only; closed Monday. **Gerry Andal's Ranch Restaurant,** 620 S.E. Everett Mall Way, tel. 355-7999, features a full American ranch-style menu .

Down in Mukilteo, just west of the intersection of highways 525 and 526, **Charles at Smugglers Cove,** 8310 53rd Ave. W, tel. 347-2700, serves highly praised yet moderately priced dinners in most elegant surroundings; closed Sundays. The **Seahorse Restaurant** at 707 Front St., tel. 353-6477, has Northwest seafood, steak, prime rib, and pasta—and captive seahorses—with dancing on the weekends. Next door to the ferry dock is **Taylor's Landing,** 710 Front St., tel. 355-2575, with waterfront dining featuring Northwest seafood, steaks, a popular clam chowder, and live entertainment Thurs. through Saturday.

One street up the hill, **Arnie's** has a view of the water at 714 Second St., tel. 355-2181. Enjoy moderately priced lunches and dinners of salmon, rockfish, ling cod, and steaks. To avoid the lunchtime crowds at the waterside restaurants, head up the hill to **Shamrock, Shillelah, and Shenanigans,** an Irish family restaurant at 8004 Mukilteo Speedway. Open for three meals, inexpensive lunches include burgers and sandwiches, Irish stew, and corned beef and cabbage; veal, chicken, and steak dinners are around $6. **Las Palmas,** 801 Second, tel. 355-6854, is a Mexican restaurant and cantina that's also open for breakfast.

ENTERTAINMENT

Nightlife

Everett has a disproportionate number of dancing and drinking establishments for a city this small. At **Klondike Kate's,** 3120 Hewitt Ave., the lounge upstairs from the steak-and-seafood restaurant has live music on Fri. and Sat. nights. **Pelican Pete's** at Everett Marina Village is lively most of the week, with comedy on Tues. and dancing Tues. through Sat. till 2 a.m. **Bacchus By The Bay,** also at the marina, has live jazz on the weekends. **Hardy's Bar & Grill** is a popular happy-hour spot, with a piano bar and dance floor at the WestCoast Everett Pacific Hotel. **Filibeck's Chuck Wagon Inn,** 6720 Evergreen Way, also has live entertainment and dancing Tues. through Sat. nights.

The **Casbah,** 2222 Everett Ave., has live music every night. Wednesday through Sat. check out **Petosa's on Broadway,** 3121 Broadway, for live music in the lounge. **Henry's Lady,** up in Marysville at 6128 Marine View Dr., has dancing to live music Tues. through Sat. nights.

Festivals

Held in early June at the Everett Yacht Basin, **Salty Sea Days** features a parade, boat tours, carnival, kayak races, and booths. The **Washington State International Air Fair,** held at Paine Field in late Aug., has civilian aerobatics, military jet demonstration teams, and other flying displays in an exciting two-day air show; tel. 355-2266. Also held in Aug. at Forest Park, **Art In The Park,** tel. 252-7469, features a juried arts show, craft booths, live performances, and hands-on activities and classes for children.

A summer-long recreational event from July to Sept. sponsored by the parks department, the annual **Jetty Island Days** "celebration" includes free scenic ferry rides to the island departing from the Marina Village Visitors Dock, guided nature walks, sailing and rowing regattas, concerts, campfire programs, and picnicking, beachcombing, and birdwatching on a saltwater beach. For a program of events call Everett Parks and Recreation at 259-0300.

The Arts

Theatrical performances are held throughout the year at **Centerstage,** tel. 252-7469, and the **College Playhouse,** tel. 259-3355. Music lovers may enjoy a performance by the Everett Symphony at the Everett Civic Auditorium on Colby Ave. or on a Sun. afternoon at the Chateau Ste. Michelle Winery in Woodinville; concerts are scheduled from Nov. to May. Phone 259-7151, ext. 313, for more information.

For those more inclined toward the visual arts, **Northlight Gallery,** at 810 Wetmore in Everett Community College, **Farrens Gallery,** 2819 Wetmore, and the **Visual Arts Center,** at 2902 Colby, have large and varied displays.

Baseball

The San Francisco Giants' Class-A farm team, the **Everett Giants,** plays at Everett Memorial Stadium from mid-June to Sept.; weekdays and Sat. games start at 7 p.m.; Sun. at 2 p.m. Call 258-3673 for schedule information.

SHOPPING

The area's largest shopping center is **Everett Mall,** with over 150 small shops, giant department stores including Frederick & Nelson and The Bon, and 10 movie theaters under one roof. Along the bay at Everett Marina Village is an 1890s-style waterfront marketplace with restaurants, gift shops, clothing stores, and more.

The **Everett Public Market,** 2804 Grand Ave., has antiques, fresh fish and produce, a coffee shop, and more in an out-of-the-way and visually unappealing location; future plans for the turn-of-the-century stable-and-storage building include restoring it to its orig-

EVERETT AND MUKILTEO

1. Legion Memorial Golf Course
2. Everett Community College
3. Firefighters Museum
4. General Hospital
5. Everett Marina Village: Pelican Pete's,
   Anthony's Home Port, Sea Charters,
   Bacchus by the Bay, Marina Village Inn,
   Bee Bee Fish & Chips
6. chamber of commerce
7. North Sound Harbor Tours
8. Civic Auditorium
9. YMCA
10. Klondike Kate's
11. public market
12. Amtrak Station
13. Providence Hospital
14. Snohomish County Museum
15. Petosa's
16. Nendel's
17. Everett Pacific Hotel
18. Seahorse Restaurant, Taylor's Landing,
    McConnel's Boathouse,
    Mukilteo-Clinton Ferry
19. Arnie's/Mukilteo Maritime Museum
20. Lighthouse and Mukilteo S.P.
21. Shamrock Shillelah & Shenanigan's
22. Charles at Smuggler's Cove
23. Gianni's Piccola Italia
24. Panivino
25. Cherry Motel
26. Walter E. Hall Golf Course
27. Everett Mall Inn
28. Northwest Motor Inn
29. Everett Mall
30. Motel 6
31. Silver Shores RV Park and
    Silver Lake Park
32. Holiday Inn

inal appearance. Open daily except Sun. in summer; tel. 252-1089.

SERVICES

The area code for Everett and vicinity is 206. For maps and brochures, stop in or call the **Everett Area Chamber of Commerce,** on the first floor of the historic Weyerhaeuser office building at 1710 W. Marine View Dr., Box 1086, Everett, WA 98206, tel. 252-5181. For specific information on the surrounding communitities, contact the **Marysville Chamber of Commerce,** 1324 Fourth St., Marysville, tel. 659-7700; or the **Snohomish Chamber of Commerce,** 116 Ave. B, Snohomish, tel. 568-2526 (closed Fri. through Sunday).

Like most developed parts of the state, the Everett area is served by 911 emergency service. For less critical emergencies, call **General Hospital** at 14th and Colby, tel. 258-6301, or **Providence Hospital** at 916 Pacific, tel. 258-7555.

Health-conscious vacationers may be interested in a one-day membership at the **Everett YMCA,** 2720 Rockefeller, tel. 258-9211; for $5 you can use the rooftop track, racquetball and squash courts, weight room, and pool.

TRANSPORTATION

Everett is 30 miles north of Seattle, a straight shot on I-5. If you're flying into Sea-Tac airport, **Everett Airporter** departs hourly from the baggage-claim area for the West-Coast Everett Pacific Hotel; fares are $20 roundtrip, $11 one way. Call 258-1955 in Everett or 743-3344 in Seattle for reservations or information.

Amtrak serves the Everett area from their Terminal St. station; tel. (800) 872-7245 or, from Seattle, 464-1930.

Everett Transit's buses and trolleys provide local transportation for $.30; phone 353-RIDE for schedule. To get out of town, **Community Transit** goes south to Edmonds and Seattle, north to Stanwood and Darrington, and east to Snohomish, Lake Stevens, and Granite Falls for $.50; call (800) 562-1375 or 778-2185 for information.

Gray Line of Seattle offers a three-hour tour of the Boeing 747-767 plant, departing Mon. through Fri., May through mid-Sept., from downtown Seattle hotels. Available only to people over 12, the tour costs $15. For more information phone 626-5208.

The Mukilteo-Clinton ferry connects the Everett area to the south end of Whidbey

Island every half-hour or better. Fares are $2.15 roundtrip for passengers or walk-ons, $3.75 one way for car and driver ($4.50 in summer), and $1.60 one way for bicycle and rider. Phone (800) 542-7052 or (800) 542-0810 toll-free statewide or 464-6400 in the Seattle area for schedule.

Charter Or Cruise
Docked at Everett Marina, **Sea Charters** on W. Marine View Dr. offers one-hour sea lion tours for $9 (with occasional $5 weekend specials) from fall to early summer, when California's migratory sea lions are splashing around the bay. Their fishing charters with gear, bait, and coffee provided are $45-65 pp, depending on the boat. Phone 252-4188

or 776-5611 24 hours for information and reservations.

Everett Northsound Harbor and Island Tours, 2815 W. Marine View Dr., tel. 339-1275, offers morning and afternoon salmon- and bottom-fishing charters for $30-50.

By Boat
You can rent canoes, rowboats, and El Toro sailboats at **Silver Lake Park,** tel. 259-0300. For adventuring into the Sound, stop at **McConnell's Boathouse,** 718 Front St. in Mukilteo, tel. 355-3411, for boat rentals and fishing gear; 15-foot-long aluminum-and-wood boats rent for $16-18 per day, plus an additional $5-7 for a motor; open March through October.

VICINITY OF EVERETT

MUKILTEO

Mukilteo was the site of the signing of the Point Elliott Treaty of 1855, whereby the leaders of 22 Indian tribes handed over their land to the white settlers. Today it's a pretty little suburb of Everett, with a scenic commute home along Mukilteo Blvd. for the city's employees. Because of Mukilteo's proximity to Everett, restaurants and hotels here are listed under "Everett," above.

Parks
Adjacent to the Whidbey Island ferry terminal, **Mukilteo State Park** has a large picnic area, beach, and a boat launch with excellent fishing in Possession Sound; open for day use only. The **Mukilteo Lighthouse,** built in 1905, is still functional and open for free tours year-round on Sat. and Sun. afternoons; tel. 355-2611.

Museum
At the corner of Third St. and Lincoln Ave., the **Mukilteo Maritime Museum,** tel. 355-2514, depicts the history of Puget Sound's ferries with photographs and models. Open

Wed. through Sun.; admission $1.50 adults, $.50 kids.

Entertainment
Held at the state park downtown, the mid-August **Mukilteo Pioneer Festival** has a parade, salmon/seafood barbecue, arts and crafts display, sailing regatta, and the state chili cook-off. From Feb. to Oct. the professional **Lighthouse Repertory Theater** stages five productions; for ticket information call 347-6783.

SNOHOMISH

Early Indians called Snohomish Sdob-dwahlb-bluh, meaning "Indian Moon," because that's where they believed their tribe came from. The town was settled in 1859 along the banks of the Snohomish and Pilchuck rivers, making it one of Washington's oldest communities. Numerous turn-of-the-century mansions in Old Snohomish bear witness to the town's earlier elegance.

Sights
Established in 1859, Snohomish has preserved a number of its elegant Victorian-era homes, particularly in the area north of Second

Street. Take a self-guided tour with a brochure available from the chamber of commerce at 116 Ave. B, or go inside on the annual Homes Tour held the first Sun. in October. The **Blackman Historic Museum,** 118 Ave. B, is an 1878 mansion built by a lumberman as a proud display of his cedar shingles; today it's filled with area artifacts and Victorian furniture. Open weekend afternoons.

Sundance Express offers an inexpensive horse-and-buggy tour of Snohomish for $1.50-5 pp, depending on destination, Fri. through Sun., beginning at noon and departing from the First St. bank clock. Just show up, or phone 334-6635 for reservations.

Bed And Breakfasts

Built in 1884 by A.H. Eddy, **Eddy's Bed & Breakfast,** 425 Ninth St., tel. 568-7081, is a beautifully restored Victorian home with a panoramic view of the Cascades, Mt. Rainier, and the Olympics. The inn features a heated pool, gourmet breakfast, and canopy or four-poster beds; rates are $55-65 d, ($10 less for singles). No indoor smoking, kids, or pets; at 119 Cedar Street.

Countryman Bed and Breakfast, tel. 568-9622, was the town's first B&B. The 28-room Victorian mansion has rooms from $39 s, $45 d, including a guided tour of Snohomish, a packet of prints, and afternoon tea. **The Cabbage Patch Inn,** 111 Ave. A, tel. 568-9091, is a farmhouse-style B&B with rooms from $35-45 d; the attached restaurant is open daily for lunch and dinner.

The Country Manner B&B, above the Country Collector's shop at 1120 First St., tel. 568-8254, has four rooms for $49-59 behind an original 1880s storefront and overlooking the Snohomish River and sawmill. No pets, kids, or indoor smoking. **Harmon House B,** 322 Ave. C, tel. 568-1078, has four rooms in an 1890 Victorian mansion, furnished in antiques and sharing one claw-foot tub, from $45-60. No pets or indoor smoking.

At 312 Ave. D, **Noris House,** tel. 568-3825, is an Edwardian B&B built in 1908 and furnished in period antiques. Rooms here are $54-65 d, including continental breakfast. No kids under 14, pets, or smoking.

Mukilteo Lighthouse

DIANNE BOULERICE LYONS

Camping

Flowing Lake Park is a 42-acre county park located on 48th St. SE, a few miles east of Snohomish. Day-use facilities include a boat launch, swimming beach, picnic area, and playground; overnight camping is available at 29 hookup and eight tent sites for $7. Ranger-guided nature hikes through the wooded portion of the park are given periodically. To reach the park take Hwy. 2 east from Snohomish; after two miles, turn left onto 99th St. SE, then turn left onto 171st Ave. SE, and right onto 48th St. SE to the park at the end of the road.

Food

The **Silver King Restaurant,** at First and B on the river in Old Snohomish, has a dreary, diner-like interior but specializes in steak and seafood, including Hood Canal oysters and the hard-to-find fried geoduck, with a view of the sawmill; prices are in the $8-16 range. For coffee or a light snack, the **Rivers Edge Café** on First St. has a comfortable, historic feeling enhanced by the absence of interior side walls—the restaurant is bordered lengthwise by the brick outer walls of the adjoining shops. For inexpensive Chinese food, try **Peking Duck,** 1208 Second Ave., tel. 568-7634. Open for lunch and dinner daily, the **Cabbage Patch Restaurant,** tel. 568-9091, offers sandwiches, salads, pasta, beef, and seafood plus homemade desserts in multiple cozy dining rooms in an old home at 111 Ave. A. Prices are $4-8 for lunch, $7-11 for dinner.

Mardini's, 1210 First St., tel. 568-8080, has pasta, quiche, steaks, seafood, stir-fry, and sauté dinners with a neat and pretty pink-and-antique-lace decor. For Mexican food, visit **Bernal's,** 515 Second St., tel. 568-7777.

Shopping

Snohomish is the self-proclaimed "Antique Capital of the Pacific Northwest." Collectors and browsers will want to spend a day at the **Star Center Antique Mall** at 821 Second St., with 110 shops open daily till 5 p.m., a restaurant, and a children's play area. There are more than a dozen other antique shops within a four-block walk of the mall.

Noncollectors might want to visit the **Old Snohomish Art & Craft Mall** at 121 Glen instead. Here more than 90 area artists and craftspersons display their goods daily except Monday; phone 568-9554 for hours.

MARYSVILLE

Though strawberries are Marysville's trademark, the economy is based on a number of other industries including lumber, dairy products, manufacturing, and high-tech enterprises.

Accommodations And Camping

Best Western's Tulalip Inn offers moderately priced luxury at 6128 Marine View Dr., off I-5 at exit 199, with an indoor pool, restaurant and lounge with entertainment and dancing, airport shuttle, and 66 rooms starting at $48-58 s, $53-63 d, plus hot tub rooms for $120 s, $132 d; phone 659-4488 or (800) 528-1234.

Eighteen miles north of Everett and six miles north of Marysville, **Wenberg State Park** on Lake Goodwin has excellent fishing with power boats permitted, a concession stand for fishing supplies and snacks, and 65 standard campsites ($6) and 10 electric-and-water hookup sites ($8) on 46 acres; tel. 652-7417.

Festivals

The third week in June brings the **Strawberry Festival,** the town's tribute to one of its major crops and the area's biggest summer event, with a parade, carnival, art show, and adult trike races. Held in Oct., **Harvest Fest** has crafts, an open-air farmers' market, hay rides, and a big farmers' breakfast. At Christmastime, Santa Claus and the **Christmas Parade** head down festively adorned State Avenue.

Bingo

Operated by the Tulalip Tribes, **Tulalip Bingo,** right off I-5 at exit 199, is open daily with three sessions daily from 11:30 a.m. and more than $100,000 in prizes every week, including special super-prize weekends where you can win campers, boats, cars, and trucks. No dingy, smoky Legion hall here—this is an enormous, landscaped, modern building with fresh air (no smoking allowed) and a restaurant. For times and other information 24 hours a day, call the Bingo Hotline at (800) 631-3313.

LAKE STEVENS

Two Snohomish County parks provide access to the waters of Lake Stevens. **Sunset Park,** on the east shore, has just a fishing dock and picnic tables on far less than an acre of land. On the west shore, **Wyatt Park** has a larger dock, boat launch for fishermen and waterskiers, picnic area, and swimming.

STANWOOD

A small village just east of the bridge to Camano Island, Stanwood prides itself on having as its chief employer the largest independent frozen-pea processor in the world: Twin City Foods. The town also hosted the world's shortest railroad—seven-eighths of a mile—until it shut down in 1938.

CAMANO ISLAND

Primarily a residential island separated from the mainland by the shortest of bridges, Camano Island was originally inhabited by the Kikialos and Snohomish Indians and later, in the mid-1850s, by European loggers and settlers. Like Whidbey Island to the west, Camano receives less than 20 inches of rain annually because of the Olympic rain shadow effect. Besides vacation homes, the island boasts **Camano Island State Park,** with 134 acres and 6,700 feet of waterfront on Saratoga Passage. The picnic tables of the park's west side provide striking views of Whidbey Island and the Olympics; hiking trails, including a half-mile interpretive loop, wind through 600-year-old Douglas firs with possible sightings of bald eagles, deer, raccoon, and opossum. Other activities here include scuba diving and fishing from the Point Lowell boat launch. The park's two camping areas have a total of 87 non-hookup sites, $6 per night.

MOUNT VERNON AND VICINITY

Disappointed gold miners settled for farming in an uneasy compromise, yet found a different kind of wealth in Mount Vernon's soil: 40% of the nation's peas are grown here, as are significant numbers of daffodils, tulips, irises, fruits, and vegetable seeds. Mount Vernon, 60 miles north of Seattle alongside I-5, was named after George Washington's plantation, both to honor him and because the town was founded on his birthday in 1877. The town grew quickly after an enormous natural logjam in the Skagit was cleared in 1879, allowing upriver travel; in 1884, Mount Vernon was chosen county seat, and by 1900, its population of 1,120 exceeded that of neighboring La Conner. Today, with a population of more than 15,000, the city is still the largest in the county, and in spring is certainly among the prettiest: tulips and daffodils are *everywhere,* from fields to yards to gas stations.

SIGHTS

Fields And Gardens
After March 1, get a map of tulip, iris, and daffodil fields (donation requested) from the chamber of commerce at the Mount Vernon Mall, corner of Riverside and College Way. The colorful spring layout is in bloom from mid-March to early May. Bring film! If you can't get a map, head west from Mount Vernon toward La Conner; most of the fields are in an area bounded on the north by Memorial Hwy. 536, on the west by La Conner-Whitney Rd., on the south by Chilberg Rd., and on the east by the Skagit River, intersected by McLean, Bennett, Calhoun, and Best roads. This is a great place to bicycle—nice, flat roads, very little traffic—except when the flowers are in bloom. A handful of farms invite the public to stroll through their display gardens; these include **Roozengaarde,** 1587 Beaver March Rd., tel. 424-8531, open year-round, daily in April and May, with a show

garden in bloom from Feb. to Oct., retail bulb sales, fresh cut flowers, and gift shop, and **West Shore Acres,** 956 Downey Rd., tel. 466-3158, with a 1½-acre show garden from mid-March to Mother's Day; they'll ship flowers or bulbs anywhere. Don't worry if you forget your map; the traffic jams will direct you to the fields.

If you miss the tulips and daffodils, all is not lost—**La Conner Flats,** 1598 Best Rd., tel. 466-3821, has an assortment of flowers in bloom from March through September. This English country garden features daffodils, rhodies, tulips, azaleas, and dogwood in spring; roses, late rhodies, dahlias, glads, and herbs in summer; and mums, summer heather, and fall foliage in early autumn. The Granary in the Garden serves lunches and high tea (reservations recommended); adjoining Hart's Nursery sells everything that grows at La Conner Flats. Admission to the garden is $2.50 adults, kids free; open daily March through Oct., 10 a.m.-6 p.m.

Parks
At 13th St. and Blackburn Rd., **Hillcrest Park** has a zoo, Oriental garden, tennis and basketball courts, picnicking, and a playground on 30 acres. Southeast of the city on Blackburn Rd. W, 927-foot **Little Mountain** affords views of the Olympics, San Juan Islands, and Skagit Valley farmland with 490 forested acres surrounding the summit observation area; to get there, follow Blackburn Rd. to Little Mountain Road.

Tours
Ask the chamber of commerce for their brochure, "Walking Tour of Historic Mount Vernon," a handy guide to historic buildings, primarily along First and Main streets.

Get a free tour and sample the products of the Washington Cheese Company, 900 E. College Way, tel. 424-3510, Mon. through Sat. 9 a.m.-5:30 p.m. The cheese shop includes gift boxes, ice cream, and other dairy products.

ACCOMMODATIONS

Hotels And Motels

The Clear Lake exit off I-5 leads you to a number of lodging choices. For budget travelers, the **West Winds Motel,** 2020 Riverside Dr., tel. 424-4224, has 40 rooms for $22 s, $28 d. A little more elegant is **Nendel's Inn,** 2009 Riverside Dr., tel. 424-4141, with 88 rooms for $38-42 s, $43-50 d, plus a pool, Jacuzzi, sauna, restaurant, and bar. The **TraveLodge,** 1910 Freeway Dr., tel. 428-7020, has 70 rooms for $38-42 s, $42-50 d, plus an indoor pool, Jacuzzi, and exercise equipment. **Best Western Motor Inn,** 300 W. College Way, tel. 424-4287, has 66 rooms, with a pool, for $35-50 s, $40-55 d; pets okay.

Bed And Breakfast

Snuggled in the middle of 90 private acres of woods bordered by Weyerhaeuser timber,

daffodil fields in bloom

DIANNE BOULERICE LYONS

Whispering Firs B&B, tel. 428-1990, offers shaded seclusion three miles south of Mount Vernon, one mile east of I-5 at 1957 Kanako Lane. Guest chambers have a private entrance and cedar deck, two queen-size beds (one's a waterbed), and private baths for $65-75 d. Prices include a big, country-style breakfast and use of the 8-by-8 hot tub. For more B&Bs, see "La Conner," p. 138.

RV Parks

Riverbend Park, 305 W. Stewart Rd., tel. 424-4480, has 120 RV and grassy tent sites for $14, plus laundry and hot showers, off I-5 exit 227; open all year. **Lake McMurray Resort,** 2294 McMurray Lane off Hwy. 9, has 45 grassy sites, 35 with water and electric hookups, for $10, with fishing, boat rentals, and swimming. Open April to Sept.; tel. 445-4555.

Big Lake Resort, 785 W. Big Lake Blvd., tel. 422-555, has eight RV hookups ($8), 4½ acres of tent sites ($8), and cabins ($150/week) on Big Lake at the foot of Little Mountain. Big Lake is reputed to have the largest freshwater bass in western Washington, so rent a rowboat here and get free advice from the proprietor. For more camping see "Burlington," p. 136, or "North Cascades National Park," p. 283.

FOOD AND DRINK

The Longfellow Café, in the historic Granary Building at 120 First St., serves excellent seafood, sandwiches, and steaks at moderate prices, accompanied by an impressive selection of wines and beers, in an informal setting. Enjoy moderately priced fresh seafood, delicious baked goods, and more at **Wildflowers,** a Victorian house at 2001 E. College Way; open for lunch and dinner Wed. through Monday. Mount Vernon's hot spot for lunch, **Café Europa** at 516 S. First St., serves great sandwiches on fresh-baked bread plus soup, salad, and pasta; open for lunch and dinner, Mon. through Friday. For inexpensive but terrific Mexican food try **La Tienda,** a combination grocery store/restaurant across the bridge at 602 Division Street.

GEORGE HOPPER INTERCHANGE EXIT 229

SKAGIT RIVER

MARTIN RD.

RIVERBEND RV PARK

OLD HWY. 99 S

DOWNTOWN MT. VERNON

NENDEL'S EXECUTIVE LODGE
MAX DALE'S
WEST WINDS MOTEL
TRUMPETER'S
MT. VERNON MALL

TRAVELODGE

WILDFLOWERS REST.

CHAMBER OF COMMERCE

W. COLLEGE WY.

528 E. COLLEGE WY.

BEST WESTERN

SKAGIT VALLEY MALL

WASHINGTON CHEESE CO.

RIVERSIDE DR.

CASCADE PIZZA INN

TO HWY. 9 & OVERLOOK GOLF COURSE

LA VENTURE RD.

FIR ST.

4 ST.

18 ST.

MEXICAN CAFE

MEMORIAL HWY.

W. DIVISION ST.

CONDENSERY MALL

LONGFELLOW CAFE

E. DIVISION ST.

LA TIENDA

SKAGIT VALLEY FOOD CO-OP

MAIN ST.

1 ST.

CASCADE SPORTS

EXIT 226

MONTGOMERY ST.

EDGEWATER PARK

KINCAID ST.

SKAGIT VALLEY HOSPITAL

GREYHOUND BUS TERMINAL

SKAGIT RIVER

1 ST.

WALTER ST.

CLEVELAND AVE.

2 ST.

3 ST.

14 ST.

15 ST.

SKAGIT CO. FAIRGROUNDS

HILLCREST PARK

BLACKBURN RD.

TO LITTLE MTN. RD. & BIG LAKE RESORT

0   0.5 mi
0   0.5 km

© MOON PUBLICATIONS, INC.

Fast-food aficionados should follow Second St. onto Riverside Dr., where McDonald's and its clones await. **Cascade Pizza Inn,** 1825 Riverside or 2083 Hwy. 20 in Sedro Woolley, has pizza, grinders, free limited delivery, and live music in the lounge. Also on Riverside are some of Mount Vernon's fancier restaurants: **Max Dale's,** 2030 Riverside Dr., tel. 424-7171, serves steak, seafood, and prime rib dinners for $11-20, with lunches in the $7 range, and entertainment and dancing in the lounge. **Trumpeters,** at the ExecuLodge on Riverside Dr., has three moderately expensive meals daily plus a lounge; tel. 424-SWAN.

ENTERTAINMENT

Festivals
The 10-day **Tulip Festival,** held annually in April by Mount Vernon, La Conner, and Anacortes, corresponds with the blooming of the tulip fields and includes bus tours, Skagit River trips, tulip pedal, rugby tournament, arts and crafts displays, belly dancing, fireworks, breakfasts, and more. The bulb farm map mentioned under "Sights," above, has a detailed list of events and phone numbers on the reverse; or phone 428-8547.

The second week in Aug. brings the **Skagit County Fair** to the fairgrounds on the southwest side of town off Blackburn Road.

Other
Six miles east of Mount Vernon on Hwy. 9, **Overlook Golf Course** is a nine-hole course with views of Big Lake; rentals and lessons available, tel. 422-6444.

See "Sedro Woolley," p.137, for bald eagle-viewing float trips, whitewater rafting, and fishing expeditions in the Skagit River.

SHOPPING

Park your car to browse through the shops in downtown Mount Vernon, particularly along First Street's bakeries, gift and clothing stores, and cafés. You don't have to be a member to shop at the **Skagit Valley Food Co-op,** 202 S. First. St.; they just charge you

more if you aren't. They have a wide selection of bulk foods, locally baked bread, wine and beer, fresh produce, plus an all-natural deli for a take-out lunch. The **Condensery Mall** at the north end of First was a Carnation condensed-milk plant from 1906-75; now it's undergoing renovation and is largely empty, but its struggling bakery and restaurant may soon be joined by other businesses. If you prefer to shop in a mall, Mount Vernon has two, one on each side of College Way at the Riverside intersection: **Mount Vernon Mall,** with Emporium and a Payless Drugstore, and **Skagit Valley Mall** with Sears, Ernst, and Payless.

SERVICES AND INFORMATION

Mount Vernon's area code is 206. For maps, brochures, and festival information, contact the **Mount Vernon Chamber of Commerce** at 325 E. College Way (Box 1007), tel. 428-8547. For information on the surrounding communities contact the **La Conner Chamber of Commerce,** Box 644, La Conner, WA 98257; **Sedro Woolley Chamber of Commerce,** 714 Metcalf St., Sedro Woolley, WA 98284, tel. 855-0770; or, farther south, the **Stanwood Chamber of Commerce,** Box 641, Stanwood, WA 98292, tel. 629-2123.

If you're headed for the mountains, **Cascade Sports,** 509 S. First St., has backpacking, bicycle, and ski equipment plus outerwear and equipment rentals. Open daily; tel. 336-6641.

For medical emergencies, Mount Vernon has **Skagit Valley Hospital,** 1415 Kincaid, off 15th; tel. 424-4111.

TRANSPORTATION

Mount Vernon is almost exactly one hour north of Seattle, straddling I-5; from Seattle, the city center and bulb fields are to the left. If you're flying into Sea-Tac, take the Bellingham Airporter, tel. (800) 235-5247, to Mount Vernon, Camano Island, and Snohomish County. Greyhound connects nationwide from their Mount Vernon terminal at 1101 S. Second; tel. 336-5111.

BURLINGTON

Downtown Burlington is just a few minutes north of Mount Vernon, so close and indistinguishable it's difficult to tell where its borders are. But it does serve as "closest civilized point" to some interesting parks and natural features.

Parks

Eight miles west of Burlington on Padilla Bay, **Bay View State Park** is small—24 acres—but has 100 campsites (nine with hookups) for $7 across Bay View-Edison Rd. from the waterfront; the waterfront picnic area is well kept, with broad views of the bay, Anacortes's smokestacks, and Hat and Saddlebag islands. The **Breazeale-Padilla Bay Interpretive Center,** just north of the state park on Bay View-Edison Rd., has natural history and marine displays (including stuffed birds and fish), hands-on exhibits and books for kids, plus Sunday films, winter kayak trips, and workshops. Borrow a guide from the center for a .8-mile nature hike through the upland cedar forest and fields, where you might see bald eagles, herons, or Pacific black brants. The interpretive center is open Wed. through Sun. 10 a.m.-5 p.m., tel. 428-1558; free.

Accommodations

The **Cocusa Motel,** 200 W. Rio Vista, tel. 757-6044, has 62 rooms for $45 s, $55 d (about $10 more in summer), with a heated pool and some refrigerators and balconies. The **Sterling Motor Inn,** 866 S. Garl, tel. 757-0071, has 34 budget motel rooms for $29 s, $34-40 d, with a great little attached restaurant and bar (see "Food," below).

For campers who don't like to rough it, the **Burlington/Cascade KOA,** 646 N. Green Rd., tel. 724-5511, is open all year with full hookup sites, grassy tent sites, an indoor heated pool, sauna, weight room, and many of the conveniences of first-class hotels for $14-18.

Food

The **Seven Countries Inn** at the Sterling Motor Inn, 866 S. Garl, is the kind of place most people glance at and drive past—but don't! The ramshackle exterior, complete with "today's special" readerboard, hides a wonderfully long menu: 42 omelettes, 20 burgers, 21 sandwiches, plus dinners, salads, and extensive beer/wine/drink list. Old-time logging and railroad photos line the walls, and they've got a bigger collection of travel brochures than the chamber of commerce; prices are moderate. For traditional Mexican food plus "fiesta hour" in the lounge, try **El Cazador,** 429 S. Garl, tel. 755-9833. **Galley 5,** at I-5 and Hwy. 20, tel. 757-4664, has a coffee shop, dining room, and Sunday brunch, next to the Cocusa Motel.

SEDRO WOOLLEY

Settlement of the area at the mouth of the Skagit River began as early as 1863, but a huge natural logjam prevented any upriver development until it was cleared in 1879. Mortimer Cook was one of the first pioneers to settle on the upper Skagit when he opened a general store in the town he named "Bug," supplying loggers and miners in the 1880s. Cook later succumbed to local pressure and changed the name to Sedro, his idea of Spanish for the "cedar" that covered the area. About the same time, P.A. Woolley built a sawmill a few miles away which became the economic basis of a small but thriving community. The towns were so close together it was difficult to determine their borders, so in 1898 the towns agreed to join forces yet retain both names. Today's Sedro Woolley is the commercial center for the farmlands that surround it and an outfitting town for adventurers on their way east into North Cascades National Park.

Parks And Recreation

Though dwarfed by the nearby mountain lakes in the national park, **Clear Lake** has swimming beaches, boating, and fishing just three miles south of town. City parks include **Bingham Park,** a small city park with picnic tables at Hwy. 20 and Cook Rd., and **Riverfront Park,** McDonald Ave., somewhat larger with picnic tables and a playground on the banks of the fenced-out Skagit.

On Hwy. 20, just east of the Sedro Woolley town line, you'll find the **Mt. Baker Ranger Station/North Cascades National Park Service Complex,** with a North Cascades relief map, books and brochures for sale, and information on road closures and conditions (see "North Cascades National Park," p. 296).

For a day-long ride on horseback to Ross Lake, overnight camp trip in the North Cascades, or fishing trips on Josephine Lake or the Chiliwak River, contact **KM Ranch,** 946 Cockreham Rd., tel. 826-3349. Daytime horseback rides cost $35-65; overnight camps are $125, including a steak dinner and cowboy breakfast. Backpackers can have fresh food, beverages, and gear dropped off at North Cascades camps and packed back out for $50 per horseload—a

VICINITY OF MT. VERNON

nice alternative to lugging pots and pans or opting for gorp and instant cocoa.

The Skagit River is one of the best places in the country to view a large winter bald eagle population, with over 300 birds stopping by for a salmon feast on their journey south from Alaska and Canada. Eagles are particularly plentiful between Rockport and Marblemount (east of Sedro Woolley on Hwy. 20), but you'll also see them soaring overhead anywhere in the Skagit Valley.

Pacific Northwest Float Trips offers bald eagle-watching trips as well as gold panning, sightseeing, and whitewater trips on a number of area rivers, ranging from five hours to overnight. Prices start at $35. For more information write them at Box 736, Sedro Woolley, WA 98284, or phone 855-0535. Operating out of Kirkland, **Rivers Incorporated,** Box 2092, tel. 822-5296, offers eagle-watching Skagit float trips and whitewater rafting on the upper Skagit, Methow, Klickitat, and other rivers. Eagle trips are $35; whitewater trips are $38-68 (depending on river and number of participants). Rivers Inc. also has two-day Klickitat whitewater trips, meals included, for $120-130.

Downstream River Runners, operating out of Bothell (just north of Seattle), also offers eagle-watching float trips from Dec. through Feb. for $40, plus a full schedule of other whitewater and float trips on western and eastern Washington rivers; they're one of the largest and most organized rafting companies around. Phone 483-0335 or, toll-free statewide, (800) 732-RAFT, or write 12112 N.E. 195th, Bothell, WA 98011 for more information.

If the idea of whitewater rafting makes you shaky, take a one-hour pontoon-boat trip up Swinomish Channel to Goat Island with **Skagit Queen River and Channel Tours,** tel. 855-0535, for just $10; or, take a longer trip to Hat Island for crab catching and lunch on Saddle Bag Island for $25.

Accommodations And Food
The **Skagit Motel,** 1977 Hwy. 20, tel. 856-6001, has 47 rooms for $25-27 d. Next door to the motel, **Angela's** serves sandwiches,

fish, and steak dinners, all under $13, in a cheerful interior. Housed in the old Bingham Bank building at 210 Ferry St., the **Gateway Restaurant,** tel. 855-0060, serves diners in a number of dark rooms, including two lounges, several dining rooms, a coffee shop, and bakery.

Festival
The Fourth of July brings the week-long **Loggerodeo** to Sedro Woolley, an annual event since 1948 with logging contests, parades, and rodeos.

Gallery
On Hwy. 9 about a mile north of Sedro Woolley at 2128 Bassett Rd., the **Lee Mann Gallery,** tel. 856-0581, has a collection of photographs of the Pacific Northwest; open Mon. through Saturday.

LA CONNER

La Conner is the most tourist-oriented town in Skagit County—too much so to suit the locals, but there's no denying it's a fun place to visit. Park the car and browse the old buildings, shops, restaurants, and bakeries all jammed into a tiny downtown area along Swinomish Channel, especially on weekends. During the Tulip Festival, La Conner

looks like a California beachfront tourist trap in July, with standing traffic, cyclists, mobs of pedestrians, full parking lots, and sidewalk hot-dog stands.

This old fishing port was settled in the late 1800s and discovered in the 1930s by Puget Sound artists, and in the 1960s by tourists. It has a population of about 600 now and a number of museums and 19th-century homes for history buffs to explore. Bright orange Rainbow Bridge, crossing the Swinomish Channel, is a good spot for photographers to get a shot of the La Conner waterfront with a Mt. Baker backdrop.

Sights And Recreation
The **Gaches Mansion** at Second and Calhoun, is a restored Victorian mansion built in 1891 and partially furnished with period furniture; the second floor houses paintings and sculpture at **The Valley Museum of Northwest Art,** mostly paintings and sculpture by artists who have lived in La Conner or have painted scenes of the Skagit Valley. The mansion is open for guided tours weekend afternoons. Admission is $1; phone 466-4288 for information. The log cabin at Second and Morris was built in 1869 by Magnus Anderson, one of the area's first settlers, but is not open for tours. At 501 Fourth St., the **Skagit County Historical Museum,** tel.

Gaches Mansion

DIANNE BOULERICE LYONS

466-3365, has Northwest pioneer artifacts including farm and logging equipment, children's toys, clothing, and a farmhouse kitchen. Open Wed. through Sun. afternoons; admission $1 adults, $.50 kids.

Boat Rentals

The Swinomish Channel is a peaceful body of water for paddling or rowing; rent a boat from **La Conner Boat Rentals,** N. Third St., tel. 466-3300. At the north end of First St., **Rainbow Enterprises,** tel. 466-4054, rents everything from boats to bikes to cars.

Accommodations

At Second and Morris, **La Conner Country Inn,** tel. 466-3101, boasts a fireplace in every room, a restaurant, **Barkley's** (see below), and a pub; rooms are $65-155 d, including continental breakfast. The renovated **Hotel Planter,** a national historic inn at 715 First St., tel. 466-4710, features 12 tastefully decorated guest rooms, all with private bath, plus a gazebo, hot tub, and garden courtyard. Rooms run $70-105 d. No pets or smoking.

The Heron, a Victorian country inn off Hwy. 20 at 117 Maple St., tel. 466-4626, has a whirlpool and 12 rooms from $60-90 s or d. **Ridgeway House,** a 1928 yellow-brick B&B in the heart of the farmland, features five guest rooms, each with a sink (two with private bath), plus complimentary appetizers and full breakfast for $45-75 d. No indoor smoking. **Rainbow Inn,** a B&B at 1075 Chilberg Rd., tel. 466-4578, is a restored turn-of-the-century farmhouse surrounded by tulip fields, a Mt. Baker view, and a hot tub on the back deck. Antique-furnished rooms are $55 d with shared bath, $65 d with private bath. No smoking; pets are accommodated as space permits. Near the tulip fields at 1880 Chilberg Rd., **Downey House,** tel. 466-3207, has five rooms; rates range from $60 s, $65 d, for the two rooms with shared bath to $75-80 s, $80-85 d for the three larger rooms with private bath. Amenities include a hot tub, full breakfast, evening blackberry pie, and a view of Mt. Baker. No pets or smoking.

Heather House B&B, 505 Maple Ave., tel. 466-4675, is a new (1979) house built to re-

semble a 1900s Cape Cod beach house, with bare oak floors and wainscoting; the three bedrooms, $45-65, share two baths. Terry robes, blow driers, flowers, candy, and a "help yourself" refrigerator add to the home's charm; continental breakfast is served at your convenience. **The White Swan Guest House,** six miles from La Conner at 1388 Moore Rd. on Fir Island (technically Mount Vernon), tel. 445-6805, is a Victorian farmhouse with guest cottage. Three guest rooms share two baths ($65 d); the cottage has a private bath and can sleep four ($85). Enjoy the wood stove in the parlor and fresh-baked chocolate chip cookies. Breakfast is continental; no pets, smoking, or small children.

Campers and RVers are welcome at the **Potlatch RV Resort,** 415 Pearle Jensen Way, tel. 466-4468, where you can relax in one of two hot tubs or the indoor pool while you're "roughing it" for $14 a night. **Pioneer Park,** adjacent to Rainbow Bridge, has camping and picnic tables.

Food And Drink

Barkley's, Second and Washington at the La Conner Inn, is a local legend serving locally produced food: sockeye salmon, Dungeness crab, geoduck, red snapper, fresh vegetables, pasta, and steaks. Open for lunch Mon. through Sat., dinner nightly, with a Sunday Champagne brunch; phone 466-4261 for reservations (highly recommended). Near La Conner, on Hwy. 20 between Anacortes and Mount Vernon, **The Farmhouse Restaurant,** tel. 466-4411, is a busy family spot. Meals here, all under $11, include steak, fried seafood, chicken and turkey dinners, burgers, and all-day breakfast, with a buffet lunch in the lounge for $4.75. **La Conner Tavern,** on the Channel at First St., has world-famous burgers, plus dancing to live music. On the Swinomish Channel waterfront, **The Lighthouse Inn,** tel. 466-3147, has outdoor-barbecued salmon, prime rib, fresh seafood, and picnic lunches to go. **The Black Swan,** First and Washington, tel. 466-3040, is open for dinner only with moderately priced seafood, pasta, and more, made with the freshest Skagit Valley ingredients. **La Conner Seafood and Prime Rib House** has fine dining and a waterfront deck at 614 S. First St., tel. 466-4014.

Entertainment And Events

Just across the Swinomish Channel bridge on Hwy. 20, **Swinomish Indian Bingo** has bingo at 7 p.m. nightly, plus a matinee session Thurs. through Sun. (times vary—phone 293-4687).

The annual **Rotary Pig Roast** is held the third Sat. in Aug. at Pioneer Park. September brings the **Fall Festival,** highlighted by a salmon barbecue, and Dec. brings the **Christmas Ships Parade** up the Swinomish Channel.

Shopping And Galleries

The most fun way to shop in La Conner is just to meander through the downtown shops, stopping for lunch or a beer and heading out again. To get you started, **Pier 7,** on First St., is a waterfront mall with gift shops, gallery, and other stores. **Town Square,** corner of First and Morris, combines modern shops and businesses with historic buildings, including the 1912 water tower and Magnus Anderson's 1869 log cabin. **Limedock Waterfront Mall** at the north end of First St. has still more shops including a gallery and seafood market. At 71750 First St., **The Cheese and Wine Shoppe** is the place to go for Northwest wines, Walla Walla pickled vegetables, local cheeses, and smoked salmon.

Established in 1885, the **Tillinghast Seed House** is the oldest operating retail seed store in the Northwest; even brown thumbs will enjoy their gallery and gift shop on Chilberg Rd., at the south entrance to town.

Transportation

By car, La Conner is about an hour north of Seattle via I-5, and 10 minutes west across the tulip fields from Mount Vernon. You can take Hwy. 20 to La Conner-Whitney Rd. and head south; or, in spring, work your way through the tulip fields southwest from Mount Vernon via McLean, Best, and Chilberg roads.

La Conner Seaplanes, tel. (800) 826-5580 or 671-1219, offers sightseeing flights over the San Juans, Mt. Baker, the Skagit Valley (another perspective on the tulip fields), the Olympic Peninsula, and the Cascades. Rates start at $20 for a 20-minute trip.

Built in Sweden in 1897, the 76-foot sailing vessel *Sylvia* still departs from La Conner, Seattle, Bellingham, and other docks for a number of scheduled and chartered cruises throughout Puget Sound. The several-day cruises can go up to $535 pp, but a number of inexpensive short trips are also available: two-hour cruises during April's Tulip Festival are $20 pp; a half-day Elliott Bay cruise to watch Ivar's July Fourth fireworks is $50 pp; a two-day "Doe Bay Bash" celebrates the summer solstice for $168 pp. Write Box 524, La Conner, WA 98257, or phone 466-4929 for schedule.

CHUCKANUT DRIVE

This seven-mile stretch of highway is among the most scenic in the state, as well it should be; it was the first route designated a scenic drive by the state. When it was built, it was part of the now-extinct Pacific Highway. It leaves I-5 just north of Burlington and heads straight as a cue stick across the black, flat soil of the Skagit Valley, passing the **Rhododendron Café** at the Bow-Edison intersection. The café serves good food and wine, and is populated on weekends by bicyclists and weekend-drive aficionados.

A short distance north, the highway runs head-on into the mountains hovering over the sound, and here the fun begins because the road doesn't have a straight stretch for seven miles as it swoops and swerves along the face of the cliff with great views across to Anacortes, Guemes Island, and farther north, the San Juans and Lummi islands. As you drive north you will pass three more good places to eat: **Chuckanut Manor,** 302 Chuckanut Dr., tel. 766-6191, at the southern end of the mountains, where you can have lunch or dinner in the bar—the best seats in the house—and on some nights partake of a smorgasbord. The **Oyster Bar,** 240 Chuckanut Dr., tel. 766-6185, is a small and expensive place clinging to the side of the mountain; it serves oysters (of course) and has a limited, mostly seafood menu. **Oyster Creek Inn**, 190 Chuckanut Dr., tel. 766-6179, in the heart of the mountainous sec-tion, also obviously serves oysters and also chicken, lamb, and other dishes.

Chuckanut Drive goes through **Larrabee State Park,** described elsewhere, and at the foot of the cliff just before you enter the Fairhaven District, you'll pass **Teddy Bear Cove,** one of the state's few nudist beaches.

BELLINGHAM

HISTORY

Bellingham Bay was named by Capt. George Vancouver for Sir William Bellingham, who provided Vancouver with supplies for his 1792 Puget Sound explorations. Captain Henry Roeder and Russell V. Peabody established the first permanent settlement here in 1852; they came north from San Francisco in search of a sawmill site to supply their hometown's growing demand for lumber. When Roeder and Peabody met Lummi Indian Chief Cha-wit-zit in Olympia, they asked him if he knew of any place with "falling water all the time from a high hill." Cha-wit-zit apparently under-stood the Americans' broken English and, speaking in kind, suggested "at Whatcom, noise all the time." With the aid of the local Lummis, Roeder and Peabody built a mill at the foot of Whatcom Falls in 1853, producing lumber until it burned down in 1873.

William H. Prattle, another of Bellingham's earliest settlers, responded to Indian tales of local coal outcroppings by opening a margin-ally successful coal mine in the settlement called Unionville in 1853. The same year, San Francisco investors opened the Sehome Mine, adjacent to the Whatcom settlement, and it became one of the two largest employ-ers in the area until the mine was flooded in 1878. Coal mining ceased until the Belling-

DIANNE BOULERICE LYONS

ham Bay Co. opened the largest mine in the state in the city's north end in 1918; it operated until 1951, when decreased demand led to its closure.

The 1850s also brought to Bellingham the aborted Fraser River Gold Stampede. About 10,000 people, most of whom had traveled north from California, came to Whatcom to await the opening of a trail to British Columbia's newfound gold. The trail was never completed, and an order from Vancouver Island's governor James Douglas that all gold diggers obtain permits in Victoria before entering the province further squelched the would-be gold rush. One remnant from the gold boom is a brick building on E St.; the first

DOWNTOWN BELLINGHAM

1. Decann House
2. Lion's Inn Motel
3. Bellingham Theater Guild
4. Maritime Heritage Center
5. Waterfront Tavern
6. Hamann's Gallery
7. Greyhound
8. Georgia Pacific Corp.
9. North Garden Inn
10. Bellingham Herald
11. Nendel's
12. Val-U-Inn
13. Visitors and Convention Bureau
14. A Secret Garden
15. KVOS TV
16. Cliff House
17. Aloha Motel
18. Pony Soldier Motor Inn
19. Park Motel
20. Motel 6
21. Bellingham Mall
22. The Castle
23. Fairhaven Bicycle shop
24. Speedy O' Tubbs and Dos Padres
25. Dirty Dan Harris/Marketplace
26. Gallery West
27. The Fairhaven
28. post office
29. library
30. Whatcom Museum of History and Art
31. Children's Museum Northwest
32. Cassidy's and Top of the Tower
33. Bristol Antiques
34. Aladdin's Lamp Antique Mall
35. Antique Mall
36. Bellingham Hardware Building/Boehm's
37. Parkade
38. Lord Cornwall
39. Il Fiasco
40. Pacific Cafe

brick building in the territory, it first served mercantile purposes and later as the Whatcom County Courthouse for 25 years.

The nearly simultaneous closures of the Whatcom Sawmill and Sehome Mine in the 1870s left the town floundering until the 1890s, when commercial attention again shifted to the timber and fishing industries. By the time the Whatcom and Fairhaven settlements combined to form Bellingham in the early 1900s, eight saw- and shingle-mills and four salmon-packing plants were providing the foundation of the city's economy. Today these industries combine with a heavy agricultural base, with dairy products, poultry, strawberries, and raspberries providing much of the county's income and supporting a population of nearly 46,000. In 1989, the Alaska Marine Highway Ferry System began docking its ships in Bellingham instead of Seattle, which should add considerably to Bellingham's tourist appeal and encourage economic growth.

Downtown Bellingham isn't among the most aesthetically pleasing of Puget Sound's cities; it's an old, squatty, congested city, much like Olympia would look without a Capitol Campus. Bellingham's treasures aren't immediately obvious, nor do they generally lie downtown; they're scattered along the

Sound, or on the lakes, or in the parks, and are worth seeking out.

SIGHTS

Fairhaven

Ninth St.—formerly Railroad Ave.—was originally the point at which the Fairhaven and Southern Railroad grade entered the town from Skagit Valley. The men working on the railroad would follow the tracks back to Ninth St. for an evening's entertainment, in rowdy bars and hotels such as "Miss Reno's" that provided much more than a bed for their patrons—and quite a hot reputation for Fairhaven. One unidentified man romanced himself into a state of exhaustion and dropped dead while walking up Ninth Street. Another, John Moore, had a few too many at the Gilt Edge Saloon and decided to sleep it off on the tracks—poor John never heard the 2:30 a.m. train pulling into town.

Today Fairhaven is considerably quieter. You can see its old buildings and Victorian homes by taking a walking tour of the Fairhaven Historic District; maps are available from the visitor and convention bureau, 904 Potter St., tel. 671-3990, and various shops and restaurants. Several shops and galleries

Western
Washington University

DIANNE BOULE-ICE LYONS

in the district are interesting, including **Fairhaven Flowers,** 11th and Mill St., tel. 676-0658, with its dried flowers, fruit baskets, and balloon bouquets, and **Gallery West,** 1300 12th St., tel. 734-8414, with fine art and crafts including oils and watercolors, sculpture, pottery, weavings, and jewelry. A new addition to Fairhaven, the restored **Marketplace** at 12th and Harris was built in 1890 and now houses shops and restaurants, including **Haven's Delight,** serving Chilean and Italian cuisine, and Boehm's Chocolates.

Western Washington University

This 224-acre campus is home to 9,500 students and a number of internationally acclaimed sculptures in an outdoor garden. Tours of the university and sculpture garden are given Mon. through Fri.; call 676-3440 for times and reservations. For a self-guided tour, pick up a brochure at the university's visitor center or the Bellingham Convention and Visitor Center on Potter St. (see "Services," p.148, for directions). Overlooking Bellingham Bay and accessible via a footpath from the university, the **Sehome Hill Arboretum** offers splendid views of the San Juans and Mt. Baker, plus 70 acres of 100-foot Douglas firs, wildflowers, and big-leaf maples preserved in their natural state. The several miles of paved trails are smooth enough for wheel-

chairs and accessible year-round; other secondary trails may be slippery when wet.

Museums

Built as the Bellingham City Hall in 1892 at 121 Prospect St., the **Whatcom Museum of History and Art,** tel. 676-6981, is recognized as one of the finest regional museums on the West Coast, with scheduled concerts and free, changing exhibits of regional history and contemporary art. The gift shop here is notable on its own merits, with a large selection of arts and crafts, Northwest foods, and books. Open Tues. through Sun. afternoons; donation.

The **Children's Museum Northwest,** 106 Prospect St., tel. 733- 8769, has many participatory exhibits for kids of all ages, including a dental center with giant walk-in mouth, infant/toddler exploration center, TV station, and puppet theater. Admission is $2 adults, $1 kids; closed Mondays.

Tours

See how a newspaper is produced at the *Bellingham Herald;* phone a week in advance for a tour of their facilities at 1125 N. State St., tel. 676-2675. Media buffs will also enjoy a tour of the **KVOS Television Station** at 1151 Ellis St.; call 671-1212 three days in advance.

PARKS AND RECREATION

Seven miles south of Bellingham on Chucka-nut Dr., **Larrabee State Park** has tidal pools for marinelife viewing, eight miles of hiking trails to two mountain lakes and viewpoints, boat launch, 61 standard campsites, and 26 hookup sites on more than 1,800 acres on Samish Bay. This became Washington's first state park when Charles Xavier Larrabee's family donated 20 acres in his honor in 1923.

A test site for the American Rose Society, **Fairhaven Park's** summer-blooming rose gardens are the highlight of the 16-acre man-icured park at 107 Chuckanut Dr., which also has picnic areas, a playground, hiking trail, and tennis courts.

Samish Park, 673 N. Lake Samish Dr., is a 39-acre county park with 1,500 feet of Lake Samish shoreline for swimming, fishing, boating, picnicking, hiking, and a children's play area. Rent canoes, paddleboats, row-boats, sailboats, or a sailboard.

Whatcom Falls Park, near Lake What-com at 1401 Electric Ave., has hiking, tennis courts, a playground, picnic area, and state fish hatchery on 241 acres. With 12 acres on the lake itself, **Bloedel Donovan Park** has a swimming beach, boat launch, playground, and picnic area at 2214 Electric Avenue.

Lake Padden Park, 4882 Samish Way, has over 1,000 acres of hiking and horse trails, a golf course, picnic areas, and a play-ground, plus swimming, fishing, and non-motorized boating on the lake.

Thirty-eight acres of practically untouched canyon wilderness is yours for the hiking at **Arroyo Park** on Old Samish Rd., with nature and horse trails and creek fishing.

ACCOMMODATIONS

Hotels And Motels
For tight-budget accommodations, the ever-present **Motel 6,** 3701 Byron St., tel. 671-4494, has 60 rooms and a pool for $30 s, $35 d. Not much more expensive is the **Aloha**

Motel, off I-5 exit 252 at 315 N. Samish Way, tel. 733-4900; the 28 rooms are $40 s, $45 d, with free continental breakfast. Also inexpen-sive is the **Lions Inn Motel,** 2419 Elm, tel. 733-2330, with 15 rooms with kitchens and refrigerators for $40 s, $42 d; pets okay. A new economy motel near the Bellis Fair Mall, **The Traveler's Inn,** 3570 Meridian St., tel. 671-4600, charges $41 s, $46 d.

For a more moderately priced room, the **Ramada Inn,** 215 N. Samish Way, has 65 rooms from $45 s, $49-51 d, plus a heated pool; tel. 734-8830 or, in Washington (800) 634-PONY. The **Park Motel,** 101 N. Samish Way, has 56 modern rooms for $54 s, $64 d, plus hot tub, sauna, and complimentary con-tinental breakfast; tel. 733-8280 or, in Wash-ington (800) 732-1225. In the same price range is the **Val-U Inn,** 805 Lakeway Dr., with 82 rooms starting at $55 s, $75 d, including complimentary continental breakfast, guest laundry, and a hot tub room; tel. 671-9600 or, statewide (800) 451-7766.

Done in colonial decor, the **Best Western Heritage Inn,** 151 E. McLeod Rd., tel. 647-1912 or (800) 528-1234, has 61 rooms from $55 s, $80 d, with a pool, plus a restaurant and movie theater across the street.

Bed And Breakfast
High on a hill above Fairhaven, **The Castle,** 1103 15th St. (15th and Knox), tel. 676-0974, offers old-world grandeur and four antique-furnished guest rooms in a 100-year-old his-toric landmark. Rooms go for $55 s up to $75 d; the two larger rooms have private bath. No pets, smoking, or kids under 12.

Housed in an ornate three-story Victorian home, **The North Garden Inn** at 1014 N. Garden St., tel. 671-7828 or (800) 922-6414, has 10 rooms (six are available in winter), many with bay views, sharing five baths for $44-54 d, including a full breakfast. A Stein-way grand piano is yours for the using; no kids, pets, or smoking.

Above Lake Whatcom surrounded by tall evergreens is **Schnauzer Crossing,** 4421 Lakeway Dr., tel. 734-2808. This B&B has two rooms for $75 and $105, both with private bath; the master suite has a Jacuzzi, double shower, sitting room, and fireplace. Special luxuries include a new outdoor spa, fresh fruit and flowers, and terry robes; borrow the owners' canoe to enjoy on Lake Whatcom, or get your exercise on their private tennis court. Children ($7.50) and pets ($10) can be accommodated with advance notice; no smoking.

A Secret Garden, 1807 Lakeway Dr., tel. 671-7850, is one of Bellingham's newer B&Bs. Close to town, the turn-of-the-century inn offers two spacious suites with private baths and Victorian breakfast for $55 and $65 d; no pets or smoking.

The **DeCann House,** 2610 Eldridge Ave., tel. 734-9172, is a Victorian B&B adorned by innkeeper Barbara Hudson's stained glass, etchings, and family heirlooms. Their two guest rooms with queen beds and private baths are $43-$59, and feature a full breakfast and views of Bellingham Bay and the San Juans. No small children, pets, or indoor smoking. Five miles east of Bellingham at 2399 Mt. Baker Hwy., **Squalicum Ranch Bed and Breakfast,** tel. 671-3868 or 733-2509, has over 300 acres of wooded hiking and riding trails, farm animals, fly-fishing in Squalicum Lake, and a big country breakfast in a turn-of-the-century farmhouse, all for just $45 d.

In a pinch, call **B.A.B's,** tel. 733-8642, a reservation service specializing in B&Bs with home and other lodging rentals. For B&Bs in the small towns north of Bellingham, see "Vicinity of Bellingham," p. 150.

Cabin
The **Seagoat** is a reasonably priced, three-bedroom cottage on the beach two miles from the Gooseberry Point ferry landing. For $75-100 for one to three persons, $125 for four, or $150 for five to six persons you get Mt. Baker views, a sunken rock fireplace, antique bedroom sets, and seclusion. Call 676-0974 or write 1103 15th St., Bellingham, WA 98225, for more information and reservations.

Sudden Valley Resort
As far as resorts go, this one isn't all that expensive. Located on 1,500 beautiful acres off Lake Whatcom Blvd., the lodging at Sudden Valley starts at $65-95 for a two-person condo and goes up to $139-154 for a six-person, three-bedroom condo. There are no telephones in the rooms so harried executives can truly escape. Enjoy the resort for a lot less by camping: 89 campsites are $8 (no hookup) to $10 (full hookup), and you can use the facilities for an extra $5. Amenities include an 18-hole golf course, movies, play barn for the kids, basketball, ice skating, swimming pools, six tennis courts, and boating, swimming, and fishing on Lake Whatcom and Lake Louise. For a brochure or more information contact Sudden Valley Resort, 2145 Lake Whatcom Blvd., Bellingham, WA 98226, tel. 734-6430.

Campgrounds
See "Parks" above and "Vicinity of Bellingham" for the cheapest campsites. Private campgrounds in Bellingham include **Diamond S RV Park,** 5330 Guide Meridian, tel. 671-2443, with 50 treed sites including electricity and showers from $12-14. Private campgrounds in neighboring towns are listed by town under "Vicinity of Bellingham."

FOOD

For the best Italian food in town, try **Il Fiasco,** across from the parkade at 1309 Commercial, tel. 676-9136. The varied menu is accompanied by a good selection of Italian and regional wines, available by the glass. **The Pacific Café,** next to the Mt. Baker Theater at 100 N. Commercial, tel. 647-0800, serves moderately priced steak, seafood, and teriyaki dishes in a warm atmosphere. Overlooking Samish Bay and the San Juans at 302 Chuckanut Dr., **Chuckanut Manor,** tel. 766-6191, specializes in steak and fresh seafood from $7-30, Friday night smorgasbord, and Sunday Champagne brunch in an atmosphere more elegant than you'd expect from the bland exterior. Open for dinner year-round, lunch spring through fall; closed Mondays.

One of Bellingham's best bay views can be yours at the **Cliff House,** 331 N. State, tel. 734-8660; open for lunch and dinner, the specialty here is salmon but the menu also covers beef, chicken, and other seafood dinners from $8-17. **The Marina,** 985 Thomas Glenn Dr., tel. 733-8292, has a terrific harbor view, indoor-outdoor lounge, and reasonably priced meals. For dinner from the rooftop, try **Top of the Tower** at 119 N. Commercial, tel. 733-3443; lunch and dinners here include steak, veal, chicken, and seafood from $11-17, complemented by an extensive wine list. On a lower floor of the same building, the more casual **Cassidy's,** tel. 734-4401, serves three meals daily from an American menu. Some of the area's best Southwest/Mexican food is at **Pepper Sisters,** 1222 N. Garden St., tel. 671-3414. Open for dinner only, Tues. through Saturday. Or, have a gyro, souvlaki, or moussaka at **Eleni's Greek Restaurant,** 1046 Lakeway Center, tel. 676-5555; also steaks, burgers, and chicken for your less adventurous companions.

Dirty Dan Harris' at 1211 11th St. in the Fairhaven District has prime rib and fresh seafood dinners in an 1800s-style saloon for $8-17; tel. 676-1011. Fairhaven's finest dining is at **The Fairhaven,** 1114 Harris Ave., tel. 676-1520, where fresh seafood, veal, and steaks—even geoduck—highlight a 40-item menu and a wine cellar filled with over 230 varieties. Or, try the Mexican food at **Dos Padres,** 1111 Harris Ave. in Old Fairhaven; it was rated "best Mexican restaurant north of L.A." by the B.C. *Sun.*

ENTERTAINMENT AND EVENTS

Nightlife
Harry O's, at Nendel's on Lakeway Dr. and I-5, has piano entertainment nightly (except Sun.) and a new dance floor. The **Lord Cornwall Restaurant** has dinner and dancing every night at 1408 Cornwall Ave., tel. 671-2031. The **Black Angus,** 165 Samish Way, also has dancing. **Speedy O'Tubbs,** 11th and Harris in Fairhaven, has a variety of live music and dancing. Formerly The Digs, the place is said to have a resident ghost, who has appeared to a number of people between 3 and 4 a.m. in the foyer. Reputedly a woman, this spirit may have once been

joined to the skeleton they found in a wall during reconstruction. More down to earth, the **Waterfront Tavern,** overlooking Bellingham Bay at 521 W. Holly St., has pool, poker, pull tabs, and punchcards.

Annual Events
Bellingham's annual **Ski to Sea Race,** held Memorial Day weekend, tests the physical endurance and athletic skills of its participants over an 85-mile course which includes a downhill ski leg, running, bicycling, canoeing down the Nooksack River, and sailing across Bellingham Bay to the finish in the Fairhaven District. The race is the highlight of a week-long festival that includes a street fair, with crafts, live music and dancing, food, and a beer garden, on Sunday after the race. For specific dates call 734-1332.

The **Lummi Indian Stommish Water Festival** is an annual mid-June event held at the Lummi Indian Reservation on Gooseberry Point. It includes war-canoe races, arts and crafts shows, Indian dancing, and a salmon bake; tel. 734-8180.

Like other Puget Sound cities, Bellingham sponsors a Christmas **Lighted Boat Parade** in Bellingham Bay in early December; tel. 733-7390.

The Arts
Western Washington University hosts a number of musical and theatrical groups in its auditorium. Some of the more notable events are the February **Jazz Festival,** tel. 676-3130, the May concert by the **Whatcom Chorale & Symphony Orchestra,** tel. 676-2170, and the Christmastime **Morca Nutcracker Ballet,** tel. 676-1864. The **Mt. Baker Theatre** hosts musical and theatrical performances from Oct. to March at 106 N. Commercial; for ticket information call 734-4950. Staffed and performed entirely by local volunteers, the **Bellingham Theatre Guild** produces five plays a year from fall to spring at the old Congregational Church building at 1600 H St.; for ticket information call 733-1811.

At 1603 N. State, **Hamann's Gallery,** tel. 733-8898, features original artwork, etchings, and limited-edition prints. In Fairhaven

The Alaska Marine Highway ferry system docks its ships in Bellingham.

SEATTLE-KING COUNTY CONVENTION AND VISITOR'S BUREAU

at 12th and Harris, **Gallery West,** tel. 734-8414, displays paintings, sculpture, graphics, pottery, jewelry, glass, and more.

SHOPPING

Bellingham's 900,000-square-foot regional shopping mall, **Bellis Fair,** was built mainly for Canadian shoppers, who save a lot of money by buying in Bellingham rather than Vancouver. The mall has five anchor stores—Bon Marché, Target, Mervyn's, JCPenney, and Sears—in addition to numerous smaller shops and a 500-seat Food Court. **Bellingham Mall,** on Samish Way at I-5 exit 252, has just 25 stores selling apparel, jewelry, fabrics, candy, and services from hairstyling to tickets for area events. The downtown **Parkade** at Holly and Commercial has covered parking for a number of small shops along Commercial St., including Nordstrom Place Two on Cornwall. If you panic and drive through the Parkade accidentally (easy to do) they won't charge you for the trip—it happens to out-of-towners all the time. On W. Holly and Bay streets, the **Bellingham Hardware Building** houses apartments, businesses, and a couple of retail shops.

Antiques

Whatcom County has a number of antique shops and malls. In Bellingham proper, **Bel-lingham Antique Mall,** 202 W. Holly St., tel. 647-1073, is open daily till 5:30 p.m. and on Sun. afternoons with a wide selection of collectibles from 20 dealers. **Aladdin's Lamp Antique Mall,** 1318 Bay St., tel. 647-0066, is open daily till 7 p.m. with heavy emphasis on comic books, furniture, glass, and books. **Bristol Antiques and Books,** 310 W. Holly St., tel. 733-7809, has small collectibles and over 650 new books on antiques; open daily till 5 p.m.

SERVICES

The area code in the Bellingham area is 206. For maps, brochures, and general information contact the **Bellingham and Whatcom County Visitor and Convention Bureau,** 904 Potter St., tel. 671-3990; open daily, year-around.

For 24-hour emergency care, contact St. Joseph's Hospital, 2901 Squalicum Parkway at exit 255, tel. 734-5400.

TRANSPORTATION

By Air

Bellingham International Airport has service to Seattle and other West Coast cities via **Alaska Air, Horizon Air, USAir, and United**

Air Express. Many Canadians use the airport because they can get more convenient flights to some U.S. destinations, cheaper tickets, and the parking, $1 a day (it used to be free) is a big savings, too. If you're flying into Sea-Tac and can't make good connections, **Bellingham/Sea-Tac Airporter** offers nine trips daily for $25 one way, $35 roundtrip to Bellingham Mall or Bellingham Airport, tel. 733-3600 or (800) BELLAIR. The Airporter also serves Blaine and Ferndale. You can charter a sightseeing flight through **Cascade Flights,** tel. 733-3727.

By Ferry
The **Alaska Marine Highway System,** tel. 676-8445, recently moved up to Bellingham from Seattle; from here you can take the ferry to southeast Alaska destinations. **AIT Waterways,** tel. 671-1137, operates a foot ferry between Bellingham's Squalicum Harbor and Orcas and San Juan islands.

By Bus
Greyhound has nationwide service from its terminal at 1329 N. State St.; tel. 733-5251 or (800) 528-0447. **Gray Line of Seattle** travels between Seattle and Vancouver, B.C., with stops at the Bellingham Cruise Terminal, Bellingham International Airport, and Semiahmoo. Locally, **Whatcom Transit** provides transportation to Ferndale, Sudden Valley, and Lynden. **Lynden Stage Line** has six roundtrips daily between the Bellingham city bus terminal to Lynden and points in between; call 734-0520 for schedule, tel. 354-1495 for other information.

By Car
Bellingham is about 86 miles due north of Seattle via I-5. If you're not in a big hurry, get off the highway near Burlington and head north on Hwy. 11, a.k.a. Chuckanut Dr., for some breathtaking vistas of the Sound after a few miles of straight 55 mph through farmland.

By Bicycle
Scenic Chuckanut Dr., historic Fairhaven, and peaceful Lake Samish are only a few places that cyclists will enjoy. If you didn't bring yours along, you can rent bicycles from **Fairhaven Bicycle Shop,** 1103 11th St., for $10 a day or $15 a weekend. Mountain bikes are also available for $12 a day, $20 a weekend; tel. 733-4433.

Cruises
For a sunset tour of Bellingham Bay coupled with a taste of local smoked salmon, cheese, and berries, take the two-hour "Taste of Washington Cruise" offered from May through Sept. by the **Maritime Heritage Center,** 121 Prospect St., 734-8866 or, statewide (800) 841-8866. Held on Mon. and Wed. evenings, these cruises include a sampling of early Bellingham history and present-day uses of the bay. The center also offers day-long and late evening whalewatching and dinner cruises to and around the San Juan Islands; **Gray Line Water Sightseeing** also offers a day-long San Juan Islands cruise and a longer one with an overnight in Victoria. Call **Gray Line of Bellingham,** 355 Harris Ave., tel. 738-7685. For information on other cruises to the islands, read "San Juan Islands," p. 174.

VICINITY OF BELLINGHAM

LUMMI ISLAND

The Lummi Indians were the first inhabitants of the island, but they had abandoned their camp even before white settlers arrived in the 1870s. Today it's a quiet island, home primarily to salmon fishermen, some of whom fish with reef-nets in the style of the original Indians.

Hiking

Hiking trails lead to the points at the north and south ends of the island, as well as to the 1,500-foot summit of Lummi Peak.

To get to **Carter Point** at the island's south end, turn left onto Nugent Rd. from the ferry dock and follow the paved road uphill to the left, then turn right onto Seacrest Dr., and right at the first fork in Scenic Estates onto Island Drive. Bear to the left when the road forks at a small lake and park just past the lake on the abandoned quarry road. Walk along the road, taking an optional quarter-mile side trail to picturesque Inati Bay. The quarry road climbs uphill and to the right, providing good views of Reil Harbor and the mainland to the east. Continue south to the knoll at the road's end for sweeping views of Bellingham, Mt. Baker, and the water below. Total hiking time is about three hours.

At the north end of the island, **Migley Point** can be reached via a two-hour roundtrip loop along little-used roads. From the ferry dock, go left on Nugent Rd., then right on Legoe Bay for just over a half mile to a fishing village on the bay; park here. Head north along the road, stopping to appreciate the westward views of Orcas Island, until you reach Migley Point; then head east down the other side of the island to Lummi Point, then back to the starting point.

For a seven-mile roundtrip hike leading to spectacular views of the San Juans, hike the 2½ hours to **Lummi Peak.** From the ferry dock go left on Nugent Rd., left again onto Sunrise Rd., and right on Seacrest Dr. for one-half mile to the top of the hill; park on a wide spot in the road a few yards up. Find the old logging road on the river, and follow it up the north side of Lummi Peak to sheer cliffs and panoramic views. As the trail progresses it gets harder to follow, as it splits and leads to knolls and viewpoints; at about the first mile, stay to the right at the fork, and at about 3½ miles, bear left to a clearing with views of Bellingham and points east. Head back here for a seven-mile roundtrip.

Accommodations

Located on the west side of the island at 2579 W. Shore Dr., **The Willows Inn,** tel. 758-2620, has B&B accommodations from $90-120, including a full three-course breakfast. The two dormer view rooms share a bath, while two rooms with antique double beds have private baths. The honeymoon cottage provides additional privacy and a magnificent view of the islands. Dining by reservation only. No kids, pets, or indoor smoking. **West Shore Farm,** 2781 West Shore Dr., tel. 758-2600, offers B&B in their unique octagonal home with a 12-sided free-standing fireplace and sweeping Georgia Strait views. Guest rooms are $50 s, $60 d, including a full breakfast; lunch ($7 pp) and dinner ($15 pp) are available on request. No indoor smoking; kids are welcome, but call for specifics. **The Loganita,** 2825 West Shore Dr., tel. 758-2651, is called "a villa by the sea." because it is quite large, with five large rooms and suites overlooking the ocean. Rates are from $85-135 s and d.

The Islander is a private campground with 10 sites, $4 up, on the water near the ferry landing at 2106 S. Nugent Rd., tel. 758-2190.

Transportation

Getting to Lummi Island is easy, via a seven-minute ferry ride from Gooseberry Point on the Lummi Indian Reservation aboard the *Whatcom Chief*. The boat departs for Lummi

VICINITY OF BELLINGHAM

Island hourly from 6 a.m. to 12:10 a.m. For further information call the Lummi Island Ferry at 676-6730.

FERNDALE

Ferndale is one of those "Main Street, U.S.A." towns, with one main drag, a couple gas stations, a few bars, and a drugstore. It is primarily an agricultural town with housing and services for the nearby ARCO petroleum refinery, a major economic factor in town.

Parks

Take a walk around a bog and interpretive displays at **Tennant Lake Natural History Interpretive Center,** 1¼ miles southwest of exit 262 from I-5. One of the park's highlights is the **Fragrance Garden,** designed so the sight-impaired can experience the variety of plants by scent. Open Fri. through Sun. afternoons in summer, tel. 733-2900; free. **Pioneer Park,** two blocks south of Main on First Ave., has museum displays in seven log cabins in a beautiful park setting. The **Hovander Homestead** is a 1903 restored home and farm on the Nooksack River with a barn, milkhouse, children's zoo, gardens, and picnic area. The park is open daily, but the homestead is open only on summer weekends. Admission is $3 per car for non-Whatcom County residents; tel. 384-3444.

Accommodations

Overlooking Nooksack Valley farmland to the Cascades and Mt. Baker, **Hill Top Bed and Breakfast,** 5832 Church Rd., tel. 384-3619, offers a twin bedroom with shared shower ($54), main-floor queen bedroom with private bath ($44), and fireside suite with private bath, shared shower, and room enough for four ($49 d). Continental breakfast. Kids are welcome (high chair and crib available); no indoor smoking. **Anderson House B&B,** 2140 Main St., tel. 384-3450, is an 1897 banker's home with four guest rooms: two with shared bath are $45 s or d, one with private bath is $55, and the Tower Suite, with refrigerator, color TV, and private bath, goes for $75. No pets, smoking, or kids under 12.

Stay on a working dairy farm at **Grandview RV Park,** 3185 Grandview Rd., tel. 366-5316. Other privately owned campgrounds in Ferndale include **Ferndale Campground,** 6335 Portal Way, tel. 384-2622,

FLORENCE BOULERICE

with 45 sites with full hookups, showers, and laundry facilities for $10-13. **Bill's RV and Mobile Home Park,** 6006 Portal Way, tel. 384-5700, is convenient if nothing else: it's 500 feet from the interstate. The 46 sites with full hookups are $15.

BIRCH BAY

Birch Bay is one of western Washington's oldest resort towns, the kind of place families go for generations, always renting the same cabin. It has managed to keep its calm in spite of numerous housing and condominium developments going on nearby, and its only street still is designed for pedestrians instead of cars.

Not far to the south is the giant ARCO refinery with its eternal flame towering above the timber, but it has no other effect on the town. **Birch Bay State Park** is on the mile-long waterfront on Birch Bay. Campsites are plentiful, with 147 standard ($7) sites and 20 hookups ($8.50), available by reservation from Memorial Day weekend through Labor Day. Other facilities include an underwater park, fishing (though there's no boat launch), a quarter-mile hiking trail, picnic area, and 40-acre Terrell Creek Estuary, home to beavers, opossums, muskrats, and great blue herons. To get there, take exit 266 from I-5, following Grandview Dr.; take a right onto Helwig, then follow the signs to the park.

BLAINE

Way up north on the Canadian border, Blaine is evolving from a quiet waterfront town to a busy tourist destination. It is the busiest of the border crossings because it is on I-5. Sometimes border traffic backs up two or three miles, so unless you are going across the border into Canada, be prepared to turn off I-5 before the main part of town.

East of town is one of the more vivid statements on the relationship between the U.S. and Canada. As you drive east toward Sum-

(top) Olympic Mountains, Olympic National Park (Washington State Tourism Division)
(bottom left) spectacular Mt. Rainier (Dianne Boulerice Lyons)
(bottom right) Diablo Lake, North Cascades National Park (Dianne Boulerice Lyons)

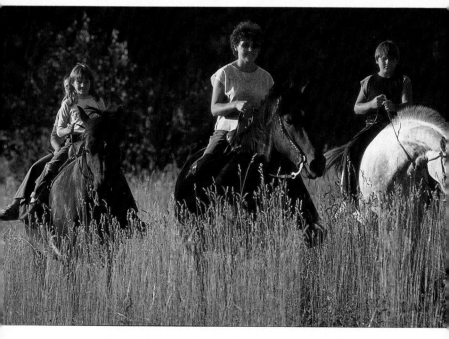

(top left) Tillicum Village salmon bake on Blake Island (Mark Hewitt/Tillicum Village)
(top right) Tillinghast Seed Co., La Conner (Dianne Boulerice Lyons)
(bottom) horseback riding in northeast Washington (Washington State Tourism Division)

Peace Arch at the
U.S.-Canadian border

as and Lynden, you can turn north off the main road and follow it until it makes a sharp right turn to the east again. Here you will notice two, two-lane blacktop highways running east and west, side by side, with a ditch separating them. That ditch is the international boundary between the largest country in the world (Canada) and America, the most powerful country in the world (as this was being written, at least). That is all the international boundary is for more than 3,000 miles, the longest unprotected such boundary in the world. When the boundary goes through forests, a swath is kept cleared by crews from both countries. But in Washington, it is separated from British Columbia by a ditch that any child can toddle across.

Parks

Open for day use only, **Peace Arch State Park** at the Canadian border has beautifully landscaped grounds and gardens surrounding the Peace Arch, a symbol of friendship between the U.S. and Canada that stands with one "foot" in each country. The parks were constructed by American and Canadian volunteers and funded by Washington and British Columbia schoolchildren, who contributed from one to 10 cents each for the project. Facilities include a picnic area, playground, and game sanctuary.

Semiahmoo County Park on the Semiahmoo Sandspit has restored salmon cannery buildings and an interpretive center open from Wed. through Sun. afternoons in summer, weekend afternoons the rest of the year; the park itself is open daily year-round.

Accommodations

Up where you'd least expect it is one of the Northwest's newest luxuries, **The Resort Semiahmoo.** A planned resort community, it is the largest of its kind in Washington. Its facilities include a 250-slip marina, athletic club, 18-hole golf course designed by Arnold Palmer, restaurants, lounges, and plenty of Puget Sound beachfront. **The Inn at Semiahmoo** has 200 rooms for $135-240 s or d. The price also includes use of the tennis and racquetball courts, jogging trails, pools, sauna, steam room, and more. The inn's restaurant, **Stars,** features Northwest cuisine in a formal setting. Call (800) 854-2608 from anywhere in the U.S. or 371-2000 locally. **Semiahmoo Rentals,** tel. 371-5700, rents motorboats, canoes, sailboats, sailboards, paddleboats, and mountain bikes at the marina.

The **Victorian Rose B&B,** housed in a 1905 Queen Anne-style cottage at 1274 Harrison Ave., serves a muffin-and-fruit breakfast with rooms priced at $30 s, $40 d; phone 332-8677 or write for reservations.

ARCHIE SATTERFIELD

Private campgrounds in Blaine include **Richmond Resort,** near the bay at 8086 Birch Bay Dr., tel. 371-2262; the 50 sites here with full utilities go for $15.50 a night. **U.S. Border RV Park** has 20 hookup sites and lots of others at 875 Johnson Rd., tel. 332-8686. Sites cost $11-14.

Festival

The annual **Peace Arch Celebration,** held at the Peace Arch the second Sunday in June, brings together veterans and scouts from the U.S. and Canada to celebrate our friendly relations; tel. 398-1356.

POINT ROBERTS

Bounded on three sides by water and on the fourth by British Columbia, it's only by political accident that Point Roberts belongs to the U.S. The small strip of land was ignored when the international boundary was drawn at the 49th parallel. The 450 Americans living in Point Roberts year-round acknowledge the reality of the situation, with many businesses accepting Canadian currency at par value to encourage the mostly Canadian tourists, though the five-square-mile point is only 23 miles (and two international borders) from Blaine.

You'll find the highway to Point Roberts clogged almost continually by Canadians coming down for cheap gasoline and other American goods. The Canadian postal system is even less efficient than America's, so Canadians doing business by mail in the States keep mailboxes at Point Roberts, Blaine, Sumas, and other border towns.

By the same token, some American couples arrange to have their children born in Canada because it is cheaper, even for aliens, and the children will have dual citizenship until the age of 18, and access to Canada's almost-free health-care system.

The border has had incidents that would cause wars between less friendly people. Several years ago a bulldozer owner from one side of the border did some work on the other

side, and when he sent the bill, the recipient of his labor refused to pay. So the dozer owner cranked up his dozer, drove it across the border, and proceeded to demolish the work he had done. This upset the client, who fired shots at the dozer, which lumbered back across the border. Authorities on both sides of the border discussed the matter, took it under advisement, and apparently decided that justice had already been done; the incident faded into legal obscurity.

Located on the southwest tip of Point Roberts, Whatcom County's **Lighthouse Park** has 22 acres and a half-mile beach, highlighted by a 600-foot boardwalk with a 30-foot lookout platform (whales are often spotted in August). The boat launch here sees a lot of use, with some of the Puget Sound's finest salmon fishing right off the point. In time-honored American tradition, the July Fourth fireworks display is held here. The park is open all year with parking (no hookups) for campers and trailers; for camping reservations call (604) 945-4911.

On the point's east side, the beaches on Boundary Bay have some of the warmest water on the West Coast as the tide comes in over a square mile of sand bars, providing safe fun for kids and waders.

Check with the **Point Roberts Chamber of Commerce,** tel. 945-2313, for the best places to eat and stay.

LYNDEN AREA

Thousands of dairy cows and chickens, berries, hops, potatoes, and—borrowing from the town's Dutch heritage—bulbs are all grown in this fertile agricultural region and taken to market in Lynden, the mini Bible Belt of the North. Calvinistic influences are seen in an unofficial ban on Sunday business and an infamous town ordinance prohibiting dancing wherever drinks are sold—leading to Saturday-night 12-mile pilgrimages to Bellingham's hot spots: Be especially careful while driving on Hwy. 539 on weekends.

Sights

Lynden's **Dutch Village Mall,** opened in 1987, reflects the area's Dutch heritage. The mall features a 72-foot windmill, 20 retail shops, indoor canal, 200-seat theater, six-room inn, restaurants, and more.

At 217 Front St., the **Lynden Pioneer Museum** exhibits Indian artifacts, horse-drawn buggies, early Chevies, and other remnants of pioneer life. Call 354-3675 for seasonally fluctuating hours; donations of $1 pp, $2 per family requested. Tractor buffs may enjoy a stop at the **Puget Sound Antique Tractor and Machinery Association** at 8825 Berthusen Rd., where a collection of steam-powered farm machinery can be viewed daily, for free; tel. 352-3754.

Located southeast of Lynden at 4298 Mt. Baker Hwy., **Mount Baker Vineyards** has tours and tastings Wed. through Sun. from 11 a.m.-6 p.m.; tel. 592-2300.

Kids 12 and older can take a tour of **Mt. Baker Mushroom Farms,** also in Everson; call 966-5915 in advance of your visit. **Edeleen Dairy Products,** 9593 Guide Meridian in Lynden, is open to the public from 8 a.m. daily for tours of their facilities. Their most important function, ice-cream processing, is carried out Mon. through Thurs. after 2 p.m.; tel. 354-5342.

Accommodations

Spend a night in a windmill at the **Dutch Village Inn,** 655 Front St., tel. 354-4440, at the Dutch Village Mall. Six hotel rooms (three are in the windmill) feature Dutch furnishings, antiques, and Dutch-style breakfast for $50-80 d. Higher-priced rooms have private hot tubs. No pets or indoor smoking; kids are welcome. They also offer seven full-hookup RV spaces; inquire for details.

Farther east in Everson, **Wilkins Farm B&B,** 4165 S. Pass Rd., tel. 966-7616, has three bedrooms with shared bath in a 100-year-old home for $20 s, $27 d, including a full breakfast and fresh flowers. The **Windmill Inn Motel,** 8022 Guide Meridian, tel. 354-3424, has 15 budget rooms from $24-30 s, $31-39 d.

For campers, **Shenandoah** at 1640 E. Badger Rd., tel. 354-5863, has eight hookup sites and five acres of tent sites, hiking, and picnicking on a wooded lot.

Fairs

An international plowing match is the highlight of Lynden's **Spring Fair and Farmer's Day Parade,** held the first week of June at the fairgrounds. Mid-August brings the **Northwest Washington Fair** to Lynden, with rides, games, food, and events; held at the fairgrounds. In December, look for **Sinterklass's** arrival! For more information on these and other events phone 354-4111.

ACME

Chug through the forests and farmlands of western Washington on an hour-long ride aboard a turn-of-the-century steam train with **Lake Whatcom Railway** in Wickersham on Hwy. 9. Normally operating Tues. and Sat. from June through Aug., the railway also hosts special "Santa Trains" two Saturdays in Dec.; all rides are $6 adults, $3 kids and students. Phone 595-2218 for reservations.

ANACORTES

Visitors know Anacortes as the jumping-off point for the San Juan Islands, but this city of more than 11,000 people is far more than a ferry dock on the tip of Fidalgo Island. White men first resided on the island in the 1850s, but William Munks, who liked to call himself "The King of Fidalgo Island," claimed to be the first permanent settler and opened a store there in 1869. Amos Bowman tried to persuade the company he worked for, the Canadian Pacific Railroad, to establish their western terminus at Fidalgo—despite the fact that Bowman had never seen the island. When they refused, Bowman came down to check out the property himself, bought 168 acres of it, and opened a store, a wharf, and the Anna Curtis Post Office, named after his wife, in 1879. Bowman was so determined to get a railroad—any railroad—into Anacortes (pronounced "Anna Cortis") that he published a newspaper, *The Northwest Enterprise,* to draw people and businesses to his town.

He was so convincing that the population boomed, even though, by 1890, the town's five railroad depots had yet to see a train pull up.

Residents gave up on the railroad idea and found financial success in lumber mills, a cannery, and box factory. The Burlington Northern Railroad eventually came—and went.

Today Anacortes relies on its oil refineries, wood products, shipbuilders, food processors, and tourism for much of its income. While other towns in Washington have hired artists to paint murals on building walls, Anacortes hired an artist to make life-sized cutouts of people, bicycles, automobiles, boats, and so forth and mount them on walls around the downtown area. The result is a lively, funky look that sets Anacortes apart.

SIGHTS

Museums And History
At 1305 Eighth St., the **Anacortes Museum,** tel. 293-5198, has local history exhibits including a doctor's and dentist's office, photographs, and period furniture. Open Thurs. through Mon. afternoons; donation. Other remnants of earlier days are scattered

throughout town, including the historic stern-wheeler W.T. Preston, on display at Eighth St. and R Ave., and the old Burlington Northern Railroad depot at seventh and R, now a refurbished community center.

Speaking of railroads, don't miss the **Anacortes Railway**. Over a 20-year period, longtime resident Tommy Thompson created an authentically scaled 0-4-4 Forney-type steam locomotive that pulls three passenger cars between the depot at Seventh St. and R Ave. and a turnaround at Ninth and Commercial every summer weekend.

The Causland Park area has a number of 1890s homes and buildings, many restored to their original splendor. The home owned and built by Amos Bowman and Anna Curtis Bowman in 1891 stands at 1815 Eighth St.; at 807 Fourth St., an architect's office is now housed in what was probably the finest bordello in the county in the 1890s. The Little Church at Fifth and R was built by its Presbyterian congregation in 1889, and is undergoing restoration; still in use is the Episcopal Church at Seventh and M, built in 1896.

Scenic Drive

Start at 36th St. and R Ave. for a scenic drive that takes you by the waterfront, through Washington Park, past Lake Erie, up Mt. Erie, and through old residential and industrial areas for an overall view of Anacortes's many faces. From 36th and R, go north on R Ave. and Q Ave. past Cap Sante Marina, then east to Cap Sante Park via Fourth St. and V Avenue. Work your way over to 12th St. through the Causland Park residential area, loaded with well-kept houses, beautiful water views, and commercial buildings from the turn-of-the-century pre-railroad population boom. Head west on 12th Ave. to Oakes Ave. for water and island views. Continue west to Washington Park via Sunset Ave., looping through the park on the scenic road; head south on Anaco Beach Dr., Marine Dr., and Rosario Rd. toward Lake Erie. Follow Heart Lake Rd. to Mt. Erie Dr., up to Mt. Erie's summit (described below). Upon your return to the base, follow Heart Lake Rd. North past Heart Lake and back to downtown Anacortes.

PARKS AND RECREATION

Three miles west of Anacortes, **Washington Park** is a strikingly beautiful picnic spot with 200 waterfront acres on the Rosario Strait affording views of the San Juans and Olympics. Walk, bike, or drive the 2.3-mile paved scenic loop, and pull in to one of many waterfront picnic areas. Other facilities include a boat launch, miles of hiking trails (see map), and a playground. Camp at one of the 46 hookup and 29 non-hookup wooded campsites from April through Oct. ($10, hookups extra). The original park acreage was donated by one of Fidalgo Island's earliest pioneers, Tonjes Havekost, who said, "Make my cemetery a park for everybody." Additional acreage was bought by the Anacortes Women's Club in 1922 from the sale of lemon pies—they paid just $2500 for 75 beachfront acres.

Five miles south of Anacortes, 1,270-foot **Mt. Erie** provides panoramic views from the Olympics to Mt. Baker to Mt. Rainier via a 1½-mile paved road to the partially wooded summit; the paths and fenced areas at the top point the way to clear viewing spots. Though the hill is small by mountain standards, the views are dizzying, perhaps because of its steep drop-offs and the oceans of water below. Take Heart Lake Rd. to Ray Auld Dr. and Mt. Erie Road.

For a good, low-elevation viewpoint of the Cascades and Skagit Valley, visit **Cap Sante Park** on the city's east side, following Fourth St. to West Avenue. Scramble up the mound of boulders for a better look.

Downtown, **Causland Park** covers a city block at Eighth and North avenues; the ornate mosaic walls and gazebo were built in 1920 with colored stones from area islands.

Hiking

Stop by the chamber of commerce, 1319 Commercial Ave., and spend $3 for a guide to trails on 2,200 acres of Anacortes Community Forest Lands around Mt. Erie and Cranberry, Whistle, and Heart lakes. All trails are numbered, rated for difficulty, and include mileage, elevation, and highlights.

ANACORTES

1. campground
2. Charlie's Restaurant
3. Burrow's Bay B&B
4. Skyline B&B
5. Slocum's Restaurant
6. Channel House B&B
7. chamber of commerce
8. Left Bank Antiques
9. Gateway Motel
10. Albatross B&B
11. Island Hospital
12. Anacortes Inn
13. Dutch Treat House B&B
14. Islands Motel and
    La Petite Restaurant

© MOON PUBLICATIONS, INC.

Five loop trails, ranging from 2.3 to 3.5 miles, start at the topographic saddle between Mt. Erie and Sugarloaf on aptly named Mt. Erie Saddle Road. Despite the short distances, these are rated all-day hikes because of the steep climb up trails #26, #207, and #21 from the individual trailheads back to Saddle Road. The longest of these, the **South-to-North Lake Loop,** circles Whistle Lake, passing an early 1900s dam and old-growth Douglas fir and cedar. For this loop, take trails #26, #207, and #21 to #22, #205, #20, #204, and back to #21. The shortest loop from Saddle Rd. is **Middle Whistle Lake Loop** at 2.3 miles. Again, take trails #26, #207, and #21, then go north on #203, looping back on #204 to #21. This hike stays on the west side of Whistle Lake but offers lake views and a summertime mid-loop swim.

From the trailhead at the intersection of Mt. Erie and Heart Lake roads, hike the .6-mile **Pine Ridge Loop Trail,** #25 and #213, for views of Mt. Erie and Sugarloaf. This moderately difficult hike takes from one to two hours. Another short hike is the **Sugarloaf Trail,** starting on Ray Auld Dr. six miles from its intersection with Heart Lake Road. Take trail #215 from the marshy trailhead straight up, ignoring side trails, to views to the west of Port Townsend, the San Juan Islands, and the Strait of Juan de Fuca, and north to Bellingham.

The Cranberry Lake area also has a number of hiking trails, ranging from .2 to 2.6 miles. The **John M. Morrison Loop Trail** starts at the end of 29th St., following trail #104 for .9 mile; steep drop-offs in the middle section of the trail allow views of Cranberry Lake and old-growth Douglas fir forests. **Old Mine Trail** is an easy, .6-mile one-way hike to an old mine entrance. Park at the end of Georgia Ave., then follow trails #100, #102, and #103 to the mines; retrace your steps to return. For experienced hikers, the 1½-mile **Cranberry Lake Loop** circles the lake from the same Georgia Ave. parking lot via trails #100, #102, and #101; the narrow trail's difficulty lies in its poor footing and its disappearance into the lake in several spots. Allow two to three hours.

ACCOMMODATIONS

Bed And Breakfast

Walking distance to downtown and the Cap Sante waterfront, the **Hasty Pudding House,** 1312 Eighth St., tel. 293-5773, is an elegantly restored 1913 Edwardian B&B furnished in antiques and lace. Home-baked full breakfasts, afternoon tea, and a cozy fireplace add to the charm. Four guest rooms (two with private bath) run $50-65 d; no pets or indoor smoking.

The Majestic, 419 Commercial Ave., tel. 293-3355, is a European-style country inn in a restored 100-year-old building. The 23 guest rooms and suites, many with view decks, have private baths, cable TV, wet bars, and in-room coffee makers, and are accented with antiques. A continental breakfast basket is delivered to your room. The dining room features Northwest seafood, and their Victorian Pub offers casual dining and imbibing. Rooms range from $89-165 d.

The **Albatross Bed and Breakfast,** 5708 Kingsway W, tel. 293-0677, features four guest rooms, all with private bath, a block away from Skyline Marina and within walking distance of Washington Park. The well-kept contemporary home offers a view of the marina, home-baked breakfasts, free transportation to and from the ferries or airport, and designated smoking areas. Rooms are $69 s or d, $84 two beds.

Dutch Treat House, 1220 31st St., tel. 293-8154, offers comfortable lodging in a 1930 Dutch Colonial home, with a full breakfast and rooms for $35 s, $50-55 d. They'll supply the wineglasses if you BYOB; kids over eight okay, smoking outdoors only.

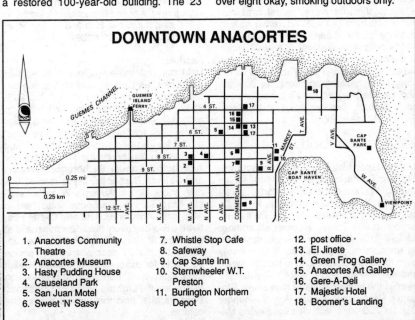

DOWNTOWN ANACORTES

1. Anacortes Community Theatre
2. Anacortes Museum
3. Hasty Pudding House
4. Causeland Park
5. San Juan Motel
6. Sweet 'N' Sassy
7. Whistle Stop Cafe
8. Safeway
9. Cap Sante Inn
10. Sternwheeler W.T. Preston
11. Burlington Northern Depot
12. post office
13. El Jinete
14. Green Frog Gallery
15. Anacortes Art Gallery
16. Gere-A-Deli
17. Majestic Hotel
18. Boomer's Landing

Burrows Bay, 4911 Macbeth Dr., tel. 293-4792, is a contemporary B&B with one luxury suite (it can accommodate up to six) for $75 s, $85 d ($10 each additional person), with a fireplace, library, private deck and entry, and a sweeping view of the San Juans; breakfast is served in your room at your convenience.

Old Brook Inn, 530 Old Brook Lane, tel. 293-4768, has two guest rooms (one can sleep five) with private baths ($50-55 s, $60-65 d) and Fidalgo Bay views amidst an old orchard, complete with babbling brook. Children welcome.

Hotels And Motels
Holiday Motel, 2903 Commercial Ave., tel. 293-6511, has 10 budget rooms from $34-38 s, $40-48 d. At Sixth and O, the **San Juan Motel,** tel. 293-5105, has 27 rooms for $29 s, $34 d. At 3006 Commercial Ave., the **Anacortes Inn,** tel. 293-3153, has 44 rooms for $48 s, $52 d, with outdoor heated pool. Some rooms have water views. The **Cap Sante Inn,** 906 Ninth St., tel. 293-0602, offers complimentary continental breakfast and rooms from $40 s, $44 d, within walking distance of the marina. The **Islands Inn,** 3401 Commercial Ave., tel. 293-4644, is one of the city's nicest motels, with rooms starting at $65 s or d, and going up to $95 for the honeymoon suite, with fireplace, Jacuzzi, and wet bar; prices for all rooms include pool, Jacuzzi, and breakfast at La Petite Restaurant (see below).

FOOD

At the Islands Motel, **La Petite Restaurant,** 34th and Commercial, tel. 293-4644, serves some of the best dinners in Anacortes, plus a hearty Dutch breakfast; open daily for breakfast, dinner daily except Monday. On the waterfront at 209 T Ave., **Boomer's Landing,** tel. 293-5108, is another of Anacortes's better restaurants, open daily for dinner, weekdays for lunch, specializing in lobster, steak, and seafood for $8-19; weekend entertainment in the lounge. Another nice one is **Slocum's Restaurant,** Skyline Way at Flounder Bay, tel. 293-0644, with views of Skyline Ma-

rina. Specialties here are steak and seafood, up to $18; an extensive wine list includes everything from $9.95 Sutter Home blush to $75 Dom Perignon. The attached chowder house serves soups and sandwiches for lunch; also open for Sunday brunch. **Charlie's Restaurant,** at the ferry dock, has a moderately priced steak and seafood menu with water and dock views; a convenient place to stop for a drink while you're waiting for your ship to come in.

For take-out food for a bike or ferry trip or casual eat-in dining, stop by **Gere-a-Deli,** 502 Commercial, tel. 293-7383, for sandwiches, salads, soups, or homemade desserts. **El Jinete** serves Mexican lunches and dinners at 509 Commercial, tel. 293-2631.

ENTERTAINMENT AND EVENTS

Theater
The **Anacortes Community Theatre,** or ACT, stages four performances from March through Nov., plus annual performances of *A Christmas Carol* and *Broadway Melodies,* at a 112-seat theater at 10th and M. For ticket information phone 293-6829.

Festivals
Held the first three weekends in April in Anacortes, La Conner, and Mount Vernon, the **Skagit Valley Tulip Festival,** tel. 293-3832, offers everything from boat rides to belly dancers to fireworks and the popular "Taste of Skagit" feed; see "Mount Vernon," p. 135, for tulip field auto/bike tours. The last weekend in July brings the self-explanatory **Anachords Annual Barbershop Concert and Salmon Barbecue.** If you missed this one, shoot for mid-August's **World's Largest King Salmon Barbecue.** Also held in Aug. is the **Anacortes Arts and Crafts Festival,** a two-day event held downtown and at the depot at Seventh and R that draws upwards of 35,000 people annually; phone 293-6211 for exact dates and times. Catch the holiday spirit, Puget-sound style: watch for the annual **Lighted Ships of Christmas Boat Parade,** held the second Sat. in December.

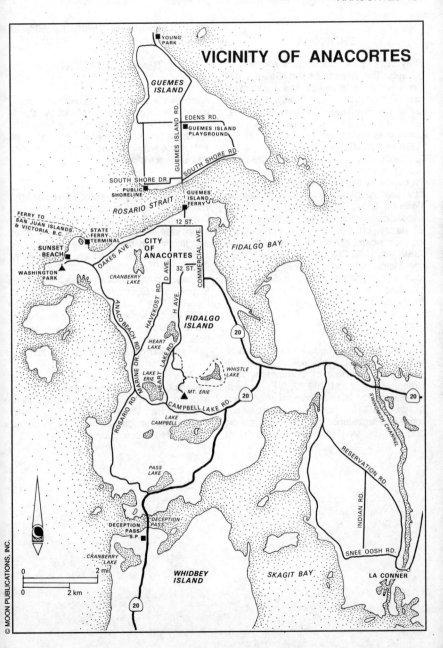

VICINITY OF ANACORTES

YOUNG PARK

GUEMES ISLAND

EDENS RD.

GUEMES ISLAND PLAYGROUND

GUEMES ISLAND RD.

SOUTH SHORE RD.

SOUTH SHORE DR.

PUBLIC SHORELINE

GUEMES ISLAND FERRY

ROSARIO STRAIT

FERRY TO SAN JUAN ISLANDS & VICTORIA, B.C.

STATE FERRY TERMINAL

12 ST.

CITY OF ANACORTES

FIDALGO BAY

SUNSET BEACH

WASHINGTON PARK

OAKES AVE.

CRANBERRY LAKE

D AVE.

32 ST.

COMMERCIAL AVE.

HAVEKOST RD.

H AVE.

FIDALGO ISLAND

ANACO BEACH RD.

HEART LAKE

HEART LAKE RD.

LAKE ERIE

WHISTLE LAKE

MT. ERIE

20

20

20

CAMPBELL LAKE RD.

ROSARIO RD.

MARINE DR. RD.

LAKE CAMPBELL

SWINOMISH CHANNEL

RESERVATION RD.

PASS LAKE

DECEPTION PASS S.P.

DECEPTION PASS

INDIAN RD.

CRANBERRY LAKE

0   2 mi

0   2 km

MOON

WHIDBEY ISLAND

SKAGIT BAY

SNEE OOSH RD.

LA CONNER

20

© MOON PUBLICATIONS, INC.

SHOPPING

They don't call it "Commercial Avenue" for nothing. The **Anacortes Art Gallery,** 414 Commercial, tel. 293-6656, has changing exhibits of area artists' work Tues. through Saturday. **The Bay Tree,** 717 Commercial Ave., tel. 293-2112, sells gifts: baskets, mugs, cards, teas, coffee, etc.

Green Frog Gallery, 516 Commercial, tel. 293-6661, has prints, etchings, gifts, and custom framing. Closed Sun. and Mondays. Pick up some Native American carvings, pottery, jewelry, prints, and more at **Samish Potlatch Gifts,** 708 Commercial, tel. 293-6404. Chocoholics won't want to miss **Sweet 'N' Sassy,** 710 Commercial, for chocolates, ice-cream bars, cards, and gifts. **Left Bank Antiques,** 1906 Commercial, tel. 293-3022, has Victorian furniture, jewelry, prints, and toys. For groceries, there's a **Safeway** at 12th and Commercial, and a **Pay Less Drug Store** at 15th and Commercial.

SERVICES

The Anacortes area code is 206. For maps, brochures, or further information, contact the **Anacortes Chamber of Commerce,** 1319 Commercial Ave., tel. 293-3832. For a medical emergency, **Island Hospital** at 24th and M, tel. 293-3183, has 24-hour emergency room and ambulance service. For a tumble and spin-dry, try **Econo-Wash Laundry** at 2022 Commercial or **Thrifty Laundry** at 1502 Commercial.

TRANSPORTATION

By Car

Anacortes is about 80 miles north of Seattle, via I-5 and Hwy. 20, or via Whidbey Island. But it would be a shame to drive to Anacortes without a quick side trip to La Conner (p. 138), especially in spring when the daffodils and tulips are blooming.

Ferries

To get to the San Juan Islands via state ferry, you have no choice but leave from Anacortes —and ferry traffic keeps a good portion of local businesses in business. For fares and other vital information see "San Juan Islands," p. 173, or phone the Washington State Ferry System toll-free at (800) 542-0810.

Skagit County operates a nearly new ferry to residential Guemes Island from Sixth and I streets. The seven-minute crossing costs $4.20 for car and driver, $1 for passengers; the boat departs daily on the hour or better, from 6:30 a.m. most days to at least 6 p.m. Take your bicycle along for a scenic tour.

By Air

Departing from Anacortes Airport at 4000 Airport Rd. or Skagit Regional Airport, 1340 Peterson Rd., **West Isle Air** offers scenic flights year-round; tel. 293-4691 in Anacortes or 757-6890 in Burlington.

WHIDBEY ISLAND

INTRODUCTION

Credit for the 1792 discovery of Whidbey Island goes to Joseph Whidbey, master of George Vancouver's flagship, the HMS *Discovery*. Apparently, however, he wasn't the first one there: while exploring the island's west side, Whidbey stumbled upon the rotted remains of another ship, too weather-beaten to identify. Wandering wild oxen in the vicinity added to the mystery. When he stepped a-shore in what is now Coupeville, Whidbey was met by a group of natives who couldn't believe he was so white! Whidbey was obliged to open his jacket to demonstrate that he was even white under his clothes.

The longest island in the continental U.S. (New York's Long Island has been declared a peninsula by the U.S. Supreme Court), Whidbey Island encompasses 208 square miles in its 45-mile length—no spot of which is more than five miles from the water. Today picturesque Whidbey Island is one of western Washington's biggest tourist attractions; attendance at Deception Pass State Park rivals that of Mount Rainier. Besides tourism, the island economy is supported by the Whidbey Naval Air Station in Oak Harbor and one of the country's largest loganberry farms near Greenbank. The movie *An Officer and a Gentleman* was filmed partly aboard the Whidbey-Port Townsend ferry *Kulshan*.

The climate is mild year-round: the temperature ranges from 40° to 60° 80% of the time; temperatures above 75° and below 20° are rare. Autumn brings late-evening and early-morning fog; winter comes with light rain or mist every other day, though the total annual rainfall ranges from less than 20 inches in Coupeville and points north to 42 inches at Goss Lake in the south part of the island.

Services
For maps, brochures, and the like contact the chamber of commerce nearest your destina-

tion: **Central Whidbey Chamber of Commerce,** 262 W. Beach Lane, Box 152, Coupeville 98239, tel. 678-5434; **Clinton Chamber of Commerce,** 6231 Galbreath Rd., Clinton 98236, tel. 321-4545; **Freeland Chamber of Commerce,** Box 361, Freeland 98249, tel. 321-5677; **Langley Chamber of Commerce,** Box 403, Langley 98260, tel. 321-6765; **North Whidbey Chamber of Commerce,** 2506 Hwy. 20, Oak Harbo, 98277, tel. 675-3535.

Located mid-island in Coupeville, **Whidbey General Hospital** at Main St. and Hwy. 20 provides emergency care; tel. 678-5151, 321-5151, or 911.

Getting There
To drive onto Whidbey Island, you've got only one option: the Deception Pass Bridge at the island's north end. To get there, go west on Hwy. 20 from I-5. Otherwise, you'll have to go by **Washington State Ferry** from Mukilteo or Port Townsend. The Mukilteo ferry leaves for Clinton about every half-hour; the 20-minute crossing costs $2.15 roundtrip for passengers, $3.75 one way for car and driver, $1.60 one way for cyclists. From the Olympic Peninsula, board the ferry in Port Townsend to arrive in the Keystone landing next to Fort Casey State Park. Ferries leave about every 50 minutes; fares are $3.30 roundtrip for passengers, $5.55 one way for car and driver ($6.65 in summer), $2.30 one way for cyclists. For information on the state ferry system call (800) 542-0810.

OAK HARBOR

Settled first by sea captains, then the Irish, and at the turn of the century by immigrants from Holland, Oak Harbor's Dutch heritage is reflected in its festivals, a windmill at City Beach, and Holland Gardens. Oak Harbor is about the only place on the island you'll find fast food, traffic, and noise—but on an infinitely smaller scale than other Puget Sound cities.

Deception Pass State Park

When Capt. George Vancouver first sighted this waterway in 1792 he called it Port Gardner. But then he realized he'd been deceived—the inlet was actually a tidal passage between two islands—so he renamed it "Deception Pass."

One of the state's most visited parks, Deception Pass has facilities that rival those of national parks: swimming at two lakes, four miles of shoreline, 18 miles of hiking trails, fresh- and saltwater fishing, boating, picnicking, rowboat rentals, viewpoints, and 251 campsites (no hookups) with hot showers and trailer dump stations. The park, nine miles north of Oak Harbor on Hwy. 20, covers 3,000 forested acres on both sides of Deception Pass Bridge.

Although only electric motors or rowboats are allowed on the park's lakes, you can observe beaver dams, muskrats, and mink in the marshes on the south side of Cranberry Lake, which also hosts a seasonal concession stand. A 15-minute hike to the highest point on the island, 400-foot Goose Rock, provides views of the San Juan Islands, Mt. Baker, Victoria, and Fidalgo Island, and possibly bald eagles soaring overhead. The trail starts at the south end of the bridge, heading east from either side of the highway; take the wide trail as it follows the pass, then take one of the unmarked spur trails uphill to the top.

Other Parks

The newest addition to the state park system, **Joseph Whidbey State Park,** just south of the Naval Air Station on Swantown Rd., is largely undeveloped, with picnic tables, pit toilets, and 400 acres of beach for day use only. **Holland Gardens,** 500 Ave. W and 30th NW, site of the annual Holland Happening festival (see below), has shrub and flower gardens surrounding its white and blue windmill. **Oak Harbor Beach Park** has a sand beach, swimming, tennis and baseball facilities, and 54 campsites on the lagoon; tel. 679-5551.

Enjoy the beaches year-round with a kite from **Pegasus Kite Shop** in the Old Town Mall on Pioneer Way, tel. 675-4655. To explore the waters around the island, charter a boat from **J&J Charters,** 5191 N. Cornet Bay Dr., tel. 675-9733. Sailboats and powerboats are available to experienced boaters from $75 per day from April through Oct.; inexperienced boaters can hire a skipper-guide for an additional $75 per day.

Whidbey Island Naval Air Station

The largest naval air base in the Northwest was placed here because Ault Field, the U.S. Navy Reserve's airstrip, has some of the best flying weather in the U.S.: it gets only 20 inches of annual rainfall, is out of the path of commercial flight routes, and is virtually isolated with little electrical interference. For in-

WHIDBEY ISLAND

FERRY TO VICTORIA B.C. & SAN JUAN IS.

TO VANCOUVER B.C.

ANACORTES

MT. VERNON

FIDALGO ISLAND

DECEPTION PASS

DECEPTION PASS S.P.

WHIDBEY

JOSEPH WHIDBEY S.P.

OAK HARBOR

WHIDBEY ISLAND

FORT EBEY S.P.

PENN COVE

COUPEVILLE

EBEY'S LANDING

KEYSTONE FERRY LANDING

FORT CASEY S.P.

ADMIRALTY BAY

GREENBANK

SOUTH WHIDBEY S.P.

STRAIT OF JUAN DE FUCA

LANGLEY

FREELAND

EVERETT

CLINTON

USELESS BAY

MUKILTEO

POSSESSION PT.

TO SEATTLE

0   5 mi
0   5 km

© MOON PUBLICATIONS, INC.

formation on air shows and driving tours through the base (two weeks' notice is required), phone 257-2286.

Accommodations

Located at 5861 Hwy. 20, the **Auld Holland Inn**, tel. 675-2288, has 28 rooms, a heated pool and whirlpool, tennis court, lawn games, and coin laundry. Rates are $38-63 s, $38-70 d. The **Coachman Inn**, 5563 Hwy. 20 at Goldie Rd., tel. 675-0727, has 96 rooms from $45 s, $49 d, with a heated pool, whirlpool, exercise room, and laundry facilities. Top of the line is the **Best Western Harbor Plaza**, 5691 Hwy. 20, tel. 679-4567. Their 80 rooms range from $50-90 s, $60-100 d (depending on the season), with a restaurant and pool.

Food

Oak Harbor's only waterfront restaurant, **Char's Cove**, 2068 200th Ave. SW, tel. 679-2515, serves lunch weekdays, dinner daily, and Sunday brunch, with entertainment Tues. through Sat. nights in their lounge. **Two Sisters Pioneer Café**, tel. 675-7981, offers lunch and dinner Mon. through Sat. plus Sunday Champagne brunch at the Old Town Mall. For something a little lighter, **Smiley's** has pizza, barbecued chicken and ribs, and steak teamed with silent movies, and a big-screen TV—at the corner of Pioneer Way and 60th Street. For Japanese food including a sushi bar, and dinner daily except Monday.

If you plan to spend the day at Deception Pass, stop by **Two Sisters Picnic Basket** near the Pass on Hwy. 20, tel. 679-0606, for family-priced picnic lunches to go, with homemade bread, salads, fruit, hard-boiled eggs, even a tablecloth.

Festivals

The last weekend in April, Oak Harbor hosts **Holland Happening**—a folk parade, arts and crafts show, international dance fest, Dutch buffet, and tulip show in Holland Gardens at 500 Ave. W and 30th NW. In mid-Dec., the **Christmas Boatlight Parade** departs from Oak Harbor, proceeding around Penn Cove to the Coupeville Wharf; caroling and hot cocoa conclude the event.

THE MAIDEN OF DECEPTION PASS

The Samish Indians told the story of the Maiden of Deception Pass, Ko-Kwal-Alwoot. The Samish beauty was gathering shellfish along the beach when the sea spirit saw her and was at once enamored; as he took her hand, Ko-Kwal-Alwoot became terrified, but the sea spirit reassured her, saying he only wished to gaze upon her loveliness. She returned often, listening to the sea spirit's declarations of love.

One day a young man came from the sea to ask Ko-Kwal-Alwoot's father for permission to marry her. Her father, suspecting that living underwater would be hazardous to his daughter's health, refused, despite the sea spirit's claim that Ko-Kwal-Alwoot would have eternal life. Miffed, the sea spirit brought drought and famine to the old man's people until he agreed to give his daughter away, with one condition: that she return once every year so the old man could be sure she was properly cared for. The agreement was made, and the people watched as Ko-Kwal-Alwoot walked into the water until only her hair, floating in the current, was visible. The famine and drought ended at once.

Ko-Kwal-Alwoot kept her promise for the next four years, returning to visit her people, but every time she came she was covered with more and more barnacles and seemed anxious to return to the sea. On her last visit her people told her she need not return unless she wanted to; and since that time, she's provided abundant shellfish and clean spring water in that area. Legend has it that her hair can be seen floating to and fro with the tide in Deception Pass.

Today this Samish legend is inscribed on a story pole on Fidalgo Island. To get there, follow Hwy. 20 to Fidalgo Island; go west at Pass Lake, following the signs for Bowman Bay and Rosario Beach, and hike the trail toward Rosario Head.

Ebey's Landing

DIANNE BOULERICE LYONS

COUPEVILLE

One of the oldest towns in Washington, the "Port of Sea Captains" was founded in 1852 when Capt. Thomas Coupe, after sailing through Deception Pass, dropped anchor and became one of the town's first white settlers (alongside 300 or so Skagit Indians). Today the little town sits amidst the nation's largest historical preservation district, operating modern businesses from Victorian-era buildings.

Parks

Fort Casey State Park, a historical Army post site three miles south of Coupeville next to the Keystone ferry dock, has two miles of beach, an underwater park, trails, picnic areas, spectacular Olympic views, and 35 campsites; good bottom, salmon, and steelhead fishing, accessible by boat launch in remarkably clear water. Check out their **Admiralty Point Lighthouse Interpretive Center,** where you can learn about coast artillery and the 1890 defense post, and climb to the top for a view of Puget Sound. Much of the fort is open for public viewing, including ammunition bunkers, observation towers, underground storage facilities, and gun catwalks.

Fort Ebey State Park, west of Coupeville on Admiralty Inlet, has 50 campsites, a large picnic area, three miles of beach, and two miles of hiking trails. Due to its location in the Olympic rain shadow, the park is one of few places in western Washington where numerous varieties of cactus can be found. Much of Ft. Ebey's popularity stems from Lake Pondilla, formed by a glacial sinkhole—a bass-fisherman's and swimmer's delight. Follow the signs from the north parking lot for a two-block hike to the lake; half a dozen picnic tables and a camping area are reserved for hikers and bicyclists.

Rockhounds frequent the area from Point Partridge to Ebey's Landing, often encountering gem-quality stones such as agate, jasper, black and green jade, plus quartz and petrified wood. The park's 226 acres serve as a wildlife preserve for bald eagles, deer, rabbits, raccoons, and ducks.

Ebey's Landing, two miles west of Coupeville center, with easily the most striking coastal view on the island, was the first national historic reserve in the country. As Ft. Ebey Rd. winds westward through acres of farmland, the glimpses of water and cliff might remind you of the northern California or Oregon coastline; the majestic Olympics add to the drama. From the small parking area at the water's edge, hike the one-mile trail to Parego's Lagoon, then wade through the lagoon and climb Parego's Bluff for a view of the coastline, Olympics, and the Strait of Juan de Fuca that shouldn't be missed.

Historical Sights

The native Skagits didn't welcome the white settlers with open arms, and their northern neighbors, the Haida Indians, were even more hostile. To protect themselves from an attack that never came, the pioneers built seven blockhouses by 1856. One of them, the **Alexander Blockhouse,** is at Alexander St. just off Front St.; another, the **Davis Blockhouse,** stands at the edge of the cemetery on Sherman Road. Call the Central Whidbey Chamber of Commerce, tel. 678-5434, for more info. The **Island County Historical Society Museum** at Alexander and Coveland streets has displays of pioneer relics as well as a brochure describing a short walking tour of the town's Victorian buildings. **Chief Snakelum's Grave** in a grove two miles east of Coupeville commemorates the chief of the Skagit Tribe and one of the town's last Indian residents.

Accommodations And Food

Built in 1907 of madrona logs, the **Captain Whidbey Inn,** 2072 W. Captain Whidbey Inn Rd., tel. 678-4097, has rooms, cottages, and houses on Penn Cove's wooded shores. Rates start at $65 s or d, going up to $150 for the one- or two-bedroom houses. Rowboat, sailboat, and bicycle rentals are available; breakfast, lunch, and dinner are served daily. **The Colonel Crockett Farm,** 1012 S. Fort Casey Rd., tel. 678-3711, is an 1855 Victorian farmhouse overlooking Admiralty Bay at Ebey's Landing and surrounded by two acres of lawn and flower beds. Their five rooms are $60-70 d per night (singles $5 less), each with private bath; a buffet breakfast is served at 9:30 a.m. No smoking or kids under 14.

For more conventional lodging, the **Coupeville Inn,** 200 N.W. Coveland St., tel. 678-6668, has 24 guest rooms with complimentary continental breakfast, from $47-65 per night s or d, along with a view of Penn Cove and the Cascades.

Festivals And Fairs

Coupeville's annual **Arts and Crafts Festival** is held the second weekend in August with a salmon barbecue and music. If you're here the first weekend in October, don't miss the Squash Festival, celebrating the 30,000-ton squash harvest with canoe races, music, squash soup and main dishes, culminating in the crowning of the King and Queen of Squash.

GREENBANK

Don't be surprised if you never see Greenbank center—the general store and post office are easy to miss—but you can't miss the acres and acres of loganberries growing just north of town. Formerly the largest loganberry farm in the U.S., Chateau Ste. Michelle uses these berries for their Whidbey Island Liqueur. Stop by the tasting room on Hwy. 20 for a short self-guided tour and a taste of Ste. Michelle wines.

Parks And Gardens

Probably the island's most underrated park, **South Whidbey State Park** on Smuggler's Cove Rd. has hiking, picnicking, clamming and crabbing on a sandy beach, 54 (non-hookup) campsites, and striking Olympic views. The 87 acres of towering firs and alders protect resident black-tailed deer, fox, raccoons, rabbits, bald eagles, osprey, and pileated woodpeckers. Late summer means salmon in the Admiralty Inlet; a public boat launch is located two miles south of the park at Bush Point.

Meerkerk Rhododendron Gardens boasts a wide variety of rhododendron species and hybrids, plus other plants such as Japanese cherries, maples, magnolia, and more, on a 53-acre site on Resort Road. Max and Anne Meerkerk built a house and started the garden upon their arrival to Whidbey Island in 1963; Max died in 1969, leaving Anne to tend the garden until 1979, when she also died and bequeathed the gardens to the Seattle Rhododendron Society. In response to one of Anne's last requests, an international rhody test garden was developed; plants from Germany, Japan, England, and other countries are added each year. The gardens are open Wed. through Sat. 9 a.m.-4 p.m.; tel. 321-6682.

Accommodations

The **Guest House,** 835 E. Christenson Rd., tel. 678-3115, features a three-room suite, four cottages, and one log home, all heavy on the romance, on 25 acres of forest and meadowland with marine and mountain views. The suite is $85; three cottages are $110, the fourth goes for $155, and the log home is $195. All accommodations except the suite include a fireplace, kitchen, VCR and complimentary movies, in-room Jacuzzi, and are for one couple only. Other facilities include a pool, exercise room, and outdoor spa. Indoor smoking, kids, and pets are not allowed.

FREELAND

South Whidbey was seemingly designed for biking. The rolling hills, clean air, and beautiful weather are inspiring enough, but occasional deer and eagle sightings add to the pleasure. Rent a bike for a day (or week) from **The Pedaler** on Hwy. 525 at Tara Village, tel. 221-5040. A boat launch and small sunny picnic area are found at **Freeland Park** on Holmes Harbor, about two streets over from "downtown" Freeland—just look for the water.

Accommodations

Get away from your troubles and your kids at the **Cliff House,** 5440 Windmill Rd., tel. 321-1566. The entire house is yours for a two-night minimum at $245 per night for a gourmet kitchen, king-size feather bed, fresh flowers, CDs, Jacuzzi, hammock for two, fireplace, beach access and water views, and continental breakfast. No kids, pets, or smoking. Those with tighter budgets will enjoy **Sea Cliff Cottage;** same owners, same seclusion, same beach, at $135 per night with a two-night minimum stay. The cottage features a small kitchen, queen-size bed, fireplace, and continental breakfast.

Pillars By The Sea overlooks Holmes Harbor at 1367 E. Bayview Ave., tel. 221-7738. The three rooms each have queen-size beds and private baths for $60 a night; add $10 for Saturday night only.

Coupeville, one of the state's oldest towns

ARCHIE SATTERFIELD

Harbor Hideaway, also on Holmes Harbor on E. Harbor Rd., tel. 321-5180, sits on an acre of grass with panoramic water views. The three rooms are $45-55 d; add $5 for kids over 12, subtract $5 for single. **Chateau la Mer,** 4946 S. Scurlock Rd., tel. 221-3753, is a contemporary B&B furnished in antiques, overlooking the beach at Bush Point. The three bedrooms are $35, $45, or $65 per night and include a gourmet breakfast, use of the Jacuzzi, two bicycles, TV, stereo, VCR, compact-disc player, deck, and fireplace. An even lower-priced alternative is the **Harbour Inn,** 1606 E. Main St., tel. 321-6900. The 20 rooms are $32-45 s; $40-55 d during summer, less off-season. **Mutiny Bay Resort/ Motel,** 5856 S. Mutiny Bay Rd. (Box 249), tel. 321-4500, has chalets for $60 d, cabins for $30 d, and full-hookup trailer sites for $12 (no tents) on 450 feet of beachfront one mile

FERRY ROUTES

STATE FERRY -----
OTHER FERRY ·········

0   10 mi
0   10 km

© MOON PUBLICATIONS, INC.

west of Freeland at the end of Fish Road. Motel guests may not have pets.

Food
Mindy's in Harbor Village Square serves breakfast, lunch, and dinner daily and specializes in fresh strawberry and raspberry pies. For seafood and steaks, try the **Island Pub** on Harbor Ave.; it is open for lunch and dinner and has entertainment on Friday and Saturday nights.

LANGLEY

If you only have time to visit one of Whidbey's towns, this is it. The shops lining the streets of this small waterfront artists' community make for good browsing, while the views of the Cascades and the Saratoga Passage provide an uplifting backdrop. Langley is the home of the **Island County Fair,** a four-day event held in late August with a logging show, local talent show, parade, music, and 4-H exhibits.

Accommodations
Langley's newest hotel, **The Inn at Langley,** 400 First St., tel. 221-3033, is an upscale getaway at the north edge of town that overlooks Saratoga Passage, which runs between Whidbey and Camano islands. The 24 guest rooms are elegantly decorated, and each has a fireplace and deck. The rates are high: $115 s, $130 d for a corner room, up to $195 d for a suite. Continental breakfast is included; a five-course dinner is $25.

Also overlooking Saratoga Passage, **The Whidbey Inn,** 106 First St., tel. 221-7115, has three rooms and three fireplace suites, each with private bath and access to the sundeck, plus some of life's little luxuries—scented bath gels, chocolates on the pillows, and a breakfast basket of homemade breads, an egg dish, juice, and coffee brought to your door. Rooms start at $70 a night. No kids, pets, or indoor smoking.

The **Saratoga Inn** is surrounded by 25 acres of forest and meadows at 4850 S. Coles Rd. (within walking distance of downtown), tel. 221-7526. The inn has five rooms

with views, private baths, and fresh flowers from $75-90; breakfast is continental, featuring muffins, croissants, and homemade blackberry jam. No pets, kids, or smoking.

Country Cottage, a B&B on three acres at 215 Sixth St., tel. 221-8709, has three rooms and two suites with private baths, a full breakfast, and a view of the Cascades and Saratoga Passage for $75-85 d; no kids, pets, or smoking.

Log Castle B&B, on the waterfront at 3273 E. Saratoga Rd., tel. 321-5483, was designed and built by the owners from material located on the property; of the four guest rooms, the third-story turret—complete with widow's walk—is the most popular. Each room has its own bath and porch with Saratoga Passage and mountain views. Rooms cost $60-80; no pets or smoking.

Food
Don't miss the **Dog House Tavern and Backdoor Restaurant,** corner of First and Anthes on the waterfront. Nothing fancy—just a great place to grab a pork sandwich, nachos, or a burger and a couple beers while enjoying the view. Nothing else comes close.

Down the street a bit at 113 First, **Café Langley** has a following of its own. Greek is the word: lamb kabobs, pita bread, soups, and other Middle Eastern dishes. Open for lunch and dinner daily. **Star Bistro** serves burgers, seafoods, salads, and more upstairs at 201½ First St.; open for lunch and dinner daily. Newly remodeled, **Mike's Place,** 215 First St., tel. 321-6575, is another popular spot, serving lunch and dinner daily from an international menu, complete with home-baked bread and pastries.

CLINTON

Driving or biking around Clinton's rural, wooded back roads provides lungfuls of fresh air and some exhilarating vistas. Take Deer Lake Rd. (watch the signs—the road takes 90-degree turns without notice) to **Deer Lake Park** for swimming, boating, and fishing in a secluded, wooded area. From Hwy. 525, go left onto Campbell Rd., then left again on Maxwelton Rd. to **Maxwelton Beach,** where you'll find the island's best Dungeness crabbing.

Accommodations
Surrounded by Deer Lagoon and Useless Bay, **Home By The Sea** at 2388 E. Sunlight Beach Rd., tel. 221-2964, has rooms for $75 d and cottages from $75-85 d with views of the Olympics and Admiralty Inlet. The cottages, one of which is available for families with children, require a two-night minimum stay.

Food
Islander Restaurant, at the Clinton ferry landing, tel. 321-4363, serves Italian and American food daily from 6 a.m.-2 a.m. plus Sunday brunch. For Chinese cuisine, **Hong Kong Gardens** is one mile from the ferry landing on Hwy. 525, tel. 221-2828, with a view of Saratoga Passage. Open daily in the summer, closed Mon. in winter. **Le Quai,** a popular French restaurant on Hwy. 525, tel. 321-1071, is open daily except Mon. for lunch and dinner.

FLORENCE BOULERICE

LOUISE FOOTE

SAN JUAN ISLANDS

Nestled between the Washington mainland and Vancouver Island, the San Juan Archipelago consists of 172 islands with names—more than 700 at low tide and 428 at high tide. People live on 60 of them and 10 are state marine parks. Four of the largest—Orcas, Lopez, Shaw, and San Juan—are served by state ferry. The pace is slow and the dress is casual, so leave your ties at home, but don't forget your binoculars (for whale- and bird-watching), camera, and bike.

More than any other part of Washington, the San Juans give one a sense of being *away*. When the ferry pulls away from the Anacortes dock, it is almost like departing on a cruise ship.

An oddity of the islands is that all of the three islands with heavy population (Shaw is out of the island mainstream even though it is a stone's throw from Orcas) manage to have their distinct personalities. Another oddity is that island people don't go out of their way to make friends on other islands. Ask someone on Orcas if they know your friend on San Juan and you'll almost invariably be told no ("We don't get to San Juan much").

Generally speaking (very generally) Lopez Island attracts the low-keyed people who care less than most about an extravagant life-style, people who are comfortable alone

or in a small community. San Juan is the county seat so that's where the lawyers and promoters and political hangers-on go. The famous novelist, Ernest K. "The High and the Mighty" Gann lives there, and so does Ruth Beebe "Hanta Yo" Hill. Friday Harbor is a hot-bed of environmentalists vs. developers.

Orcas is something of the Kiwanis Club of the islands. Several industrialists have built homes there, and it continues to attract successful writers (Richard "Jonathan Livingston Seagull" Bach lives there), and members of the Kaiser family and some of Seattle's wealthiest citizens.

Climate
The San Juans do most of their tourist business between Memorial Day and Labor Day when the weather is warm—rarely above 85°—and sunny, but for the locals September and October are the nicest months of the year: the tourists are gone, and the weather is still warm and dry, with highs in the 60s and lows in the 40s or 50s, and the salmon are running. Because the islands are shielded by the Olympic and Vancouver Island mountains, rainfall amounts to less than 25 inches per year; December is the wettest month, with 4½ inches of rain on the average and temperatures in the low 40s.

HISTORY

Because of inexact wording in the U.S.-Canada boundary treaty, the San Juan Islands were not only the subject of a territorial dispute, but also the stage for an international incident commonly referred to as the "Pig War." During the mid-1850s, the ownership of the San Juan Islands was in doubt because Capt. George Vancouver claimed them in 1791 and Capt. Charles Wilkes did the same in 1841. The islands were occupied by both American and British citizens and military; the British built a stockade and encampment about midway on the west side of the island in a beautiful cove. The Americans built their camp at the very southern tip on the most windy, exposed part of the island. Both camps are part of the San Juan Islands National Historic Park.

The military units arrived because in June of 1859 one of 25 American settlers on San Juan Island, Lyman A. Cutler, got tired of a British-owned hog rooting in his potato patch, so he shot and killed it. The Englishman who owned the pig insisted that Cutler pay for the pig, and when he refused, the Englishman insisted that he be brought to trial in Victoria. The American refused to participate. The soldiers, bored most of the time because no shots were fired, remained there until the matter was settled by arbitration 13 years later by Kaiser Wilhelm I, who gave the San Juans to the United States. Fortunately, the pig was the only casualty.

SERVICES

The area code in the San Juan Islands is 206. For maps and information, write or call the **San Juan Island Chamber of Commerce**, Box 98, Friday Harbor, WA 98250, tel. 378-5240, or the **Orcas Island Chamber of Commerce**, Box 252, Eastsound, WA 98245, tel. 376-2273.

Fitness fanatics might want to take advantage of the $10 one-day memberships offered by **San Juan Fitness and Athletic Club**, open daily in Friday Harbor; tel. 378-4449. Facilities include racquetball courts, exercise equipment, sauna, steam room, spa, and juice bar.

For groceries, film, and other essentials stop by **King's Market** in Friday Harbor or **Templin's General Store** in Eastsound. You can do your laundry at **Wash Tub Laundromat**, San Juan Inn Boardwalk in Friday Harbor, tel. 378-2070, or **Airport Center Self Service Laundry** in Eastsound, tel. 376-2478.

For medical emergencies, call 911 in Friday Harbor or Lopez, or 376-2341 on Orcas Island.

TRANSPORTATION

By Air

Air San Juan/Chart Air connects to major carriers via Seattle, Bellingham, and Anacortes; call them at 378-3133 or, toll-free in Washington, (800) 237-1101. You can also fly to Rosario Resort on Orcas Island from Seattle via seaplane four times daily with **Lake Union Air;** call (800) 826-1890 or 284-2784. **West Isle Air,** tel. 293-4691 or (800) 874-4434, flies daily from Anacortes and Bellingham to several of the San Juans—Lopez, Orcas, Waldron, Stuart, Decatur, and San Juan, and as needed to Boeing Field or Sea-Tac Airport. **Kenmore Air,** tel. (800) 543-9595, serves the San Juans three times daily by floatplane from its base at the north end of Lake Washington with pick-ups on Lake Union. **Orcas Flight** offers scenic airplane rides from $45 for 30 minutes out of Orcas's Eastsound Airport; call 376-2771 for reservations or information.

By Ferry

If you can only take one ride aboard a **Washington State Ferry,** the trip from Anacortes to the San Juans should be the one. The scenery is so beautiful that even amateur photographers can get spectacular sunset-over-the-islands shots. Ferries leave Anacortes five times daily (seven times on Fri.)

SAN JUAN ISLANDS

(map labels: PATOS I., SUCIA I., MATIA I., LUMMI I., BELLINGHAM, WALDRON I., STUART I., EAST SOUND, CLARK I., MORAN S.P., TO SIDNEY B.C., SPIEDEN I., WEST SOUND, ROSARIO, ORCAS ISLAND, DOE BAY, POSEY I., ROCHE HARBOR, DEER HARBOR, OLGA, DOE I., SINCLAIR I., HENRY I., SAN JUAN I. NAT'L HIST. PARK (ENGLISH CAMP), ORCAS, OBSTRUCTION PASS, CYPRESS I., SHAW I., SHAW I. C.P., ODLIN C.P., GUEMES I., SAN JUAN ISLAND, FRIDAY HARBOR, TURN I., SPENCER SPIT S.P., BLAKELY I., LIME KILN PT. S.P., LOPEZ, HUMMEL, JAMES I., ANACORTES, HAVEN BICYCLE CAMP., DECATUR I., LOPEZ ISLAND, SAN JUAN I. NAT'L HIST. PARK (AMERICAN CAMP), FIDALGO ISLAND, WHIDBEY I.)

STATE FERRY ——————
OTHER FERRY ------------

0 5 mi
0 5 km

© MOON PUBLICATIONS, INC.

from 6:45 a.m.-9 p.m., stopping at Lopez, Shaw, Orcas, and Friday Harbor, in that order; it takes roughly an hour and 50 minutes from Anacortes to Friday Harbor. Fares to Friday Harbor are $4.65 for passengers, $15.85 car and driver ($19 in summer), and $6.25 bicycle and rider; car-and-driver fares to the other islands are a few dollars less, and carry-on kayaks go free.

Once a day this ferry continues on to Sidney, B.C.; fares are $6.05 passenger, $26.05 car and driver ($31.25 in summer), and $8.55 bicycle and rider. For exact departure times or special fares call 464-6400 from Seattle or (800) 542-0810 statewide.

The *Victoria Clipper*, tel. (800) 888-2535, the passenger-only vessel running between Seattle and Victoria in the summer, makes flag stops at Port Ludlow on the Olympic Peninsula and Rosario Resort on Orcas Island, in addition to its usual stops at Port Townsend and Friday Harbor.

Day Cruises

Gray Line Water Sightseeing, of Bellingham, 355 Harris Ave., Ste. 104, tel. 738-8099, provides daily San Juan Islands cruises, departing Bellingham's cruise terminal from May to mid-Oct. for $42 adults, $20 kids 5-12. Gray Line also offers an overnight cruise to Victoria through the San Juans May through mid-Sept., from $140-180 for one night to $275 for two nights, hotels included. A San Juan overnight trip can be arranged.

Once you're on San Juan Island, **Western Prince Cruises** offers trips for $40 aboard the 46-foot *Western Prince,* departing from the dock across Front St. from the museum. The cruises are narrated by a wildlife naturalist who knows all of the San Juans' 76 orcas by name. Prepayment is required for the four-hour cruise, which includes lunch and a photo souvenir. Phone 378-5315 for more information.

Longer Cruises
Catalyst Cruises, 515 S. 143rd St., Tacoma, tel. 537-7678, offers several 5- to 14-day San Juan Island cruises, departing from Seattle, aboard their 55-foot motor cruiser *Sacajawea.* Catalyst is one of few Northwest charter outfits that offer scheduled cruises, meaning your group doesn't need to fill up the whole boat. Five- and six-day cruises stop at several San Juan islands plus Victoria, B.C., and La Conner; a two-week Canadian cruise visits the American San Juans and heads up to Campbell River, Big Bay, and Desolation Sound. Five- and six-day cruises run June through Aug. ($662-950 pp); the 14-day San Juan/Canadian cruise is held once or twice each summer for $1590-1855 pp. Onboard

meals are included with all cruises, and the fresh seafood is legendary.

Departing weekly mid-July through Sept. from Vashon Island in south Puget Sound, **Gallant Lady Cruises** offers a six-day San Juan Islands cruise aboard a 65-foot 1940s teak-and-mahogany yacht with stops at Rosario Resort, Friday Harbor, Sucia Island, and La Conner. The *Lady* is quite stable and the cruises are through protected waters, so seasickness is generally not a problem. The $699 pp pricetag includes all meals, featuring fresh seafood and low-fat meats served Northwest, continental, and Oriental style. For more information call or write Box 1250, Vashon, WA 98070, tel. 463-2073.

Another six-day cruise leaves from La Conner on the 62-foot fiberglass sailboat *J. Marie.* Sailing May through Oct., these cruises visit a number of the smaller islands, including Stuart and Sucia, with stops at Friday Harbor and Rosario Resort. All meals are

Sailboats provide photographic opportunities in the San Juans.

included for $825; no kids under 12. For more information write or call **J. Marie Sailing Cruises,** Box 722, La Conner, WA 98257, tel. 466-4292.

Take a seven-day sail in spring or fall aboard the *Norden,* an 83-foot-long wooden Baltic schooner. Departing from Friday Harbor, the cruise visits a number of smaller islands plus the larger resorts and, because of the size of the ship and the stillness of the water, even landlubbers won't get queasy. All meals are included for $685 pp, and families are welcome; call 842-2803 or write Box 10642, Bainbridge Island, WA 98110, for reservations or special family rates.

Sea Kayaking
Shearwater Sea Kayak Tours has half-day kayak trips paddling around East Sound or out to Point Doughty and overnighters to Matia, Sucia, or Jones island; no experience necessary, but you must be at least 16. One-day tours start at $45; two-day tours are $119-129; and three-day trips are $169. Kayaking gear and most camping equipment are included.

Requiring somewhat more effort are the three- and six-day sea kayak tours offered from May through Sept. by **Northwest Sea Ventures,** Box 522, Anacortes, WA 98221. Led by an experienced guide well versed in local history and wildlife, these tours are open to anyone 15 or over in good physical

condition; those with no previous experience will be assigned to stable two-person kayaks. The group is limited to eight, covering 5-10 miles a day, with occasional side trips into small towns. The $165 and $325 prices include all camping and kayaking equipment, three meals a day, and instruction; just bring your sleeping bag. They also sell and rent kayaks and offer private and group lessons at their shop at 2114 Commercial St. in Anacortes. For more information call 293-3692.

Boat Rentals
Boat and kayak rentals are easy to find on the islands; rates are generally $30-40 a day for small outboard motorboats, increasing with the size of vessel. In Friday Harbor try **Different Strokes Boat Rentals,** tel. 378-2342; on Orcas, **Black Bottom Boat Rental** in Eastsound, tel. 376-4032.

By Bicycle
Bicycle rentals are available on the four major islands by the day, hour, or week; they're cheaper to bring on the ferry than a car. Rentals cost about $4 an hour, $12-16 a day; most shops also rent 15-speed mountain bikes (for trips up Mt. Constitution), panniers, child carriers, and helmets. On Lopez try **Lopez Bicycle Works,** Fisherman Bay Rd., tel. 468-2847; on Orcas, **Island Chain Saw** in the Sears building in Eastsound, tel. 376-

2586; on San Juan, **Island Bicycles,** 180 West St. in Friday Harbor, tel. 378-4941.

By Moped
For all the fun of biking without the effort, rent a moped from **Susie's Mopeds** in Friday Harbor, tel. 378-5244, or **Key Moped Rentals** on Orcas Island at the ferry landing, Deer Harbor Marina, or in Eastsound, tel. 376-2474.

Other
Shuttle bus service between Friday Harbor, Roche Harbor Resort, Lakedale, and other San Juan Island destinations is available from **San Juan Island Tow and Transit,** tel. 378-5545. The 14-passenger vans make three loops of the island, departing hourly or so until 8 p.m.; one-way fares start at $3 adults, half price for kids. Taxi service is available before and after bus service.

SAN JUAN ISLAND

The largest island in the archipelago, San Juan Island is about 20 miles long and seven miles wide, covering 55 square miles. Friday Harbor, the only incorporated town in the chain, is the also county seat, the commercial center of the San Juans and home to half of the island's 4,000 residents.

Sights
The American and English encampments from the 1859 "Pig War" are now national historic parks. **American Camp** is located in the southeast corner of the island, five miles from Friday Harbor, with two buildings and other remains of the original post and an interpretive trail; it's also home to thousands of rabbits whose ancestors were brought to the islands as a food source, but the inevitable happened and they keep multiplying. The only nesting skylarks in the state can be found at American Camp, too.

English Camp, eight miles from Friday Harbor on the northwest side of the island, includes a restored hospital, the picturesque blockhouse, commissary, and barracks, plus hiking trails to the top of Mt. Young, which has good views of the archipelago. Both sites have picnic areas and beach access for day use only. The grounds are open year-round with rangers at both sites in summer, but the buildings close in winter.

The **University of Washington** operates a marine biology research laboratory a mile north of Friday Harbor with an aquarium and display tanks. Free tours are given Wed. and Sat. afternoons in July and Aug.; phone 378-2165 for information.

Probably the most exciting sights in the San Juans, orca, or "killer" whales are usually minding their own underwater business while tourists anxiously peer out their ferry windows. What some visitors think are schools of baby orcas escorting their boat are actually full-grown black-and-white Dall's porpoises. On the island, a good spot to watch for whales is from **Lime Kiln Point State Park** on Haro Strait on the island's west side; it's the only park in the country dedicated exclusively to whalewatching. Bald eagles also live on the island year-round; look for them between Eagle Cove and Cattle Point on the island's east side.

Museum
The Whale Museum, 62 First St., Friday Harbor, tel. 378-4710, has whale and porpoise displays including full skeletons of a baby gray whale and an adult killer whale, paintings, photographs, and carvings. You can also adopt a whale for $20; you get your whale's photo and ID number plus a subscription to the museum's newsletter. Open daily till 5 p.m. in summer, till 4 p.m. in winter; admission is $2 adults, $.75 for kids. If you're intrigued by the museum and wildlife cruises (see "Cruises" above), consider attending the museum's week-long university-accredited "Whale School," offered three times in July and Aug. for $767. By the way, if you spot a whale anywhere around the San Juans, swimming or stranded, be a sport and call the museum's 24-hour hotline: tel. (800) 562-8832.

Winetasting
Sample San Juan Cellars' variety of wines created exclusively for **The Island Wine**

Company at Cannery Landing (at the ferry dock) in Friday Harbor; open 10 a.m.- 6 p.m. daily, tel. 378-3229.

Accommodations

Bed-and-breakfast accommodations are popular in the islands, with San Juan leading the pack. The **San Juan Inn**, just a half block from the ferry at 50 Spring St. (Box 776), tel. 378-2070, has been in the B&B business since 1873 and still retains its original Victorian charm. Ten guest rooms with shared baths, a harbor view parlor, and continental breakfast start at $34 s, $52-60 d in winter, up to $60-64 d in summer. The **Moon and Sixpence**, 3021 Beaverton Valley Rd., tel. 378-4138, is a country inn with three guest rooms, a suite, and a rustic cabin from $65-95, with full Dutch breakfast, plus visiting eagles and swans outside for no extra charge. No pets; children by arrangement. Next to American Camp at 4531-A Cattle Point Rd., **Olympic Lights**, tel. 378-3186, has five rooms, one with private bath, for $60-90 including Olympic views, goosedown comforters, and full breakfast with eggs from the resident hens. **Duffy House**, 760 Pear Point Rd., tel. 378-5604, overlooks Griffin Bay on the east side of the island surrounded by flower and vegetable gardens, with five rooms (shared baths) for $70-80 in summer, $60-70 in winter, with full breakfast. Two-night minimum stay; no kids or smoking. A waterfront cabin with laddered loft is also available in summer; call for rates and info. **Tucker House**, walking distance from the ferry at 260 B St., tel. 378-2783, has three rooms furnished in turn-of-the-century charm for $70 d (shared bath), including full breakfast and use of the hot tub; three private rooms with separate entrance and bath, wood stove or fireplace (two with kitchens) go for $80-90. Kids are okay in the private rooms. For a real waterfront room, **Wharfside B&B** has two cabins aboard the 60-foot sailing vessel *Jacquelyn,* docked at K dock at the Friday Harbor Marina, for $65-70 d, including a hearty seaman's breakfast and shared bath. Captain Clyde also offers custom-tailored sightseeing/whalewatch cruises and sportfishing charters ($65 pp for a half day of fishing) aboard his 27-foot cruiser. Call 378-3404 or 378-5661 for reservations and information.

For more conventional accommodations, **Friday Harbor Motor Inn,** 410 Spring St., tel. 378-4351, has 72 rooms, some with kitchens, and a shared Jacuzzi for $50-60 d in winter, $65-75 d in summer, within walking distance of the ferry dock. **Island Lodge,** 1016 Guard St., tel. 378-2000, is a little less expensive at $36 d in winter, $52-60 d in summer, including a whirlpool, with moped and car rentals and free ferry or airport pickup.

Follow Roche Harbor Rd. to **Roche Harbor Resort,** tel. 378-2155, with 100-year-old Hotel de Haro, cottages, condos, and a popular by-reservation-only restaurant on the island's north end. Other facilities at the resort include a marina, seaside tennis courts, musical entertainment, and a historic walking tour. Hotel rooms and suites cost $85-145; cottages and condos are $85-190 d with a four-night minimum in July and August.

Food

Café Bissett, 170 West St., tel. 378-3109, serves elegant yet moderately priced dinners at this tiny side-street location. Open for dinner only, daily in summer, Thurs. through Mon. rest of year. For elegant dining, **Winston's,** 95 Nichols St. in Friday Harbor, has seafood, steak, and international cuisine plus a good wine and beer selection. Open for dinner only; tel. 378-5093 for reservations. A tad more expensive, the **Duck Soup Inn,** 3090 Roche Harbor Rd., tel. 378-4878, specializes in superbly done local seafood, chicken dishes, and regional wines. **Springtree Eating Establishment,** Spring St. in Friday Harbor, tel. 378-4848, serves a varied menu including steak, seafood, chicken, pasta, salads, and more in a pretty Victorian setting; open for three meals daily.

Downrigger's, tel. 378-2700, at the Friday Harbor ferry landing, is open for lunch and dinner with seafood, steak, burgers, pasta, including salmon ravioli, and a choice of 30 wines available by the glass. **The Cannery House,** overlooking the port at 174 First St., tel. 378-2500, specializes in "homemade" Mexican meals, sandwiches, soups, and chowders. Open for lunch, dinner, and Sunday brunch (in summer). For deep-dish pizza and Italian food in a family atmosphere, try **The Friday Harbor Bistro** in the Elite Hotel at 35 First St.; phone 378-3076 for orders to go.

Entertainment

Friday Harbor and Roche Harbor gather 15 West Coast bands for their **Dixieland Jazz Festival,** held annually the third weekend in July; tel. 378-5509. A large, contemporary gallery in Friday Harbor, **Waterworks Gallery,** 315 Argyle at Spring St., tel. 378-3060, has paintings, prints, watercolors, and sculpture by island and international artists.

ORCAS ISLAND

Many believe that Orcas Island is the chain's most beautiful island. It is definitely the hilliest: drive, hike, or bike to the top of 2,409-foot Mt. Constitution for a panoramic view from Vancouver, B.C., to Mt. Rainier. Orcas's most prominent mansion, Rosario Resort, regularly graces the pages of national travel magazines and employs almost 200 people, making it the county's largest private employer.

Park

Located near Eastsound, 5,000-acre **Moran State Park** is most popular for its paved road and hiking trails to the summit of Mt. Constitution. Other hiking trails include a 1½-mile straight downhill trek from the summit to Twin Lakes, and a two-miler from Mountain Lake (park here) to Twin Lakes. Another option—with three waterfalls along the way—is the 2½-mile trail from Mountain Lake to Cascade Lake, following Cascade Creek. Or hike the four-mile loop trail around Mountain Lake for a chance to see some deer, particularly in the morning and early evening. The park's lakes also provide freshwater fishing and boating, with boat rentals and fishing supplies available at a concession stand. Campers can stay at one of 136 non-hookup sites, but all sites are preassigned, so check in at the pay station across from Cascade Lake when you first arrive, or call or write Moran State Park, Star Route Box 22, Eastsound, WA 98245, tel. 376-2326, as much as a year in advance of your trip.

Museum

Located in Eastsound, the **Orcas Island Historical Museum,** tel. 376-4840, has a collection of relics from 1880s pioneer homesteads. Open Tues. through Sat. afternoons in summer, donations gladly accepted.

Accommodations

Situated on 80 acres in the shadow of Turtleback Mountain, **Turtleback Farm Inn** on Crow Valley Rd. in Eastsound, tel. 376-4914, has seven rooms, all with private bath, in a comfortable, farmhouse atmosphere. On warm days the full country breakfast is served outdoors on the valley-view deck. Rates are $145 d. Kids by special arrangement, but no pets. The **Orcas Hotel,** on a knoll above the ferry dock in Orcas, tel. 376-4300, is a three-story Victorian built in the early 1900s overlooking the ferry landing, Shaw Island and Harney Channel; extensively restored in 1985, it's on the National Register of Historic Places. Rooms, including continental breakfast, are $65-170 d, some with private baths, and kids are okay. The **Kangaroo House,** on approximately two acres north of Eastsound Village on N. Beach Rd. (Box 334), tel. 376-2175, was built in 1907 and bought in the '30s by a sea captain, Harold Ferris, who picked up a young female kangaroo on one of his Australian voyages and tamed her with the music he frequently played onboard. Once home on Orcas, the captain found Josie could "dance," predict the weather, and keep the geraniums well trimmed. The neighborhood kids gave Josie's house the name it still bears. Today the inn has five guest rooms from $60-70 d ($10 less off-season), plus a large sitting room with fireplace, period furnishings, and gourmet breakfasts. Sorry, no pets or indoor smoking.

Over in Deer Harbor, **Palmer's Chart House,** Box 51, tel. 376-4231, was the first B&B on Orcas Island when it opened for business in 1975, and still is one of the few with water views. Rooms here include a hearty breakfast, tea and coffee in your room, private entrance and bath, for $45 s, $60 d; dinner may be arranged for $7.50 pp. No pets, but they'll make arrangements with a local kennel. See "Longer Cruises," p. 175, for information on their overnight and afternoon sails.

For a resort atmosphere, try **Smuggler's Villa Resort** in Eastsound, tel. 376-2297. Their 20 condominiums cost $88-94 (one-four people) and include use of the hot tub, sauna, outdoor pool, tennis and pickleball courts, 400 feet of private beach, and moorage. The condos themselves have all the comforts of home: washer and dryer, microwave, fireplace, TV, and dishwasher, plus sunset views over Haro Strait. Weekly rates are available.

Around Eastsound from Orcas, past Moran State Park, is the little town of Olga and, farther south, **Obstruction Pass Resort,** tel. 376-2472. Cabins on the protected bay start at $40 a night; for something a little different, their 104-foot tug has five private staterooms that sleep two comfortably from $50 d. Boat rentals are available.

Deer Harbor Inn, tel. 376-4110, has units from $55 and up available year-round on Deer Harbor, so named by the island's earliest settlers for its swift, black-tailed inhabitants. Deer still live on many of the islands and swim between them. The resort also has a heated indoor pool, restaurant, gift shop, and overnight moorage. In winter, your second night is free. Write Box 176, Deer Harbor, for more information. In the heart of Eastsound Village, **The Outlook Inn,** tel. 376-2200, offers a bay view, comfortable country surroundings, restaurant, and bar, plus 30 rooms in a choice of styles: European-type (at the inn) with shared bath for $55 d, or American-style (in the annex) with private bath and TV for $68 d. Breakfast is not included, but the Inn's restaurant opens at 8 a.m.

Rosario Island Resort And Spa
This is a nationally known getaway, and the largest resort in the state, housed in Seattle shipbuilder Robert Moran's turn-of-the-century mansion in Eastsound. Moran wasn't blessed with musical talent so he played the 1,972-pipe organ like a player piano and none of his guests were the wiser; organ concerts are still held Tues. through Sat. at 5 p.m. The building has been beautifully restored, offering fine dining, exercise equipment and classes, and salons featuring massage therapy, facials, body wraps, tanning beds, nail care, and more—all for a fee, of course. Room rates start at $85 s or d in summer with assorted winter packages, including a weekend "bargain" for $189 d for two nights' accommodations plus Friday night seafood buffet and Sunday brunch. Phone 376-2222 or, toll-free statewide, (800) 562-8820 for reservations.

Food
The **Outlook Inn,** Main St. in Eastsound, tel. 376-2200, serves three meals daily (moderately priced) in a relaxed and pretty Victorian setting with a bay view. Their world-class East Coast chef, Antony Vincenza Carbone, changes the dinner menu daily to ensure the freshest seafood, and also shows considerable expertise in his beef, lamb, and poultry dishes, soups, and vegetarian fare. For Mexican food, **Bilbo's Festivo** on A St. in Eastsound is something of a local legend. They're open daily (except Mon.) for dinner, Thurs. through Sat. for lunch (summer only), plus Sunday brunch, with fresh-fruit margaritas and espressos; tel. 376-4728. For inexpensive Italian meals and fresh seafood, try **La Famiglia Ristorante,** also on A St. in Eastsound. Open daily for dinner, lunch daily except Sun.; call 376-2335 for reservations. Enjoy waterfront dining at **Christina's,** on Horseshoe Hwy. in Eastsound, tel. 376-4904, with fresh seasonal cuisine including Crescent Bay oysters and a nice wine selection. Open for dinner daily in summer, Thurs. through Mon. in winter, plus Sunday brunch. Stop by **Café Oga** near Moran State Park for a beer and an inexpensive, home-style lunch.

Theater
The **Orcas Theatre and Community Center** hosts a variety of events nearly year-

*Fisherman's Bay,
Lopez Island*

ARCHIE SATTERFIELD

round in Eastsound, from concerts to theatrical performances to lecture series; for ticket and schedule info, phone 376-4873.

Arts And Crafts

Orcas has a number of craft shops and galleries kept well supplied by the artists and craftspeople who live there. Olga's artist co-op is **The Artworks,** tel. 376-4408, with an assortment of locally made arts and crafts; next door is **Café Olga,** a country café with homemade pies, beer, wine, and espresso. **Otters Lair Pottery** in Eastsound Square, tel. 376-4708, specializes in functional stoneware and porcelain pottery. See how candles are made from May to Oct. at **Orcas Island Candles,** Eastsound, tel. 376-2645. **Darvill's Rare Print Shop** in Eastsound has, naturally, rare prints from the 18th and 19th centuries plus limited-edition prints by contemporary Northwest artists; tel. 376-2351. **The Right Place** on West Beach, tel. 376-4023, has an assortment of crafts from pottery to hand-knit and woven items to blown glass.

LOPEZ ISLAND

Because of its gently rolling hills, Lopez is the most popular with cyclists; views of the surrounding islands and mountains to the east and west poke out from every turn. Despite being one of the largest San Juan islands, Lopez is probably the friendliest—waving to passing cars and bicycles is a time-honored local custom, and failure to wave will mark you as a tourist as surely as a camera around your neck and rubber thongs.

Parks

On the east side of the island, **Spencer Spit State Park** has a mile-long beach for good year-round clamming and beachcombing, 28 campsites, and a trailer dump station; camping is also available at **Odlin County Park** at the north end of the island.

Accommodations

For inexpensive camping far from civilization, bike out to **Hummel Haven Bicycle Camp,** 4½ miles from the ferry landing, off Center Rd. at Hummel Lake, tel. 468-2217. No motor vehicles are allowed within the 40-acre campground (though parking spaces are available for those who arrive by car), and each secluded campsite is equipped with a fire pit, picnic table, and bike rack for just $2.50 pp. If you need to, you can rent a bike for $10 a day; boat rentals are also available for trout fishing in the lake for $3.50 per hour.

For secluded log cabin living, try **Marean's Blue Fjord Cabins** at Elliott Rd. on Jasper Bay (Route 1 Box 1450). Nestled among 16 acres of forest, each cabin has a fully equipped kitchen and deck, and is situated to assure complete privacy just a short walk from the rocky beach. The smaller cabins, built for two, are $55; a larger cabin with fireplace, water view, dishwasher, and space for six is $95 d ($10 per additional person). Call 468-2749 for reservations—they're required—and detailed directions (you'll need them to find the unmarked dirt road).

MacKaye Harbor Inn, a B&B on MacKaye Harbor Rd., tel. 468-2253, has five antique-furnished rooms on the water for $60-85 d, including full gourmet breakfast.

Food And More
There's more than one way to make a living, and the owners of **Jeanna's Seafood Gallery** in Lopez Plaza, tel. 468-2114, are trying three at once, with a seafood restaurant, art gallery, and fish market all rolled into one. Open daily 10 a.m.-9 p.m. **The Bay Café,** across Main St. from the post office in Lopez Village, tel. 468-2204, opens Wed. through Sun. for Mexican, Indonesian, Thai, American—you name it—lunch and dinner. The **Galley Restaurant and Lounge,** tel. 468-2713, on Fisherman's Bay, is best known for its omelettes, prime rib, and abalone. **Gail's,** tel. 468-2150, serves soups, deli sandwiches, burgers, quiche, plus wine and beer; open for three meals daily (dinner on weekends only in winter).

OTHER ISLANDS

Shaw Island
The least visited of the ferry-served islands, Shaw is primarily residential and known mostly for the Franciscan nuns who operate the ferry dock and general store, "Little Portion." **Shaw Island County Park,** two miles south of the ferry landing, has eight campsites, a picnic area, and a rope swing, but no drinking water.

State Parks
A number of the smaller islands in the archipelago are preserved as state parks, accessible only by private boat and largely undeveloped, with primitive campsites and no drinking water. Sea kayaks are a popular island-hopping mode of transportation, but since some of the smaller islands are several miles out, be careful not to overestimate your ability.

Blind Island State Park, on a small, unforested island about .2 mile from the north shore of Shaw Island in Blind Bay, has a rocky shoreline and four primitive campsites.

Doe Island State Park, about one mile southeast of Orcas Island, has five primitive campsites on a small, secluded island with a rocky shoreline.

About .4 mile east of Decatur Island, **James Island State Park** has 13 primitive campsites on a small, forested island with sunny beaches on the Rosario Strait.

Two miles northeast of Orcas Island is **Clark Island State Park,** with eight primitive campsites—no garbage cans, so take it out with you—and beautiful beaches for walking, sunbathing, fishing, or treasure-hunting offshore. **Matia Island State Park,** three miles northeast of Orcas Island, has six primitive campsites near the dock and is home to a large population of puffins. It also once was home to a hermit who got a regular workout rowing the three miles to Orcas and walking another two miles to Eastsound to buy his groceries. **Sucia Island State Park,** 2½ miles north of Orcas Island, is among the more beautiful of the "lesser" islands with crabbing, clamming, and scuba diving plus 51 primitive campsites. Popular for its hiking and good salmon and bottom fishing, **Patos Island State Park** has four primitive campsites about five miles north of Orcas Island and two miles northwest of Sucia.

Close to San Juan Island are **Posey Island State Park,** about .6 mile west of San Juan's northwest shore, recommended for kayaks and canoes, with just one primitive campsite; **Stuart Island State Park,** five miles northwest of Roche Harbor with good harbors for larger boats and 19 primitive campsites; and **Turn Island State Park,** .3 mile from San Juan's east shore, with 10 campsites, two beaches, and wooded hiking trails.

BOB RACE

OLYMPIC PENINSULA

KITSAP PENINSULA

The Kitsap Peninsula is a quiet appendage to the Olympic Peninsula—in fact, visitors and locals alike sometimes confuse the two, thinking that anything west of Seattle must be the Olympic Peninsula, but the Kitsap is separated from the Olympic Peninsula by Hood Canal. The only cross-Sound connections are by ferry from Seattle and Edmonds, or by Tacoma's Narrows Bridge, preventing the Kitsap Peninsula from becoming another Bellevue.

Much of the Kitsap Peninsula shares the inaccessibility of Whidbey Island a short ferry ride across Admiralty Inlet.

SERVICES AND INFORMATION

The area code on the Kitsap Peninsula is 206. The people at the **Bremerton/Kitsap County Visitor and Convention Bureau** at 120 Washington Ave., Suite 101, Bremerton, tel. 479-3588, can answer most of your questions and provide you with maps and brochures. For more specific information, contact the individual towns' chambers of commerce and public relations departments: **Central Kitsap Chamber of Commerce,** 9191 Bay Shore Dr. NW, Silverdale, tel. 692-6900; **Greater Poulsbo Chamber of Commerce,** 19044 Jensen Way NE, Poulsbo, tel. 779-4848; **Bainbridge Island Chamber of Commerce,** 123 Madrone Lane W, Bainbridge Island, tel. 842-3700; and for Port Gamble info, contact **Pope and Talbot,** Public Relations Dept., Box 217, Port Gamble, WA 98364, tel. 297-3341.

For fire, police, or medical emergencies, dial 911. The area's major medical center is **Harrison Memorial Hospital,** 2520 Cherry Ave., Bremerton, tel. 377-3911.

(top) the Seattle skyline (Seattle-King County News Bureau, Walter Hodges)
(bottom left) Mukilteo Lighthouse, Mukilteo (Dianne Boulerice Lyons)
(bottom right) historic downtown Port Townsend (Dianne Boulerice Lyons)

(top) Deception Pass Bridge (Archie Satterfield)
(bottom) burly trees in Olympic National Park (Dianne Boulerice Lyons)

TRANSPORTATION

Arriving By Air
Serving Port Orchard, Bremerton, Silverdale, and the Tacoma area, **Bremerton-Kitsap Airporter,** tel. 876-1737 or (800) 562 7948, provides transportation to and from Sea-Tac Airport for $10-18 one way; reservations are required.

Arriving By Car
From Tacoma, take Hwy. 16 across the Narrows Bridge and follow it to Port Orchard and Bremerton on the Kitsap Peninsula. Highway 3 takes over at this point, leading you to Poulsbo (off Hwy. 3 onto Hwy. 305) and Port Gamble, where the Hood Canal Floating Bridge connects the Kitsap and Olympic peninsulas.

Arriving By Ferry
Four points in Kitsap County are served by the **Washington State Ferry** system. From the Seattle waterfront you can take a 60-minute trip to Bremerton or a 35-minute crossing to Winslow on Bainbridge Island; from the Fauntleroy dock in West Seattle, take the 35-minute ride to Southworth on the southeast side of the peninsula, or the 30-minute crossing between Edmonds and Kingston. Ferries depart about every 70 minutes for Bremerton, every 50 minutes for Winslow, and every 40 or 50 minutes for Southworth and Kingston. Fares are the same for all three crossings: $5.55 one way for car and driver ($6.65 in summer), $3.30 roundtrip for passengers, and $2.30 one way for bicycle riders.

Horluck Transportation Co. Inc., tel. 876-2300, provides ferry service across the Sinclair Inlet between Bremerton and Port Orchard for foot traffic only; the 10-minute crossing costs $.60 one way, available daily.

Getting Around By Bus
Kitsap Transit, tel. 373-2877 or 697-2877, provides daily service to Bremerton, Silverdale, Bangor, and Poulsbo.

Bus tours of the Kitsap Peninsula are available from **Open Rode Tours,** 738 Bay St., in Port Orchard. Among trips are four museum tours ranging from six hours to two days, a two-day Kitsap Circle tour, and an eight-hour Hood Canal/Shelton tour. For specific information on dates and prices call 876-9305.

Getting Around By Bicycle
Lack of traffic and congestion make Kitsap County an excellent place for cyclists. A map of recommended bike routes throughout the county is available for $1 from the Bremerton-Kitsap County Visitor and Convention Bureau (see above). This "Kitsap County Bike Map" shows bike routes, other good roads, circular bike tours, uphill sections, difficult intersections, bike shops, campgrounds, and other points of interest, plus rules of the road.

BREMERTON

Surrounded by water on three sides, Bremerton has sweeping views of both the Cascades and the Olympics, and is close to the metropolitan areas of Puget Sound without having the problems of a suburb. Even though Bremerton was suffering its own recession while other Puget Sound cities were thriving, Money magazine still selected Bremerton the most livable city in America in 1990, much to the chagrin of Seattle, which had been given that honor a few times in the past.

With all the water around it and the deep harbor at its doorstep, Bremerton is a natural place for the Puget Sound Naval Shipyard, the "Welcome Aboard City's" economic mainstay since 1891. Since the U.S.S. Missouri no longer uses Bremerton as its home port, there isn't much for the tourist to see here, with the exception of the **Naval Shipyard Museum,** in the Ferry Terminal Bldg. at 151 First Street. The museum has American and Japanese naval artifacts, ship models, and historical naval displays. Open Tues. through Sun.; donation. Call 479-7447 for information.

The only other taste of the Navy that visitors can enjoy is during Armed Forces Week in May, when a parade, memorial services, softball tournament, and crowning of Miss Armed Forces highlight the festivities.

KITSAP PENINSULA

© MOON PUBLICATIONS, INC.

Parks

Eighty-one acre **Belfair State Park,** 15 miles southwest of Bremerton on Hwy. 3, has camping and trailer hookups, swimming, and fishing on Hood Canal. Make reservations by mail from Memorial Day through Labor Day: N.E. 410 Beck Rd., Belfair, WA 98528, tel. 478-4625.

Illahee State Park, three miles northeast of Bremerton on Hwy. 306, has 25 campsites on 75 acres close to the urban area, with swimming beaches, boat launch, and pier for salmon and bottom fishing.

Hikers will enjoy the two-mile trek to the summit of 1,700-foot **Green Mountain** for spectacular views of the Kitsap Peninsula, Puget Sound, and the Seattle skyline. From Seabeck go west on Holly Rd., then take a left onto Tahuyeh Rd. for 1¼ miles to Gold Creek Rd.; turn left onto Gold Creek and follow it for 1½ miles to the trailhead on the left, before Gold Creek Bridge. Be sure to wear proper footwear: the trail is rocky and often wet.

Accommodations

Once the private residence of Colonel Julian Wilcox, the 1936 10,000-square-foot waterfront **Wilcox House,** 2390 Tekiu Rd., tel. 830-4492, Bremerton, was described in historical accounts as "the grand entertainment capitol of the Canal region." Five marble and copper fireplaces and the original oak parquet floors are accented by antique and period furniture, and every room is angled to capture a water and Olympic view. Outdoors, a 300-foot pier can accommodate guests' boats. Clark Gable once stayed in the room that now bears his name. Five rooms each have private bath and king bed for $90-145 d. No pets, indoor smoking, or kids under 15.

At **North Bay Inn,** E. 2520 Hwy. 302 in Belfair, tel. 275-5378, enjoy a stay in an antique-furnished farmhouse on the north end of Case Inlet. A fireplace, shoreline view, and sweeping lawn enhance your visit. Three guest rooms share a bath for $50-60 d. No kids or pets.

For budget lodging, rooms at the **Super 8 Motel,** 5068 Kitsap Way, tel. 377-8881, start at $35 s, $38-41 d, and pets are allowed. The **Midway Inn,** next to the Black Angus on Hwy. 303 at 2909 Wheaton Way, tel. 479-2909, is just as cheap: their 60 rooms cost $39 s, $39-42 d with free continental breakfast, laundry facilities, and some kitchen units. **Oyster Bay Inn,** 4412 Kitsap Way, tel. 479-2132, is a step up in quality with 100 rooms, a heated pool, and small balconies overlooking tranquil Oyster Bay. Rooms start at $40 s, $44-54 d. **Nendel's,** 4303 Kitsap Way, tel. 377-4402, has free continental breakfast, pool, and adjacent restaurants; their 102 rooms cost $36-58 s, $46-64 d. **Quality Inn Bayview,** 5640 Kitsap Way, tel. 373-7349 or (800) 422-5017, is the town's nicest hotel, with Mt. Rainier views, restaurant, two lounges with nightly entertainment, two movie theaters, an indoor pool, jacuzzi, and free child care for kids 3-12. They offer a variety of weekend discount rates with Champagne and other amenities; their standard room rates start at $63 s, $70 d.

Food

Next to the Oyster Bay Inn, the **Hearthstone** restaurant at 4312 Kitsap Way, tel. 377-5531, has moderately priced lunches and dinners specializing in prime rib, seafood, and steak; entertainment and dancing in the lounge daily except Sunday. **Sinclair's,** a block from the ferry landing at 232 Washington Ave., tel. 479-7799, features moderately priced seafood with a waterfront view; open for three meals. For a Chinese Sunday Champagne brunch, or a daily selection of over 200 Cantonese and Mandarin items plus steak and seafood, try **Yee's,** overlooking Oyster Bay at 4180 Kitsap Way, tel. 479-8222. Have nachos, a sandwich, or salad over the water at the **Boat Shed,** a mile from the ferry dock at 101 Shore Drive.

Entertainment and Events

The oldest outdoor theater in the Northwest, **Mountaineers' Forest Theater** on Seabeck Hwy. holds outdoor productions in late May or early June. The amphitheater's log ter-raced seats are beautifully backdropped by rhododendrons, Douglas firs, and hemlocks; be prepared for a one-third-mile hike from your car to the theater. For tickets and information write 300 Third Ave. W, Seattle, WA 98119, or phone 284-6310.

Every August the **Kitsap County Fair and Rodeo,** tel. 692-3655, comes to the Kitsap County Fairgrounds five miles north of Bremerton center off Hwy. 303. Highlighted by a rodeo, the fair also includes a carnival, circus, and entertainment. Younger cowboys and cowgirls display their talents at the annual **Little Britches Rodeo,** held at the Fairgrounds in mid-June; tel. 876-2040.

PORT ORCHARD

Across the Sinclair Inlet from Bremerton, Port Orchard is a small waterfront community with an antique mall and other shops within walking distance of the marina and "foot ferry" dock.

Sights

Follow Beach Dr. from Port Orchard for a scenic approach to **Manchester State Park,** at the entrance to the Sinclair Inlet, six miles northeast of Port Orchard and just north of Manchester. The park's 111 acres include 50 campsites, trailer dump stations, hiking and interpretive trails, and swimming, fishing, and scuba diving in Rich Passage. You can rent a 13-foot aluminum boat with motor for $35 a day or $12.50 for the first hour, $5 each additional hour, from **Manchester Boatworks,** 9001 Main St. E, Manchester, tel. 871-4040, daily in summer, weekends and holidays in winter. To fish from a pier, try the Harper Fishing Pier on Hwy. 160 on the way to the state park.

East of Port Orchard on Banner Rd., **Coolen Wine Cellars,** tel. 871-0567, produces sulfite-free premium red wines and an estate-bottled Champagne. The tasting room is open weekends, noon to 5 p.m., or by appointment.

Housed in a 1913 pioneer log home, the **Log Cabin Museum** has rotating exhibits of Kitsap Peninsula history. At the corner of Sidney and DeKalb, the museum is open Sunday afternoons and Monday mornings; free.

Accommodations

Overlooking the Sinclair Inlet, **Ogle's Bed and Breakfast,** 1307 Dogwood Hill SW, tel. 876-9170, has two guest rooms in a comfortable, rambling one-story home in wooded hills; breakfast is served indoors before view windows or on the outdoor deck. You can't beat the price: $35 s, $45 d. Kids over 10 okay; no pets or indoor smoking. The **Vista Motel,** 1090 Bethel Ave., tel. 876-8046, has Spartan, inexpensive rooms from $27 s, $32 d.

Food

For a semi-scenic view of the Bremerton shipyards with your breakfast, lunch, dinner, or Sunday brunch, try **Tweten's Lighthouse,** on the water at the intersection of Bay St. and Port Orchard Blvd., tel. 876-8464. Their steaks, seafood, veal, chicken, and pasta dinners are around $12; for breakfast, be sure to try one of their enormous cinnamon

VICINITY OF BREMERTON

rolls. **The Clambake,** on Hwy.160 just west of Port Orchard, tel. 876-3545, serves dinner every day and lunch daily except Sunday, featuring steak-and-seafood combinations, oysters, red snapper, salmon, and prime rib in less-than-elegant surroundings.

Shopping
The **Olde Central Antique Mall,** 801 Bay St. at Sidney, tel. 895-1902, has 60 shops specializing in collectible glassware and furniture; open daily from 10 a.m. Every Saturday morning from April to October brings the **Farmer's Market** to Port Orchard, where fresh Northwest produce can be purchased at the waterfront on Frederick Street.

BLAKE ISLAND

Accessible only by boat, Blake Island has 476 acres of state park land with 30 standard campsites and 11 primitive sites, with excellent bottom fishing, scuba diving, a three-

quarter-mile loop nature trail and eight miles of other hiking trails. To get there, you can rent a boat from Manchester Boatworks (see "Port Orchard" above). Organized tours to Tillicum Village for an Indian salmon bake, craft displays, and interpretive dances depart daily from Seattle and Tacoma, but only by special charter from Kitsap departure points. These charters are generally offered by **Open Rode Tours,** 738 Bay St., Port Orchard, tel. 876-7292, or **Horluck Transportation,** Sidney Dock, Box 87, Port Orchard, tel. 876-2300.

SILVERDALE

Silverdale's Kitsap Mall (see below) and surrounding restaurants and plazas have helped turn the town into the peninsula's commercial center. Just north of town is the Bangor Annex, a nuclear submarine base.

Sights
West of Silverdale in the small town of Seabeck, **Scenic Beach State Park** has 50 campsites, salmon fishing and oyster gathering in season, with Olympic Mountain views on Hood Canal. To get there take Anderson Hill Rd. W to Seabeck Highway, particularly pleasant when the spring rhodies are in bloom.

Kitsap County Historical Society Museum, 3343 N.W. Byron St., tel. 692-1949, has musical instruments, photographs, toys, clocks, and nautical artifacts from the Kitsap Peninsula plus area information; open daily, free. After visiting the museum have a picnic lunch at the adjacent waterfront park on Dyes Inlet.

Accommodations And Food
Just south of the Bangor Submarine Base, **Seabreez Cottage,** 16609 Olympic View Rd. NW, tel. 692-4648, features two loft bedrooms, sleeper sofa, washer/dryer, fully equipped kitchen, TV, spa, continental breakfast, and Olympic views, all for $99 d weekends, $89 d weekdays ($20 less in winter), with a two-night minimum stay (or add $20 for a one-night stay).

The **Poplars Motel**, 9800 Silverdale Way, tel. 692-6126, has 53 rooms at $36-41 s, $44-56 d, heated pool, and attached steak-and-seafood restaurant, appropriately named the **Poplars Restaurant,** tel. 692-5564, with dinners in the $8-13 range and dancing in the lounge. A giant step up in price and quality, the **Best Western Silverdale on the Bay Resort Hotel,** 3073 N.W. Bucklin Hill Rd., tel. 698-1000, has 151 rooms from $65-75 s, $70-80 d, plus a glassed-in heated pool, sauna, Jacuzzi, exercise room, pickleball and tennis courts, and room and patio service. Their **Mariner Restaurant** features excellent Northwest seafood; open for three meals.

At Silverdale Village, **O'Malley's Pub and Eatery,** 9447 Silverdale Way NW, tel. 692-6976, features Irish food and drink plus steaks and seafood.

Festival
Silverdale's **Whaling Days** festival, held in late July, is the town's biggest event: a parade, arts-and-crafts displays, boat races, air show, sidewalk sales, five- and one-mile runs, and carnival.

Shopping
The first major shopping mall on the Kitsap Peninsula, the **Kitsap Mall,** just south of the junction of Highways 305 and 3, has over 200 stores, including Sears, Lamonts, and The Bon. The mall is surrounded by smaller shopping centers, fast-food restaurants, and **Silverdale Cinemas,** a four-theater complex at 9923 Clear Creek Rd. NW, tel. 698-1510.

POULSBO

Poulsbo's first settler was a Norwegian who rowed across the Sound from Seattle and was reminded of his homeland's mountains, fjords, and valleys. Today, Scandinavian architecture and festivals perpetuate the culture of "Little Norway's" first immigrants, at least enough to add the tourist dollar to its mainstay industries of fishing and oystering. Poulsbo is also the "Geoduck Capital of the World." Pronounced "gooey-duck," the large,

BOB RACE

unattractive clams commonly weigh in at 3-12 pounds and live up to 50 years or longer. Because of its less-than-appetizing appearance, the geoduck is used in chowders. In an effort to make it more appealing, some have tried to change the geoduck's name to "king clam," following the line of thought that changed the spider crab into Alaskan king crab—but so far the name hasn't stuck.

Sights
You can get friendly with a sea cucumber in its saltwater touch-tank or learn about other Puget Sound sea creatures at the **Marine Science Center,** 215 Third Ave. S, tel. 779-5549. Open Tues. to Sun. in summer, Mon, through Fri. during the school year; donation.

Stroll down the boardwalk at the edge of Liberty Bay connecting **Liberty Bay Park** to the small arboretum at **American Legion Park.** Both parks have picnic areas, restrooms, and water access.

Sea Kayaking
Tours, kayak rentals, and instruction are available from Poulsbo Sea Kayaking Co., **Liberty Bay Marina,** 17791 Fjord Dr. NE, tel. 697-2464, including a kayak tour of the Dungeness Wildlife Refuge (see "Sequim," p. 205) with all equipment and lessons provided for $26.

Accommodations
Poulsbo's **Evergreen Motel,** 18680 Hwy. 305, tel. 779-3921, has 60 rooms, some with kitchens and/or mountain and water views, from $42-46 s, $46-50 d, plus a heated pool, whirlpool, and playground. **Cypress Inn,** 19801 N.E. Seventh, tel. 697-2119, has 65 rooms for $48-58 s, $53-63 d, plus a small pool. For a more luxurious stay, try the **Man-**

or Farm Inn, a B&B at 26069 Big Valley Rd. NE, tel. 779-4628, where fresh-squeezed orange juice, a hot tub, and a three-course farm breakfast are just part of the pampering you'll receive at this working farm. The eight guest rooms (all but two with private bath) are $90-120 d. A two-bedroom farm cottage across the street goes for $165 d; a two-bedroom beach cottage two minutes up the road has Olympic views, private beach, fireplace, and more for $230 d. Four- and six-course dinners are available from $25-35 pp. No kids, pets, or indoor smoking.

Food
Open daily for breakfast, lunch, and dinner, **The Viking House,** on the waterfront at Poulsbo's Wharf, tel. 779-9882 or 283-0920, serves steak, pasta, and seafood with the town's best-stocked liquor cabinet. **Larry's Best BBQ,** 19559 Viking Way at the south end of town, barbecues pork, chicken, beef and more in Old-West style.

Festivals
Poulsbo is a lively little town, with festivals and fairs occurring year-round. More than 50 bands compete in the annual **Viking Jazz Festival,** the largest event of its kind in the state. Held at the North Kitsap Community Center Auditorium, bands compete for two full days in Feb. starting at 9 a.m.; finals begin at 7:30 p.m. Admission is $3.50 adults, $2.50 kids; tel. 779-5777. The **Viking Fest,** held in mid-May, has a parade, food, and games. The **Scandia Midsommarfest** in June brings Scandinavian food, music, and folk dancers to Frank Raab Park. The **Poulsbo Boat Rendezvous** in late July is a gathering of Poulsbo-built wooden boats at the marina, while the holiday season brings the annual **Yule Log Ceremony,** held sometime after Thanksgiving, featuring Norwegian folk dancers and a guest appearance by Santa Claus.

SUQUAMISH

The name "Suquamish" came from the Indian word *d'suq'wub* (apparently after much mispronunciation), meaning "place of clear salt water." The Suquamish were a peaceful people and as the white man took over, they were forced to surrender their own culture: children were sent to Tacoma schools, where boys learned trades and girls provided cheap kitchen labor, while the Suquamish men went to work at Port Madison lumber mills.

Historical Sights
The **Suquamish Museum** off Hwy.305 is a good place to start a tour of Suquamish and the Port Madison Indian Reservation. Chief Seattle, his Suquamish descendants, and Pacific Northwest history come to life in this shoreline museum with award-winning exhibits and slide presentation, narrated by Suquamish elders. Open daily spring and summer, Tues. through Sun. the rest of the year; admission is $2.50 adults, $1 kids under 12, tel. 598-3311.

DIANNE BOULERICE LYONS

Chief Sealth's (Seattle's) grave

Chief Seattle's Grave overlooks Puget Sound with a glimpse of Seattle's skyscrapers in a small, peaceful cemetery on the Port Madison Indian Reservation. It's not hard to tell which grave is his: painted canoes are positioned high above the headstone to honor this leader of the Suquamish Nation and friend to the early settlers.

A cedar longhouse 500-1,000 feet long and 60 feet wide, the communal home of eight Suquamish chiefs and their families, stood at the waterfront site now called "Old Man House" until 1870, when federal agents torched it in an effort to subtly discourage this form of accommodation. Today a Washington State Heritage site, a small historical display marks the location of the original longhouse on a lot surrounded by housing developments at the west end of Agate Passage. After seeing the slide show and displays at the Suquamish Museum depicting the peaceful, everyday Suquamish life, this tiny historical remembrance will break your heart.

Festival

Chief Seattle Days, an annual weekend affair held in August at the downtown Suquamish waterfront park, has been going strong since 1911 with canoe racing, arts and crafts, traditional Indian dancing, storytelling, and salmon bake.

BAINBRIDGE ISLAND

When Vancouver sailed through Puget Sound in 1792, he never realized that Bainbridge Island was an island; it wasn't until 1841 that Charles N. Wilkes found Agate Pass, the waterway separating the island from the Kitsap Peninsula. Wilkes named the island for Capt. William Bainbridge, a Naval hero from the U.S.S. *Constitution*. Within 15 years of its charting, Bainbridge Island was home to one of Puget Sound's greatest lumber mills, and soon thereafter its ports were world renowned. Port Blakely had the biggest sawmill in the world, employing over 1,000 men, and the shipyard there built the largest stern-wheeler at that time in the Pacific Northwest, the *Julia*.

Today the four- by 12-mile island is almost entirely privately owned, by the wealthy, by politicians, artists, a lot of stockbrokers, a few fishermen, and a lot of ordinary folks, 85% of whom commute by ferry to their Seattle-area jobs.

Parks

Two state parks make this island worth a visit: **Fort Ward State Park,** six miles from the Winslow ferry terminal at the island's south end, has 137 acres for day-use pic-

BAINBRIDGE ISLAND

© MOON PUBLICATIONS, INC.

nicking, boating, and scuba diving on a mile-long beach; **Fay Bainbridge State Park,** with a mere 17 acres, has 26 hookup camp-sites, hot showers, and beach access with scuba diving and boating facilities at the island's northeast end.

City and district parks include **Strawberry Hill Park** on High School Rd., 18 acres with ball fields and a museum; **Battle Point Park,** on the island's west side on Battle Point Dr. NE, with 90 acres of jogging trails, ball fields, tennis courts, gardens, and a pond; **Manzanita Park,** on Day Rd. on the northwest side of the island, with 120 acres of hiking and equestrian trails, but, unfortunately, no horse rentals; and **Eagle Harbor Waterfront Park** with picnic tables, play areas, trails, and a boat launch on the waterfront in Winslow.

Winery

Family-operated **Bainbridge Island Winery,** one-quarter mile from the ferry terminal at 682 Hwy. 305 in Winslow, is the only place (outside of a restaurant) to buy their limited-run western and eastern Washington wines, including their increasingly popular "Ferry-boat White." The outdoor picnic area is a refreshing spot for a lunch break. Tours and tastings are held Wed. through Sun. from noon to 5 p.m.; tel. 842-9463.

The history of former mill towns Port Madison and Port Blakely is preserved in exhibits and displays at the **Bainbridge Island Historical Museum** at Strawberry Hill Park on High School Road. Open Saturday 11 a.m.-4 p.m.; free.

Accommodations

The Captain's House, 234 Parfitt Way (four blocks west of the Winslow ferry terminal), tel. 842-3557, is a turn-of-the-century B&B overlooking Eagle Harbor with rowboats, tennis courts, and an old-fashioned porch swing. Rooms are reasonably priced at $35 s, $40 d, and include a European pastry and fruit breakfast.

For a vacation from the kids try **The Beach Cottages,** 5831 Ward Ave. NE on Eagle Harbor, tel. 842-6081. Their two-night minimum stays are $75 d per night, but look at what you get: one of four cottages, either right on the water or 40 feet back, with Olympic and Cascade views; a queen-size bed, TV, stereo, fireplace, robes, and ingredients for a cook-it-yourself breakfast; and a waterfall outside your door. Weekly rates are $422, and off-season specials include a three-nights-for-the-price-of-two midweek deal. No kids or pets.

The Bombay House in southeast Bainbridge Island at the corner of Beck and W. Blakely roads overlooks Rich Passage; country antiques, flowers, and a widow's walk add to the home's turn-of-the-century charm. Rooms are $50-68 d; phone 842-3926 or write 8490 N.E. Beck Rd., Bainbridge I., WA 98110.

Food

Noted for serving some of the best Mexican food in the Northwest is the **San Carlos Restaurant,** two blocks from the Winslow ferry terminal at 279 Madison N, tel. 842-1999. Open for lunch Tues. through Fri., dinner daily. On the waterfront at the Winslow Wharf Marina, the **Saltwater Cafe,** 403 Madison Ave. S, tel. 842-8339, features seafood, pasta, and Cajun dishes daily from 11:30 a.m. The **Streamliner Diner,** Winslow Way and Bejune, is famous for its hearty breakfasts.

Festival

May brings the **Scotch Broom Festival** to Bainbridge Island, highlighted by a Rotarian-Kiwanian Tiddlywink contest held in the middle of Winslow's main street.

PORT GAMBLE

A native of East Machias, Maine, Captain William Talbot founded North America's oldest continuously operating sawmill here in 1853. Modeling the city after his hometown, he built traditional New England-style homes and imported trees from back East. The town has since been restored by the Pope and Talbot Lumber Company and preserved as a historic district. Walking down these quiet streets, shuffling through the fallen leaves, you'd swear you were in Vermont.

The Pope and Talbot Lumber Co. is still Port Gamble's economic mainstay.

TACOMA PUBLIC LIBRARY

Park

Located four miles south of town on Hwy. 3, **Kitsap Memorial State Park** has saltwater swimming, hiking, fishing, oyster- and clam-gathering, boating, picnicking, scuba diving, and 43 campsites on 58 acres; tel. 779-3205.

Hood Canal

The 80-mile-long Hood Canal is not a canal at all, but a tidal channel; Capt. George Vancouver originally named it "Hood's Channel" when he sailed through it in 1792, but faulty records copying resulted in the name change. Today the 6,471-foot-long **Hood Canal Floating Bridge** connects the Kitsap and Olympic Peninsulas. The world's third-longest floating bridge (the longest over tidewater) was opened in 1961 and served the peninsulas well until February 13, 1979, when a violent storm with 100-mph gusts broke off and sank nearly a mile of the western portion of the bridge. Ferry service took over the job for the more than three years it took to rebuild the structure. Today you can cast a line for salmon or bottom fish from the fishing pontoon; there's a special angler's parking lot at the Kitsap end of the bridge. Just north of the bridge, **Salsbury Point County Park** has a boat launch.

For information on towns on the west side of the canal such as Hoodsport, Union, and Shelton farther south, see "Shelton And The Lower Hood Canal," p. 236.

Museums

The **Port Gamble Historic Museum,** downhill from the General Store on Hwy. 104, tel. 297-3341, houses exhibits from the timber company, original rooms from hotels and houses, and a Forest of the Future display. Open daily from Memorial Day to Labor Day.

Of Sea and Shore Museum, housed in the General Store, has a bookshop and the largest shell collection in the country. Open daily in the summer, weekends only the rest of the year; donations requested.

Nursery

The **Cyrus T. Walker Tree Nursery and Forest Research Center,** on the edge of town off Hwy. 3 (follow the signs), was established in 1976 to grow more than three million trees annually on Pope and Talbot lands. Tours of the facility include a look at four greenhouses, a water reservoir, pump house, a tree shade house, and a film about tree growing; free, tel. 297-3292.

HANSVILLE

The **Hansville Recreation Area** occupies the northernmost tip of the Kitsap Peninsula, northeast of Port Gamble and the Hood Canal Bridge. This is the place to catch salmon in Puget Sound—most fishing is done quite close to shore, rarely more than a half mile out. The facilities here are all geared toward fishermen: the accommodations are sparse and the lone restaurant isn't fancy. The historic **Point No Point Lighthouse** is here, so named by the Wilkes expedition because the point that was visible from one approach disappeared from the other. Tours of the light station are available Wed. through Sun. afternoons with a day's notice required; call 638-2261. The beach here provides good views of Hood Canal, the Admiralty Inlet, and Whidbey Island, but picnicking and fires are not allowed.

Accommodations
Captain's Landing has rustic cabins, a trailer and RV park, waterfront restaurant, pub with weekend entertainment, and boat and fishing equipment rentals. Open year-round, the cabins run $47-60 with a maximum six persons in each. Trailers and RVs can park for $18.50 for waterfront space, $14 off waterfront; non-hookup spaces are available for $10-12 per night. Boat rentals are $75 per day with motor, $25 without motor. Call 638-2257 or write Box 113, Hansville, WA 98340.

PORT TOWNSEND AND VICINITY

Standing on the northern tip of Quimper Peninsula—a thumb off the northeast corner of the Olympic Peninsula—Port Townsend is best known for its generous helping of Victorian architecture; it has more authentic remnants of this period than any other town north of San Francisco. Wealthy merchants of the late 1800s built these beauties, many of which have been restored and are located in one of the town's two national historic districts.

The main port of entry to Puget Sound and the first townsite on the Olympic Peninsula, Port Townsend started off with a bang. Platted in 1852, by the late 1880s the town prospered as a busy seaport; it reached its all-time peak population of 7,000 in 1890. An official port of entry, Port Townsend hosted consulates and agencies from Chile, Sweden, Norway, Germany, France, Great Britain, and Hawaii during its prime.

From there, however, it was all downhill: the transcontinental Union Pacific railroad opted for a Seattle junction rather than in Port Townsend, and Seattle and Tacoma siphoned off most of the town's shipping. Over the years, military bases and a pulp and paper mill restored Port Townsend's economic stability; today, tourism accounts for most of the town's prosperity.

SIGHTS

Parks
On Point Wilson on the Strait of Juan de Fuca, **Fort Worden State Park** (named for John L. Worden, the Union commander during the *Monitor-Merrimac* battle on March 9, 1862, which makes it the only Army fort named for a Navy man), houses a collection of Victorian homes, historical Army barracks, and hidden bunkers. Modern facilities include a campground with 50 hookup sites, underwater park, boat launch, tennis courts, and hiking trails, including a 30-minute self-guided historic walk. If it looks familiar, it may be because the movie, *An Officer and a Gentleman,* was filmed here.

Also at the park is the **Port Townsend Marine Science Center,** tel. 385-5582, located on the dock. "Wet tables" offer intimate, hands-on relationships with local sea creatures; beach walks, evening slide shows and lectures, seaweed workshops, and fish-printing classes are given for an optional donation. Lodging is available in the officers' quarters and camping is permitted with advance reservation or preregistration upon arrival; write Fort Worden State Park, Box 574, Port Townsend, WA 98368, or call 385-4730.

DIANNE BOULERICE LYONS

Jefferson County Courthouse, 1892

Chetzemoka Park on the Admiralty Inlet at Jackson and Roosevelt streets remembers Chief Chetzemoka, friend to the town's earliest settlers. Today the small, shady park offers picnicking, gardens, a bandstand (often used for weddings), and beach access.

At 12th St. near Sims Way, **Kah Tai Lagoon Nature Park** encompasses 85 acres of wetlands, grasslands, and woodlands—great for birdwatching—plus picnic and play areas, exercise equipment, and 2½ miles of trails. No camping or swimming.

Four miles south of town, 377-acre **Old Fort Townsend State Park** has seven miles of hiking trails and 40 shady tent sites under tall firs, sloping to a 150-foot cliff on Port Townsend Bay. The fort was established in 1856 to guard against possible Indian attacks, and in 1859 troops were sent from the fort to assist England in the San Juan Island boundary dispute commonly known as "The

Pig War" (see "San Juan Islands," p. 173). Fort Townsend saw sporadic activity through the 1800s until a fire, started by an exploding kerosene lamp and unstoppable due to lack of water, destroyed the barracks in 1895 and the fort was decommissioned. During WW II the fort was used as an enemy munition defusing station; in 1958 it was turned over to the State Parks Commission. A short self-guided historical walk starts at the display board near the park entrance.

Museums And Homes

Housed in the city's 1891 City Hall Complex, **Jefferson County Historical Society Museum,** 210 Madison St., tel. 385-1003, has three floors of marine antiques, 5,000 historical photographs, a Victorian bedroom, and a research library. Open daily 11 a.m.-4 p.m., Sunday 1-4 p.m.; donation requested.

The **Rothschild House** on Franklin and Taylor streets was built by D.C.H. Rothschild, a Port Townsend merchant, in 1868. Notable for its simplicity of style, the house belonged to the Rothschild family for nearly 90 years; the last remaining son, Eugene, donated it to Port Townsend in 1959 and it is on the National Register of Historic Places. Now restored, housing period furniture and surrounded by herb and flower gardens, the Rothschild house is open to the public daily from May to Oct., weekends the rest of the year, for a donation; tel. 385-2722.

Historic Home Tours are held the first weekend in May and the third weekend in Sept.; owners of private Victorian residences open their doors to the public. Tickets are $10 adults, $5 kids under 12, and may be purchased up to one month in advance from the visitor information center, 2437 Sims Way, Port Townsend, WA 98368, tel. 385-2722.

RECREATION

Excursions

Inn Deering, a Victorian B&B at 1208 Franklin St., tel. 385-6239, offers personalized excursions in and around Port Townsend for $250 per couple. Let them do the planning while you kick back and enjoy! For the price

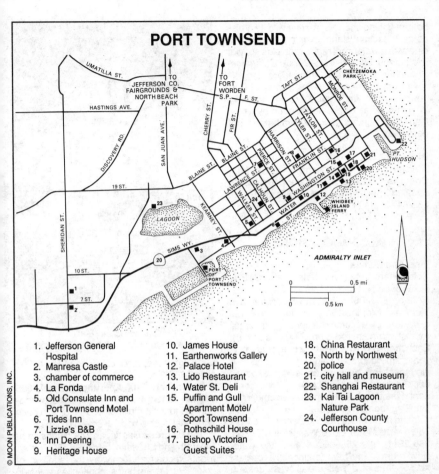

PORT TOWNSEND

1. Jefferson General Hospital
2. Manresa Castle
3. chamber of commerce
4. La Fonda
5. Old Consulate Inn and Port Townsend Motel
6. Tides Inn
7. Lizzie's B&B
8. Inn Deering
9. Heritage House
10. James House
11. Earthenworks Gallery
12. Palace Hotel
13. Lido Restaurant
14. Water St. Deli
15. Puffin and Gull Apartment Motel/ Sport Townsend
16. Rothschild House
17. Bishop Victorian Guest Suites
18. China Restaurant
19. North by Northwest
20. police
21. city hall and museum
22. Shanghai Restaurant
23. Kai Tai Lagoon Nature Park
24. Jefferson County Courthouse

of two nights' lodging at other inns, here's what you get: two nights' accommodations plus breakfast at Inn Deering, one picnic lunch, one dinner, and one activity of your choice: windsurfing, fly/cruise to the San Juans, fishing on Puget Sound, massage therapy, Champagne moonlight cruise, or music and theater.

On The Water

Sport Townsend, 215 Taylor S., tel. 385-6470, offers kayak tours, windsurfing les-sons, bicycle tours and rentals, a video li-brary, and an assortment of outdoor gear. No kayaking experience is necessary to enjoy a three- to four-hour Mystery Bay wildlife pad-dle ($35 pp), a two-hour historical tour ($25 pp), or a day-long Dungeness National Wild-life Refuge trip ($65 pp). Or, come home from vacation with a new skill—learn to windsurf in two full lessons, guaranteed! Try it out with a 2½-hour mini-lesson for $25.

Sport Charters, Box 805, Port Townsend, WA 98368, tel. 385-3575, offers salmon and bottom-fishing charters, marine wildlife cruises to Protection Island, evening cruises with dinner at a waterfront restaurant, plus special excursions aboard the 42-foot *Cheyenne*. Phone for dates, prices, and reservations.

Anderson Lake State Park, south of Port Townsend on Anderson Lake Rd. off Hwy 20, is an isolated lake surrounded by trees. Camping, hunting, and swimming are not permitted.

Bicycling
Tour historic Port Townsend on a bike from **Coast to Coast** at 1102 Water St., tel. 385-5900, or **Sport Townsend,** 215 Taylor S., tel. 385-6470.

ACCOMMODATIONS

Inns And Motels
Somewhere between a hotel and a B&B is the **Palace Hotel,** 1004 Water St., tel. 385-0773 or (800) 962-0741. Newly renovated in Victorian style, the 100-year-old inn features a variety of accommodations, from small rooms with a shared bath ($44-95 s and d). Each room has a name and a unique identity: some are decorated with antiques and ceiling fans, some have water views or exposed brick walls. All include cable TV and continental breakfast. Children are welcome; non-smoking rooms available.

In the heart of the historic district, **The Port Townsend Motel,** 2020 Washington St., tel. 385-2211, has 25 units, scenic and water view rooms, and free continental breakfast for $67-89 s or d; pets are allowed. Just up the road at 2333 Washington St., **Aladdin Motor Inn,** tel. 385-3747, has rooms starting at $58-99 s and d for rooms with refrigerators and microwaves; every room has a Sound view. **Tides Inn,** 1807 Water St., tel. 385-0595, has 21 units with complimentary breakfast, also allows pets, and was part of the filming of *An Officer and a Gentleman;* prices start at $68-120. **The Bishop Victorian Guest Suites,** 714 Washington St., tel. 385-6122, offers 13 one- or two-bedroom suites with mountain and water views, com-

James House (1881)
was the Northwest's first bed and breakfast.

plete kitchens, and continental breakfast from $68-98 d.

Puffin and Gull Apartment Motel, 825 Washington St., tel. 385-1475, can accommodate up to six people for $59-75 d, $10 each additional double bed; no smoking or pets.

The **Manresa Castle,** an 1892 mansion at Seventh and Sheridan, tel. 385-5750, has 41 rooms modernized only by the addition of color TVs, private baths, phones, and electric heat. Prices run from $70-175 d; many rooms have bay views. Restaurant and lounge on the premises. Tours of the castle are $1.25 adults, $1 kids, which may be applied toward your room charge.

Lido Restaurant and Inn, 925 Water St., tel. 385-7111, is a 100-year-old Victorian inn with four rooms from $70-175 d- _., better yet, enjoy the Take-Over-The-Inn Special with your loved one and four other couples for $240. If you can't make the inn, be sure you don't miss the restaurant (see below).

Cabin

Enjoy a romantic getaway at **The Cabin,** 839 N. Jacob Miller Rd., tel. 385-5571. Surrounded by woods and water views, the cabin features a complimentary bottle of champagne, fire pit, fresh-baked goods, and a stocked refrigerator for a full make-it-yourself breakfast, all for $70 d.

Bed And Breakfasts

A Victorian B&B at 731 Pierce St., **Lizzie's,** tel. 385-4168, has eight guest rooms from $55-98 d ($6 less), some with private bath. Enjoy the two parlors with fireplaces, leather sofas, library, and grand piano. Smoking permitted; kids over 10 welcome. Two-night minimum weekend stay.

James House, 1238 Washington St., tel. 385-1238, a Victorian mansion built in 1891, was the first B&B in the Northwest and is still going strong. Commanding views of the town and waterways, 12 guest rooms and suites range from $50-120, with shared or private bath; a secluded cottage with two beds and private bath goes for $75 d, $85 t. Limited accommodations for children in garden suites and cottage; no pets.

Another Victorian B&B, **The Old Consulate Inn,** 313 Walker St., tel. 385-6753, overlooks Port Townsend from atop a high bluff, providing mountain and water views in comfortably elegant surroundings. The inn was built in 1889 by F.W. Hastings, son of Port Townsend's founding father Loren B. Hastings. Enjoy the fireplaces in two parlors or hone your skills in the large billiard and game room. Eight guest rooms all have private bath; rates range from $59-145 d. No smoking or pets.

Three short blocks from downtown, the elegant **Ravenscroft Inn,** 533 Quincy St., tel. 385-2784, features a gourmet breakfast (served when *you're* ready), a great room with an always-lit fireplace, columned piazza with Sound and mountain views, and five guest rooms, all with private bath, for $65-150 d. No pets or kids under 12.

An annual part of the Historic Homes Tour, **Heritage House,** tel. 385-6800, furnishes its rooms with museum-quality antiques and of-fers unparalleled views of the surrounding waters and mountains from its location at 305 Pierce Street. The six guest rooms are $55-99 s or d. No pets or smoking, but kids over eight are welcome.

Built in 1871 by Captain Henry L. Tibbals as a home for his family, the house and guest quarters at 1208 Franklin were completely renovated in 1984 and became **Inn Deering** three years later. Three bedrooms in the main house are decorated with antiques and Victorian furnishings; the two rooms with shared bath are $60, the third, with private bath, is $60. The self-contained guesthouse ($90) features private bath, kitchen, double bed, and rollaway. Kids are welcome, non-smokers preferred; tel. 385-6239. See "Recreation" above for Inn Deering excursions.

Holly Hill House, 611 Polk, tel. 385-5619, built in 1872, has been beautifully maintained and renovated to provide four guest rooms, each with queen bed (Lizette's room can accommodate three persons) and private bath ($72-86 d, singles $5 less). Full breakfast included. No pets or kids under 12; smoking outdoors only.

Built in 1889, the historic Victorian mansion at 744 Clay St. is now an elegant B&B, the **Starrett House Inn,** tel. 385-3205. Five of the 10 guest rooms have private bath; some boast Sound and mountain views. Rates are $68-125; no kids under 12, pets, or smoking.

FOOD

Lido Restaurant and Inn on the waterfront at 925 Water St., tel. 385-7111, is a 100-year-old establishment serving lunch and dinner daily (no lunch on Saturday) featuring fresh seafood and Italian specialties, plus a four-room inn upstairs. The **Fountain Cafe,** 920 Washington St., tel. 385-1364, is popular with visitors and locals alike, specializing in seafood (most notably oysters); open for lunch and dinner daily.

The **Shanghai Restaurant** at Point Hudson, tel. 385-4810, is the place to go for good, inexpensive Chinese food. If you're biking or enjoying a summer picnic, design your own sandwich at the **Water Street Deli,** 926 Water St.; wine, beer, salads, and home-made desserts also available. Stop by **Elevated Ice Cream,** 627 Water St., for espresso, Italian ices, chocolates, and fresh, home-made ice-cream treats.

Just out of town, the **Hadlock House,** 141 Chimacum Rd., Hadlock, tel. 385-3331, specializes in jumbo prawns and weekend-only prime rib. Open daily for lunch and dinner. **The Discovery Bay Restaurant and Lounge,** 5781 Hwy.101 in Discovery Bay, tel. 385-1711, serves lunch and dinner with dining and dancing on the waterfront.

ENTERTAINMENT

The **Centrum Foundation,** a nonprofit arts organization, sponsors seven major festivals and events from mid-June through Labor Day including Jazz Port Townsend, American Fiddle Tunes, Port Townsend Writers' Conference, dance workshops, and performances by the Tacoma Actors' Guild, all at Fort Worden State Park. Phone 385-3102 or write Box 1158, Port Townsend, WA 98368, for information.

Festivals
The **Rhododendron Festival** is held the third weekend in May, with parades, dances, antique and art shows, a carnival, rhododendron displays, and the crowning of the Rhododendron Queen, whose handprint and signature are forever captured in the cement sidewalk downtown. The end of July brings the two-day **Jazz Festival,** a Centrum event held at Fort Worden State Park. The second weekend in August is reserved for the **Jefferson County Fair,** the old-fashioned kind with livestock shows and 4-H displays. The **Wooden Boat Festival** is held the second weekend in Sept., an educational affair with displays, lectures, and classes to promote interest in the dying art of wooden boat building and restoration. Early Oct. brings the **Kinetic Sculpture Race** to Port Townsend; human-powered mechanical sculptures race over land *and water* to the finish. This race is

a derivation of the Ferndale, California, three-day 37-mile world championship contest.

SHOPPING

Galleries
Water and Lawrence streets house numerous art galleries and antique shops. **North By Northwest,** 918 Water St., tel. 385-0995, features Indian and Eskimo art, artifacts, baskets, and jewelry. **Earthenworks,** 1002 Water St., 385-0328, has native photography and other works of American art. Other galleries offer original bronze, wood, and stone sculptures, pottery, custom jewelry, prints, porcelains, and plates. Gallery Walks are held the first Sat. of each month, from 5:30-8 p.m. March through Dec., during which galleries hang their new shows, serve refreshments and often have artists on hand.

The Main Street Project
Not on Main St. at all but covering Water St. and intersecting Tyler, Taylor, Adams, and Quincy streets, this waterfront historic district houses antique and gift shops, bookstores, restaurants, clothing stores, and an ice-cream emporium.

Military Surplus
It's fitting that an area surrounded by old forts and military installations would be a good source of Army surplus material; there are a few such shops along Hwy. 20 approaching Port Townsend.

INFORMATION

The Port Townsend area code is 206. For a self-guiding historic tour map or other information contact the **Port Townsend Chamber of Commerce,** Tourist Information Center, 2437 Sims Way, Port Townsend, WA 98368, tel. 385-2722. For medical emergencies, dial 911 or contact **Jefferson General Hospital** at Ninth and Sheridan, tel. 385-2200.

TRANSPORTATION

Arriving By Ferry
Port Townsend is served directly by the Keystone ferry, departing from the west side of Whidbey Island about every 50 minutes. Fares are $3.30 roundtrip passenger, $5.55 one way car and driver ($6.65 in summer), $2.25 one way cyclist. Other cross-Sound connections are the Edmonds/Kingston, Seattle/Bremerton, and Seattle/Winslow ferries; the fares are the same as the Keystone/Port Townsend route, but considerable driving is involved; cross the Hood Canal Bridge, then take Hwy.104 west to Hwy. 20 north to Port Townsend.

Ferry To The San Juans
P.S. Express, tel. 385-5288, provides charter-passenger service between Port Townsend and Friday Harbor on San Juan Island. The boat leaves Port Townsend twice daily, May through Sept.; fares are $27.50 round-trip, $18.50 one way.

Bus Service
Jefferson Transit, tel. 385-4777, serves Port Townsend and Jefferson County, connecting with Clallum Transit to Port Angeles and Greyhound to Seattle and Port Angeles.

Arriving By Air
Ludlow Aviation, tel. 385-6554, flies to Seattle and elsewhere from Jefferson County International Airport; sightseeing flights are also available for $68 per hour for one to three persons.

MARROWSTONE ISLAND

The island's biggest attraction is **Fort Flagler State Park,** at the northern tip of Marrowstone Island and surrounded by water on three sides. Boating, picnicking, crabbing, salmon and bottom fishing, wooded hiking trails, and camping in 116 beach sites are available in this 783-acre park.

Since it is in the Olympic rain shadow, the park only gets 17 inches of rain per year. With Fort Worden and Whidbey's Fort Casey, Fort Flagler formed what old-timers called the Iron Triangle, the trio of forts guarding the narrow Admiralty Inlet between Port Townsend and Whidbey Island against attack of Puget Sound. They were equipped with the 10-inch "disappearing rifles," the cannons you can see today at Fort Casey. When these cannon were fired, the recoil would cause them to swing down out of sight behind the cement walls for reloading, giving the gun sighter a wild ride, and usually a

wooden boats at
Port Townsend

PAUL BOYER

PROTECTION ISLAND

ADMIRALTY INLET

PT. WILSON

FORT WORDEN S.P.

THE CABIN

HASTINGS ST.

F ST.

PT. HUDSON

ARCADIA COUNTRY INN

IRISH ACRES

WATER ST.

PORT TOWNSEND MAP

VICINITY OF PORT TOWNSEND

PORT TOWNSEND

MARROWSTONE PT.

CHEVY CHASE RD.

OLD FORT TOWNSEND S.P.

FORT FLAGLER S.P.

MARROWSTONE ISLAND

DISCOVERY BAY

DISCOVERY RD.

JEFFERSON CO. AIRPORT

INDIAN ISLAND

U.S. NAVAL RESERVE

MYSTERY BAY

NORDLAND

TO PORT ANGELES

101

20

ANDERSON LAKE

HADLOCK

HADLOCK HOUSE

ANDERSON LAKE RD.

DISCOVERY BAY RESTAURANT

CHIMACUM

SUMMER HOUSE

THE ECOLOGIC PLACE

DISCOVERY BAY

CHIMACUM-CENTER RD.

CENTER

104

PORT LUDLOW

RESORT AT PORT LUDLOW

KITSAP PENINSULA

TEAL LAKE RD.

LUDLOW-PARADISE RD.

HOOD CANAL FLOATING BRIDGE

104

101

MOON

0   2 mi

0   2 km

3

TIMBER HOUSE RESTAURANT

QUILCENE

TO OLYMPIA

HOOD CANAL

TO BREMERTON

© MOON PUBLICATIONS, INC.

shiner from being repeatedly struck by the eyepiece. As an aside, Battery Russell at Fort Stevens south of the Columbia River estuary was equipped with these "rifles" when the Japanese submarine fired several rounds at it in 1942. The battery commander knew his artillery was too weak to hope to hit the sub, so he wisely held fire and didn't give away the exact position.

The Iron Triangle forts also had enormous mortars that were proven impractical at the first test: the concussion was so great that windows were broken, pictures fell off walls, and foundations cracked.

Today Fort Flagler is on the National Register of Historic Places. Campsites may be reserved in advance; write Fort Flagler State Park, Nordland, WA 98358, for information.

On the road to Fort Flagler, the park on **Mystery Bay** has a picnic area, beach, boat moorage, and protected waters for small boaters, along with striking Olympic views.

Lodging
The Ecologic Place, 10 Beach Dr. in Nordland, tel. 385-3077, has 11 rustic cabins with Oak Bay and Olympic views, accommodating one to six people for $30-65 per night, $180-395 by the week; each comes with complete kitchen and bath facilities, plus a wood stove. The owners stress that they are not a motel and prefer not to rent cabins for a single night. No pets, campers, or trailers, and only small boats can be launched at the beach; kids under eight are okay in July and August. Canoes are available for rent for Oak Bay paddling, where waterfowl and other wildlife can be seen.

CHIMACUM

Fifteen minutes south of Port Townsend, this wide-open, slow-paced farming community doesn't have a great deal to offer; but **The Summer House,** 2603 Center Rd., tel. 732-4017, provides B&B luxury without a B&B price. The two guest rooms in this Victorian farmhouse share a bath for $30 s, $40 d, including a simple fresh fruit and pastry breakfast. Smoking is not permitted, but children over three are welcome.

PORT LUDLOW

The Resort at Port Ludlow *is* Port Ludlow. Once a major sawmill and shipping town, the sawmill closed and shipping with it, and the town diminished until the resort arrived. Owned by Village Resorts, which also owns the **Sun Mountain,** Port Ludlow offers the utmost in luxury: heated outdoor and indoor pools, Jacuzzi, saunas, squash and tennis courts, paved bike paths, an award-winning golf course, a marina on Port Ludlow Bay complete with rental sailboats, and the **Harbormaster** restaurant, serving breakfast, lunch, and dinner with entertainment nightly (except Mon.) in the lounge. Rooms range from $90 d for economy rooms, $99 d for a view bedroom, and one- to four-bedroom suites start at $130 d. Children under 12 are free in their parents' room. Call (800) 732-1239 toll-free statewide, or 437-2222 for reservations.

You don't have to be a guest at the resort to take advantage of some of their offerings, however. **Bicycle rentals** are available for $3 per hour; tel. 437-2222. **Rowboat rentals** are $2 per hour, $6 for a half day, $10 full day; **sailboats** are $6, $18, and $35, while **power-boats** are $10, $30, and $60. Six people can employ **Captain Mel** for a full-day sightseeing trip aboard his 40-foot sailboat for $100; call 437-2222 for info.

QUILCENE

The **Olympic Music Festival** is an annual summertime concert series held weekends from late June to mid-August. The Philadelphia String Quartet and guest artists perform their "Concerts in the Barn" one-quarter mile south of Hwy. 104 on Center Rd.; tickets are sold through Ticketmaster, at the Timber House (see below), or at the gate when available. For a free festival brochure write Friends of the PSQ, Box 45776, Seattle, WA 98145, or call 527-8839.

Prime rib, seafood, and Mexican food on Monday distinguish the **Timber House,** a restaurant on Hwy. 101 one-half mile south of Quilcene, tel. 765-3339. Open for lunch and dinner daily except Tuesday.

SEQUIM

The weather in Sequim (pronounced SKWIM) is odd for the soggy Olympic Peninsula: 17 inches of annual rainfall and habitually clear skies are caused by the town's location in the "blue hole," a locally famous weather pattern. As storms pass over the peninsula, they split in two; one part clings to the Olympics and the other is blown along by the strait's air currents, bypassing Sequim like an island in the stream. The pleasant temperate climate and lack of hustle and bustle make this town of 3,180 an ideal retirement community, while the tourist trade and natural features of the area provide a disproportionate number of visitor attractions.

SIGHTS

Museums
One block north of Hwy. 101 at 175 W. Cedar, the **Sequim-Dungeness Museum,** tel. 683-8110, was built to store the 12,000-year-old bones and artifacts unearthed at Sequim's world-famous Manis Mastodon Site (see "History," p.15, for background on the dig). Other displays include Indian and Eskimo artifacts, pioneer farming, and timber exhibits. Open Wed. through Sun., noon to 4 p.m.; donation. **Sequim Natural History Museum** in the Peninsula Cultural Arts Center, 503 N. Sequim Ave. Room 4, features dioramas of Olympic Peninsula birds and wildlife from seashore to the subalpine zone. Donation requested.

Wineries
Although Sequim's arid climate would seem to make it a natural place for wineries, the majority of the grapes used here are grown east of the Cascades. Maria and Eugene Neuharth have been producing only naturally fermented fine dinner wines since 1978 at **Neuharth Winery** on Still Rd., tel. 683-9652 or 683-3706. Their tasting and sales cellar is open daily noon to 5 p.m. **Lost Mountain Winery,** 730 Lost Mountain Rd., tel. 683-5229, produces robust red wines from California and Washington grapes; open for tastings and tours by appointment or during special periods when new wines are released.

Other Attractions
The **Olympic Game Farm,** a vacation and retirement home for Hollywood stars, is a 90-acre preserve where Gentle Ben and over 200 other animals of TV and movie fame can be visited. If you're lucky, you may witness the stars rehearsing their scenes or actually being filmed. Guided walking tours are available daily from June to Sept. for $4 adults, $3 kids; the park is open all year for driving tours (two loop roads) for the same prices. Combined walking and driving tour tickets are $5 adults, $3.50 kids. Follow the signs from Sequim five miles northwest to Ward Rd.; tel. 683-4295.

"The Duke" loved the Strait; he often explored the waters with his refurbished Navy minesweeper, the *Wild Goose.* He liked it so much he bought land on Sequim Bay and donated it to of Port Angeles for a marina. Many years and much paperwork later, the **John Wayne Marina** has 422 slips, a landscaped park and picnic area, and a bronze statue of the Duke as he appeared in the 1949 flick, *She Wore A Yellow Ribbon.*

Gourmet cooks and craftspeople might enjoy a visit to **Cedarbrook Herb Farm,** 986 Sequim Ave. S, tel. 683-7733, where over 150 varieties of herbs, teas, and flowers are organically grown. The gift shop here sells books, herb vinegars, potpourri, decorative straw hats, catnip mice, and herbal moth repellents. Open daily March through Sept., weekends Oct. through December.

PARKS AND RECREATION

The **Dungeness National Wildlife Refuge** provides habitat for 250 species of birds on the world's longest natural sandspit: seven-mile-long Dungeness Spit. As many as 40,000 birds rest at this saltwater lagoon during their migratory journeys. Admission is $2 per party. Hike to the lighthouse at the spit's tip, or rent a horse. **Quarter Moon Ranch,** Spath Rd., tel. 683-5863, rents horses for trail, beach, or mountain riding for $7.50 per hour, including a mandatory lesson. Clamming, fishing, and canoeing are permitted in the protected bay, but not camping, dogs, firearms, or fires.

Dungeness Recreation Area, a 216-acre Clallam County park at the base of the refuge, has camping from Feb. through Oct. in 65 campsites ($6 county residents, $8 nonresidents) with showers and a dump station; tel. 683-5847.

Sequim Bay State Park, just east of Sequim on Hwy. 101, has 60 wooded tent sites ($6), 26 hookup sites ($8.50), a boat launch, scuba diving, hiking, tennis courts, and superb views of Sequim Bay.

Golf

Two 18-hole public golf courses in the area are: the **SunLand Golf Course,** tel. 683-6800, just north of Sequim at 109 Hilltop Dr., and the **Dungeness Golf Course,** tel. 683-6344, adjacent to the Dungeness Inn Restaurant, north of Carlsborg on Woodcock Road. Green fees are $11 weekdays, $12-13 weekends.

Fishing

Departing from the John Wayne Marina at daylight, **Lucky Strike Charter Service,** Box 2288, tel. 683-2416, provides tackle and gear (but not lunch) for an eight-hour salmon, halibut, or bottom-fishing excursion. Trips cost $55; punch cards are available on the boat.

ACCOMMODATIONS

Five miles from Hwy. 101 and one-half mile from the beach, **Groveland Cottage,** 1673 Sequim Dungeness Way, tel. 683-3565, features four comfortable guest rooms (two with private bath) from $55-75 s, $60-80 d (lower in winter), plus a country store with gifts by local artists, wine, and groceries. Enjoy the morning paper delivered to your door, then head down for a full breakfast. Older children only, please. **Granny Sandy's Orchard Inn,** 405 W. Spruce, tel. 683-5748, has guest rooms with two shared baths for $35-50 d ($10 less in winter); fresh flowers and family-style breakfasts are evidence of Granny's personal touch. No pets or smoking. Children are welcome. **Brigadoon B&B,** 105 Brigadoon Blvd., tel. 683-2255, is a fairly new B&B in a 1920 farmhouse, set back from the highway on a knoll on the way to Three Crabs Restaurant. Rooms are $65 ($5-10 less in winter), with full breakfast and use of the outdoor spa.

The **Greathouse Motel,** a half mile east of town on Hwy.101, tel. 683-7272, has 20 rooms for $38-75 s, $34-48 d. **Sequim West Motel,** 740 W. Washington St., tel. 683-4144, has a restaurant and 21 rooms from $56-62. **The Red Ranch Inn,** tel. 683-4195, adjacent to the restaurant of the same name at 830 W. Washington St., has 31 motel rooms furnished in Western decor for $56-80 d. **Best Western Sequim Bay Lodge,** 1788 Hwy. 101 E (three-qyarters of a mile from John Wayne Marina), tel. 683-0691, offers two-room suites with hot tubs and/or fireplaces, plus on-site restaurant and pool, from $ 68-175 d.

Campers should check out the numerous campgrounds at Olympic National Park, p. 214.

FOOD

The Three Crabs has served Dungeness crab and other local seafood specialties such as red snapper, halibut, and salmon for over 25 years at their waterfront location on Three Crabs Rd.; they also have a retail seafood

SEQUIM

1. Three Crabs
2. Groveland Cottage
3. Brigadoon B&B
4. Casoni's
5. Red Ranch Inn
6. Bandits Pizza
7. Sequim-Dungeness Museum
8. Granny Sandy's Orchard B&B
9. Sequim Gallery
10. Greyhound
11. visitor information
12. Old Sequim Depot
13. Cedarbrook Herb Farm
14. Neuharth Winery
15. Lamplighter's Restaurant
16. Best Western Sequim Bay Lodge

© MOON PUBLICATIONS, INC.

market. Open daily at noon; take Sequim-Dungeness Way from Hwy. 101, then go right on Twin View Dr. at the Three Crabs sign. Reservations are recommended, tel. 683-4264. The **Oak Table Cafe,** 292 W. Bell, tel. 683-2179, serves gourmet breakfasts and light lunches. For pizza and beer, sandwiches, and spaghetti in a family atmosphere, try **The Bandit's Pizza Parlor** at 392 W. Washington, tel. 683-3388. **Casoni's,** 105 Hooker

Rd., tel. 683-2415, offers something a little fancier: seafood, veal, steak, and sautées. Open for lunch and dinner at the intersection of Hwy.101 and Carlsborg Road. **The Lamplighter Restaurant,** 1292 Hwy. 101 E, tel. 683-4134, serves moderately priced Mexican and American lunches and dinners. The **Dungeness Inn,** tel. 683-3331, overlooking the Dungeness Golf Course at 491A Woodcock Rd., serves breakfast, lunch, and dinner Tues. through Sun., specializing in prime rib, steak, seafood, and bouillabaisse. Another steakhouse, **The Red Ranch Restaurant,** has a 50-item salad bar to accompany their mesquite-broiled grain-fed beef. On Hwy. 101 in Sequim, they're open daily for dinner, tel. 683-6622.

The area's only dinner theater is the **Old Sequim Depot,** 710 S. Sequim, tel. 683-6840, where your choice of three dinners precedes the live production in a 76-year-old restored railroad station. Open for lunch and dinner Tues. through Saturday.

ENTERTAINMENT AND EVENTS

Established over 90 years ago and still going strong, the **Sequim Irrigation Festival** celebrates the beginning of Dungeness Valley agriculture thanks to the hand-dug ditch that first brought water from the Dungeness River to the arid prairie in 1896. The first festival (May 1, 1896) was a picnic in a shady grove; today a parade, art and flower shows, and the crowning of a May Queen commemorate the annual event.

For something a little different, hear old-time Southern gospel music every night except Mon. at 7 p.m. (weekends only Oct. through April) at the **Olympic Peninsula Retreat Center,** 309 Kitchen Dick Lane, tel. 683-2780.

Gallery
Olympic Peninsula artists are represented at **Sequim Gallery,** 130 N. Sequim Ave., tel.

683-6503. Drawing and watercolor classes are taught by resident artist Judy Priest.

INFORMATION

The area code in Sequim and all of the Olympic Peninsula is 206. For maps, brochures, and further information contact the **Sequim-Dungeness Valley Chamber of Commerce,** 1192 E. Washington, tel. 683-6197.

For fire, medical, or police emergencies, dial 911. The nearest hospital with 24-hour emergency service is Olympic Memorial Hospital, 939 Caroline in Port Angeles, tel. 457-8513.

TRANSPORTATION

Arriving By Car
From the Puget Sound area, take Hwy. 16 north from Tacoma to Hwy. 3 in Bremerton; cross the Hood Canal Bridge (Hwy.104) at Port Gamble, then connect with Hwy.101 to Sequim.

Arriving By Air
Coastal Airways, tel. 683-4444, has daily half-hour flights from Sequim Valley Airport to Seattle's Sea-Tac Airport. Farther west, Port Angeles's Fairchild International Airport offers daily scheduled commuter service to Sea-Tac, Bellingham, Hoquiam, the San Juan Islands, Vancouver and Victoria, B.C., via San Juan Airlines, tel. 452-1323 or (800) 438-3880.

Getting Around By Bus
Clallam Transit, tel. 452-4511 or (800) 858-3747, operates a daily commuter route between Sequim and Port Angeles, including a stop at Fairchild International Airport, and regular routes as far west as Forks and Neah Bay. **Greyhound,** tel. 683-4343, offers nationwide service from their station at 117 E. Washington.

OLYMPIC NATIONAL PARK

The diversity of climate and geography in Olympic National Park's 908,720 acres of wilderness is one reason it was among the 100 parks in the world named a "World Heritage Park" by the United Nations in 1981: rugged glaciated peaks, damp low-lying rainforests, and 57 miles of virgin shoreline provide some of Washington's most spectacular (and most photographed) scenery.

Paved roads only skirt the park, allowing the largest coniferous forest in the Lower 48 to remain the undisturbed home of 180 species of birds and 50 species of animals, including Roosevelt elk, black bear, deer, bald eagles, and Olympic marmots. Noticeably absent are the grizzly bear, red fox, pika, porcupine, and other species common to the Cascade Range. The reason for this difference between the ranges dates back to the Pleistocene Ice Age, when a Canadian glacier isolated the Olympics from the rest of Washington. It's taken 11,000 years for the red fox and porcupine to advance to the park's southern boundary. Mountain goats native to the Cascades were artificially introduced to the Olympics in the 1920s and now thrive in the park's interior. They thrive so well, in fact, that the National Park Service has been capturing them and removing them from the park because they are causing so much damage to the plantlife. The park service has also talked about shooting many of the goats, which has fed the flames of this controversial issue.

Today Olympic National Park ranks 10th in attendance among U.S. national parks, with over three million visitors a year; because of its enormous size and preserved interior, it's not hard to find peaceful solitude on its lakes and trails.

Climate
Weather in Olympic National Park is as varied and unpredictable as its geography. Rain is an ever-present threat, particularly on the western "wet" side, although three-quarters of the park's precipitation falls from Oct. through March. In summer, park temperatures may be in the 80s—or the 60s; at sea level mild temperatures prevail, summer 70s to winter 40s.

SIGHTS

Hwy. 101 circles the park, with paved or dirt roads leading to attractions around the park's periphery. The park is open year-round, although some roads may be closed in winter. A $3 park entrance fee, good for seven days, is charged at Staircase, Hoh, Heart o' the Hills, Mora, Elwha, and Soleduck entrances in summer.

Hurricane Ridge
One of the park's most scenic areas and by far the most visited, Hurricane Ridge rises over 5,200 feet seemingly straight up from the Strait of Juan de Fuca, providing an awesome contrast from sea level and breathtaking 360-degree views from the summit. The paved road starts at Race St. in Port Angeles, becoming Hurricane Ridge Rd. as it snakes up mountainsides for 17 miles at an easy seven percent grade; frequent turnouts allow for photo breaks. At the top, **Hurricane Ridge Lodge** provides food service, a gift shop, summer naturalist programs, winter ski rentals and ski-tow service; summer hiking trails and winter cross-country ski and showshoe trails start here as well (see "Outdoor Activities," p. 211). One of the park's best areas for spotting wildlife, black-tailed deer often bound across the parking lot and black bear are sometimes visible from a distance. The ridge's name isn't without basis in fact: the first lodge at the summit lost its roof in a strong winter blast.

If the drop-offs and absence of guardrails on Hurricane Ridge Rd. made your palms

Hurricane Ridge,
Olympic National Park

ARCHIE SATTERFIELD

sweat, you're in for a real treat on **Obstruction Point Road.** Starting from the Hurricane Ridge parking lot, this narrow gravel road follows the ridge for eight miles without a rail or fence, providing spectacular views for the strong-hearted. The road, constructed in the 1930s by the Civilian Conservation Corps, went as far as it could until a steep talus slope prohibited any further roadmaking.

Hoh Rainforest
Nearly 140 inches of rain per year keep this slug haven perpetually green and damp under towering conifers over 200 feet tall and up to 10 feet wide. The **Hoh Visitor Center,** located 18 miles east of Hwy. 101 on the Hoh River, offers interpretive exhibits and summer guided walks; nearby are three short interpretive trails.

Lake Crescent
According to Indian legend, Mount Storm King once became so fed up with the bickering between the Clallams and Quileutes that he broke a rock off his head and threw it down at the warring tribes, damming a river and thereby creating Lake Crescent. The scientific view of the lake's origin isn't much different, it's attributed to an ancient landslide blocking the Lyre River. Today, freshwater Lake Crescent, 624 feet deep and 8½ miles long, is famous for its Beardslee trout, a subspecies that is large and a hard fighter when hooked. Swimming, boating, camping, picnicking, and, of course, fishing are popular lake activities.

Marymere Falls
This 90-foot unspoiled waterfall is off the southern shore of the lake. To get there, hike the three-quarter-mile trail starting behind the Storm King Ranger Station or from Lake Crescent Lodge.

Sol Duc Hot Springs
Bask in 102-109° natural hot springs, throwbacks to the area's volcanic ancestry. Located 12 miles from Hwy. 101 just south of Lake Crescent, facilities include 84 year-round campsites, nature trails, and summer evening programs at the amphitheater.

Quinault Valley
Surrounded by steep mountains and dense rainforest, **Lake Quinault** is bordered on the northwest by Olympic National Park and on the southeast by Olympic National Forest; the lake and land to the southeast are part of the Quinault Indian Reservation and subject to Quinault regulations. The Quinault Rain Forest is one of three major rainforests on the Peninsula; here the annual average rainfall is 140 inches, manifested in enormous trees and lush vegetation. Quinault Valley Loop Auto Tour, a 25-mile trip con-

necting South Shore Rd., North Shore Rd., and Hwy. 101, boasts views of Lake Quinault, the rainforest, and possible glimpses of Roosevelt elk; not recommended for those with trailers in tow.

The Pacific Coast

To preserve the natural habitat, automobile access to the park's Pacific Ocean beaches is severely limited, but the picturesque cliffs and sea stacks are worth the effort to get there. At the northwest corner of the park, three-mile hiking trails lead from the Ozette Visitor Center to Cape Alava and Sand Point on the Pacific coast. Cape Alava and the beaches near Ozette Lake and La Push are known for fruitful beachcombing, particularly for collectors of the colored glass balls used in the Orient to float nets. All along the coast are millions of flat, round rocks, remarkable in their uniformity, worn smooth by the ceaseless pounding of the surf. At the park's southern coastal reaches, beach access, summer naturalist programs, and tidepool walks are available at Mora and Kalaloch campgrounds.

Near the north park boundary, Point of Arches is a testimony to the relentless pounding of the Pacific where, with a force of two tons per square inch, the ocean carves giant arches out of ancient rock. Neighboring Shi Shi (pronounced shy-shy) Bluffs provide a vantage point for watching the spring and fall gray whale migrations; the best viewing season is from March to May. Both Shi Shi Bluffs and Point of Arches are accessible only through Neah Bay and with permission from the Makah Indians, whose reservation you must cross. The beach is reached after a mile hike from road's end. The Arches, legendary children of Destruction Island and Tatoosh Island, were pushed from Mother Tatoosh's canoe when she deserted her husband because, she said, "You'd probably grow up just like your father!"

Be prepared for soggy, windy weather; 100 inches of annual rainfall combine with sometimes violent winds for less-than-pleasant hiking weather, although thanks to the warming effect of the Japanese Current that flows past the Olympic coast, the temperatures are mild year-round.

OUTDOOR ACTIVITIES

Naturalist Programs
Guided walks, campfire programs, and demonstrations are held daily or on weekends at Elwha, Fairholm, Heart o' the Hills, Hoh, Kalaloch, Mora, Soleduck, and Staircase campgrounds, July Fourth through Labor Day. Check the campground bulletin board for times and topics.

Field Seminars
Olympic Park Institute, a nonprofit educational organization, offers field seminars for would-be naturalists, photographers, and anyone interested in the ecology or geography of the park. Course offerings in the past have included Birds of the Olympic Peninsula, Nature Photography, Wilderness Medicine, Watercolor in the Olympics, Geology of Olympic National Park, and more. Seminars last two to five days (over a weekend), cost $110-220, and may be taken for college credit. For information and registration, write Olympic Park Institute, HC 62 Box 9T, Port Angeles, WA 98362, or phone 928-3720.

Hiking
More than 600 miles of hiking trails crisscross the park, covering the park's virgin forest core. These short trails provide maximum reward for minimum hiking effort (mileages are one way).

From Lake Crescent Lodge, follow the **Marymere Falls Trail** one-quarter mile for a spectacular view of the 90-foot falls. For a similar experience, try the **Soleduck River Trail** from the Sol Duc Ranger Station; after one mile you reach Soleduck Falls and a footbridge over a deep gorge.

Take the Elwha River Trail for two miles to **Humes Ranch,** built in 1889 by Grant Humes, who made his living leading wilderness expeditions and by hunting and trapping game. Today his cabin is on the National Register of Historic Places.

A four-mile hike starting at Lyre River Rd. or North Shore Rd. at opposite ends of Lake Crescent, the **Spruce Railroad Trail** follows the tracks of the 1918 Spruce Railroad, built to supply spruce for WW I aircraft. The war was over before the railroad was completed, however, and the spruce was no longer needed. Two tunnels and depressions from the never-used railroad ties remain. Besides a taste of local history, the hike provides a view of Lake Crescent.

A number of trails begin at Hurricane Ridge, including 1½-mile **Hurricane Hill Trail,** a paved walk to the top of 5,757-foot Hurricane Hill passing picnic areas, marmot colonies, and spectacular vistas. A longer hike, the **Klahanee Ridge Trail,** follows the ridge's summit for two miles after leaving the paved trail near the marmot colonies.

For an all-day hike, the 14-mile **Colonel Bob Trail** provides views of Mt. Olympus, Quinault Valley, and the Pacific Ocean from its 4,492-foot summit. Drive past Lake Quinault on South Shore Rd. till you see the trailhead on the right.

The four-mile Quinault Loop Trail, accessible from Willaby and Falls Creek campgrounds and the Lake Quinault Lodge, provides an easy two-hour trek along the shore and into the rainforest. Easier still is the one-half-mile Quinault Rain Forest Nature Trail, where signs explain the natural features. A good hike for those traveling with small children begins at North Fork Campground, following the **Three Lakes Trail** for the first mile to Irely Lake.

Backpacking

The only way to cross the park is on foot; auto roads barely penetrate it. Backcountry use permits are required for trail or beach camping; pick one up at the ranger station nearest your point of departure. Because of overuse, reservations are required for Flapjack Lakes and Lake Constance trails; call the Staircase Ranger Station at 877-5569.

For a south-to-north 44-mile hike, start at the North Fork Ranger Station (follow North Shore Rd. from Lake Quinault); the North Fork Trail follows the North Fork Quinault River for 16½ miles, then joins the Elwha River Trail terminating at Lake Mills near Elwha (just west of Port Angeles). You'll be hiking in reverse the route of James Halbold Christie, leader of the Seattle Press expedition across the then-unexplored Olympic Peninsula. It took Christie and his party six months and one black bear to complete the route in 1890; it should take you only four days and a packful of gorp. Bring binoculars for a closer look at the mountain goats near Elwha.

enjoying the sun and sand at Olympic National Park

A somewhat shorter loop trail follows the Soleduck River Trail to Seven Lakes Basin, then shifts uphill to the summit of Bogachiel Peak and out for a roundtrip of 22 miles. For a 24-mile one way, relatively level hike on the more remote east side, start at Graves Creek on the south side of the park, follow the east fork of the Quinault River for 13 miles, passing Enchanted Valley Ranger Station and Anderson Pass, then travel alongside the Dosewallips River to the Dosewallips Ranger Station and campground.

Climbing

When English sea captain John Meares first sighted Mt. Olympus from aboard ship in 1788, he reputedly said, "If that be not the home where dwell the gods, it is certainly beautiful enough to be, and I therefore will call it Mt. Olympus." He seemed to have forgotten (or never knew) that Juan Perez named the four peaks "Sierra Nevada de Santa Rosalia" in 1774. George Vancouver used Meares's name for the mountain, following a trend caused by the waning of Spanish influence in the Northwest.

Climbing 7,965-foot Mt. Olympus is a 44-mile roundtrip. From the Hoh Ranger Station—the closest and most popular departure point—hike 12 flat miles along the Hoh River Trail, then another four to the Olympus base camp, Glacier Meadows. Crossing Blue Glacier and the Snow Dome requires rope, ice axe, crampons, and mountaineering skills; a hard hat is advised because of rock falls near the summit. The eight-mile climb from Glacier Meadows to the summit takes about 10 hours. The best months for climbing are late June through early Sept., driest months in the park; prior to that time mud and washouts may slow you down. *A Climber's Guide to the Olympic Mountains,* published by The Mountaineers, gives detailed information on this and other climbs in the park. This book, other trail guides, and quadrangle maps can be obtained from The Pacific Northwest National Parks and Forests Assn., Olympic Branch, 3002 Mt. Angeles Rd., Port Angeles, WA 98362; write for prices.

Fishing, Boating, And Rafting

The clear, turquoise waters of Lake Crescent are open to fishing and boating; rowboats can be rented from Lake Crescent Lodge. Salmon fishing is popular in the Strait of Juan de Fuca and along the coast; no license is necessary within park limits, though salmon and steelhead punch cards are required. These punch cards are not available in the park, but sporting goods stores statewide have them.

Boating is permitted at nine-mile-long Ozette Lake (the state's largest totally natural lake) in the park's northwest corner; in fact, boating in is the only way to get to Ericson's Bay Campground on the west shore. Boat over to the lake's south end and hike the 2.3-mile trail to Norwegian Memorial, a tribute to the victims of a 1903 shipwreck on the Pacific coast. You're practically assured of

isolation, since the only other way to get there is by miles of beachwalking.

Olympic Raft and Guide Service offers summer raft trips on the Elwha River for $25 adults, $15 kids, leaving from Elwha Resort. For reservations and information, phone 457-7011 or write Box 846, Port Angeles, WA 98362.

Winter Sports

Ski rentals, two rope tows, poma lift, and cross-country ski trails provide Nordic and Alpine skiing at Hurricane Ridge; nonskiers can enjoy the sights via a naturalist-led snowshoe walk (snowshoes provided). Snow-tubing is another popular winter activity at the Ridge. The road is plowed and the lodge and ski facilities are open for holiday and weekend day use only from mid-Dec. to late March; tel. 452-9235.

Giant trunks covered with moss are a rainforest staple.

ACCOMMODATIONS

Indoors

The following accommodations are located in or very near the park. For meals, lodging, and sights in Sequim or Port Angeles, see pp. 205 and 217.

At the base of Storm King Mountain, **Lake Crescent Lodge** has fireplace cottages (built for Franklin Roosevelt's visit in 1937), modern motor lodge rooms, and new cottages with views of the mountains and Lake Crescent. Rates are $50-99 for historic lodge rooms with shared bath, motor lodge rooms and three-bedroom Roosevelt cottages. Open May to Nov., write National Park Concessions, Lake Crescent Lodge, HC 62, Box 11, Port Angeles, WA 98362-9798, or call 928-3211 for reservations. **Log Cabin Resort,** at the northeast end of the lake, has motel units, cabins, campground, and boat rentals three miles from Hwy. 101 on E. Beach Road. Lodging rates range from $40-59 for cabins, motel rooms, and waterfront A-frame chalets. Open all year; contact Manager, 6540 E. Beach Rd., Port Angeles, WA 98362, tel. 928-3245.

About 12 miles south of Hwy. 101 and 28 miles west of Port Angeles, **Sol Duc Hot Springs Resort** has a restaurant and cabins from $47 and up, s or d, and trailer hookups for $9. Swim in warm mineral pools and a freshwater pool for $3.75 a day, or enjoy a massage. Handicapped-accessible cabins are available; the lodge, two pools, and three cabins are wheelchair accessible. Open mid-May through Sept,; write Sol Duc Hot Springs Resort, Box 2169, Port Angeles, WA 98362-0283, or call 327-3583 for reservations.

Kalaloch Lodge, 35 miles south of Forks or 70 miles north of Aberdeen on Hwy. 101, has motel and cabin accommodations overlooking the Pacific. Open year-round, cabins range from $54-82 d; motel and lodge rooms go for $34-68 d. Pets are allowed in the cabin area for an additional $4 charge. Contact the Kalaloch Lodge Reservation Clerk, HC Route 80, Box 1100, Kalaloch, WA 98331, tel. 962-2271, for reservations.

Seventy miles south of Forks and 40 miles north of Aberdeen on S. Shore Rd., the **Lake Quinault Lodge** has an indoor pool, sauna, Jacuzzi, and rooms ranging from $70-95 Write to them at S. Shore Rd., Box 7, Quinault, WA 98575, or call 288-2571 or, toll-free in Washington, (800) 562-6672 for reservations. Also on Lake Quinault with some of the least expensive lodging in the area is **Rain Forest Resort Village,** 3½ miles off Hwy. 101 on S. Shore Road. Rooms at the inn, with private bath and TVs, are $28-34 s, $38-40 d; simple wooden cabins range from $38-79 d, some with fireplaces and/or Jacuzzis; 31 trailer hookups are available for $9 a night. Write them at Route 1, Box 40, Lake Quinault, WA 98575, or call 288-2535 or, toll-free in Washington, (800) 562-0948. Around the other side of the lake, four miles north of Hwy. 101 on N. Shore Rd., Lochaerie Resort, 288-2215, has six cottages, all different, built from 1926-41, for $40-60 d per night. All have lake views and fireplaces; some also have porches and lofts.

Outdoors

Camping in the park is available on a first-come, first-served basis for $5 a night (free in primitive campgrounds). No showers or laundry facilities are available at any campground; if you really miss bathing, Sequim Bay State Park, Bogachiel State Park, and Dosewallips State Park have showers you can use. Although lacking trailer hookups, some campgrounds do have trailer dumping stations. Trailers over 21 feet in length will have a tight fit. The camping limit is 14 days.

The following campgrounds are open year-round for tents and trailers: Elwha, 41 sites; Fairholm, 87 sites; Heart o' the Hills, 95 sites; Hoh, 95 sites; Kalaloch, 179 sites; Mora, 91 sites; Ozette, 14 sites; and Staircase, for small trailers only. Open year-round for walk-in campers are Erickson's Bay, 15 sites, and July Creek, 31 sites.

These campgrounds for tents and trailers are classified as closed-if-it-snows: Graves Creek, 45 sites, and Soleduck, 84 sites. Same category, no trailers: Deer Park, 18 sites. Boulder Creek's 50 sites are walk-in only.

Summer-only campgrounds for tents are Dosewallips, 33 sites; North Fork, eight sites; Queets, 26 sites. The only summer-only campground for trailers is Altaire, with 29 sites.

FOOD

Lake Crescent Lodge, 20 miles west of Port Angeles on Hwy. 101, serves moderately priced salmon, steak, scallop, and oyster dinners as well as daily breakfast and lunch in the Lodge Dining Room; the cocktail lounge opens daily at 5 p.m. The restaurant at **Sol Duc Hot Springs Resort** serves breakfast, lunch, and dinner daily, with limited service early and late in the season. **Lake Quinault Lodge** offers gourmet dining and cocktails with a broad lake view; neighboring **Rain Forest Resort Village** serves fresh seafood, steaks, and cocktails year-round.

TRANSPORTATION

Arriving By Car
From Tacoma take Hwy. 16 north to Hwy. 3 in Bremerton; join Hwy. 104 at Port Gamble, connecting with Hwy. 101 to Port Angeles. Hwy. 101 continues to circle the park, finally joining I-5 near Olympia.

Arriving By Ferry
From the Seattle area, access to the Olympic Peninsula is provided via the Seattle/Winslow and Edmonds/Kingston ferries; take your pick. The Kingston ferry runs a little more often, leaving about every 40 minutes as opposed to Winslow's more or less hourly schedule. From the north, the Keystone/Port Townsend ferry leaves Whidbey Island about every 50 minutes. The fares are the same for all three: $3.30 roundtrip passenger, $5.55 one way car and driver ($6.65 in summer).

The MV *Coho* sails between Victoria, B.C., and Port Angeles four times a day (twice daily off-season); the 1½-hour crossing costs $22 for car and driver, $5.50 for passengers, $2.75 for kids, and $2.40 for bicycles one way. For more info on the *Coho* contact Black Ball Transport, 106 Surrey Bldg., Bellevue, WA 98004, tel. 622-2222, or check at the ferry dock at the foot of Laurel St. in Port Angeles, tel. 457-4491.

Arriving By Air
San Juan Airlines, tel. 452-9500, offers scheduled flights from Seattle to Fairchild International Airport in Port Angeles.

Bus Tours
Seattle's **Gray Line,** tel. 624-5813, offers two-day bus tours of the Olympic Peninsula. Included in the $114 pp double-occupancy price are overnight accommodations at the Red Lion Bayshore Inn in Port Angeles and lunch at the Alderbrook Inn Resort on Hood Canal. Departing from downtown Seattle hotels, the tour circles the Peninsula on Hwy. 101, providing views of Hurricane Ridge, the Pacific Ocean, and a rainforest.

SERVICES

The area code on the Olympic Peninsula is 206. For additional information, phone the visitor center or ranger station nearest your destination: on the north side, Pioneer Memorial Visitor Center, tel. 452-4501; on the west, Hoh Visitor Center, tel. 374-6925; and on the east, Hoodsport Ranger Station, tel. 877-5254. For general information on camping, hiking, accommodations, etc., write the Superintendent, Olympic National Park, 600 E. Park Ave., Port Angeles, WA 98362, or stop by the Pioneer Memorial Visitor Center, about one mile from Hwy. 101 on Race Street.

PORT ANGELES

A population of 17,100 makes Port Angeles the largest city on the northern Olympic Peninsula. Its busy harbor, protected by the strong arm of Ediz Hook, is visited daily by logging ships, fishing boats, and the MV *Coho* from Victoria. The view from the Port Angeles city pier is breathtaking: rocky Hurricane Ridge, made more ominous by a wispy cloud cover, seems to rise straight out of the turbulent waters of the Strait of Juan de Fuca, creating an overwhelming contrast of land and water, height and depth.

In 1610 this strait was discovered by Greek pilot Apostolos Valerianus, sailing under the Mexican flag and the Spanish name of Juan de Fuca. De Fuca's claim was thought to be something less than the truth until 200 years later when Capt. John Kendrick, an American, found the Greek's observations to be quite accurate. The town of Port Angeles was named by an early Spanish explorer—literally "Port of Our Lady of the Angels"—and although it changed names a number of times in the interim, Port Angeles was organized under its original name in 1890. The town's first white settler, Angus Johnson, traded with Hudson's Bay Company in Victoria across the Strait in 1857; in 1862 President Lincoln named Port Angeles and Ediz Hook as military reservations. Port Angeles was the second town site (after Washington D.C.) to be planned by the federal government, probably because of the attractiveness of its deep harbor—though the town's population at the time was only 10.

The military influence held on for decades, as parts of the Pacific Fleet anchored in Port Angeles every summer in the 1920s and '30s, providing the town with 30,000 eligible bachelors and attracting unattached women from all over for a little summer fun. Today the city caters to tourists; it feeds, shelters, and entertains many of Olympic National Park's three million annual visitors.

SIGHTS

Municipal Pier And Marine Laboratory

The best part of Port Angeles, outside of its proximity to Olympic National Park, is clearly the city pier. An observation tower at pier's end provides 360-degree views of the city, harbor, and majestic Olympic mountains, while a sandy beach with picnic area is available for day use. Also located on the pier near the *Coho* ferry dock, the **Arthur D. Feiro Marine Laboratory,** operated by Peninsula College, has hands-on displays and exhibits of the area's sealife with volunteers to answer questions. Open daily in summer, weekend afternoons the rest of the year. Admission is $1 for adults, $.50 kids under 13. For specific hours or a guided tour call 452-9277, ext. 264.

Ediz Hook

Drive west on Marine Dr. to a mile-long natural sandspit, or sandbar, protecting one of the world's deepest harbors. Watch as freighters are guided in, or take out your own boat for fishing or sightseeing; motorboat rentals are available at Thunderbird Boathouse for $6 per hour ($20 minimum) or $45 per day including fuel. Picnicking and beachcombing are also popular activities. The U.S. Coast Guard Air Station occupies the far end of the spit; slightly closer to the mainland, the Puget Sound Pilots Association assigns a pilot to each commercial ship passing this point to steer it on its way through Puget Sound.

Clallam County Courthouse
And Historic Museum

A state historic site (built in 1914), the county courthouse houses the Clallam County Museum's displays of Olympic Peninsula history, including local genealogy and a completely stocked old country store. Located at

DIANNE BOULERICE LYONS

Municipal Pier and observation tower

Lincoln and Fourth streets, the museum is open Mon. through Sat. 10 a.m.-4 p.m.; donation.

ACCOMMODATIONS

Hotels
Lodging is plentiful in Port Angeles, and fortunately much of it is inexpensive. If you're not too particular, a few downtown motels of truck-stop quality post their under-$20 rates on readerboards outside their offices. For familiar, yet still inexpensive, lodging, the **Super 8 Motel** at 2104 E. First St., tel. 452-8401, is within walking distance of several restaurants and three miles from the B.C. ferry; rooms are $35-40 s, $38-48 d. **Royal Victorian,** 521 E. First St., tel. 452-2316, a small motel without a lot of extras, has 11 rooms in a wide range of prices, from $34-58 s or d. **Aggie's Inn,** 602 E. Front St., tel. 457-0471, has an indoor pool, sauna, and 114 rooms for $44 and up. The **Uptown,** 101 E. Second, tel. 457-9434, has some view rooms from $47-110. **Hill Haus,** 111 E. Second St., tel. 452-9285, has 23 rooms (some with balconies) going for $36-75 s or d. On Port Angeles Harbor, the **Red Lion**

Bayshore Inn has 187 guest rooms (some with bayside balconies), a heated pool, and adjacent restaurant; rooms are $57-83 s, $67-91 d.

Bed And Breakfasts
Built in 1910 of English Tudor design, **The Tudor Inn,** 1108 S. Oak, tel. 452-3138, has five bedrooms with views of the Olympics or the Strait of Juan de Fuca, a lounge, library, and private baths; room rates are $55-85 d. Hosts Jane and Jerry Glass have made arrangements with local companies offering salmon charters and guided hiking or backpacking trips, and also offer a winter cross-country ski package. The **Glen Mar,** 318 N. Eunice, tel. 457-6110, has two rooms and two suites for $75-87—one overlooking the water, one with a mountain view—and a two-room suite with a harbor view. Breakfast on the patio, use of the grand piano, and coffee or tea in your room are among the options here; but no indoor smoking, please.

Kennedy's B&B, 332 E. Fifth, tel. 457-3628, has five rooms from $50-70 d in one of Port Angeles's oldest homes, built in 1896. Included in the price is a full bacon-and-eggs breakfast, fresh flowers and fruit in your room, and courtesy car service to the airport or ferry dock.

Camping
The **Port Angeles/Sequim KOA,** 2065 Hwy. 101 E, tel. 457-5916, is nestled at the base of Hurricane Ridge; facilities include hookups, pool, laundry, and hot showers. There's plenty of camping at nearby Olympic National Park, albeit *without* hookups, pool, laundry, or hot showers; see p. 208.

FOOD

Part of Red Lion Bayshore Inn, **Haguewood's** has an extensive menu with over 75 salads, sandwiches, and entrees; breakfast runs about $4, lunch $4-8; dinners, $8-15, feature crab and steak. Forget atmosphere—Denny's is more elegant. The challenge here

1. Harbor House
2. Tudor Inn
3. Inside Stuff
4. Chowder House and Carriage House Wines
5. chamber of commerce
6. Kennedy's B&B
7. museum
8. county courthouse
9. coin laundry
10. Hill Haus
11. Harbor Towne Mall
12. The Greenery
13. Red Lion Bayshore Inn
14. Haguewood's Restaurant
15. Jim's Pharmacy
16. Royal Victorian
17. Olympic Memorial Hospital
18. Bushwhacker Restaurant

is to take more than 40 seconds to finish your food, though getting a harbor-view window seat will remove you from most of the hash-slinging commotion. Served at a more re-laxed pace, the specialties at the **Bush-whacker,** 1527 E. First St., tel. 457-4113,

include seafood, steak, chicken, and a chow-der bar; open from 5 p.m.

The Greenery Restaurant, in the midst of the downtown shopping area at 117-B E. First St., tel. 457-4112, serves three meals a day Mon. through Sat., specializing in cioppino, fresh-baked French bread, and home-made pasta in a plants-and-wood decor catering to the city's businesspersons; prices here are about the same as Haguewood's. If you prefer diner-style, the tiny **Chowder House,** 117 N. Oak St., offers breakfast all day, plus clam chowder, chili, soups, and sandwiches till 4:30 p.m. **First Street Haven,** First and Laurel, serves hearty breakfasts and inexpensive sandwiches, quiche, and salads for lunch. Just east of Port Angeles at 2300 Hwy. 101 E, highly acclaimed **C'est Si Bon** prepares local seafood with a French accent, with Olympic and rose garden views adding to the ambience; fortunately, you can't see the dark-flamingo paint job from the inside. Open for dinner Tues. through Sun.; call 452-8888 for reservations. And for the old reliable, **Pizza Mia,** 3033 Hwy. 101 E, tel. 452-3131 or 452-1111, is open till 2 a.m. and delivers.

RECREATION

Parks

Eighty-seven campsites, a marinelife sanctuary, hiking trails, beach, and picnic areas occupy 196-acre **Salt Creek Recreation Area** off Hwy. 112, west of Port Angeles; open year-round.

Near the William R. Fairchild International Airport at W. Lauridsen Blvd. and Bean Rd., **Lincoln Park's** authentic pioneer cabins and an Indian longhouse accompany tennis courts, baseball diamond, campsites, nature trails, picnic area, and children's fishing pond at this 144-acre park.

The 17-acre county park at **Freshwater Bay** on the Strait of Juan de Fuca is primarily a saltwater boat launch with minimal recreational facilities.

Fishing

Depart at 6 a.m. for a five-hour salmon-trolling trip on the Strait of Juan de Fuca with **Carousel Charters,** 1030 Mt. Pleasant Rd., tel. 457-3000. No fishing expertise is required; the knowledgeable skipper provides fishing tackle, salmon punch card and stamp,

coffee and doughnuts (even nets and cleans your catch) for $55 per person.

Fish Bear Charters, Box 1424, tel. 457-7029, operates daily from mid-June to mid-Sept. (and some April and May weekends) with an all-day fishing excursion, including gear, cleaning, and bagging, for $60 (no kids under 12), maximum six persons; tel. 457-7029. If it's salmon you're after, July through mid-August is the best time, according to Fish Bear's Skipper John Willits.

One of the most popular charter trips is offered by **Satin Doll Charters,** operating every day, year-round with winter blackmouth, halibut, and ling cod fishing in Port Angeles waters, and summer deep-sea fishing for salmon, bottom fish, halibut, or ling cod from Big Salmon Resort in Neah Bay, about 60 miles west of Port Angeles. All tackle is furnished; bring your own lunch. A full day of fishing costs $50, plus a buck for a one-day license. For information on the winter Port Angeles trips write Box 2108, Port Angeles, WA 98362, or call 457-6585 after 5 p.m.; for summer charters, write Big Salmon Resort, Neah Bay, WA 98357, or call 645-2374.

Blue Dolphin Charters runs salmon and bottom fish charters year-round (weekends only Sept. to June) for $55 per person, with everything but lunch included (they provide continental breakfast) aboard their 32-foot cruiser with heated cabin. Call 928-3709 for reservations.

For more fishing charters departing from towns west of Port Angeles along the Strait of Juan de Fuca, see "West of Port Angeles," p. 222.

Experienced anglers may want to participate in **Derby Days,** a 10-day late-August festival highlighted by two parades and culminating in a two-day salmon fishing derby with prizes totaling $50,000.

Horse Riding

Four Winds Equestrian Center, 787 N. Arnette Rd., three miles southeast of Port Angeles off Monroe Rd., has guided trail riding by appointment only for $10 per hour with a $20 minimum; call 457-4385 for reservations.

Auto Racing

From May through Sept. **Port Angeles Speedway,** five miles east of Port Angeles on Hwy. 101, has stock and hobby-car races every Sunday afternoon. Gates open at 11 a.m., with time trials at 1 p.m. and races at 2 p.m. For prices and additional info call 457-6063.

ENTERTAINMENT

The **Port Angeles Symphony Orchestra** begins its six-concert season in Oct. but holds other special-occasion concerts throughout the year at various locations. Tickets can be purchased at Angeles Music in Port Angeles or Carlson's Hallmark in Sequim; season tickets and other info are available from PASO, Box 2148, Port Angeles, WA 98362, tel. 457-5579.

DIANNE BOULERICE LYONS

sculpture outside Arthur D. Feiro Marine Laboratory

SHOPPING AND SERVICES

Port Angeles's downtown shopping district is centered on First St., where shops, restaurants, galleries, and movie theaters can keep your wallet out all day. **Inside Stuff,** 301 W. First, carries out-of-the-ordinary, innovative home and bath accessories. Across the parking lot from the Red Lion and just off the waterfront, **Harbor Towne** at 222 N. Lincoln is a small shopping mall with clothing shops, a candy store, and assorted boutiques. Wine lovers won't want to miss **Carriage House Wines,** located in a tiny old white house just off the waterfront at 219 N. Oak. They have a good selection of imported and domestic wines, a winetasting area, and home wine-making and brewing supplies. Open Mon. through Sat. till 5:30 p.m.; call 452-WINE for their extended summer hours.

INFORMATION AND SERVICES

The area code on the Olympic Peninsula is 206. For maps, brochures, and further information on Port Angeles contact the chamber of commerce, 121 E. Railroad Ave., tel. 452-2363. Olympic National Park Headquarters at 600 Park Ave. can give you hiking, camping, and other park info, but first read "Olympic National Park," p. 208.

Campers and backpackers will appreciate **Peabody Street Coin Laundry** after getting back to nature in Olympic National Park; open seven days a week, 24 hours a day, at 212 S. Peabody.

For medical emergencies, contact **Olympic Memorial Hospital,** 939 Caroline St., tel. 457-8513.

TRANSPORTATION

By Air

Horizon Airlines, tel. (800) 547-9308, provides daily commuter service to Victoria, B.C., and Seattle's Sea-Tac Airport from Fairchild International Airport on the city's west side.

*stained-glass art displayed
at the chamber of commerce*

and marina, while the "Panorama Tour" takes you to the Olympic National Park Visitor's Center with views of the Strait of Juan de Fuca, Vancouver Island, San Juan Islands, and the Olympics. Tours leave hourly in the summer, less often in the off-season, from the chamber of commerce office on Railroad Ave. at the waterfront. Fares are $2 adults, kids under 12 free when accompanied by an adult. For more information call the chamber of commerce at 452-2363 or Clallam Transit, (800) 858-3747.

Arriving By Ferry
The Port Townsend, Kingston, Winslow, and Bremerton **Washington State Ferries** deposit you at various points on the west side of Puget Sound for $5.55 one way car and driver ($6.65 in summer), $3.30 roundtrip passenger, or $2.30 one way bicycle rider; from each of these destinations you can connect, after varying amounts of driving, with Hwy. 101 to Port Angeles. From Seattle, the most direct route is via the Kingston ferry, over the Hood Canal Bridge, and onto Hwy. 104, connecting to Hwy. 101 near Discovery Bay. For specific info on departure times or fares call the ferry system at (800) 542-0810, or (800) 542-7052 toll-free statewide.

Ferry To Victoria
For a side trip, the MV *Coho* leaves Port Angeles for Victoria, B.C., four times daily in summer, twice daily in winter. One-way fares for the 1½-hour crossing are $24 car and driver, $6 passengers, $3 kids, and $2.75 for bicycles. This route across the turbulent strait has been known to make landlubbers severely seasick; stop by **Jim's Pharmacy,** 221 S. Peabody St., for *free* seasick pills before you go. For specific departure times contact the ferry terminal at the foot of Laurel St. in Port Angeles, tel. 457-4491, or **Black Ball Transport,** 106 Surrey Bldg., Bellevue, WA 98004, tel. 622-2222.

Getting Around By Bus
Clallam Transit, tel. 452-4511, provides hourly service throughout Port Angeles, east to Diamond Point and as far west as Forks, Neah Bay, and Clallam Bay, including Olympic National Park's Sol Duc Hot Springs and Lake Crescent. Connect with **Jefferson Transit** in Sequim for Port Townsend, Port Ludlow, Quilcene, and other Jefferson County points.

Trolley Tours
Clallam Transit operates two 50-minute trolley tours: the "Waterfront Tour" shows you Ediz Hook, the port, paper and wood mills,

WEST OF PORT ANGELES

JOYCE

Joyce is the easternmost in a series of small towns on the Strait that cater primarily to commercial and recreational fishermen. Accommodations and restaurants here and in neighboring fishing towns are no-frills enterprises.

Museum

Housed in a former railroad station on Hwy. 112, the **Joyce Museum,** tel. 928-3568, has relics from the town's early days plus logging and railroad equipment, photos, and driftwood carvings. Open afternoons Tues. through Sunday.

Accommodations

Five miles west of Joyce, **Harrison Beach,** tel. 928-3006, has furnished cabins and trailers for $22-45 d (no bedding supplied in the trailers). Right next door, **Lyre River Park,** tel. 928-3436, has 60 hookup sites for $11-12 and 15 non-hookup campsites for $10-11 on the Strait and Lyre River. Other facilities include hot showers, laundry, dump station, and boat ramp. **Whiskey Creek Beach,** three miles west of Joyce, tel. 928-3489, has primitive (no electricity, pit toilets) camping on the beach for $5; trailers are available for $13-15 a night. Cabins are available on a monthly or yearly basis only.

CLALLAM BAY

Once a commercial logging center, today Sekiu (pronounced SEE-kew) and Clallam Bay, like the other Strait towns, depend on fishermen for their livelihoods.

Parks

The Clallam County Parks Department has two parks in the Clallam Bay area: **Clallam Bay Spit** is a 33-acre waterfront park for day use only; **Pillar Point Fishing Camp,** just east of Clallam Bay, is a four-acre park with 35 campsites (small fee) and boat launch, open for camping from mid-May through mid-September.

Resorts

Curley's Resort, tel. 963-2281, has lodging in motel units for $28-55 or cabins for $20-26; trailer space, with full hookups, is also available at $8 a night. More importantly in these parts, Curley rents 14- and 16-foot fiberglass boats for $16 bare, $45 with motor and a tank of gas.

Herb's Motel and Charters, tel. 963-2346, has 12 motel rooms from $24-52. Their six-person charter boat runs from March through Sept.; a six-hour trip costs $55 pp with all gear included.

NEAH BAY

At the end of Hwy. 112, 72 miles from Port Angeles, Neah Bay sits on the Makah Indian Reservation in virtual isolation, at the northwesternmost point of the continental United States. Fishing is the big business here as well, with charter boats, commercial fishermen, and vacationing anglers competing for the resident salmon and bottom fish.

In 1970 tidal erosion unearthed old Ozette Indian homes that had been preserved in a mudslide some 500 years earlier. After 11 years of digging by Washington State University archaeologists the excavation site was closed, and the thousands of artifacts thus uncovered are now on display in the **Makah Cultural and Research Center** in Neah Bay. The museum is open 10 a.m.- 5 p.m. daily in summer, Wed. through Sun. the rest of the year, for a $3 admission; tel. 645-2711.

Makah Days is the town's big annual festival, celebrating its citizenship grant. Held in late August, dances, a parade, fireworks show, salmon bake, canoe races, and Indian gambling highlight this three-day event.

*Charley Swan dressed to impress
for Neah Bay's Makah Days*

Motels
Makah Motel is right in Neah Bay and has 11 units from $45; tel. 645-2366.

Charter Information
For information on fishing charters out of Neah Bay, call **Big Salmon Fishing Resort,** tel. 645-2375, or **Far West Fishing Resort,** tel. 645-2270.

FORKS

The westernmost incorporated city in the Lower 48, Forks is the economic center and logging capital of the western Olympic Peninsula—a big handle for this town of 3,000 with one main drag. Since the spotted-owl controversy began, logging in this area has been severely curtailed and Forks has been in something of a depression as loggers search for alternate means of earning a living. For travelers, the town's big selling point is its proximity to the west side of Olympic National Park and Pacific coast beaches.

Sights
Forks proudly displays the world's largest western red cedar—19 feet wide, 170 feet tall, and still growing in a cleared field. To see the tree go east on Nolan Creek Rd., about six miles south of the Hoh River Bridge on Hwy. 101. Stay on Nolan Creek Rd. for about 1¼ miles, then go right for 1½ miles on forest road N-1100. Turn right for one-half mile, then take another right for another half mile—it's hard to miss.

The **Forks Timber Museum,** tel. 374-9666, has historical logging and Indian cultural exhibits, including a steam donkey, a logging camp bunkhouse, and various pioneer implements.

Parks And Recreation
Six miles south of Forks on Hwy. 101, **Bogachiel** (Indian for "Muddy Waters) **State Park** encompasses almost 200 acres on the usually clear Bogachiel River. Enjoy the short nature trail through a rainforest, or swim, paddle, or fish in the river—famous for its summer and winter steelhead, salmon, and trout. The park has 41 standard ($7) campsites; no hookups, but RVs up to 35 feet long will fit.

Operating near Forks out of the virtually uncharted town of Beaver, **West Side Guide Service,** tel. 327-3671, runs year-round steelhead and salmon charters on Olympic Peninsula rivers. All tackle and bait is furnished as part of the $100 for one, $170 for two price tag.

Accommodations
The **River Run Lodge,** west of Forks on the La Push road, is an all-inclusive resort with four rooms with twin beds, three meals, transport to the airfield or bus stop, and several other amenities. From $115 per person per day, tel. 374-6295.

Miller Tree Inn, just east of Forks's only stoplight, tel. 374-6806, has six rooms (two with private half-baths, one with full bath) in a comfortable three-story homestead on three acres. Rates are $30-35 s, $40-60 d, including a full breakfast. Kids over six welcome; smoking limited to one bedroom and kitchen area, or outdoors. The **Forks Motel,** four blocks south of town on Hwy. 101, tel. 374-6243, has a heated pool and 58 rooms from $38 s, $38-47 d, plus eight rooms with kitchens for an additional $6.

In **La Push,** which is on the Quileute Indian Reservation, two places have been opened for fishermen and tourists. **Ocean Park Resort,** on the beach, has 43 units, including cabins, townhouses, and a motel. Rates range from $59-92 d.; tel. (800) 487-1267. **Shoreline Resort** has 14 cabins with kitchens ranging from $42-79. Also has RV spaces for $13; tel. 374-6488.

Food

In Forks get the best Chinese food for miles at **South North Gardens,** Sol Duc Way. For pizza, lasagne, spaghetti, and deli sandwiches try **Pacific Pizza** at Forks Ave. and C Street. Open daily; call 374-2626 for takeout. **Clark's Vagabond,** 142 Forks Ave. N, is open daily for all meals (24 hours on Fri. and Sat.) offering steaks, seafood, and dancing in the lounge. A mile north of Forks at the La Push road junction on Hwy. 101, the **Smokehouse Restaurant,** tel. 374-6258, is open daily for lunch and dinner with a full menu specializing in seafood.

DIANNE BOULERICE LYONS

THE PACIFIC COAST

The northern half of Washington's coastline—from the state's northwest corner at Neah Bay to the Quinault Indian Reservation—is a picture of how the Pacific coast looks in brochures and calendar photos: pristine beaches, pounding waves, trees sculpted by relentless sea breezes. This area looks natural because it's protected: the Quinault beaches are off-limits to the public; farther north, most of the coastline is part of Olympic National Park (see p. 208) and thereby protected.

Investors haven't even done a good job of commercializing these areas. Ocean Shores, at the south end of what's referred to as "North Beach," was developed as a summer resort area in the '60s and '70s. Perhaps because of its newness, it still lacks the beach-resort atmosphere that you'd find on the East Coast, Florida, or California. The failure of these Pacific coast towns to develop may be due in part to overcast, damp, windy weather; western Washington is not the best place to go for a tan, and thanks to the California current, summer temperatures are cooler than one would expect at this latitude.

OCEAN SHORES TO TAHOLAH

Quinault Indian Reservation beaches, from just south of Queets almost to Moclips, have been closed to the public since 1969 in an effort to forestall further destruction of the natural landscape. However, you can arrange for an escorted tour of Point Grenville or Cape Elizabeth, two good birding spots, by calling 276-8211, ext. 323. As you drive north from Ocean Shores toward Moclips, you'll notice that the beaches look better and better all the time. The area from Moclips to Pt. Brown, "North Beach," includes the hub of summer activity, Ocean Shores.

Built on a 6,000-acre, six-mile-long peninsula, Ocean Shores was Indian clam-digging grounds until May 7, 1792, when Robert Gray's ship *Columbia Rediviva* found the harbor entrance. Gray's discovery led to a slow settlement of the area, started in 1860 by the peninsula's original homesteader, Matthew McGee, and followed shortly thereafter by A.O. Damon, who bought the southern tip of the peninsula from McGee. It wasn't until 1970 that Ocean Shores became an incorporated city, after investors bought the 6,000 acres from Damon's grandchildren and started selling lots. The development still has lots of empty lots and there's lots of beachfront property available.

Farther north, Copalis Beach and Ocean City are "Home of the Razor Clam." The State Department of Fisheries sponsors clam-digging clinics throughout the summer at Ocean City State Park and neighborhood schools to better prepare you for the short, intense razor clam season; phone 249-4628.

Parks And Beaches
To get to any of the central or southern Washington beaches, just follow the green or brown "Beach" signs pointing seaward from the beachfront highway, in this case Hwy. 109. The advantages of state parks are rest rooms, camping facilities (usually), and sometimes no vehicle access to the beach—a plus or a minus depending on your perspective.

Starting from the south—a logical point since Ocean Shores is the center of North Beach civilization—Ocean City State Park, two miles north of Ocean Shores on Hwy. 115, has 178 campsites (29 with hookup) near Ocean Shores' restaurants and shops. No beach access for vehicles here; however, there are numerous access points in Ocean Shores; from the end of Chance à la Mer, you can drive onto the beach or rent a horse. With all that ocean out there, it's easy to overlook Ocean Shores' six-mile-long **Duck Lake,** but it's a haven for small boats, fishermen, and waterskiers. You can launch your boat from City Park, at Albatross and Chance à la Mer, or Chinook Park Boat Launch on Duck Lake Drive.

Just west of Copalis Beach, **Griffiths-Priday State Park** is a day-use facility for picnicking, kite flying, beachcombing, and bird-watching at the mouth of the Copalis River. The Copalis Spit is one of three snowy plover

breeding grounds on the Washington coast; in 1985, only 15 pairs nested in the state. These birds are very sensitive to human intrusion. To protect them, large areas of the beach north of the park entrance are closed to the public, from the high-tide mark to the dunes, from mid-March to late August. The restricted areas are marked on the map at the park entrance.

Pacific Beach State Park in Pacific Beach offers surf fishing, clamming, and beachcombing with 138 beachfront campsites (20 with hookups).

Accommodations
Ocean Shores has several motels to choose from, but the best are booked up in advance—phone ahead. Starting with the least expensive, the **Oceanside Motel,** Ocean Shores Blvd., has a pool, sauna, and rooms

from $20-36; tel. (800) 562-6373 or 289-3323. The **Sands Resort,** Ocean Shores Blvd., tel. 289-2444, has 80 rooms starting at $38-42, up to $42-45 for kitchenettes, plus a game room, heated pool, hot tub, and sauna. At the **Discovery Inn,** five miles south of town on Point Brown Ave., tel. 289-3371, prices start at $42 d for a motel-type room, $50 for a studio, and $55-60 for a one-bedroom fireplace suite; facilities include a pool, hot tub, and playground. In the same price range, **The Polynesian,** 291 Ocean Shores Blvd., tel. 289-3361, starts at $49 for a motel unit, $66 d for a studio with view balcony, up to $89-109 for one- and two-bedroom suites (lower in winter); amenities include an indoor pool, lounge, and restaurant serving seafood, steaks, and Polynesian cuisine. On the beach at Ocean Shores, **The Canterbury Inn,** tel. 289-3317 or (800) 562-6678, has luxury accommodations with an indoor pool, hot tub, and private balconies, and suites with full kitchen and fireplace. Summer rates (April through Sept.) are $70-102; winter rates are $56-82. **The Grey Gull,** tel. 289-3381 or (800) 562-9712, has efficiencies ($75 and up d), one- and two-bedroom suites ($100-150 d), and penthouses ($200 d), all facing the ocean with kitchens, fireplaces, heated outdoor pool, and sauna. Winter rates (Oct. through March) are $13-40 less. If all else fails, call **Ocean Shores Reservations Bureau,** tel. (800) 562-8612 or 289-2430, or **Ocean Front Beach Rentals and Reservations,** tel. (800) 544-8887, for information and reservations.

Just north of Ocean Shores at Ocean City, the **West Winds Resort Motel** has budget accommodations from $28-32 d. Open all year; tel. 289-3448. Also in Ocean City, **Pacific Sands Resort Motel,** tel. 289-3588, has rooms with no kitchen from $35 d, with kitchen $40-45 d.

Three miles north of Copalis Beach on Hwy. 109, **Iron Springs Resort,** tel. 276-4230, is open all year with fireplace cottages ($40-68 d) and studio apartments ($34-42 d) nestled among spruce trees on a low bluff overlooking the ocean. Facilities include a heated indoor pool, gift shop, and playground,

though kids generally prefer to splash in the shallow creek running out to sea.

Open year-round, the **Sandpiper Beach Resort,** tel. 276-4580, 1½ miles south of Pacific Beach on Hwy. 109, has studio apartments from $42 d and suites from $59 d up to $132 for three bedrooms, right on the beach; most rooms feature fireplaces and full kitchens. A kite shop at the office guarantees cloudy-day fun.

Ocean Crest Resort, on Hwy. 109 at Sunset Beach in Moclips, tel. 276-4465, has economy rooms with no view; studios with fireplaces, ocean-view balconies, and refrigerators; and one- and two-bedroom apartments for $49-110 d. Facilities include a recreation center with indoor pool, sauna, hot tub, exercise equipment, tanning bed, and children's play area, plus a restaurant (see below) and ocean-view lounge. On the ocean three miles north of Moclips on Hwy. 109, **Hi Tide Resort Condominiums,** tel. 276-4142, has 24 one- or two-bedroom suites with kitchens for $44-64 s or d, some with view balconies, most with fireplaces; larger two-bedroom housekeeping units are $84-94 s or d.

Camping And RV Parks

Campers can park their tents or RVs for $8 at one of the state parks (above), or these commercial RV parks: **Tidelands,** $12 a night, on the beach at Copalis Beach, tel. 289-8963; **Surf and Sand RV Park,** $14, also at Copalis Beach, tel. 289-2707; **Blue Pacific Motel and Trailer Park,** $10, Ocean City, tel. 289-2262; **Marina View RV Park,** $9, at the Ocean Shores marina, tel. 289-3391.

Food

Most of the notable food on this stretch of beach is in Ocean Shores. At Ocean Shores Blvd. and Chance a La Mer, **Ocean Shores Inn** serves three meals daily and Sunday brunch overlooking the beach, with live weekend entertainment and dancing in the lounge; tel. 289-2407. The **Misfit Restaurant** at the municipal golf course is open for lunch and dinner with prime rib, steak, and seafood; tel. 289-3376. **The Home Port**

Restaurant, just past the city entrance on Pt. Brown Ave., tel. 289-2600, serves three meals; specialties include salmon, Dungeness crab, steak and lobster dinners ($8-16), and fish and burger lunches ($4-7). For Chinese food, try **Look's Village Chinese Restaurant,** Pt. Brown Ave., tel. 289-2152; open for lunch and dinner daily (closed Mon. in winter).

For ocean-view quality dining at the north end, try **Ocean Crest** at the resort in Moclips, tel. 276-4465. Open for three meals, the varied dinner menu features Northwest specialties such as Willapa Bay oysters, trout, quail, steak, and seafood for $9-18, with entertainment weekends in the lounge.

Mopeds
Scoot around town on a moped rented from **O.W.W. Inc.** on Chance à la Mer, tel. 289-3830. Mopeds and bicycles can also be rented at the Shores Mall in Ocean Shores (see below).

Fishing
Although Westport is usually thought of as Washington's fishing capital, **Ocean Shores Marina** has a few charter boats offering fishing, whale- and birdwatching, and sightseeing cruises; phone tel. (800) 562-7720 for reservations and information. Or, take the summer passenger ferry from Ocean Shores to Westport and depart from there. **Olympic Adventures,** headquartered in Copalis Beach, offers steelhead, salmon, and trout fishing excursions in the Copalis River; tel. (800) 824-0936.

Golf
At Canal and Albatross in Ocean Shores, the 18-hole **Ocean Shores Golf Course** is open to the public, with restaurant, lounge, and complete pro shop; tel. 289-3357.

Events
Ocean Shores hosts an annual **Beachcombers Fun Fair** at the Convention Center in March. See displays of glass floats and driftwood art, or listen to speakers on marine topics. **"Undiscovery Day"** or the "Hey George Festival" is an annual April 27 event, commemorating the fact that Capt. George Vancouver *didn't* discover Ocean Shores on his 1792 exploration; patrons of local taverns run to the beach at midnight and shout "Hey, George!" April brings the **Kite Flying Festival** to Griffiths-Priday State Park in Copalis Beach; another kite-flying and **Sandsculpture Contest** is also held here in July. A kite festival is part of Ocean Shores' annual **Festival of Colors,** held each May; another kite-flying contest is held here each October. Ocean City sponsors the area's Fourth of July fireworks and picnic.

Shopping
Ocean Shores' **Shores Mall** has bike and moped rentals, kite shop, bank, clothing store, and state liquor store on Chance à la Mer, just before the beach. In Homeport Plaza on Pt. Brown Ave., Ocean Shores' **Gallery Marjuli,** tel. 289-2858, is open daily with art and gifts created by Northwest artists. **Tide Creations Gift Shop,** near the marina on Pt. Brown Ave., has thousands of items, from kites and windsocks to fudge; tel. 289-2550. On Hwy. 109 in Copalis Beach, **The Jail House Gift Shop** is housed in a jail built in 1937, and sells Washington arts and crafts plus kites and toys.

Services And Information
With an information center at Hogan's Corner on Hwy. 109, the **Ocean Shores-Olympic Coast Chamber of Commerce,** tel. 289-4552, can provide maps and current festival and tour information. Across the street from Shores Mall on Chance à la Mer in Ocean Shores, the **Ocean Shores Convention and Information Center,** tel. 289-2451, has brochures, local menus, and other information, as does the **Ocean Shores Chamber of Commerce** on Pt. Brown Ave., just inside the entry archway.

For medical emergencies, 911 territory extends as far as the 289 exchange. Near Pacific Beach and Moclips, 911 won't work; phone 276-8375 for emergencies. In less dire situations, the **North Beach Health Care Clinic,** Hwy. 109 in Copalis Beach, has

LOUISE FOOTE

To celebrate the state's centennial in 1989, a full-scale replica of Robert Gray's *Lady Washington* was constructed to serve as the central part of Aberdeen's new **Grays Harbor Historical Seaport;** a replica of Gray's *Columbia Rediviva* may be added in the future. The **Lady Washington** has been sailing to various seaports along Washington's coastline since.

Mansions And Museums

In 1897, lumber baron Robert Lytle built **Hoquiam's Castle,** a 20-room Victorian beauty at 515 Chenault Ave. in Hoquiam. The mansion has been restored to its original luster, completely furnished in antiques, Tiffany lamps, and cut-crystal chandeliers, and is open for tours daily in summer, weekends in winter, closed in Dec.; $3 adults, $2 kids, tel. 533-2005. Another wealthy lumber magnate, Alex Polson, owned the 26-room mansion at 1611 Riverside Ave. in Hoquiam. **Polson Museum,** tel. 533-5862, housed in the mansion, is filled with Grays Harbor history and logging exhibits, and is surrounded by a small park with rose gardens and exotic trees. Open Wed. through Sun. in summer, weekends in winter; donation.

In the National Guard Armory at 111 E. Third, the **Aberdeen Museum of History,** tel. 533-1976, has exhibits of local history including a turn-of-the-century kitchen and bedroom, pioneer church, photographs, antique fire trucks, canoe collection, and a continuous slide show; open Wed. through Sun. in summer, weekends in winter. Donation.

Wildlife Refuge

Due west of Hoquiam off Hwy.109, **Grays Harbor Wildlife Refuge,** tel. 533-5228, is a 500-acre wetland in the northeast corner of Grays Harbor Estuary that attracts up to half a million migrating shorebirds in spring and fall. The two dozen shorebird species that visit the basin include the western sandpiper, dunlin, short- and long-billed dowitcher, and red knot; other birds seen here are the peregrine falcon, northern harrier, and red-tailed hawk. The best viewing time is one hour before and one hour after high

doctors on call 24 hours a day, plus a dentist; tel. 289-2427.

Transportation

To drive to the coast from Seattle, take I-5 south to Olympia, then follow the "Ocean Beach" signs to Hwy. 101, then join Hwy. 8, which merges into Hwy. 12 at Elma. Despite the highway number changes, it's a straight shot. At Hoquiam, take Hwy. 109 north. For Ocean Shores, turn left at Hogan's Corner onto Hwy. 115; for all other North Beach cities, follow Hwy. 109. Ocean Shores is about 130 miles from Seattle, 102 from Tacoma.

Grays Harbor Transportation Authority route 50 serves North Beach from Ocean Shores to Taholah from Aberdeen and Hoquiam; Route 51 is the local Ocean Shores service. Fares are $.25 adults, kids under five free; (800) 562-9730 or 532-2770.

ABERDEEN/HOQUIAM

Aberdeen and Hoquiam are twin cities on the easterly tip of Grays Harbor; Aberdeen is the larger of the two, with a population of 18,700 doubling that of Hoquiam. Heading west from Olympia, you'll notice acres and acres of clearcut; this is the most heavily logged area of the state—some of these hills have been clearcut three times.

ABERDEEN AND HOQUIAM AREA

© MOON PUBLICATIONS, INC.

tide. The arrival of the spring shorebirds in mid-April is cause for the annual **Festival of Shorebirds,** featuring slide programs and displays by state and local wildlife organizations, usually held in one of the city's shopping malls.

Parks
At E. Ninth and N. I streets, Aberdeen's **Samuel Benn Park** has rose and rhododendron gardens, tennis courts, playground, and picnic facilities. **Lake Aberdeen** at the east entrance to town has swimming and nonmotorized boating plus play equipment.

East of Aberdeen, about a mile north of Montesano off Hwy. 12, **Lake Sylvia State Park** has swimming, trout fishing, boat launch and rentals on a small lake, plus 35 wooded campsites. Follow the signs for 10 miles north of Elma to **Schafer State Park** on the Satsop River. Formerly a park for Schafer Logging Company employees, today it has 47 public campsites (six with hookups), riverside picnic areas, and a fine collection of mossy trees. Weyerhaeuser's **Swinging Bridge Park** is also about 10 miles from Elma in the middle of nowhere, forking left off the road to Schafer; here you'll find free camping with a five-day limit, free firewood, and secluded picnic and play areas.

Accommodations
Lytle House, 509 Chenault in Hoquiam, tel. 533-2320, is a Victorian B&B next door to Hoquiam's Castle with four nonsmoking guest rooms (expanding to seven in summer 1990) with shared bath for $40 s, $50 d, including full breakfast buffet. More than just a B&B, the antiques, collectibles, and furniture here are for sale, as are small gifts of lace, flowers, and potpourri. No indoor smoking; call regarding kids under 10.

The M Street House, 82 M St., tel. 532-4262, has two guest rooms with private entrance in a 1912 home. Breakfast is served in your room or the dining room. Rates are reasonable: $35 s, $40 d.

Also in Hoquiam, the **Westwood Lodge,** 910 Simpson Ave., tel. 532-8161 or (800) 562-0994, has 65 motel rooms starting at $36-42 s, $43-55 d, with some kitchens and two-bedroom suites.

The **Nordic Inn Motel,** next to the South Shore Mall at 1700 S. Boone in Aberdeen, tel. 533-0100, has 66 rooms from $30 s, $34-44 d, attached restaurant, coffee shop, and lounge with live entertainment six nights a week. The **Red Lion Motel,** 521 W. Wishkah just off Hwy. 101 in Aberdeen, is a little nicer; rooms here are $45 s, $55 d; tel. 532-5210 or (800) 547-8010. The **Olympic Inn,** 616 W. Heron in Aberdeen, tel. 533-4200, has some kitchens, laundry facilities, and rooms starting at $38 s, $48 d.

Just south of Aberdeen, **Cooney Mansion B&B,** 802 E. Fifth in Cosmopolis, tel. 533-0602, was built by lumber baron Neil Cooney at the turn of the century, and sits adjacent to woods and a golf course on a dead-end street. Five of the nine guest rooms have private bath; rates are $55 d, including use of the whirlpool, sauna, and common fireplace.

Food
At 112 N. G St. in Aberdeen, **Bridge's,** tel. 532-6563, has prime rib, steak, and seafood dinners, including razor clams, from $7-18; lunch runs about $4-9. The atmosphere is elegant but not stuffy, with a wide selection of nonalcohol drinks in addition to a full bar; open for lunch and dinner daily plus Sunday brunch. **Billy's,** a restored saloon at 322 E. Heron, also serves delicious steaks, seafood, and sandwiches; with that gold and bright green paint job you can't miss it. At 116 W. Heron in Aberdeen, **Misty's,** tel. 533-0956, has a good assortment of Washington wines and micro-brewery beers, plus American-menu lunches and dinners; kids are welcome. Aberdeen's **Nordic Inn,** at the motel of the same name at 1700 S. Boone St., serves moderately priced steak and seafood; open for three meals. **Duffy's** is the local family restaurant, featuring a varied, inexpensive-to-moderate menu and great pies. There are three Duffy's in an incredibly small area: 1605 Simpson Ave. and 1212 E. Wishkah St. in Aberdeen, and 825 Simpson Ave. in Hoquiam. Also in Hoquiam, the **Levee Street Restaurant,** 709 Levee St., tel. 532-1959,

serves fine sautés, fettucine, and steaks with a European flair and a river view.

Festival
Hoquiam's **Loggers Playday,** held the second weekend in September, is an opportunity for sedentary executives to see what real work is all about. After kicking off the event with a parade, loggers compete in ax-throwing, log-chopping, tree-climbing, and more. Thelma is Elma's **Slug Festival** mascot, welcoming thousands to the annual event in August. Elma is also home to the Grays Harbor Fairgrounds, where you can take in horse racing in July, the county fair in August, and horse shows and auto races year-round.

Shopping
In Aberdeen, follow Hwy.105 over the bridge and around the corner to **Safeway,** at Boone and Scott, and the **South Shore Mall,** featuring Sears, JCPenney, K mart, and four cinemas. The smaller **Wishkah Mall,** on Hwy.12 at the east end of Aberdeen, has 30 stores including Ernst, Pay 'N' Save, and Lamonts.

Services And Information
The **Grays Harbor Chamber of Commerce,** tel. 532-1924, is open weekdays at 2704 Sumner Ave. in Aberdeen. For emergencies, dial 911 or head for **St. Joseph's Hospital,** 1006 N. H St. (near Samuel Benn Park), for 24-hour service; tel. 533-0450 or (800) 634-0030.

Transportation
Aberdeen and Hoquiam are well served by **Grays Harbor Transportation Authority,** tel. 532-2770 or (800) 562-9730. Route 20 is the local service, running from W. Hoquiam to Aberdeen and Cosmopolis. You can take bus 40 east to Olympia, 60 to Quinault Lake, 55 to Westport, 50 to North Beach, and 51 to Ocean Shores. The **Grays Harbor Passenger Ferry** operates daily from Memorial Day through Labor Day, with weekend service in September, connecting Aberdeen and Hoquiam with Westport; tel. 268-0047.

BEACH DRIVING

Most of Washington's Pacific shoreline south of the Quinault Indian Reservation is open to vehicular traffic. This fact causes considerable debate among the residents, many of whom feel it's unnatural to have to look both ways before going for a swim, or don't want to have their kids flattened by RVs. In any case, it's legal, so here are a few rules, regulations, and driving tips.

The shoreline is considered a state highway; therefore, only registered vehicles driven by licensed drivers are allowed.

Pedestrians have the right of way; cars and horses must yield.

Drive only on the higher hard sand, not in the water, on the clam beds, or in the dunes, and observe the 25 mph speed limit.

If you get stuck, put boards or other hard, flat material under your tires and pull out slowly.

WESTPORT TO NORTH COVE

This section of coastline is known as "The Cranberry Coast"; the bogs east of Hwy.105 near Grayland produce much of the state's berries, which come from plants imported from Cape Cod in the early 1930s. Westport, the principal Cranberry Coast city, calls itself "The Salmon Capital of the World," and it does seem that there's nothing to do there but fish: charter boat services line the waterfront, where locations are marked not by street address but by proximity to numbered floats. You'll be hard pressed to find a luxurious hotel room here; the bare-bones, bed-and-shower motels cater to sportsmen who are out to sea by five a.m.

Parks And Viewpoints
Open for day use only, **Westhaven State Park,** on Hwy. 105 just north of Westport, is popular with rockhounds, beachcombers, and divers; look for agates and Japanese glass floats. The jetty was built here to in-

crease the velocity of the seagoing water, collected from six rivers flowing into Grays Harbor. Prior to the construction of the jetty, deposits of sediment mandated annual channel dredging. The jetty worked—the channel hasn't required dredging since 1942. **Westport Light State Park,** about a mile south of Westhaven off Hwy. 105 (continue straight when 105 goes left), is another day-use park good for kite flying, rockhounding, and fishing for ocean perch. The lighthouse here was built in 1898. There's vehicular beach access here, but the sand is considerably softer than at other driveable beaches; be careful if you don't have 4WD. **Westport Observation Tower and Ramp,** on opposite ends of Revetment Dr. north of Westport Marina (head for the neon Islander Restaurant sign), are good places to view freighter activity, scenery, sunsets, or an occasional whale.

On Hwy.105, two miles south of Westport, **Twin Harbors State Park** has over 17,000 shoreline feet in its 317 acres; facilities include 332 campsites (49 with full hookup), a three-quarter-mile sand dune nature trail, picnic areas, and playground. Between Grayland and North Cove on Hwy. 105, **Grayland Beach State Park** has 4,000 feet of ocean frontage, a self-guided nature trail through huckleberry, sitka spruce, and lodgepole pine, and 200 acres for picnicking and camping with 60 full-hookup sites. Other beach access points are marked with "Beach" signs on Hwy.105.

Historical Sights
A historical bus tour departs Sat. afternoons in summer from the Westport Observation Tower; adults $2, kids $1.50. Phone the chamber of commerce, tel. 268-9422, for specifics.

At 2201 Westhaven Dr. in Westport, the **Historical Maritime Museum** is housed in a former Coast Guard station and includes photographs of the early Aberdeen-Westport plank road, cranberry and logging industry exhibits, Coast Guard memorabilia, and the Whale House, with whale, sea lion, and porpoise skeletons. Open weekends in spring, Wed. through Sun. afternoons in summer,

and by appointment in fall and winter; tel. 268-9692.

Aquarium
The **Westport Aquarium,** 321 Harbor St., tel. 268-0471, is open daily from April through Dec. with large display tanks holding octopus, sharks, bottom fish, and anemones, plus performing seals and a gift shop.

WESTPORT AND LONG BEACH PENINSULA

© MOON PUBLICATIONS, INC.

Accommodations

Bed-and-breakfast establishments aren't as common on the newly commercialized coast as in other, older parts of the state. **Glenacres Inn,** built around 1898 on nine acres at 222 N. Montesano, tel. 268-9391, is one of few. This B&B has five beautifully decorated inn rooms, all with private bath ($55-65), three motel-like rooms with TVs and private bath ($45-50), and four cottages that can sleep up to 14 people. Continental breakfast and use of the outdoor hot tub included for inn guests only.

Most Cranberry Coast accommodations are in motel form, closer to Motel 6 than the Sheraton. Expect a heavy summer surcharge after Memorial Day. **Chateau Westport Motel,** 710 Hancock, tel. 268-9101, offers the only luxury accommodations in Westport, with 110 rooms (some with kitchens or view balconies) from $55 s or d to $125 for a three-bedroom suite, with indoor heated pool, hot tub, and free continental breakfast; winter rates are half off. For less expensive, fisherman-style lodging in the $20 range try the **Frank L. Motel,** 725 S. Montesano St., tel. 268-9200, one of many low-priced motels lining Montesano. The **Albatross Motel,** 200 E. Dock St., is a short walk to the floats, with rooms for $35-45 d (some with kitchens); tel. 268-9233. **The Islander,** Westhaven and Revetment, tel. 268-9166, combines a budget motel, RV park, restaurant, lounge, and charter service; rates start at $37 s, $46-47 d in winter, up to $60 s, $63-67 d in summer. South of Westport, **Ocean Gate Resort** in Grayland has cabins ($27-37 d) and RV spaces ($10) on the ocean; tel. 267-1956. Other than that, there's virtually nothing but houses between Westport and Tokeland (see below).

Food

At the corner of Westhaven and Cove, tiny **Arthur's,** tel. 268-9292, is *the* quality restaurant in town, open for lunch and dinner daily with seafood, prime rib, and burgers. **Dee's Restaurant,** 203 S. Montesano St., tel. 268-9737, is open for three meals and popular with locals; grab a box lunch here for your fishing trip, or have just-caught seafood for dinner. **The Islander** is across the street from Arthur's, with an overpriced dinner menu ($10-15) considering the so-so cooking; to keep it cheap, order from the Java Shop sandwich menu and stay late for the musical entertainment.

Festivals

The third weekend in March, Grayland-area artists display their driftwood and shell creations at the town's **Driftwood Show.** Westport's **Blessing of the Fleet,** held annually in May, includes a memorial service for people lost at sea and demonstrations of Coast Guard sea-air rescues. The **Cranberry Blossom Festival,** held annually in June, celebrates the blooming of the tiny pink flowers with festivities including the crowning of "The King of the Bog." Held in early June, the two-day **Westport Kite Meet** has contests for the youngest and oldest kite flyers, best crash event, longest train of kites, and more, sponsored by Pic a Patch Kites, tel. 268-0877. Westport's two-week-long **Saltwater Festival** starts with a late-June parade and ends with July Fourth fireworks, interspersed with kite-flying contests, treasure hunt, bicycle race, and more.

Fishing And Whalewatching

You don't have to charter a boat to go fishing; the whole stretch from Westport to North Cove is popular for surf fishing. The jetty near Westhaven State Park (see above) is a good spot for catching salmon, rockfish, ling cod, surf perch, and crabs. Clam-digging is seasonal and requires a license. The 1,000-foot-long **Westport Fishing Pier,** off the end of Float 20 at the Westport Marina, is another landlubber fishing option.

Offshore rocks and reefs are feeding grounds for salmon, bottom fish, even halibut; take a charter boat to find the best spots, not to mention having your fish cleaned and ready to cook by the time you get back to shore. The charter services all charge about the same amount, so when you call for reservations be sure to check whether the price includes bait and tackle, cleaning, sales tax, etc., to see if

FLORENCE BOULERICE

*Charter boats
operate year-round.*

your "bargain" is really a good deal. All of the following charters depart from Westport.

Westport Charters schedules trips for salmon, bottom fish, or albacore tuna from April through Oct., plus winter Puget Sound and Strait of Juan de Fuca salmon and bottom fish charters from Neah Bay, Sequim, Everett, and Seattle, aboard a fleet of 40- to 50-foot charter boats. Their office is across the street from Dock 8; tel. (800) 562-0157 or 268-9120. **Neptune/Rainbow Charters,** tel. (800) 562-0165 or 268-0124, also has charters for salmon, tuna, sea bass, and bottom fish, in addition to spring and fall gray whale-watching trips. **Deep Sea Charters,** across from Float 6, tel. (800) 562-0151, has salmon fishing June through Sept., bottom fishing March through Oct., and whalewatching excursions from March through May. Other Westport outfits offering similar services are **Cachalot Charters,** across from Float 12, tel. 268-0323; **Sea Horse Charters,** across from Float 5, tel. 268-9100 or (800) 562-0171; **Bran Lee Charters,** Westhaven Dr., tel. 268-9177 or (800) 562-0163; and **Salmon Charters, Inc.,** tel. 268-9150 or (800) 562-0145.

Shopping
Across from Westport's Float 12, **Cachalot Kites** has kites of every description, plus windsocks and toys, as does **Pic a Patch,** almost next door, reputedly the best kite shop on the coast. For one-day film processing, prescriptions, seasickness pills, and camping supplies, stop by **Twin Harbor Drug,** 421 N. Montesano in Westport; tel. 268-0505. There's very little else here for the shopper. Poor fishing in previous years led to an economic depression in town, with the numbers of shops and charter services dwindling; changes in fishing seasons and limits have made vast improvements in both fishing and the tourist trade, so you should see growth in tourist shops and services here before long.

Services And Information
At 1200 N. Montesano St. in Westport, the **Westport-Grayland Chamber of Commerce,** tel. 268-9422, is open daily in summer, weekdays in winter, and has maps, brochures, and festival and tour information.

Transportation
The **Westport-Hoquiam Passenger Ferry** operates in summer only, providing service to Hoquiam and Ocean Shores with three trips each way daily; tel. (800) 562-9730. **Grays Harbor Transit** Route 55 serves Westport, Grayland, Aberdeen, and Hoquiam for $.25 adult, kids under five free; tel. (800) 562-9730 or 532-2770. If you're driving to Westport, take Hwys. 101, 8, and 12 west from Olympia; then head southwest on Hwy. 105 to Westport. The trip takes about two hours from Tacoma, 2½ hours from Seattle.

SHELTON AND THE LOWER HOOD CANAL

Mason County, of which Shelton is the county seat, is one of the nation's largest Christmas tree-producing areas; every year, over three million trees are shipped worldwide. Originally named Sheltonville, the town was founded in 1855 by David Shelton, although its plat wasn't officially recorded until 1884. Forestry, farming, fishing, and oystering were and still are the primary industries here, beginning in 1878 when the first shipment of oysters left Kamilche. Shelton, a blue-collar town of about 7,600, is the only incorporated city in the county. Lake Cushman is a popular fishing and summer recreation spot, just east of the Staircase entrance to Olympic National Park (p. 208), and the dam at the lake's southeast end produces a part of Tacoma's electricity. Hoodsport's winery and Union's waterfront resort attract some visitors, but for the most part the lower Hood Canal area is undeveloped.

SIGHTS

Parks

Eight miles west of Belfair on Hwy.106, **Twanoh State Park** is a popular spot for swimming and waterskiing on Hood Canal. The park also has tennis courts, a concession stand for snacks and groceries, and camping at 30 standard ($7) and nine hookup ($9.50) sites.

Enjoy diving, clamming, crabbing, and fishing in Hood Canal at **Potlatch State Park,** 12 miles north of Shelton on Hwy. 101. Have a picnic on the water, or explore the underwater park; camp across the street at 17 standard ($7) and 18 full-hookup ($9.50) sites.

You'll need a boat to get to two other Shelton-area state parks: **Squaxin Island State Park,** between Shelton and Hartstene Island, has 20 primitive campsites ($3 plus a boat moorage fee from $4-6); **Stretch Point State Park,** 12 miles north of Shelton, has no camping, showers, toilets, or drinking water, but has one of the best sandy beaches around Puget Sound.

Lake Cushman was a popular resort area at the turn of the century, offering fishing, hiking, and hunting. By the 1920s, the two lakeside resorts had shut down and the city of Tacoma had planned a dam on the Skokomish River. When completed, the dam increased the lake's size tenfold to 4,000 acres. Though private summer homes are springing up around the lake, the area still has a decidedly remote feel, thanks in part to its protected neighbor, Olympic National Park, about 10 miles up the road. **Lake Cushman State Park,** seven miles west of Hoodsport, is a popular spot with fishermen: cutthroat, kokanee, and rainbow trout inhabit the lake, the home of the only known entirely freshwater king salmon run. Hikers will enjoy the four miles of hiking trails at the park, leading from lake's edge to deep woods; swimming, waterskiing, and, in winter, cross-country skiing, are also popular. Camp at one of 50 standard ($7) campsites or 30 hookup ($9.50) sites.

A mile south of Brinnon on Hwy. 101, **Dosewallips State Park** covers 425 acres at the foot of the Olympic Mountains, offering both fresh- and saltwater activities at the confluence of Hood Canal and the Dosewallips River. Enjoy fishing for salmon and bottom fish in the canal, steelhead in the river, or clamming, crabbing, and oystering on the shores of the canal; there's a public boat launch six miles north of the park at Whitney Point. Stay at one of 113 campsites, 40 with full hookup, for $7-9.50 per night. Two miles south of Brinnon, **Pleasant Harbor State Park** has a dock adjacent to a private marina; no camping, boat launch, or swimming facilities.

Hiking Trails And Scenic Drives

Stop at the **Hood Canal Ranger Station** on Lake Cushman Dr. in Hoodsport for a map of trails and forest roads in the Olympic National Forest ($1), and current campground and hiking trail information.

The most popular viewpoint along the canal is 2,804-foot **Mt. Walker,** about five miles south of Quilcene and five miles west of Hwy. 101. Two viewpoints along the route provide panoramic views of Seattle, Mt. Rainier, and the Cascades to the east, and the majestic Olympics to the northwest. Bring a lunch to enjoy at the summit picnic area; in early summer, you'll be met by blooming rhodies.

Webb Lookout is another popular high spot, although it offers no Olympic views, just a broad shot of the canal. Take Hwy. 101 to Hamma Hamma River Rd. #249, two miles north of Eldon. Turn right on a logging road at about 2½ miles and follow the signs. Park along the road and hike the half-mile trail to the lookout.

Follow Lake Cushman Rd. to a "T" at road's end; go left and follow the lake's edge to 70-foot **Cushman Falls,** near the lake's northwest end, about 11 miles from Hoodsport. Or, turn right at the "T," then turn left in another 1½ miles onto Big Creek Rd. #2419 for six miles to **Big Creek Viewpoint** for a sweeping view to the east. Continue on for another mile for a waterfall off Mt. Washington. The **Mt. Ellinor Trail** leaves Rd. #2419 at the five-mile point; the trail heads up one mile for a view of Lake Cushman.

Winery

Stop in at **Hoodsport Winery,** N. 23501 Hwy. 101 in Hoodsport, tel. 877-9894, for a sip of wine produced from Puget Sound fruits and berries, such as their loganberry, rhubarb, and raspberry wines, or their gewürztraminer, riesling, merlot, or chardonnay, produced from eastern Washington grapes. Open daily 10 a.m.-6 p.m.

Tollie And Caboose 700

Tollie, the locomotive in downtown Shelton between Second and Third on Railroad Ave., is a 90-ton shay engine that saw most of the

Hood Canal

ARCHIE SATTERFIELD

country in its heyday; today the caboose houses the Shelton-Mason County Chamber of Commerce. Tollie and Caboose 700 were placed on the National Register of Historic Places in 1984.

ACCOMMODATIONS

Motels

At Shelton's north exit, the **Super 8 Motel,** 6 Northview Circle, tel. 426-1654 or (800) 843-1991, has budget rooms from $34 s, $37-40 d. Downtown, the **Hallmark Motel,** N. Seventh and W. Railroad, tel. 426-4468 or (800) 345-5676, has a heated pool and rooms from $33 s, $38 d.

Resort

On Hwy. 106 in Union, the **Alderbrook Inn Resort** is a full-service resort with 83 motel

TO
PORT
TOWNSEND

WEBB
LOOKOUT

LENA
CREEK

OLYMPIC
NATIONAL
FOREST

HAMMA
HAMMA

HOOD CANAL

101

ELDON

MT.
WASHINGTON
(6,250 ft.)

MT
ELLINOR
(5,940 ft.)

BIG CREEK
VIEWPOINT

STAIRCASE
R.S.

CUSHMAN
FALLS

LAKE
CUSHMAN

LAKE
CUSHMAN
S.P.

THE LOWER
HOOD CANAL

LILLIWAUP

TO
BREMERTON

BELFAIR

N. MASON
CHAMBER OF
COMMERCE

LAKE
CUSHMAN
GOLF
COURSE

HOOD
CANAL
R.S.

HOOD CANAL

106

HOODSPORT

ALLYN

BELLAGAMBA
RESTAURANT

POTLATCH

POTLATCH
S.P.

ALDERBROOK
INN
RESORT

TWANOH
S.P.

MINERVA
BEACH
R.V. PARK

UNION

MASON
LAKE

GRAPEVIEW

STRETCH
POINT
S.P.

SKOKOMISH RIVER

PICKERING PASSAGE

LAKE
LIMERICK

3

101

HARTSTENE
ISLAND

MASON GEN.
HOSPITAL

MASON CO.
FAIRGROUNDS

SHELTON

SQUAXIN I.
INDIAN
RESERVATION

0   5 mi

0   5 km

TO
OLYMPIA

SQUAXIN
ISLAND
S.P.

© MOON PUBLICATIONS, INC.

rooms, 21 cottages, restaurant, lounge, heated indoor pool, jacuzzi, saunas, 18-hole golf course, tennis courts, and moorage on the Hood Canal. Rooms start at $66-79 s, $72-85 d (higher rates are for water views); suites are $130 and cottages are $110-175 for up to four adults. For reservations phone 898-2200 or, toll-free from Seattle, (800) 622-9370.

Bed And Breakfast

Stay close to the Alderbrook for a fraction of the price at **Highland House,** E. 31 Hyland Dr. in Union, tel. 898-4862. Enjoy the resort's golf, tennis, and other facilities while you stay at this cozy B&B for $24-36 d in winter, $30-45 d in summer, including continental breakfast; the highest-priced master bedroom has a private bath.

Campgrounds And RV Parks

Glen-Ayr RV Park, N. 25381 Hwy. 101 in Hoodsport, tel. 877-9522, has RV parking and motel rooms on a rocky Hood Canal beach, good for clamming and oyster gathering. Open year-round, rates for RV parking are $14 d including hookups; motel units are $40-50 per night. Pets are not allowed in the motel; RVers must keep their dogs on a leash. About 3½ miles south of Hoodsport

DIANNE BOULERICE LYONS

Tollie and Caboose 700

on Hwy. 101, **Minerva Beach RV Park,** tel. 877-5145, is open all year with sites from $11 per night across the highway from the Hood Canal.

Real campers may prefer to stay at the free or very inexpensive national forest campgrounds, though these are usually closed during the off-season. **Collins,** eight miles west of Brinnon, has free camping at nine tent and five trailer sites; on Hamma Hamma Rd., stay at **Hamma Hamma,** seven miles in, or **Lena Creek,** nine miles in, for $3. None of the national forest campgrounds charge more than $8, and most are in the $3-6 range; get a complete list, including location, fees, and numbers and types of sites, from the ranger station in Hoodsport.

FOOD

Shelton's **Capital Restaurant,** 102 W. Railroad, tel. 426-1101, serves three meals daily, specializing in low-priced steak and seafood; the food is much better than the atmosphere. For Chinese food plus lunch and dinner buffet, try **Dragon Palace,** near McDonald's at 2503 Olympic Hwy. N; tel. 426-7975 for orders to go. Enjoy Mexican lunches and dinners Tues. through Sat. at **Hacienda,** 1927 Olympic Hwy. N, tel. 426-7070. On Lakeland Dr. at the Lakeland Golf and Country Club in Allyn, **Bellagamba,** tel. 275-2871, serves moderately priced steak, seafood, veal, and pasta for lunch and dinner Tues. through Sunday. The restaurant at the **Alderbrook Inn Resort** in Union, tel. 898-2200, serves three meals daily from a varied menu that includes steak, seafood, chicken, and veal dishes. Lunch runs $4-9, dinner $8-20.

ENTERTAINMENT

Festivals

Early June's **Mason County Forest Festival** in Shelton began as an effort to prevent forest fires; today the event includes a Paul Bunyan parade, an appearance by Smokey Bear, a carnival, musical entertainment, an arts-and-crafts show, and logging competition.

The **Mason County Fair** is held annually the last weekend in July at the fairgrounds, one-half mile north of downtown Shelton off Hwy. 101. Highlights of the fair include the Olympic Peninsula Draft Horse Show, live entertainment, and traditional county fair favorites such as 4-H exhibits and cake and preserve competitions.

The **West Coast Oyster Shucking Championship and Seafood Festival,** a.k.a. "Oyster Fest," is held annually in early Oct. at the Mason County Fairgrounds. The fair's main event, high-speed oyster shucking, lasts about two minutes; the national record, set here in 1984, is held by Diz Schimke, who shucked 24 oysters in 2:41.31 minutes. Surrounding the competition are two days of winetasting, a cook-off, art and boating exhibits, dancers, bands, and magicians. Admission is $2 adults, $1 kids.

The holiday season brings Santa to Shelton during the annual **Christmas Parade and Bazaar,** held the first weekend in December. Santa lights the Christmas tree, then visits the kids at the 100-booth bazaar; the parade is set for Sat. at 5 p.m.

Golf

Golfers can enjoy the summer sunshine at the 18-hole courses at the **Alderbrook Inn,** tel. 898-2200, or the **Lake Cushman Golf Course,** four miles west of Hoodsport on Lake Cushman Rd., tel. 877-5505.

GETTING THERE

By Car

Shelton is about 50 miles from Tacoma via I-5 and Hwy. 101; continue north on Hwy. 101 to downtown Hoodsport, then turn left to Lake Cushman and Olympic National Park's east side. An alternate route from Seattle would be to take the ferry to Bremerton (see "Bremerton," p. 185), then head south on Hwy. 3.

By Boat

For a scenic alternative to driving, take the *Spirit of Alderbrook* from Seattle's Pier 56 for a day-long excursion through Hood Canal with a stop at the Alderbrook for lunch; fares are $30 adults, $20 kids. Phone 623-1445 or see "Seattle," p. 70, for more details.

SERVICES AND INFORMATION

The Shelton and Hood Canal area code is 206. For maps or festival information, contact the **Shelton-Mason County Chamber of Commerce** (located in the caboose on Railroad Ave. between Second and Third streets), Box 666, Shelton, WA 98584, tel. 426-2021, or the **North Mason Chamber of Commerce,** Theler Center, Box 416, Belfair, WA 98528, tel. 275-4898.

For ambulance, police, or fire emergencies, dial 911. **Mason General Hospital,** 2100 Sherwood Lane in Shelton, tel. 426-1611, has 24-hour emergency-room service.

BOB RACE

SOUTHWESTERN WASHINGTON

CENTRALIA/CHEHALIS

At first glance, Centralia and Chehalis seem like overgrown rest areas on the long stretch of highway between Seattle and Portland. Although these working-class towns aren't known as vacation destinations, they share a rich and colorful history, some of the best antique and factory-outlet shopping around, and are one of the biggest baseball centers in western Washington. Centralia's population of nearly 12,000 makes it about twice as big as Chehalis, the county seat.

HISTORY

Centralia is the only city in Washington founded by a black man. George Washington was the slave of James C. Cochran, a Missourian who, in 1850, filed a claim on the land where Centralia now sits. Washington, set free and adopted by Cochran, later bought the land for $6000. He platted a town, sold lots, built a home, and donated a parcel of land for the development of George Washington Park. Within 15 years, Washington had sold 2,000 lots and named the thriving town "Centerville." During the 1893 depression, Washington hauled supplies up from Portland for his neighbors, offered interest-free loans, found work for Centerville's residents, and saved the town from economic disaster. Though a respected businessman, not everyone liked him, or his color: someone tried to kill him by putting carbolic acid in his wine. But Washington lived to be 88, when he died from being thrown out of a buggy.

Centralia is best known for what is often referred to as the "Centralia Case." The early

1900s brought a long, hard-fought labor struggle to the Pacific Northwest. Dominated by a Chicago union, the Industrial Workers of the World were called "Wobblies" after a Chinese member reputedly tried to pronounce I.W.W. and came up with "Eye-Wobbly-Wobbly." The radical Wobblies wanted to unite the workers of the world into one great union, take possession of production machinery, and abolish the wage structure. Though they tried to relieve the horrible working conditions of the times, the Wobblies allegedly resorted to violent means and spread out into political affairs. They strongly urged members not to enlist when the U.S. declared war on Germany in WW I. Their stance drew fire from the *L.A. Times* and others, who stated that I.W.W. stands for "I won't work" and "I want whiskey." In Sept., 1918, 100 Wobbly leaders were convicted of obstructing the war effort, and the Wobblies were finished as a major labor force.

Wesley Everest was a Wobbly leader who died a hero's death. In 1919, lumbermen decided to rid Centralia of Wobblies, and warned the organization through ads in the local paper. On Armistice Day, 1919, Everest was sitting in the I.W.W. Hall, on Tower Ave. between Second and Third streets, when members of the American Legion marched through the streets, armed; Legion members claim it was part of the Armistice Day Parade. Someone fired a shot; each side said the other fired first. The Legion stormed the building, Everest shot into the crowd, and was chased into the woods by the mob. He waded up to the waist in the turbulent Skookumchuck River and surrendered. The crowd came after him, dragged him back to town tied to a car's bumper, and put him in jail. After dark, they came back for him, and castrated, hanged, and shot him at the Chehalis River bridge. Only Wobblies were tried for the massacre that left four Legionnaires dead; no one was tried for Everest's lynching. Three witnesses who claimed the Legionnaires stormed the hall were arrested for perjury. The case was not discussed by the community for decades, and nobody would give interviews about it. But as the 75th anniversary of the event neared, the few remaining people who were alive then have begun talking about it more freely.

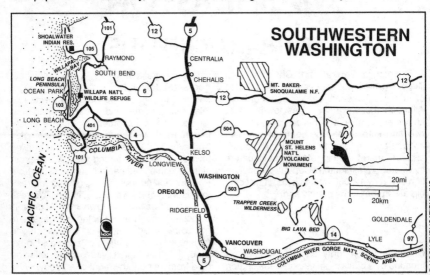

SIGHTS

Historic Sights And Museums

Take exit 81 off I-5, then follow Mellen St. west for one-quarter mile to the bridge where Wesley Everest was hanged on Nov. 11, 1919.

Mrs. George Washington named Iron, Maple, Pearl, Silver, and First streets, on which you can now find elegant turn-of-the-century homes, though often not restored to their earlier splendor.

The **Magyar Museum,** 2228 Harrison Ave., tel. 736-4178, is open daily from April through Oct. with displays of Indian artifacts, woodcarvings, antiques, dolls, and ivory.

Murals

Fourteen murals decorate the outside walls of downtown Centralia's buildings, modeled after historic photographs. The murals depict Buffalo Bill Cody, Centralia's founder George Washington, railways, ferries and sternwheelers, and buildings and scenes from Centralia's past. Get a map and guide to the murals from the chamber of commerce.

Power Plant Tour

Lewis County is the largest producer of electric power in the state, thanks to **Pacific Power and Light Co.,** a coal-fired plant 12 miles north of town. Phone 736-9901 to reserve a spot in their two-hour guided tour, given Tues. and Thurs.; kids under 12 must be accompanied by an adult.

ACCOMMODATIONS

Bed And Breakfast

The 6,500-square-foot home built in 1903 for lumber baron J.P. Gurrier is now Centralia's only B&B, the **Candalite Mansion,** 402 N. Rock, tel. 736-4749. Six guest rooms with full breakfast run from $50-100 d; lower rates have double beds and shared bath, higher rates are for larger rooms with king-sized bed and private bath. Enjoy the ping-pong and pool tables or just cozy up by the fireplace. No smoking or pets. Well-behaved kids OK only by arrangement; not a good place for rambunctious toddlers (breakables and handmade rugs!).

Motels

Just off I-5 at 1310 Belmont, **Motel 6,** tel. 330-2057, is always the cheapest: rooms here are $21 s, $27 d, including a pool. **Peppertree West Motor Inn and RV Park,** 1208 Alder just off exit 81, tel. 736-9362, also has budget rates ($20-22 s, $22-26 d) plus RV parking and a pool; pets are welcome. Across from Fort Borst Park, the **Park Motel** at Belmont and Harrison, tel. 736-9333, has 31 rooms for $22-24 s, $25-29 d. Another bargain is the **Lake Shore Motel,** 1325 Lake Shore Dr., tel. 736-9344, with 34 rooms for $25-27 s, $29-31 d, on Plummer Lake. The **Hallmark Motel,** 702 Harrison Ave., tel. 736-2875 or (800) 345-5676, has a heated pool and 93 rooms starting at $31 s, $35-39 d. The **Ferryman's Inn,** just off I-5 at 1103 Eckerson Rd., tel. 330-2094, charges $34 s, $36-40 d, and has a pool and spa; pets OK for a fee.

FOOD

Centralia caters to the tight-budget diner; expensive restaurants are scarce. At 1054 Harrison Ave., the **Country Cousin** serves three meals daily at inexpensive prices, specializing in chicken and steak; tel. 736-2200. At 202 W. Locust next to Centralia Square, the **Antique Mall Cafe** is among the best, serving steak, seafood, pasta, and chicken from $7-13, plus Sunday brunch for $9; open daily for lunch and dinner, tel. 736-1183. **Casey's Pizza Mill** has pizza, lasagne, and a salad bar at two locations: in Centralia at 1326 Harrison, tel. 736-1156, and in Chehalis at 1340 N.W. Maryland, tel. 748-7111. For Mexican food, try **Casa Ramos,** just off I-5 at 929 Harrison, tel. 330-2045; open seven days for

CENTRALIA

TO SEATTLE

TO CENTRALIA STEAM ELECTRIC PLANT

ZENKNER VALLEY RD.

DOWNING RD.

SHAFFER PARK

PEARL ST.

MAGYAR MUSEUM

HARRISON AVE.

SCHEUBER RD.

REYNOLDS AVE.

SKOOKUMCHUCK RIVER

MARION

1

3

5

2

14

4

EXIT 82

BORST AVE.

RIVERSIDE PARK

6 ST.

4 ST.

3 ST.

2 ST.

1 ST.

GOLD ST.

6

7

M ST.

FORT BORST PARK

Borst Lake

OAKLAND AVE.

BRYDEN AVE.

RHODODENDRON GARDEN & ARBORETUM

BORST HOME

CHEHALIS RIVER

PLUMMER LAKE

MAPLE ST.

LOCUST ST.

WALNUT ST.

PEAR ST.

WASHINGTON AVE.

MAIN ST.

PEARL ST.

TOWER AVE.

AMTRAK DEPOT

CENTRALIA ELKS GOLF COURSE

13

12

10

11

GOLD ST.

BERRY

SEMINARY HILL

COOKS HILL RD.

CENTRALIA HOSPITAL

EXIT 81

MELLEN ST.

ALDER ST.

SEMINARY HILL RD.

8

9

LONG RD.

AIRPORT RD.

SOUTH ST.

KRESKY AVE.

FLORAL

GOLD ST.

RACETRACK

GRAND AVE.

TO VANCOUVER

SW WASHINGTON FAIRGROUNDS

0   0.5 mi

0   0.5 km

MOON

CENTRALIA

1. Casey's Pizza Mill
2. Country Cousin Restaurant
3. Motel 6
4. Park Motel
5. Ferryman's Inn
6. Casa Ramos Restaurant
7. Hallmark Motel
8. Lake Shore Motel
9. Peppertree West Motor Inn
10. Centralia College
11. Centralia Square
    and Antique Mall Cafe
12. Washington Park and Library
13. Candalite Mansion
14. factory outlets

lunch and dinner. For more dining, see "Chehalis" below.

ENTERTAINMENT

Fairs
Late July's **Pioneer Days** brings a street fair, arts and crafts, sidewalk sales, and music to downtown Centralia; tel. 736-0300. Since 1909, the **Southwest Washington Fair** has been one of the largest summer festivals in the state, attracting crowds of over 125,000 annually on the third weekend in August to the fairgrounds at the south end of town on Gold Street.

PARKS AND RECREATION

George Washington Park, downtown between Pearl and Silver streets, was donated by the city's founder and houses a library and playground.
  At **Fort Borst Park,** a mile west of town off Harrison Ave., visit the 1852 Borst Blockhouse, which was a strong defense against Indian attacks, originally built at the confluence of the Chehalis and Skookumchuck rivers. The house that Joseph Borst, an early

Centralia settler, built for his young bride Mary in 1860 still stands here; Borst boasted that the house was so well built it would last for 80 years! Tours of the home are given Mon. through Fri. by appointment only, tel. 736-7687. The park is open daily, and also offers an arboretum, rhododendron garden, playground, and trout fishing for kids under 14.
  Although Centralia has a number of noteworthy parks, they can be difficult to find, tucked behind shopping centers and motels. **Riverside Park,** on the Skookumchuck River, has a large grassy play and picnic area, hidden behind the Hallmark Motel on Harrison Avenue.

Golf
Three golf courses serve the area: **Centralia Elks,** 1012 Duffy, tel. 736-5312, has nine

Rainbow Falls State Park

DIANNE BOULERICE LYONS

holes; **Newaukum Valley,** 3024 Jackson Hwy. in Chehalis, tel. 748-0461, and **Riverside Golf Course,** near Centralia's airport at 1451 N.W. Airport Rd., tel. 748-8182, are 18-hole courses.

SHOPPING

Centralia's newest designation is Factory Outlet Capital of the Northwest. Just off I-5, over 40 factory-owned and -operated stores include London Fog, Gitano, Corning Glass, and Hanes. Downtown's **Centralia Square Antique Mall,** 201 S. Pearl, tel. 736-6406, is an antique collector's paradise, with 50 dealers displaying estate jewelry, furniture, and other collectibles; open daily till 5 p.m.

SERVICES AND INFORMATION

The area code in and around Centralia is 206. The **Twin Cities Chamber of Commerce,** I-5 and National Ave., Chehalis, tel. 748-8885, or toll-free statewide, (800) 525-3323, has information on both Centralia and Chehalis and all of the surrounding area.

For police and fire emergencies, dial 911. For medical emergencies, **Centralia General Hospital,** 1820 Cooks Hill Rd., tel. 736-2803, has 24-hour emergency service.

TRANSPORTATION

Steam Railroad
Take a ride on the **Centralia/Chehalis Steam Railroad,** either between Centralia and Chehalis or out to a railroad junction called "Ruth" in the Boistfort Valley. The railroad expects to operate on weekends, May through Sept.; phone the chamber of commerce for details.

By Car
Centralia is halfway between Seattle and Portland (about 85 miles each way), with Chehalis about five miles farther south. Driving south from Seattle, you'll know you're near Chehalis when you see the Hamilton Farms billboard, proclaiming a political message on both sides that is usually of the angry conservative persuasion.

By Train
Amtrak, tel. 736-8653 or (800) 872-7245, serves Centralia from Union Depot, located (appropriately enough) on Railroad Avenue.

By Bus
Centralia's bus service is provided by **Greyhound,** 2604 N.E. Kresky Rd., tel. 736-9811. **Twin Transit,** tel. 330-2072, has service connecting Centralia and Chehalis hourly.

LONGVIEW/KELSO

Alhough Longview's first settlers paddled up the Columbia River in 1849, it wasn't until the 1920s that the city experienced its first growth spurt. Engineers from the Long-Bell Lumber Company sought a new supply for timber as their resources were running out in Texas and Louisiana. Southwest Washington had an abundant supply of old-growth timber and, from a logging viewpoint, Longview's location—on a major river and rail lines—was ideal.

Lumber baron R.A. Long founded the city in 1923, and Longview became the first planned city in the Pacific Northwest, designed with ample room for future development and an eye toward the aesthetic. Today, Longview has a population of about 35,000. In addition to its thriving lumber business, Longview and its close neighbor, Kelso, comprise one of southwestern Washington's largest retail shopping centers.

Kelso (pop. 11,000) is much older than Longview. It got its start in the 1840s when the Hudson's Bay Co. used Cowlitz and Columbia river ports to export beef from the Kelso wharves. Settlement began in 1847, with Peter Crawford's donated land claim on the Cowlitz River giving rise to the town of Crawford, renamed Kelso in 1884 after the founder's Scottish birthplace. Kelso was incorporated in 1889, became county seat in 1923, and has since been an important logging, milling, and fishing town, called "The Smelt Capital of the World" in honor of the abundant winter run of these fish up the Cowlitz River. The first Cowlitz County cannery was built in 1886, and the smelt is still a dominant force in Kelso's economy as tons of fish are shipped annually to the Orient.

PARKS AND RECREATION

Longview's early planning is made evident by **Lake Sacajawea Park,** a 120-acre greenbelt that bisects the city along Nichols Boulevard with a string of serene lakes surrounded by grassy hillsides, shady trees, and a jogging path.

The **Civic Center** is a grassy green in the city's core, at the intersection of Olympia and Washington ways. Surrounding the green are many of the city's oldest buildings, including the **Public Library,** finished in 1926 and now on the National Register of Historic Places, and the **Monticello Hotel,** built in 1923 and still the town's most elegant building.

A small park at 18th, Maple, and Olympia avenues in Longview marks the **Monticello Convention Site,** where Washington residents met to petition the government to separate Washington Territory from Oregon.

Golf

The area's two major public golf courses are **Mint Valley,** 4002 Pennsylvania in Longview, tel. 577-3395, and Kelso's **Three Rivers,** 2222 S. River Rd., tel. 423-4653. Both are 18-hole courses with covered driving ranges, restaurants, and equipment sales and rentals.

SIGHTS

The Nutty Narrows

Just up Olympia Way from the Civic Center, the Nutty Narrows is the world's only skybridge for squirrels. Builder and developer Amos J. Peters built it in 1963 to save the critters as they attempted to cross the busy street. Peters is honored for his effort with a many-times-greater-than-life-size squirrel sculpture between the library and skybridge.

Mt. St. Helens Informsation

The **Kelso Volcano Tourist Information Center,** one-half mile east of town on Minor Rd. (next to the Kelso Chamber of Commerce), is a small-time exhibit for those who may have missed the *real* St. Helens visitor center up near Castle Rock. This one has a

Lake Sacajawea Park

DIANNE BOULERICE LYONS

15-foot model of the volcano and Toutle River valley, plus photos and exhibits of the 1980 eruption. Open daily; adults $.50, kids free, tel. 577-8058. For more information on the national monument, see p. 322.

Museum

Visit the **Cowlitz County Historical Museum,** 405 Allen St. in Kelso, to see Chinook and Cowlitz Indian artifacts, relics from the Oregon Trail, war items, dolls, and changing exhibits. Open Tues. through Sat. until 5 p.m.; tel. 577-3119.

Tour

The **Reynolds Metal Company,** 4029 Industrial Way, tel. 425-2800, offers a free tour of its aluminum-reduction plant every Thurs. at 1 p.m. for kids over 12.

ACCOMMODATIONS

Motels And Hotels

Quality lodging in Longview is scarce. The **Monticello Hotel,** 17th and Larch in Longview, tel. 425-9900, is a stately building flanked by gardens across from the Civic Center green. The hotel is mostly offices and apartments, but rooms in the adjacent motel are inexpensive—$31 s, $35 d, with two fireplace rooms for $39 d—with an ele-

gant restaurant (see below). **Town Chalet,** 1822 Washington Way, Longview, tel. 423-2020, has budget rooms for $65-30 s, $30-38 d; many rooms have kitchens. In the same price range, **Lewis and Clark Motor Inn,** 838 15th Ave., tel. 423-6460, has 32 rooms for $30-32 s, $34-38 d, opposite the Medical Center.

Kelso is the better choice for quality accommodations, largely because its location along I-5 has drawn some of the larger chains to the area. The predictable but inexpensive **Motel 6,** 106 Minor Rd., tel. 425-3229, has 64 budget rooms for $26 s, $32 d, plus heated pool. The **Best Western Aladdin,** 310 Long Ave., tel. 425-9660 or (800) 528-1234, has an indoor pool, whirlpool, and guest laundry, plus 79 rooms starting at $34-50 s, $40-53 d. The **Red Lion,** 510 Kelso Dr., tel. 636-4400 or (800) 547-8010, is the best in town, with a heated pool, room and poolside service, restaurant, and dancing in the lounge; rooms start at $65-72 s, $73-80 d.

RV Parking

RV campers can stay at **Oaks Trailer and RV Park,** open year-round at 636 California Way in Longview, tel. 425-2708. Facilities include more than 60 hookups, laundry, kids' play area, and free cable TV for $10.50 a day; monthly rates available. For more camping in the Mt. St. Helens area, see p. 328.

1. St. John's Hospital
2. Town Chalet
3. chamber of commerce
4. Monticello Hotel
5. Civic Center
6. library, Nutty Narrows, and Monticello Convention Site
7. Triangle Cinema and Columbia Theater
8. Casa Azteca
9. Broadway Gallery
10. Monticello Medical Center
11. fairgrounds
12. Best Western Aladdin
13. Cowlitz County Historical Museum
14. Peter's Gay' 90s Restaurant
15. Three Rivers Mall
16. Red Lion
17. Motel 6
18. Lewis & Clark Motor Inn

FOOD

Henri's, 4545 Ocean Beach Hwy. in Longview, tel. 425-7970, is a popular spot for business lunches or an evening out, specializing in moderately priced steak and seafood dinners and an impressive wine collection; open weekdays for lunch, Mon. through Sat. for dinner. The dining room at the **Monticello Hotel,** 17th and Larch in Longview, tel. 425-9900, serves primarily steak and seafood in an elegant 1920s decor; open for lunch and dinner (dinners run $7-14). **Hillman's Restaurant,** 1125 Commerce Ave. in Longview, tel. 423-7040, also serves moderately priced seafood and steak for lunch and dinner daily, with dancing nightly in the lounge. For Chinese food, try **The Paragon,** 1311 15th Ave. in Longview, tel. 423-7830; closed Mondays.

Enjoy Mexican lunches and dinners at **Casa Azteca,** 1124 Washington Way, Longview. Over in Kelso, **Peter's Gay '90s Restaurant,** 310 S. Pacific, tel. 423-9620, specializes in steaks in an 1890s atmosphere highlighted by a solid marble bar, antique lamps, and stained glass.

ENTERTAINMENT

Festivals
After the annual winter smelt run comes to a close, Kelso hosts a season finale in the form of a comical **Smelt Eating Contest** the first Sunday in March. The Independence Day **Go-4th Celebration** is one of the largest in the country. Held at the fairgrounds in Longview in late July or early August, the **Cowlitz County Fair** has exhibits and entertainment; tel. 577-3121. The **Kelso Highlander Festival,** held in August each year, features a parade, Scottish bagpipe music, truck pull, and more.

Symphony And Movies
The **Columbia Theater,** 1231 Vandercook Way, tel. 423-1011, another legacy from the prosperous 1920s, hosts local theater and dance groups as well as national acts. For now, the **Southwest Washington Symphony** gives a handful of performances there from Nov. through May; tel. 425-5346 or 425-5887.

The **Triangle Cinema,** 1228 Washington Way, tel. 425-5448, has four screens showing first-run films.

SHOPPING

Kelso's newest shopping center is the impressive **Three Rivers Mall,** just off I-5 at Longview/Kelso exit 39 with The Bon, JCPenney, Emporium, and scores of smaller specialty shops.

Stop by downtown Longview's **Broadway Gallery,** 1418 Commerce Ave., tel. 577-0544, to see an outstanding collection of southwestern Washington art produced by more than 30 area artists, including jewelry, pottery, watercolors, weaving, baskets,

sculpture, and more. Open Mon. through Sat. till 5:30 p.m., with extended Christmas hours.

SERVICES AND INFORMATION

The Longview/Kelso area code is 206. For more information, contact the **Longview Chamber of Commerce,** near the Civic Center at 1563 Olympia Way, Longview, tel. 423-8400, or the **Kelso Chamber of Commerce,** just east of the I-5 entrance ramp at 105 Minor Rd., Kelso, WA 98626, tel. 577-8058.

For medical, fire, or police emergencies, dial 911. For other medical problems, the **Monticello Medical Center,** Broadway and Seventh in Longview, tel. 636-7253, has a 24-hour physician-staffed emergency room; or try **St. John's Hospital,** 1614 E. Kessler Blvd., Longview, tel. 636-4818 for emergencies, tel. 423-1530 for the switchboard.

TRANSPORTATION

By Car
I-5 passes right over Kelso on its way to Portland; Longview sits just to the west. The cities are about 125 miles, or just over two hours, from Seattle.

By Bus
Community Urban Bus Service (CUBS), 254 Oregon Way, provides local service; phone 577-3399 for schedule information. **Greyhound,** tel. 423-7380, provides cross-country connections from their 1109 Broadway station.

By Train
Take **Amtrak's** *Pioneer, Coast Starlight,* or *Mount Rainier* into Kelso from Seattle, Los Angeles, and other major West Coast cities; tel. (800) 872-7245.

LOWER COLUMBIA

The stretch of river from Bonneville Dam to the ocean is the only part of the river still subject to the ebb and flow of the tides. The tidal force is so strong in the river that tugs pulling log booms upstream must tie up when the current and the tide are flowing in the same direction. The river below the Willamette has a distinct saltwater ambience to it. Seagoing ships steam back and forth in the 40-foot channel, loading and unloading in Portland, Kalama, Longview, and Astoria. Seagulls wheel overhead with their rusty-hinge cries and fishing boats share the waterway with the ships and tugs.

As you drive west along the Columbia on Hwy. 4, or the Ocean Beach Hwy., you will notice that it grows to four miles wide in places and the lower river is marked by a series of islands, many little more than sandbars with a fringe of willows and grass. Most are named but some are not. Only one is inhabited; Puget Island, which is between Cathlamet and the Oregon side. It is connected to the Washington side by a bridge across the narrow channel, and to Oregon by a small ferry.

Puget Island was settled by dairy farmers from Switzerland and fishermen from the Scandinavian countries. Some of the best commercial fishing boats used on the Columbia River were built on Puget Island. Over the years many of the boats were taken to Bristol Bay, Alaska, where they can still be found.

Cathlamet, with a population of about 600, is the largest town between Longview-Kelso and the Pacific Ocean. It was built on the side of a steep hill overlooking Puget Island, and was a favorite haunt of Ulysses S. Grant when he was a lieutenant stationed at Fort Vancouver before the Civil War.

Before WW II this area was one of the most remote in America; many immigrants never bothered to learn English because they had little use for it, and their children born along the Columbia still speak with Scandinavian and Finnish accents.

Accommodations

Cathlamet has two places to stay: **Country Keeper,** 61 Main St., tel. 795-3030, is a former mansion that more recently became a former library in favor of becoming an elaborate inn with five rooms named for the artist whose work decorates them: Chagall, van Gogh, Degas, Renoir, and Monet. Rates are $60-70 d, breakfast included.

Our Place, 305 N. Welcome Slough Rd., Puget Island, tel. 849-4328, is a former fishermen's net shack redecorated and with a full kitchen, bath, wood stove, and bedroom on the main floor beneath a loft with a total of two double beds, one twin, and a cot. For $3 per person, the owners, ElRose and Everett Groves, will have you in for a dinner in their home nearby. Rates are $39 Mon. through Thurs., $49 Fri. through Sun. nights.

Just downstream from Cathlamet is the 4,400-acre Columbian White-tailed Deer National Wildlife Refuge, established in 1972 to protect the few remaining members of this subspecies. You can drive through the refuge on your way downriver and will see the small deer sharing grazing rights with dairy cattle and lots of birds. For information on the refuge, write to P.O. Box 566, Cathlamet, WA 98612, tel. 795-3915.

The western end of the refuge stops at the next town, Skamokawa, which is built partly on the Columbia and partly on Skamokawa Creek. Skamokawa has no lodging and dining is limited to the local tavern, but it is as picturesque as it is small. Its most notable building is the **Redmen Hall** on a steep bluff overlooking the creek and river. Formerly a school, it was taken over by the Redmen, a fraternal organization that has since died out. The hall has been taken over by a local group to preserve it.

A few miles west on Hwy. 4 brings you to Grays River, and a short distance west of the one- or two-store town you will see the only covered bridge in Washington still in use. The Grays River Covered Bridge, on the National Register, was built in 1905 and has been repeatedly shored up.

Two miles west of it is the country store-post office town of Rosburg. Here you can turn south on Hwy. 403 and follow Grays River down to the broad Grays Bay. Out on the open river are the remains of three cannery towns; Cottardi, Altoona, and farther upriver on a dirt road, Pillar Rock. All three were built as canneries and the houses and dormitories were for workers, often Chinese brought in almost as endentured servants.

Back on Hwy. 4 again, you will go through Naselle, the largest town in the area, before swinging back down to the river at Knappton, also a former cannery town, and finally to the Long Beach Peninsula.

LONG BEACH PENINSULA

The Long Beach Peninsula feels a lot like North Beach at first, with the drive-on, littered beaches and waterfront hotels, but on closer inspection you'll see something that's missing from Ocean Shores: character. The town of Long Beach has the only walkable downtown area on the coast, with little shops and the required souvenir joints—like a *real* beach town. At the north end of the peninsula, things are drastically different too, with beautifully restored turn-of-the-century homes in Oysterville, and an isolated natural area at Leadbetter Point.

Parks

At the north end of Long Beach Peninsula on Hwy. 103, **Leadbetter Point State Park** is a protected natural area and wildlife refuge, providing sanctuary for waterfowl, particularly during spring and fall migrations; birdwatchers will enjoy the foot trails through dunes and woods. The ocean side of the point is off-limits from April to Aug. to protect the fragile nests of the snowy plovers, but you'll see thousands of black brants in the marshes during their spring migration from Mexico to Alaska. Getting there can be an adventure; the bumpy road seems endless, but keep your chin up—the gravel part goes for two miles, followed by three-quarters of a mile of hard-packed dirt. There are hiking trailheads at road's end and at end of the gravel section. The mosquitoes are thick out here—bring insect repellent! No fires, camping, or off-road driving allowed.

Fort Canby State Park, 2½ miles west of Ilwaco, is the peninsula's most scenic state park, as well as home to the **Lewis and Clark Interpretive Center,** with photos, au-

thentic journal entries, and multimedia presentations of the explorers' historic trip from Illinois to Cape Disappointment at the southern tip of the Long Beach Peninsula. The cape got its name from British fur trader John Meares, after a number of failed attempts at crossing the Columbia River bar. It's not that Meares wasn't a good sailor: more than 230 ships were wrecked or sunk here before jetties were constructed to control the bar. Several have piled up since the jetties arrived.

You can see the mouth of the Columbia by turning right at the concession area and driving to the road's end; park here and walk through the sand to the lookout atop North Jetty. The Cape Disappointment Lighthouse is the Northwest's oldest, built in 1856; follow the quarter-mile path from the Coast Guard Station or a quarter-mile trail from the Interpretive Center. The North Head Lighthouse was built in 1898 and stands above Dead Man's Hollow, commemorating the sailors of the ill-fated *Vandelia,* which sunk here in 1853; it's a short walk from the upper parking lot or a 2.1-mile hike from the trailhead.

Another hike, the Waikiki Trail, climbs the bluffs for one mile to an old radar station and lookout, affording great ocean views. The beach was named Waikiki in honor of a Hawaiian sailor whose body washed ashore here after a failed attempt to cross the bar in 1811, aboard Capt. Jonathan Thorn's *Tonquin.* Other park activities include camping at 250 sites (60 hookup), surf and jetty fishing, hiking trails, and a concession for snacks and fishing supplies.

Loomis Lake State Park, south of Klipsan Beach, has picnic tables and restrooms on the ocean, not the lake; the real Loomis Lake is

Long Beach

about a quarter mile north, open at 4 a.m. for public fishing. No camping at either facility.

Two miles southwest of Chinook on Hwy. 101, **Fort Columbia State Park** is a national historic site, constructed in 1895 but never engaged in battle; an interpretive center in the enlisted men's barracks features coastal artillery. Hike up Scarborough Hill behind the fort for a view of the Columbia River. Open for day use only.

Museums And History

Oysterville boomed in the late 1800s with the discovery of Willapa Bay oysters; a number of homes constructed during this era have been restored and are included in a self-guided historic walking tour. For a map, stop by the Oysterville Church or phone 665-4575. Take a weekend guided tour through the Tom Crellin House, built in 1869; also tel. 665-4575.

Visit the **Ilwaco Heritage Museum,** just east of Hwy. 101 at 115 S.E. Lake St., tel. 642-3446, for a look into Pacific coast history via models, exhibits, and photographs of early settlers' fishing, oystering, and forestry methods and Cape Disappointment shipwrecks.

Rhododendron Garden

The **Clark Rhododendron Nursery** is a visual treat with over 1,000 varieties of rhodies in bloom in spring and early summer,

6½ miles north of Long Beach on the bay. The nursery is open daily in spring and summer, weekdays fall and winter; tel. 642-2241.

Tours

Nahcotta has several oyster canneries, all kept in business by the abundance of Willapa Bay oysters. Tour the **Nahcotta Shellfish Laboratory** weekdays and hear a tape about oyster biology. The actual oyster beds are closed to the public. About a mile northeast of Long Beach, the **Washington State University Research Center,** Pioneer Rd., studies the private lives of cranberries; take a tour to see the bogs, picking equipment, and slide show. Try to time your visit for June, the peak bloom season, or Oct., to see the harvest; open 9 a.m.-4 p.m., Mon. through Friday.

Accommodations

The highly acclaimed **Shelburne Inn,** Hwy. 103 and 45th St. (Box 250) in Seaview, is an elegant 1896 Victorian hotel and restaurant definitely worth at least a mealtime visit, if you can't swing an overnight stay. The 16 guest rooms are cheerfully furnished in antiques, five have private bath; rates range from $69 for a double with shared bath, $79-140 for a double with private bath, to $135 for a suite with private bath. A full country breakfast is included; for many, it's the highlight of

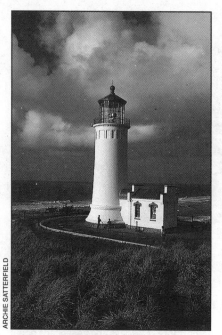

ARCHIE SATTERFIELD

the North Head Lighthouse

their stay. Dinners here are superb as well, with Northwest seafood and game enhanced by in-season vegetables and berries, Northwest wines, and homemade breads, pastries, and desserts. Open in summer for Sunday brunch, and daily for lunch and dinner; closed Wed. in winter, open for lunch Thur. through Saturday. For room reservations, phone 642-2442; for dinner, 642-4142.

A 1926 Presbyterian church was restored by two Seattle couples and converted into **The Inn at Ilwaco,** 120 Williams St. NE, tel. 642-8686. The inn's guest quarters occupy the old Sunday school rooms and the sanctuary is now a playhouse, welcoming concerts and theater as well as receptions, reunions, and other events. Ten guest rooms run $45-70 d; well-behaved children are welcome, but no smoking or pets. **Scandinavian Gardens Inn,** a block west of Hwy. 103 between 16th and 17th (Rt. 1 Box 36), tel.

642-8877, is a quiet hideaway featuring a Scandinavian breakfast buffet, four double rooms and a two-room suite, all with private bath, plus sauna and spa for $75-145 d.

Even the nicest beachfront motels and resorts in Long Beach are reasonably priced. **The Breakers,** a mile north of town on Hwy. 103, tel. 642-4414, is one of the largest, with 106 rooms, heated pool, hot tub, and private balconies starting at $39 d, $44 d with kitchen, and $65 for a one-bedroom suite. **Chautauqua Lodge,** a block west of Hwy. 103 at 304 14th St. NW, tel. 642-4401, has 120 rooms from $28 d (no view) to $40 with an ocean view and $50 with a kitchen, plus an indoor pool, hot tub, sauna. Their **Potlatch Restaurant** serves fine seafood for lunch and dinner, and the bar has weekend dancing. The **Surfside Inn,** three miles north of Ocean Park at 31512 J Pl., tel. 665-5211, has 96 rooms starting at $32 d, an indoor pool, hot tub, restaurant and bar with weekend dancing, view balconies, and golf course. The new **Super 8,** 500 Ocean Beach Blvd., tel. 642-8988, has 51 rooms for $37-40 s, $41-49 d. **Nendel's Inn,** 409 10th St. SW, tel. 642-2311 has similarly priced rooms: $53 s, $53-71 d.

Resort
About midway on the Long Beach Peninsula, **Ocean Park Resort,** 259th Ave. and R St. in Ocean Park, tel. 665-4585, has accommodations to suit everybody, with 12 motel rooms ($36-41 s or d), eight cabins, 140 tent and RV spaces, pool, Jacuzzi, and other extras like clam-digging equipment rentals, kids' play area, and sports courts.

Food
Some of the best food on the peninsula is at the **Shoalwater Restaurant** at the Shelburne Inn (see above). **The Sanctuary Restaurant,** corner of Hazel St. and Hwy. 101 in Chinook, tel. 777-8380, serves fresh local seafood (including Willapa oysters), steaks, veal, and homemade desserts in a converted Methodist/Episcopal church built in 1906. Open for dinner Wed. through Sunday. **The Ark Restaurant,** tel. 665-4133, is another local legend, located in Nahcotta on Willapa

Bay 12 miles north of Long Beach on Sandridge Rd., or just turn right at the Ocean City light. The building is rustic at best but the seafood is famous, especially after publication of *The Ark Cookbook* and attendance at food fairs and festivals. **B.J. Squidley's** in Ocean Park, tel. 665-5261, features fresh seafood and home-baked goods, $12 and less; open for three meals daily.

Shopping

Long Beach is the commercial core of the peninsula, with all the typical beachfront services including bike and moped rentals, candy stores, an amusement park, and the oh-so-tacky **Marsh's Free Museum,** a huge souvenir shop. **Gray Whale Gallery & Gifts,** 105 Pacific Ave., has Northwest art, cards, jewelry, and cranberry products made from the local crop. **Bergkvist Scandia Gifts,** 504 Pacific Ave. S, sells Scandinavian imports, crystal, jewelry, and more. Don't miss **Pastimes,** a collectibles shop and espresso bar at S. Fifth and Pacific Hwy., tel. 642-8303. Clocks, china, and glassware for antique hounds; cappuccino, hot chocolate, iced egg creams, and baked goods for the rest. The **Charles Mulvey Gallery,** a few doors north of the Shelburne, is open weekends with Northwest coast watercolors. In Ocean Park, the **Potrimpos Gallery,** Bay Ave. between Hwy. 103 and Sandridge Rd., tel. 665-5976, features watercolors, sculpture, and photography in a Victorian house.

Festivals

Long Beach hosts the annual Independence Day **Fireworks on the Beach,** as well as the week-long **International Kite Festival** in late August. The annual **Cranberry Festival,** held in Ilwaco in Oct., celebrates more than a century of coastal cranberry farming. Cranberries were originally called "crane berries" by early settlers, who thought the blossoms resembled cranes' heads.

Fishing

Ilwaco is a scaled-down version of Westport, with charter boats leaving daily for deep-sea rockfish, flounder, sole, and ling cod, migrating albacore tuna, and sturgeon and salmon near the mouth of the Columbia. Salmon punch cards are available on the boats themselves or in the charter offices. A few charter services include **Pacific Salmon Charters,** tel. 642-3466, **Ilwaco Charter Service,** tel. 642-3232, and **Coho Charters,** tel. 642-3333.

Services And Information

For information on area festivals, maps, and more, stop by the **Megler Information Center,** tel. 777-8388, a mile east of the Astoria Bridge on Hwy. 401, or the **Long Beach Peninsula Visitors Bureau** at the junction of Hwys. 101 and 103, tel. 642-2400. You can't miss Ilwaco's **Ocean Beach Hospital,** just off the main drag; tel. 642-3181 or 642-2316 for fire or ambulance only. Long Beach is the place to go to do your laundry, buy groceries, get your car washed, or rent a moped; bike rentals are also available in Seaview.

Transportation

Unlike North Beach, the Long Beach Peninsula is served by two parallel main roads: Hwy. 103, going through the commercial centers on the ocean side, and Sandridge Rd., passing the largely residential sections on the bay side. The roads intersect at Oysterville, where only one road continues up to Leadbetter Point. To get to Long Beach from Seattle, you can take the scenic route along Hwy. 101, after traveling on Hwy. 12 to Aberdeen, or the freeway route, south to Longview/Kelso on I-5, then west on Hwy. 4; it's about the same distance either way.

A public bus system runs every hour, Mon. through Saturday. For personalized service, call **Beach Cab,** tel. 642-3905.

WILLAPA BAY

Raymond, on the Willapa River just east of the bay, began as a booming milltown, with 20 lumber mills processing Pacific coast trees. Today they're still harvesting the same hills, thanks to years of reforestation, with just two mills, including a new Weyerhaeuser plant. Just south of Raymond, South Bend,

*a good day's
catch at Ilwaco*

the city that calls itself "The Oyster Capital of the West," is the highlight of the Willapa Bay area. Founded in 1869, South Bend started out as a sawmill town; when the Northern Pacific Railroad extended a spur to South Bend in the late 1880s, it became "the Baltimore of the Pacific." Victorian homes, churches, and an ornate glass-domed courthouse attest to the prosperity of the times. The Panic of 1893 put an end to South Bend's grandiose logging plans, while the Willapa Bay oysters that had brought great sums of wealth to a few shrewd businessmen were just about farmed out.

Aquaculture had its start in the early 1900s, when 95 carloads of Chesapeake oysters were "planted" in the bay. Oyster-processing plants flourished until 1919, when a mysterious pestilence wiped out the crop. In 1924, the Japanese oyster was introduced, spawning faster than they could be harvested. When the Great Depression finished off South Bend's lumber business, the oyster plants were still going strong—as they are today. South Bend's other major contribution to the state is Helen Davis; she composed the state song, "Washington, My Home."

Historic Sights
In South Bend, follow the "Courthouse" signs up the hill to the **Pacific County Courthouse,** built in 1911 and covered by an im-

mense, multicolored glass dome over mosaic-tile flooring. The parklike grounds surrounding the courthouse offer views of Weyerhaeuser-shaved hills and the town below. Tours of the courthouse may be arranged in advance by phoning the Pacific County Historical Society, tel. 875-5224, or just explore on your own during normal working hours.

Also in South Bend, the **Pacific County Historical Museum** has an impressive collection of local artifacts at 1008 W. Robert Bush Dr.; tel. 875-5224.

Just east of Raymond, off Hwy. 6 in Menlo, **Willie Keil's Grave** is testimony to a father's devotion to his son. The elder Keil was founder and titular head of a Christian Communist organization and they called themselves the Bethelites in honor of the town they founded in northern Missouri. They became very wealthy on the community-owned farms and town, so that when the great migration over the Oregon Trail occurred, the Bethelites decided to form a branch of their belief and business empire at the opposite end of the Oregon Trail. Young Willie (he was 19) was excited about the trip but as the departure date neared, he fell ill with malaria, from which there was no cure. In his final delirium he imagined himself at the head of the wagon train going across the continent.

Willie's brokenhearted dad promised the boy he *would* lead a wagon train west; when

Willie died in Bethel, in 1855, his father put the body in a lead-lined, alcohol-filled casket and carried his remains to Washington in honor of his pledge, and he was buried on the little knoll where the park stands today. After a short time in the area, the Bethelites gave up on the Willapa Bay site and moved south of Portland and founded Aurora.

Tokeland, protruding into the north end of Willapa Bay off Hwy. 105, is the site of a number of turn-of-the-century homes and commercial buildings, including the **Tokeland Hotel.** Built as a home in 1885, it became an inn in 1899 and is now on the National Register of Historic Places.

Parks
The 12,000-acre **Willapa National Wildlife Refuge** encompasses all of Long Island plus parts of Leadbetter Point State Park and Shoalwater Bay. Long Island can be reached only by boat from launch areas at refuge headquarters (12 miles north of Ilwaco on Hwy. 101, tel. 484-3482), Nahcotta, or other points on the Long Beach Peninsula. The island has five primitive campgrounds, but getting there can be tough due to tidal fluctuations—during low tide, you can practically walk out to it. The resident deer, elk, grouse, and bear may argue with the "refuge" designation, since archery hunting is allowed. No motorized travel is permitted. You don't have to get out to the island to enjoy the wildlife, though; there are numerous turnouts along Hwys. 105 and 101 where you can pull off and watch herds of elk or black-tailed deer.

Just west of South Bend, **Bruceport County Park** has RV parking ($6) and Willapa Bay beach access.

Accommodations And Food
South Bend is the big city around Willapa Bay, but the food here isn't particularly nota-ble. Best bets are **Boondocks,** Willapa and W. Robert Bush Dr., tel. 875-5155, a steak and seafood restaurant on the bay (open for three meals), and **O'Sheridan's** next door at 1011 W. Robert Bush Dr., a tavern that serves the ever-present oysters on the half shell.

Festivals
South Bend's Memorial Day weekend **Oyster Stampede** starts off with a winetasting to get you in the spirit, and continues with oyster shucking and eating contests, oyster cook-off, Reno night, and dancing. Menlo, southwest of Raymond on Hwy. 6, sponsors the annual **Pacific County Fair,** a four-day event in late August. Naselle, east of the refuge on Hwy. 4, sponsors the two-day **Finnish-American Folk Festival,** with dramatic performances, dancing, food, music, and arts and crafts, in late July; tel. 484-7759. Fifteen miles east of Raymond, Frances is a ghost town that comes to life twice each year for Swiss festivals: **Schwingfest** in July, a tribute to Switzerland's national sport, wrestling, and autumn's **Oktoberfest,** with beer, polka music, and lots of bratwurst; tel. 934-6321.

Services
The **South Bend Chamber of Commerce,** W. First and Alder, tel. 875-5231, has maps and other current information on the Willapa Bay area. For medical emergencies, South Bend has **Willapa Harbor Hospital** at Alder and Cedar, tel. 875-5526.

Getting There
For most people, the Willapa Bay area is something you pass through on your way to Long Beach, Westport, or Ocean Shores. Highways 105 and 101 outline the bay, with occasional wildlife spottings and peaceful tideflat scenery.

THE COLUMBIA GORGE

Driving along Hwy. 14 on the Washington side of the Columbia River, the scenery takes a dramatic turn, from the green, forested hills of the western section to the dry, yellow, barren hills of the eastern half. Temperature extremes on the east side range from zero or less in winter to 110° F of dry heat in summer. The area from Maryhill Museum near Goldendale to the Ste. Michelle Winery in Paterson is the least traveled stretch of the gorge, but it has its own rugged, sun-baked beauty. From Maryhill downstream to Vancouver has some of the Northwest's most photographed scenery.

HISTORY

When Capt. George Vancouver's 1792 expedition sailed up the Northwest coast, they must have been napping as they passed the Columbia River—George never saw it. That same year, American trading captain Robert Gray discovered this great river on his journey to become the first American to sail around the world. Gray claimed the river and its huge drainage area for the U.S., naming the river after his ship, the *Columbia Rediviva,* "Columbus lives again." After Gray's discovery, Vancouver sent William Broughton out to explore the upriver territory; Broughton asserted that Gray hadn't found the true channel, and claimed the river for England. Canadian traders searched western Canada for the Columbia's source. Finally, in 1811, David Thompson found it, and canoed to the confluence of the Snake and Columbia where he erected a sign, stating, in part, "Know thereby that this country is claimed by Great Britain." The conflicting claims weren't settled until the U.S.-Canada boundary treaty of 1846.

The most famous Columbia River explorers were Meriwether Lewis and William Clark. Selected by Thomas Jefferson in 1803 to lead an expedition from St. Louis to the Pacific coast, they were to keep extensive logs of the flora, fauna, and geography of this unknown territory, and to establish friendly relations with the native Indians. The 28 members of the expedition set out on May 13, 1804, accompanied by an Army detachment, in several canoes and a 55-foot barge powered by 22 oars and men towing it along the bank. When they ran out of river, the party of 28 got horses from the Indians and headed for the mountains, where they nearly starved to death. The Plateau Indians helped them find the Columbia River, where they built canoes and paddled downstream, arriving at Fort Clatsop on the Pacific coast in late November 1805.

Northwesterners won't be surprised to hear that Lewis and Clark recorded 31 consecutive days of rain during their visit to the Northwest! In March 1806, the party headed home. After a two-year absence, many had given them up for dead, but only one member of the party died en route, apparently of appendicitis.

SIGHTS

Parks, Dams, And Viewpoints
If you have a boat, visit **Reed Island State Park** on the Columbia River, three miles east of Camas-Washougal Marina. There are five primitive campsites here (no water).

On Hwy. 14 between Washougal and North Bonneville, the **Cape Horn Viewpoint** offers a good spot for photographing the dramatic west entrance to the Gorge.

Beacon Rock State Park is 35 miles east of Vancouver on Hwy. 14 (near North Bonneville). The core of an ancient volcano, 848-foot-high Beacon Rock is the largest monolith in North America and the second largest in the world (after Gibraltar). The rock was named by Lewis and Clark in 1805. It was a "beacon" informing river travelers that there were no further obstructions in the river from here to the Pacific Ocean, 150 miles away! Henry J. Biddle bought the rock in 1915 to

DIANNE BOULERICE LYONS

Columbia Gorge

preserve it, and spent two years blazing the trail to the summit; his heirs donated the rock to the state in 1935. Hike Biddle's one-mile trail for spectacular views of the Gorge; the trail boasts a 15% grade, but handrails make the hiking both easier and safer. This and other trails provide 14 miles of hiking in the park. Advanced climbers only may attempt to climb on the south side of the rock; register at the trailhead. Fishermen can launch their boats here to catch Columbia River sturgeon, and campers can stay in one of 33 standard forested sites (no hookups).

Visit the **Bonneville Second Powerhouse** visitor center, opened in 1983 on the Washington side of the Bonneville Dam, to see the inner workings of the powerhouse and informative displays. You'll feel dwarfed by the enormity of the river, dam, and surrounding hills. The dam is referred to as "the bottleneck of the Columbia," but a proposed new lock will bring Bonneville's capacity up to that of other Columbia River dams. Cross "The Bridge of the Gods" into Oregon and visit the original **Bonneville Lock and Dam,** a popular tourist spot with continuous presentations, exhibits, and a fish-eye view of the Columbia's inhabitants. The bridge crosses the river at the site of the former Cascade Rapids. According to Indian legend, a stone arch once spanned the river at this point, and

its collapse created the Cascade Rapids, damming the Columbia and causing considerable trouble for upriver travelers until the creation of the Cascade Locks in 1896. You can see these locks, no longer in use, at **Cascade Locks Marine Park,** on the Oregon side of the river. A small museum here relates Columbia River history, and includes the Northwest's first steam locomotive, the Oregon Pony.

The **Klickitat Gorge,** just north of Lyle, is a strikingly scenic area accented by rope bridges, where you can often see local Indians fishing with dip nets.

Cross over into Oregon via Hwy. 197 to see **The Dalles Dam.** Take the free train for a guided tour of the dam, displays, and fish ladders. "The Dalles" is from the French "Le Dalle," meaning "The Trough," the most dangerous point in the river for early navigators. Just east of The Dalles on Oregon's I-84, the **Fort Dalles Historical Museum** boasts a number of intact 1850s structures, including the 1856 Surgeon's Quarters that now houses the museum, and the original 1859 Wasco County Courthouse, now housing the visitor center. Stop here for a free walking-tour map.

Horsethief Lake State Park, 28 miles west of Goldendale on Hwy. 14, has good trout and bass fishing from your boat or one of the park's rentals, with two boat launch-

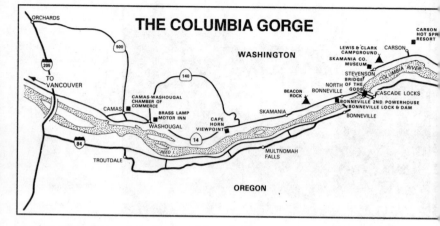

THE COLUMBIA GORGE

es—one on the lake, one on the river. The park is surrounded by Indian petroglyphs on natural rock formations; other facilities include a divers' underwater park and 12 standard (non-hookup) campsites.

Just east of Horsethief and 12 miles south of Goldendale on Hwy. 97, **Maryhill State Park** offers Columbia River access for boating, windsurfing, and fishing, plus 50 full-hookup campsites.

A mile north of Goldendale, **Goldendale Observatory State Park,** tel. (509) 773-3141, has the country's largest telescope open to public viewing, a 24½-inch reflecting Cassegrain. Take a tour and enjoy free audiovisual programs, displays, and demonstrations Wed. through Sun., 1-5 p.m. and 7-11 p.m.; winters Fri. through Sun. only. The camping facilities here are for group use only, but you can stay instead at **Brooks Memorial State Park,** 15 miles north of Goldendale on Hwy. 97, with 22 standard sites and 23 hookup sites on 700 forested acres. Enjoy the nine miles of hiking trails and good trout fishing in the Klickitat River, or snowmobiling in winter; tel. 773-4611.

The **John Day Lock and Dam,** 24 miles upriver from The Dalles, gave birth to Lake Umatilla and produces enough electricity for two cities the size of Seattle. Here you'll find one of the largest single-lift locks in the world,

hefting vessels 113 feet. At the dam on Oregon's I-84, enjoy the fish-viewing room, visitor's gallery, and Giles French Park, with a boat launch, fishing, and picnic area.

Farther west on the Columbia, **Crow Butte State Park** also offers boating, fishing, and waterskiing, with 50 hookup sites, 30 miles west of the McNary Dam along a virtually unpopulated stretch of Hwy. 14.

Museums

The well-known **Maryhill Museum of Art,** tel. 773-3733, was billed by *Time* magazine as "the loneliest museum in the world" when it opened in 1940. Housed in Sam Hill's 1926 "Castle on the Columbia" 100 miles from any major city, the museum is one of the country's finest, drawing more visitors than either the Seattle or Portland art museums with an impressive collection of drawings and plasters by French sculptor Auguste Rodin, French fashion mannequins, paintings, Russian icons, antique chess sets, and Native American artifacts. The museum's cafe serves lunch and snacks to eat in or take on the road. Open 9 a.m.-5 p.m., daily from mid-March to mid-Nov.; admission $3 adults, $1.50 kids.

Three miles east of Maryhill is the nation's first WW I memorial, a replica of England's Stonehenge, but with all the rocks neatly in

place rather than scattered around. It was
built by Sam Hill between 1918 and 1930.

Stevenson's **Skamania County Historical Museum,** tel. (509) 427-5141, has displays of pioneer life, Indian artifacts, and the
world's largest collection of rosaries—nearly
4,000, gathered from around the world and
fashioned from a variety of materials—in the
Courthouse Annex basement on Vancouver
Ave.; open every afternoon, free. The Historical Society also has an outdoor museum,
at Rock Creek Park and Fairgrounds on
Second Ave., with a Corliss steam engine
and caboose.

Goldendale's 20-room **Presby Mansion,**
127 W. Broadway, tel. (509) 773-4303 or
773-5779, is the home of the Klickitat County Historical Museum. Accurately restored
and filled with pioneer furniture and other
exhibits, it's open Tues. through Sun., May
through Oct., the rest of the year by appointment.

Wineries
Mont Elise Vineyards, 315 W. Steuben in
Bingen, specializes in pinot noir and offers
tours and tastings Thurs. through Sat. afternoons; tel. (206) 493-3001. Eleven miles
north of White Salmon on the road to Trout
Lake, the family-run **Charles Hooper Winery** produces 2,000 gallons of riesling, char-

donnay, gewürztraminer, and pinot noir blanc
every year; open weekends, 10 a.m.-6 p.m,
and most summer weekdays, tel. (509) 493-
2324. On the Columbia River in Paterson,
the state's largest winery, **Chateau Ste. Michelle,** offers tours and tastings of its Columbia Crest line daily, 10 a.m.-4 p.m.; tel. (509)
875-2061.

ACCOMMODATIONS

Hotels And Motels
Take Hwy. 14 to Washougal's **Brass Lamp
Motor Inn,** 544 Sixth St., tel. (206) 835-8591.
The 14 rooms start at $32 s, $34.50 d, and
include a heated pool, whirlpool, sauna, and
laundry facilities.

The **Inn of the White Salmon,** two miles
east of the bridge at 172 W. Jewett in White
Salmon, tel. (509) 493-2335, is a 50-year-old
European-style B&B featuring an outdoor hot
tub and antique-furnished rooms starting at
$59 d with breakfast, up to $116 d for the
deluxe suite; weekday singles are a bargain at
$44. Enjoy the locally famous country break-
fast without lodging for $13—but be sure to
phone ahead for reservations. Kids are not
encouraged; call ahead for restrictions.

Also in White Salmon, **Orchard Hill Inn,**
tel. (509) 493-3024, is a secluded country inn

surrounded by forests and apple orchards. Rooms are $33 s, $48 d, including a sideboard breakfast of breads, cheeses, cereal, and fruit, and use of the whirlpool and 1,000-book library; kids are welcome ($3 extra for toddlers and babies, $15 extra for older kids), but pets are not. Groups or large families can rent a six-bed bunkhouse. Smoking is allowed in the sitting room or outside. Take Hwy. 141 from White Salmon to Husem, then turn right on Oak Ridge Rd. for 1.8 miles to the inn.

The Grand Old House, across the bridge from Hood River in Bingen, tel. (509) 493-2838, is a Victorian B&B built in 1860. Rooms are $30-65, including a full breakfast and hot tub, and the proprietors will be happy to help you arrange for sailboard rentals and lessons, or cross-country ski tours. The inn serves dinners Tues. through Sun., emphasizing fresh seafood, steak, and chicken entrees.

The historic **Carson Hot Springs Resort,** tel. (509) 427-8292 in Carson, has been drawing visitors to its 126° F natural mineral baths since the springs were discovered in 1876. At that time, the baths were seen as a cure for everything from arthritis to kidney disorders. The St. Martin Hotel was built in 1897 to replace the tents that had accommodated the droves of guests; cabins were added in the 1920s. Today you can stay in the same lodgings—and enjoy the same relaxing bath plus a massage. Hot baths are $5 each, $12-18 for a massage; rooms start at $22-27 s, cabins are $24-29 s (add $5 each additional person), and hot tub suites are $90 d. Full-hookup RV spaces are $8 per day, with tent spaces available for just $3 a day. The restaurant here serves three home-style meals daily.

Three Creeks Lodge has individual, duplex, and four-plex chalets and Creekhouses (hillside condos that sleep two to six) scattered through 60 acres of forest and streams in the Simcoe Mountains on Hwy. 97 near Goldendale, tel. (509) 773-4026. All units have color TVs, skylights, handcrafted pine furniture, and an outdoor deck or patio; most have private spas, fireplaces, and kitchenettes. Rooms start at $46 d, up to $135 d for a deluxe unit and $155 d for a Creekhouse; with a seven-course, candle-lit, European-style dinner included, rates are $213-245 d. This is a wildlife-protection area: no pets, no hunting, no off-road vehicles.

For budget Goldendale lodging, stay at the **Ponderosa,** 775 E. Broadway, tel. (509) 773-5842; the 28 rooms here are $28 s, $32-34 d.

At 333 Vancouver Ave. in Stevenson, **Evergreen Inn B&B,** tel. (509) 427-4303, offers cozy comfort in the heart of the Columbia Gorge. Kids are welcome—a rollaway or crib is available upon request—and a room with full breakfast is $45 d. Lunches and dinners by arrangement; no pets or indoor smoking.

You can also find plentiful mid-Columbia food and lodging in The Dalles, Oregon; visit The **Dalles Area Chamber of Commerce,** 404 W. Second St., tel. (503) 296-2231, for suggestions and Oregon information.

Camping

Aside from state park campgrounds and resorts mentioned above, camping and RV parking in the Columbia Gorge are available at **Beacon Rock Trailer Park** 12 miles east of Stevenson on Hwy. 14, tel. (509) 427-8473, for $8.50; open all year.

FOOD

Three Creeks Lodge, Hwy. 97 in Goldendale (see above for lodging), is one of the finest restaurants you'll find in the Columbia Gorge area. Local fresh seafood, steak, and produce are complemented by Yakima Valley and Columbia Basin wines. Open for three meals daily, with Sunday Champagne brunch; tel. (509) 773- 4026. Other inns listed above also serve meals.

The Camas/Washougal area features a number of small restaurants and pizza places, including a **Dairy Queen** (527 N.E. Cedar in Camas). Mexican food aficionados will enjoy **Juanita's,** 231 Third in Camas, tel.

834-5856; open for lunch and dinner Mon. through Saturday.

ENTERTAINMENT

Festivals And Events

July Fourth brings the usual fireworks, picnics, and concessions to Skamania County; the best way to see the fireworks is aboard the sternwheeler *Columbia Gorge* (see below). July also brings the **Columbia Gorge Blue-** grass Festival, with foot-stompin' music, gospel and stage shows, and plenty of food all day long at the Rock Creek Fairgrounds. The annual **Skamania County Fair and Timber Carnival,** held the Fourth weekend in Aug., offers entertainment, contests, exhibits, and food. The **Klickitat County Fair and Rodeo** is held annually in Goldendale over Labor Day weekend; contact the City Clerk, tel. 773-4288, for specific information.

BRIAN BARDWELL

Windsurfing

The wind blowing through the Columbia Gorge provides some of the best windsurfing conditions in the country—but not for beginners. Gusty winds, large waves, a strong current, and frigid water make the Gorge challenging for even experienced sailors. The most protected waters in the Gorge are at Horsethief Lake, but even here strong winds may make it difficult for the beginner to return to the upwind launch area. If you're sitting this one out, expert-level conditions at **Swell City,** four miles west of the Bingen Marina, and the **Fish Hatchery,** 3½ miles west of Hood River, make for exciting sailboard-watching, as does **Maryhill State Park,** where the river is less than a half mile wide.

SERVICES AND INFORMATION

For more information on Columbia Gorge area towns and events, stop at the downtown Stevenson Visitor Center (open year-round) or contact the **Goldendale Chamber of Commerce,** Box 524, Goldendale, WA 98620, tel. (509) 773-3400; the **Skamania County Chamber of Commerce,** Box 1037, Stevenson, WA 98648, tel. (509) 427-8911; **Camas-Washougal Chamber of Commerce,** 422 Northeast Fourth Ave., Camas, WA 98607, tel. (206) 834-2472; or the **Skamania Parks and Recreation Dept.,** tel. (509) 427-5141, ext. 217. For more information on the Oregon attractions along the Columbia, contact the **Columbia Gorge Visitors Association,** Box 118, Hood River, OR 97031, tel. (503) 386-6262.

For emergencies, phone 911 in the Camas-Washougal area, tel. (509) 427-5626 in Skamania County. You'll have to travel to Vancouver for a hospital: **St. Joseph Community Hospital**, 600 N.E. 92nd Ave., tel. (206) 256-2064, or **Vancouver Memorial Hospital**, 3400 Main St., tel. (206) 696-5232

TRANSPORTATION

By Car

While the trip along Hwy. 14 does offer some beautiful Gorge scenery, by the time you arrive at Maryhill Museum you'll realize this Columbia River trek is a lot longer than it looks on the map—especially if your destination is Tri-Cities, more than 200 miles from Camas. The crowds at Maryhill probably have less to do with art appreciation than with sore fannies. This is truly a God-forsaken part of the state, so stock up on Cokes, chips, or whatever gets you through the drive.

Scenic Drive

A drive from Carson to the east side of Mt. St. Helens provides ample photographic and recreational opportunities. See the Mt. St. Helens map on p. 323 for access roads.

Scenic Cruises

Take a cruise on the Columbia, with views of steep basalt cliffs and stops at Cascade Locks, Bonneville Dam, and Stevenson, aboard the stern-wheeler *Columbia Gorge*, tel. (503) 374-8427 or (503) 223-3928. The boat can accommodate 599 people (400 indoors), and has full food and beverage services. Cruises depart daily, mid-June to Sept., from Cascade Locks, Oregon, across the toll bridge between North Bonneville and Stevenson, Washington. Daily two-hour cruises depart three times a day and cost $9 for adults; Thurs. through Sat., enjoy a sun-

set dinner cruise for $26 adults, or watch the fireworks aboard a special July Fourth cruise.

For a longer cruise, check out one- and two-day tours aboard *The Whatever,* Box 3, North Bonneville, WA 98639, tel. (509) 427-4347. Take an eight-hour cruise for $60, including two meals, to Sauvie Island and Portland Harbor, Longview via Sauvie Island, or Jantzen Beach to Beacon Rock; for $75, with three meals, see the Columbia Gorge from Camas, through the Bonneville Dam, on to Bradford Island. Two-day tours travel from Portland to Astoria or the Columbia Gorge from Portland for $169 s, $149 pp d; if time and money are no object, take the seven-day tour from Portland to Lewiston (return by chartered bus) through eight locks for $749 s, $649 per person d.

Board **YachtShip CruiseLine's** four-deck *Executive Explorer* for a six-day cruise following Lewis and Clark's route through the Columbia and Snake rivers. Starting in Portland, the cruise takes you to Astoria, Tri-Cities, Whitman Mission, Lewiston and Hell's Canyon, Maryhill Museum, and the Columbia Gorge, starting at $995 pp. Cruises run April through May and Sept. through early Nov.; write YachtShip CruiseLine at 523 Pine St., Suite 808, Seattle, WA 98101, or phone (206) 623-4245 for more information.

By Train

Bingen/White Salmon is the closest Amtrak station to the Columbia Gorge. Contact the station at 800 N.W. Sixth, tel. 248-1146, or phone Amtrak's toll-free number, (800) 872-7245, for information.

By Bus

The cruises listed above are as close as you'll come to an organized tour of the Gorge. Bus service to these parts is close to nonexistent: Vancouver's **C-Tran,** tel. 695-0123, will get you as far east as Camas.

VANCOUVER

A two-time winner of the All-America City Award, Vancouver's population of over 43,000 is supported by wood products, electronics, and the neighboring Portland economy, where many of Clark County's 215,000 residents are employed. Besides serving as a Portland suburb and Washington's I-5 gateway city, Vancouver enjoys a colorful history, kept alive by the Fort Vancouver National Historic Site, Officers' Row, and recreational opportunities at nearby Mt. St. Helens and the Columbia River.

SIGHTS

Fort Vancouver
The United States and Great Britain had been unable to come to terms on the ownership of Oregon Country, a fur- and lumber-rich land that included the Northwest coast of North America. By 1818, the two powers had agreed to share the land until an agreement could be reached—but in 1825, the British Hudson's Bay Co. moved its headquarters from Fort George, at the mouth of the Columbia, to Fort Vancouver, 100 miles inland, in hopes of solidifying the British claim to the region.

Fort Vancouver became the Pacific Northwest's commercial center for fur trading from Utah to Hawaii; shops, fields, pastures, and mills made the fort a self-sufficient, bustling pioneer community. Droves of pioneering Americans were drawn to Oregon's fertile farmland in the 1830s and '40s, leading to the division of the territory along the 49th parallel in 1846—a boundary that put Britain's Fort Vancouver squarely on American soil. By 1860 all of Fort Vancouver was in the hands of the U.S. Army, but decay and a fire in 1866 destroyed all of the remaining structures.

Beginning in 1948, archeologists recovered more than a million artifacts, leading to the accurate reconstruction of five of Fort Vancouver's buildings on the original location, now preserved as a national historic site. The three-story bastion, the fort's unofficial trademark, was originally built in 1845 as protection from Americans and to salute arriving ships with its eight cannons. It was a peaceful place, however, and the occupants never had to hide in fear. Other reconstructed buildings include a blacksmith's shop, bakery, Indian trade shop, and the elegant residence of John McLoughlin, the chief factor who looked so fearsome with his hard stare and great head of white hair, but who was one of the most generous men in those pioneer years.

Fort Vancouver is open daily year-round. Guided tours are given by Park Service rangers throughout the day as demand requires, and visitors may also enjoy the slide programs and exhibits at the interpretive center. From downtown, drive east for a half mile on E. Evergreen Blvd.; tel. 696-7655, $1 fee mid-May to September.

Parks, Birds, And Trees
The **Ridgefield National Wildlife Refuge,** just off I-5 in Ridgefield, has over 4,615 acres of fields, woodlands, and marshes for the protection of otters, deer, beavers, as many as 180 species of birds and, in winter, up to 10,000 geese and 40,000 ducks. Hiking and fishing are permitted—the mile-long "Oaks to Wetlands Wildlife Trail" is popular with all ages; no fires or off-road vehicles (ORVs).

Vancouver Lake Park is a local hot spot for both windsurfers and fishermen. The nearly 300-acre strip of land on the south and west shores of 2,800-acre Vancouver Lake has picnicking, swimming, grassy and shady areas, plus fishing for shad, sturgeon, steelhead, and more. Take Hwy. 501 (a.k.a. Fourth Plain Blvd.) west for about three miles; bear right at the giant arrow, just after you see the huge lake on your right, a few hundred feet to the parking lot.

Fort Vancouver National Historic Site

Five miles south of Woodland just off I-5, **Paradise Point State Park** offers fishing in the East Fork Lewis River, a two-mile hiking trail, and camping at 70 standard ($7) sites. **Battle Ground Lake State Park** is the more popular summer getaway, 21 miles northeast of Vancouver on Hwy. 503. The sandy beach and snack bar attract swimmers; riders will enjoy the equestrian trails; 35 standard ($8) sites.

Museums And Historic Buildings

The only fully restored row of officers' homes in the nation is at Vancouver's **Officers' Row National Historic District.** The city of Vancouver paid the hefty $10 million price tag for the restoration of these 21 turn-of-the-century homes, the two most famous of which are the **Marshall House** and **Grant House,** named for their onetime residents General George C. Marshall and President Ulysses

S. Grant. The Marshall House, 1313 Officers' Row, tel. 693-3103, is open for touring (free); the Grant House, 1101 Officers' Row, tel. 696-9699, is a fine restaurant (see below).

The **Clark County Historical Museum,** 1511 Main St., tel. 695-4681, is open Tues. through Sun. afternoons; free exhibits include an 1890 country store, 1900 doctor's office, Indian artifacts, and the first piano in Washington Territory, built in 1836.

The **Covington House,** 4201 Main St., tel. 693-9571, is one of the state's oldest log cabins. Built in 1848, it housed the area's first school; open to the public June through Aug., Tues. and Thurs. 10 a.m.-4 p.m.; free.

Exhibits at **Pearson Air Museum,** 101 E. Reserve St., include Lindbergh's 1927 flight and the 1937 Soviet landing in Vancouver from the world's first transpolar flight, plus operating vintage aircraft. Admission is $2 adults, $1 kids, tel. 694-7026.

Out in Yacolt, the **Pomeroy House/Living History Farm,** N.E. Lucia Falls Rd., gives visitors a look into Clark County's rural lifestyle in the 1920s. Tour the working blacksmith shop, herb garden, and historic log home the first full weekend of each month, May through Oct.; tel. 686-3537.

Winery

Just north of Vancouver, **Salishan Vineyards,** North Fork Rd. in La Center, tel. 263-2713, produces dry wines including award-winning pinot noirs and rieslings. Open for tours and tastings Sat. and Sun. 1-5 p.m. from May through Dec., or by appointment. Take I-5 exit 16 onto N.W. La Center Rd., following it north onto Main St. and N. Fork Road.

ACCOMMODATIONS

At I-5 exit 4, the **Value Motel,** 708 N.E. 78th St., tel. 574-2345, has over 100 rooms starting at $16-18. The **Guest House Motel,** 11504 N.E. Second St. (off I-205 and Chkalov Dr.), tel. 254-4511, has 47 rooms starting at $31 s, $36 d. **Nendel's Suites,**

1. Amtrak
2. The Crossing Restaurant
3. Columbia Arts Center
4. Esther Short Park
5. Slocum House Theater
6. Red Lion Inn at the Quay
7. Who-Song and Larry's Cantina
8. TraveLodge
9. Hidden House Restaurant
10. Clark County Historical Museum
11. Shilo Inn
12. Greater Vancouver Chamber of Commerce
13. Chart House

© MOON PUBLICATIONS, INC.

7001 N.E. Hwy. 99, tel. 696-0516, has a pool, guest laundry, and all kitchenette rooms from $36-41 s, $40-45 d.

The **Vancouver Lodge,** downtown at 601 Broadway, tel. 693-3668 or (800) 255-3050, has moderately priced lodging for $36-40 s, $42-50 d. Off I-5 exit 4 at 7901 N.E. Sixth Ave., the **Best Western Ferryman's Motel,** 574-2151, has 132 rooms from $43 s, $49 d, plus a heated pool, spa, and laundry facilities. At 221 N.E. Chkalov Dr., the **Mark 205 Motor Inn,** tel. 256-7044 or (800) 562-2205, has 120 rooms from $48 s, $55 d, plus an indoor pool and jacuzzi, near the Vancouver Mall. Downtown's **Shilo Inn,** 401 E. 13th St., tel. 696-0411 or (800) 222-2244, has 120 rooms from $55 s, $55-61 d, plus a heated pool, hot tub, sauna, laundry, valet service, and free continental breakfast. Another **Shilo Inn,** this one at 13206 Highway 99 (the 134th St. exit off I-5) in Hazel Dell, tel. 573-0511 or (800) 222-2244, has 66 rooms from $49 s, $49-55 d, indoor pool, hot tub, steam room, sauna, valet service, coin laundry, and free continental breakfast.

Enjoy top-of-the-line accommodations at the **Red Lion Inn at the Quay,** 100 Columbia St., tel. 694-8341, overlooking the Columbia River. The 160 rooms here cost $69-99 s, $83-105 d, and include a heated pool with poolside service, restaurant (see below), bar with dancing nightly (except Sun.) and a Columbia River view, room service, and bellhops. For a home away from home, try **The Residence Inn,** near the Vancouver Mall at Hwy. 500 and N.E. Thurston Way, tel. 253-4800 or (800) 331-3131. Apartment-style rooms include fully equipped kitchens (complete with popcorn popper), separate living rooms (some with fireplaces), free continental breakfast and newspaper, pool, hot tub, sport court, and guest laundry. Rates start at $53-63 per night; $10 extra for roll-away, $5 for a pet.

FOOD

Enjoy black-tie service in an elegant historic setting at **The Grant House,** 1101 Officers' Row, tel. 696-9699. Antiques, fireplaces, and a list of 250 regional wines complement the high-priced Northwest and continental menu. **The Chart House,** 101 E. Columbia Way, tel. 693-9211, overlooks the Columbia and features moderate to expensive steak, seafood, and prime rib, with an oyster bar and a good wine list. Have dinner in a railroad diner car at **The Crossing,** 900 W. Seventh St., tel. 695-3374. Open weekdays for lunch, Mon. through Sat. for dinner; entrees of prime rib, seafood, steak, and chicken run from $9-15.

Hidden House, 100 W. 13th St., tel. 696-2847, was built in 1885 for a prominent Vancouver citizen, L.M. Hidden, and still retains the original stained glass, shutters, and woodwork—but now it offers a moderately priced, largely French menu. Open for lunch weekdays, dinner Tues. through Sat. Enjoy the Columbia River view with your Mexican food at **Who-Song and Larry's Cantina,** 111 E. Columbia Way, 695-1198. **The Quay,** the restaurant at the **Red Lion Inn at the Quay,** 100 Columbia St., tel. 694-8341, specializes in steak and seafood in a nautical decor. Open for three meals daily, plus Sunday brunch. **The Olive Garden,** one of a chain of Italian restaurants, has popular and moderately priced pasta, veal, chicken, and seafood dishes, plus their famous breadsticks, at 8000 N.E. Parkway Dr., Orchards.

ENTERTAINMENT AND SHOPPING

Festivals
The **Fourth of July** celebration held at Fort Vancouver has one of the best fireworks displays in the Northwest, food, crafts, and live music. Held the last Sun. in July, the **International Festival** has ethnic food, dancing, and entertainment, and best of all, it's free. August's **Clark County Fair** is the fifth largest in the nation, held at the fairgrounds at 17402 Delfel Rd. in Ridgefield; phone 573-1921 for a schedule of events.

The Arts
At 400 W. Evergreen Blvd., the **Columbia Arts Center** offers a full, year-round schedule of theatrical productions, art shows, and concerts. For information on current events or a copy of their latest newsletter with calendar, phone 693-0351 Mon. through Saturday. Listed on the National Register of Historic Homes, the 60-seat Slocum House Theater was built in 1867 and moved to Esther Short Park at W. Sixth and Esther in 1966. The theater is now most famous for its August Victorian Festival, though it stages productions year-round.

Shopping And Movies
The two-level **Vancouver Mall** has over 115 shops, restaurants, and services, including five major department stores—JCPenney, Nordstrom, Mervyn's, Sears, and Meier and Frank—at the junction of I-205 and Hwy. 500, or from downtown, follow Fourth Plain Blvd. east. Just outside the mall, the Vancouver Mall Cinemas features four first-run films; phone 254-0000 for listing.

SERVICES AND INFORMATION

The Clark County area code is 206. For maps or other information, visit the **Vancouver/ Clark County Visitor and Convention**

Bureau at 404 E. 15th St. (left off the I-5 Mill Plains exit 1D), tel. 693-1313.

For all fire, police, or medical emergencies, dial 911. For emergency-room services, try **St. Joseph's Hospital,** 600 N.E. 92nd Ave., tel. 256-2064, or **Vancouver Memorial,** 3400 Main St., tel. 696-5232.

TRANSPORTATION

Horse And Buggy
Take a covered wagon or horse-drawn carriage ride through Officers' Row with the **Palmer House Carriage Company.** Horse-drawn carriages pick up at the Grant House; covered wagon rides start from the front of Fort Vancouver on E. Fifth Street. For current schedules and fares phone (503) 284-5893.

Scenic Train
Enjoy a 2½-hour train ride through the Cascade foothills and along the Lewis River to Moulton Falls County Park with the **Lewis & Clark Railway Co.,** 1000 E. Main St., Battle Ground, tel. 687-2626. Along the way you'll pass through a 340-foot rock tunnel, travel over three wooden trestles, and see waterfalls and acres of countryside. Fares are $9 adult, $5 kids; trains run Feb. through Nov. (phone for schedule). A special December Christmas Tree Train takes passengers to an Amboy tree plantation, where they can cut their own tree to take back home; fares are $12 adults, $6 kids, not including tree.

By Car
From Seattle, Vancouver is about 165 miles south on I-5. The speed limit shifts back and forth from 55 mph to 65 mph, so stay alert—the metropolitan areas are heavily patrolled.

By Bus
The local transit system is **C-TRAN,** 108 E. Seventh, tel. 695-0123, providing service throughout Clark County. For cross-country trips, phone **Greyhound,** 512 Columbia St., tel. 696-0186 or (800) 528-0447.

By Train
Amtrak provides daily service to Vancouver from its station at the foot of W. 11th St.; phone (800) 872-7245 or 694-7307 for information.

By Air
The Vancouver area is served by most major carriers at **Portland International Airport** just across the Columbia River. Make cross-country or international connections with **United,** tel. 696-0155, **American,** tel. (800) 433-7300, or **Continental,** tel. (800) 525-0280; **Alaska Airlines,** tel. (800) 426-0333, primarily serves West Coast cities.

BOB RACE

THE CASCADE RANGE

INTRODUCTION

In addition to creating almost opposite climates on either side of the state, the Cascades also serve as a political and psychological barrier between east and west, resulting in what could easily be two states within one. With the wisdom of hindsight, many historians have said the founding fathers erred in creating the states, and that they should have used the crest of the Cascades as state boundaries. Perhaps, but that would have robbed the state of much of its diversity, and diversity is conducive to cultural and geographical richness.

The two halves of the state are different not only in appearance but also in other less immediately obvious ways. Speaking very generally, western Washington is urban-oriented, with an emphasis on industry and

manufacturing, while eastern Washington is mainly rural and agricultural. While this division is blurring, and in spite of the difficulty in crossing the Cascade passes in winter (an adventure many Washingtonians prefer to forgo), increasing numbers of Puget Sounders are commuting across the Cascades. Like the thousands of avid skiers who look forward to the snow, these commuters have learned to live with the snow-tire and chain requirements, snowpacked and icy roads, and infrequent pass closures.

In summer, the Cascades take on a more benign image and become a popular destination for all manner of travelers, who have a wide variety of places and experiences from which to choose because millions of acres have been set aside for recreation: the

THE CASCADE RANGE

CANADA

MT. BAKER WILDERNESS

ROSS LAKE

MOUNT BAKER

NORTH CASCADES

BAKER L.

20 CONCRETE

MT. BAKER N.F.

NAT'L PARK

WINTHROP 20

530

DARRINGTON

153

150

GRANITE FALLS

RANGE

LAKE CHELAN MANSON

92

2

97

SKYKOMISH

LEAVENWORTH

WENATCHEE

KACHESS L.

CLE ELUM L.

28

169 18

90

97

KEECHEUS L.

CLE ELUM

164

410

410

ELLENSBURG 90

MOUNT RAINIER NAT'L PARK

82

MOUNT RAINIER

410

97

7 706 123

12

ASHFORD

7

CASCADE

12

MOUNT ST. HELENS

MT. ADAMS WILDERNESS

97

MOUNT ADAMS

MOUNT ST. HELENS NAT'L VOLCANIC MON.

0   20mi

INDIAN HEAVEN WILDERNESS

14

0   20km

WASHINGTON

OREGON

COLUMBIA RIVER

14

© MOON PUBLICATIONS, INC.

North Cascades and Mt. Rainier national parks, Mt. St. Helens National Volcanic Monument, numerous wilderness areas carved out of the national forests, several wildlife refuges, the areas around Mt. Baker and Mt. Adams, all comprise the backbone of Washington's outdoor recreation.

The Cascade Range is about 25 million years old, but the range's volcanos in Washington—Rainier, St. Helens, Glacier Peak, Adams, and Baker—plus another 15 or so in Oregon and California, are less than a million years old. Although none can be declared totally dead, only two have erupted in this century: northern California's Mt. Lassen in 1914, and Mt. St. Helens in 1980. Not long before Mt. St. Helens came to life in such a violent manner, Mt. Baker began heating up and sent out clouds of steam and melted some of the glaciers, but Mt. St. Helens stole the show in 1980.

The only break in the Cascade Range is the Columbia Gorge, which lets the Columbia River flow through, and also permits an exchange of air between east and west that is impossible elsewhere along the range. Because it is the only such corridor for hundreds of miles, the resulting winds are strong and almost constant and provide some of the country's best windsurfing conditions.

The rest of the range continues uninterrupted, shielding the interior from storms coming off the ocean and resulting in two vastly different climates: wet on the west side, dry on the east. This weather variation is caused by what is commonly called "the rain-shadow effect": incoming storms dump most of their rain and snow on the western side of the ridge as the air is forced up and over the mountain range.

MOUNT BAKER

Mount Baker, the northernmost of the Cascade volcanos, towers dramatically over the surrounding hills. It is bathed in glaciers and snowfields and serves as a scenic backdrop for Bellingham and Vancouver, B.C., photographers. Besides improving the scenery, Mt. Baker-Snoqualmie National Forest has a wealth of recreational activities, from skiing to hiking to whitewater rafting, with more than 200 miles of trails in over a half-million acres.

The four "life zones" on the mountain, from sea-level forest to alpine meadows, have a wide variety of wildlife including coyotes, black bear, black-tailed deer, porcupines, elk, marmots, and mountain goats. Forest birds include grouse, gray jays (the black-and-white equivalent of the eastern blue jay), ptarmigan, and a large winter population of bald eagles on the Skagit and Nooksack rivers. Five species of salmon spawn in the rivers, and the insect population is well represented by three of its least popular members, the mosquito, black fly, and "no-see-um."

HISTORY

Discovered in 1792 by Capt. Vancouver's first mate, Joseph Baker, Mt. Baker had been known for centuries to local Indians as Koma Kulshan, meaning "Broken One," a reference to an early eruption that blew out part of its summit. Like other Cascade volcanos, Baker is asleep—but not dead. In 1843 it awoke from its slumber, spewing vast amounts of smoke and ash and causing a major forest fire on the east shore of Baker Lake. The mountain lay dormant from 1884 to 1975, when it again began to release steam, leading seismologists to believe it would erupt, but it was upstaged in a grand manner in 1980 by Mount St. Helens.

The mountain has been a source for year-round recreation since 1868, when librarian-turned-mountaineer Edmund Coleman and his party climbed to the summit after two failed attempts. Either poor planners or extremely conscious of pack weight, the entire climbing party shared one plate and spoon and ate only bacon, bread, and tea during the 10-day ascent. By 1911, the mountain had become an integral part of the Mt. Baker marathon, a 118-mile roundtrip between Bellingham and the summit using any mode of transportation in addition to at least 24 miles on foot. The marathons were discontinued in 1913 after one competitor fell into a crevasse, though he did live to tell about it.

RECREATION

Mt. Baker-Snoqualmie National Forest covers an area far broader than just the peak and its immediate vicinity; it spreads east to the border of North Cascades National Park and intermittently southeast past the towns of Concrete and Darrington to Snoqualmie National Forest.

Skiing

Downhill skiing at **Mt. Baker** lasts from early Nov. to mid-May, the longest ski season in the state. Six chair lifts put 1,500 vertical feet of slope underfoot, from machine-groomed intermediate runs to open powder bowls. Nordic skiing is also available. Other facilities include child care, ski school, rentals, restaurant, and bar; no night skiing. Lift tickets are $20 adults, $14 youth (ages 7-15). For a ski report, phone 671-0211 from Bellingham or 634-0200 from Seattle; the business office number is 734-6771.

Glacier Nordic Ski School offers cross-country skiing along the Nooksack River at Salmon Ridge with trails, equipment rentals, lessons, and backcountry tours. Open Fri. through Sun. plus holidays, they're located in Glacier on the way to Mt. Baker. Call 671-4615 or write Resort-Salmon Ridge, Box 2974, Bellingham, WA 98227.

MT. BAKER

CANYON RIDGE TR.

BOUNDARY WAY TR.

WINCHESTER MTN.
(6,521 ft.) TWIN
LAKES

DAMFINO
LAKES

EXCELSIOR
PASS

WELCOME
PASS

HIGH DIVIDE TR.

TWIN LAKES RD.

TO
BELLINGHAM

DOUGLAS NOOKSACK EXCELSIOR

GLACIER

SILVER
FIR

HANNEGAN
PASS

SKYLINE DIVIDE TR.

HEATHER
MEADOWS
AREA

AUSTIN
PASS

MT. BAKER
LODGE

ARTIST
PT.
VISTA

LAKE
ANN

MT. SHUKSAN
(8,268 ft.)

MT.
BAKER
VISTA

COLEMAN GLACIER

MT. BAKER
(10,778 ft.)

0 ——— 3 mi
0 ——— 3 km

© MOON PUBLICATIONS, INC.

Rafting

North Cascades River Expeditions, tel. (800) 634-8433 or 435-9548, offers advanced glacial whitewater raft trips on the Nooksack from July to Sept. for participants over 12. A hearty lunch is included in the price, which ranges from $37-49 pp depending on day and group size. **Downstream River Runners,** 12112 N.E. 195th in Bothell, tel. 483-0335, offers a whitewater Nooksack trip (minimum age 12) for $45-60 pp; their prices may be a bit higher than other companies, but include wetsuits, lunches, and shuttle, and *all* guides have certified Swiftwater Rescue training.

Hiking

More than 200 miles of hiking trails meander through the Mt. Baker district, and, fortunately for hikers, all of them are closed to ORVs. The variety is enormous; backpackers and one-milers alike can find striking sce-

nery within their reach. Hikers and photographers would do well to pick up a copy of Norm and Diane Perreault's *Photographers Guide To Mt. Baker*. This small, self-published book is the best Mt. Baker guide in print, fun to read and full of beautiful photos and been-there tips on hiking trails and scenic viewpoints. Send $2.95 plus $1 postage to Norm and Diane Perreault, Box A, Glacier, WA 98244, or buy a copy at the Glacier Creek Motel, Forest Service information centers, or Village Books in Bellingham.

First the short, though not necessarily easy, hikes. Take Rd. #3060 off Mt. Baker Hwy. to the trailhead for a 1.8-mile one-way hike to **Welcome Pass;** this route gains 2,200 feet in elevation via 67 switchbacks to an open meadow with sweeping views of the surrounding area. From the end of Mt. Baker Hwy. at Artist Point, follow the 1.8-mile loop trail up lava cliffs to the appropriately named flat-topped **Table Mountain;** a complete re-

SKIING IN WASHINGTON

The best ski areas in Washington are stretched along the Cascades from Mt. Baker to Mt. Rainier. Snow on the western slopes of the Cascades is usually wet and heavy while some ski areas on the eastern slopes, such as Mission Ridge, have powdery snow. The telephone numbers with each resort are for information on the resort, leaving messages, etc. A list of numbers for recorded information on snow conditions for skiing, road conditions, and pass reports, avalanche dangers, etc., are at the end.

Beginning at the northernmost ski area and working south toward the Columbia River, **Mt. Baker,** tel. (206) 734-6771, is 56 miles east of Bellingham on Route 542. It has an elevation range from 3,500 to 5,040 feet and a vertical drop of 2,200 feet. It has seven double chairs, three rope tows, day lodge, and food services.

North Cascade Heli-Hiking, tel. (509) 996-3272, operates out of Mazama. Clients are dropped off at varying elevations up to 8,000 feet.

Stevens Pass, tel. (206) 973-2244, is 80 miles east of Seattle on Route 2 and has an elevation of 3,800 to 5,800 feet with a vertical drop of 1,800 feet. It has 10 chairs, schools, shop, rentals, restaurant, and cafeteria.

Echo Valley, tel. (509) 684-4002, is 10 miles northwest of Chelan on a dirt road off Route 150. It has an elevation of 3,000 to 3,500 feet with a vertical drop of 500 feet. It has a poma lift, three rope tows, day lodge, food services, school.

Leavenworth Ski Hill, tel. (509) 548-5115, is one mile north of Leavenworth and has an elevation of 1,300 to 1,850 feet with a vertical drop of 400 feet. It has two rope tows, day lodge, school, and coffee shop.

Mission Ridge, tel. (509) 663-7631, is 13 miles southwest of Wenatchee on Squilchuck Creek Road. It has an elevation of 4,600 to 6,740 feet with vertical drop of 2,140 feet. Four chair lifts, two rope tows, snowmaking equipment, shop, school, lodge and cafeteria.

Snoqualmie Pass is 47 miles east of Seattle and has four major ski areas in a space of two miles: **Alpental, Ski Acres, Snoqualmie,** and **Hyak.** The average summit elevation is 5,400 feet and a base of 3,000 feet, for a vertical drop of 2,200 feet. The four have 25 chair lifts among them, and 11 rope tows. Snowboarders are welcome only at Ski Acres and Snoqualmie. All have ski shops, day lodges, food service, and bus service to the area. For bus reservations to all areas call (206) 232-8162. For Alpental: tel. (206) 434-6112; Ski Acres: tel. (206) 434-6671; Snoqualmie: tel. (206) 434-6161. Snow conditions for all four: tel. (206) 976-7623.

do in 1988 made this trail, though still steep, accessible to most hikers. One of the most popular—and overused—hikes is the 2½-mile one-way **Heliotrope Ridge Trail** to the edge of **Coleman Glacier,** the starting point for Mt. Baker summit climbs. The trail starts from Rd. #39 off Mt. Baker Hwy. and gains 1,500 feet along the way. An easy two-mile one-way hike leaves from the end of Twin Lakes Rd. off Mt. Baker Hwy. to a lookout atop **Winchester Mountain,** with excellent views of Mounts Baker and Shuksan and the North Cascades.

Popular with equestrians and hikers is the six-mile roundtrip **Skyline Divide** trail, beginning 13 miles up Rd. #37 and providing ample Baker views and wildflower meadows. Starting at Austin Pass near the end of Mt. Baker Hwy., the four-mile one-way hike to **Lake Ann,** one of the Cascades' most beautiful high-country lakes, is a popular route with day-hikers and the major approach trail to Mt. Shuksan. Physically fit day-hikers should try the nine-mile roundtrip hike to **Excelsior Pass** for spectacular views of Baker and Shuksan after a 3,800-foot gain in elevation.

Backpacking

Only a few loop trails are suitable for over-night trips; most Mt. Baker trails are in-and-out propositions. Still, the scenery here is good enough to see twice.

SKIING IN WASHINGTON (CONTINUED)

Crystal Mountain, tel. (206) 663-2265, is 40 miles east of Enumclaw just off Route 410 and in the shadow of Mount Rainier. The summit elevation is 7,000 and base elevation is 3,100; the vertical drop is 3,100 feet. Crystal has 32 major runs and 1,000 acres of backcountry for cross-country skiing. Open Mon.-Fri. 9 a.m.-4:30 p.m., weekends 8:30 a.m.-10 p.m. It has 10 chair lifts, ski shop, rentals, school, lodge, food services, lounges, hotels, condominiums, swimming pool, groceries.

White Pass, tel. (509) 453-8731, is 20 miles east of Packwood on Route 12 southeast of Mount Rainier. It has a summit elevation of 6,000 with the base at 4,500 and a vertical drop of 1,500. It has four chair lifts, a poma lift, rope tow, ski shop, school, day lodge, food services, condominiums, groceries, and service station.

Cross-country, or Nordic, skiing is particularly popular on the eastern slopes of the mountains, in part because the snow is more powdery and the weather is usually sunny and clear.

Some of the best is in the Methow Valley, where some 150 km of trails are marked, the majority of which is groomed. The **Methow Valley Ski Touring Association,** P.O. Box 147, Winthrop, WA 98862, provides a hotline for ski-touring information, tel. (800) 422-3048, and a brochure showing the major trails. The

Methow was recently voted the best for Nordic skiing in eastern Washington in *Pacific Northwest* magazine.

Two ski centers are near Chelan: **Echo Valley,** tel. (509) 682-4002, seven miles north of Chelan has both cross-country and downhill skiing, and **Bear Mountain Ranch,** Rt. 1, Box 63B, Chelan, WA 98816, tel. (509) 682-5444, is five miles downlake from Chelan and has 55 km of groomed trail.

The following toll-free numbers are for Seattle-area callers. Outside the Seattle area, all calls must be prefixed by either 1-206 or 1-509 if outside the 206 area code.

  Cascade Ski Report: tel. 634-0200
  Snowline: tel. 976-7669
  Info Line: tel. 464-2000. Ask for category 5600 for directory of ski information.
  Ski Report Hotline: tel. 634-2754
  Crystal Mountain: tel. 634-3771 (Seattle number)
  Mount Baker: tel. 671-0211
  Cross-country skiing areas: tel. 632-7787
  Avalanche information: tel. 526-6677
  Mountain pass information from the State Department of Transportation: tel. 434-7623
  Mount Rainier National Park: tel. 569-2211
  Olympic National Park: tel. 452-9235
  North Cascade National Park: tel. 873-4590 or 873-4500

One loop, perhaps too short for the more robust, starts on Mt. Baker Hwy. for a 4½-mile hike to **Excelsior Pass** (see above), follows the **High Divide** trail for four miles, and returns to Rd. #3060 via Welcome Pass for 1.8 miles (see above). To stretch it out, travel north for three miles past the Excelsior Pass/High Divide junction to **Damfino Lakes** and Rd. #31. To continue north, take the poorly maintained old bootleggers' route, **Boundary Way,** for three more miles to the Canadian border. A trail turns west off Boundary Way just past Damfino Lakes; this is **Canyon Ridge,** heading back to Rd. #3140, but the trail is hard to follow and the rangers discourage its use.

From the campground at the east end of Rd. #32, **Whatcom Pass** trail starts with four level miles, climbing abruptly up to Hannegan Pass, then back down to a fork at the entrance to North Cascades National Park. The right fork continues east over Whatcom Pass and eventually to Ross Lake. Permits are required for overnight stays in the national park; you can get one in Glacier at the Public Service Center.

Climbing
Thousands of people annually reach the snow-and-ice summits of Mt. Baker and smaller, but no less challenging, Mt. Shuksan (elev. 9,127 feet). Inexperienced climbers

ARCHIE SATTERFIELD

Mt. Baker provides the backdrop for a Lutheran church.

can register for a six-day summer alpine mountaineering class with **American Alpine Institute** and acquire all the skills they need, starting on gentle terrain and working up to more challenging slopes, for the end-of-week summit climb. Cost is $380. Contact them at 1212 24th St., Bellingham, WA 98225, tel. 671-1505, for information on this and other Mt. Baker and Mt. Shuksan climbs.

Northwest Wilderness Guides offers two-day ascents of Mt. Baker for $85 or less, depending on group size, in July and August. Included in the price is all climbing gear, instruction, tents and stoves, ice axe practice, breakfasts and dinners; you supply clothing, lunches, pack, sleeping bag, and boots. All that's required is *good* physical condition—don't kid yourself on that one— and proficiency in ice axe self-arrest, which you'll acquire through the practice sessions.

Call 733-7014 at least a week in advance for reservations or more info.

Picnicking
Sightseeing and sandwich-chomping are as athletic as some of us like to get. Picnic areas are located at the **Mt. Baker Viewpoint,** past the trailhead on Rd. #39; **Shuksan Picnic Area,** at the beginning of Rd. #32; and at **Austin Pass,** a.k.a. Heather Meadows, at the end of Mt. Baker Highway. **Heather Meadows,** stuck between Baker and Shuksan, has been drawing tourists since the first lodge was built here in the 1920s, although it has since burned to the ground. The lakes, meadows, and rock formations surrounded by snowcapped peaks were the setting for Clark Gable's *Call of the Wild* and Robert DeNiro's *The Deer Hunter.* The view of Mt. Shuksan across Picture Lake is one of the world's most photographed scenes.

ACCOMMODATIONS

See "Bellingham" and "Vicinity of Bellingham" for a wide selection of B&Bs, motels, hotels, and campgrounds within an hour of Mt. Baker; accommodations at or near the mountain are quite limited.

Bed And Breakfast
Twenty-six miles east of Bellingham in Maple Falls, **The Yodeler Inn,** 7485 Mt. Baker Hwy., tel. 599-2156 or (800) 642-7334, is a countrified B&B, built by an early settler in 1917. The inn's five guest rooms share three baths, a hot tub, and a living room with a fireplace; rates are $48 s, $55 d.

Cabins
Open year-round, **Glacier Creek Motel,** tel. 599-2991, has nine motel rooms and a number of small creekside cabins accommodating up to six people on Hwy. 542. Rates are $34 d for the motel rooms, $45 d for cabins.

Camping
Four campgrounds are maintained by the ranger district, although one, **Excelsior,** is

open only to large groups with reservations. Two offer camping for a small fee: **Douglas Fir,** two miles east of Glacier on Mt. Baker Hwy., has 30 sites; **Silver Fir,** 13 miles east of Glacier, has 21 sites.

FOOD

For fine dining after a tiring romp in the woods, **The Cookhouse,** 7521 Kendall-Sumas Rd. in Kendall, tel. 599-2594, is open for three meals daily, with country cooking and a good beer and wine selection. Also on the classier side is the **Innisfree Restaurant,** 31 miles east of Bellingham on the Mt. Baker Hwy., tel. 599-2373, serving regional foods with seasonally changing hours. The **Chandelier** in Glacier, tel. 599-2949, has family dining and the largest dance floor at Baker. **Paisano's** has pizza (for there or to go) and other Italian food at 6186 Mt. Baker Hwy. in Deming, tel. 599-2380.

SERVICES

The area code in the Mt. Baker area is 206. For further information, contact the **Mt. Baker Ranger District,** Box 232, Sedro Woolley, WA 98284, tel. 856-5700. In case of emergency, call the ranger district at 856-1324, or the Mt. Baker-Snoqualmie National Forest Supervisors Office, tel. 442- 5400. The Whatcom County Sheriff, tel. 676-6911 or 384-5390, or the Skagit County Sheriff, tel. 336-3146, can also help. To report a forest fire call (800) 562-6010.

The Outpost in Glacier, tel. 599-2991, rents cross-country skis, backpacking equipment, gold pans, mountain bikes, and more. Outdoor equipment, clothing, maps, and cross-country ski rentals are available in Bellingham at **Base Camp, Inc.,** 901 W. Holly, tel. 733-5461.

DARRINGTON/GRANITE FALLS

Darrington, in the foothills of the Cascades northeast of Everett, was home to the Sauk and Suiattle Indians until white miners arrived in the late 1800s and early 1900s, in search of silver and gold. Though some deposits were found, the real money in this area was in logging; Swedish, Irish, Welsh, and Norwegian loggers, plus a very large group from North Carolina, founded a community that still reflects its ethnic origins.

Granite Falls, with a population of just over 1,000, sits at the southwest end of the "Mountain Loop Highway," an impressive title for a half-paved, half-gravel road connecting Granite Falls and Darrington. This rainy logging town at the base of the Cascades provides a jumping-off point for hikers, campers, cross-country skiers, and snowmobilers exploring the Mt. Baker National Forest.

Monte Cristo, south of Darrington and east of Granite Falls, was established in the 1890s when gold and silver strikes lured over 1,000 people to the boomtown, connected by rail to the port of Everett. The ore turned out to be of poor quality, and within 20 years Monte Cristo had become a ghost town. The fireplace and foundation of the Big Four Inn, a luxurious turn-of-the-century resort that burned to the ground in 1949, stand as reminders of the town's earlier glory. During the Depression, the railroad to Monte Cristo was replaced by the Mountain Loop Highway; today, the only access to the town is via a four-mile hike from the end of the paved section of "highway"—the neglected bridges into town can't stand up to vehicular traffic.

Climate

The Darrington District is an anomaly in the Cascades. Whereas the Seattle area receives 30-40 inches of rain per year, Darrington gets an average of 80 inches while Monte Cristo gets over 140 inches, creating a dense rainforest much like those of the Olym-

DARRINGTON/GRANITE FALLS

© MOON PUBLICATIONS, INC.

pics. The low elevation here means questionable snowfall, though cross-country skiing and snowmobiling are popular area activities.

RECREATION

Hiking
More than 300 miles of trails are within the Darrington Ranger District. Due to budget cuts, many of these trails are maintained by volunteers, so do your part to keep them clean. Parking-area theft is a major problem in this isolated area, so don't assume your valuables are safe in the trunk—leave them at home or carry them with you whenever possible, and report all thefts to a ranger station or the county sheriff.

The closest of the area peaks to Granite Falls is 5,324-foot **Mt. Pilchuck,** offering a number of good day-hikes. For a 360-degree view of the Cascades and Puget Sound from an abandoned lookout atop Mt. Pilchuck, head toward the tiny Mt. Pilchuck ski area via Mt. Pilchuck Rd. #3014, a half mile east of the Verlot Ranger Station, and park near the sign marking the trailhead. Allow four hours for the two-mile one-way hike, and be prepared for a 2,300-foot gain in elevation; best in late summer.

The virgin forest is as much the attraction as the clear mountain lake on the four-mile roundtrip hike to **Heather Lake.** To reach the trailhead, take Rd. #3014 for 1½ miles, then hike up an old logging road before reaching the forest and open meadows. Allow three hours; elevation gain is 1,100 feet.

Late spring is a good time to hike the 2½ miles to Lake 22 to see the numerous waterfalls along the way in their most turbulent state. The trail, starting 2¼ miles east of the Verlot Ranger Station, also passes through an old-growth cedar forest to the mountain lake. Allow four hours for the mild 1,400-foot elevation gain.

For a short, three-quarter-mile hike, take Rd. #3013 for 1½ miles to the trailhead for *Maiden of the Woods*. A Seattle sculptor, Dudley Carver, carved this woman (who was to be accompanied by various animals and wood spirits) into the side of a giant cedar as

The Darrington area is popular with hikers and backpackers.

TACOMA/PIERCE COUNTY VISITOR AND CONVENTION BUREAU

part of a proposed park. The park plan was abandoned, as was the sculpture.

The **Big Four Ice Caves** are a popular two-mile roundtrip hike, starting 22½ miles from Granite Falls at the Big Four Picnic Area. The hike begins at a marshy area inhabited by beavers, then heads through a dense forest and over the South Fork of the Stillaguamish River to the ice caves and a view of 6,135-foot Big Four Mountain. The caves are generally exposed in August and are visible through October, but admire them from afar: the caves are very dangerous to enter, as tons of ice may separate from the ceiling at any time, and in winter and spring the snowfield is susceptible to avalanches.

A full-day hike to alpine meadows starts 26 miles from Granite Falls and heads up **Mt. Forgotten** for an eight-mile roundtrip hike. Take the Mountain Loop Hwy. for 15¼ miles from the Verlot Public Service Center, then go north on Perry Creek Rd. #4063 for a mile to the trailhead. The trail passes waterfalls at about two miles, heading through an old-growth forest for another 1¾ miles to the first meadow. Allow seven hours to reach the meadows at 5,200 feet, an elevation gain of 3,100 feet. The trail continues through meadows to Mt. Forgotten's climbing route (for experienced alpine climbers only).

The rangers at the **Darrington Ranger Station** or the Verlot Public Service Center (see "Services and Information," below) can provide you with excellent printed material on these and many other trails in the Darrington District.

Backpacking

The ultimate backpacking experience, the **Pacific Crest Trail,** crosses the Glacier Peak Wilderness at Dishpan Gap, accessible via Bald Eagle Trail #650. Drive east on Mountain Loop Hwy., 27 miles from the Verlot Public Service Center to Sloan Creek Rd. #49; turn left, and stay on Rd. #49 for 8½ miles to Cadet Creek Rd. #4920. Go right, staying on the road for two miles to Sloan Creek. Park here and cross the bridge by foot, hiking another 2½ miles to the trailhead. From here, it's 9½ miles to Dishpan Gap through clearcut, forest, and meadows with a 2,300-foot gain in elevation. In the Glacier Peak Wilderness, you're likely to see deer, blue grouse, and hoary marmots, plus an occasional lynx, mountain goat, and cougar.

The 6.7-mile one-way trail to **Tin Pan Gap** and Three Fingers Mountain is a popular overnight hike. From Verlot, go west on Mountain Loop Hwy. for four miles, then head north on Tupso Pass Rd. #41, following it for 18 miles to the trailhead. The trail passes through dense forest for 2½ miles to four-acre Saddle Lake; continue for another 2½ miles through meadows to Goat Flat, a popular camping spot. Use only a campstove; fire rings leave near-permanent scars in these fragile meadows. The trail reaches Tin Pan Gap after about six miles; from here, the hike becomes a technical climb over Three Fingers Glacier and a scramble to the top of Three Fingers Mountain and lookout.

Climbing

The Pacific Crest Trail approaches 10,541-foot **Glacier Peak,** a popular alpine climb in summer and fall. Climbers typically take White Chuck Trail #643 to the Pacific Crest Trail #2000, scrambling to the timberline and following the Sitkum Glacier to the summit; consult with a North Cascades climbing guide (see "Booklist," p. 417) for a detailed description of the route. In spring, phone (206) 527-6677 for avalanche information.

Boating And River Running

Enjoy a half- or full-day whitewater or scenic float trip on the Sauk, Suiattle, or Skagit rivers with **Downstream River Runners.** A full-day whitewater trip on the Suiattle, including all gear, costs $50-65 adults, (minimum age 12); a 10-mile class III-IV whitewater trip on the Sauk costs $55-70 (minimum age 14). In winter, enjoy a half-day float trip on the Skagit to see the wintering bald eagles for $40 adults; OK for kids as young as five. (For more Skagit River eagle trips, see "The North Cascades And Lake Chelan," p. 290). Prices include wetsuits (drysuits $10 extra), lunch, and shuttle. For a brochure or reservations, write 12112 N.E. 195th, Bothell, WA 98011, or phone (206) 483-0335.

Rivers Incorporated, Box 2092, Kirkland, WA 98033, tel. (206) 822-5296, offers a Suiattle trip for novice or advanced river runners in July and Aug. for $38-60, depending on group size (lunch and wetsuit available but not included in price). They also offer Upper Skagit whitewater ($38-60) and Skagit eagle trips ($35), plus runs on the Wenatchee, Methow, and Klickitat rivers.

Experienced, do-it-yourself river runners will enjoy the challenges of the Sauk and Suiattle rivers. The Suiattle is the more tame of the two, rated class II to III from Boundary Bridge to the Sauk River; it's unnavigable within the national forest boundary due to logjams, hidden stumps, and debris. Put in at Boundary Bridge or William Dearinger State Park. The Sauk River ranges from class I to V; from the White Chuck launch area to Clear Creek it's a IV or V, with difficult rapids through narrow passages. From Bedal to White Chuck, the river is classified as a class III to IV, and below Clear Creek it ranges from class III to I. North of Darrington, the river is considerably calmer and is popular for canoeing.

Paddlers and rubber rafters will enjoy exploring six-acre **Coal Lake,** a subalpine lake at 3,600 feet elevation. Go east on the Mountain Loop Hwy. for 15 miles from the Verlot Public Service Center, then go north on Coal Lake Rd. #4060 for 4½ miles to the trailhead. Carry your boat for about 50 feet to the lake, where you'll find a toilet and a limited number of campsites (that fill up very quickly).

Another lake with easy canoe and raft access is five-acre **Canyon Lake.** From the Verlot Public Service Center, drive four miles on the Mountain Loop Hwy. to Rd. #41; turn right, continuing for two miles to Green Mtn. Rd. #4110. Turn right again (heading east now), driving 1⅓ miles to Rd. #4111; follow this road for 10¾ miles to the trailhead on the left side of the road. Carry your boat along the 50-foot trail to Canyon Lake, surrounded by trees and a few campsites; fair fishing.

The Darrington District boasts a large number of small lakes, some of which provide excellent fishing. Check at the ranger station or public service center for a list of lakes and suggestions on the best for boating, fishing, or paddling.

Cross-country Skiing And Snowshoeing
Skiers and snowshoers can count on solitude when exploring the Darrington District; most roads aren't plowed and snowfall is unpredictable at this low elevation, and what snow there is often wet and difficult to ski through. Still determined? Take these routes as suggestions; if the roads themselves aren't snow-covered, keep driving along the route until you come to some.

From Hwy. 530 on the way to Darrington, go south on French Creek Rd. #2010 through dense forest and switchbacks for great views and a fast, downhill trip back. Or, from the Darrington Ranger Station, drive north on Hwy. 530 for 6½ miles to Suiattle River Rd. #26; ski on the road or follow the road till you hit snow.

On the Granite Falls side, the Big Four area is very popular with skiers, snowshoers, snowmobilers, and winter hikers; take the Mountain Loop Hwy. 23 miles from Granite Falls to the end of the maintained road at Deer Creek Rd. #4052. Ski two miles from the parking area to Big Four Picnic Area, following the South Fork of the Stillaguamish River; continue another mile to the snowfield near the Big Four Ice Caves. The avalanche danger here is severe; don't travel beyond the edge of the clearing—it's the force of avalanches that created and maintain that clearing! Allow three to five hours roundtrip; suitable for beginninfg skiers.

ACCOMMODATIONS

Motels
Darrington's **Stagecoach Inn,** 1100 Seaman St., tel. (206) 436-1776, is an attractive, though small, motel with rooms from $32 s, $43 d. A greater variety of lodging is available in Arlington, about 25 miles west on Hwy. 530. **Smokey Point Motor Inn,** 17329 Smokey Point Dr. at Arlington exit 206 off I-5, tel. 659-8561, has rooms from $30 s, $35-50 d, plus a year-round heated pool and whirlpool. The **Arlington Motor Inn,** 2214 Hwy. 530 off exit 208, tel. 652-9595, has rooms from $29-32 s, $38-42 d. Granite Falls doesn't offer much; best to stay in Marysville or Everett (see p. 123), or better yet, go camping.

Camping
The Forest Service operates 13 campgrounds in the Darrington District, most on a first-come, first-served basis; no electrical hookups or dump stations. Campgrounds are open from Memorial Day through Labor Day weekends, and campers are limited to a 14-day stay in campgrounds.

From Granite Falls, neighboring **Turlo** and **Verlot** campgrounds have 19 and 26 spaces respectively near the Verlot Public Service Center; **Gold Basin** Campground, 2½ miles east of the service center, has 93 campsites. All three have piped well water, trailer space, flush or vault toilets, and garbage service and charge a $6 fee. **Red Bridge Campground,** seven miles east of the Verlot Service Center, has 16 sites with vault toilets; no well water or garbage collection, but no fee either.

From Darrington on the Mountain Loop Hwy., **Clear Creek** Campground has 10 sites and trailer space 3½ miles from the Darrington Ranger Station; **Bedal** has 18 units and trailer space 18 miles from the ranger station. Both have vault toilets; no fee. From Darrington via Suiattle River Rd. #26, **Buck Creek,** 23 miles in with 51 spaces, and **Sulphur Creek,** 28 miles from Darrington with 29 campsites, have trailer spaces and vault toilets; no fee.

These four campgrounds are available by reservation only (contact the Darrington office, tel. 436-1155): **Esswine,** five miles east of the Verlot Service Center, $15; **Boardman Creek,** about six miles east of Verlot, $25; **Marten Creek,** nine miles east of Verlot, $15; **Coal Creek Bar,** 12½ miles east of Verlot, $15; and **Beaver Creek,** 13½ miles east of Verlot, $15. These are smaller campgrounds, with three to eight campsites each; Boardman and Coal Creek have trailer spaces.

FOOD

Aside from a handful of diner-style restaurants and backwoods taverns in Darrington and Granite Falls, food in these parts is scarce. Head back to Arlington for good food in surprising surroundings: two restaurants right off I-5 at the Hwy. 530 exit, **Weller's Chalet Inn** and **O'Brien's Manor,** are remarkably good considering their right-off-the-interstate location. Weller's has good sandwiches for about $5, steak and seafood dinners for $6-14. O'Brien's has sandwiches, salads, and light dinners (heavy on the turkey) for under $6. Travel east on Hwy. 530 for fast food in downtown Arlington. Off I-5 exit 206 (Smokey Point), the shopping center adjacent to the Smokey Point Motor Inn offers pizza, Mexican food, and a family restaurant, plus banks, state liquor store, drugstore, and mini-post office.

ENTERTAINMENT

The last weekend in June brings the annual **Timber Bowl Rodeo** to the rodeo grounds four miles west of Darrington. In mid-July, enjoy Darrington's three-day annual **Bluegrass Festival and Street Fair.**

SERVICES AND INFORMATION

The area code in Darrington, Granite Falls, and surrounding area west of the Cascades is 206. For up-to-date information on trail conditions, campgrounds, fishing, and other outdoor activities contact the **Verlot Public Service Center,** tel. 691-7791, or the **Darrington Ranger Station,** tel. 436-1155. For other area information, call or write the **Granite Falls Chamber of Commerce,** Box 28, Granite Falls, WA 98252. Hikers and campers can stock up on forgotten supplies at **Forrister's Sport Shop** on Hwy. 530 in Darrington; for groceries, the **IGA** is across the street. The closest hospital to Darrington is **Cascade Valley Hospital,** 330 S. Stillaguamish in Arlington; call 911 or 435-2133.

TRANSPORTATION

By Car
The **Mountain Loop Highway** from Darrington to Granite Falls is a 55-mile-long, largely unpaved road through valleys and forests, offering numerous glimpses of snowy peaks. From Darrington, the road is paved for the first 9⅓ miles, becoming a narrow dirt road for the next 23½ miles; the remaining 22 miles to Granite Falls are paved. The highway and logging roads are popular snowmobile routes in winter.

By Bus
Based in Everett, **Community Transit** goes south to Edmonds and Seattle, north to Stanwood and Darrington, and east to Snohomish, Lake Stevens, and Granite Falls for $.50; tel. (800) 562-1375 or 778-2185.

THE NORTH CASCADES AND LAKE CHELAN

North Cascades National Park is an outdoor lovers' paradise. Few roads spoil this pristine wilderness, where rugged peaks, mountain lakes, and waterfalls greet the determined backcountry hiker. A total of 318 glaciers, more than half of those in the Lower 48, are found on this national park's half-million acres. Although Hwy. 20 is one of the country's most scenic routes, the park and surrounding national forests can best be experienced close up, on foot or horseback; in fact, many campgrounds and one entire resort town are not accessible by car. So don't just drive through; bring your hiking boots, map, and a flexible schedule to really experience the North Cascades.

Climate
The weather on the west side of the North Cascades is cooler and wetter than the eastern portion, protected by the rain-shadow effect. The middle section of Hwy. 20 is closed in winter, usually from mid-Nov. to late April or beyond, although it is open to snowmobile traffic from Colonial Creek to Early Winters. Lower-elevation hiking trails, such as those along Ross Lake and Lake Chelan, are generally accessible from April through mid-Oct.; at higher elevations, trails are open from mid-July through September. The glacier-fed waters of Ross, Diablo, and Gorge lakes are too cold for swimming, but boating and fishing are popular activities.

HISTORY

The earliest white men to explore the North Cascades were Alexander Ross and his party, who crossed today's southern park boundary at Cascade Pass in 1814. In 1859, Henry Custer, working as an assistant of reconnaissances for the International Boundary Commission, traversed the region and commented: "Nowhere do the mountain masses and peaks present such strange, fantastic, dauntless and startling outlines as here. . . . [It] must be seen, it cannot be described." From 1880 to 1910, prospectors struck gold, platinum, lead, and zinc, but mountain travel was too difficult to justify the modest return.

Although logging and early settlement of the area began around 1900, the potential of the Skagit River wasn't harnessed until 1924, when the first of three dams was built by Seattle City Light. This rugged area was preserved as the North Cascades National Park Service Complex in 1968, incorporating Ross Lake and Lake Chelan National Recreation Areas, and North Cascades National Park.

SIGHTS

Scenic Drives
Highway 20 joins Hwy. 153 at Twisp, Hwy. 97 near Pateros, and Hwy. 2 near Wenatchee to form the northwest portion of the "Cascade Loop." This 400-mile scenic drive winds through the North Cascades, past Ross Lake and Lake Chelan, through Leavenworth on its approach to Stevens Pass, and returns to western Washington and Whidbey Island. Highway 20, the **North Cascades Scenic Highway**, was originally commissioned in 1893, when state legislators set aside $20,000 for the completion of the Cascade Wagon Route. Some 79 years and $4.5 million later, the highway was completed. Along the route are numerous pulloffs for viewing the striking scenery, plus access to self-guiding trails, campgrounds, and informational displays. Be sure to make at least two stops: at **Diablo Lake**, for lunch in a cozy lodge with a lake view, and at 5,447-foot **Washington Pass Overlook**, where a short paved trail

DIANNE BOULERICE LYONS

The North Cascades are among the most rugged mountains in the U.S.

leads to over-the-highway viewpoints of Liberty Bell, the symbol of the North Cascades Hwy., and surrounding mountains. There are no gas stations, restaurants, or other facilities (except restrooms at Washington Pass) for the 75 miles between Ross Dam and Mazama; but those with fuel-efficient cars can fill up in Sedro Woolley and have plenty of gas to get to Lake Chelan.

On the north shore of Lake Chelan, drive the 12-mile scenic loop from downtown Manson along the shore of Lake Chelan, up into apple orchards and past smaller lakes in the foothills, with striking views all along the way. From Manson drive west on Lakeshore Dr. and Summit Blvd., north on Loop Ave. and Manson Blvd., east on Wapato Lake Rd., then south on the Chelan-Manson Hwy. back to Manson. Another scenic spot is on the south shore of the lake; follow Hwy. 97 for nine miles west of Chelan to **Chelan Butte Lookout,** across the street from the Park

Lake Motel. The road curves upward with pullouts for photos of the lake, surrounding hills, and acres of apple orchards.

Baker Lake
Nine-mile-long Baker Lake was created by the upper dam on the Baker River; the Lower Baker Dam created Lake Shannon, just off Hwy. 20 near Concrete. Baker Lake is very popular with campers, boaters, and water-skiers, despite the enormous stumps that lurk just below the water's surface. To get there, take Baker Lake-Grandy Lake Rd. north from Hwy. 20.

Ross, Diablo, And Gorge Lakes
The second-largest lake in the North Cascades after Lake Chelan, **Ross Lake** is 24 miles long and up to two miles wide, covering 12,000 acres from the Skagit River up to and beyond the Canadian border. You can see the lake from the Ross Lake Overlook on Hwy. 20 or area hiking trails (see below), but the only vehicle access and boat launch is at the lake's north end, via a 39-mile Canadian gravel road. A boat taxi can get you to **Ross Lake Resort** (see below). Two smaller lakes created by Seattle City Light dams are **Gorge Lake,** 210 acres, and the emerald-green **Diablo Lake,** covering 910 acres just west of Ross Lake along the Skagit River; both are accessible from Hwy. 20. Diablo and Gorge lakes get their deep-green color from the minerals in the glacial runoff, much more evident here than at bluer Ross Lake. Boat rentals are available at all three lakes; see "Transportation" below.

Lake Chelan
Glaciers carved the 1,500-foot-deep trough that forms one of the deepest lakes in the country: Lake Chelan (pronounced sha-LAN). At its deepest point, the glacier- and stream-fed lake dips 400 feet below sea level. A dam built here in 1927 to increase electrical production raised the lake's level by 21 feet; the lake is now a popular year-round resort, with swimming, boating, and water-skiing in summer and cross-country skiing in winter. The town of Stehekin (ste-HE-kin), at

BAKER
LAKE
AREA

MT. BAKER
(10,778 ft.)

PARK CR.

SHANNON CR.

PANORAMA PT.

PARK BUTTE

BAKER LAKE

HORSESHOE COVE

MAPLE GROVE

LOOMIS MTN.
(5,587 ft.)

KOMA KULSHAN F.S. STATION

PUGET POWER

UPPER BAKER DAM

LAKE SHANNON

CREEKSIDE RV PARK

GRANDY CREEK

GRANDY LAKE

BAKER DAM

TO BURLINGTON

BIRDSVIEW

20

CONCRETE

20

0   3 mi.
0   3 km

© MOON PUBLICATIONS, INC.

the northwest end of the 55-mile-long lake, can be reached only by boat, plane, or foot; thousands of visitors take the four-hour boat trip for lunch or an overnight stay at one of the Stehekin resorts. Or, rent and launch a boat in Chelan and do your own exploring; see "Transportation," p. 296.

Winthrop

Winthrop's Main Street buildings have been remodeled with an "Old West" theme to reflect the town's 1890s mining boom—and to encourage hungry, tired Hwy. 20 drivers to stop for a meal, gas, and souvenirs. A visitor information building on the corner of the highway and main drag can help you with lodging, camping, restaurants, and other area facilities. Winthrop also hosts annual festivals and rodeos (below) that reflect the western mood.

Seattle City Light Tours

Seattle City Light has been offering regularly scheduled tours of their Skagit facilities since 1928. Today, a four-hour guided tour begins with a slide presentation at the Skagit Tour Center in Diablo, followed by a 560-foot ride up Sourdough Mountain on an antique incline railway used to haul supplies during the construction of the Diablo Dam. Then, enjoy a cruise across deep-green Diablo Lake and back to an all-you-can-eat dinner. Tours leave three times a day, Thurs. through Mon., from late June to early Sept.;

Liberty Bell at
Washington Pass
in the North Cascades

DIANNE BOULERICE LYONS

the total cost of the tour and dinner is $21
adults, $10 kids and seniors, kids under five
free (but mention them when making reservations). Contact the **Seattle City Light
Tour Desk,** 1015 Third Ave., Seattle, WA
98104, tel. (206) 684-3030, or from late
June to Labor Day, stop by the Skagit Tour
Center.

A 90-minute tour is also given Thurs.
through Mon. afternoons. This 1½-hour version includes a slide show, ride on the incline lift, and tour of the Diablo Powerhouse
(sorry, no boat ride) for $5 for everyone over
12.

State Parks

About 10 miles east of Baker Lake on Hwy.
20, **Rockport State Park** has five miles of
wooded hiking trails (including one with
wheelchair access), Skagit River steelhead
fishing, and camping at 50 hookup sites and
eight standard sites under an old-growth
Douglas fir forest.

Pearrygin Lake State Park, five miles
north of Winthrop off Hwy. 20, offers a sandy
beach, fishing, and boat launch on a small
lake, winter snowmobiling, plus camping at
57 full- or water-only hookup sites and 26
tent sites.

Another park popular with the summer
crowd is **Alta Lake,** two miles southwest of
Pateros off Hwy. 153. Fish, swim, and boat in

east-of-the-mountains sunshine, and enjoy
the mile-long trail for a scenic view. Lots of
camping here: 16 partial-hookup sites, 164
tent sites.

Two state parks provide camping along
Lake Chelan. **Lake Chelan State Park** is
right on the lake, nine miles west of Chelan,
with an underwater park, docks for campers,
boat launch, and concession stand. Camp at
one of 127 tent sites or 17 full-hookup sites.
Twenty-five Mile Creek State Park, 18 miles
north of Chelan, has camping at 52 tent sites
and 33 hookup sites, plus a swimming pool
for campers and Lake Chelan boat launch.

All state park campgrounds charge $8 for
a standard site, up to $9.50 for a full-hookup
site. For more information on camping in the
state parks, see p. 29.

Museums

Winthrop's **Shafer Museum** on Castle Ave.,
tel. (509) 996-2817, is housed in an 1897 log
cabin built by the town's founder, Guy War-
ing. Displays include pioneer farming and
mining tools, bicycles, furniture, and other
relics from the early days in the Methow
Valley. Open daily, Memorial Day through
mid-Oct.; donations appreciated. Visit the
Lake Chelan Museum at Woodin Ave. and
Emerson St. in Chelan, tel. (509) 687-3470,
to see displays of pioneer and Indian relics.
Open Mon. through Sat. afternoons, June

through Sept., by appointment the rest of the year.

OUTDOOR RECREATION

Hiking

More than 300 miles of maintained trails provide ample opportunities to explore this rugged wilderness area. Trails below 3,000 feet are generally open by mid-April or May; high-

er up, you may meet snow in July so be prepared. Wear bright colors when hiking in the recreation areas so hunters won't mistake you for a deer.

In the Baker Lake area, hike through a rainforest along the **Baker River.** To reach the trailhead for this six-mile roundtrip hike, drive north on Baker Lake-Grandy Lake Rd. for 14 miles to the Komo Kulshan Guard Station. Follow the Forest Service road for 11½ miles, then left a mile, then right on the

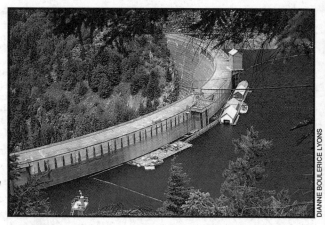

Diablo Dam

DIANNE BOULERICE LYONS

first side road for half a mile to the start of Trail #606. This level, low-elevation trail affords views of glaciers and beaver ponds on the way to Sulphur Creek. Stop at the creek and retrace your steps for a three- to four-hour hike, snow-free from early spring to late fall.

Another Baker Lake hike takes you to **Park Butte,** a 5,450-foot summit with views of Mt. Baker glaciers. This summer-only trek is seven miles roundtrip, but with an elevation gain of over 2,200 feet it'll take a good part of the day to complete. Go north for 12½ miles on Baker Lake-Grandy Lake Rd., then turn left on Loomis-Nooksack Rd. #13 for nine miles to road's end. The trail is west of the road, crossing Sulphur Creek before the switchbacks begin.

Some of the park's most spectacular scenery can be seen at **Cascade Pass.** This is a day-use-only area; no camping is allowed between the end of Cascade River Rd. and Cottonwood Camp on the south side of the pass. Drive to the trailhead at the end of Cascade River Rd., a 25-mile trip from Marblemount. The first two miles of the seven-mile roundtrip hike climb steadily through forest and meadows to the 5,400-foot pass at 3½ miles. Allow about five hours for this summer-only hike.

Drive to Hart's Pass from Mazama, then go right for 1½ miles on Slate Peak Rd. to the **Windy Pass** trailhead for another high summer-only hike. This seven-mile roundtrip hike starts at 6,800 feet with little additional elevation gain for striking views of peaks and meadows all along the route. Get an early start; hiking at this elevation may be a little slower than your normal pace.

To hike to **Cascade Pass** from the south side of the park, take *Lady of the Lake* to Stehekin and hop the shuttle bus to road's end at Cottonwood Campground. From here climb the talus slope to Doubtful Creek (that is, doubtful if you can cross it in spring); continue uphill for a one-way trek of 5½ miles to the pass, with a total elevation gain of 2,600 feet. For a shorter Stehekin-based trip, take the shuttle to High Bridge for a 1¼-mile uphill hike to **Coon Lake** for excellent views of Agnes Mountain and good birdwatching.

For detailed descriptions of these and many other North Cascade hikes, see Ira Spring and Harvey Manning's *101 Hikes in the North Cascades,* published by The Mountaineers in Seattle. Fifteen hikes accessible by the Stehekin shuttle are described in the park brochure, "Day Hiking in Stehekin," available at any ranger station; be sure to pick up a map to accompany the brochure.

Backpacking

A backcountry permit is required for all overnight trips, in an effort to reduce overcrowding and preserve the fragile alpine environ-

ment. Pick one up at the information or
ranger stations at Marblemount, Hozomeen,
Chelan, Stehekin, Early Winters, or Concrete
(summer only). The North Cascades are
among the most rugged mountains in the
Lower 48, so plan accordingly: lots of wool
clothing, extra food, a waterproof tarp, and a
flexible schedule for waiting out storms or
resting feet and muscles sore from all the ups
and downs.

From June to Nov., enjoy the 31-mile trip
from Panther Creek to Hozomeen along
Ross Lake's **East Bank Trail.** The trailhead
is on Hwy. 20, eight miles east of the Colonial
Creek Campground at the Panther Creek
bridge. The trail leads through low forest and
along the lakeshore for 18 miles, when you
have the option of continuing to Hozomeen
or taking a side trip up 6,085-foot **Desolation
Peak.** The roundtrip up the peak is nine
miles, almost straight up, with an elevation
gain of 4,400 feet; you'll be rewarded with
views of Mt. Baker, Shuksan, Jack Mountain,
and The Pickets. To get right to the peak, skip
the first 18 miles of hiking by taking the water
taxi to the Desolation Peak trailhead; stay
overnight at Lightning Creek Campground,
since you probably won't return in time to
catch the boat.

Use the *Lady of the Lake* to make a 38-
mile loop trip from Prince Creek, past Lake
Juanita and 6,900-foot Purple Pass, to Stehekin. Lot of ups and downs on this hike,
through forests and alpine meadows with
striking views of mountain peaks, including
8,690-foot Star Peak. The upper Lake Chelan area has a fair number of rattlesnakes, so
watch your hand-holds.

The **Pacific Crest Trail** enters the park
from the south from Glacier Peak Wilderness, crossing Hwy. 20 at Rainy Pass and
heading north through the Okanogan National Forest to the Canadian border.

Climbing

The **American Alpine Institute** offers six-
and 12-day alpine mountaineering courses in
the North Cascades for those with little or no
climbing experience; tuition is $380 and
$670. Their basic rock course, also for begin-

ners, is $100 for two days. The group also offers scheduled guided climbs, individual instruction, and classes in other climbing-related subjects. For a brochure or more information, write 1212 24th St., Bellingham, WA 98225, or phone (206) 671-1505.

Hunting And Fishing

You can rent a small motorboat at Baker Lake Resort, Diablo Lake Resort, Ross Lake Resort, Stehekin's North Cascade Lodge, or from private operators in Chelan (see "Transportation" below). Diablo Lake has boat-launch ramps at Diablo Lake Resort and Colonial Creek Campground; at Gorge Lake, there's a small ramp near Diablo. At Lake Chelan, launch from Chelan, Manson, or Twenty-five Mile Creek or Lake Chelan state parks. Catch rainbow, brook, golden, and Dolly Varden trout in mountain lakes and streams, or kokanee salmon in Lake Chelan.

Hunting is not allowed within national park boundaries; however, hunting is permitted in season at Ross Lake and Lake Chelan national recreation areas. Licenses are required and all state laws apply.

Pack Trips

North Cascade Outfitters leads horseback trips into the Pasayten Wilderness. "Economy" trips include riding horses and a guide; you provide food, tents, kitchen gear, and sleeping bags, for $60 a day. With a "first-class" trip, pay $90 a day and get riding horses, guide, meals, tents—everything but your sleeping bag and toothbrush. Kids eight and over are welcome; some exceptions are made for younger children. For more information write Box 397, Brewster, WA 98812, or phone (509) 689-2813 during normal working hours or (509) 689-3131 evenings and weekends.

Sightseers, photographers, hunters, and fishermen will all find a package to suit their needs from **Early Winters Outfitters.** Day-long horseback trips start at $60. For more information write or phone Star Route Box 28, Winthrop, WA 98862, tel. (509) 996-2659.

Claude Miller Pack Trips offers horseback trips into the Pasayten and Sawtooth wilderness areas. Hiking trips, in which the outfitter

---

NORTH CASCADES NATIONAL PARK RULES AND REGULATIONS

- Vehicles are not permitted in the park except on the North Cascades Hwy. and Cascade River Road.
- No dogs or other pets, except on the Pacific Crest Trail, Ross Lake, and Lake Chelan national recreation areas, and vehicle-access campgrounds, where they must be on a leash.
- No hunting or firearms in the national park; hunting is allowed according to state seasons and regulations at Ross Lake and Lake Chelan national recreation areas.
- No backpacking groups over 12.
- Backcountry permits—required for all overnight trips—are issued on a first-come, first-served basis. Areas that fill up fast are Fireweed, Copper Ridge, Thorton Lakes, Basin Creek, Monogram Lake, and McAllister Camp.
- Don't bury your trash; pack it out.
- Campground quiet hours are 10 p.m. to 6 a.m.
- Don't pick, dig, cut, or remove any plants or trees; berry and fruit picking for your personal consumption is okay.

---

carries the equipment, start at $65 per day; saddle horse trips, including tents, start at $75 a day if you do the cooking, $95 if they do. For more information write Box 250, Winthrop, WA 98862, or phone (509) 996-2350.

If you're traveling with young children, your best bet may be a trip with **Back Country Burro Treks,** Box 150, Malo, WA 99150, tel. (509) 779-4421 (evenings). A burro is gentle and cooperative enough to carry a two-year-old on its back, relieving you of having to carry the child on long trips or settle for two-mile hikes. The outfitters will supply you with a burro for the child, packing all of your camping equipment and meeting you at a designated campsite; at camp, you can cook your own meals ($35 per person per day) or leave the food preparation to the outfitters ($75 per person per day). Kids are $5 per day under

50 pounds, $10 per day up to 75 pounds. Scheduled treks last from three to 14 days, averaging nine to 10 miles of hiking per day.

Bald Eagle Float Trips
Just east of Rockport, the **Skagit River Bald Eagle Natural Area** is a haven for wintering bald eagles. The eagles arrive in October and feast on the Skagit River salmon run through March. The best way to see the eagles is on a scenic float trip down the Skagit with one of the area organizers. One of these, **Downstream River Runners,** claims to encounter at least 50 of these majestic birds perched in trees along the route. Their nine-mile trip from Marblemount to Rockport is held Dec. through February. The river is so gentle that wetsuits are not necessary (just warm winter clothing), and kids over five are welcome; $40 pp includes a post-float picnic lunch. Write 12112 N.E. 195th, Bothell, WA 98011, or phone (206) 483-0335 for more information.

Other companies offer essentially the same scenic float trip, with varying prices and departure dates. **Pacific Northwest Float Trips,** operating out of Sedro Woolley, tel. (206) 855-0535, offers a Skagit River float for $35 adults, from Dec. through Feb. or early March. **Rivers Inc.,** Box 2092 in Kirkland, WA 98083, tel. (206) 822-5296, also offers Dec. through March eagle-watching trips on the Skagit for $35. **North Cascades River Expeditions**, Box 116, Arlington, WA 98223,

tel. (206) 7435-9548, or (800) 634-8433 has 10½-mile Skagit River trips, year-round, for $37-49 with a riverside lunch included; minimum age six.

Winter Sports
The Methow Valley, from Mazama to Pateros, is known throughout the state for its fine cross-country skiing. The Methow Valley Ski Touring Assn. maintains over 150 km of trails, many of which are accessible from area inns (see above), as well as providing rentals, lessons, and hut-to-hut skiing. Phone (800) 422-3048 for information.

The Lake Chelan Valley is another heavily skied area. Ten minutes from Chelan, **Bear Mountain Ranch Nordic Ski Center** offers 40 km of groomed trails and 2,500 acres of forest and meadows for your cross-country skiing enjoyment. Open Fri. through Sun. and holidays from Dec. through Feb., daily during the Christmas holiday season. For ski conditions, phone (509) 682-5444 or (206) 453-5785. Other Chelan-area Nordic ski trails include five km of groomed runs at **Lake Chelan Golf Course** and another five km of groomed trails plus plenty of backcountry touring at Stehekin; the *Lady of the Lake* runs all winter (see "Transportation" below).

In Echo Valley, 12 miles northwest of Chelan, **Lake Chelan Nordic Skiers** has 20 km of groomed cross-country trails for every skill level. Rent cross-country equipment for $10

BRIAN BARDWELL

a day or $25 for three days at **Lake Chelan Sports,** 137 E. Woodin Ave., tel. (509) 682-2629. In Echo Valley, **Lake Chelan Ski Club** has day and night downhill skiing on 3,000-foot Echo Mountain, served by three rope tows and a poma lift; open Wednesday, and weekends.

Liberty Bell Alpine Tours, tel. (509) 996-2250, offers helicopter downhill skiing for the truly adventurous, flying skiers to deep powder on over 80 downhill runs in the Okanogan National Forest. Ski from Dec. to May; five runs will set you back $245.

For information on skiing at Mission Ridge, see "Wenatchee," p. 337; for Okanogan Valley skiing, see "Vicinity Of The North Cascades," below.

Snowmobilers will enjoy the 125 miles of trails on both sides of Lake Chelan, accessible from three Sno Parks, or the 150 miles of trails in the Methow Valley, with five Sno

Parks and snowmobile rentals; for information contact the Lake Chelan Ranger Station, tel. (509) 682-2576, or the Okanogan County Engineers, tel. (509) 422-3350.

Waterslide
Take advantage of Chelan's sunshine and enjoy the waterslides, hot tub, sunbathing, games, and concessions at **Slidewaters,** 102 Waterslide Dr. on the lake's south shore, tel. (509) 682-5751. Open Memorial Day weekend through Labor Day; admission is $9 adults, $6 kids four to seven.

Golf
Winthrop's **Bear Creek Golf Course** is a nine-hole course; tel. (509) 996-2284. In Pateros, **Alta Lake Golf Course** on Alta Lake Rd. also has nine holes; tel. (509) 923-2359. For 18 holes, try **Lake Chelan Golf Course,** a championship course at 1501 Golf Course Dr., tel. (509) 682-5421.

ACCOMMODATIONS

Inns And Resorts
Six miles past the Koma Kulshan Guard Station on the west shore, **Baker Lake Resort** has cabins, camping, boat rentals, a store, and a restaurant. The resort is generally open from the first day of fishing season in April through October. Cabins with bathrooms are $35 s, $40 d; without bathroom, $25 s, $30 d; camping is $10 d, plus $3 per day for hookups. Write Box 100, Concrete, WA 98237, or phone (206) 853-8325 or 424-0943 for reservations.

Seven miles east of Newhalem, **Diablo Lake Resort** has lodging in housekeeping cottages supplied with linens, pots and pans, and electric heat. Rates are $45-50 s or d for cabins; camping is available for $8 per night; Visa and MasterCard accepted. You'll also find a snack bar, restaurant, grocery store, and motorboat and canoe rentals. No public telephone; pets okay for an additional $5. Open year-round. Write Diablo Lake Resort, 503 Diablo, Rockport, WA 98283, or phone (206) 386-4429.

Diablo Lake

DIANNE BOULERICE LYONS

You can't drive to **Ross Lake Resort;** you'll have to hike in, boat in from Hozomeen, or take the boat taxi that leaves the Ross Dam Powerhouse parking lot twice a day. Lodging comes in "modern units," housing up to six people for $52, "rustic units" that can fit four people for $33, and "bunkhouse units" for $75 for one to six people, $7 for each additional person up to 10. You can rent a motorboat or canoe here (see "Transportation" below for details), but there are no telephones, groceries, food service, or pets, and they don't take credit cards. Write Ross Lake Resort, Rockport, WA 98283.

North Cascades Lodge in Stehekin can be reached only by floatplane or tour boat from Chelan (see "Transportation" below). Lodge rooms cost $46-68 s or d; furnished housekeeping units are $82 s or d (available Oct. through May). Amenities include a restaurant, bar, boat rentals, gasoline, and groceries; credit cards okay, but no pets. Write Box W, Chelan, WA 98816, or phone (509) 682-4711 for information and reservations. For general information on these four resorts, write or phone North Cascades National Park, 800 State St., Sedro Woolley, WA 98284; tel. (206) 855-1331.

The **Mazama Country Inn,** just off Hwy. 20 in Mazama, tel. (509) 996-2681, has 10 guest rooms in the newly completed lodge plus additional rooms in the restored farmhouse. Winter may be the best time to visit; miles of cross-country ski trails are accessible from the door of the inn, and a full line of rental equipment, guided tours, and lessons are available. Summer rates are $65 s, $75 d; winter rates are $95 s, $145 d, and include all meals, served family-style. All rooms have private bath; outdoor hot tub and sauna available. No smoking, pets, or kids under 10. For more information, write Box 223, Mazama, WA 98833.

Atop a 5,000-foot peak with 360-degree views into the North Cascades and the Methow Valley is **Sun Mountain Lodge,** one of the premier resorts in Washington. Its restaurant is one of only four to be given the AAA four-diamond rating. It has almost every amenity: tennis, swimming, hiking,

biking, the largest string of saddle horses in the region, cross-country skiing, canoeing. At the end of Patterson Lake Rd. nine miles southwest of Winthrop, tel. (509) 996-2211, it has 78 units, plus a cluster of new housekeeping cabins on Patterson Lake just below. All have mountain views. Rooms are $90-200 s or d in summer, $65-200 s or d after Labor Day.

At **Stehekin Valley Ranch,** your meals, lodging, and local transportation are included in the price of your cabin: $49 per person, $10-39 for kids under 12 (depending on age). The ranch is open from late May through Sept. and offers a variety of activities: 2½-hour horseback rides for $25, 10-mile raft trips down the Stehekin River for $35, several-day mountain hiking and horseback trips, day-hikes, fishing, boating, and more. For more information write Stehekin Valley Ranch, Box 36, Stehekin, WA 98852, or phone the answering service during normal working hours at (509) 682-4677.

At Stehekin's **Silver Bay Inn,** enjoy broad views of the lake and mountains while breakfasting in the solarium. Couples can enjoy the master suite for $85 d; families will enjoy one of two waterfront cabins, $85 d ($7.50 each additional up to four total). Two-night minimum; no pets or credit cards. Transportation to and from the boat landing is provided. Write Box 43, Stehekin, WA 98852, or phone (509) 682-2212 Mon. through Fri. during working hours.

Relax in Victorian splendor at the romantic **Whaley Mansion,** 415 Third St., Chelan, tel. (509) 682-5735. The 1911 frame house has been restored with French wallpapers, custom carpeting, and elegant draperies, plus modern conveniences like private baths. Rooms are $65-95 d; Champagne breakfast included. No kids, pets, or smoking. In Manson at Rt.1, Box 424, **Lee's,** tel. (509) 687-3942, is a modern B&B just off Totem Pole Road. Lake Chelan and mountain views, plus privacy and low rates: $40 s, $55 d.

The town of Pateros also has B&Bs; these are described, along with Lake Pateros, Bridgeport, and Brewster, under "Vicinity of the North Cascades," below.

Motels And Hotels

At the south end of Winthrop on Hwy. 20, the cedar-log **Virginian,** tel. (509) 996-2535, has motel rooms and cabins (some with fireplaces) and a heated pool in summer; rooms are $50-65 d, up to $150 for a one-bedroom house and $200 for a three-bedroom fireplace unit.

In Chelan, the **Apple Inn Motel,** 1002 E. Woodin Ave., tel. (509) 682-4044, has a heated pool, hot tub, and budget rooms from $29-55 s or d.

Most of the rooms in Chelan are considerably more expensive. The **Caravel Motor Hotel,** 322 W. Woodin, tel. (509) 682-2715, has 92 rooms from $92 s to $138 d for suites in summer including a pool, boat moorage, playground, airport and bus depot transportation, on the waterfront. **Campbell's Lodge,** 104 W. Woodin Ave., tel. 682-2561, has 106 rooms plus 17 cottages; rates are $52-86 s, 54-96 d in summer, $28-64 s, $32-68 d after Labor Day. Amenities include two heated pools, hot tub, poolside service, boat moorage, and a sandy beach. See "Food," below, for the hotel restaurant, the Campbell House. **Darnell's Resort Motel,** off Hwy. 150 on the lake's north shore, tel. (509) 682-2015, features luxury accommodations with heated pool, hot tub, sauna, exercise room, lighted tennis courts, putting greens, rowboats, bicycles, moorage, kids' play area—you name it. One-bedroom suites are $135-145 per day for a family of four; two-bedroom suites for a family of six are $165; the budget two-person loft is $60, and the four- to six-person penthouse, complete with two fireplaces, Jacuzzi, wet bar, and sundeck is $275 a day. No pets.

Hotels at Lake Chelan fill up fast in summer, so be sure to have reservations to stay on the lake. Bargain hunters who don't mind traveling can pick and choose from several reasonably priced hotels in Wenatchee, a half hour south on Hwy. 97, even when Chelan is booked solid; for example, the Wenatchee's Red Lion Thunderbird is a first-class hotel (room service, pool, restaurant, and the all-important shower caps and sewing kits) with rooms for about $50 s, $60 d.

Bed And Breakfast

The **Cascade Mountain Inn,** 3840 Pioneer Lane, Concrete-Birdsview, tel. (206) 826-4333, has six guest rooms, each furnished in the theme of a different country. Most rooms have views of Sauk Mountain, and each has a private bath. Rooms are $70 s, $84 d; no pets or kids under 10. Lunch and dinner are available to guests and others with reservations.

Camping And RV Parks

The west side of Baker Lake has numerous campgrounds: **Boulder Creek, Baker Lake, Lower Park Creek,** and **Shannon Creek** are right on the main drag, while **Puget Power, Depression Lake, Horseshoe Cove,** and **Morovitz Creek** are off the beaten path. Campgrounds accessible by car on the North Cascades Hwy. include **Goodell, Newhalem, Colonial Creek, Rainy Pass, Cutthroat Creek,** and **Lone Fir.** Fees from $3-5 are collected at the larger campgrounds: Goodell (22 sites, open year-round), Newhalem (116 sites, mid- June to Labor Day), and Colonial Creek (162 sites, mid-April through October). No hookups are available. Along Cascade River Rd., camp at **Cascade Island, Marble Creek,** or **Mineral Park.**

Brave the 39-mile gravel road from Canada and camp at **Hozomeen** at the north end of Ross Lake, from mid-May through Oct. or take a boat up Lake Chelan and camp at **Stehekin.** In summer, a shuttle bus drives campers from Stehekin to **Harlequin, High Bridge, Tumwater, Dolly Varden, Shady,** and **Cottonwood** campgrounds along the Stehekin River for a real escape from the crowds. Enjoy summer naturalist activities including nature walks and evening programs at Colonial Creek, Newhalem, Hozomeen, and Stehekin.

Private RV parks include **Creekside,** 761 Baker Lake Rd. in Birdsview, tel. (206) 826-3566, with 25 trailer sites for $8 on the banks of Grandy Creek. **Wilderness Village,** on the Skagit River in Rockport, tel. (206) 873-2571, has RV parking for $8-9, $2-3 additional for hookups; leashed pets are welcome. Marblemount's **Alpine RV Park and Campground,** 1½ miles east of town on Hwy. 20, tel. (206)

873-4142, has 30 full-hookup trailer sites for $8 a night; open all year. At **Rocking Horse Ranch** in Mazama, tel. (509) 996-2768, stay at one of 25 tent sites (10 suitable for RVs) for $8 from April through Oct. Two miles north of Twisp on Hwy. 20, **River Bend Trailer Park,** tel. (509) 997-3500, is open from mid-April through Oct. with 56 trailer sites for $9; hook-ups extra. In Pateros, the **Outpost RV Park** on Hwy. 97, tel. (509) 923-2200, is open all year with 20 trailer sites for $9.

Check "State Parks" above for more camping.

FOOD

Food, like gasoline and diesel, is hard to come by between Sedro Woolley and Winthrop. For a midday stop, try the **Hidden Inn** at Diablo Lake Resort for pizza, sandwiches, and other low-priced items with a lake view; open for three meals daily.

Most Hwy. 20 travelers stop at Winthrop for lunch, as evidenced by the town's parking problem even on midweek summer afternoons. For casual dining, downtown's **Duck Brand Restaurant,** tel. (509) 996-2192, serves moderately priced Mexican food, on the deck on sunny days; open for three meals daily. To find it, look up from the "Hotel and Restaurant" sign on the east side of the street. For pizza, snacks, sandwiches, and ribs, the over-21 crowd will enjoy **3 Fingered Jack's Saloon,** also downtown. **The Virginian,** the restaurant at the motel just south of Winthrop on Hwy. 20, tel. (509) 996-2536, serves three meals daily from a menu that includes pork, seafood, steak, and chicken; dinner runs $8-13.

The **Stehekin Valley Ranch Restaurant** is open every night from mid-June through Sept., Fri. and Sat. nights from late May to mid-June. The menu includes steaks, burgers, salad bar, and homemade desserts— all of which will taste pretty good after a week of backcountry travel or a long day in the saddle! Reservations are required. The restaurant is nine miles up the valley from Stehekin, but free transportation is provided from the Stehekin Valley Ranch.

Chelan has a large number of restaurants from which to choose. For Mexican food overlooking the lake, try **Cosina del Lago** on the Manson Hwy. next to Chelan Shores; tel. (509) 682-4071. The **Campbell House** at Campbell's Lodge, 104 W. Woodin Ave., tel. (509) 682-2561, offers elegant dining from a continental menu specializing in steak and seafood; prices are moderate, with dinners in the $7-18 range. Open for three meals; closed Dec. to March. **Katzenjammers** on Wapato Point in Manson, tel. (509) 687-9541, serves moderately priced steak and seafood; open weekdays for lunch, daily for dinner, plus Sunday brunch.

FESTIVALS

May is the start of Winthrop's rodeo season and **49ers Days,** with a parade, drawings, dance, and baseball tournament. **River Rat Days,** held in Winthrop on the July Fourth weekend, features a 12-mile race on the Methow River from Winthrop to Twisp on rafts, inner tubes, and canoes. Enjoy the **Apple Blossom Festival,** held the second weekend in May in Manson (on the north shore of Lake Chelan). The Fourth of July brings fireworks and a watermelon-seed-spitting contest to Manson. See Chelan's **rodeo** the third weekend in July, or visit their **Harvest Festival** in mid-September.

SHOPPING AND SERVICES

At the North Cascades Visitor Center in Concrete, visit the **Saturday Market,** where fruit, crafts, houseplants, and baked goods are offered for sale 9 a.m.-5 p.m. every Sat. from Memorial Day to Labor Day. Visit **The Mountain Gallery,** 114 Riverside Ave. in Winthrop, tel. (509) 996-2166, for paintings, woodcarvings, photographs, and prints of Western and North Cascades scenery and wildlife.

For up-to-date information on trail conditions and weather forecasts, contact the ranger stations at Marblemount, tel. (206) 873-4500, or Chelan, (509) 682-2549. Maps and other information may be obtained at these and other ranger stations at Stehekin, Early Winters, Concrete, and Sedro Woolley.

On the north side, gasoline and oil are available at Marblemount, Diablo Lake Resort, and Ross Lake Resort. Do your laundry at Diablo Lake Resort. Marblemount, Newhalem, and Diablo Lake Resort also stock limited groceries and supplies. **Methow Valley Central Reservations,** tel. (800) 422-3048, can help you find lodging from cabins to motels and provide information on helicopter skiing, ski rentals, steelhead fishing, and more. On the south side, Chelan is a bustling tourist town with all the services you'll ever need. For maps or other information, contact the **Lake Chelan Chamber of Commerce,** Box 216, Chelan, WA 98816, tel. (800) 4-CHELAN in Washington or (509) 682-2022.

For medical emergencies, contact a ranger station in the more remote areas or **Lake Chelan Community Hospital,** 503 E. Highland, tel. (509) 682-2531, in Chelan. Though "safety first" is always good advice, be especially careful when hiking in the Stehekin area; there are no doctors or medical facilities outside the ranger's first-aid kit, and it's a long boat ride to Chelan.

TRANSPORTATION

By Car
North Cascades National Park and Ross Lake National Recreation Area are about 100 miles, or 2½ hours, from Seattle via I-5 and Hwy. 20. Remember to gas up at or before Diablo Lake (Sedro Woolley is cheapest if you get lots of miles per tank), since there are no services for 75 miles between the dams and Mazama.

By Bus
No bus service goes to the north side of the park; the closest you'll get is Mount Vernon. On the south side, however, Chelan is served twice daily from Wenatchee by **Empire Bus Lines,** tel. (509) 682-2022, connecting with Greyhound and Trailways for countrywide service.

Take the boat up Lake Chelan (see below) and the summer shuttle bus from Stehekin to campgrounds and hiking trails along Stehekin

Valley Rd. for an extensive, no-car journey into the Cascades backcountry. The shuttle runs to the end of the road near Cascade Pass three times daily; the roundtrip fare is $8 adults, $4 kids and seniors, or buy an annual pass for $20 adults, $40 for the family. Be sure to get a shuttle schedule at the Chelan or Stehekin ranger station before setting out; seats are not reserved or guaranteed for the return trip, so be prepared to spend the night in case you miss the late afternoon bus.

By Boat
The *Lady of the Lake II* departs from Chelan for Field's Point, Lucerne, and Stehekin in the heart of the Cascades. In summer, the boat leaves daily at 8:30 a.m., arriving in Stehekin at 12:30 p.m.; after a 1½-hour layover for lunch and exploring, the boat heads back for a 6 p.m. return to Chelan. From mid-Oct. to mid-April, the boat departs on Sun., Mon., Wed., and Fri., shortens the layover to a half-hour, and returns to Chelan by 4:30 p.m. No reservations are necessary. Fares to Stehekin are $12 roundtrip adults. The boat will stop at any Forest Service campsite upon request. No pets allowed in summer; in winter, they must be in travel cages. One barge trip a week is made to transport cars, bicycles, horses, pets, canoes, and other large cargo. Shorter dinner cruises popular in the past have been discontinued, but may start up again in 1988 or later. For more information, write the Lake Chelan Boat Company, Box 186, Chelan, WA 98816, or phone (509) 682-2224.

Boat Rentals
Baker Lake, Diablo Lake, and Ross Lake resorts rent small boats, with or without motor, for about the same fee: $30-35 a day or $7-8 an hour for a boat with motor, $15-17 per day or $3-4 per hour for a row-it-yourself model. Ross Lake also rents 17-foot canoes for $15 per day, $4 per hour. At Lake Chelan, **Chelan Boat Rentals** on the lake's south shore at 1210 W. Woodin Ave., tel. (509) 682-4444, rents motorboats, Hobie cats, jet-skis, and mopeds. Boats cost $40-50 per

hour, and include gas, skis, life jackets, and knee-boards, and require a $100 cash deposit. Hobies are $20 per hour, jet-skis are $25-40 per hour, and mopeds are $12 per hour, all requiring a deposit of $20-30.

By Air
Chelan Airways offers daily seaplane service to Stehekin, Domke Lake, and other uplake destinations aboard four- and six-passenger planes. Fares to Stehekin are $40 one way, $75 roundtrip, two-passenger minimum. Or, fly one-way and take *Lady of the Lake* the other direction for $45 pp, minimum two people. Sightseeing flights of the Chelan basin start at $15; the Stehekin Valley tour is $25, and a 110-mile tour of all of Lake Chelan with a stopover at Stehekin is $50. For more information write Box W, Chelan, WA 98816, or phone (509) 682-5555 or 682-5065.

LEAVENWORTH

HISTORY

Although preceded by prospectors and Hudson's Bay fur traders, the first settlers in the Leavenworth area didn't arrive until the late 1880s, with the news that the Great Northern Railway planned to lay tracks through the valley. The resulting population "boom" brought Leavenworth about 300 people by the turn of the century. They were mostly railroad men or lumberjacks employed by the Lamb-Davis Lumber Co., operators of one of the state's largest sawmills. The after-hours rowdiness of these laborers gave little Leavenworth a somewhat unrefined reputation that took years to live down. Even so, by the early 1920s a wave of families bought tracts of land to grow "Wenatchee Big Red" apples.

When the railroad moved its switching yard from Leavenworth to Wenatchee, and the sawmill closed its doors after logging all its waterfront land, these family-based fruit farms provided much of the town's income. But by the 1960s, it was clear that Leavenworth needed more than apples to survive. A committee on tourism was formed to brainstorm and it suggested a fall festival and a major remodeling job.

Suggestions for the town's new theme ranged from a Gay '90s theme to a Western town, but with the impressive mountain backdrop, an alpine village seemed the best answer. The renovation was financed with private funds, and backed by local bankers, and it quickly earned national attention for its attention to detail, its aggressive promotion, and bootstraps efforts.

SIGHTS

The Bavarian Village
Start your tour of the Bavarian Village on Front St., the heart of town, where there's plenty of on-street parking. Shops, restaurants, taverns, and hotels are squeezed side by side, all beautifully decorated with carved wood, flower boxes, and murals—even the automated teller machine is surrounded by a painted alpine scene! There are shops that sell wooden toys, clocks, music boxes, wool clothing, and a bakery, **Hoelgaard's** (731 Front St.), that will tempt even the strongest-willed. Work your way back through the numbered side streets and onto Commercial for more shops. Don't miss **Obertal Mall** on Ninth St.; it contains galleries, high-quality craft and gift shops, boutiques, and a coffee shop.

PARKS AND RECREATION

Riverfront Park, on the banks of the Wenatchee River off Eighth and Commercial, has walkways over and around the river, benches for a respite from shopping, plus beautiful views of the peaks surrounding Ici-

LEAVENWORTH

0   0.25 mi

0   0.25 km

1. Haus Rohrbach
   Pension
2. Der Ritterhof Motor Inn
3. Enzian Motor Inn
4. Casa Mia
5. Gustav's
   Onion Dome Tavern
6. Hoelgaard's Bakery
7. Cascade General
   Hospital
8. Hansel 'n' Gretel Deli
   and Reiner's Gasthaus
9. chamber of commerce
10. city park
11. Der Sportsman,
    Edelweiss Restaurant,
    and Europa Hotel
12. Obertal Mall
    and Baren Haus
13. Edel Haus Inn
14. Haus Lorelie Inn
15. U.S. Forest Service
16. Evergreen Inn
17. Greyhound station
18. Brown's Farm B&B
19. Bavarian Meadows
20. Bayern Village
    Motor Inn
21. Chalet Trailer Park
22. Pine Village KOA
23. River's Edge Lodge
24. Mountain Home Lodge

cle Canyon. Cross-country ski from here to the golf course. **City Park,** across Front St. from the shops, is a relaxing, sunny spot for a picnic lunch or noontime break.

Twenty-three miles north of Leavenworth on Hwy. 207, **Lake Wenatchee State Park** is a popular year-round recreation area, with cross-country skiing in winter, plus swimming, fishing, and canoeing on over 12,000 feet of spectacular Lake Wenatchee waterfront, set against a backdrop of majestic snow-covered peaks. Other facilities include boat rentals, weekend-evening interpretive programs, and 197 wooded campsites (no

hookups). Summer camping is $6 per site; a number of sites are plowed for winter camping at $4.50 a night. Rent a horse from **Icicle Outfitters and Guides** for a guided one- or two-hour ride from their barn at the park for $8 an hour, Memorial Day through Labor Day; no reservations necessary.

Cross-country Skiing
Leavenworth is a popular spot with cross-country ski enthusiasts, with more than 30 km of groomed trails within minutes of downtown. Four ski areas are maintained by the Bavarian Nordic Club: one mile from Leaven-

worth on Icicle Rd., 13 km of groomed tracks traverse a golf course and gravel pit with mountain and river views. A few miles out of town at the mouth of Icicle Canyon, a 10-km level trail goes through meadows and forests above the Fish Hatchery. Ski Hill Dr. has a five-km track, with two km lighted for night skiing, rolling over the hills adjacent to the downhill ski area. Here you get the added benefit of a lodge and weekend food service. Lake Wenatchee State Park, 23 miles north of Leavenworth, has a minimum of five km of maintained trails. Trail fees for the first three areas are $4 per day for adults, kids under 12 free; skiing is free at Lake Wenatchee State Park. For more information contact the Bavarian Nordic Club at Box 573, Leavenworth, WA 98826, tel. (509) 548-5983.

Eagle Creek Ranch has 10 km of groomed trails, ski rentals, and instruction on Eagle Creek Rd., two miles north of town on Hwy. 209, as well as wilderness hut-to-hut ski trips and Saturday night "moonlight ski and barbecues" in Jan. and Feb.; call 548-7798 for specifics.

The **Leavenworth Nordic Center** on Hwy. 2 just east of the downtown area offers ski equipment rentals and lessons in everything from the basics to telemark techniques, plus a Kiddies Kamp where your four- to eight-year-old can learn to ski from a patient expert.

Cross-country ski rentals are available from the ski areas themselves or the following retail outlets: **Der Sportsman,** 837 Front St., tel. 548-5623, or **Gustav's Onion Dome Tavern,** Hwy. 2, tel. 548-4509.

For overnight cross-country skiing or alpine hiking in the high Cascades, stay in semiluxury at **Scottish Lakes Nomad Camps,** tel. 548-7330. Two rustic camps, one halfway up and one at the top of 5,000-foot McCue Ridge, provide warmth, company (up to 35 people), and a ride down for $56 d at Midway (no meals) and $120 d at High Camp (three meals); prices one-third off in summer. Write Box 312, Leavenworth, WA 98826, for details.

Downhill Skiing
Leavenworth has its own tiny ski area, Leavenworth Ski Bowl, with two rope tows providing

uphill transportation for the handful of runs. The ski season here is generally shorter than at the bigger areas because of the lower elevation; call (509) 548-5115 for conditions.

Two larger ski areas are close by: **Stevens Pass,** 35 miles to the west on Hwy. 2 (see "Skykomish," p. 306), and **Mission Ridge,** 35 miles in the other direction near Wenatchee (see p. 337).

Raft Trips
The rivers in the central Cascades support a number of whitewater outfitters in the Leavenworth-Skykomish area. **Quiet Water Outfitters & Guides** operates out of Leavenworth over Gustav's Onion Dome, providing scenic float trips for people four and over on the upper Wenatchee from April to Aug. and exciting white water trips for adults from mid-April to about mid-July; prices are in the $30-45 range. Canoe rentals are also available, with the outfitters getting you started and picking you up at a predetermined point downriver. For info and reservations call (509) 763-3733.

The **Northern Wilderness Co.,** a somewhat bigger operation, provides all the necessary equipment and a gourmet lunch for their river trips, ranging from slow float trips to wild whitewater rides on the Wenatchee, Skykomish, Naches, Tieton, and other rivers throughout central and western Washington. Call them toll-free at (800) 848-8001 for specific trip dates and reservations.

For more central Cascade raft trips see "Skykomish," p. 307.

Pack Trips

From July through Sept. **Eagle Creek Ranch** offers a number of pack trips to Alpine Lakes, Glacier Lakes, and Henry M. Jackson wilderness areas in the Cascades. Their standard pack trips and their "you hike and we pack" trips—meaning you provide and cook the food—cost $60-70 pp per day. "Drop camp" packages, in which the wrangler takes you to a favorite spot for as long as you like and then comes back to get you out, include pack and saddle horses and cost $250 pp. They also offer day-long horseback rides along mountain trails from April through Sept. at 9 a.m. everyday. For a brochure or additional info contact them at Box 719, Leavenworth, WA 98826, tel. (509) 548-7798.

Icicle Outfitters and Guides offers hourly horse rides at Lake Wenatchee State Park for $8 an hour, guided day rides into the Cascades for $45 a day, and an assortment of two- to five-day pack trips, including combination horseback-and-raft or -canoe trips, from $50 pp per day for the hike-and-pack trips, $160 for an overnight campout and barbecue in the high country, to $350 for a five-day horseback trip. Write or call them at Box 322, Leavenworth, WA 98826, tel. 784-1145 or 763-3647.

Hiking

The Lake Wenatchee Ranger District, centered around Lake Wenatchee and Fish Lake at the north end of Hwy. 207, has an extensive system of hiking trails. Popular with hikers and photographers is the **Dirtyface Trail,** a steep 4½-mile one-way trail from the Lake Wenatchee Ranger Station to the Dirtyface Lookout at 6,000 feet, with views of the lake and surrounding scenery. Backpackers may want to try the **Nason Ridge Trail,** a 22-mile one-way scenic trail along the length of the Nason Ridge, starting at South Shore Rd. off Hwy. 207; check at the ranger station for possible closures due to trail reconstruction. A number of other one-day or longer hikes start from various points along a complicated network of numbered forest roads; best bet is to check at the ranger station for detailed maps and printed trail descriptions. This is black bear country; hikers and campers should use standard bear precautions (see "Flora and Fauna," p. 8).

Climbing

Good physical condition is the only requirement for participation in one of **Leavenworth Alpine Guides'** guided climbs and rock- and ice-climbing courses. Prices range from $25 for the half-day basic rock course to $310 for a five-day alpine climbing camp with an ascent of 9,415-foot Mt. Stuart. A number of other courses and climbs are offered, including other central Cascade peaks, Mt. Baker, the Alps, and Mt. Everest. For a brochure write Box 699, Leavenworth, WA 98826, tel. (509) 548-4729.

ACCOMMODATIONS

Bed And Breakfast

Brown's Farm B&B, tel. (509) 548-5863, is a three-gabled log home surrounded by woods and farm animals at 11150 Hwy. 209. Antique-furnished rooms are $55-65 d; kids ($5-10 more) are welcome to hike the wooded trails, gather farm-fresh eggs, or play with Barney, the family dog. Winter guests can rent cross-country skis, then warm up with hot cider by the rock fireplace. Bring a sleeping bag and pillow for the kids; foam pads are provided. No pets or smoking in the guest rooms.

Haus Rohrbach Pension, 12882 Ranger Rd., tel. 548-7024, is a European-style inn overlooking the Leavenworth Valley. Their 10 rooms begin at $70 d. The complimentary breakfast features sourdough pancakes and home-baked cinnamon rolls, and an outdoor pool and hot tub are also available. Their Alm Haus offers a bedroom, dining area, kitchen, and bath, and can accommodate six to eight people for $98-118. Kids are welcome; outdoor smoking only, and no pets.

*Leavenworth's streets
have a Bavarian flair.*

ARCHIE SATTERFIELD

Above the Wenatchee River, the **Haus Lorelei Inn,** 347 Division St., tel. 548-5726, was built in 1903 and retains a turn-of-the-century charm with its architectural detail and Elisabeth's German furniture. The inn is located on the riverfront cross-country ski trail and a short walk from a sandy swimming beach, just two blocks from downtown. The six rooms (four with private bath) are $70 d, including a full breakfast and use of the hot tub and tennis court. No smoking.

Mountain Home Lodge, tel. 548-7077 (Box 687), is in a category by itself: located just three miles from downtown, this lodge is a true escape, particularly in winter when transportation from parking lot to lodge is via snowcat. Half a mile up into the Cascades, rates begin at $70 d. Cross-country skiing, snowshoeing, and sledding are outside the back door. Other activities, such as downhill skiing, horseback riding, snowmobiling, whitewater rafting, and mountain tours can be arranged. Smoking outdoors only.

Located between Waterfront Park and the shopping district at 320 Ninth St., **Edel Haus Pension** is a B&B with five guest rooms furnished with antiques; children can be accommodated in the Family Room on the main floor. Rates are $60 and up d for rooms with shared bath. A full breakfast and private use of the hot tub are included; tel. 548-4412.

Housed in the Old Blewett Pass Stage Stop that served as a B&B in the early 1900s, the **Old Blewett Pass Bed and Breakfast,** tel. 548-4475, came back to life in 1986, offering food and lodging "country-western style" about 10 miles south of downtown at 3470 Hwy. 97. Rooms are $30 s, $38 d with shared bath, $40 s, $48 d with private bath; a four-person family suite is also available for $60. A full breakfast is served; children are welcome to enjoy the enclosed playground, and babysitting is available with advance notice. Other extras include a pool, sauna, and recreation room.

About a mile out of town on the Icicle River is **Run of the River,** 9308 E. Leavenworth Rd., tel. 548-7171. The beautiful log lodge has four rooms with private baths, and is believed to be the only bed-and-breakfast exclusively for nonsmokers. Smoking isn't only banned inside; you can't smoke *anywhere* on the property. The cathedral-ceilinged rooms have windows with views of the Icicle River and the Cascades. True to its theme, the furniture is of handcarved logs and the quilts are handmade. Prices begin at $70; if you stay five nights, the last night is free.

Hotels And Motor Inns

Leavenworth is a popular getaway, particularly in winter, so room rates are generally higher on weekends; try to time your visit from Sun. through Thursday.

The **Enzian Motor Inn,** 590 Hwy. 2, tel. (509) 548-5269 or (800) 223-8511, is a cross between a conventional motel and B&B: its 77 rooms, convention facility, and heated pool and hot tub are standard hotel equipment, but the German architectural design, imported furniture, continental breakfast, and complimentary cross-country ski rentals give the inn a warm, homey feeling. Rates are $59 and up. The **Europa Hotel,** downtown at 833 Front St., tel. 548-5221, has 12 rooms with full baths, TV, and continental breakfast in European style for $36-46 s or d. **Der Ritterhof Motor Inn,** Hwy. 2, tel. 548-5845, has 52 rooms, heated pool, hot tub, outdoor volleyball, horseshoes, and badminton areas, and a putting green from $54.

Bayern Village Motor Inn, 1505 Alpen See Strasse, tel. 548-5875, has rooms with private decks overlooking the Wenatchee River, swimming pool, and barbecue pits for $55. The **Evergreen Inn,** 1117 Front St., tel. (800) 327-7212 or 548-5515, is less than two blocks from the downtown commercial center and has cottage-like rooms from $50-120.

Between Leavenworth and Cashmere on Hwy. 2, **The River's Edge Lodge,** tel. 548-7612, has 23 rooms on the Wenatchee River with outdoor pool and hot tub starting at $50 s or d; some rooms include kitchenettes.

Camping

Stretched out along the Wenatchee River at 11401 River Bend Dr., the **Leavenworth Pine Village KOA,** tel. (509) 548-7709, operates from April through mid-Oct. with a heated pool, cabins, laundry, groceries, and Sat. hay rides; rates are $13.50 per night; hookups extra. **The Chalet Trailer Park,** one-half mile east of town on Hwy. 2, has 24 sites for $10.50, including all hookups. Open from May to Oct.; tel. 548-4578. About 15 miles northwest of Leavenworth near Lake Wenatchee, **Midway Village RV Park** has 10 tent sites and 23 hookup sites for $8. Open all year; tel. 763-3344. For camping in Lake Wenatchee State Park, see "Parks and Recreation," above.

FOOD

The village has a number of restaurants, all very Bavarian from the outside but often with largely American menus fortified by a token bratwurst or Wiener schnitzel. You'll get the real thing at **Reiner's Gasthaus,** 829 Front St., tel. (509) 548-5111, serving authentic Austrian, Bavarian, and Hungarian cuisine with live accordion music, all at low to moderate prices. The **Edelweiss Restaurant,** 843 Front St., tel. 548-7015, is open for three meals with a mixed American/German menu; lunch runs $2-9, dinners up to $22 for twin lobster tails, but generally $12 or less. Grab a beer and burger at **Gustav's Onion Dome Tavern,** at the west end of town on Hwy. 2. **Hansel 'N' Gretel Deli,** 819 Front St., has German sausages, sandwiches, homemade pies, 18 flavors of ice cream, and picnics-to-go. Perhaps a little out of place, **Casa Mia** has Mexican food (under a Bavarian disguise) across from the fire station at 703 Hwy. 2; tel. 548-5621. Or, for pizza, try **Baren Haus** at Ninth and Front streets. If you're headed up to Lake Wenatchee, try the **Cougar Inn Resort** at the end of Hwy. 207 for steaks, seafood, prime rib, chicken, and Sunday Champagne brunch with stunning lake and mountain views; call 763-3354 for reservations.

ENTERTAINMENT

Festivals

The people in Leavenworth always find something to celebrate, with festivals and fairs circling the calendar. January brings **The Great Bavarian Ice Fest,** with a snowman contest, kids' cross-country ski day, fireworks, and Sasquatch dance in mid-month. Smaller festivals fill the months until the big **Maifest,** held on Mother's Day weekend, when costumed Bavarian dancers circle the maypole, and concerts, a fun run, volksmarch, and Saturday night street dance are accompanied by oompa music from the band stand. This weekend marks the start of **Art in the Park,** with area artists displaying their talents

*the festival capital
of the state*

every weekend from May through Oct. in City Park. The **Washington State Autumn Leaf Festival,** a week-long event held at the end of Sept., starts with a grand parade and includes daily oompa music, a street dance, hootenanny, fun run, flea market, and casino night. But Christmas is Leavenworth's most festive holiday: the **Christmas Lighting Festival,** held the first and second Saturdays in Dec., when all the Christmas lights go on simultaneously at dusk. Mr. and Mrs. Claus appear in their house in the park, and caroling, sleigh rides, concerts, and food booths add to the holiday festivities.

Sleigh Rides And Hay Rides

The people at **Red-Tail Canyon Farm** at 11780 Freund Canyon Rd. operate hay rides and sleigh rides year-round through scenic Red-Tail Canyon. One-hour sleigh rides are $7 adults ($10 in the evening), $4 for kids; hay rides are $6 and $4. To get there, take Hwy. 209 north for 2½ miles; call 548-4512 for reservations. **Eagle Creek Ranch,** tel. 548-7798, also offers hay and sleigh rides over the meadows and through the woods surrounding the ranch two miles north of town off Hwy. 209.

Snowmobile Tours

See the Cascades and the Leavenworth valley from a unique perspective on one of **Cascade Snowmobile Safaris'** snowmobile tours. All cold-weather clothing from snowsuits to boots to helmets is included in the price of $35 for a two-hour tour, $45 for a three-hour tour, starting off Hwy. 2 and heading almost to the top of Wedge Mountain and/or Boundary Butte. Two tours are scheduled every day, weather permitting, with occasional twilight tours; riders must be 16 or over. For reservations call 548-5162 or 548-4337.

SERVICES AND INFORMATION

All Leavenworth-area phone numbers are preceded by area code 509. For maps, brochures, and additional information contact the **Leavenworth Chamber of Commerce,** Box 327, Hwy. 2, Innsbrucker Bldg., Leavenworth, WA 98826, tel. 548-7914.

Hikers and campers will find **Die Wascherei** on Front St. a relief: laundry facilities and hot showers in the same place! Open daily 7 a.m.-10 p.m. Places as beautiful as Icicle Canyon and Tumwater Canyon should be heavily photographed; take your rolls to **Der Darkroom,** 819 Front St., for one-hour processing.

The Leavenworth area, unlike some mountain communities, is equipped with emergency 911 service. For less critical medical emergencies, contact **Cascade Hospital,** 817 Commercial St., at 548-5815.

TRANSPORTATION

Getting There

Driving to Leavenworth via Hwy. 2 through Stevens Pass has been described as "driving through a Christmas card." Rocky, snow-covered peaks surround the highway as you approach the 4,061-foot pass; then, closer to Leavenworth, the Wenatchee River rushes alongside the road. The trip from Seattle is about 125 miles. From late fall to early spring, be sure to call 976-7623 for pass conditions before setting out—and have your chains ready! As an alternate route, take I-90 over Snoqualmie Pass to Hwy. 97 north over Swauk Pass; these passes are generally drier, and snow-free earlier, than Stevens. From Wenatchee the trip is an easy one: 30 miles northeast on Hwy. 2.

Greyhound Bus Lines serves Leavenworth from their Kountry Kitchen "station" at the east end of town on Hwy. 2; they have three eastbound and three westbound departures every day, year-round. The nearest real airport (outside the airstrips at Lake Wenatchee and Cashmere) and railroad station is in Wenatchee; see p. 339 for information.

Bus Tours

Gray Line of Seattle offers tours from Seattle to Leavenworth for Maifest ($34) in early May and the Christmas Tree Lighting Ceremony ($30) on the first two Saturdays in December. Prices for both one-day trips include a snack on the bus. For more information call Gray Line at (206) 624-5813. Also operating out of Seattle, **Don & Diane Fun-Tours** has one-day bus tours in late Sept. or early Oct. to the Autumn Leaf Festival, and the first Sat. in Dec. to the Christmas Lighting Festival; both tours are $34. For reservations or information call (206) 282-3508.

Departing from Tacoma, **Cascade Trailways** offers one-day Autumn Leaf Festival tours for $28.50, including snack; call (206) 383-4615 (Tacoma) or (206) 838-3465 (Seattle), or toll-free statewide (800) 824-8897 for information and reservations.

SKYKOMISH AND VICINITY

The little towns of Skykomish, Index, Gold Bar, and Monroe serve mainly as jumping-off points for the wealth of recreational opportunities in the nearby Cascade wilderness areas. The Skykomish District of the Snoqualmie National Forest encompasses more than 315,000 acres of national forest land and 41,000 acres of state and private lands, with striking natural features from glaciers and alpine meadows to dense forests intersected by clear, clean rivers. The Alpine Lake and Henry M. Jackson wilderness areas and the Mt. Index Scenic Area are within the district's boundaries; access to Glacier Peak Wilderness Area is via the Pacific Crest Trail. Much of the area's beauty can be seen through your car windows and from short roadside paths, but over 140 miles of hiking trails let you experience its splendor at close range.

OUTDOOR RECREATION

Scenic Drives

U.S. Hwy. 2, the main access to the area, is one of the state's most beautiful drives and is the western end of the transcontinental two-lane route that runs east to Maine. From the Skykomish Ranger Station, one mile east of Skykomish center on Hwy. 2, west to the small town of Scenic, the two-lane road gains 1,000 feet in elevation; from there to the summit of Stevens Pass it gains another 2,000 feet to reach a height of 4,061 feet, passing rugged snow-covered peaks and waterfalls along the way.

Other scenic drives in the Skykomish District are on numbered gravel forest roads. Create your own loop route from the roads on the map below, or try the **Maloney-Sobieski Mountain Rd.** for views of Glacier Peak and deep valleys. To get there, head east from the ranger station for a half mile, then turn left onto Foss River Rd. #68. Drive about 5½ miles to the intersection of #68 and #6840;

go right onto #6840. When you reach the next fork, stay to the right onto #6846 until the next fork; then go left to Sobieski Mountain or right to Maloney Mountain, with spectacular views on either route.

Waterfalls

The Hwy. 2 planners must have loved waterfalls: several raging falls are right along the roadside. **Bridal Veil Falls,** a quarter mile east of the Index junction, vary with the season: summer brings two distinctive "veils" while winter freezes the falls into a glistening sheet of ice. Five miles east of the ranger station, **Alpine Falls** drop 50 feet into the Tye River below; park on the south side of the highway and follow the can't-miss path. About 1½ miles from Alpine Falls are **Deception Falls,** right on the south side of the highway. To see the biggest falls you've got to exert a little more effort: **Wallace Falls,** a 265-foot waterfall, is a seven-mile roundtrip hike from the trailhead two miles northeast of Gold Bar.

Nature Trails

If you're not up for a long hike, these two half-mile nature trails through Douglas fir forests will give you a breather from mountain driving. **Deception Falls Nature Trail** begins at the north end of the picnic area about 6½ miles from the ranger station on Hwy. 2; **Troublesome Creek Nature Trail** starts 10.8 miles northeast of Index next to the Troublesome Creek Campground on North Fork Skykomish Rd. #63.

Hiking Trails

Check in at the ranger station for information on trail conditions before you start any of the longer hikes described below.

For a short trip, try the one-mile one-way hike from Hwy. 2 just east of Index to Heybrook Lookout for views of Mt. Index, Baring Mountain, and the Skykomish Valley. An-

SKYKOMISH

other lookout, **Evergreen Mountain,** can be reached via a 1½-mile one-way hike from the end of Evergreen Mountain Rd. #6554. The trail gains 1,300 feet in elevation, but on a clear day the 360-degree view includes Glacier Peak and Mt. Rainier. Regrettably, this trail is open to ORVs. Slightly longer (2.2 miles one way) but with little elevation gain is the **Barclay Lake** trail, following the course of Barclay Creek to the lake with a nice view of Baring Mountain. To get to the trailhead, take Barclay Creek Rd. #6024 for four miles.

Backpackers have quite a few options. A good two-day roundtrip hike (9.7 miles one way) starts from North Fork Skykomish Rd. #63 to **Bald Eagle Mountain,** via a loop from trail #1050 north to Trail #650, east to Trail #1051, and southeast to the end of Forest Rd. #63. Switchbacks take you to ridgetops for most of the hike, through masses of hillside wildflowers. Serious backpackers can hook up with the **Pacific Crest Trail** and hike clear up to Canada or down to Mexico if they like—or, more likely, just hike a short chunk of the trail. It crosses Hwy. 2 near Stevens

Pass, about 15½ miles east of the ranger station. Head north on the Pacific Crest Trail for 16 miles to the Henry M. Jackson Wilderness Area; the first 1½ miles are level, but don't get discouraged—the switchbacks are coming! Heading south from Hwy. 2, it's just over 19 miles to the Alpine Lake Wilderness Area, passing a number of lakes and climbing over Surprise Mountain.

Skiing

About halfway between Skykomish and Lake Wenatchee is **Stevens Pass,** a full-size ski area, popular with Seattleites, with 10 lifts serving 1,125 acres of beginner through expert terrain. Stevens Pass is open mid-Nov. through late April (snow permitting), offering ski rentals and lessons, ski shop, restaurant, cafeteria, cocktail lounges, and weekend child care. Lift tickets are $24 adults, $18 kids, $20 seniors; six and under, 70 and older ski free. Phone (206) 973-2441 or (206) 634-1645 for conditions.

See "Wenatchee," p. 337, for information on **Mission Ridge Ski Area.**

Raft Trips

Operating out of Bothell, **Downstream River Runners** offers one- to five-day whitewater or float trips on numerous rivers throughout eastern and western Washington and Oregon, including the popular and challenging Skykomish River with its class V "Boulder Drop" ($55-70, minimum age 14) and an Upper Skykomish trip on an inflatable kayak ($70, minimum age 16). Write them at 12112 N.E. 195th in Bothell, WA 98011, or phone (206) 483-0335, for a brochure.

North Cascades River Expeditions, Box 116, Arlington, WA 98223, tel. (206) 435-9548 or (800) 634-8433, also offers a variety of one- and two-day river trips, including the Skykomish, Wenatchee, Skagit, Klickitat, and more. Prices are $37-40 pp for one-day trips, $82-159 for a two-day expedition, and include shuttle and riverside lunch.

For a do-it-yourself trip, the lower Skykomish is a peaceful river to raft or kayak, rated class II from Index to Sultan and class I from Sultan to Monroe with a few small, generally avoidable rapids. The Upper Skykomish from Skykomish to Baring and the South Fork from Skykomish to Boulder Drop are not for beginners; before attempting them it's a good idea to consult *Water Trails of Washington* by Werner Furrer, published by Signpost Books, 8912 196th SW, Edmonds, WA 98020, for $5.95. The guide has detailed maps, cautionary notes, and loads of useful information.

ACCOMMODATIONS AND FOOD

Camping

The four area campgrounds provide minimal facilities—toilet, fireplace, and table—for tents and trailers under 15 feet in length. All campgrounds generally close in Sept. after a late spring opening; all sites are available on a first-come, first-served basis for a small nightly fee. **Beckler River,** 2½ miles from the ranger station, has 24 sites; **Money Creek,** just over four miles away, also has 24; **Miller River,** about 6½ miles from the station, has 15; and **Troublesome Creek,** 20 miles away, has 35 primitive sites (no well water or garbage pick-

up) for no fee. As in virtually all natural areas today, giardiasis is a problem; boil all drinking water for three to five minutes to prevent this "backpacker's diarrhea."

Motels

Skykomish has a gas station, two motels, two restaurants, a tavern, and a liquor store. Following the Skykomish River west along Hwy. 2, you'll pass a number of other bare-bones establishments between Skykomish and Monroe that consider a four-foot sign reading "MOTEL" or "RESTAURANT" sufficient advertising. One of the cleaner and more modern is the **Dutch Cup Motel** at 918 Main St. in Sultan, with rooms going for $31 s, $35-41 d; tel. (206) 793-2215.

Food

The **Dutch Cup Restaurant,** up the street at 927 Hwy. 2, is open daily from 5 a.m.-2 a.m. (a courtesy to the skiers passing through) with steaks and weekend specials. When you arrive in the thriving commercial center of Monroe (pop. 3,000), you'll be overwhelmed by the choices: Dairy Queen, McDonald's, and Rax have brought fast food to the foothills, but locally owned establishments provide a welcome change of tastes. **Nina's Soup Kitchen,** 113 East Fremont, is open daily for breakfast and lunch, and the **Holiday Inn Country Eatery and Lounge,** 612 East Stevens Pass Hwy., serves homemade chili, steaks, soups, and desserts.

SERVICES

The Skykomish Ranger Station provides recreation and topographic maps, books, and current information on trail conditions and campground closures. The ranger station is open daily in summer, Mon. through Fri. in winter.

The Skykomish area code is 206. For medical emergencies call 677-2222 in Skykomish; for first aid or search and rescue, call the King County Sheriff at (800) 344-4080 or the Snohomish County Sheriff at 258-2484. To report a forest fire, call the Skykomish Ranger

Station at 677-2412 or the Dept. of Natural Resources at (800) 562-6010.

TRANSPORTATION

Skykomish is on the good-road-conditions side of Stevens Pass, often a challenge to traverse (and sometimes closed) in winter. If you're going to ski at Stevens Pass Ski Area or continue west to Leavenworth or Wenatchee, be sure to phone 976-7623 (there's a $.35 toll for the call) for road conditions before you set out; you don't want to have to buy chains at the only gas station in Skykomish.

SNOQUALMIE AREA

When most Washington residents hear "Snoqualmie," they think first of the pass and ski areas, then the falls; the tiny town is only an afterthought. Snoqualmie Pass is the easiest way through the Cascades in winter, sporting the widest highway and lowest elevation of any of the mountain passes; the four ski areas at the summit bring a lot of vehicular traffic through the region.

Snoqualmie Falls is an attraction both for the falls itself and for the restaurant and new hotel that sit atop it. But the little town of Snoqualmie, with about two blocks of civilization on either side of the tracks, draws tourists only for its scenic railroad. The bigger town in the rural Snoqualmie area is North Bend, a pseudo-Bavarian village at the foot of Mount Si, one of the state's most hiked mountains.

SIGHTS

Snoqualmie Falls

One hundred feet taller than those at Niagara, Snoqualmie Falls in Fall City has been awe-inspiring since probably the last ice age, and electricity-generating since 1898, when Puget Power built the world's first totally underground generating facility. Though the land is all owned by the utility, they've made a great deal of it available for public use with a landscaped park and picnic area, hiking trail, view platforms, and a snack bar. To get there, drive about four miles north on Hwy. 203 from Snoqualmie; open all year.

Carnation Research Farm

North of Snoqualmie and Fall City on Hwy. 203 is the Carnation Research Farm, owned and operated by the Carnation milk-and-ice-cream, dog- and cat-food people. Free, self-guided tours of the plant include the milking carousel, maternity barn and recovery room, and research kennels where beagles, Scotties, and fox terriers sample new flavors of dog food. Because of their susceptibility to airborne illnesses, the kitties are kept in a "cattery" closed to visitors. The rest of the place is open Mon. through Sat. 10 a.m-3 p.m.; tel. (206) 788-1511.

Museum

In North Bend, the **Snoqualmie Valley Historical Museum,** 320 North Bend Blvd. S, has permanent displays of Indian artifacts, pioneer and logging history, and a small gift shop. Open weekend afternoons from April through Oct.; tel. (206) 888-3200 or 888-0062.

Winery

The **Snoqualmie Winery,** 1000 Winery Rd. in Snoqualmie (take a right off the Snoqualmie Falls exit from I-90), produces seven varieties of wine, including johannesburg riesling, merlot, and cabernet sauvignon. Besides the usual gift shop, this one has a big picnic area with panoramic views of the Cascades and Snoqualmie Valley. Open for tours and tastings 10 a.m.-4:30 p.m. daily, year-round, with occasional extended hours during the summer and ski seasons; tel. (206) 888-4000.

Herbfarm

More than a decade ago, Lola Zimmerman put out a few pots of her home-grown herbs at a roadside stand. Today, The Herbfarm boasts over 400 kinds of live herb plants, 120 species of succulents, and classes in everything from Medicinal Gardening to Herbal Vinegars. Pick up an herbal flea collar, beer bread mix, live plants, book, herbal deodorant, or gourmet coffee bags at the farm's country store. Or, plan ahead and enjoy their immensely popular weekend luncheon, served Fri. through Sun., April through Christmas. The two-hour luncheon is a six-course meal featuring fresh local game and fish, accompanied by vegetables from The Herbfarm's garden; $24.95 per person, and reservations are required. The Herbfarm is open daily, March to Oct., with reduced days and hours in fall and winter; 32804 Issaquah-Fall City Rd., Fall City, tel. 784-2222.

OUTDOOR RECREATION

Skiing

Snoqualmie Pass offers probably the best skiing in the state, with more choices than in any other region. There are four major ski areas here, virtually side by side. Three of them operate as one, calling themselves "The Big Three" and requiring only one lift pass: **Alpental, Ski Acres,** and **Snoqualmie Summit.**

Snoqualmie, in the center, emphasizes beginner and intermediate terrain serviced by eight chairs and five rope tows. Ski Acres is the next step up in difficulty, with a good showing of intermediate and expert as well as beginner terrain, with seven chairs and six rope tows. Alpental is the most challenging with a 2,200-foot vertical drop, and while novices and intermediate skiers have some territory, the emphasis here is clearly on difficult and expert-only slopes, serviced by four chairs, four ropes, and a platter. You can ski between Ski Acres and Snoqualmie via expert-level terrain, but you'll have to board the free shuttle bus to get to Alpental.

Lift tickets are $15 weekends, $12.50 midweek; night skiing, available on almost all of Snoqualmie and Ski Acres' slopes and about a third of Alpental's, costs $11-12. Child care is available at Ski Acres for kids two and over, daily except Tues. and by appointment; call

(206) 434-6400 for reservations. Naturally, all three areas provide ski school, equipment rentals, restaurants and/or snack bars; in addition, Ski Acres has 20 km of cross-country trails, including 1½ km of lighted track for night skiing. Snoqualmie and Alpental are closed Mon., Ski Acres is closed Tues., except during the Christmas season. Call 236-1600 for the Snoqualmie report; or from Seattle, call 634-0200; from Tacoma, tel. 572-4300; and from Everett, tel. 353-7440.

Pacific West Mountain Resort, otherwise known as Pac West, is just west of The Big Three. Members of the Pac West Sport & Racquet Club receive a 25% discount on the $12 day lift pass, but you don't have to be a member to ski here. The mountain has a 1,143-foot vertical drop, making it slightly higher than Ski Acres and Snoqualmie; the beginner through expert terrain is served by four double chairs and two rope tows. Night skiing goes on till midnight. Besides the usual ski school, rentals, restaurant, and lounge,

VICINITY OF SNOQUALMIE FALLS

© MOON PUBLICATIONS, INC.

Pac West has extensive cross-country ski terrain. For information call 633-2460.

Hiking

North Bend's 4,167-foot **Mount Si** is one of the most climbed mountains in the state; 10,000 people a year take the eight-hour roundtrip hike. It's not just the length of the hike that's tough—the elevation gain of 3,100 feet keeps you puffing. The views west to Puget Sound, Seattle, and the Olympics, however, are worth the effort. To get there go left on 432nd SE (Mt. Si Rd.), about a mile from the east edge of North Bend. After you

cross the Middle Fork Snoqualmie River, go right at the first intersection, then drive 2½ miles to the parking lot, trailhead, and picnic area. The trails are generally snow-free from April to November.

ACCOMMODATIONS

Hillwood Gardens B&B, 41812 S.E. 14 Second St. in North Bend, tel. (206) 888-0799, features mountain views in an Oriental atmosphere; rooms cost $35, no children. For simple, inexpensive lodging, the **North Bend Motel,** 322 East North Bend Way, has rooms for $27 d; tel. 888-1121. Cheaper still, the **Sunset Motel,** 227 West North Bend Way, will keep you warm and dry for $22 d; tel. 888-0381. On the way to Snoqualmie Pass, just off I-90 at exit 34, the **Edgewick Inn,** 14600 468th Ave. Southeast in North Bend, tel. 888-9000, has 43 modern rooms plus a whirlpool and laundry facilities for $33 s, $37-42 d.

In 1988, the long-awaited **Salish Lodge,** tel. (800) 826-6124, opened at Snoqualmie Falls. This luxury hotel features a fireplace, spa, and refrigerator in every room, plus a balcony in most. A great place for a honeymoon or a getaway weekend, the rooms here are pricey: $150 s or d for a courtyard room, $165 s or d for a room with a river and mountain view.

FOOD

The Salish Lodge Restaurant atop Snoqualmie Falls has been in operation (under various names) since 1916. The new dinner menu features six entrees in the $15-24 range, and the farm-style Sunday brunch has always been a regional favorite. The homey lodge atmosphere, with overstuffed chairs surrounding a warm fire in the lounge, is worth the price of admission. Don't waste it on the kids. Reservations are recommended: tel. (800) 826-6124.

Atop Snoqualmie Pass, the **Restaurant Continental,** tel. 434-6343, specializes in fondues; open daily for breakfast, lunch, and dinner. Also at the pass, **Traveler's Restaurant** has inexpensive sandwiches, burgers, light meals, take-out food, and public restrooms.

ENTERTAINMENT

Set amongst towering evergreens at the foot of the falls, the **Snoqualmie Falls Forest Theater** in Fall City has stage performances every weekend from late June to about Labor Day, plus a special Easter Passion Play. For current productions and ticket information call 222-7044.

SERVICES

The area code in the Snoqualmie area is 206. For maps, brochures, and other information contact the **Snoqualmie Falls Chamber of Commerce,** Box 356, Snoqualmie, WA 98065, tel. 888-2320, or the **North Bend Chamber of Commerce,** 320 S. Bendego, North Bend, tel. 888-1678.

Dial 911 for medical, fire, and police emergencies. **Snoqualmie Valley Hospital** is easy to find from the I-90 Snoqualmie Falls exit, at 1505 Meadowbrook Way SE, for 24-hour emergency service; tel. 888-1438.

TRANSPORTATION

Arriving By Car
Carnation, Snoqualmie, Fall City, and North Bend lie to the west of the mountains, actually just east of Bellevue and Issaquah, so getting there from Seattle isn't a problem in winter. Although Snoqualmie Pass is the easiest pass to traverse, it does get snowy up there and sometimes closes during heavy storms; call 976-7623 for road conditions and information on snow tire or chain advisories or requirements.

Arriving By Bus
The Big Three ski areas offer bus service from Seattle and Bellevue via the *Snoqualmie Flyer*. For information call 232-8182. Seattle's **Metro** serves Fall City (right to the falls), Snoqualmie, and North Bend; call 447-4800 for schedule.

Bus Tours
For a "Wines and Antiques" tour, call **Gray Line of Seattle** at 624-5813. The bus leaves downtown Seattle for a tour of Snoqualmie Winery, then, well-oiled, you head for the Putnam Antique Mall, making a final stop at Woodinville's Chateau Ste. Michelle for more vino. This tour operates monthly from Jan. through June for $28.

Steam Train Tour
The **Puget Sound & Snoqualmie Valley Railroad** operates steam trains between Snoqualmie and North Bend, at the base of Mount Si, through the Snoqualmie Valley, passing the top of Snoqualmie Falls and offering other viewpoints along the way. The 1¼-hour ride departs about every 1½ hours on Sun. from April through Oct., and on Sat. from Memorial Day through Sept.; fares are $5 adults, $3 for kids 5-15, and lap-sitters under five are free. Two special "Santa Trains" run the first two weekends in Dec. for $2; also, a Halloween "Spook Train" operates the last weekend in Oct.—anyone dressed in full costume rides for half price. Call 888-3030 weekends, or tel. 746-4025 24 hours a day.

STATE OF WASHINGTON, TOURISM DIVISION

MOUNT RAINIER

The Indians wouldn't climb it; "Tahoma" was sacred ground, inhabited by a vengeful deity who didn't welcome visitors. But Hazard Stevens, the Union's youngest Civil War general, was determined to be the first to reach Rainier's summit. So in 1870 he began assembling his climbing party: an unemployed miner, Philomon Beecher Van Trump, and landscape artist Edward T. Coleman would accompany him to the summit; James Longmire, a local farmer, would guide them as far as Bear Prairie, at 2,630 feet; but the group needed someone with expertise. They found it in Sluiskin, a nomad Indian who had taken up residence at Bear Prairie, and whose grandfather, going against Indian tradition, had once attempted a summit climb—without success.

The first day out after Bear Prairie, Coleman turned back. He'd found himself in a precarious position on a precipice where he could go neither forward nor back with his 40-pound pack; so he chucked it, along with most of the party's food. Stevens, Van Trump, and Sluiskin continued.

As the climbers progressed, Sluiskin began losing his nerve. Stevens wrote about the Indian in an article for *Atlantic Monthly* in 1876:

> *Takhoma, he said, was an enchanted mountain, inhabited by an evil spirit who dwelt in a fiery lake on its summit. No human being could ascend it or even attempt its ascent and survive . . . at first, indeed, the way was easy . . . but above [the broad snow fields] the rash adventurer would be compelled to climb up steeps of loose, rolling rocks, which would turn beneath his feet and cast him headlong into the deep abyss below. . . . Moreover, a furious tempest continually swept the crown of the mountain, and the luckless adventurer, even if he wonderfully escaped the perils below, would be torn from the mountain and whirled through the air by this fearful blast.*

Begging off, Sluiskin promised to wait three days for the climbers to return; then he'd go to Olympia to tell their friends they were dead.

Sluiskin's description of the mountain wasn't far from the truth. Stevens wrote,

> *Our course . . . brought us first to the southwest peak. This is a long, exceedingly sharp, narrow ridge springing out from the main dome for a mile into mid-air. The ridge affords not over ten or twelve feet of foothold on top, and the sides descend almost vertically. . . . The wind blew so violently that we were obliged to brace ourselves with our Alpine staffs and use great caution to guard against being swept off the ridge.*

After reaching the true summit of the mountain, Stevens and Van Trump found a volcanic steam cave where they huddled for the warmth, and in spite of the rotten-egg stench of the sulfuric steam, they spent the night. The next day the two men returned to Sluiskin, who was *really* surprised to see them, and expressed his deep admiration for the men who had conquered Takhoma: "Strong men," he said; "brave hearts."

Though the Indians called it "Tahoma" or "Ta-cc-bet," Captain George Vancouver renamed the mountain in 1792 after his friend, Rear Admiral Peter Rainier (who had never seen it). About 10 years after Stevens's climb, James Longmire built his mineral springs resort on what is now national park land, and the awesome beauty of the sleeping volcano has been drawing visitors ever since: over 1.5 million people visit Mount Rainier National Park every year. The park is located about 60 miles southeast of Tacoma; visitor centers are open year-round at Longmire, May to mid-Oct. at Paradise, and during the summer at Ohanapecosh and Sunrise; here you can view exhibits (slide shows and films at Paradise), purchase assorted publications, or get additional information. The Paradise Visitor Center's circular glass-walled structure offers 360-degree views of the park. The visitor center at **Sunrise,** at 6,400 feet the highest auto-accessible point in the park, offers one of the best views. Admission to the park is $5 (good for seven days).

Climate

Because of the incredible height of the mountain (recently recalculated at 14,411 feet), Rainier creates its own weather by interrupting the air flow around it, producing massive amounts of snowfall—a world-record 1,122 inches at Paradise in 1971-72. The mountain's height also accounts for its lenticular clouds—the upside-down, saucer-shaped clouds that obscure or hover just above the summit on otherwise clear days. Throughout most of the park, temperatures are not much different from those around Puget Sound; the nasty summer heat will sometimes follow you right up to Paradise, although generally the higher elevations enjoy cooler temperatures. Spring and fall are the times to be careful; rain at Longmire can very often translate to snow at Paradise.

SIGHTS

Even when the mountain isn't "out," driving through the park provides numerous sightseeing and photographic opportunities; the surrounding mountains, waterfalls, forests, and canyons alone justify the trip. Be sure to call ahead at (206) 569-2211 to see which roads are open. All park roads are closed from late Nov. to June or July, with the exception of the section from the Nisqually entrance to Paradise, on which chains are frequently required.

Another way to view the area west of the mountain, with an occasional peek at it through the timber, is from the **Mount Rainier Scenic Railroad,** tel. 569-2588. The steam train leaves Elbe Station for a 14-mile, 1½-hour ride over bridges and through forests, with live music accompanying the spectacular views. The train runs weekends beginning Memorial Day, daily between June 15 and Labor Day; fares are $6.50 adults, $5.50 seniors, $4.50 teens, and $3.50 for

MT. RAINIER
NATIONAL PARK

© MOON PUBLICATIONS, INC.

kids, or buy a family pass for $17. The train leaves three times daily from Elbe on Hwy. 7.

Gray Line offers bus tours of the park; see "Getting There" below for details.

OUTDOOR ACTIVITIES

Hiking

Rainier's hiking season is quite short: most trails are snow-free from mid-July to mid-Oct., though trails at the lower elevations may be clear earlier and later in the year. It's also advisable to dress for *all* seasons, with cotton under wool under rain gear, and strip as needed. A booklet of info for hikers and backpackers, called "Fragile, Handle With Care," is available at visitor centers or through the mail. About 305 miles of hiking

trails crisscross the park, many miles of which are suitable for day-hikes. Best bet is to contact a ranger upon your arrival, who has up-to-date info on trail conditions and will be happy to suggest a trail suited to your experience and physical condition.

To get the best for less, here are five short (one- to 5½-mile) easy hikes that provide superior mountain views:

The **Pinnacle Peak** trail starts at the Reflection Lake parking lot (southeast of Paradise) on Stevens Canyon Rd.; hike the 1½-mile trail to the saddle between Pinnacle and Plummer peaks.

For **Dege Peak,** start between Sunshine Point and the Sunrise parking area; this one-mile trail climbs 7,006-foot Dege Peak in the Sourdough Mountains.

To get to **Mt. Fremont Lookout** from the Sunrise picnic area, follow the Wonderland trail 1½ miles to a junction of five trails; the lookout trail is well marked. This 5½-mile trail takes about three hours round trip.

From Mowich Lake in the northwest part of the park, hike the three-mile trail to the **Tolmie Peak** fire lookout (5,939 feet).

Gobbler's Knob is another fire lookout (5,500 feet) which can be reached from Round Pass on Westside Rd., near the Nisqually (southwest) entrance. This 2½-mile trail passes Lake George.

More challenging day-hikes with Rainier views: for **Shriner Peak** trail start from Hwy. 123, 3½ miles north of the Stevens Canyon entrance, or 7½ miles south of Cayuse Pass, and park on the west side of the road about a half mile from the Panther Creek bridge. This eight-mile hike—about five hours round-trip—is almost completely devoid of shade, ending in a lookout/ranger station at Shriner Peak.

The 12½-mile **Sunset Lookout** hike begins from the end of Westside Road. Enjoy a two-mile descent to a river, then climb 3½ steep miles to a fork at Sunset Park; take the right fork to Lookout Point. Allow about eight hours.

Backpacking

The **Wonderland Trail** is a backpacker's dream: 93 miles of mountain passes, forests, streams, and alpine meadows, completely encircling the mountain. Campsites are strategically placed about 10 miles apart, resulting in a good 10 days of hiking. You can start almost anywhere—Mowich Lake, Longmire, White River, Box Canyon—but Ipsut Creek may be the best choice, since you'd be hitting the only showers in the park at Paradise about halfway through. Also for marathon packers, the **Pacific Crest Trail** touches the east edge of the park at Tipsoo Lake on Hwy. 410, continuing north to British Columbia and south to Mexico. Backcountry permits are required for all overnight trips, and are available free from any ranger or visitor center.

For a rewarding overnight trip, **Seattle Park** trail starts from the far end of Ipsut Creek Campground, continues along the Carbon River, approaches Cataract Falls (a quick side trip), and crosses Marmot Creek. Camping is permitted about one mile below Seattle Park in Cataract Valley. Hike across a permanent snowfield into Spray Park, doubling back to return on the same route, or continue to Mowich Lake, turning northeast

Snow drifts permit skiing on roof of Paradise Lodge.

TACOMA PUBLIC LIBRARY

*Longmire's mineral
springs resort*

TACOMA PUBLIC LIBRARY

to follow Ipsut Creek back to the starting point. It's about 16 miles roundtrip.

Another good overnighter, though not a circular route, is **Indian Bar.** This 14½-mile hike starts at Box Canyon on Stevens Canyon Rd., crosses Nickel Creek, then turns left to follow the Cowlitz Divide. At Indian Bar the Ohanapecosh River divides a meadow; the shelter is on the west side, just above Wauhaukaupauken Falls. Return by the same route.

Climbing

Despite Sluiskin's vengeful deity, more than 4,000 people reach Rainier's summit every year—of some 7,000 who attempt it. Two days are usually required for the trek: the first day involves a four- to five-hour hike over trails and snowfields to Camp Muir, the south side base camp at 10,000 feet, or Camp Schurman, on the north side at 9,500 feet; the second day starts early (about 2 a.m.) for the summit climb and the return to the Paradise starting point. Reservations are not accepted for the high camps, so be prepared to camp outside: Muir's 25-person capacity is frequently filled, and Schurman has no public shelter—your only luxury is a pit toilet.

Above the high camps climbers are roped, using ice axes and crampons to inch their way over glaciers to the summit. All climbers must register at a ranger station before and after their climb; solo climbers need the park superintendent's approval.

But even inexperienced climbers can conquer the mountain: snow- and ice-climbing seminars are offered for climbers of all skill levels at Paradise by Rainier Mountaineering, Inc. They charge $50 for their one-day snow- and ice-climbing school (no reservations necessary), $230-260 for a three-day summit climb package (one day of instruction plus the two-day climb), and $350 for a four-day Emmons Glacier package (one day of instruction plus a three-day roundtrip). RMI also offers seminars in crevasse rescue, mountain medicine, and basic rock-climbing, plus winter ski programs and a two-day avalanche course. Some of the required equipment is available for rental at Paradise. RMI recommends that persons under 15 not attempt the summit climb, and that climbers be in top physical condition. Call RMI at tel. (206) 627-6242 (535 Dock St., Ste. 209, Tacoma, WA 98402) in winter (Oct. to May) or 569-2227 (at Paradise) in summer.

Interpretive Programs

The National Park Service schedules nature walks, slide programs, and other organized activities from late June through Labor Day. Program schedules are posted at the visitor centers and campgrounds. Snowshoe walks are offered at the Paradise Visitor Center weekends and holidays from late Dec. through March.

Field Seminars

The Pacific Northwest National Parks and Forests Assn. offers one- to three-day seminars in glaciology, alpine ecology, photography, geology, and more at Mt. Rainier, plus similar courses at Mt. St. Helens. Tuition ranges from $85-100; participants are responsible for their own lodging, food, and equipment. Seminars fill up fast; to get on the mailing list write Pacific Northwest Field Seminars, 83 S. King St., Ste. 212, Seattle, WA 98104, or phone (206) 442-2636.

Others

Fishing is generally disappointing at Rainier; the fish, if you get any, are small. Park waters are not stocked—the trout and char are native, so restrictions are plentiful. Waters closed to fishing are Klickitat Creek above the White River entrance, Ipsut Creek above the Ipsut Creek Campground, Frozen Lake, Shadow Lake, Reflection Lakes, and Tipsoo Lake; the Ohanapecosh River and its tributaries are okay for fly-fishing only. Lakes and ponds are open late-April through Oct.; rivers, streams, and beaver ponds from late-May through late-November. Bait fish, dead or alive, are forbidden, as are amphibians, roe, and nonpreserved fish eggs. No license is required. Stop at any ranger station for info on limits and closures.

Nonmotorized **boating** is allowed on all park lakes except Frozen Lake, Reflection Lakes, Ghost Lake, and Tipsoo Lake; rowboating is a great way to view the wildlife.

Facilities are open for **winter sports** at Paradise from Dec. to April. Soft platters and inner tubes may be used in designated play areas only. Most ski-touring routes begin at Paradise, where rental equipment and instruction are also available; for maps and conditions contact a ranger. Growing weekend skiing and tubing crowds at Paradise—and the resulting parking problems—may force rangers to turn visitors away in the

future, but so far no limits have been imposed.

ACCOMMODATIONS

Campgrounds

All campsites in the park (except Class-C group sites, which may be reserved) are available on a first-come, first-served basis only, with a limit of 14 days from June 15 through Labor Day, and 30 days from Labor Day to June 14. Class-A campgrounds (running water and flush toilets) are located at Ohanapecosh, White River, and Cougar Rock for $6/night. Class-B sites (running water and pit toilets) are at Sunshine Point and Ipsut Creek for $5/night. Class-C multiple-tent sites, at Ipsut Creek and Cougar Rock, have a central fireplace and tables for $1 pp. Sunshine Point is the only year-round camping area; the others are open only for the season. While no trailer hookups are available, holding-tank disposal stations are located at Ohanapecosh and Cougar Rock.

Inns

There are two inns within the park itself. The **National Park Inn** at Longmire is open daily year-round. This small inn has rooms with private baths from $44 s or d to $68 for the larger two-room unit; rooms with shared baths go for $35 s or d. **Paradise Inn,** with unsurpassed mountain views from its elevation of 5,400 feet, and a spacious dining room, is open daily from late May to early October. Rooms with shared bath are $44 s or d; with private bath, $57-77. Contact Mount Rainier Guest Services, Box 108, Ashford, WA 98304, tel. (206) 569-2275, for reservations.

For accommodations outside the park, see "Vicinity of Mount Rainier," p. 317.

FOOD

The dining room at Paradise Inn opens at breakfast, lunch, and dinnertime, plus Sunday brunch during its season of operation. Paradise also offers a cafeteria, while Longmire has a sit-down restaurant. The snack bar at Sunrise operates only during the summer. Groceries can be bought during the summer at Longmire and Sunrise.

For food outside park limits, see "Vicinity of Mount Rainier," p. 319.

SERVICES

For brochures and information on camping, hiking, fishing, climbing, or other activities in the park, contact the National Park Service at Tahoma Woods, Star Route, Ashford, WA 98304, tel. (206) 569-2211.

Backpackers can obtain topographic maps from the Mount Rainier Branch of the Pacific Northwest National Parks and Forest Assn., Longmire, WA 98397; for prices write or call (206) 569-2211, ext. 295. Camping supplies in the park are limited; better to bring yours in from the outside. Public showers are available at Paradise, but there are no laundry facilities within park boundaries.

GETTING THERE

For year-round access to the park, take I-5 south to Hwy. 7; follow the Mt. Rainier signs as Hwy. 7 joins 706 and enters the park near Longmire. To get to the White River entrance (closed in winter) take Hwy. 18 east to Auburn; exit onto Hwy. 164 and follow that to Hwy. 410 and Mt. Rainier. From Yakima, take Hwy. 12,

PARK RULES AND REGULATIONS

- Pets must be confined or on a leash at all times; they are not allowed in the backcountry, on park trails, or in public buildings.
- No hunting. Firearms must be broken down and out of sight.
- No off-road vehicles.
- Leave rocks, plants, and animals where you find them.
- Firewood may be purchased at the Longmore service station or you can bring your own; collection of wood for fires is not permitted, except for dead wood from riverbeds at Ipsut Creek and sunshine Point campgrounds.
- No trash in the toilets, please.

joining Hwy. 123 to the Stevens Canyon entrance, or Hwy. 410 over Chinook Pass.

Gray Line offers 10-hour Mt. Rainier bus tours for $29 adults, $15 for kids 5-12, daily from May through October. The bus leaves from downtown Seattle hotels—Sheraton, Westin, Crowne Plaza, and more—and the Space Needle. Backpackers can arrange to be dropped off at the park and picked up a day or two later for no additional charge. Their "Mt. Rainier Overnight," offered May through Sept., includes one night at Paradise Lodge for $106 s, $70 pp d, $61 pp triple. Call 626-5208 for info and reservations.

VICINITY OF MOUNT RAINIER

CRYSTAL MOUNTAIN RESORT

This year-round resort on Hwy. 410, just outside the north park boundary, has winter Nordic and Alpine skiing, plus hiking, fishing, swimming, tennis, horseback riding, and chairlift sightseeing rides the rest of the year. The ski resort boasts 3,120 vertical feet, 10 lifts serving 2,300 acres, plus 34 expert backcountry trails. With a top height of 7,002 feet, you'll have a fantastic view of nearby Mt. Rainier. Lift tickets are $26 adults, $16 kids, $12 seniors; under five and over 70 ski free. Adults can ski Mon. or Tues. for just $14. Forewarned is fore-filled: there's no gas at Crystal Mountain!

Their **Summit House,** accessible only by chairlift, is the highest restaurant in the state and offers a phenomenal view of Mt. Rainier; watch for climbers approaching the summit. **Crystal Mountain Corral,** tel. (206) 663-2589, has group trail rides, overnight barbecues, fishing, hunting, and photography trips; prices start at $25 for a short trail ride, $55-95 for a full-day ride, and $135 for an overnight ride with steak fry and cowboy breakfast. You can stay at the **Crystal House Motel** for $40 d. For more info on the resort write Crystal Mountain, Box 1, Crystal Mountain, WA 98022, or phone 663-2265 or (800) 852-1444.

CHINOOK PASS

The highest of the mountain passes, Chinook Pass rises almost a mile above sea level (5,440 feet) on Hwy. 410. This is a fair-weather route, closed in winter and often dusted with snow as late as June.

At the summit of Chinook Pass, **Tipsoo Lake** is one of the most beautiful, easily accessed Cascade alpine lakes. Enjoy a picnic lunch here against a striking Mt. Rainier backdrop.

Accommodations And Food

Off Hwy. 410 in Goose Prairie, **Double K Mountain Ranch** is hidden in the William O. Douglas Wilderness, often under feet of snow. No pools, phones, or pavement here—just the indescribable natural beauty of the Cascades and high mountain lakes, with plenty of time for fishing, swimming, hiking, and skiing. The cabin and ranch house can accommodate up to 16 people; $275 per week gets you a room, meals, and use of the motorboat. Aside from July and Aug., when rooms are rented by the week only, you can stay for $60 per night with a two-night minimum. Write Double K Mountain Ranch, Goose Prairie, WA 98929, for reservations.

Whistlin' Jack Lodge, 18936 Hwy. 410 on the way to Chinook Pass, tel. (509) 658-2433, borders on the sunny side of the mountains, with just 12-15 inches of rain annually and 312 days of sunshine. Open year-round, the lodge includes a motel, cottages, restaurant, lounge, gas, and groceries. Rooms cost $50-60 d for motel units, $65 d for a fireplace bungalow, and $75-100 d for cottages (the more expensive ones have hot tubs). In winter, rent cross-country skis or a snowmobile ($60-85 a day for one or two); in summer, enjoy hay rides and trail rides. The food is good: fresh blueberry pancakes for breakfast, a buffet lunch, and prime rib, mountain trout, or tenderloin tails for dinner.

WHITE PASS

Highway 12 between Yakima and Mt. Rainier traverses 4,500-foot White Pass. The route passes through heavily forested areas with a few clear views of Rainier.

Skiing

White Pass Ski Area, off Hwy. 12 about 55 miles west of Yakima, offers a 1,500-foot vertical drop and 650 acres of skiing, served

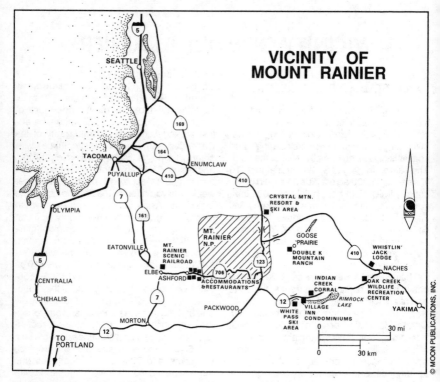

VICINITY OF MOUNT RAINIER

© MOON PUBLICATIONS, INC.

by four double chairs, a poma, and rope tow. Amenities include a ski school, child care, cafeteria, bar, and privately owned condos. Lift tickets are $20 adults, $15 kids ($5 less midweek). Phone (509) 453-8731 for more information.

Horseback Riding

Eight miles east of White Pass Ski Area on Hwy. 12, **Indian Creek Corral** offers horseback rides from one hour to three days long, Memorial Day to Oct. 1. Take a guided trail ride for one to three hours for $10 an hour (kids must be over 12 or experienced), an all-day scenic trip for $50 per person, or a three-day wilderness pack trip for $250. Groups are limited to five to keep it personal. Hikers can take advantage of their dropcamp service; they'll drop up to 75 pounds of gear at a selected site and pick it up whenever you like for $75. Write Star Route Box 218, Naches, WA 98937, or phone the owner at (509) 925-2062.

Lake

Traveling along Hwy. 12, you can't miss **Rimrock Lake,** just east of White Pass. The massive blue-green lake was created in 1927 by what was then one of the largest earth-filled dams in the country. Today Rimrock is popular with fishermen in search of good-sized silvers, mid-May to late June, and with boaters, swimmers, and campers.

On the lake, **Twelve West** has 35 campsites (all but four with RV hookups), a marina with boat rentals, and a quality restaurant serving three meals daily, including steak and seafood dinners accompanied by Washington and imported wines. For reservations, phone (509) 248-2276 or write Star Route, Box 206, Naches, WA 98937.

Elk Feeding

During most winters, the large White Pass elk population and a small herd of bighorn sheep are fed at the **Oak Creek Wildlife Recreation Area,** two miles west of the intersection of Hwys. 410 and 12 near Yakima. Keep an eye out for wildlife as you pass, particularly during early morning or late afternoon, when the animals are most active.

Backpacking

The **Pacific Crest Trail** (PCT) intersects White Pass as it continues north to Chinook Pass and south through the Goat Rocks Wilderness, on its long path to Canada and Mexico. The PCT follows the crest of the Cascades through the Goat Rocks Wilderness, passing through some alpine meadows but generally following rough terrain 4,200 to 7,500 feet in elevation. Plan on two nights and three days to get through the Wilderness; the two miles between Elk Pass and Packwood Glacier are the most hazardous, but the scenery here is the most spectacular.

The trail is usually snow-free from late July to mid-Sept., but even in late Aug. you can expect to cross snowfields up to a half mile across, so bring your ice axe and warm clothing—several hikers have died from hypothermia on these exposed ridges. Be sure to contact the Packwood Ranger Station, Box 559, Packwood, WA 98361, tel. (206) 494-5515, when planning your trip for updated information on snow levels and trail conditions. You can send your supplies to yourself, General Delivery, White Pass Rural Branch, U.S. Post Office, Naches, WA 98937, marked "PCT Hiker" with your anticipated date of arrival; the post office is located in the Cracker Barrel store and may be reached by asking the operator for White Pass #5.

The trail from White Pass north to Chinook Pass is about 26 miles of more ridgetop hiking, passing a number of alpine lakes; allow three nights for this leg.

ASHFORD

Ashford is your last chance for food, lodging, and gas before you enter the national park. Rather than being a "last resort," some of the hotels, cabins, and restaurants here are as good or better than park facilities.

Accommodations

Lodging abounds in Ashford, just outside the southwest park entrance. Listed on the National Register of Historic Places, **Ashford Mansion** is a 12-room turn-of-the-century inn on an old mountain road just six miles from the national park entrance. A wraparound porch, two second-floor verandas, and nearby Ashford Creek make this a delightful retreat. The four guest rooms share two baths; rooms are $48-80 d (singles $8 less). No kids or smoking. Write Box G, Ashford, WA 98304, or phone (206) 569-2739.

Alexander's, tel. (206) 569-2300, boasts immaculate rooms, handmade quilts, large fireplaces, stained-glass windows, a hot tub, free breakfast, and a quality restaurant featuring salmon fresh from Tacoma docks and rainbow trout from the pond out back. There are 11 rooms: $49.50 without bath, $66 with, and $82.50 for the "tower room," a two-story, two-room mini-paradise. **Growly Bear B&B,** tel. (206) 569-2339, has two upstairs guest rooms with shared bath in an 1890s homestead; rates are $40-50 s, $50-60 d. **Rainier Country Cabins** has cedar cabins with fireplaces, electric heat, kitchens, and alpine views. A basic cabin goes for $36-39; with kitchen, $43-46; with fireplace, $47-50. Call (206) 569-2355 or write Box IRS, Ashford, WA 98304 for reservations.

The **Gateway Inn,** tel. (206) 569-2506, features log cabins with rock fireplaces, a restaurant, cocktail lounge, and gift shop. Open year-round, the cabins are $31.50 s, $41.50 d. **The Lodge,** tel. (206) 569-2312, has cottages capable of handling large groups, from $40-60 s or d (add $5.50 pp, up to six) with full kitchen and fireplace. **Mounthaven** has nine cabins ($37-63, up to four persons) with kitchens and fireplaces as well as 20 full-utility RV hookups and a group lodge. Write Mounthaven, 38210 SR 706 E, Ashford, WA 98304, or phone (206) 569-2594.

Food
Alexander's, tel. (206) 569-2300, specializes in homebaked bread and fresh salmon and trout. The **Copper Creek Restaurant,** (206) 569-2326, is open March through Oct. for breakfast, lunch, and dinner, with dinners starting at $10. For pizza, sandwiches, nachos, and over 60 beers and wines, try **Wild Berry Restaurant,** open 365 days a year—the food is better than you'd expect, and the prices are reasonable.

MOUNT ST. HELENS

Prior to May 18, 1980, Mt. St. Helens had the most perfectly shaped cone in the Pacific Northwest volcanic chain. Often called "the ice-cream cone in the sky," and compared constantly with Japan's Mt. Fujiyama, 9,677-foot Mt. St. Helens was viewed as a sleeping beauty, popular with hikers, climbers, and other outdoor adventurers. It was silent for as long as any of them could remember—the volcano had been dormant for 123 years.

On March 20, 1980, Mt. St. Helens began to rumble. By March 30, steam was rising from two brand-new craters, which had merged by April 4 into one huge crater measuring 1,700 feet across. Seven weeks of minor earthquakes followed. At 8:32 a.m. on May 18, 1980, Mt. St. Helens blew her top; the eruption had the explosive power of several atomic bombs.

Triggered by an earthquake that measured 5.1 on the Richter scale, the eruption blew 1,312 feet off the volcano's summit in a lateral blast that shot northeast across the mountains, searing the forest and flattening it. This blast, similar to the one at Mt. Lassen earlier in the century, was the one that killed most of the victims. This was followed by a vertical plume of ash that rose 16 miles. Temperatures 15 miles away reached 572° F; the eruption killed 57 people and destroyed more than 220 homes and 17 miles of railroad. The wildlife death toll was upward of 5,000 black-tailed deer, 1,500 Roosevelt elk, and millions of birds and fish; the economic loss included 4½ billion board feet of usable timber.

The damage wasn't limited to this 15-mile area: 60,000 acres not destroyed by the blast were covered with more than eight inches of ash. Six hours after the eruption, the water at Castle Rock, 40 miles downstream, was over 100° F; towns in eastern Washington were coated with up to three inches of ash, clogging carburetors on cars, trucks, and farm vehicles and shrouding the towns in thick darkness at noon. Traces of ash were detected as far away as mid-Montana, Vancouver, B.C., and the Washington and Oregon coasts.

Mount St. Helens isn't ready for another long nap. Since the eruption, the volcano has had numerous smaller, dome-building eruptions and irregular spurts of activity. Plant and animal life is slowly returning to the devastated area. Hiking trails are being cleared, and a new visitor center relates the mountain's volatile history. But the mountain has permanently shed its light-hearted "ice-cream cone" reputation.

SIGHTS

Scenic Drives And Viewpoints
Until 1987, the area immediately surrounding Mt. St. Helens' crater was closed to the public because of sporadic volcanic activity, logging, and construction, but now the "forbidden zone" is open. You don't have to be a climber to enjoy the view; you can get close enough for some striking photographs without even leaving your car. The close-up views are all on the east and south sides of

the volcano. Be sure to fill your gas tank before you start your final approach to the visitor center or any of the Mt. St. Helens access roads; gas stations are few and far between.

Forest Service Rd. #26 and some of the viewpoint roads are not recommended for trailers or boats; these are narrow, single-lane roads with turnouts. For easier driving, drop off your trailer at the Woods Creek Information Station or Iron Creek Picnic Site on Forest Service Rd. #25 if traveling from the north, or at the Pine Creek Information Station if you're coming from the south.

For a quick trip, or for a good starting point from the north, take exit 49 to the new visitor center on Silver Lake for maps and current trail and road conditions. From there, continue east on Hwy. 504 to the end for a west-side viewpoint. If you get off I-5 at exit 68 instead, you'll find the old visitor center is closed, but follow Hwy. 12 toward Randle for a binocular view of the crater opening and lava dome, three miles west of Morton on Short Road. From Hwy. 12, shoot down Rd. #25 to #99; this will lead you past several viewpoints, picnic areas, trailheads, and Spirit Lake on its way to **Windy Ridge,** the closest access on the east side at the very edge of the restricted zone, just three miles from the crater. Prior to the #99 cutoff you'll see Rd. #2516 to **Strawberry Mountain;** another good viewpoint, but not recommended for those in bulky motor homes. Continuing south on #25 (after backtracking from the Windy Ridge lookout), get a good view of mudflow deposits along **Muddy River.** If you're not in a motor home, take Rd. #2588 to the **Lahar** viewpoint, located on a mudflow close to the mountain's southeast side. From Lahar take Rd. #83 southwest—or, if you skipped this one, stay on #25 and go west at the Rd. #90 junction, *then* take #83 north—to everyone's favorite, **Ape Cave.** You don't want to miss this one; see "Spelunking" and "Hiking" below. From here you can take #83 south to #90, continue south to Hwy. 503, and eventually return to I-5 at Woodland, exit 21. Start early for this long loop trip: it takes about 2¾ hours to get

from exit 68 to Windy Ridge, and another 2½ hours to get to Woodland—not including cave explorations, photo stops, and potty calls. Forewarned is forearmed: the only concession along the way is at Independence Pass in summer, so pack some Cokes and cookies. The all-important restrooms are located at the visitor center and information stations (see below), plus Ryan Lake (Rd. #2612), Bear Meadow (Rd. #99), Windy Ridge, Lava Cast (Rd. #83), and Ape Cave.

Winter travelers will likely be thwarted in their loop attempt; roads #25, #26, and #99 are generally closed by snow from November to May, and the Ape Cave road is closed till April 1, regardless of weather, to protect deer and elk in their winter range. Call the visitor center's 24-hour info line at 274-4038 for road conditions before you set out. A parking lot, shuttle bus staging area, and ticket booth are located at the intersection of roads #99 and #26. Buses to the end of the road, the closest you can get to the volcano, run daily in summer (including holidays), departing about every 20 minutes; fares are $1.50, kids under six free.

A new Spirit Lake Memorial Highway is being built to extend Hwy. 504 eastward to Coldwater Lake. The road will climb 3,800 feet above the valley floor, providing panoramic viewpoints and hiking access to Johnston Ridge, where you'll be able to peer into the volcano's crater.

Visitor Centers

The $3 million **visitor center** on the shores of Silver Lake, completed in 1986, features an impressive $800,000 walk-in model volcano, a theater featuring an eight-minute slide show, a mural, and numerous displays. This center, at exit 49 (Castle Rock) off I-5, replaces the visitor center at exit 60 or 68 near Lewis and Clark State Park. From late June to early Sept., park rangers give talks and lead nature hikes and car caravans from various information stations and viewpoints throughout the day; get a copy of the *Volcano Review* at the visitor center or information stations for a schedule. At **Windy Ridge,** a ranger tells the story of the eruption hourly, every summer afternoon. The **Pine Creek Information Station** is open daily in summer on the mountain's southeast side with educational videos and books for sale; the **Iron Creek Information Station** on Rd. #25 also has up-to-date information on conditions and viewpoints. At **Ape Cave,** naturalists lead a lantern walk through the lava tube every summer afternoon.

OUTDOOR ACTIVITIES

Spelunking

Located on the south side of the mountain, **Ape Cave** is the longest lava tube cave in North and South America, and among the longest in the world at about 12,810 feet. Despite widely circulated stories to the contrary, there are no apes nor Bigfoots around Mt. St. Helens; the "ape-like creatures" that threw rocks at Mt. St. Helens miners in 1924 turned out to be a pair of local youths, not Sasquatch. Prior to the 1980 eruption, there were reports of 12- to 18-inch footprints attributed to Sasquatch, but no such evidence has surfaced since the eruption. The cave actually got its name from a group of local conservationist Boy Scouts in 1952 who liked to call themselves the "Mt. St. Helens Apes," in fond memory of the creatures of rock-throwing fame.

Tube caves are formed when fluid basaltic lava, called pahoehoe (pah-hoey-hoey), is crusted over with cooler lava during an eruption; afterward, the more liquid pahoehoe drains out, leaving a tunnel. Ape Cave is of the "unitary" or "throughway" type; other tube caves, such as the ones at Lava Beds National Monument in California, are of a more complex, intertwining structure.

The roof of Ape Cave is as much as 60 feet thick in some places and quite thin in others—spots which will eventually give way, creating a trench. The cave's most famous feature is the "Meatball," a round ball of lava that got stuck above the present floor level when the lava was flowing through the cave; it's located about 2,500 feet from the metal stairway.

The main entrance to the cave is a lava sink, with cemented stairs leading down to the small upper level, and metal stairs down to the main level. The temperature in the cave is about 42° F, year-round, so wear warm clothing, gloves, and hiking boots, or comfortable walking shoes if you intend to stay only in the dry, lower part. This is not a tacky, well-lighted, guided tour; you're on your own, so bring *at least* two sources of light (a headlamp will free your hands). Avoid torches and flares because the smoke harms cave-dwelling insects and thoroughly annoys other visitors; same goes for smoking. Keep food, beverages, and pets out of the cave; removing pieces of the cave for "souvenirs" is thoughtless and strictly prohibited. Ape Cave now has its own **visitor center,** offering sound spelunking advice and lantern rentals.

Hiking

Mount St. Helens hiking trails are still undergoing clearing, reconstruction, and rerouting. Don't use an out-of-date guidebook or map

VICINITY OF MOUNT ST. HELENS

TO SEATTLE

MOUNT RAINIER N.P.

ELBE 706

7

6

PACKWOOD R.S.

PACKWOOD

IKE KINSWA S.P.

5

EXIT 68

4

MORTON

Mayfield Reservoir

5

RANDLE

12

RANDLE R.S.

GOAT ROCKS WILDERNESS

MOSSYROCK

7

LEWIS & CLARK S.P.

8

1

2

12

3

MOSSYROCK DAM

RIFFE LAKE

21

MAYFIELD DAM

MAYFIELD

EXIT 60

TOLEDO

MOUNT ST. HELENS NAT'L. VOLCANIC MONUMENT MAP

IRON CREEK INFORMATION STATION

23

505

SEAQUEST S.P.

TOUTLE

TOUTLE RIVER

CASTLE ROCK

TRAVEL INFORMATION

EXIT 49

MT. ST. HELENS VISITOR CENTER

SILVER LAKE

26

MOUNT ADAMS WILDERNESS

MOUNT ST. HELENS

WINDY RIDGE

90

KELSO

LONGVIEW

APE CAVE VISITOR CENTER

PINE CREEK INFORMATION STATION

23

YALE VISITOR INFORMATION

COUGAR

TROUT LAKE

YALE RESERVOIR

503

MERWIN RESERVOIR

WOODLAND

EXIT 21

AMBOY

30

141

503

502

BATTLE GROUND

WIND RIVER R.S.

5

CARSON

14

WHITE SALMON

EXIT 9

ORCHARDS

STEVENSON

205

VANCOUVER

14

CAMAS

COLUMBIA RIVER

0   10 mi

0   10 km

PORTLAND

© MOON PUBLICATIONS, INC.

1. Lake Mayfield Motel and Restaurant
2. Mayfield Lake County Park
3. Mountain Road Inn
4. Short Road Viewpoint
5. Main's Gift Shop
6. Resort of the Mountains
7. St. Helens Manorhouse
8. Jackson House

(particularly pre-1980), and check in at a ranger station for current trail conditions and routes. Inquire at visitor centers about sources of fresh water for canteens.

A short, ⅛-mile paved trail at **Meta Lake** on the northeast side of the mountain takes you through a grove of trees that survived the 1980 blast by virtue of a deep snowcover. Another easy trail is the one-mile loop at **Cedar Flats,** three miles north of the Pine Creek Information Station on Rd. #25. Here you'll see a preserved old-growth forest, with Douglas firs and western red cedars topping 600 years old.

On Rd. #26 on the east side you'll find the **Norway Pass** trailhead. This new, 2.2-mile one-way hike takes about 1¾ hours each way and passes a "blowdown" forest (leveled by the force of the eruption) on its way to spectacular views of crater waterfalls, the lava dome, and Spirit Lake. **Ape Canyon Trail** is a long, 5½-mile one-way hike well worth the effort. Starting at the Lahar viewpoint, the trail climbs a ridge to the pumice Plains of Abraham, upward to the treeless top of Ape Canyon, with striking views of mounts Adams, Rainier, Hood, and St. Helens.

Not far from Mt. St. Helens is **Goat Rocks Wilderness,** about an hour east of Randle on Hwy. 12; see "Mt. Rainier," p. 314, for hiking and camping here. Mt. Adams, due east of Mt. St. Helens on the opposite side of Gifford Pinchot National Forest, is covered in a separate chapter beginning on p. 330.

Climbing

After the eruption, Mt. St. Helens' summit was closed to climbers until early 1987, although scores of climbers, clad in white to blend in with the snow, completed the illegal ascent in the interim. The earliest "legal" climbers described the accomplishment as a good winter day-hike, with no technical climbing involved, although a snow precipice at the crater rim invites disaster as it tempts you farther and farther over the edge for a closer look.

A permit is required for travel above 4,800 feet or for entry into the crater. Travel on the crater floor is permitted when the ground is snow-covered, but camping in the crater is not allowed. From Nov. to mid-May, climbers need only register before and after their climb at Yale Park, two miles west of Cougar on Lewis River Rd.; from mid-May through Oct., 100 permits will be issued per day on a first-come basis. Forty of these will be available at Yale Park on the day of the climb; the other 70 may be reserved in advance by mail or in person at the Monument Headquarters. Even with a permit, climbers must still sign in and out at Yale Park. Conditions change frequently so always check with the monument before planning a climb: call 274-4038 for a recorded message.

Even though the climb is not technically difficult, don't underestimate the steep slopes and severe weather. Climbing boots, ice axe, sunscreen, crampons, rope, and a hard hat are suggested, and climbers should rope up near the crater rim.

Winter Sports

Forest Service Rd. #83's two Sno-Parks offer a wide area for winter activities from cross-country skiing and snowshoeing to snowmobiling. To use the area you'll need a Sno-Park permit, available at Cougar area stores. **Shoestring Glacier Lahar,** 4½ miles east of the Sno-Park, is another popular cross-country skiing and snowmobiling spot, made more exciting by dangerously steep gullies. For good skiing and beautiful views, take Forest Service Rd. #81 west for one mile beyond the #83-#81 junction, then go north on Rd. #8100830. On the park's north side, **Ryan Lake** is usually accessible year-round on Rd. #26, 20 miles south of Randle, with open, flat areas for skiing or snowmobiling.

Seminars

If you're clever enough to plan ahead, you can get in on one of the field seminars at Mt. St. Helens offered by the Pacific Northwest National Parks and Forests Association. Scheduled in late summer, these three-day weekend seminars cost $60-100 and include such topics as Mt. St. Helens photography, geology, and elk recolonization. For a descriptive brochure write or phone Pacific

Northwest Field Seminars, Mt. Rainier National Park, Longmire, WA 98397, tel. 569-2211 ext. 295.

Fishing
Salmon, trout, steelhead, bass, sturgeon, and smelt fishing is popular along the Lewis River from the Columbia to Mt. Adams, with access to Yale, Swift, and Merwin reservoirs and numerous recreation sites (contact a ranger for current limits and regulations). Unfortunately, boat rentals are rare in these parts; best bet is to rent from one of the RV parks or motels below.

Area Parks
If you get to the monument and the roads are closed, or the mountain's covered by a thick cloud, don't despair! Get yourself a picnic lunch and visit the parks and dams along Hwy. 12 instead. **Lewis and Clark State Park,** home to the defunct visitor center, has a 1¼-mile nature trail, plus 25 campsites. Across the street is **Jackson House,** a log cabin built in 1844 that was a popular stopping place for Oregon Trail travelers. **Mayfield Lake County Park,** about ¼ mile off Hwy. 12 just before Mossyrock, is open for day-use only with a boat launch, small picnic area, and playground. Follow Hwy. 12 east to Mossyrock and the **Mayfield Dam;** there's a nice roadside viewpoint about three miles east of Mossyrock on Hwy. 12. To get to **Mossyrock Dam Park,** turn south at the Mossyrock light and follow the signs three miles east. Here you'll find hundreds of campsites, picnic tables, and boat launches on beautiful green-blue Riffe Lake. The 23½-mile-long lake was dam-created in 1968; originally named Davisson Lake after Ira S. Davisson, a public power pioneer. The lake was renamed Riffe Lake in 1976 to honor the settlers of Riffe, founded in 1898 and now covered by about 225 feet of water. If you turn north at the Mossyrock light you'll eventually get to **Ike Kinswa State Park,** about three miles off the highway. The park is open year-round for trout fishing on Mayfield Lake, with swimming, picnicking, and 101 campsites on the lake (41 with hookups).

Across from the new visitor center on Silver Lake, **Seaquest State Park** has 54 tent sites and 16 hookup sites on one of the best bass fishing lakes in the state.

All state park campgrounds charge $7-9.50 per night. For other specific information on camping in the state parks, see p. 29.

ACCOMMODATIONS

Bed And Breakfast
Six miles east of Morton on Hwy. 12, **St. Helens Manorhouse,** tel. 498-5243, is a 1910 three-story Douglas fir home, with four bedrooms (private and shared baths) for $38 s, $49 d. A full breakfast is included. No kids, pets, or indoor smoking.

Resort
Five miles north of Morton on Hwy. 7, **Resort of the Mountains** is a natural health center with motel accommodations, a natural foods store and restaurant, exercise room, and organic garden—definitely not for the Cheetos-and-beer crowd. Rooms all have fireplaces, kitchens, and dishwashers for $40 s, $50 d. Reservations are required; write 1130 Morton Rd., Morton, WA 98356, or phone 496-5885.

Cabins And Motels
In Morton, the **Evergreen Motel,** tel. 496-5407, has budget rooms for $21 s or d. On Hwy. 12, 13 miles east of exit 68, **Lake Mayfield Motel and Restaurant,** tel. 985-2484, has eight rooms for $30 d, with a full-service family restaurant specializing in homemade rolls and desserts. The **Mt. St. Helens Motel,** 227 Spirit Lake Hwy. in Castle Rock, tel. 274-7721, has 32 rooms for $30 s, $32 d, and laundry facilities just five miles from the visitor center. At 3201 Spirit Lake Hwy. in Silver Lake, **Silver Lake Motel and Resort,** tel. 274-6141, has motel rooms, rustic two-bedroom cabins, RV and tent sites, plus boat rentals for fishing. Open year-round. Rooms are $45 d, $60 for two to four persons, with a porch over the water; full RV hookups are $12.50, tent spaces $9; motorboats are $30 per day, rowboats $12.50.

Camping

Forest Service campgrounds are concentrated on the south and southeast sides of the monument. Near the town of Cougar, **Cougar** and **Beaver Bay** provide tent camping, first-come, first-served, for $4 a night on the Yale Reservoir on Rd. #90; go north on #81 to **Merrill Lake,** a Department of Natural Resources campground; **Speelyai Hill** has camping and an RV park. Go east on #90 to **Swift** campground, for $4 tent and RV sites just south of the Pine Creek Information Station; reserve a spot by calling Pacific Power and Light, tel. (503) 243-4778. Farther east, **Lower Falls** has camping on Rd. #90. The only park campground on the north side is **Iron Creek,** open in July with 96 sites ($5 per night) 10 miles south of Randle on Rd. #25. **Tower Rock,** near Iron Creek on Rd. #76, has 22 sites. Cougar, Swift, and Iron Creek all have summer campfire programs from June or July through Aug., when a park naturalist gives talks, shows slides, or leads sing-a-longs.

Private RV parks in the area include **Harmony RV Park,** 2½ miles north of the Mossyrock caution light on Harmony Rd. in Silver Creek. They have 52 trailer sites plus 14 tent sites for $9, overlooking manmade Mayfield Lake on the Cowlitz River; for reservations phone 983-3804. On the southwest side of the mountain, **Volcano View Campground,** 230 Hwy. 503 in Ariel, tel. 274-7087, is open all year with 26 trailer sites and 15 tent sites for $12 near Merwin Lake.

See "Area Parks" above for camping in state and county parks on the north and west sides of the monument.

FOOD

You'll have to go into one of the neighboring towns to find something to eat; the monument has just one snack bar, at Independence Pass, open only in summer. In Morton, the **Wheel Cafe** has steaks, seafood, a salad bar, and chicken and sandwiches to go, plus a lounge, and is almost always open (7 a.m.-2 a.m.). Also in Morton, the **Roadhouse Inn** is strictly sit-down, serving steak and seafood

dinners plus breakfast and lunch; tel. 496-5029. In Mossyrock, the **Mountain Road Inn** at the caution light on Hwy. 12 has nightly dinner specials and live entertainment Fri. and Sat. nights. On the west side, Toutle has a restaurant, drive-in, souvenirs, groceries, and gas on Hwy. 504. See "Longview/Kelso," p. 248, for more food and lodging on the west side of the monument.

SHOPPING

It wouldn't be a trip to Mt. St. Helens without picking up some ceramic or glass ornaments made from St. Helens' ash. **Marti's Ceramics,** 630 Westlake Ave. in Morton, has a wide assortment of souvenirs and also conducts tours of the ash-ceramic factory. Open daily April-Sept. till 4:30 p.m. **Mains Gift Shop,** four miles west of Morton on Hwy. 12 at the foot of the Hopkins Hill viewpoint, has a variety of Mt. St. Helens glass ornaments, ceramics, petrified wood, gemstones, and the usual T-shirts, with a free video showing the eruption.

SERVICES AND INFORMATION

The **visitor center** at Silver Lake has all the maps and current trail and road information you'll probably need; they're open daily, year-round, and have a 24-hour recording for road conditions and other information at 274-4038. Another visitor center at Ape Cave can provide assistance and lantern rentals. The ranger stations can also help; they're located at **Packwood,** northeast of the monument, tel. 494-5515; at **Randle,** tel. 497-7565; and at **Wind River,** tel. 427-5645. For emergencies, 911 only works from the phone at the Pine Creek Information Station; otherwise, call the Washington State Patrol at 577-2050 or the Skamania County Sheriff at 427-5047, 24 hours. All Mt. St. Helens area phone numbers are preceded by area code 206.

For more general area information, visit the small travel information building just west of I-5 at exit 49 in Castle Rock.

TRANSPORTATION

By Car
The Silver Lake Visitor Center is about two
hours south of Seattle via I-5, or about 1½
hours north of Portland, Oregon.

Bus Tours
With pickup points in Olympia, Castle Rock,
the old visitor center, and Randle, **Capital
Aeroporter** has narrated bus tours to Windy
Ridge from June through September for $20-
30, depending on point of departure. This is
a good deal for people who don't want to take
their enormous motor homes over miles of
gravel roads, or anyone who'd rather soak up
the scenery than drive; call 754-9544 or
(800) 225-3966 toll-free.

Departing from Tacoma, **Cascade Trailways** offers a full-day Mt. St. Helens
motorcoach tour about every two weeks from
late June through August for $28 pp, includ-
ing a box lunch; call 383-4615 or (800) 824-
8897 statewide toll-free.

A little later in the season, **Gray Line of
Seattle** offers a two-day "Mountain Connection" trip to Eatonville's Northwest Trek, Mt.
Rainier, and Mt. St. Helens' Windy Ridge with
overnight accommodations at Rainier Country Cabins (see "Mt. Rainier National Park,"
p. 317). Offered about every other week from
mid-Sept. to early Nov., the excursion costs
$133 pp s or d; phone 624-5813 in Seattle or
write 720 S. Forest, Seattle, WA 98134 for
more details.

Scenic Flights
A number of small aviation companies offer
scenic flights over Mt. St. Helens for $25-35
pp, depending on the type of aircraft and
length of flight, affording passengers a view
of the crater and lava dome that you just
can't get otherwise. **Sunrise Aviation** is the
closest to the mountain, operating out of
Morton from 9 a.m. to dark; phone 496-5510
or 496-5207 for information and reservations. Departing from Vancouver, WA, **Vancouver Aviation,** tel. 695-3821 offers one-
hour flights from Pearson Airpark. Departing
from the same airport, **Aircraft Specialties,
Ltd.,** tel. 694-8971, also has one-hour flights
on an appointment basis. **Aero West Aviation,** tel. 423-4902, departs from Kelso, and
also offers Columbia Gorge and Pacific
Coast air tours.

MOUNT ADAMS

Measuring in at 12,276 feet, Mt. Adams is no peanut; its snow-covered peak is as worthy of oohs and aahs as Rainier's. If it stood alone, Adams would be a prime recreation site, silhouetted on license plates and keychains. But from a Seattle viewpoint, Adams is geographically behind and below its attention-getting neighbors: Mt. Rainier, a heavily used national park, and Mt. St. Helens, a rumbling national volcanic monument. The lack of any good access roads (you've got to drive behind Mt. St. Helens along gravel Forest Service roads) and the Yakima Indian Reservation bordering on the east, make Mt. Adams an isolated, underutilized mountain. Those willing to venture out onto remote forest roads will find trails, unusual geologic formations, and scenic areas; if your goal is to escape civilization, this is the place to do it.

SIGHTS AND RECREATION

Viewpoints

Approaching Trout Lake on Hwy. 141, the **Indian Sacred Viewpoint** provides a spectacular view of Mt. Adams. For a closer look, take Forest Service Rd. #23—the main Mt. Adams access road—about eight miles from Trout Lake. Just before the pavement gives way to gravel, you'll have a good view of the mountain to the east.

Ice Cave

Ancient volcanic activity formed this 650-foot-long, four-section lava tube cave, which during pioneer times supplied ice for the towns of The Dalles and Hood River. Accessible from Ice Cave Forest Service Campground, 10 miles west of Trout Lake, the cave entrance is a collapsed sink, 15 feet across and 14 feet deep, connected to three other collapse sinks by passageways of varied diameter. Wear warm clothing and boots, and bring at least two light sources and a helmet or other head protection.

Lava Beds

The **Big Lava Bed Geologic Area** encompasses 12,500 acres of lava beds, remains of an ancient volcano. In the north section of the beds, the crater, now covered by trees, rises 800 feet; inside, the walls slope down almost to lava-bed level; a small meadow covers the bottom of the bowl. Another visually interesting feature is the 100-foot-deep trough or sink of unknown geologic origin, northeast of the crater. When exploring the lava beds, be sure to bring your own water; by mid-June, all the creeks are dry. Take Hwy. 14 from White Salmon to Cook; at Cook, go north on the county road for seven miles to Willard; then take Forest Service Rd. #66 north for seven miles along the east side of the lava bed.

Hiking

Mt. Adams Wilderness, north of Trout Lake, and **Indian Heaven Wilderness,** just northwest of the lava beds, offer miles of little-used hiking trails; you won't find Mt. Rainier's crowds here because the average day-hiker isn't willing to drive this far into the woods on beat-up forest roads. So if it's seclusion you want, check at the ranger station (see "Services" for locations) for a map ($1) and rudimentary—but free—trail guide.

For a good view of the area's peaks, take a short hike to the top of **Little Huckleberry Mountain,** best hiked mid-July to October. Take Forest Service Rd. #66 (along the east edge of the lava bed) to the #49 trailhead; climb the steep grade for 2½ miles to the summit and a refreshing berry break.

The most heavily used trail in the Mt. Adams Wilderness is **South Climb,** a 2.2-mile trail from Cold Springs Campground to timberline, from where climbers depart for routes to the summit. Take Forest Service Rds. #80, #8040, and #500 (about 13 miles) to Cold Springs Campground at road's end.

Beginning at Morrison Creek Horse Camp on the south side of Mt. Adams, 2.7-mile **Crofton Butte** trail follows the mountain's

Novice mountaineers often use Mt. Adams as a first climb.

DIANNE BOULERICE LYONS

lower slopes for scenic views of the butte. Take Forest Service Rds. #80 and #8040 for about 10 miles from Trout Lake.

Thomas Lake is a well-used 3.3-mile trail through Indian Heaven Wilderness, starting near Dee Lake and passing Thomas, Naha, Umtux, and Sahalee Tyee lakes before intersecting with the Pacific Crest Trail near Blue Lake. Head north on the main road from Carson, then turn right onto Forest Service Rd. #65 for about 17 miles to the trailhead.

Backpacking

The **Pacific Crest Trail** passes through Indian Heaven, Mt. Adams, and Goat Rocks wilderness areas—some of Washington's most scenic and God-forsaken real estate—on its way to the Canadian border. The PCT hooks up with civilization near Bridge of the Gods on the Columbia River on the south, and at White Pass on the north. The 18 miles of the trail that pass through Mt. Adams Wilderness are accessible from Forest Service Rd. #23, near its intersection with Forest Service Rd. #8810, on the south; on the north, the PCT crosses Forest Service Rd. #5603 near Potato Hill. Subalpine meadows, glacial streams, dense forest, wildflowers, and scenic viewpoints reward the adventurous hiker. The PCT traverses Indian Heaven Wilderness from south to north: start at Crest Horse Camp, just south of the wilderness

boundary on Forest Rd. #60 (right off Forest Service Rd. #65); the trail passes lakes, meadows, and forest for 17 miles through the wilderness area, then connects with Forest Service Rd. #24 near Surprise Lakes on the north side.

Climbing

Mt. Adams is one of the easiest Northwest volcanic peaks to climb; in fact, it's often used as a first climb by area mountaineering clubs. Before you begin, be sure to register with the Mt. Adams Ranger Station in Trout Lake. The south slope route is least difficult: it begins at the end of the road at Cold Springs Camp, at an elevation of 6,000 feet; follow the old road for two miles to Timberline Camp. From here the trail leads to a large snowfield. Bear right across the snowfield to the ridge, following the ridge to the false summit at 11,500 feet. A zigzag trail leads through pumice to the summit, for a six- to eight-hour one-way trip. Other, more difficult routes are described in the American Alpine Club's Climber's Guide.

ACCOMMODATIONS

Mio Amore Pensione, on the southern edge of Trout Lake, is one of the better places to stay and eat in the Mt. Adams-Columbia Gorge area. The converted farmhouse has three

MOUNT ADAMS AND VICINITY

TO RANDLE

21

ADAMS FORK

5603

POTATO HILL

23

YAKIMA INDIAN RESERVATION

PACIFIC CREST TRAIL

MOUNT ADAMS WILDERNESS

MT. ADAMS (12,326 ft.)

SOUTH BUTTE

CROFTON BUTTE

TILLICUM

MORRISON CR. HORSE CAMP

COLD SPRINGS

24

MORRISON CREEK

8810

SURPRISE LAKES

65

CULTUS CREEK

INDIAN HEAVEN WILDERNESS

23

80

24

MT. ADAMS R.S.

TROUT LAKE

DRAPER SPRINGS

GLENWOOD

FLYING L RANCH

INDIAN SACRED VIEWPOINT

PETERSON PRAIRIE

60

66

ICE CAVE

141

BIG LAVA BED

LITTLE HUCKLEBERRY MTN.

OKLAHOMA

CREST HORSE CAMP

65

PACIFIC CREST TRAIL

86

WIND RIVER R.S.

MOSS CREEK

WILLARD

0   5 mi

0   5 km

TO VANCOUVER

CARSON

86

41

WHITE SALMON

14

COOK

COLUMBIA RIVER

© MOON PUBLICATIONS, INC.

rooms in the main house and room for four in the former icehouse outside. The owners, Tom and Jill Westbrook, also operate an excellent restaurant, serving dinners only (guests get a mountainous breakfast free but have to make dinner reservations like everyone else). The first person to call and make a dinner reservation sets the menu for the evening. Rooms are $65-135 d; dinners begin at $20.

Flying L Ranch

Glenwood's 160-acre Flying L Ranch sits in a secluded valley on the eastern slope of the Cascades, with a spectacular skyline dominated by Mt. Adams. Open from April through Oct., the electric-heated inn and adjacent cabin can accommodate at least 15 people. Inn rooms start at $49 d for a small room, up to $64 d for the suite, including a family-style breakfast; the two-room cabin goes for $50 per night. Dinners may be arranged for large groups; otherwise, you can eat in Glenwood or cook your own in a kitchenette unit. Kids can swim or raft in their small lake, or take a short ride on the owners' horse. Special summer naturalist programs are held by **Mount Adams Institute,** a nonprofit organization dedicated to the preservation of Mt. Adams; also, an annual **Artists' Retreat** features a slide show, two nights' lodging, two days' breakfasts and dinners, and plenty of time for painting and sketching the majestic mountain, all for just $75. Write Route 2, Box 28, Glenwood, WA 98619, or call (509) 364-3488 for more information.

Camping

The Mt. Adams Ranger District has 20 developed campgrounds. Most are free; there is a $4 fee at the larger campgrounds, including **Cultus Creek,** with 53 trailer and 10 tent sites, **Moss Creek,** with 18 trailer sites, **Oklahoma,** 23 trailer and three tent sites, **Peterson Prairie,** 19 trailer sites, and **Tillicum,** with 37 trailer and 12 tent sites. See the ranger at Trout Lake for a complete list of campground locations and facilities.

SERVICES AND INFORMATION

Trout Lake has minimal services, in the form of one restaurant, a small grocery store, and a gas station. For more dining variety and other services, head south to White Salmon or, better still, The Dalles, Oregon.

The area code for the Mt. Adams Ranger District and surrounding area is 509. Get maps, camping information, and current trail conditions at the Mt. Adams District Ranger Station in Trout Lake, tel. 395-2501.

GETTING THERE

There are two ways to approach Mt. Adams: from Seattle, take I-5 south to I-205 near Vancouver, then follow I-205 to Hwy. 14 and head east. At Underwood, take Hwy. 141 north to Trout Lake. An alternative is to take I-5 south past Chehalis, then head east on Hwy. 12 to Randle and take Forest Service Rd. #23 south for 56 miles to Trout Lake. The two ends of Forest Service Rd. #23 are paved, but the middle section—about 25 miles' worth—is gravel. It's also very isolated so be sure your vehicle is in sound working order and full of gas before you set out.

BOB RACE

CENTRAL WASHINGTON

WENATCHEE AND VICINITY

Driving east on Hwy. 2 from the damp Puget Sound area, the transition to the "dry side of the mountains" is an abrupt one. The heavily forested, snowcapped Cascades give way to bone-dry hills, blanketed by snow in winter but covered only by dry brown grass in summer. You'll experience few of Puget Sound's mostly cloudy days here: Wenatchee gets over 300 sunny days and only 10-15 inches of rain per year. The warm sunny days, cool nights, and volcanic ash soil combine to provide ideal apple-growing conditions.

Philip Miller was Wenatchee's pioneer apple grower. In 1872, Miller took squatter's rights on a parcel of land in the Wenatchee Valley and planted a handful of apple seedlings. The trees flourished, and when the railroad came to Wenatchee in 1892, Miller drove in the silver pike to link the last rails—and to help determine Wenatchee's econom-

ic future. Miller's ranch shipped its first full carload of apples to Seattle in 1901. Irrigation projects, beginning with the Highline Canal in 1904, brought much-needed water to this arid region, and helped the apple industry blossom. Today, an average of 30,000 carloads of apples are shipped from the Wenatchee Valley every year.

SIGHTS

Ohme Gardens
Located just north of Wenatchee on a bluff overlooking the Wenatchee Valley, Ohme Gardens is a testimony to over 50 years of watering and weed-pulling by the Ohme family that transformed a barren hillside of sagebrush into one of America's most highly acclaimed gardens. Originally created for the

Ohmes' personal use, the patch of green on the otherwise desolate hillside attracted visitors' attention. Now covering nine acres, the gardens resemble natural alpine scenery: evergreens, grass, ponds, and waterfalls blend with the existing rock—a cool reprieve from the scorching Wenatchee sunshine. A lookout from the gardens' highest point provides broad views of the valley, Cascades, and Columbia River. The gardens are near the junction of Hwys. 2 and 97, three miles north of Wenatchee, at 3327 Ohme Rd., tel. (509) 662-5785; open daily from 9 a.m. to dusk, early April through October. Admission is $3 adults, $1.50 kids under 18; steep dropoffs make this a hazardous place for uncontrollable toddlers.

Rocky Reach Dam

The 4,800-foot-long Rocky Reach Dam, seven miles north of Wenatchee, was built across the Columbia in 1962. Picnic tables and elaborately landscaped areas are on 15 acres of grounds. Visitors may visit the fish-viewing room and two exhibits: **The Gallery of the Columbia,** contains the pilothouse of the late 1800s steamer *Bridgeport* and replicas of Indian tools and villages, lumbermen, and turn-of-the-century railroaders; **The Gallery of Electricity** relates the history of electricity in displays and photos, and allows visitors to generate their own electricity. To get there, follow Hwy. 97 north from Wenatchee.

Museum

The **North Central Washington Museum,** 127 S. Mission, tel. 662-4728, has two floors of exhibits; pioneer life in the Wenatchee area, the first trans-Pacific flight, and the Great Northern Railway are the main attractions. Joined to the museum by a skybridge, the Apple Industry Exhibit includes a working antique apple sorter and assembly line. Open weekdays 10 a.m.-4 p.m., weekends 1-4 p.m.; donation.

More Apples

At 2900 Euclid Ave., the **Washington State Apple Commission Visitor Center,** tel. 663-9600, has a film and displays about the

CENTRAL WASHINGTON

© MOON PUBLICATIONS, INC.

apple industry, and, better still, samples of a variety of apples and juices. Open daily May through Oct.; free.

ACCOMMODATIONS

Hotels And Motels

For budget lodging (from $22-25 s, $28-36 d) with a year-round heated pool and sauna, try **Scotty's Motel,** 104 N. Wenatchee Ave., tel.

DIANNE BOULERICE LYONS

Ohme Gardens

(509) 662-8165. The **Imperial Inn,** 700 N. Wenatchee Ave., tel. 663-8133 or (800) 368-4400, is also inexpensive, with 40 units from $20-23 s, $26-35 d. Among the nicest of the area's budget motels is the **Orchard Inn,** 1401 N. Miller across from the Valley North Shopping Center, tel. 662-3443 or (800) 368-4571. Rooms start at $35 s, $35-41 d, and include a heated pool and hot tub, available year-round.

Nendel's Inn, on the Columbia River in E. Wenatchee at 11 W. Grant Rd., tel. 884-6611, has 101 rooms from $40-58 with a pool, sauna, whirlpool, and adjacent restaurant and lounge. The **Chieftain,** 1005 N. Wenatchee Ave., tel. 663-8141 or (800) 572-4456, has a heated pool, hot tub, attached restaurant, and 105 rooms from $40 s to $60 d. The **Best Western Rivers Inn,** 580 Valley Mall Parkway in E. Wenatchee, tel. 884-1474 or (800) 528-1234, has 55 rooms from $40 s, $43-53 d, with Jacuzzi, heated pool, restaurant, and lounge.

More elegant is the **Red Lion Motor Inn,** 1225 N. Wenatchee Ave., tel. 663-0711. Rooms are reasonably priced, $60 s, $70-80 d, and include all the niceties of more expensive hotels: a heated indoor pool and Jacuzzi, room service, and a restaurant and lounge with nightly entertainment. Another quality hotel is the **West Coast Wenatchee Center Hotel,** 201 N. Wenatchee Ave., tel. 662-1234, with 146 rooms and suites from $51-59 s and $57-69 d. Extras include free airport shuttle, swimming pools and Jacuzzis indoors and out, exercise room, glass elevators, room and valet service, and a rooftop restaurant serving breakfast, lunch, and dinner with mountain and river views.

Camping

About 15 miles north of Wenatchee, **Entiat State Park** has tent and trailer camping on the Columbia River. The **Wenatchee River County Park,** six miles west of Wenatchee on Hwy. 2, has playgrounds, picnic areas, and camping for 64 trailers and RVs (40 full hookups, 24 water and electric only) and 20 tent sites; overnight fees are $7-9. The park is open from April through Oct., and all camping is on a first-come, first-served basis.

FOOD

The **Horan House Restaurant,** 2 Horan Rd., tel. 663-0018, serves international cuisine in a home built in 1896 by John Horan, one of the valley's "Apple Kings"; open for dinner only, Tues. through Sat.; reservations are suggested. **The Windmill,** 1501 N. Wenatchee Ave., tel. 663-3478, has been one of the Northwest's prime steak houses for the past 65 years, featuring charbroiled steak, pork, and seafood. Open for dinner Tues. through Saturday. At 928 S. Mission, the **New Orleans Kitchen,** tel. 663-3167, serves moderately priced Cajun, creole, and catfish for dinner only, Wed. through Saturday.

The Chieftain Restaurant, at the motel of the same name at 1005 N. Wenatchee Ave., tel. 663-8141, specializes in moderately priced seafood and prime rib ($7-13), and is open for three meals daily; they also feature live entertainment Tues. through Sat. nights. **Magnum's,** 1112 N. Wenatchee Ave., tel. 662-9121, serves prime rib, seafood, pasta, and steaks at family prices, generally under $10; open for three meals daily. **The Cottage Inn** has been serving chicken, steak, and seafood at the 134 Easy St. location since 1940. Open for dinner only, Tues. through Sat.; tel. 663-4435. **Viscounti's Italian Restaurant,** 1737 N. Wenatchee, serves Northern Italian food. Open for lunch and dinner 11 a.m.-2 and 5-10 p.m.; tel. 662-5013.

ENTERTAINMENT

Festivals
The self-proclaimed "Apple Capital of the World" is the only proper place to hold the annual **Apple Blossom Festival,** going strong since the "Blossom Days" of 1919. This 10-day event starts at the end of April and is highlighted by the Apple Blossom Parade on the first Saturday in May; other festivities include carnivals, circuses, horse shows, gem and mineral exhibits, and a production staged by local talent.

The **Wenatchee Youth Circus,** perhaps the best amateur youth circus in America, opens in July in Wenatchee, then travels throughout the Pacific Northwest all summer. The end of summer brings the **Wenatchee Valley Arts Festival,** a juried sidewalk fine arts display, to downtown Wenatchee in late September. For more information call the Allied Arts office at 662-1213.

Leavenworth, the Bavarian village nestled in the Cascades just 22 miles away, hosts numerous festivals throughout the year; see p. 302.

PARKS AND RECREATION

On the east side of Rocky Reach Dam, six miles north of Wenatchee on Hwy. 2, **Lincoln Rock State Park** has swimming and a boat launch popular with fishermen and water-skiers. Camping facilities here include 27 non-hookup sites. Nine miles southwest of Wenatchee on Squilchuck Rd., **Squilchuck State Park** has winter cross-country skiing amidst a forested mountain setting, plus a small downhill ski area with two rope tows, ski school, and coffee shop. Camping here is limited to large groups with advance reservations; call 662-1651.

Skiing
Just 12 miles from Wenatchee, **Mission Ridge** is the area's largest ski area, with four double chairs serving 33 runs—70% of which are intermediate—and a 2,140-foot vertical drop. One chair and the beginner's rope tow serve the area lighted for night skiing on Wed. through Sat. and holidays. There are also 42 km of marked cross-country trails on rolling terrain, and spaces available for RVers. All the big-time ski area extras—ski school, cafeteria, rentals and repairs—are available here. For snow conditions, call 663-7631; to get there, take Hwy. 2 to S. Mission Street.

For information on the tiny **Squilchuck Ski Bowl,** see "Parks" above.

SHOPPING

The **Wenatchee Valley Mall** is the area's largest, with 47 stores including Sears, Lamonts, and Ernst, across the bridge in E. Wenatchee. The **Valley North Shopping Center,** Miller St. in N. Wenatchee, is a smaller version, highlighted by JC Penney. At Second and Mission, **Mission Square** has an assortment of boutiques, including a kitchen shop, fine art and custom-framing shop, craft supply store, deli, and restaurant. Skiers and other outdoors enthusiasts will want to visit **Asplund's,** a sporting goods store at 1544 N. Wenatchee Ave., tel. 662-6539. Here you'll find everything from swimsuits to bicycles to backpacking supplies, plus cross-country ski equipment, rentals, and lessons.

SERVICES

All phone numbers in Wenatchee and points east are preceded by area code 509. For maps, brochures, or specific information on the Wenatchee area, contact the **Wenatchee**

WENATCHEE

1. Cottage Inn
2. Horan House Restaurant
3. Windmill Restaurant
4. Asplund's Sporting Goods
5. Orchard Inn
6. Valley North
   Shopping Center
7. Red Lion Motor Inn
8. Magnum's
9. Chieftain Motel
   and Restaurant
10. Imperial Inn
11. Steven's at
    Mission Square
12. West Coast Wenatchee
    Center Hotel
13. Scotty's Motel
14. Greyhound Depot
15. David Brown's 2nd Story
16. visitor information
17. Central Washington
    Hospital
18. Wenatchee Valley Mall
19. Best Western Rivers Inn
20. Nendel's Inn
21. New Orleans Kitchen

© MOON PUBLICATIONS, INC.

Area Visitor and Convention Bureau, Box 850, 2 S. Chelan Ave., Wenatchee, WA 98801, or call 662-4774 or toll-free statewide (800) 57-APPLE.

For fire or police emergencies, dial 911. For medical emergencies or problems, phone **Central Washington Hospital,** 1300 Fuller, tel. 662-1511.

TRANSPORTATION

Arriving By Air

Wenatchee's airport, Pangborn Field, was named in honor of Clyde Pangborn, a pilot who piled up aviation record after record in the '20s and '30s. Pangborn's most notable feat was accomplished on Oct. 6, 1931, when he and Hugh Herndon completed the first nonstop flight over the Pacific Ocean, landing at the Wenatchee airport—minus the landing gear they had intentionally dropped when excess weight threatened to shorten their flight. The trip was an eventful one—the pair was charged with spying and held in Tokyo for several weeks before being released with a hefty fine; then, while crossing the Pacific, icy wings and an empty gas tank nearly ended the flight prematurely.

Today Pangborn Field connects Wenatchee with Seattle, Spokane, Tri-Cities, and Portland by commuter airlines **Horizon Air,** tel. (800) 547-9308, and **United Express,** tel. (800) 241-6522.

Arriving By Bus

Greyhound, tel. 662-2183, provides daily service to Seattle, Spokane, and other cities from the depot at 301 First Street. Also, **Link Transit,** tel. 664-5565, serves most of the towns surrounding Wenatchee, and so does **Empire Stage Lines,** tel. 624-4116.

Bus Tours

Gray Line of Seattle has two-day bus tours from downtown Seattle to Wenatchee for the May Apple Blossom Festival; prices of $137 s, $110 pp d include roundtrip transportation, hotel accommodations, dinner, and a snack. For information and reservations call (206) 624-5813.

Arriving By Train

Amtrak serves Wenatchee daily via the Seattle/Chicago train, The *Empire Builder,* connecting to Ephrata and Spokane to the east and Everett, Edmonds, and Seattle to the west. For reservations and information call (800) USA-RAIL.

CASHMERE

Tucked between Wenatchee and Leavenworth on Hwy. 2, the tiny town of Cashmere (pop. 2,300) is famous—at least statewide— for its Aplets and Cotlets and Grapelets. These gooey, all-natural confections are made of fruit juices (apple, grape, and apricot) and walnuts and coated with powdered sugar.

Sights

Tours of the downtown Cashmere **Aplets and Cotlets** plant (just off Hwy. 2) include free samples and are available Mon. through Fri. and most summer weekends, from 8-11:45 a.m. and after lunch from 1-5 p.m., tel. 782-2191.

Reputedly among the top five restored pioneer villages in the country, the **Chelan County Historical Museum,** 5698 Museum Dr., tel. 782-3230, has restored and furnished 18 of the oldest buildings in Chelan County, all built prior to 1900, to create an authentic Old West atmosphere. A blacksmith shop, school, gold mine, mission building, and hotel are part of the Pioneer Village; there's also a sizable collection of Indian artifacts. Open 10 a.m.-4:30 p.m. weekdays, and Sunday afternoons; closed mid-Oct. to April 1. Donation.

Food

Among Cashmere's more elegant restaurants is **The Pewter Pot,** a colonial-style restaurant featuring fresh-baked bread and locally grown produce. Open for lunch and dinner; tel. 782-2036. The **Coachman Inn,** 128 Cottage Ave., tel. 782-3213, is open daily from 6 a.m.; prawns, steaks, and prime rib are the specialties here. The lounge, open till 2 a.m., features live country-western music nightly. Open weekdays from 5 a.m., the

Parkside Restaurant at Cottage and Division serves three meals daily from an omelette/sandwich/seafood/steak menu; tel. 782-4317.

To ship eastern Washington apples home to your relatives, stop in at **Bob's Apple Barrel** on Hwy. 2 for a gift pack; tel. 782-3341.

Festivals

Celebrated the first week in July, **Founder's Days** is a creation of the local chamber of commerce, inspired by the 1979 celebration of Cashmere's 75th year of incorporation, the "Diamond Jubilee." The town had such a good time they made the fair an annual event. One of the highlights is the "Stillman Miller Hill Climb," inspired by an early resident who claimed he could pour himself a beer in the local tavern, run up Numbers Hill, and be back before the head settled. Whether or not he actually made it is anybody's guess, but the concept was so appealing that runners are still trying it today. Other events include a parade, barbecue, arts and crafts show, and street dance.

Cashmere is also home to the **Chelan County Fair,** a four-day event beginning the first Wed., after Labor Day, highlighted by rodeos, musical entertainment from area bands, a carnival, and youth group exhibits.

The second weekend in Oct. brings **Cashmere Apple Days,** the primary fund-raising event of the Chelan County Museum. Apple bin races, an apple-pie-baking contest, music, dancing, and staged shoot-outs are all part of the pioneer days fun.

For specific festival dates, maps, or other info contact the **Cashmere Chamber of Commerce,** 99 N. Division, Cashmere, WA 98815, tel. 782-1511.

Raft Trips

Rafters from the daring to the scared-skinny can find a raft trip to their liking with **Wenatchee Whitewater and Scenic River Trips.** Real whitewater enthusiasts will enjoy their September Tieton River trip, the fastest, narrowest river they run, plunging 50 feet per mile over its 15-mile course; children and more timid rafters may prefer their two-hour to two-day scenic float trips, with plenty of photographic, birdwatching, and gold-panning opportunities on the upper Wenatchee River. Prices range from $21 for a two-hour meander, $25-33 for a full-day scenic, $39-49 for a full-day whitewater; Visa and MasterCard are okay. Wetsuits, tents, and sleeping bags may be rented for a small fee. For a brochure or reservations, call 782-2254 or write Box 12, Cashmere, WA 98815.

ELLENSBURG AND VICINITY

Ellensburg's biggest claim to fame is the popular Labor Day weekend rodeo, attracting thousands of spectators and top rodeo talent from across the country. The town isn't particularly Western in appearance; the Western clothing stores, tack shops, and country-western bars that you might expect in a rodeo town just aren't there. Instead you'll find an old, quiet town of fewer than 12,000 with progress squeezing in on a historic city center. Ellensburg is at the more or less geographic center of the state, serving as commercial center for the small mining towns and cattle ranches surrounding it. Besides the rodeo, Ellensburg has something found nowhere else in the world: the beautiful "Ellensburg Blue" agate, fashioned at local jewelry stores into earrings, necklaces, and rings.

Driving toward Ellensburg from Puget Sound, the change in weather and geography is dramatic. From Seattle to Snoqualmie Pass, you'll pass forested hills and snow-covered peaks, often under a thick cloud cover. When you're about 20 miles west of Ellensburg, the clouds thin out, the temperature rises in the summer and falls in the winter, and the landscape flattens to low, rolling hills dotted with bushes and an occasional tree. Out here the summers are sunnier and hotter—nearly every motel has a pool—but the winters are harsh, with snow and bitter cold that the Puget Sound region rarely sees.

HISTORY

From the beginning, the Kittitas Valley has been blessed with an abundance of fish and wildlife. From the earliest days, Indians from the otherwise hostile Nez Percé, Yakima, and Wenatchee tribes tolerated each others' presence as they hunted and fished the area peaceably. White settlers first arrived in the Ellensburg area in 1867. By 1870, Jack Splawn and Ben Burch had built the town's first store, "Robber's Roost," and the town took on the store's name until a few years later, when John Shoudy bought the store and platted the town, naming it for his wife, Mary Ellen.

Ellensburg's population grew rapidly in the late 1880s, when the Northern Pacific Railroad finished its line through town to Puget Sound. Ellensburg was a contender for the state capital seat until a fire in July 1889 destroyed its new commercial center and 200 homes; but the town fought back, rebuilding the community in brick before the year was out. One of the first colleges in the state, Central Washington University, was established here in 1891. Since then, the town hasn't seen a great deal of growth, but it remains the hub of the central Washington cattle business and commercial center of the mining and agricultural region.

SIGHTS

Museum And Historic District

At E. Third and Pine streets, the **Kittitas County Historical Museum,** tel. (509) 925-3778, has Indian artifacts and displays of pioneer tools, photographs of early Ellensburg, and an impressive collection of petrified wood and gemstones, including a six-pound Ellensburg Blue agate. The museum is housed in the 1889 Cadwell Building, a two-story brick structure with horseshoe-shaped windows. Open afternoons Tues. through Sat.; donation.

Pick up a map at the museum or chamber of commerce for a self-guided tour of 18 Victorian-era buildings, most located within a five-block area between Sixth and Third avenues and Main and Pearl streets. The **Davidson Building** at Fourth and Pearl is probably the first you'll notice because of its proud tower and ornate windows. Next door, the

ELLENSBURG

TO AIRPORT

WALNUT ST.
ALDER ST.

15 AVE.

14 AVE.

RANDALL HALL

OKANOGAN ST.

CENTRAL
WASHINGTON UNIV.

CASCADE WAY

A ST.
B ST.
C ST.
D ST.

OLD VANTAGE HWY.

1

GREYHOUND
DEPOT

BARGE
HALL

TOWER
THEATER

REED
PARK

2

8 AVE.

KITTITAS CO.
FAIRGROUNDS

DOLLARWAY

MAIN ST.

3

5 AVE.

5 6
5 7

CHAMBER
OF COMMERCE

CRAIG AVE.

AMTRAK

4

3 AVE.

SPRAGUE ST.

8

9

KITTITAS ST.
WATER ST.
MAIN ST.
PEARL ST.
PINE ST.
RUBY ST.

CAPITOL AVE.

CHESTNUT ST.
MAPLE ST.

MANITOBA AVE.

KITTITAS VALLEY
COMM. HOSP.

MOUNTAIN VIEW AVE.

ANDERSON RD.

TO
CLE ELUM

DAMMAN RD.

10
11
12

IRENE
RINEHART
PARK

MATTOON
LAKE

YAKIMA RIVER

CANYON RD.

90

13
14

MOON

1. Rainbow Motel
2. Thunderbird Motel
3. Regalodge Motel
4. Valley Cafe
5. Lynch Block
6. Stewart Building
7. Davidson Building
8. Kittitas County Museum
9. The Castle
10. Nites Inn Motel
11. The Buckboard
12. Casa de Blanca
13. Super 8 Motel
14. Best Western

0   0.5 mi

0   0.5 km

TO
MOSES
LAKE

TO
YAKIMA

© MOON PUBLICATIONS, INC.

1889 **Stewart Building** now houses the Community Art Gallery. **Lynch Block,** at Fifth and Pearl, is the only remaining structure that survived the 1889 fire; when it was built, its front windows were the largest in central Washington. Travel down to Third and Chestnut to see **The Castle,** optimistically built in 1888 to be the governor's mansion when Ellensburg won the contest for state capital; it's lost much of its elegance since, and now houses apartments. Built in 1893-94, four-story **Barge Hall,** Eighth and D at CWU, is the oldest building on campus.

Galleries
At 408½ N. Pearl, the **Ellensburg Community Art Gallery,** tel. 925-2670, is open Tues. through Sat., with seven display and sales rooms surrounding a central atrium in the 1889 G. R. Stewart Building. Central Washington University's **Sarah Spurgeon Art Gallery,** tel. 963-2665, has regional artists' and students' work displayed in Randall Hall; open Mon. through Friday. The newest is **The Clymer Museum,** 416 N. Pearl, tel. 962-6416. It honors Clymer, an Ellensburg native and well-known Western artist. It is connected with the annual **National Western Art Show and Auction,** which has been held in Ellensburg since 1972. Information: P.O. Box 893, tel. 962-2934.

ACCOMMODATIONS
For budget-minded travelers, the **Rainbow Motel,** 1025 Cascade Way, tel. 925-3544, has a playground, laundry, and rooms from $29 s, $38-40 d. The **Regalodge Motel,** 300 W. Sixth Ave., tel. 925-3116, has rooms starting at $26 s, $35-40 d, plus an indoor pool. At 1500 Canyon Rd., the **Super 8 Motel,** tel. 962-6888, has an enclosed pool and spa, laundry, and RV hookups; rooms cost $31-37 s, $35-45 d. The **Nites Inn Motel,** 1200 S. Ruby, tel. 962-9600, is one of the newer motels in town, with laundry, RV parking, and rooms from $34 d. The **Thunderbird Motel,** 403 W. Eighth, tel. 962-9856, has a pool and live music Wed. through Sat. in the lounge; rooms are $38-40 d. Ellensburg's largest hotel is the **Best Western Ellensburg Inn,** 1700 Canyon Rd., tel. 925-9801, home of the Western Art Show. The 105 guest rooms start at $45 s, $40-49 d, and include an indoor heated pool, putting green, restaurant, and lounge with nightly dancing.

FOOD
Downtown, **The Valley Cafe,** 103 W. Third, tel. 925-3050, serves sandwiches and salads, Mexican and Italian dishes in '30s art deco surroundings. **Casa de Blanca,** Canyon and Ruby roads, tel. 925-1693, has Mexican specialties plus moderately priced American-style steak and prime rib.

PARKS AND RECREATION
Four miles south of town off Kittitas Hwy., see one of the first Kittitas Valley farms at **Olmstead Place State Park.** The log cabin dates back to 1875; you can tour the eight buildings, including a granary, dairy barn, and wagon shed, daily in summer, rest of year by appointment; tel. 925-1943 or 856-2700. A three-quarters of a mile trail leads from the red barn to the Seaton Cabin Schoolhouse, originally located farther away in a meadow; the kids didn't trudge miles through blizzards—they rode horseback.

In the city, **Irene Rinehart Park,** on the Yakima River off Damman Rd., is a welcome relief from the relentless summer sunshine. You can cool your toes in the swift green river, take a walk along shaded paths, or enjoy a riverside picnic. **Reed Park** at the end of Craig Ave. has a small shaded green for reading and relaxing, plus superb views of the county below and the snow-covered Stuart Range to the northwest.

River Trips
River Excursion Co. offers a four-hour, 16-mile raft trip on the upper Yakima, where you can view striking canyon scenery and wild-

life. Write Box 543, Ellensburg, WA 98926, or phone 925-9117.

CWU's **Tent-N-Tube/Outdoor Programs** offer Yakima River float trips as demand requires; tel. 963-3537. If you'd rather do it yourself (and the Yakima is a good place to do that—it drops just 14 gentle feet per mile), their rental shop is the cheapest around (they claim they're not in it for the money). You can rent anything from inner tubes and canoes to cross-country skis and ice axes, as well as VCRs and instructional videos on golf, fishing, skiing, racquetball, and more. They also have a resource center with books, maps, and other outdoor information.

Rockhounding
Kittitas County is the only place on Earth that you'll find the "Ellensburg Blue" agate. Most finds are made on private or leased land northwest of Ellensburg (you'll need permission to hunt there), but you can check Dry Creek, on Hwy. 97, or Horse Canyon Road. Here are the rules: no digging—surface hunting only; respect property lines and fences; and don't bother the cows. If you come up empty handed, Ellensburg stores sell the uncut stones as well as jewelry. For some nice handcrafted rings and necklaces visit **Art of Jewelry** on Pearl Street.

ENTERTAINMENT

Festivals And Events
Visit the **National Western Art Show and Auction,** tel. 962-2934, in mid-May to add to your collection of Western paintings. The Western Art Association reserves the entire Best Western Ellensburg Inn for the event, renting out rooms to various artists to display their work. Three auctions give you a chance to purchase your favorites, but the highlight for many is the "Quick Draw," when about a dozen artists create a work of art in 45 minutes.

The **Whiskey Dick Triathlon,** held annually in July, consists of a one-mile swim, 35-mile bicycle ride, and 8.1-mile run—not impossible, even though the swim is in the 60° Columbia River and the bike leg climbs

1,900 feet in the first 12 miles. At least the running leg is on level ground! Superb athletes can get an entry form by writing Whiskey Dick Triathlon, 436 N. Sprague, Ellensburg, WA 98926 ($40 for an individual entry); regular people can contact the chamber of commerce, tel. 925-3137, for exact dates and places to set your lawn chair.

Labor Day weekend's **Ellensburg Rodeo** is one of the top rodeos in the nation, attracting high-priced cowboys from all over with a $100,000 purse. You can watch calf roping, Brahma bull riding, and wild cow milking during this four-day event, held in conjunction with the carnival, exhibits, and entertainment of the **Kittitas County Fair** at the fairgrounds at the east end of Sixth Avenue. Rodeo tickets include admission to the fair and cost $6-11; you can order in advance by writing the Ellensburg Rodeo Ticket Office, Box 777, Ellensburg, WA 98926, or phone 925-5381 or (800) 637-2444.

Held in September at Olmstead Place State Park, the **Threshing Bee and Antique Equipment Show** gives city slickers an opportunity to see blacksmithing, plowing, and steam and gas threshing; tel. 925-3137.

Theater
CWU's **Laughing Horse Summer Theatre** presents four professional productions, early July through mid-August, in Tower Theatre at Eighth Ave. and Anderson Street. For schedule information, phone 963-3400 or write Box 1412, Ellensburg, WA 98926; you can purchase tickets at the box office at the Rotary Pavilion on Pearl St. or at Berry's department store at Fifth and Ruby.

Nightlife
Aside from lounges at the Best Western Ellensburg and the Thunderbird Motel (see above), you can hear live music weekends at **The Buckboard,** 1302 S. Ruby, tel. 925-9921.

SERVICES AND INFORMATION

Ellensburg's area code is 509. The **Ellensburg Chamber of Commerce** is located at

436 N. Sprague; tel. 925-3137. For emergencies, dial 911 or 925-5303 for the State Patrol. **Kittitas Valley Community Hospital** is located at 603 S. Chestnut; tel. 962-9841.

TRANSPORTATION

Ellensburg sits at the junction of I-90 and I-82, an easy 107-mile, 65-mph drive on I-90 from Seattle. **Greyhound Bus Lines** can get you out of town from their 801 Okanogan depot; tel. 925-1177. The nearest commercial airport is in Yakima, 36 miles to the south.

CLE ELUM

Cle Elum, an Indian name meaning "Swift Water," was settled in 1870 by Thomas L. Gamble, but growth was slow until geologists working for the Northern Pacific Railroad discovered coal in 1884. A forest fire in the late 1880s wiped out a large part of the mining town, but coal veins discovered in 1889 gave Cle Elum four quite prosperous years. Today the town is a jumping-off point for hiking, fishing, and other recreational activities in the Wenatchee National Forest. Stop by the Forest Service Ranger Station at the west end of

VICINITY OF ELLENSBURG

Second St. for maps ($2), detailed trail descriptions, and camping information.

Parks

East of Cle Elum off I-90, **Iron Horse State Park** is the start of the 25-mile-long John Wayne Pioneer Trail, extending to the Yakima-Teanaway River Canyon on property that once belonged to the Milwaukee Railroad. Open to hikers, skiers, mountain bikes, and horses (closed to motorized vehicles), the trail begins in a Douglas fir and pine forest and follows the Yakima River through canyons and farmland. No overnight camping. Day-hikers can reach the trail at either Easton or South Cle Elum. In Easton, take I-90 exit 71 and follow the signs; park at the trailhead gate; in South Cle Elum, park at the end of Seventh St. to reach the trailhead east of the old depot. There are no restrooms or facilities of any kind here yet, so plan ahead.

About 15 miles west of Cle Elum just off I-90, **Lake Easton State Park** encompasses almost 200 forested acres on the west and north sides of Lake Easton. The mile-long reservoir is good for swimming, boating, trout fishing, and waterskiing; hiking, cross-country skiing, and snowmobiling are popular dryland sports. There are 100 tent sites and 45 trailer-hookup sites here, plus a Big-Toy playground, picnic tables, and bathhouse with hot showers.

Continue west from Cle Elem on I-90 to **Kachess Lake** (pronounced ka-CHEES), a national forest campground and recreation area about 10 miles east of Snoqualmie Pass. The beautiful blue-green lake offers swimming, boating, picnicking, a nature trail through old-growth forest, and 183 campsites ($6-12).

Hiking

The Cle Elum Ranger District of the Wenatchee National Forest has a plethora of hiking trails; some are also open to motorized vehicles but, fortunately, a lot of them aren't. Take Hwy. 903 from Cle Elum northwest to Cle Elum Lake; a number of forest roads leave it for wilderness hiking trails. From the north end of the lake, take Forest Rds. #4308 and #4312 to the Thorp Creek

CLE ELUM AREA
HIKING TRAILS

© MOON PUBLICATIONS, INC.

trailhead for a 3.1-mile hike to Thorpe Lake and Kachess Ridge. Backpackers or sturdy day-hikers (with two cars) can follow Trail 1315 along the ridge for about 1½ miles to its intersection with Trail 1330, a 6.7-mile hike up Red Mountain and back to Forest Rd. #46 near Salmon la Sac. Take Forest Rd. #4308 to French Cabin Trail 1305, a 1.3-mile hike up to Kachess Ridge and Trail 1315. A 6.2-mile one-way hike on Trail 1307 leaves Salmon la Sac and follows a ridge to an excellent view atop **Jolly Mountain.** Be sure to get a map at the Cle Elum Ranger Station before you set out, and don't hike without your compass; many of these trails are poorly maintained and hard to follow.

Snowmobile Tours
Tour the Cle Elum Lake Wilderness (near Roslyn) on snowmobile with **Sasse Moun-**

tain **Outdoor Experiences,** tel. 649-2794 or 925-3334. Tours for four to eight people include the "Deluxe Package," a six-hour guided ride that includes the snowmobile and gasoline plus trail lunch and steak dinner with wine and dessert, for $125 pp. For tighter budgets, the standard night ride is a four-hour guided trip with snowmobile and gasoline only for $60 pp.

Museum
The **Cle Elum Historical Telephone Museum** at First and Wright, tel. 674-5702, exhibits the area's first phone system. Open daily except Mon. in summer, Tues. through Fri. mornings the rest of year; donation.

Accommodations
Now a B&B on the National Historic Register, the **Moore House,** tel. 674-5939 or (800)

572-2877, was built in 1909 by the Chicago, Milwaukee, Pacific, and St. Paul railroads to serve the men who worked on some of the most treacherous mountain tracks in the country. The 10 restored inn rooms are named after some of the railroad men who lived there; photographs and antique toy trains complete the decor. Covered wagon rides, mystery weekends, and sleigh rides are all part of the fun here. Rooms vary greatly in price, from $41 for a two-bunk room to $95 for a honeymoon suite with private bath and two-seat whirlpool, up to $75 (one to three people; $85 for four to five people) for the caboose, with queen bed, private bath, TV, refrigerator, and deck. All rooms include a full breakfast and use of the outdoor hot tub. Kids welcome; smoking in the lobby only.

Hidden Valley Guest Ranch, off Hwy. 97, is the state's oldest dude ranch. Here you can indulge your cowboy fantasies while still enjoying heated cabins, hot showers, a heated pool, and someone else's cooking. Horseback rides leave twice daily, last 1½ hours, and cost $15; you don't have to be an overnight guest to join the rides. In winter, the ranch is generally open on Jan. and Feb. weekends for cross-country skiing; call ahead to check on conditions. Cabins cost $45-55 pp including ranch-style meals; families of up to four can stay in a housekeeping unit and cook their own meals for $110 per day. Babysitting is available with advance notice. Write Route 2, Box 111, Cle Elum, WA 98922, or phone 674-2422 for more information.

Food

For German food, beer, and wine try the Bavarian **Matterhorn Restaurant,** 212 W. Railroad St. (a block off the main street), tel. 674-5863. Potato pancakes, homemade soups, sauerbraten, and Wiener schnitzel highlight the menu; open Wed. through Mon. for lunch and dinner. **Cavallini's** on the main drag serves predictable food in a dressed-up diner; but at least it's cheap, with even their best steak dinners under $10. For a donut or cinnamon roll for the road, stop by the **Cle Elum Bakery,** First and Pennsylvania;

closed Sunday of all days! Past Roslyn on Lake Cle Elum on Hwy. 903, the **Skookum Inn,** tel. 649-3409, caters to hikers and snowmobilers. Dinners here include prime rib, steaks, seafood, and a handful of others, all under $11; sandwiches are under $5, and breakfast is a steal at less than $3.50. The lounge is a good spot for a post-hike brew.

VANTAGE

Vantage is a tiny town on the shores of Wanapum Lake, created in 1959 by the Wanapum Dam on the Columbia River. The dam was named for the Wanapum Indians, a peaceful and religious tribe that lived along the river from Pasco to Vantage. The tiny village has a park, gas station, snack bar, rattlesnakes, and some breathtaking views of the river and surrounding brown hills. From Ellensburg, it is east on I-90 about 30 miles.

Parks

You won't see many trees here, except those several million years old. These are in **Ginkgo Petrified Forest State Park.** Fifteen to 20 million years ago, this area was first covered by lakes and swamps and then by molten lava, which poured out of fissures in the Earth's crust. Submerged logs were preserved intact by the lava cover; water eventually leaked through to the logs, and the silica in the groundwater replaced the natural structure of the wood. The tremendous erosion of the last ice age exposed 259 species of petrified wood, including the prehistoric ginkgo, which are now on display in outdoor "cages" or indoors at the interpretive center (open daily in summer), as are Indian petroglyphs.

The real beauty of the park is evident when walking the three-quarter-mile interpretive trail or the 2½-mile hiking trail; the dry, windblown hills host an assortment of scrappy wildflowers, sagebrush, and broad views. Watch for bald eagles, hawks, deer, elk, coyote, and a variety of lizards and snakes, including the poisonous Northern Pacific rattlesnake. You can also fish or waterski on the Columbia, and camp in one of 50 sites.

Get a close-up look at a Columbia River dam at the **Wanapum Dam Tour Center,** tel. 754-3541, 32 miles east of Ellensburg on Hwy. 243. The center is open April through Oct. for free self-guided tours, and also has a fish-viewing room and Indian and pioneer exhibits.

YAKIMA

Yakima, a far cry weatherwise from its neighbors to the west, averages 300 sunny days per year with just eight inches of precipitation. The "wet" season—Nov. to Jan.—accounts for almost half of the annual rain- or snowfall. Summer temperatures on the dry side of the mountains generally run 10 or more degrees higher than in Puget Sound cities, explaining why virtually every motel, no matter how cheap, has a pool. Despite the dry, brown hills surrounding the city, Yakima's suburbs are green, due to the constant chit-chit-chit of lawn sprinklers.

The Yakima Valley's volcanic soil is twice as productive as ordinary soil—teamed with irrigation and a 200-day growing season, it's hard to beat. The county ranks first in the country in apples, fruit trees, hops, and mint, and fourth in all fruits, with pears, grapes, cherries, peaches, and apricots as major crops. Though among the largest cities in eastern Washington and the commercial hub of the valley, Yakima's population is just under 50,000.

HISTORY

Yakima-area Indians defended their ground, preventing any permanent white settlement here until the end of the 1855-57 Indian War. With the Indians' acceptance of the Yakima Reservation in 1858, pioneer cattlemen settled in the valley—farmers weren't interested in this arid region. In 1861, Fielding M. Thorpe and his wife Margaret became Yakima's first homesteaders. Dry soil was the area's biggest drawback, so in the 1860s Sebastian Lauber and Joseph and Charles Schamo built an irrigation ditch to shift some of the Yakima River's water into town, paving the way for agriculture. In 1870, John W. Beck planted 50 apple trees and 50 peach trees in the region's first orchards, marking the end of the cattle era and the start of a major fruit industry. With a population of 400, "Yakima City" was incorporated in 1883. The Northern Pacific Railroad had a problem acquiring land from some of the property owners, so they built their Yakima Valley station four miles north of town. Since the railroad couldn't come to the city, the townspeople put their houses on skids and rollers and moved the city to the railroad—in time to meet the first train pulling into town on Dec. 14, 1884.

SIGHTS

Wine Tour
If you're a wine lover, visit **The Wine Cellar,** 5 N. Front St., for a good selection of Yakima Valley and other wines; staffed by a friendly, knowledgeable staff, the shop always has a few bottles open for you to taste. See below for information on the many wineries in the area.

Brewery
In a region known for its wineries, it's easy for beer drinkers to feel left out—but there's a place here for you too! The **Yakima Brewing and Malting Co.,** 25 N. Front St., became the Northwest's first microbrewery

YAKIMA

TO MT. RAINIER

NACHES RIVER

YAKIMA RIVER

TO ELLENSBURG

TERRACE HEIGHTS RD.

LINCOLN AVE.

EXIT 33

DOWNTOWN YAKIMA DETAIL

YAKIMA RIVER GREENWAY

YAKIMA SPORTSMAN S.P.

GILBERT PARK

W. YAKIMA AVE.

FRANKLIN PARK

CENTRAL WASHINGTON STATE FAIRGROUNDS & RACETRACK

YAKIMA ARBORETUM

WESTWOOD GOLF COURSE

TIETON DR.

YAKIMA VALLEY COMM. COLLEGE

E. NOB HILL BLVD.

EXIT 34

FISHER PARK & GOLF COURSE

DOWNTOWN YAKIMA DETAIL

LINCOLN AVE.

POST OFFICE

YAKIMA MUNIC. AIRPORT

YAKIMA AVE.

E. CHESTNUT AVE.

E. WALNUT AVE.

VALLEY MALL

TO YAKIMA VALLEY WINERIES

UNION GAP

0   1 mi
0   1 km

(1-13 see insert map)
1. Yakima Brewing and Malting Co., Wine Cellar, and Greystone Restaurant
2. Track 29 Dining Co. and Shops
3. Golden Wheel
4. Santiago's
5. House of Art
6. Yakima Mall
7. Capitol Theater
8. Casa de Blanca
9. TraveLodge
10. Greyhound
11. Towne Plaza
12. visitor center
13. chamber of commerce
14. Best Western Rio Mirada
15. Meadowbrook Garden
16. Meadowbrook Miniature Golf
17. Warehouse Gallery and The Attic
18. Red Robin
19. Tudor Guest House
20. Memorial Hospital
21. H.M. Gilbert Homeplace
22. Yakima Valley Museum
23. Ichiban
24. St. Elizabeth Hospital
25. Comfort Inn
26. Bali Hai Motel
27. Red Lion Inn
28. Colonial Motor Inn
29. Nendel's Inn
30. Motel 6
31. Gasparetti's
32. Gallery Gage
33. Red Lion Motel
34. Black Angus
35. Imperial Inn
36. Marti's

when investors got a taste of Bert Grant's home brew in 1981. Grant's Scottish Ale launched the brewery, which now also produces Grant's Imperial Stout, India Pale Ale, and others from locally grown Cascade hops. You can tour the brewery daily at 2 and 3 p.m., or visit **The Brewery Pub** in the same building, where you'll find at least five different brews on tap at all times, plus Cornish pasties, sausage rolls, pub pies, and Scotch eggs in British-pub fashion. Smoking is not allowed.

Dinner Train
Take a ride through the Yakima River Valley aboard the **Spirit of Washington Dinner Train.** Enjoy the scenery from one of five stainless-steel cars, including a vista dome (with a bar). Three-hour roundtrip brunch ($30) or dinner ($45) rides run Fri. night be-

tween Kennewick and Prosser, Sat. night and Sun. morning between Yakima and Ellensburg. Reservations and meal selections must be made in advance; phone 452-2336 or (800) 876-RAIL or write 1 E. Yakima Ave., Yakima, WA 98901, for more information.

Bridges And Scenic Drives
Driving on I-82 between Ellensburg and Yakima, you'll realize that eastern Washington isn't the flat desert wasteland that it's sometimes made out to be—a desert wasteland, maybe, but not flat. As the road snakes up treeless ridges over 2,000 feet high, the brown hills in the distance look as if they're covered with velvet; up close, sagebrush dots the brown grass (in an imitation of a scruffy three-day beard). Pull in at the "view point" sign for broad vistas of green valley farmland below and the snowcapped Stuart Range to the north. Along the way, you'll cross the largest single concrete span bridge in North America. The **Fred Redmon Memorial Bridge** twin spans are 1,336 feet long and 330 feet high. Pull into the rest stop at the south end of the bridge for a striking view of the summits of Mt. Adams and Mt. Rainier.

The **Jacob Durr Wagon Road** was the only route linking Yakima and Ellensburg in the 1880s; today it's surely the most scenic, climbing over Umtanum Ridge for a 360-degree view of the Cascades and Yakima Valley. Drive north from Selah on N. Wenas Ave. and Wenas Creek Rd. for six miles, then turn right onto Sheep Company Rd.; in two miles you'll reach Durr Road.

Museums And History
The N. Front St. Historical District boasts some of Yakima's oldest buildings, including the 1898 Lund Building, which once housed a saloon (now the Greystone Restaurant) directly across from the Northern Pacific Railroad depot. Be sure to visit **The Wine Cellar** and **Brewery Pub** (mentioned above), also in the district.

Visit the **Yakima Valley Museum,** 2105 Tieton Dr., tel. 248-0747, at the edge of

view from Umtanum Ridge, midway between Yakima and Ellensburg

Franklin Park to see Yakima Indian clothing, beadwork, and artifacts, a replica of Chief Justice William O. Douglas's office, and the most comprehensive collection of horse-drawn vehicles west of the Mississippi. Open Wed. through Sun. till 5 p.m., year-round; admission is $2.50 adults, $1.25 students and seniors.

Union Gap's **Central Washington Agricultural Museum** displays tractors, pea pickers, and other early Yakima Valley farm equipment on 15 acres in Fulbright Park.

The **H.M. Gilbert Homeplace,** 2109 W. Yakima Ave., was built in 1898 amidst 20 acres of sagebrush by Horace M. Gilbert, a farmer, land developer, and one of the pioneers in the irrigation of the Yakima Valley. You can tour this early Yakima Valley farm home on Fri., March through Dec., 10 a.m.-3 p.m., for $2.50; tel. 248-0747.

Three miles northwest of Yakima on Hwy. 12 you'll find the mysterious **Indian Painted Rocks,** a state historical site. Although the pictographs were partially destroyed by an early irrigation project, some remain at Naches Hwy. and Powerhouse Road.

The **Ahtanum Mission,** east of Yakima along Ahtanum Creek, was built in 1852 by Oblate priests. Though it burned down in the Indian War, the church was rebuilt in 1869 and is still used. You can visit the mission and surrounding park for a small fee.

Planetarium

Every Mon. at 7 p.m. the planetarium at Yakima Valley Community College puts on a stellar performance; S. 16th Ave. and W. Nob Hill, tel. 575-2356 or 575-2209; free.

ACCOMMODATIONS

Bed And Breakfasts

At 3111 Tieton Dr., the stately **Tudor Guest House,** tel. 452-8112 or 452-6015, is an elegant bargain. Constructed in 1932, this English Tudor mansion is surrounded by parklike grounds and furnished in early 19th-century antiques (plus color TVs). All rooms are on the second floor with shared baths and start at $40 d; breakfast is continental.

Eighteen miles east of Yakima on Hwy. 24, **The Desert Rose B&B,** 18170 Hwy. 24, tel. 452-2237, is an English country manor surrounded by thousands of acres of rolling hills and views of the valley and Mt. Rainier. The greatest concentration of great horned owls in the state live nearby, and the night skies out here are dark and clear—great for stargazing. Peace and quiet are ensured with just two guest rooms ($50 s, $60 d); families are welcome, and you can choose your breakfast when you make your reservation.

For more B&Bs, see "Vicinity of Yakima" below.

Hotels And Motels

Take the N. First St. exit off I-82 for "hotel row." See the charts on pp. 353 and 358 for a comprehensive list of these and other hotels in and around Yakima.

FOOD

Yakima's finest is **Birchfield Manor Gourmet Restaurant,** tel. 452-1960, a restored 1912 farmhouse two miles east of the city on Birchfield Road. Dinners are served Fri. through Sun., for $22.50, complemented by a vast selection of Yakima Valley wines; the owners ask that you leave the kids with a sitter. For Italian food from simple to fancy plus Northwest specialties, try **Gasperetti's,** 1013 N. First St., tel. 248-0628; open for dinner only, Tues. through Saturday. **Marti's,** 1601 Terrace Heights Rd., serves everything from steak to seafood to pizza, and three meals daily, overlooking the Yakima River; tel. 248-2062. In the historic district, **The Greystone Restaurant,** 5 N. Front St., tel. 248-9801, has moderately priced Northwest cuisine, fresh seafood, and homemade pasta in an elegant atmosphere; open for dinner only, Tues. through Saturday.

The **Track 29 Dining Co.,** Yakima Ave. and N. First St., serves moderately priced steak, chicken, pasta, and Mexican dishes for lunch and dinner daily in two restored 1920s railroad cars; or, enjoy a beer and appetizers on their sunny patio. **Santiago's,** 111 E. Yakima Ave., tel. 453-1644, is a popular Mexican restaurant open for lunch and dinner daily; or, try **Casa de Blanca,** 402 E. Yakima Ave., tel. 248-3501. For delicious Hawaiian and Polynesian fare, try **Haleaina,** 1406 N. 16th Ave., tel. 248-1965, open daily for dinner, weekdays for lunch, plus Sunday brunch.

For Cantonese and American cuisine, try the **Golden Wheel,** 9 S. First St., tel. 457-8400. Get authentic Japanese food with a sushi bar at **Ichiban,** 1107 Tieton Dr., tel. 248-2585. Enjoy good-old American steak and seafood, priced $7-17, at **Black Angus,** 501 N. Front St., tel. 248-4540. **Red Robin,** 2706 W. Nob Hill Rd., features gourmet hamburgers, sandwiches, and light meals; open for lunch and dinner daily. For a great little English-style pub, see "Brewery" above.

The lounge at **Meadowbrook Garden** at the Meadowbrook Mall, 72nd and Nob Hill, has live music Wed. through Sat., with free dance lessons every Wed. at 7:30 p.m.; tel. 965-0384.

PARKS AND RECREATION

About a mile east of town off I-82, **Yakima Sportsman State Park** has a stocked pond for kids to fish—adults can try their luck in the Yakima—plus 28 standard and 36 hookup campsites along the greenbelt; a great spot to escape the summer heat. The **Yakima River Greenway**, currently being developed, will encompass 3,600 acres east of the city, connecting existing parks along a 10-mile paved bike path. Already completed is the riverside trail at the **Yakima Area Arboretum**, I-90 and Nob Hill Blvd., a partially developed, 70-acre park with Japanese garden and bird sanctuary. At **Eschbach Park,** five miles past the fish hatchery on the Old Naches Hwy., rent a tube ($1) and take a lazy float down the Yakima River. The day-use, 175-acre county park offers boating, swimming, picnicking, and play areas. **Randall Park,** south of Nob Hill Blvd. on S. 48th Ave., has a picnic area, trails, duck pond, and creek on 40 grassy acres. **Franklin Park,** behind the museum at Tieton Dr. and 20th Ave., has tennis courts and grassy hills for romping or winter sledding. Seventeen miles east of Yakima on Hwy. 24, the 244-acre **ORV Park** has motorcycle, jeep, and three-wheeler race tracks, and trapshooting station. Open Sat. through Wed. till 6 p.m.

Across the Yakima River from Union Gap, **Moxee Bog,** a spring-fed preserve, is home to a rare breed of monarch butterfly that feeds on the violets that grow here. Birders will want to visit the **Boise Cascade Bird Sanctuary** in the Wenas Valley, five miles west of Selah on Wean Road. The corporation donated 40 acres for the campground and sanctuary where over 100 species of birds have been sighted.

Golf
Yakima has three public golf courses: **Sun Tides,** 2215 Pence, tel. 966-9065, has 18 holes, eight miles west of town on Hwy. 12; **Fisher Golf Course,** S. 40th Ave. and W. Arlington, tel. 575-6075; and **Westwood Golf Course,** 6408 Tieton Dr., tel. 966-0890, are nine-hole courses.

ENTERTAINMENT

Festivals
Held in mid-June at the Central Washington State Fairgrounds on Fair Ave., the **Washington State Open Horse Show** is one of the largest in the country. The most popular fairgrounds event (aside from the horse racing, below) is the **Central Washington State Fair and Rodeo,** held in late September.

Horse Racing
For quarter horse and thoroughbred racing, check out **Yakima Meadows Racetrack** at the fairgrounds on Fair Avenue. The horses usually run Fri., Sat., and Sun., March through May and Sept. through Nov., with a scanty summer schedule; tel. 248-3920.

Auto Racing
The **Yakima Speedway,** 1600 Pacific Ave., has NASCAR racing every Sat. night; tel. 248-0647.

Theater
The historic **Capitol Theater** at 19 S. Third St. first opened its doors in 1920, featuring vaudeville and feature films. Today the theater hosts a full schedule of theatrical productions nearly year-round; tel. 575-6267.

Movies
Yakima is one of few cities where you can still find drive-ins; in fact, they have two: **Country Drive-In,** 4309 W. Nob Hill, tel. 966-5340, and **Fruitvale Triple Drive-In,** 1819 Fruitvale, tel. 248-3650. Indoor theaters include **Uptown Plaza** at 202 E. Chestnut, tel. 248-0245, **Mercy 6-Plex** at the Valley Mall, tel. 248-0242, and **Cinema West,** 2706 W. Nob Hill, tel. 248-0243.

DOWNTOWN YAKIMA ACCOMMODATIONS

Name	Address	Phone	Rates	Comments
Bali Hai Motel	710 N. 1st St.	452-7178	$19-25 s $24-32 d	pool
Best Western Rio Mirada Motor Inn	1603 Terrace Heights Dr.	457-4444	$49 s $54-59 d	on the river, Jacuzzi, pool, exercise facilities, adjacent restaurant, rooms have river views
Colonial Motor Inn	1405 N. 1st St.	453-8981	$33 s $38-43 d	heated pool, two hot tubs
Comfort Inn	1700 N. 1st St.	248-5650	$45 s $50-58 d	pool, sauna, airport and bus shuttle
Imperial Inn	510 N. 1st St.	457-6155	$34 s $34-42 d	pool
Motel 6	1104 N. 1st St.	454-0080	$28 s 32 d	pool
Nendel's Inn	1300 N. 1st St.	248-6666	$43 s $48-50 d	pool, playground, lounge, restaurant
Red Lion Motel	818 N. 1st St.	453-0391	$43 s $53-65 d	pool, airport and bus shuttle
TraveLodge	110 S. Naches Ave.	453-7151	$40 s $50-56 d	pool
Towne Plaza	N. 7th and E. Yakima	248-5900	$63-78 s $73-88 d	two pools, poolside service, lounge, cafe, airport and bus shuttle
Red Lion Inn	1507 N. 1st St.	248-7850	$55-65 s $65-72 d	two pools, poolside service, airport and bus shuttle, cafe, lounge

SHOPPING

Usually the giant covered shopping malls are found in suburbia, but Yakima's biggest shopping center is in the heart of downtown: the **Yakima Mall** has over 75 shops including The Bon, Nordstrom, JC Penney, and Mervyn's, plus 1,200 covered parking spaces to keep your car cool. At Yakima Ave. and N. 1st, two 1920s railroad cars house the **Track 29 Dining Co.** (see "Food" above) and serve as a backdrop for numerous gift shops and eateries. Just over the line into Union Gap, **Valley Mall** on S. First St. has 44 stores including Sears, Lamonts, and Pay Less Drug Store.

Art galleries abound in Yakima. Visit **Gallery Gage**, 1007 N. First St., **Warehouse**

Gallery and The Attic at 5000 W. Lincoln, and House of Art, 106 N. Fifth Avenue.

Grocery stores are all over town, but the biggest and easiest to find are Fred Meyer and Safeway, both on S. First Street.

SERVICES AND INFORMATION

The area code from Chinook Pass to the eastern border is 509. For maps, brochures, and current festival information, contact the Yakima Valley Visitors and Convention Bureau, 10 N. Eighth St., Yakima, WA 98907, tel. 575-1300, or the Greater Yakima Chamber of Commerce, 10 N. Ninth St., tel. 248-2021. For information on the surrounding towns, contact the Toppenish Chamber of Commerce, 219 S. Toppenish Ave., tel. 865-3262; the Sunnyside Chamber of Commerce, 340 S. Sixth Ave., tel. 837-5939; the Zillah Chamber of Commerce, 111 Seventh St., tel. 829-6994; or the Prosser Chamber of Commerce, 611 Sixth St., tel. 786-2626.

No 911 service here; in an emergency, phone 248-1010 for police or 248-2100 for fire. For medical emergencies, phone Yakima Valley Memorial Hospital, 2811 Tieton Dr., tel. 575-8000; St. Elizabeth Hospital, 110 S. Ninth Ave., tel. 575-5060; or Yakima Ambulance Medic 1, tel. 248-3610.

Post offices are located at 205 W. Washington and 112 S. Third Avenue.

TRANSPORTATION

By Car
Coming from Seattle, the fastest and best winter or bad-weather route to Yakima is on I-90 over Snoqualmie Pass, turning south onto I-82 in Ellensburg. If you have time to spare, the routes through or near Mt. Rainier National Park are more scenic. In the best weather, pick up Hwy. 410 in Enumclaw, following it through the park and over two mountain passes; or continue south from Cayuse Pass onto Hwy. 123, then go east on Hwy. 12 over White Pass. (See "Vicinity of

Fred Redmon Memorial Bridge

Mount Rainier," p. 319). Before you try these routes in winter, phone 976-7623 for pass conditions from Nov. to March.

Getting oriented after you've arrived in Yakima can be difficult, until you figure out the system. North Front St., along the railroad tracks, divides the downtown area; from here, street numbers ascend, starting with "1," in both directions, leading to a confusing situation in which Sixth St. and Sixth Ave. are 12 blocks apart.

Here's the key: "streets" are on the east side; "avenues" are on the west. East Yakima Ave. runs perpendicular to N. Front St. and divides the numbered streets into North and south sections, e.g. S. Second Street. Simple?

By Air
The Yakima Municipal Airport off Washington Ave. is the largest in the area, served by Horizon Airlines, tel. (800) 547-9308.

By Trolley
Ride the Yakima Trolley Line's restored 1906 trolley cars through orchards, over the Naches River, and past Congdon's Castle. Trains depart hourly on weekends from 44th Ave. and Nob Hill Blvd., late April through Labor Day, for a 45-minute ride; fares are $3 adults, $1.50 for kids, or $9 for the whole brood; phone 575-1700 for recorded information.

By Bus

Yakima Transit, tel. 575-6175, has nine routes serving the Yakima area, including the Municipal Airport. Fares are $.35 adults, $.20 kids. To get out of town or across the country, hop aboard **Greyhound** from their station at 602 E. Yakima Ave., tel. 457-5131. Other Yakima-area Greyhound stations are at 602 W. First in Toppenish, tel. 865-3773, and at 13th St. and Hwy. 12 in Sunnyside, tel. 837-5344.

Tours

Since no one wants to be the "designated driver" on a day-long winery tour, leave the driving to **Custom Tours,** Route 1, Box 1474, Zillah, WA 98953, tel. 865-3353 or 575-6595. **PW Charter Service,** Box 2455, Yakima, WA 98907, tel. 575-3655 or (800) 572-2877, also offers local sightseeing and winery tours.

VICINITY OF YAKIMA

TOPPENISH

Toppenish, about 25 miles southeast of Yakima, is the home of the Yakima Indian Agency and the commercial center for the Yakima Indian Reservation.

Yakima Nation Cultural Center

About 23 miles southeast of Yakima, the Yakima Nation Cultural Center, tel. (509) 865-2800, features a museum that tells the story of the Yakima Nation from its beginnings to the present; a library specializing in the American Indian; and a theater that presents first-run movies and stage productions. Open daily; admission is $2 adults, $1 kids, or $5 for the family.

   As you're driving near the reservation, keep an eye out for UFOs! The Yakima Indian Reservation, made the *National Enquirer* in late 1986 because of their alleged high frequency of UFO sightings, reportedly "an everyday part" of their culture. (And as a historical aside, the very first UFO sighting that was reported to officials was in the Mount Rainier area.)

Fort Simcoe State Park

About 30 miles west of Toppenish in the heart of the Yakima Indian Reservation, Fort Simcoe State Park, tel. 874-2372, is a day-use park surrounding Fort Simcoe, erected by the Army in 1856 and named a national historic site in 1956. Two blockhouses and a barracks have been reconstructed, and five of the original buildings have been restored and furnished. Tour the buildings and interpretive center, then enjoy a picnic lunch on the landscaped grounds. The grounds are open Wed. through Sun., April through mid-Oct., weekends the rest of the year; the museum and interpretive center are open Wed. through Sun., April through October.

Festival

Held annually in June, the **Toppenish Western Wine Fest** is a day-long feast of Yakima Valley wines and beers, food, arts and crafts, and country and western music.

Food

A tiny joint on W. First St., **El Paso Cafe** serves inexpensive Mexican lunches and dinners. Closed Sun.; no alcohol. Enjoy a root beer float and chili dog at **A&W,** 433 S. Elm.

YAKIMA VALLEY

While Toppenish is virtually a world—or a nation—apart, the rest of the Yakima Valley blends together to form a single conceptual region, basing its reputation, if not its economy, on the wineries that line the Yakima River.

   For a pleasant side trip, drive south from Mabton on the Bickleton-Goldendale Hwy. across the Horse Heaven Hills to the tiny town of Bickleton. It is a very small town with a friendly cafe and tavern across the street, and a few Victorian homes, some no longer occupied. But it does have another kind of home, perhaps hundreds of them, that are seasonally occupied. Bickleton is the bluebird capital of the Northwest. It has houses for bluebirds on fence posts, on mailboxes, on trees, and virtually everywhere you look. There's even one in front of the community church, a mirror-image (although considerably smaller) of the church. The bluebird housing project started many years ago when a resident built one, then another and another, and soon it was a community project. When the birds leave for the winter, the houses are taken down, cleaned and painted if they need it, and everyone has the pleasure of watching for the first arrivals each spring.

YAKIMA VALLEY WINERIES

Museum

In Prosser City Park, the **Benton County Historical Museum** has a natural history display, 1900 homestead, 1913 school-house, ladies' gowns from the 1840s to 1920s, and an 1867 Chickering Square grand piano you can play. Open daily except Mon., 10 a.m.-4 p.m., Sun. 1 p.m.-5 p.m.; admission is $1 adults, $.50 for kids.

Bed And Breakfasts

In the heart of wine country, **Cottage Court Bed & Breakfast,** 1824 Meade Ave., tel. 786-1430, offers continental or full breakfast with three guest rooms (shared bath) for $30 s, $35-40 d. No pets; smoking permitted in the lounge. The **Rinehold Cannery Homestead,** Route 1, Box 1117, on Gurley Rd. in Granger, tel. 854-2508, provides lodging and continental breakfast in a country setting for $45 s, $55 d.

Wine Tours And Barrel Tasting

The Yakima and Columbia valleys comprise the premier wine-growing regions in Washington, located along the same latitude as France's Burgundy and Bordeaux regions. The 13 wineries along the Yakima River pro-

vide more than a day's touring; all of these wineries have tasting rooms, and all but Hinzerling have picnic facilities.

From Yakima, your first stop will be **Staton Hills,** 2290 Gangl Rd. in Wapato, tel. 877-2112, open for tastings Tues. through Sun., 11 a.m.-5 p.m. Here you'll get a nice view of the Yakima Valley.

Next stop is **Covey Run,** formerly named Quail Run, at Route 2, Box 2287, in Zillah, tel. 829-6235; this is one of the area's big-name wineries (meaning you can find their wine in most Northwest grocery stores). Quail Run was the first major Washington winery to use only Yakima Valley grapes. Eighty-five percent of their production is white wine, most of it riesling. The mezzanine tasting room affords a nice vineyard view; open daily from 11 a.m.-4:30 p.m., Sun. from noon to 5 p.m.

A newer addition to the Valley is **Bonair Winery,** off Highland Dr. in Zillah, tel. 829-6027. Their first productions were a 1985 riesling, chardonnay, and cabernet sauvignon. Visitors are welcome Thurs. through Mon., April through Nov., 10 a.m.-5 p.m.

Also in Zillah, at Route 2, Box 2396, is **Horizon's Edge,** tel. 829-6401, another of

ACCOMMODATIONS—VICINITY OF YAKIMA

Name	Address	Phone	Rates	Comments
UNION GAP				
Best Western Tapadera Motor Inn	12 Valley Mall Blvd. Yakima	248-6924	$49 s $54-59 d	next to mall, restaurant
Super 8	2605 Rudkin Rd.	248-8800	$31-34 s $35-41 d	indoor pool, laundry, pets okay with notice
Days Inn Motor Inn	2408 Rudkin Rd.	248-9700	$34-40 s $38-44 d	pool, cafe, room service, airport and bus shuttle
SUNNYSIDE				
Nendel's Motor Inn	408 Yakima Valley Hwy.	837-7878	$43 s $48-50 d	pool
Red Apple Motel	412 Hwy. 12	839-2100	$30 s $33-36 d	kitchen $3 extra
Town House	509 Hwy. 12	837-5500	$27 s $27-27 d	playground, pets okay
GRANDVIEW				
Apple Valley Motel	Hwy. 12	882-3003	$30 s $30-34 d	pool
Grandview	522 E. Main St.	882-1323	$20-24 s $26-35 d	pool

the valley's newest wineries. Future releases will include cabernet sauvignon and pinot noir. (Their chardonnay and riesling releases started in 1984). The tasting room is open daily from April 1 to Christmas, 11 a.m.-5 p.m.

Stewart Vineyards, tel. 854-1882, is at Route 3, Box 3578, in Sunnyside. Their production includes rieslings, chardonnay, muscat canelli, gewürztraminer, and cabernet sauvignon; open daily at 10 a.m., Sun. at noon.

Also in Sunnyside, **Tucker Cellars,** Route 1, Box 1696, tel. 837-8701, is a family winery established in 1981 which now produces nine varieties and over 20,000 gallons annually. This is a good first or last visit: the tasting room is open daily 9 a.m.-6 p.m. in summer (10 a.m.-4 p.m. in winter).

Chateau Ste. Michelle, W. Fifth and Ave. B in Grandview, tel. 882-3928, is Washington's oldest winery. Established in the 1930s, it has come to represent the Washington wine industry across the country. Grandview is the site of all Ste. Michelle red wine fermentation; two other facilities are located in Woodinville and Paterson. Try their award-winning cabernet sauvignon and merlot daily from 10 a.m.-5 p.m.

Pontin del Roza, Route 1, Box 1129, in Prosser, tel. 786-4449 was established in 1984 and produces chardonnay, white riesling, and chenin blanc; open daily 10 a.m.-5 p.m.

Also in Prosser at Route 1, Box 1657, **Yakima River Winery,** tel. 786-2805, was started in 1978 by the John W. Rauner family and produces a wide variety of wines from

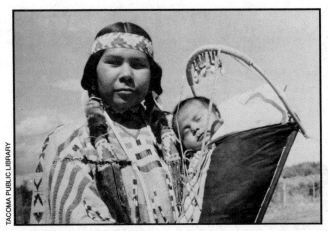

Rosalie Harry and Annie May of the Yakima tribe

dry and semidry whites and reds to dessert and ice wines, including some that are available only at the winery. The tasting room is open daily 10 a.m.-5 p.m.

Your next Prosser winery is **Hinzerling Vineyards,** 1520 Sheridan, tel. 786-2163. The vineyard here was planted in 1972, the winery founded in 1976; their specialties include estate-grown cabernet. Tastings are usually held in the wine cellar, Mon. through Sat. 10 a.m.-4 p.m. (closed for the noon hour); in winter, Sun. noon to 4 p.m.

You probably won't find **Chinook Wines** in your grocery store, so stop by the winery at Meade and Wittkopf roads in Prosser for some sparkling riesling, sauvignon blanc, chardonnay, or merlot. Open Thurs. through Mon. noon to 5 p.m.

The Hogue Cellars, Route 2, Box 2898, tel. 786-4557, is the big-name Prosser winery, with a range of products from rieslings to merlot along with a very nice, summery cabernet blush. Hogue Farms grows asparagus, concord grapes, hops, and scotch mint along with wine grapes on 1,200 acres. Their tasting room, gift shop, and art gallery are open daily 10 a.m.-5 p.m.

One of the newer Prosser wineries is **Mercer Ranch Vineyards,** in the Horse Heaven Hills on Alderdale Rd., tel. 894-4741. Premium reds are the specialty here, including cabernet sauvignon and limberger. Open Mon. through Sat. 9:30 a.m.-5:30 p.m. in summer, Sun. by appointment; phone for off-season hours.

Your wine tour ends with two Benton City wineries. **Kiona Vineyards,** Route 2, Box 2169E, tel. 588-6716, sits on Red Mountain with a nice tasting-room view of the vineyards. In business since 1980, Kiona produces a full range of varietal wines; open daily noon to 5 p.m. You'll need an appointment to taste the wines at Benton City's **Blackwood Canyon,** Route 2, Box 2169H, tel. 588-6249. It may be worth your while, since their chardonnays, cabernets, and late harvest wines are available only at the winery and select restaurants.

The **F.W. Langguth Winery,** tel. 932-4943, out in Mattawa is open to group tours by appointment only; if you don't have a group or don't want to drive that far, you can easily find their riesling and chardonnay in area stores.

Barrel Tasting: During the April **Yakima Valley Spring Barrel Tasting,** all the valley wineries pour samples of their new releases straight from the barrel, and offer tours, hors d'oeuvres, and educational exhibits. All 15 wineries are open 10 a.m.-5 p.m. during the three-day event.

Get a brochure describing the Yakima Valley wineries by sending a long, self-addressed, stamped envelope to the Yakima Valley Wine Growers Assoc., Box 39, Grandview, WA 98930, or phone 837-8701.

News
Pick up a copy of *The Wine Almanac of the Pacific Northwest* from area wine shops or by mail ($10.50 a year) from NWA Subscriptions, Box 85595, Seattle, WA 98145-1595. The *Almanac* has winery news and a calendar of events for festivals and competitions.

Cheese
Cheese is a natural accompaniment to good wine, so it's no surprise to find the **Yakima Valley Cheese Co.,** Alexander Rd., producing 1,300 pounds of gouda (they pronounce it "GOW-da") daily. No tours are available, but you can pick up a pound or two at the sales room Tues. through Sat. 9:30 a.m.-5:30 p.m.; tel. 837-6005.

Food
For Mexican food, antiques, gifts, or tortillas to take home (made on the premises), try **El Ranchito,** just off the Zillah exit, tel. 829-5880; sorry, no alcohol. Or, stop by **Doc's Pizza,** 505 First Ave. in Zillah, tel. 829-6259.

In Sunnyside, the **Tillicum Restaurant,** 410 Hwy. 12, serves only Yakima Valley wines with their steak and prime rib dinners; tel. 837-7222. For Szechuan and Mandarin cooking, try China Grove, 325 Hwy. 12, tel. 839-3663.

BOB RACE

EASTERN WASHINGTON

MOSES LAKE

When you cross the Columbia River on I-90 headed toward Spokane, you are entering the northernmost reaches of the Great American Desert, which runs through eastern Washington, eastern Oregon, Nevada, eastern California, and Arizona and down into Mexico. It ends with the trees of the Spokane area and the Okanogan Highlands. However, the Columbia River almost defines the northern rim of the desert when it makes its turn to the west where the Spokane River enters, and when it turns south again at Grand Coulee, it forms most of the western boundary of the desert.

In spite of the scarce rainfall and open country that alternately freezes in the winter and sears in the summer, and precious few year-around streams, this basaltic desert has always had several small, natural lakes scattered through it. Their numbers increased

dramatically when the Columbia Basin Irrigation Project was created. One such lake is Moses Lake.

Moses Lake was considerably smaller before the Columbia Basin Project occurred and the area was already being irrigated on a smaller scale by water from artesian wells. When Columbia River water was pumped onto the fields, reclamation engineers didn't know exactly what to expect from the water; whether it would simply stand and create lakes, or if it would flow underground. The irrigation water in the Moses Lake area and farther north toward Grand Coulee generally seeps southward, following the natural slope of the land, and collects in Potholes Reservoir behind O'Sullivan Dam. The original Moses Lake is at the northern end of the reservoir, its level controlled by the smaller Moses Lake Dam.

EASTERN WASHINGTON

You would expect that two large bodies of water in such a hot and arid climate would be surrounded by time-share condos and RV parks, and they probably would be if they were in a more populated part of the state. But in lonely central Washington the lakes are often just a pit stop on the way to somewhere else, except for fishermen who come for trout, perch, and the sunshine. Although a lot of the area remains in its natural state of basaltic outcroppings, sand, and sagebrush, irrigation water is being put on more and more land through the area and it is losing its desert look.

Like most of eastern Washington, Moses Lake gets little rainfall—about nine inches a year—an average of 15 inches of snow, and some of the state's highest summer temperatures. Though eastern Washington is best known for its wheat production, the Columbia Basin leads the country in potato production per acre, with alfalfa and corn as other major crops.

SIGHTS

Parks And Lakes

The **O'Sullivan Dam,** on Hwy. 17 at the south end of Potholes Reservoir, is one of the largest earth-filled dams in the country. **Potholes State Park,** at the west end of O'Sullivan Dam, is a popular spot for launching a boat to catch the reservoir's trout, walleye, and perch. Waterskiers, picnickers, and swimmers also enjoy the sunny east-of-the-mountains weather at this 2,500-acre park. Camp at one of 66 standard ($7) or 60 hookup ($9.50) sites; tel. (509) 765-7271.

Eighteen-mile-long Moses Lake, the state's second-largest lake, is two miles west of town. **Moses Lake State Park** has swimming, fishing for trout, crappie, and catfish, a grassy picnic area, and a snack bar; open for day use only.

Cascade Park, on Valley Rd. and Cascade Valley on Moses Lake, also offers swimming, boating, waterskiing, and camping for $7.50, $9 with hookups. Open daily from mid-April through mid-Oct.; tel. 766-9240.

Sand Dunes/ORV Park

Hike, slide, or ride your off-road vehicle on the 3,000 acres of sand dunes south of town. Crab Creek, adjacent to the dunes, is good for paddling. Go south on Division St., which becomes Potato Hill Rd., to its end, then follow the signs—and six miles of gravel road—to the ORV park.

Museums

At 421 Balsam St. in the Civic Center, the **Adam East Museum** displays fossils from prehistoric animals and marinelife and early man in North America. Open Mon. through Fri. from mid-March through Oct., phone 766-9240 for hours; free.

Wildlife Refuge

The **Columbia National Wildlife Refuge** on the south shore of the reservoir is in the famous Pacific Flyway; over 200 species of birds stop at the more than 50 seep lakes, making for good birdwatching throughout the area. Hunting for waterfowl, rabbit, and deer is permitted on about half of the refuge's 28,000 acres; stop by the refuge headquarters at 44 S. Eighth St. in Othello for maps and other specifics.

Wineries

Three wineries are scattered around the Moses Lake area. In Othello, stop by **Hunter Hill Vineyards,** 2752 W. McManamon Rd., tel. 346-2607. **Saddle Mountain/Langguth Winery** is at 2340 Winery Rd. in Mattawa, tel. 932-4943. Enjoy a tour and sample the variety of wines produced at the **Champs de Brionne Winery,** 98 Rd. NW in Quincy, tel. 785-6685. The winery has a terraced amphitheater and hosts summer evening concerts with big-name stars such as Rod Stewart, Bob Dylan, and the Judds. Open daily 11 a.m.-5 p.m.

Petting Zoo

Sponsored by the Moses Lake/Grant County Humane Society, the Petting Zoo at the Grant County Airport on Randolph Rd. is home to a pony, sheep, goats, rabbits, chickens, and other livestock. Open Mon. through

MOSES LAKE

GRANT CO. FAIRGROUNDS

CASCADE PARK

EL PAPAGAYO

TO AIRPORT

VALLEY RD.

SCOTT RD.

CASCADE MARINA

GREYHOUND DEPOT

ADAM EAST MUSEUM

CHAMBER OF COMMERCE

VELTRI'S

SAMARITAN HOSPITAL

BROADWAY AVE.

3 AVE.

DIVISION ST.

PIONEER WAY

17

MOSES LAKE

BEST WESTERN HALLMARK INN

MOSES LAKE S.P.

TO POTHOLES S.P. & COL. NAT'L. WILDLIFE REC. AREA

90

POTATO HILL RD.

0   1 mi

0   1 km

© MOON PUBLICATIONS, INC.

Fri. 10 a.m.-4 p.m., Sat. 1-4 p.m.; donations accepted.

ACCOMMODATIONS

Motels
The **Motel 6,** 2822 Wapato Dr., tel. (509) 766-0250, has budget lodging for $21 s, $27 d, plus a pool. **TraveLodge,** 316 S. Pioneer Way, tel. 765-8631 or (800) 255-3050, has 39 rooms from $29 s, $36-39 d, with heated pool and hot tub. The **Imperial Inn,** 905 W. Broadway, tel. 765-8626, has 29 rooms for $26-30 s, $30-36 d, plus a heated pool. The **Interstate Inn,** 2801 W. Broadway, tel. 765-1777, has 30 rooms from $28 s, $33 d, an indoor pool, hot tub, and sauna. **Super 8,** 449 Melva Lane at I-90 exit 176, tel. 765-8886, has 62 rooms from $31-34 s, $35-41 d, with indoor pool and guest laundry. The best in town, the **Best Western Hallmark Inn,** 3000 Marina Dr., tel. 765-9211, has 132 rooms from $47-57 s, $51-61 d, plus swimming and wading pools, restaurant, lounge with dancing (nightly except Sun.), room service, and tennis courts.

Camping
At the west end of O'Sullivan Dam, **Mar Don Resort,** tel. 346-2651, has 250 sites for RV and tent camping, plus a motel, restaurant, lounge, and more, for $13 per night; open year-round. **Willows RV Park,** 2½ miles south of I-90 exit 179 off Hwy. 17, tel. 765-7531, has 64 trailer sites for $10 per night; open all year. See "Parks And Lakes" above for more camping.

FOOD

One of Moses Lake's best family restaurants, **The Pantry,** 3001 W. Broadway Ave. just off I-90, tel. 765-8385, looks like a highway chain from the outside, but inside boasts a blue and pink interior and good food from a varied menu that includes burgers, chicken, steaks, pasta, and Mexican entrees for $10 and less; open 24 hours every day. A little more elegant with a lake view, **Cade's** at the Best Western Hallmark Inn, 3000 Marina Dr., tel. 765-9211, serves three moderately priced meals daily from a varied American menu. Enjoy Japanese and American cuisine at the **Flight Deck Restaurant** at Grant County Airport's main terminal building, tel. 762-2404; open for three meals weekdays, dinner only on Sat., closed Sunday. **The Porterhouse,** 217 N. Elder, tel. 765-6041, is open for three meals daily, specializing in steak and seafood dinners in a casual atmosphere for under $7. For Mexican food and dancing Tues. through Sun. nights, try **El Papagayo,** Hwy. 17 and Stratford Rd., tel. 765-1265.

ENTERTAINMENT

Festivals And Fairs
The Memorial Day weekend **Spring Festival** features a carnival, arts and crafts, torchlight boat parade, antique cars, fireworks, ATV races, and a 10-km run; tel. 765-8248. The rodeo is the highlight of the **Grant County Fair,** held for five days in mid-Aug. at the Grant County Fairgrounds just north of town off Hwy. 17.

Golf
Play 18 holes in the sunshine at **Warden Golf Course,** 12 miles south of Moses Lake on Hwy. 17, tel. 349-7794.

SERVICES AND INFORMATION

The area code in Moses Lake, Ephrata, and points east is 509. For more information on current festivals and events, contact the **Moses Lake Chamber of Commerce,** 324 S. Pioneer Way, tel. 765-7888; open Mon. through Fri. during normal working hours.

Dial 911 for medical, fire, and police emergencies in Moses Lake, Ephrata, Othello, and the surrounding area. **Samaritan Hospital,** 801 E. Wheeler Rd., tel. 765-5606, has 24-hour emergency room service.

TRANSPORTATION

Moses Lake is 180 miles—a three-hour drive from Seattle on I-90, all 65 mph after Issaquah.

The Moses Lake area is part of **Greyhound's** national network, served by bus stations at 630 E. Broadway in Moses Lake, tel. 765-6441, 741 Basin NW in Ephrata, tel. 754-3322, and 1176 S. Division in Ritzville, tel. 659-1792.

The nearest **Amtrak** station is in Ephrata at its First St. depot; tel. (800) 872-7245.

Horizon Air, tel. (800) 547-9308, has scheduled passenger service to Seattle, Portland, Spokane, and other major Northwest cities from Grant County Airport, north of town off Randolph Road. The airport is frequently used by Boeing to flight-test new planes, and by major foreign and domestic airlines, including Japan Air Lines, to train pilots and crews (look out below!). Besides contributing to the local economy, JAL shows its community spirit by hosting two flights over the Columbia Basin each fall on its 747s for Moses Lake sixth graders and senior citizens.

Explore the islands in Potholes Reservoir on a motorboat rented from **Cascade Marina,** 2242 Scott Rd., tel. 765-6718; open daily in summer.

VICINITY OF MOSES LAKE

RITZVILLE, EPHRATA, OTHELLO, AND SOAP LAKE

Ritzville is a small wheat-farming town about 45 miles northeast of Moses Lake on I-90. It is the main town in an area settled by Volga Germans during the latter part of last century. These Germans were descendants of German citizens lured to the Volga River Valley in Russia by Catherine the Great, a German herself. The Volga Germans were harshly discriminated against by the Russians after Catherine died, and all had to flee the country. Many managed to immigrate to America, and most settled across the northern part of the country. Odessa, a nearby town, was also settled by many Volga Germans.

Ephrata is a tidy town of 5,000 set amidst a sprinkling of trees, surrounded by miles of green and beige landscape. It has the headquarters of Columbia Basin Reclamation Project, which is the irrigation arm of the Grand Coulee Dam undertaking. Few towns in Washington were more desolate than Ephrata before the irrigation project.

Othello is about the same size and is about 20 miles south of O'Sullivan Dam. Other than the hotel gallery listed below, and a grassy park with swimming pool, Othello has few visitors' facilities.

Though you'd never suspect it today, Soap Lake, about five miles northeast of Ephrata on Hwy. 28, was once a bustling resort area surrounding the Soap Lake Sanitorium, a health retreat that capitalized on the lake's legendary medicinal qualities. The Smokiam Indians sent their sick to soak in the Great Spirit's *smokiam* or "healing waters"; early white explorers called it Soap Lake because its 17 natural minerals and oils give the water a soapy feel and create a suds-like foam on windy days.

In the early 1900s, great crowds of people from around the country came here to drink and bathe in the water to cure joint, skin, digestive, and circulatory ailments. Most of the visitors weren't too sick: they found time for drinking, dancing, and general hell-raising, leading the local newspaper to admonish them to "be more careful" about remembering their swimsuits! The drought and Depression of 1933 brought an end to the revelry, turning Soap Lake into a curiosity in the midst of a desolate region. It has been making a steady comeback, though, and the chamber of commerce actively promotes the curative powers of the lake's water. Local shops sell Soap Lake Salts and the water is piped into several motels for your convenience.

Parks

For a reprieve from the heat in Moses Lake, head to aptly named **Oasis Park,** 5103 Hwy. 28, for a picnic and swim in a cool lake, enjoy the par-three, nine-hole golf course next door, or camp overnight for $7 (tents), $10 for full hookup; tel. 754-5102.

The **Ritzville City Park,** just off I-90 at the Washtucna exit, covers 2.6 acres and has a public swimming pool, playground equipment, an outdoor kitchen, restrooms, and horseshoe pits. No overnight camping.

Enjoy some healing or just a quick swim at **Soap Lake,** just off Hwy. 28 about five miles northeast of Ephrata. Follow the signs for Notaras Lodge up First St. to East Beach, with play equipment, lake access, and rest rooms; the Soap Lake Chamber of Commerce is also here if you need maps or directions. **Smokiam Campground,** adjacent to the chamber of commerce, has waterfront camping for $8.50 for all sites.

Eight miles west of Quincy off Hwy. 28, **Crescent Bar Park** on the Wanapum Reservoir offers swimming, boating, waterskiing, picnicking, fishing, a playground, tennis courts, a nine-hole golf course, and camping; tel. 787-1511.

Museums

Dr. Frank R. Burroughs Home, 408 West Main in Ritzville, was built in 1890 and served for 37 years as the physician's office, containing records of house calls, births, and fees charged. The 1907 **Andrew Carnegie Library,** also in Ritzville at 302 W. Main, houses photos and artifacts from Ritzville's history, as well as the city's public library and a time capsule buried in its front lawn in 1981.

The little town of Ephrata has an excellent collection of Indian and pioneer artifacts, clothing, tools, diaries, documents, and relics arranged chronologically from prehistoric to modern times, at **Grant County Historical Museum and Pioneer Village,** 742 N. Basin St., tel. 754-3334. An 18-building pioneer village has a saloon, dress shop, barbershop,

printing office, blacksmith, and more. Guided tours are available Thurs. through Tues. afternoons from May through mid-September. Demonstrations of pioneer crafts are given each year during the **Living Museum,** held the last weekend in June.

Gallery

Browse through the arts and crafts displays at **The Old Hotel,** a 1912 hotel-boarding house now dedicated to the arts, at 33 E. Larch St. in Othello, tel. 488-5936. Open Tues. through Sat., 10:30 a.m.-4:30 p.m.

Accommodations

In Moses Lake, the **TraveLodge,** 31 Basin St. SW, tel. (509) 754-4651, has 28 rooms from $28 s, $34-40 d, and a heated pool.

Cheaper still is the **Sharlyn Motel,** 848 Basin St., tel. 754-3575, with 19 no-frills rooms for $22 s, $30-35 d.

In Ritzville, the **Comfort Inn,** 1405 Smitty's Blvd., tel. 659-1007, has 40 units in the $46-60 price range. The **Coldwell Motor Inn,** 501 W. First Ave., tel. 659-1620, has 25 units in the $38-44 range.

In Soap Lake, everyone talks about the log **Notaras Lodge,** 231 Main St., tel. 246-0462. It features rooms named after the famous, and decorated with their belongings, such as the Bonnie Guitar Room, with one of the singer's guitars encased in plastic and used as a coffee table; the Ben Snipes Room, named for the pioneer cattle man. Rooms cost from $32 up to $100; the more expensive units feature in-room whirlpools with Soap Lake water piped in for medicinal use, bathroom phones, skylights, and balconies.

See "Parks" above for camping options.

Food
Downtown Ephrata is no bustling commercial hub, but you can get a pizza at **Pizza Extravaganza** or Mexican food at **El Charro Cafe,** both on Basin St., the main drag. Up in Soap Lake, **Don's,** 14 Canna St. at the Notaras Lodge, tel. 246-1217, specializes in steak, seafood, and Greek dishes; open daily for dinner.

Entertainment
Moses Lake's annual **Sage and Sun Festival,** held in June, features a parade, arts and crafts, antique cars, and a circus.

As part of the state's Centennial Celebration in 1989, Moses Lake built an outdoor amphitheater on the lake's shore and holds free concerts throughout the summer. Artists such as Glenn Yarbrough, The Platters, and Ranch Romance give performances. For information, tel. (800) 992-6234.

The **Grant County Fair** is held in Moses Lake each August and it features the usual fair events, plus a Rooster Crowing Contest and a Goat Milking Contest. For information, call 765-3581.

Services And Information
For maps or other area information, contact the **Ephrata Chamber of Commerce,** 12 Basin St. SW, Ephrata, tel. 754-4656, or the **Soap Lake Chamber of Commerce,** 300 Beach E, Soap Lake, tel. 246-1821. Dial 911 for police, fire, or medical emergencies.

Getting There
Ephrata is about 20 miles northwest of Moses Lake on Hwy. 282; Quincy is about 15 miles southwest of Ephrata on Hwy. 28, and Soap Lake is about five miles northeast of Ephrata. For train and bus information, see "Moses Lake," above.

BOB RACE

COULEE DAM
NATIONAL RECREATION AREA

The construction of Grand Coulee Dam, "at that time the biggest thing built by the hand of man," employed thousands of workers during the Great Depression. Twice as high as Niagara Falls and nearly a mile long, the dam is the world's greatest producer of hydroelectric power, supplying energy to cities in several states and water to irrigate more than a half-million acres of farmland. The enormous Franklin D. Roosevelt Lake, which stretches more than 150 miles from the dam to beyond Kettle Falls, was designated the Coulee Dam National Recreation Area in 1946, and is popular with boaters, water-skiers, swimmers, anglers, and campers. Banks Lake and the parks to the southwest of the dam, in the coulee formed by the Columbia River during the last ice age, are also scenic summer playgrounds.

The dry, sunny climate is perfect for lake activities; summer temperatures range from the mid-70s to 100°, with evenings cooling off to the 50s or 60s. The area is a popular winter recreation spot as well, with cross-country skiers, ice fishermen, and snow-mobilers enjoying the off-season, along with the 200 bald eagles who winter here before heading north to British Columbia for the spring. Like many noteworthy sites in eastern Washington, the national recreation area is barely developed—a plus for those seeking privacy and unspoiled settings, but a definite minus for people who enjoy plush hotels and fine dining.

SIGHTS

Grand Coulee Dam
Start your visit to the recreation area with a self-guided tour of the dam itself. A film is shown on the hour at the visitor arrival center, tel. 633-9265. A highlight of the dam tour is riding the glass incline elevator to the face of the third powerplant for a spectacular view of the spillway from an outside balcony. An artifact room displays the Indian tools and arrowheads uncovered during the construction of the dam.

In summer, the visitor center is open from 8:30 a.m.-10 p.m; guided tours of the third powerplant are available from 9 a.m.-6 p.m. Water is released over the dam for about a half hour daily at 1:30 p.m. The evening laser light show, an elaborate high-tech program that packs the house, is held from 9:30 p.m.-10:20 p.m. Memorial Day through Labor Day. Winter visitors can take a self-guided tour and enjoy the free educational film from 9 a.m.-5 p.m. daily, with guided tours held four times a day.

Fort Spokane
From 1880-98, the U.S. Army post at Fort Spokane served to keep the peace between the Indian tribes to the north and the white settlers to the south. The fort was built at the confluence of the Spokane River and the Columbia River. These were peaceful years, in this area at least, so the soldiers practiced their drills and played a lot of baseball. Take a walking tour through the grounds to see four of the original buildings and a number of trailside displays relating the fort's history. For information, call 725-2727.

St. Paul's Mission
This small Catholic chapel in Kettle Falls, built in 1846, is one of the oldest churches in the state. Missionaries held services here for the Indians who often fished for salmon in these waters. The chapel was closed from 1858 to 1862 due to Indian hostilities at other Northwest missions, but reopened for the summer salmon runs in the 1870s and '80s, after which it fell into disrepair. Restoration of

COULEE DAM NATIONAL RECREATION AREA

CURLEW

396

25

CURLEW LAKE

NORTH GORGE

SUMMER ISLAND

EVANS

TO OROVILLE

20

ST. PAUL'S MISSION

MARCUS ISLAND

REPUBLIC

SHERMAN PASS (5,575 ft.)

SCENIC DRIVE

KETTLE FALLS

KETTLE FALLS

COLVILLE

COULEE DAM INSET

CROWN POINT VISTA

COULEE DAM

NAT'L. REC. AREA H.Q.

CURLEY'S TRAILER PARK

GRAND COULEE

VISITOR CENTER GRAND COULEE DAM

LAKEVIEW TERRACE MOBIL PARK

ELECTRIC CITY

SPRING CANYON

BANKS LAKE GOLF COURSE

SANPOIL RIVER

21

HUCKLEBERRY RANGE

DAISY

COLVILLE INDIAN RESERVATION

RAINBOW BEACH RESORT

NORTH TWIN LAKE

SOUTH TWIN LAKE

INCHELIUM

CHEWELAH

396

GIFFORD

155

COLUMBIA RIVER

SCENIC DRIVE

HUNTERS

WILMONT CREEK

HUNTERS

HUCKLEBERRY MTN.

HUNTERS CREEK

231

292

COULEE DAM INSET

KELLER FERRY MARINA

McCOYS

SPOKANE INDIAN RESERVATION

BANKS LAKE

STEAMBOAT ROCK S.P.

ROOSEVELT LAKE

KELLER FERRY

SEVEN BAYS MARINA

DETILLION

FORT SPOKANE VISITORS CENTER

PORCUPINE BAY

174

HAWK CREEK

SPOKANE RIVER

2

25

TO SPOKANE

DRY FALLS DAM

COULEE CITY

TO DRY FALLS S.P.

0   10 mi

0   10 km

© MOON PUBLICATIONS, INC.

the mission began in 1939, and in 1974 the site was turned over to the National Park Service. Phone 633-1360.

Kettle Falls's falls are now submerged beneath Lake Roosevelt, but at one time they dropped 33 feet in less than a half mile. They were named Les Chaudieres ("The Kettles") by French-Canadian fur traders in reference to the bowl-shaped rocks carved by the water's force.

Banks Lake

Banks Lake, which lies outside the national recreation area on the southwest side of the dam, is a 31-mile-long, wide, clear-blue beauty surrounded by the deep sides of the coulee. In the early '50s, the coulee was dammed on both ends and filled with water from the Columbia. As well as being a popular recreational alternative to Lake Roosevelt for fishermen and waterskiers, water from Banks Lake irrigates over a half-million acres of farmland stretching south to the Oregon border.

State Parks

Eight miles south of Grand Coulee on Hwy. 155, **Steamboat Rock State Park** has 100 full-hookup campsites ($9.50), swimming, good fishing, play equipment, and an underwater park on Banks Lake. Steamboat Rock, an island in the Columbia River during the last ice age, is now a scenic butte rising 1,000 feet above Banks Lake. You can hike to the top of the butte for a panoramic view, and then explore the 640 acres on the flat top. Bring repellent to combat the vicious mosquitoes. Winter sports are also popular here, from ice fishing to snowmobiling and cross-country skiing.

Farther south, **Sun Lakes State Park,** seven miles southwest of Coulee City on Hwy. 17, is a large park famous for its "dry falls." When the Columbia ran through the coulee, Dry Falls were 400 feet high and 3½ miles wide. Look out across the "falls" from a lookout at the interpretive center on Hwy. 17. The main part of Sun Lakes Park, just south of the dry falls interpretive center, boasts 3,300 acres with 175 standard campsites (18 with hookups), horse trails, boating,

swimming, and trout fishing. Concessions offer snacks, fishing supplies, horse rentals, and groceries.

Nine miles south of Coulee City on Pinto Ridge Rd., **Summer Falls State Park** is an appropriately named park, as the irrigation falls are operated only in summer. This is a cool spot for a picnic or fishing in Billy Clapp Lake.

South of Sun Lakes State Park and just north of Soap Lake, hike the short, uphill trail to **Lake Lenore Caves.** These caves, carved out of the coulee's walls by rushing meltwaters during the ice age, served as temporary shelters for prehistoric man's hunting trips.

Scenic Drives

One popular scenic drive starts at Keller Ferry and follows Hwy. 21 and the Sanspoil River north toward Republic, where two gold mines are still in operation and where the Stonerose fossil beds are found. Here you can turn east on Hwy. 20 to cross Sherman Pass, the state's highest at 5,575 feet. In spite of the elevation, you won't see dramatic snowcapped peaks, just thousands of acres of pine, fir and deciduous trees covering rolling hills. The drive ends on the shores of Lake Roosevelt at Kettle Falls.

Another scenic route starts at Fort Spokane, heading north on Hwy. 25 along the lake's eastern shore through the Huckleberry Mountains. One of the best views of the dam and the evening spillway light show is from **Crown Point Vista,** 626 feet above the river, about three miles west of the Grand Coulee four corners on Hwy. 174.

Museum/Gift Shop

The **Colville Confederated Tribes Museum/Gift Shop,** Birch St., tel. 633-0751, sells moccasins, beaded goods, turquoise jewelry, baskets, and has limited exhibits relating to the Colville Indians. Museum admission is $1; the gift shop is free.

ACCOMMODATIONS

Houseboat Rentals

The best way to explore the reaches of Lake Roosevelt is to rent a houseboat. Swimming and fishing are just outside your bedroom window; no noisy neighbors to contend with; and you'll see parts of the lake you just can't get to in a Winnebago. Each houseboat is at least 46 feet long and comes equipped with a kitchen, bath, sleeping areas for up to 13, swim slide and ladder, gas grill, and more. You can also rent 18-foot ski boats or 14-foot fishing boats to take along. Weekly rates range from $1100-1245; weekend: three days and two nights will run $915-1035. For more information phone (509) 647-5755, (800) 648-LAKE (in Washington), or write Roosevelt Recreational Enterprises, Box 587, Grand Coulee, WA 99133.

Motels
Lodging is mostly unpretentious in the coulee area. At the east end of the Columbia River Bridge on Hwy. 155, the **Coulee House,** tel. 633-1101, overlooks the Grand Coulee Dam with 61 rooms from $42-50 s, $42-56 d, with heated pool and coin laundry. Every room has a view of the dam at the **Ponderosa Motel,** 10 Lincoln St. in Coulee Dam, tel. 633-2100, and the rates are low, from $30 s, $37 d. The **Sky Deck Motel,** Hwy. 155 in Electric City, sits on the shore of Banks Lake with a heated pool and waterfront rooms from $38-42 s or d, plus five kitchen units for $60-70.

Camping
Campers can stay at one of 579 campsites at 32 campgrounds that line both sides of Lake Roosevelt and the Spokane River arm. None of the campgrounds offer hookups; all of them have restrooms, and all but the most primitive have water. A $6 fee is charged at Evans, Fort Spokane, Gifford, Hunters, Keller Ferry, Kettle Falls, Porcupine Bay, and Spring Canyon; the rest are free. Summer evening programs are often offered at the fee campgrounds. Most campgrounds are open year-round; Porcupine Bay, Hunters, and Detillion are open May through October. There is a 14-day camping limit.

Private RV parks in the area charge $8-10 per night and are open year-round; these include Lakeview Terrace Park, 3½ miles east of Grand Coulee on Hwy. 174, tel. 633-

2169, and **Curley's Trailer Park,** one-half mile northwest of Grand Coulee on Hwy. 174, tel. 633-0750. Farther uplake, **Rainbow Beach Resort** has 100 sites for $9, 10 miles west of Inchelium on Bridge Creek/Twin Lakes Rd.; open year-round, tel. 722-5901.

FOOD

The Coulee Dam area is not for gourmands, but you will find good food, generous portions and usually genuinely friendly service. Try Grand Coulee's **Sage Inn,** 415 Midway Ave., tel. 633-0550, for sandwiches and meals in dark, diner-style surroundings. A block up the street, **The Wild Life Restaurant,** 113 Midway Ave., tel. 633-1160, serves moderately priced steak and seafood and three meals daily. For Chinese, Thai, and American food, visit **Siam Palace,** open daily for lunch and dinner at 213 Main St., Grand Coulee; call 633-2921 for orders to go. Up in Kettle Falls, **Barney's at the Junction** serves three meals daily, featuring moderately priced steak and seafood, on Hwy. 20; call 738-6546. For a quick meal, there are snack bars at Spring Canyon, Porcupine Bay, Keller Ferry, and Kettle Falls.

OUTDOOR RECREATION

Swimming
Swim at beaches protected by lifeguards from July through Labor Day at Spring Canyon and Keller Ferry in lower Lake Roosevelt, at Fort Spokane and Porcupine Bay on the Spokane River arm, and at Kettle Falls and Evans on upper Lake Roosevelt. The water in the Spokane River arm tends to be five to eight degrees warmer than the rest of the lake, which averages about 60° in June, rising to the 70s in August. If you're swimming outside a protected area, keep an eye out for boats!

Boating And Fishing
Sixteen free public boat launches line Lake Roosevelt. From April through June only a

DIANNE BOULERICE LYONS

Steamboat Rock
State Park

few of them are usable, because the lake is lowered about 100 feet in late winter or early spring to accommodate the spring runoff; from late June through Oct., all boat launches are accessible. The lowest-elevation launches are at Kettle Falls, Hunters, Keller Ferry, and Porcupine Bay, at 1,230-1,240 feet; the highest launches are at about 1,280 feet at Hawk Creek, Marcus Island, Evans, and North Gorge. Phone the reservoir hotline at (800) 824-4916 for an estimate of current and future water levels. Be sure to stay clear of protected swimming beaches and the waters near the dam.

A state fishing license is required to fish in the recreation area; you can pick one up, along with current fishing regulations, at most area hardware or sporting goods stores or marinas. The 30 species of fish inhabiting these waters include one- to four-pound walleye (more than 90% of the annual catch), one- to three-pound rainbow trout, and enormous white sturgeon, averaging 100-300 pounds but growing up to 20 feet long and 1,800 pounds.

Other residents include the kokanee salmon, yellow perch, bass, cutthroat trout, perch, and pike. The best months for fishing are Sept. through Nov. and May and June; in midsummer, the fish retreat to cooler waters in streams or deep in the lake. Popular fishing spots are at the points where rivers and streams meet the lake—the Sanpoil River, Wilmont Creek, Hunters Creek, Kettle River, and others—or the waters near high shoreline cliffs, such as those near Keller Ferry.

Golf

About a mile south of Electric City on Grand Coulee Airport Rd., **Banks Lake Golf and Country Club** is a nine-hole public course, open from March until the first snow; tel. 633-0163.

EVENTS

The second weekend in May, the **Colorama Festival & WRA Rodeo** brings a rodeo, flea market, arts and crafts show, carnival, and cowboy breakfast to the Coulee Dam area; tel. 633-3074. The annual **Memorial Day Festival** features arts and crafts, music, food, a fun run, and the grand opening of the laser light show followed by a fireworks display off the top of the dam; most events are held at the park below the visitor arrival center. See the **Junior Rodeo** at the Colorama Rodeo Grounds in Grand Coulee the last weekend in June. The Colville Confederated Tribes sponsor a July Fourth **American Indian Pow Wow** with traditional dances, costumes, and Indian fry bread; tel. 634-8212. Mid-August brings the nationally known **Golden Over the Dam Run,** with five-km and 10-km races;

contact the Grand Coulee Dam Chamber of Commerce for registration information.

SERVICES AND INFORMATION

Services in the recreation area are generally open from June to September. There are small stores with groceries and supplies at Daisy and McCoys, and at Seven Bays, Keller Ferry, and Kettle Falls marinas.

The Coulee Dam area code is 509. For information on programs, park brochures, or books on the area's natural history, contact the Coulee Dam National Recreation Area Headquarters, 1008 Crest Dr., Box 37, Coulee Dam, WA 99116, tel. 633-9441, or the ranger stations at Kettle Falls, tel. 738-6266, and Fort Spokane, tel. 725-2715. The Coulee Dam station is open weekdays year-round; the others are open in summer with varied winter hours. For information on events in the surrounding area, contact the Grand Coulee Dam Area Chamber of Commerce, Box 760, Grand Coulee, WA 99133, tel. 633-3074.

TRANSPORTATION

By Car

Perhaps inaccessibility is one reason Coulee Dam NRA isn't the tourist trap it could be; there's just no quick and easy way to get here from the state's more populous cities. From Seattle, the quickest route is to take I-90 to George (between Ellensburg and Moses Lake), then go northeast on Hwys. 283, 28, 17, and 155 to the dam—about 220 miles. For a slower, more scenic route, try Hwy. 2 through Leavenworth to Coulee City, then head north on 155 to the dam. From Spokane, it's an easier drive: due west on Hwy. 2 to Wilbur, then northwest on Hwy. 174 for a total of less than 150 miles.

Cross-lake Ferries

Two ferries cross Lake Roosevelt year-round: the **Keller Ferry** connects Hwy. 21 in the south part of the recreation area, and, farther north, the **Gifford Ferry** joins Hwy. 25 near Inchelium. Both ferries are free, carry passengers and vehicles, and take about 15 minutes for the crossing.

OKANOGAN VALLEY

Omak and Okanogan, the valley's largest cities, are separated only by name and are strung along the west bank of the Okanogan River. The Colville Indian Reservation comes down to the river on the opposite bank, with Hwy. 97 running along that side of the river.

Nestled between the east and west sections of the Okanogan National Forest, the twin towns serve as the commercial hub for a sparsely populated area dominated by apple orchards along the river valleys and outdoor recreation in the national forest. Okanogan, the older of the two towns, was established in 1907 and serves as the county seat as well as headquarters for governmental and state departments. Omak, the modern-day commercial center, was chartered in 1910 but was slow to develop until a sawmill was built there in 1922.

Omak has a slightly larger population—almost 4,000 residents, compared to Okanogan's 2,400—though the entire county consists of just 31,500 people. The Okanogan Valley is a dry area surrounded by mountains, with 28 inches of annual snowfall and a hot, sunny summer.

Okanogan National Forest
The Okanogan National Forest offers a plethora of recreational activities, from hiking to camping to cross-country skiing. The area from the eastern border of North Cascades National Park, from Rainy Pass to Winthrop and south to Chelan, is covered under "North Cascades And Lake Chelan," p. 283, but the Okanogan National Forest Headquarters is located in Okanogan, just over the bridge from the Cedars Inn on Hwy. 97, tel. (509) 422-2704; stop here for backcountry permits, maps, or other information if you're entering the forest or national park from the east.

Parks
For camping, fishing, and swimming at two lakes, visit **Conconully State Park,** 22 miles

northwest of Omak on Hwy. 97. Seventy-five campsites ($8) include 10 with water hookup ($.50 extra); hike the half-mile nature trail. Okanogan's **Legion Park** offers overnight camping on the Okanogan River and a Farmer's Market in summer.

Three miles northeast of Bridgeport on Rufus Woods Lake, **Bridgeport State Park** offers boating, fishing, golf, and 28 standard ($6) campsites. Nine miles farther north on Hwy. 17, **Fort Okanogan State Park** is open for day use only from late June through August; enjoy a picnic lunch and visit the fur-trading post at the interpretive center.

St. Mary's Mission
This Jesuit mission was founded in 1896 by Father Steven DeRouge to bring Christianity to the Okanogan and Chelan Indians. DeRouge's presence met with resistance until he saved an Indian child who had fallen into the swift waters of the creek; he was then accepted. The church was completed in 1915, with local settlers and Indians cooperating in the building of the altar; the side altars were shipped around the Horn from France. Take Hwy. 155 east of Omak for four miles, then go 1½ miles south. Open daily; tel. 826-2097.

Museum
The **Okanogan County Historical Museum,** 1410 Second N. in Okanogan, tel. 422-4272, is open from May through Sept. with displays depicting pioneer life in the county; free.

Dam
Though overshadowed by the Grand Coulee to the east, Bridgeport's **Chief Joseph Dam** boasts a 2,000-foot-long powerhouse—the largest in the world. No visitor center has been built yet, but visitors are welcome to enjoy the sights from the designated viewpoint. The dam was named after Chief "I shall fight no more forever" Joseph, leader of the

Time moves just a little more slowly in Okanogan country.

ARCHIE SATTERFIELD

Nez Percé Indians during a fighting retreat in 1877 that military strategists praise as a classic tactic; he took his people, including the elderly, the ill, and women and children, on the 600-mile series of battles and end runs, trying to get them to Canada. He was almost successful, but the Army in 1877 caught the 200-member party just 30 miles from the Canadian border. Joseph and his people lost all of their land down in the Blue Mountains and in Oregon's Wallowas and he spent the rest of his life on the Colville Reservation and was buried there.

Accommodations

The **Cedars Inn,** at the junction of Hwys. 97 and 20 in Okanogan, tel. (509) 422-6431, has 78 rooms for $36 s, $41 d, plus a heated pool, restaurant and bar, and free airport and bus station transportation. Across the bridge into Okanogan, the **Ponderosa Motor Lodge,** 996 Second S., tel. (509) 826-9971, has modest motel rooms with kitchenettes plus RV hookups; rooms are $25 d, with or without kitchen. The **Motel Nicholas,** a half mile north of Omak on Hwy. 215, tel. 826-4611, has 22 rooms for $30 s, $30-40 d.

Campers and RVers can stay in town at **Log Cabin Trailer Court,** Hwy. 215, tel. 826-4462. Open year-round; sites cost $8. Three resorts northwest of Tonasket near Loomis are open from April through Oct. or Nov., for $9-10 per night: **Spectacle Lake Resort,** 12 miles northwest of Tonasket on Loomis Hwy., tel. 223-3433; **Rainbow Resort,** 14 miles northwest of town on Loomis Hwy., tel. 223-3700; and **Spectacle Falls Resort,** another mile northwest on Loomis Hwy., tel. 223-4141.

Pateros has an abundance of lodging for Methow Valley cross-country skiers and fishing enthusiasts. One of the area's best places to stay is **The French House,** 206 W. Warren in Pateros, tel. 923-2626. The country home is decorated with antiques, crafts, and handmade quilts, and room rates of $32 s, $45-50 d, include a full breakfast. Kids under four are free; for older kids ($4 additional), bring a sleeping bag and pillow and the owners will provide a foam pad or cot. No pets or indoor smoking.

Another Pateros B&B is **Amy's Manor,** five miles northwest of town on Hwy. 153, tel. 923-2334 (Box 411, Pateros, WA 98846). The 170-acre estate overlooks the Methow River and features four guest rooms, fireplace, basketball and tennis courts, and a small farm with goats, chickens, rabbits, and cows; rooms are $40 s, $50 d, with continental breakfast. No kids under 12, indoor smoking, or pets.

Whistlin' Pine Resort, off Hwy. 153 on the west shore of Alta Lake in Pateros, tel. (509)

923-2548 or (509) 923-2448 (winter only), has accommodations ranging from tent spaces to deluxe cabins, and entertainment from boating to windsurfing to pack trips. Camp for $7 a night in a tent space, $9 per night for an RV hookup, or stay in a primitive cabin for $15 or a cabin with modern conveniences, like kitchen and bath, for $39 per night. Rent a sailboard for $8 an hour, $11 an hour with a lesson, or rent a rowboat or canoe for $12 a day to fish or explore in Alta Lake. Horse enthusiasts can enjoy a guided trail ride ($6.50 an hour) or a pack trip for $80-95 per day.

For conventional motel accommodations, try the **Lake Pateros Motor Inn,** 115 S. Lakeshore Dr. in Pateros, tel. 923-2203. Their 30 lakeshore rooms cost $29-44 s, $33-52 d.

Food
Most of the area's restaurants, including the only Dairy Queen for miles, are in Omak. Omak's **Breadline Cafe,** 102 S. Ash, tel. 826-5836, serves inexpensive lunches and dinners of soups and sandwiches Mon. to Sat., and Fri. night ethnic dinners. **Cafe di Midi,** 17½ N. Main St. in Omak, serves an inexpensive breakfast and lunch daily, with heavy emphasis on vegetarian fare. Out in Loomis, **Palmer Mountain Barbecue,** 116 E. Palmer Ave., tel. 223-3311, serves barbecued steak, chicken, brisket, seafood, and ribs; open for three meals daily.

Festivals
Omak is famous for its annual **Stampede and Suicide Race,** held in Aug. at East Side Park. Festivities include two parades, Western art show, carnival, a professional rodeo, and a horse race down a steep cliff and across the Okanogan River. Animal-welfare organizations speak out against this race every year because often a horse will break a leg during what's seen as a cruel and senseless form of entertainment; but the race goes on. Tickets for the three-day event cost $4-10 and are available in advance from Omak Stampede, Inc., Box 916, Omak, WA 98841, tel. 826-1983. The weekend before

the Stampede, Omak's **Not Quite White Water Race** is a slow float down the lazy Okanogan River. Rafters display their creative talents in their costumes and raft design while spectators bomb the participants with water balloons.

Skiing
The Okanogan Valley boasts an abundance of winter sports areas. **Loup Loup,** between Okanogan and Twisp on Hwy. 20, has Alpine skiing on a 1,250-foot vertical drop served by two pomas and a rope tow, plus two km of groomed cross-country trails. Rentals and lessons are available; open Wed., Sun., and holidays, tel. (509) 997-5334. About 12 miles northeast of Tonasket, **Sitzmark** offers alpine skiing on a small, 650-foot vertical drop served by one chair, one poma, and one rope tow, plus six km of groomed cross-country trails; open Wed. through Sun., and holidays, tel. (509) 488-3323. **Highland Park Snow Park,** 10 miles northeast of Tonasket, has 12 km of groomed cross-country trails; open daily.

Snowmobilers will enjoy over 100 miles of groomed trails at six snow parks in the Okanogan Valley; for specifics, phone the Okanogan County Engineers, tel. (509) 422-3350.

Information
The area code on this side of the mountains is 509. For groceries, gas, and other necessities, Omak, the area's thriving metropolis, is the better choice. For more information on Okanogan County events, contact the **Omak Chamber of Commerce,** 401 Omak Ave., Omak, WA 98841, tel. 826-1880. For medical, fire, or police emergencies, dial 911.

OROVILLE

Oroville lies just south of the Canadian border on Hwy. 97. One of the county's oldest cities, Oroville's first pioneer, Hiram Okanogan Smith, settled here in 1858, planting apples and mining for gold. Apple orchards are still a prominent feature in the valley, as

OKANOGAN HIGHLANDS

10,000 acres of farmland are irrigated from Oroville to Tonasket.

Parks

A mile north of Oroville center on Hwy. 97, **Osoyoos Lake State Park** offers year-round fishing, swimming, waterskiing, and concessions on a lake shared with our Canadian neighbors. Stay at one of 80 campsites for $7; no hookups. **Palmer Lake,** south of Nighthawk, a popular spot with fishermen, is managed by the Bureau of Land Management; a boat launch and picnic area are at the south end of the lake.

Accommodations And Food

Visit **Sun Cove Resort** on two-mile-long Wannacut Lake for a family retreat. The remote area offers hiking, swimming, and fishing in a trout-stocked mineral lake, plus a playground, heated swimming pool, boat, kayak, and canoe rentals, and guided horse-trail rides. Groups up to eight can stay in a large cottage for $395 per week; up to six people, $310 per week. The smaller cabins require a two-day minimum stay for $48 d. Tent campers can stay for $10, $11 for trailers (hookups extra). Open April through October. Write Rt. 2, Box 1294, Oroville, WA

98844, or phone (509) 476-2223, for reservations.

For conventional motel accommodations, try the **Red Apple Inn,** Hwy. 97 and 18th, tel. 476-3694. Rooms are $20-29 s, $27-35 d (the higher-priced rooms have kitchenettes) and include a heated pool, riverfront picnic area, and laundry facilities. Down in Tonasket, another **Red Apple Inn** at Hwy. 97 and First, tel. 486-2119, charges $25-32 s, $30-

39 d for similar facilities.

Try **Don Ernesto's,** 806 Central, tel. 476-2339, for Mexican and American lunch and dinner daily, breakfast on the weekends.

Festival
Early May means **May Day,** a two-day festival with parades, dancing around the Maypole, arts and crafts and a race.

THE THREE FACES OF MOLSON

Few towns or cities in Washington—or anywhere else for that matter—have such an eccentric history as the almost-ghost town of Molson in the Okanogan Country northeast of Oroville near the Canadian border.

Like most western ghost towns, Molson began with a gold mine. The Poland China Gold Mine was two miles south of the Canadian border in countryside too rugged for a town. Instead, a site four miles west of the mine was selected, a place with rolling hills, a seasonal stream, and a supply of woods within walking distance.

John Molson of the Canadian brewing family, a heavy investor in the mine, and George Meacham, a promoter, pooled their resources to build the town.

In 1900 Molson put up $75,000 in the new town. He built a drugstore, a newspaper, and the town's showpiece, the three-story Tonasket Hotel.

More than 300 people flocked to the instant town, but the Poland China Mine coughed up rocks and dirt—no precious metals. As quickly as they came, people moved on; those who stayed went into farming and livestock. But then homesteaders began arriving in the area, and in 1904 a store and grain warehouse were built, along with a mercantile store.

A small railroad came through town, and soon Molson had eight saloons. A deputy sheriff was sent up from the county seat at Okanogan to keep peace in the small but booming town.

Then along came J.H. McDonald, surely one of the most insensitive and greedy men in

Washington history. McDonald filed for a homestead of 160 acres. It included nearly the entire city of Molson, including the Hotel Tonasket.

Nobody had bothered to file for the land on which Molson stood. McDonald had them cold. McDonald further endeared himself by posting notices to the "squatters." Thus, the storekeepers had to move a half mile north, where they built a new town. By 1906, Old Molson and New Molson were about the same size, and the hatred between the two towns was deep and permanent. Residents fought over every imagined slight and threat.

McDonald kept up his campaign of diplomacy by fencing the entire town of Old Molson. That same year (1908), a man named Work built a bank and placed it in Old Molson. However, McDonald wouldn't permit him to obtain legal ownership of land on which to put his bank, so Work put the bank on skids and moved it each day—or night—and his customers never knew from one day to the next where they would find the bank. Fortunately, Old Molson was quite small, and it was usually a matter of walking down the main street and watching for it.

Finally Work was able to find a permanent resting place and when he had it firmly anchored, he had a grand opening party which became a free-for-all street fight.

Old Molson had kept the post office, which rankled New Molsonites, and they tried several legal avenues to get their own post office. Nothing worked, so one day when the

THE THREE FACES OF MOLSON (CONTINUED)

postmaster was at lunch, New Molsonites stole the whole post office and moved it.

This rancor continued year after year, and the only truce the two towns recognized was the matter of a school. Since neither town had enough children to support its own school, they built a brick school roughly halfway between the two towns. And it was grand: a large auditorium on the main floor, steam heat, two floors of classrooms, and an indoor gymnasium.

The school generated a small building boom as people who hated the continual bickering looked for a middle ground. A theater was built there, and so was a mercantile store and a pool hall and barbershop. The fighting continued, though, and each town tried to outdo the other. When one got a theater, the other built one. The same happened with nice homes, and finally with auto dealerships.

By the 1950s, very few citizens were left. By the 1960s Molson—all three, actually—were relegated to ghost towns.

Today Molson consists of a few scattered buildings and farm equipment in an open-air museum, a brick school building that is now a museum, and a small cluster of modest homes and a store with gas pumps out front, closed.

ARCHIE SATTERFIELD

Molson today

THE NORTHEAST CORNER

Washington's northeast corner, north of Spokane and east of Roosevelt Lake, is dominated by Pend Oreille (pon-do-RAY) County, a "sportman's paradise" with good fishing in 55 lakes and 48 streams, all-season recreation from swimming to snow skiing, an abundance of wildlife, and very few people. The largest city in this not-quite-urban sprawl is Newport, pop. 1,700; the other four incorporated towns combined muster up another 1,300 bodies.

This uninhabited forestland gives wildlife photographers plenty of opportunities: the Pend Oreille River attracts osprey, ducks, cranes, and geese, and bighorn sheep, bear, cougar, elk; a rare moose or grizzly may also be seen. For the most part, the area's beauty is understated and its resources must be sought out; it's easy to drive right by and miss trails, lakes, and wildlife. This corner of the state isn't on the way to anywhere else in Washington, so only a determination to escape civilization or a strong exploratory drive brings visitors out here.

RECREATION

Rivers And Lakes

Small lakes are scattered throughout Pend Oreille County. Many are circled by summer cabins, modest year-round homes, or low-budget resorts and RV parks. As is common in eastern Washington, the natural features here aren't played up or exploited to the degree they would be on the more crowded, beach-hungry East Coast or other more populous areas of the country; yours is likely to be the only boat on the lake. With this serenity comes a corresponding lack of services, so keep the fuel tank full and the ice chest filled.

While traveling Hwy. 395, between Spokane and the Canadian border, you can pull off at several lakes; Loon, Deer, and Waitts in particular; on Hwy. 2, between Spokane and Newport, you'll find Diamond, Eloika, Trout, Sacheen, and Davis lakes. These and other lakes are generally clearly marked and easily accessible from the highway, though facilities are often limited to a boat ramp and portable toilet. The Pend Oreille River, popular for fishing and boating, follows Hwys. 31 and 20 from the Canadian border to Newport and on into Idaho's Pend Oreille Lake.

Cave

You can tour one of the largest limestone caves in the state, Gardner Cave, at **Crawford State Park,** 11 miles northwest of Metaline Falls off Hwy. 31. Guided tours are held daily in summer; camping is limited to 10 primitive campsites.

Hiking

Contact any Colville National Forest ranger station for a map and detailed, printed descriptions of these and many other day-hikes. This is bear country—even a few grizzlies have been spotted—so make noise, keep your food in the trunk, and don't be too proud to choose another route if you encounter bears, bear tracks, or droppings.

In the Colville District, a popular 2½-mile-loop trail, **Springboard Trail #149,** begins at the east end of the Gillette Campground, 26 miles east of Colville off Hwy. 20. This is a self-guided interpretive trail relating the history of an early homesteader and leading to a viewing platform at 3,600 feet.

Abercrombie Mountain Trail #117 is a 3.2-mile one-way hike to a ridgetop with panoramic views of the Pend Oreille and Columbia river valleys from 7,300 feet. From Colville, take Aladdin Hwy. north for 23 miles to Deep Creek Rd.; turn north onto Deep Creek Rd. for seven miles, then turn right on Silver Creek Rd. #4720 to the junction with Rd. #7078. Take #7078 north to Rd. #300, then follow #300 to the road's end. Most of the 3.2

NORTHEAST CORNER

BRITISH COLUMBIA

CRAWFORD S.P.

METALINE FALLS

IONE

PRIEST LAKE

COLVILLE NATIONAL FOREST

KETTLE FALLS

COLVILLE

PEND OREILLE RIVER

CHEWELAH

CUSICK

USK

SACHEEN LAKE

ROOSEVELT LAKE

WAITTS LAKE

DEER LAKE

TROUT LAKE

LOON LAKE

DIAMOND LAKE

NEWPORT

WASHINGTON / IDAHO

COLUMBIA RIVER

DEER PARK

SPOKANE RIVER

SPOKANE

© MOON PUBLICATIONS, INC.

0   10 mi
0   10 km

miles is wooded, crossing several streams and huckleberry bushes on the way to the ridge. This trail is also popular with hunters because of the abundance of deer—so look conspicuous!

Another hike with good views of the Pend Oreille and Columbia river valleys is the 3.6-mile one-way **South Fork Silver Creek Trail #123.** Take Silver Creek Rd. #4720 east from Leadpoint to the junction with Rd. #070; follow #070 to the trailhead at the road's end. The trail parallels and sometimes crosses the south fork of Silver Creek along an old jeep road on its way to the 5,400-foot ridge, at the saddle between Abercrombie and Sherlock mountains; the last mile is quite steep.

In the Sullivan Lake District, **Nature Trail #509** is a 2½-mile interpretive loop through trees and lush vegetation. From County Rd. #9345, go east on Rd. #22 for one-half mile, then turn right onto Rd. #241 to the trailhead

for Sullivan Lake Trail #504; the loop trail starts .1 mile in. **Sullivan Lake Trail #504** is a four-mile one-way hike along the eastern shore of Sullivan Lake through aspen and forested areas, ending at the Noisy Creek Campground. The clear, blue lake is the main attraction, but keep your eyes peeled for big-horn sheep, black bear, and whitetail deer.

A short half-mile loop trail beginning at Newport's Warren Ave. affords views of Ashenfelder Bay as it passes through forest and wildflowers, and is wheelchair-accessible. To reach **Wolf Barrier Free Trail #305,** go north on Warren Ave. at the junction of Warren Ave. and Hwy. 20, continuing about a mile to the trailhead.

Backpacking

Two good overnight trips are in the Sullivan Lake District; other trails can be combined to form loops of virtually any length. Get a map from one of the ranger stations (see "Services and Information" below) and ask for suggestions; the rangers have a wealth of printed material on hiking trails in the national forest.

Shedroof Divide Trail #512, begins off Rd. #22, which leaves Rd. #9345 just north of Sullivan Lake. Follow Rd. #22 for six miles, then turn right onto Pass Creek Pass Rd. #22 for one-quarter mile to the trailhead. The first 15¾ miles go through timber stands and occasional clearings, with old, difficult look-out trails to the tops of Round Top, Thunder, Helmer, and Shedroof mountains. At the intersection of trail #535, the trail begins an 18-mile loop (Salmo Loop Trails #535, 506, and 512) traversing the most scenic part of the area through numerous switchbacks. This loop can be reached from the 15¾-mile Shedroof Divide Trail, described above, or by road: go east about six miles on Rd. #22 from Sullivan Lake; at the junction with Pass Creek Pass Rd., the road number changes to #2220. Drive along #2220 for a one-half mile beyond the junction with Rd. #270. The trail passes through old-growth forest and along a ridge with views of Crowell Ridge, Gypsy Peak, the Sullivan Creek drainage, and part of Priest Lake. Much of the trail is at 6,000

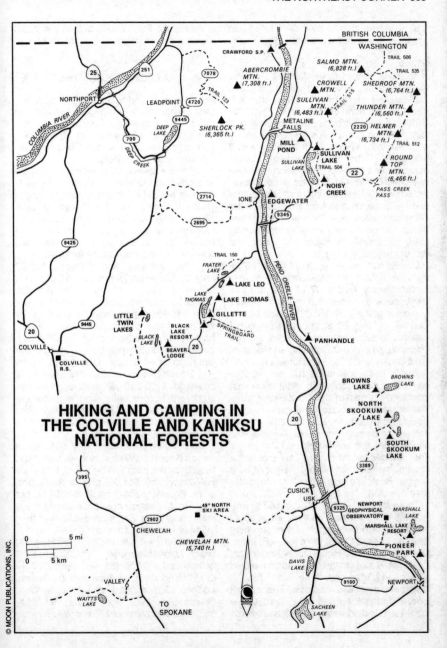

HIKING AND CAMPING IN THE COLVILLE AND KANIKSU NATIONAL FORESTS

feet elevation, so sea-level dwellers should expect to hike a little more slowly than usual.

Skiing

Nine miles east of Chewelah, **49 Degrees North** has day and night skiing on 1,900 vertical feet of slope from four chairlifts, about an hour north of Spokane off Hwy. 395. Sixteen runs offer beginner through expert skiing; terrain is set aside for powder skiing on weekends. Weekend lift tickets are $20 adults, $17 kids; lower midweek. Snowboarders and cross-country skiers are also welcome. Phone 924-5252 for ski conditions, tel. 935-6649 for other information. Be sure to drive to the ski area from Hwy. 395 on the Chewelah (west) side; the road in from Hwy. 20 on the east is a narrow gravel logging road, impassable in winter and no fun the rest of the year.

Colville National Forest has miles of hiking trails that double as cross-country ski trails in winter. **Sherry Trail #147** is a set of three short loops that total 3.8 miles in length, beginning at the trailhead 23½ miles east of Colville on Hwy. 20 at the entrance to the national forest. The route passes through lodgepole pine and Douglas fir, with views of Lake Sherry and Little Pend Oreille River.

Frater Lake Trail #150 has two loops— one three miles long, the other two—that start 29 miles east of Colville at Frater Lake. The shorter blue-blazed trail cuts through Douglas fir close to the lake on gentle terrain, and should be traveled in a counterclockwise direction for the easiest skiing. The longer and steeper yellow-blazed trail crosses a stream, meadow, and has a viewpoint from Coyote Rock; it's less difficult in the clockwise direction.

Three ski trails—#300, 301, and 302—provide 5.6 miles of skiing on three loops about 10 miles north of Newport. From Newport, take the Leclerc Creek Hwy. for eight miles, then turn right onto Indian Creek Rd., following it for 1½ miles to the trailhead on the right side of the road. All three wind through lodgepole pine and fir trees. The easiest loop, #300, is 2.1 miles long; the 2.6-mile loop, #301, is moderately difficult and affords a view of the Pend Oreille Valley; trail #302, nearly a mile in length, is the most difficult.

ACCOMMODATIONS

For an area as underpopulated as the northeast corner, there are lots of lodging and camping options—no Sheratons or Red Lions, but quite a few small motels, RV parks, and campgrounds, most bordering on Spartan, plus a delightful B&B.

Lakeside Manor, 25 miles east of Colville at 2425 Pend Oreille Lake, tel. (509) 684-8741, is nestled in the evergreens of Colville National Forest, on the shores of Lake Sherry. Enjoy a soak in the hot tub and huckleberry croissants at breakfast; the guest rooms ($50 s, $65 d) have king-sized waterbeds. No pets, kids, or smoking.

At the southwest end of Deer Lake, off Hwy. 395 between Chewelah and Deer Park, **Styman's Resort,** W. Deer Lake Rd., tel. 233-2233, has five cabins from $34-55 per night and RV parking with full hookups for $12.50 ($1 less for tents). Services include a boat launch, motorboat rentals for $30 a day, a swimming beach, playground, and grocery store. On the north side of Deer Lake, **Pearl-Ray Beach Resort,** tel. 233-2166, rents five cabins for $150-200 per week, and also has boat rentals, groceries, and a swimming beach. **Sunrise Point Resort,** N. Deer Lake Rd., tel. 233-2342, has seven cabins renting for about $200 per week.

Up in Valley, six miles off Hwy. 395, **Silver Beach Resort** on Waitts Lake, tel. 937-2811, has six cabins from $34-44 per night and 55 RV spaces for $11.50, plus a restaurant, store, and motorboat rentals for $34.50 per day. The largest rainbow trout caught in the state came from Waitts Lake; excellent fishing here for trout, perch, and bass.

Eighteen miles east of Colville off Hwy. 20, **Black Lake Resort,** tel. 684-2093, has 20 campsites for $7.50 ($9 with electric hookup), fishing dock, and swimming. **Beaver Lodge,** 25 miles east of Colville on Lake Gillette (Box 196, Tiger Route), tel. 684-5657, has six cabins for $30 per night for four, six full-hookup and seven partial-hookup sites for $10, and 19 no-hookup spots for $7. The lodge is open all year, with access to 193 miles of groomed snowmobile trails and cross-country ski trails. Summer activities include, of course, trout fishing—you can rent a motorboat for $28 a day—and paddleboating ($4 an hour or $22 a day). There's also a store, deli, and laundromat.

Blueside Resort, 37 miles north of Newport on Hwy. 20, tel. 445-1327, has a motel ($16-20 d), cabins ($24 d), and RV spots ($7-8) on the Pend Oreille River. Facilities include a boat ramp and dock, swimming pool, and store. On Hwy. 20 between Cusick and Ione, **Outpost Resort,** tel. 445-1317, has five cabins for $16-35 and RV parking and tent sites for $8-10, plus a restaurant, groceries, and boat launch. **North Skookum Lake Campground,** eight miles north of Usk, tel. 447-4158, has 27 campsites for $5.50, with boat and canoe rentals for $6.50 a day. **Marshall Lake Resort,** 6½ miles north of Newport on Leclerc Rd., tel. 447-4158, has 30 campsites (20 with hookups) for $6.50-7.50; rent a boat or canoe for $6.50 a day or hike the trails around the lake.

Newport has two budget motels close to downtown. The **Newport Motel,** 220 N. Washington (Hwy. 2), tel. 447-3463, has 12 rooms starting at $23-27 s, $28-33 d. The **Golden Spur Motel,** one-half mile south of town on Hwy. 2, tel. 447-3823, has a restaurant and 20 rooms for $25-28 s, $27-31 d.

The Forest Service maintains four campgrounds each in the Colville Ranger District, the Newport Ranger District, and the Sullivan Lake Ranger District. All but three charge a $5 fee; most have water and fishing or other water sports. In the Colville District, the campground at **Lake Leo** has eight sites, **Lake Thomas** has 15, and **Lake Gillette** has 43; **Little Twin Lakes** has 20 campsites and no fee; in the Newport District, **Brown's Lake** has 10 sites, **South Skookum Lake** has 13 (no water), **Pioneer Park** has 14, and **Panhandle** has 11 sites and no fee; at Sullivan Lake, **Mill Pond** has 10 sites, **Sullivan Lake** has 35, **Noisy Creek** has 19, and **Edgewater** has 23 campsites and no fee.

One of the newer and ambitious places to stay is **My Parents Estate,** tel. 738-6220, one mile east of Kettle Falls on Hwy. 395. It was a Catholic mission and convent that was turned into a boys' school, then closed. The present owners, Bev and Al Parent, have three rooms available now, each named for its period decor: the Queen Anne Lace, English Cottage Room, and the French Country Room. Rates are $75 d.

FOOD

Eating out in the northeast corner probably won't give you an urban dining experience, but you can find good food and low prices in any of the small towns; Colville, Kettle Falls, Chewelah, or Newport. Colville is the agricultural and business center of the region, with the only McDonald's for at least 100 miles and a handful of other choices, including the **Roadhouse,** a restored farmhouse one-half mile south of town on Hwy. 395, tel. 684-3021, open for dinner, served family style, Thurs. through Sun.; reservations are appreciated. In Chewelah, try the **Parkside Restaurant,** next to the city park on Hwy. 395, for inexpensive sandwiches and light meals; get it to go and eat in the park, where there's plenty of shade and play equipment for the kids. Or, get Chinese food at the **Shanghai Inn** downtown, or try **Polanski's Pizza,** just south of downtown on Hwy. 395. Newport has a Chinese restaurant and a pizza place on Hwy. 2, the main drag, plus a coin laundry at the junction of Hwys. 2 and 20; have a quick meal while your clothes are tumbling. Farther south on Hwy. 2, try **Al's Restaurant** south of Eloika Lake for German food and live music on the weekends.

ENTERTAINMENT

Festival
The annual **Poker Paddle,** held the third weekend in July, consists of a 40-mile canoe trip down the Pend Oreille River; participants collect Poker Paddle cards at various stops

along the two-day route. Spectators can take the easy way out and join the fun on a paddle-wheeler, and a crowd congregates at the finish to greet the paddlers and enjoy food and game booths; phone 445-1212 for more information.

SERVICES AND INFORMATION

The area code is 509. For more information on events and activities in Pend Oreille County, contact **Pend Oreille Scenic,** Box 21-A, Usk, WA 99180, tel. 445-1212. For more specific information on hiking, camping, and other recreational activities in the Colville National Forest, write or phone the **USDA Forest Service,** Colville National Forest, Colville Ranger District, 755 S. Main, Colville, WA 99114, tel. 684-4557; at Sullivan Lake, contact the Forest Service at Sullivan Lake Ranger District, Metaline Falls, WA 99153, tel. 446-2681; in Newport, write the Newport Ranger District, Box 770, Newport, WA 99156, tel. 447-3129.

The Colville area has no 911 emergency service; phone 684-2211 for fire, 684-2525 for police, and 684-2555 for an ambulance. For the Stevens County Sheriff, phone 684-2555 or (800) 572-0947. Dial the Washington State Patrol (for emergencies only) at (800) 572-3222. To report a forest fire, phone (800) 562-6010.

TRANSPORTATION

To reach Pend Oreille County from Seattle, take I-90 to Spokane, then head north on Hwy. 2 to Newport or Hwy. 395 to Chewelah and Colville. You'll need your own car because no buses, trains, or planes service the area.

bighorn sheep

FLORENCE BOULERICE

SPOKANE

HISTORY

Spokane's population of 172,000 makes it the largest city between Seattle and Minneapolis and the second-largest city in Washington. Though Spokane is less than half as large as Seattle, and has little of the latter's vertical sprawl, the two cities have had much in common from their earliest days: both were leveled by great fires, after which both towns were rebuilt in brick; both cities attribute some of their early growth to outfitting gold and silver miners; both have impressive park systems designed by the same firm; and both cities hosted a World's Fair.

Probably the most exciting event in Spokane's history was witnessed by no one: the Spokane Flood, which occurred 18,000 to 20,000 years ago. As the last ice age came to an end, the glaciers melted and water backed up behind the ice-dammed Clark Fork River in the great basin where Missoula, Montana, stands now. The ice-and-earthen dam created an enormous lake covering more than 3,000 square miles, larger than Puget Sound, and marks from its shoreline can still be seen along the mountains above the basin.

As the ice dam melted, the great pressure from the backed-up water caused it to suddenly collapse, sending an unimaginable rush of water over all of eastern Washington, flattening the landscape, digging coulees, washing away soil, and emptying the great lake in as little as two days. Evidence of the flood is shown on the landscape between Spokane and the Columbia River around the Tri-Cities area, an area known as the Channel Scablands. Most protruding rocks and mesas are ship-shaped, all pointing in a northeasterly direction, and there's no evidence that the erosion process was caused streams, the normal source of such erosion. Some geologists theorize that there may have been more than one of these floods.

The next several thousand years were relatively uneventful ones for Spokane, but the first white settlers came to the area in 1810—very early in Washington's history—when David Thompson built Spokane House, the first trading post in the state. The War of 1812 and turbulent times that followed led to the abandonment of the post in 1826, and white settlers didn't return until 1838, when Elkanah Walker and Cushing Eels established a Protestant mission that lasted until 1847. Though Spokane County was created in 1859, which included all of the land between the Columbia River and Rocky Mountains, north of the Snake River, the first permanent settlers didn't arrive at "Spokane Falls" until 1871.

By 1880, Spokane's population had grown to only 350, and the town competed hotly with neighboring Cheney for the county seat. Vote counters announced Spokane as the winner, but Cheney residents suspected the officials of lying about the results, so they came at night, kidnaped the election official and his records, and proclaimed Cheney as the winner of the ballot. Spokane's population grew dramatically by the next election, and in 1886 the city had the votes it needed to win the county seat back.

Like Seattle, Spokane experienced tremendous growth when the railroad came to town: from a population of 350 in 1880 to almost 20,000 by 1890. The Northern Pacific was the Northwest's first railroad, but its monopoly drove transportation prices sky-high; though eastern Washington was the cheapest place to grow wheat, the farmers paid the highest prices getting it to market. The city of Spokane was so determined to get a second railroad, they gave the land, free of charge, to the Great Northern Railroad Co. to be sure it would pass through town—and loosen the Northern Pacific's grip on the farmers.

As in Seattle and Ellensburg—and most cities in the pioneer West—a devastating fire

GREATER SPOKANE

© MOON PUBLICATIONS, INC.

ripped through Spokane in the summer of 1889, putting an end to the all-wood construction that had previously been so popular in these forested regions. Henceforth, all downtown areas were rebuilt in brick. Though farming was a large part of the Spokane economy, the turn-of-the-century gold and silver strikes throughout the Northwest also sparked the city's economic growth.

The event that put Spokane on the map for most of the country was Expo '74, the city's World's Fair. The theme for the fair, "Celebrating Man's Fresh, New Environment," was a real problem for the developers, since the location chosen was Havermale Island in the middle of the polluted Spokane River, in a dirty, run-down section of town. The governing bodies of Washington and Idaho combined their efforts to clean up the river, while grass and trees were planted and buildings torn down to prepare for the fair. The result was a world-class expo that won international attention and served to gear up the country for the bicentennial celebration.

SIGHTS

Riverfront Park
The site of Expo '74 has been preserved as a striking city park covering over 100 acres in downtown Spokane, with many of the original displays still intact on both sides of the Spokane River. Outdoors, visit the Japanese Garden, Canada Island, and suspension bridge and skyride over **Spokane Falls,** illuminated at night. Indoors, enjoy the **Eastern Washington Science Center,** featuring a planetarium and 150 hands-on exhibits; open Memorial Day through Labor Day, admission is $2.50 adults, $1.50 kids. The five-story-high **IMAX Theater,** one of only 40 in the world, has shows on the hour from 1 p.m., featuring dazzling, sharp images and stereo sound for $4 adults, $3 kids; phone 456-5511 for schedule. Riverfront Park boasts the **Spokane Opera House,** home to the Spokane Symphony Orchestra. The **Pavilion** amusement park features the Dragon Coaster and other rides for the daring, plus tamer attrac-

tions for the kids. Be sure to take a spin on the hand-carved 1909 **Looff Carousel** on the park's south side; the fare is $1. Take a gondola ride over the Spokane River, park, and falls from the west side of the park for $3 adults, $2 kids. The park also features an ice-skating rink, miniature golf course, restaurant, picnic areas, and more. All-inclusive park admission is $8.50 adults, $7.50 kids.

Every weekend from May to Sept., Riverfront Park hosts an arts and crafts show, and every Wed. and Sat. it sponsors a public market with fresh produce near the north park entrance. The **Flour Mill,** adjacent to the park at W. 621 Mallon, was the most modern mill west of the Mississippi when it was built in 1890; today it houses shops, restaurants, and galleries; tel. 838-6541.

Historical Sights And Museums
Visit the magnificent sandstone **Cathedral of St. John the Evangelist,** 1125 S. Grand

Looff Carousel

DIANNE BOULERICE LYONS

Blvd., tel. 838-4277, to see an impressive example of Gothic architecture complete with stained-glass windows and stone- and wood-carvings. Forty-nine-bell carillon concerts are held Thurs. at noon; Aeolian-Skinner organ recitals are scheduled regularly (phone for times). Take a guided tour on Sun. following morning services or most summer afternoons; phone 838-4277 for times. The bookstore and gift shop are open daily; admission is free.

Browne's Addition, on the city's west side along W. Pacific and W. First, boasts some of the city's finest homes from the 1890s; stroll through the tree-lined neighborhood and stop at **Patsy Clark's** (see "Food" below) for a drink at the grandest mansion on the block, or let the kids enjoy the Big Toys and swings at shady **Coeur d'Alene Park** on W. Second Street. Also in the neighborhood, the **Eastern Washington State Historical Society,** W. 2316 First Ave., houses its enormous collection in two buildings: the **Cheney Cowles Memorial Museum** has regional artifacts dating to prehistoric times as well as rotating exhibits in the Fine Arts Gallery; the **Campbell House,** built in 1898, is a restored mansion from Spokane's turn-of-the-century "age of elegance." Open Tues. through Sat. 10 a.m.-5 p.m. and Sun. afternoons; free, tel. 456-3931.

At E. 200 Cataldo Ave., the five-story **Museum of Native American Cultures** houses the largest collection of Indian artifacts in the Northwest, including beads, paintings, ceramics, plus Western art. Admission is $2 adults, $1 kids, or $5 for the family. Open Tues. through Sun.; tel. 326-4550.

The **Crosby Library,** E. 502 Boone Ave. at Gonzaga University, houses a large collection of Bing Crosby records, trophies, awards, pipes, and other memorabilia. The library was Crosby's gift to his alma mater. Open daily Sept. to April, Mon. through Fri. rest of the year; phone 328-4220, ext. 6133, for hours or a campus tour.

The **Fort Wright Museum and Cemetery,** W. 4000 Randolph Rd., tel. 328-2970, is on the site of the Fort George Wright Army post built in 1899. The museum displays include military memorabilia and a totem pole relating the history of the fort; open weekend afternoons.

Twelve miles northwest of Spokane on Aubrey White Parkway, the **Spokane House Interpretive Center,** tel. 325-4629, is built on the site of the first structure built by white men in the Pacific Northwest. Erected in 1810, the fur-trading post sat at the confluence of the Spokane and Little Spokane rivers; today's interpretive center relates trading post's history in photos and artifacts. Open Wed. through Sun., free; tel. 466-4747.

See **Indian Painted Rocks** 30 miles northwest of Spokane, between Spokane House and the Spokane Country Club near Rutter Bridge.

Eastern Washington University

Sixteen miles southwest of Spokane on Hwy. 904 in Cheney, EWU enrolls 8,000 undergraduates and 1,600 graduate students in over 100 majors, both on the 350-acre campus and by extension in downtown Spokane. The Gallery of Art has changing exhibits throughout the school year. Phone 359-6200 for information on these or other university events.

Wineries

Enjoy a picnic with a bottle of award-winning wine at **Worden's Winery,** Washington's oldest at 7217 W. 45th, tel. 455-7835. Open daily noon to 4 p.m. for tours and tastings. **Latah Creek Wine Cellars,** off the I-90 Pines exit at E. 13030 Indiana Ave., also features tours, tastings, and a picnic courtyard. Open daily from 10 a.m., Sun. from noon; tel. 926-0164. **Arbor Crest,** E. 4506 Buckeye, tel. 484-9463, also has a tasting room and gift shop open daily from noon to 5 p.m. **Steven Thomas Livingston Winery,** E. 14 Mission, tel. 328-5069, near the downtown district, features a Victorian setting and Pacific Northwest gift items in the tasting room.

Zoo

Nine miles east of the city at 12600 Euclid Ave., just off Pines Rd., **Walk in the Wild** is a 240-acre zoo and park with nature trails, animal petting area, and weekend trained parrot shows. Though not a world-class zoo,

LOUISE FOOTE

you can see flamingos, eagles, bears, bison, and more. Open daily, year-round. Admission is $1 adults, $.50 kids; tel. 924-7220.

ACCOMMODATIONS

Bed And Breakfast

Enjoy homelike surroundings in one of two guest rooms at the **Blakely Estate B&B,** E. 7710 Hodin Dr., tel. (509) 926-9426. The reasonable rates—$38 s, $43 d—include continental breakfast and use of the hot tub and shared sitting room with fireplace. No pets, smoking, or drinking on the premises; two-night minimum stay on weekends and holidays.

Stay in an 1891 Victorian home in historic Browne's Addition at the **Fotheringham House B&B,** across the street from Patsy Clark's at W. 2128 Second Ave., tel. 838-4363. The home was built by the first mayor of incorporated Spokane. Rooms have queen or double beds and period furnishings; rates are $40-45 s, $45-50 d (the higher-priced rooms have private bath) including continental breakfast. No kids, pets, or indoor smoking.

Three doors down from the Clark Mansion, **The Georgian,** W. 2118 Second Ave., tel. 624-7107, offers two guest suites in a home built for Moses Phelps in 1901 and now listed on the National Historic Register. The Lunette Suite has a parlor with fireplace, queen-sized bed, and bath, overlooking Coeur d'Alene Park; the Americana-Lee Suite features a 100-year-old oak bedroom set (double bed), tile bath, and extra bedroom for a guest or children over 12. Both include full breakfast; rates are $65-75 s, $85 d in summer, $65 in winter. Smoking on the veranda only; no pets.

Marianna Stoltz House, 427 E. Indiana, tel. 483-4316, was built in 1908 on a tree-lined street five blocks from Gonzaga University. Today the B&B features four guest rooms with private or shared bath from $45 s, $50 d, with a full breakfast and complimentary evening wine or homemade liqueurs. No pets (there's a kennel nearby) or indoor smoking; kids over six okay.

Waverly Place, W. 709 Waverly Place off Division, tel. 328-1856, is a Victorian B&B on Corbin Park. Built in 1902, the home features hardwood floors, gas chandeliers, and a wraparound porch, plus three guest rooms for $35-55 s, $40-60 d. Kids are okay (for an extra $10); no pets, but smoking is allowed in the living rooms.

Hillside House B&B, E. 1729 18th St., tel. 535-1893 or 534-1426, is a cozy country home on Spokane's South Hill, near Lincoln Park. Antique-furnished rooms cost $35 s, $48 d, with shared bath, and feature a gourmet breakfast (served in bed if you like). No smoking, pets, or kids under 10.

Just north of Spokane in Deer Park, enjoy **Bed and Breakfast with Love's,** N. 31315

*Patsy Clark's
Restaurant*

DIANNE BOULERICE LYONS

Cedar Rd., tel. 276-6939. The Victorian-style home with wraparound porch sits amidst five acres of pine trees for peaceful seclusion just minutes from bustling Spokane. Two rooms with shared bath go for $40 s, $45 d, with a full breakfast, evening snack, library, and private hot tub room. No indoor smoking or pets; kids by prior arrangement. From Spokane, take Hwy. 395 north to Dennison Rd., then follow Dennison for 2¾ miles.

Twenty minutes to downtown and 15 miles to Mt. Spokane skiing, **Town and Country Cottage,** N. 7620 Fox Point Dr., tel. 466-7559, offers reproduction nostalgia pieces and oak period furniture alongside a sitting room with a cozy fireplace and TV. Rooms are inexpensive—$28 s, $38 d—including continental breakfast (served in your room if you like). No pets, smoking, or small children.

Hotels And Motels
Be it ever so humble, the **Motel 6,** 1508 S. Rustle St. (on the west side of Sunset Hwy., near the airport), tel. 459-6120, is still the cheapest in town: the 122 rooms cost $24 s, $30 d, and include a pool. The **Super 8 Motel,** N. 2020 Argonne Rd., tel. 928-4888 or (800) 843-1991, has a game room and coin laundry, plus rooms from $34 s, $36-42 d. Other lodging bargains include the **Days Inn,** 1919 Hutchinson Rd. (at the I-90 Argonne

Rd. exit), tel. 926-5399, with 92 rooms from $40 s, $45 d, and the **Liberty,** N. 6801 Division St., tel. 467-6000, with a heated pool and rooms from $32 s, $35-44 d.

A step up the ladder is the **Best Western Thunderbird Lodge,** W. 120 Third Ave., tel. 747-2011, with 90 rooms from $36-46 s, $36-52 d, plus a heated pool and hot tubs. The **Best Western Trade Winds-Downtown,** W. 907 Third Ave., tel. 838-2091, features rooms for $36-44 s, $36-52 d, plus a hot tub, weight room, and continental breakfast. The **Best Western Trade Winds-North,** N. 3033 Division St., tel. 326-5500, is a bit more expensive ($48-56 s, $50-56 d) but has a year-round pool, hot tub, and continental breakfast. Make reservations at any Best Western hotel by phoning tel. (800) 528-1234.

The **Quality Inn,** east of town at N. 905 Sullivan Rd., tel. 924-3838, and the **Quality Inn Oakwood,** 7919 N. Division St., tel. 467-4910, have rooms from $44-52 s, $46-52 d, plus a heated pool; the N. Division inn also has an exercise room. The **Quality Inn Spokane House,** 4301 W. Sunset Hwy., tel. 838-1471, has 90 rooms from $35-49 s, $50-54 d, as well as a heated pool, hot tub, sauna, room and poolside service, restaurant and bar, and driving range. The **Holiday Inn-Downtown,** E. 110 Fourth Ave., tel. 838-6101, has 153 rooms from $45-54 s, $49-60 d; amenities include a heated pool, poolside and room service, and bellhops. Downtown's **Shilo Inn,** 923 E. Third, tel. 535-9000, has a restaurant, exercise room, hot tub, indoor pool, and sauna; rooms start at $41-46 s, $46-58 d.

Stepping up in price, **West Coast Ridpath,** W. Sprague and First Ave., tel. 838-6122 or (800) 426-0670, with 350 rooms from $59-72 s, $65-78 d, plus all the usual features as well as a barbershop, drugstore, and some bathroom phones. **Cavanaugh's River Inn,** N. 700 Division St., tel. 326-5577, features two heated pools, a wading pool, whirlpool, and sauna, restaurant, bar, and room and poolside service, tennis courts, and dancing nightly except Sun.; rooms start at $63-79 s and d. Its sister operation, **Cavanaugh's Inn at the Park,** W. 303 N. River Dr., tel. 326-8000 or (800) 843-4667, has rooms from $68-95 s, $77-1054 d, most of the other Cavanaugh's amenities, plus an exercise room.

At I-90 and Sullivan Rd., the **Red Lion Inn,** tel. 924-9000 or (800) 547-8010, has 241 rooms, a heated pool, restaurant, lounge with dancing, barbershop and beauty salon; rates start at $70-85 s, $80-95 d. The enormous **Sheraton,** N. 322 Spokane Falls Ct., tel. 455-9600, has 388 rooms, a heated pool and exercise room, restaurant, bar, dancing, and more on the Spokane River; a good weekend getaway, rates here are $69-87 s, $78-87 d weekdays with regular weekend specials for about $60 d.

Camping
Spokane is an urban area, but it's amazing how abruptly the city stops and the country begins. **El Rancho RV Park,** W. 3000 Sunset Blvd., tel. 455-9400, is open year-round and has full hookups for $15-18; tent spaces for $6-10. **Peaceful Pines Campground,** a mile southwest of Cheney on Hwy. 904, tel. 235-4966, is also open year-round with 20 sites from $10.50. Other resorts and trailer parks in the area are off I-90 exits 264, 270, and 272, though most are closed in winter. See "Parks And Recreation" below for more—and cheaper—camping.

FOOD
One of the most elegant mansions in the Northwest is now home to **Patsy Clark's Restaurant,** W. 2208 Second St., tel. 838-8300. Patsy came to America in 1870, made millions in mining, and commissioned an architect to build him a nice little home—and money was no object. The resulting structure features stained-glass windows from Tiffany's, Italian marble, and carved wood from England. Enjoy a dinner of duck, lamb, prime rib, or seafood (at about $20 a head), or just have a drink in the bar and tour the interior. Open daily for dinner plus Sunday brunch.

In the Flour Mill near Riverfront Park, **Clinkerdagger's,** 621 W. Mallon Ave., tel. 328-5965, serves up a well-prepared American menu with a view of Spokane Falls. **Ankeny's,** at W. 515 Sprague Ave. atop the Ridpath Hotel, tel. 838-6311, specializes in prime rib with a panoramic view; open for lunch and dinner daily except Sunday. Another hotel restaurant with a view is the **Spokane House,** at the Quality Inn at 4301 W. Sunset Hwy., tel. 838-1475, serving steak, seafood, veal, and chicken; open for three meals daily plus Sunday Champagne brunch.

For a varied menu from burgers to seafood, try **Dewey, Cheatam, and Howe,** E. 12909 Sprague, tel. 928-7688, or N. 3022 Division, tel. 326-7741; lunch runs about $5, dinners $7-13. **Auntie's Bookstore and Cafe,** 313 Riverside Ave., serves a good homemade lunch (breakfast and dinner on weekends) in a bookstore! Across Spokane Falls Blvd. from Riverfront Park, **Cyrus O'Leary's,** W. 516 Main, tel. 838-6822, has a book-length, moderately priced menu with everything from seafood and pasta to burgers and quiches in a lighthearted atmosphere; fun for lunch, dinner, or just some beers and appetizers. For cheap eats, try the **Old Spaghetti Factory,** S. 152 Monroe St., tel. 624-8916. Like its Seattle and Tacoma clones, the converted warehouse features a pasta menu that stays under $8; open daily for dinner only.

DOWNTOWN SPOKANE

1. Civic Theater
2. Flour Mill and Clinkerdagger's
3. Cavanaugh's Inn at the Park
4. Cavanaugh's River Inn
5. Imax Theater
6. Looff Carousel
7. Sheraton
8. Casa Blanca
9. River Park Square
10. Morelands Restaurant
11. C.J. Timothy's Comedy Underground
12. Cyrus O'Leary's
13. Niko's II Greek Cafe
14. Sherwood Mall
15. Azar's Cafe
16. Auntie's Bookstore and Cafe
17. Henry's Pub
18. Greyhound Depot
19. Ankeny's Restaurant and Ridpath Hotel
20. Old Spaghetti Factory
21. Europa Pizzeria
22. Amtrak Station
23. Gatsby's
24. Best Western Tradewinds
25. Deaconess Hospital
26. Best Western Thunderbird Lodge
27. Holiday Inn
28. Sacred Heart Medical Center
29. St. Lukes Hospital

Spokane is not without its ethnic restaurants as well. **Azar's Cafe,** N. 3818 Nevada, tel. 487-0132, or W. 410 Sprague, tel. 838-4783, serves inexpensive Lebanese sandwiches and kebabs; open for three meals daily except Sunday. **Peking Garden,** E. 3420 Sprague, tel. 534-2525, is among the city's best Chinese restaurants—and inexpensive to boot. For pizza, calzones, and Yugoslavian treats, try the **Europa Pizzeria And Bakery,** S. 125 Wall St., tel. 455-4051.

Mexican food is the mainstay at **The Casa Blanca,** next to the Sheraton at W. 200 Spokane Falls Blvd., tel. 456-0350. Enjoy Greek food in Spartan surroundings at **Niko's Greek and Middle East Restaurants.** Open for lunch and dinner at S. 321 Dishman-Mika Rd., tel. 928-9590, and for breakfast and lunch at W. 720 Sprague, tel. 624-7444, the food at this popular spot is inexpensive, and lamb is their specialty; enjoy belly dancing on Thurs. or a Moroccan dinner on Sunday.

SHOPPING

Downtown, the **Skywalk** connects 15 blocks of shopping and dining on two levels, including two shopping malls plus large department stores such as Nordstrom, The Bon, The Crescent, Lamonts, and JCPenney. **River Park Square** is at the northeast end of the Skywalk at Main and Post, and connects to **Sherwood Mall** at Riverside and Stevens. Parking is available at Main and Stevens, and Howard and Sprague.

The restored **Flour Mill** overlooking the Spokane River at Riverfront Park is home to 26 shops, including galleries, restaurants, gifts, and candy stores. At Wellesley and Division, the **Northtown Shopping Center** has a Sears, The Crescent, and a number of smaller shops.

PARKS AND RECREATION

Stroll through the **John A. Finch Arboretum,** 3404 Woodland Blvd., to see 65 acres of maples, rhododendrons, and ornamental trees along Garden Springs Creek, or walk the interpretive trail with signs in braille and print. Open daily; free.

See more blooms and bushes at **Manito Park,** Grand Blvd. at 18th Ave., tel. 456-4331. Have a picnic and enjoy the changing fountain displays, rose, lilac, and Japanese gardens, duck pond, and conservatory.

For a view from the highest point in the city, visit Review Rock at **Cliff Park,** 13th Ave. and Grove St., tel. 456-4381. The rock, a half-acre wide at the base, was once a volcanic island.

Mt. Spokane State Park, 30 miles northeast of the city on Hwy. 206, encompasses over 16,000 acres including 5,878-foot Mt. Spokane and 5,306-foot Mt. Kit Carson. Enjoy downhill skiing at Mt. Spokane (see below), or cross-country skiing, snowmobiling, hiking, and huckleberries throughout the park. Have lunch at Vista House, a restaurant atop Mt. Spokane; drive up in summer, take the chair lift in winter. Camping at this enormous park is limited to 12 standard ($7) campsites.

Riverside State Park, six miles northwest of town, rents horses for trail rides and has an off-road vehicle area. A lava formation in the river here is typically referred to as "bowl and pitcher." Camping is plentiful, with 12 standard ($8) sites.

Liberty Lake, near the Idaho border at the I-90 Liberty Lake exit, has public swimming, picnicking, and boating.

Wildlife Refuge

Twenty-one miles south of the city, 17,000-acre **Turnbull National Wildlife Refuge,** tel. 235-4723, has miles of trails and roads for walking, skiing, horseback riding, or driving through the protected lake area. This refuge, unlike others in eastern Washington, is not open to hunting; this is strictly an observation-only area, and nature lovers will be rewarded with sightings of grebes, hawks, shorebirds, deer, coyote, owls, badgers, herons, and an occasional bald eagle or peregrine falcon. The refuge is open every day during daylight hours.

Trail Riding

Enjoy a trail ride with **Last Chance Riding Stable** from Indian Canyon Park, 4812 W. Canyon Dr., tel. 624-4646. The one-hour ride costs $7 and includes Spokane views, waterfalls, and creeks; open every day from 9 a.m. to dark.

Skiing

Thirty miles northeast of town on Hwy. 206 at Mt. Spokane State Park (above), **Mt. Spokane** offers Alpine skiing, including a 1½-mile-long run, five chair lifts, and a 2,000-foot vertical drop. Night skiing draws the crowds here, as does the dry snow and 360-degree view of the Cascade, Selkirk, and Rocky mountains. Other features include ski school and rentals, restaurant, and bar (no child care). Cross-country ski trails are adjacent, as are **Snowblaze Condominiums,** tel. 238-4543. Lift tickets are $18 adults, $12 kids; ski midweek for just $5! Phone 238-6281 for more information. For information on **49 Degrees North** in Chewelah, see "The Northeast Corner," p. 384.

Golf

Spokane is proud of its three beautiful city-owned 18-hole golf courses, all within 10 minutes of downtown. **Downriver,** N. 3225 Columbia Cir., tel. 327-5269, is just south of Riverside State Park and affords views of the Spokane River. **Esmeralda,** E. 3933 Courtland, tel. 487-6291, is a relatively new course suitable for all skill levels. **The Fairways,** off I-90 exit 272 on Milville Rd., tel. 747-8418, is the Spokane area's newest 18-hole course. (actually, it's in Cheney.) **Indian Canyon,** S. Assembly and West Dr. at the top of Sunset Hwy., tel. 747-5353, was rated among the top 10 public courses in the U.S. by Golf Digest, and is the site of many major golf tournaments.

ENTERTAINMENT

Festivals

Enjoy the roping and riding at the **Diamond Spur Rodeo,** held in the Spokane Coliseum in March; tel. 328-6761. In Feb., the **Western Art Show and Auction** brings hundreds of paintings to the Convention Center for browsers and buyers to enjoy. Mid-May's **Lilac Festival** features parades, exhibits, a flower show, and concerts. The **Bloomsday Run,** also in May, attracts over 30,000 runners and up to 100,000 spectators with a downtown 7½-mile course. Cheney's mid-July **Rodeo Days** features bronc and bull riding, calf roping, and a parade at one of the largest amateur rodeos in the Northwest; tel. 235-4848. The **Spokane Interstate Fair,** tel. 535-1766, held for nine days in mid-Sept. at the fairgrounds at Broadway and Havana, features live musical entertainment and a rodeo; admission is $4 adults, $3 students, $.50 kids.

Nightlife

Enjoy music from the '60s plus a good beer and cooler selection at **Henry's Pub,** W. 230 Riverside. **Gatsby's,** S. 152 Browne, has rock 'n' roll nightly except Sunday. For Top 40 and jazz, try **Ankeny's** atop the Ridpath Hotel at W. 515 Sprague, nightly except Sunday. Other hotel bars with entertainment include the **Ramada Inn** at the airport with a singalong piano bar; J.J.'s Lounge at the **Sheraton** with local bands on Sun. and Mon. and dancing the rest of the week; and light jazz and music from the '50s and '60s at the **Spokane House Restaurant,** W. 4301 Sunset Highway. Hear Top 40 dance tunes at **Casa Blanca,** W. 200 Spokane Falls Blvd., next door to the Sheraton. Country-western music lovers will want to head east to **Kelly's,** tel. 773-5003, at the Idaho state line, for Grand Ole Opry-style music Wed. through Sat. and free dance lessons on Wed. nights. Try **C.J. Timothy's Restaurant and Comedy Underground,** across from Riverfront Park at W. 525 Spokane Falls Blvd., for live comedy Tues. through Sun.; call 456-6565 for reservations.

Music And Theater

Riverfront Park sponsors concerts and other entertainment during the summer months; phone 456-5511 for schedule. The **Spokane Symphony Orchestra** presents classical and pops concerts and *The Nutcracker* at the Spokane Opera House, W. 334 Spokane Falls Blvd., plus a number of free summer concerts in city parks; tel. 624-1200. The **Spokane Civic Theater,** 1020 N. Howard, hosts performances from drama to comedy

Spokane Opera House

nearly year-round; phone 325-1413 or 325-2507 for schedule and ticket information. For information on the **Spokane Interplayers Ensemble,** a resident professional theater group, phone 455-PLAY.

Baseball

The Northwest League's **Spokane Indians** play Class-A ball at the Interstate Fairgrounds Stadium, on Havana St. between Sprague and Broadway. The stadium, which seats 10,000, was designed for Class-AAA ball, played here until 1982; it's now the classiest ballpark in the league. The Indians play 38 home games each season; phone 535-2922 for ticket and schedule information.

Horse Racing

From May to Oct., take a chance on a horse at the **Playfair Race Course,** Altamont and Main streets, every Wed., Fri., Sat., Sun., plus holidays; phone 534-0505 for post times. Admission is $1.75 general, $4 turf club; kids under 10 free.

SERVICES AND INFORMATION

The Spokane area code is 509. Visit the **Spokane Regional Convention and Visitors Bureau,** W. 926 Sprague, tel. 747-3230, for up-to-date information on festivals and events, maps, brochures, and other information.

In case of emergency, dial 911 for police, fire, or ambulance, or 456-4100 for the Washington State Patrol. Medical emergencies can be handled at **St. Luke's Memorial Hospital,** S. 711 Cowley, tel. 838-4771, **Sacred Heart Medical Center,** W. 101 Eighth Ave., tel. 455-3131; or **Deaconess Medical Center,** W. 800 Fifth Ave., tel. 458-5800. For nonemergency medical questions, dial 455-7611, 24 hours, for "Ask a Nurse."

TRANSPORTATION

Arriving By Air

Spokane International Airport, just west of town, is served by several major commercial airlines, including **United,** tel. 838-4711, with international service; **Alaska Airlines,** tel. 838-6320, serving Seattle, Pasco, and western states from Alaska to Arizona; and **Horizon Air,** tel. (800) 547-9308.

Arriving By Train

Amtrak's *Empire Builder* serves Spokane with daily service from Chicago, Minneapolis, and other Midwest cities, continuing west to Wenatchee, Everett, and Seattle or southwest to Pasco, Vancouver, and Portland, Oregon. Stop by their station at West 221 First St. or phone 747-1069 or (800) 872-7245 for schedule and fares.

Getting Around By Car
Spokane is 280 fast highway miles from Seattle via I-90, most of which is 65 mph after leaving the densely populated Puget Sound area.

Spokane is not as taken with the numbered street system as Seattle and Tacoma, so a good map is a necessity; Rand McNally's Spokane street map is one of the best, and is available at most area drugstores, bookstores, and department stores. Spokane addresses can be a little confusing, but rest assured—W. 410 Sprague and 410 W. Sprague are one and the same.

By Bus
Spokane Transit serves downtown Spokane and the Cheney area; call 328-7433 for routes and schedule information. **Greyhound** provides nationwide connections from their terminal at W. 1125 Sprague; phone 624-5251 for schedule and fares. **Empire Stage Lines** serves most larger towns in the area; tel. 624-4116.

Tours
Departing from the Flour Mill adjacent to Riverfront Park, the **Spokane Tour Train,** tel. 455-5921, features a one-hour tour of Spokane's attractions aboard an 1890-style train. Trains depart four or five times daily from June through Labor Day, weekends only through Sept.; fares are $3 adults, $1.50 kids under 12.

Gray Line, tel. 455-5055, offers 2½-hour bus tours through Spokane, with special emphasis on the city's museums and parks. Tours depart from downtown hotels Tues. through Sun. mornings from June through Aug.; fares are $6 adults, $3 kids under 12. A combined bus and train tour includes both of the above trips on the same day for $7.50 adults, $3.75 kids.

From June through Aug., **Gray Line** also offers a 4½-hour winery tour, with 45-minute stops at Worden's, Arbor Crest, and Latah Creek wineries. Tours depart on Mon. only, from June through August. Fares are $6 adults, $3 kids; tel. 455-5055.

THE PALOUSE COUNTRY

The Palouse Country is a broad area of low hills that are often steep and nearly all are barren of trees; you'll see an occasional fringe of trees but mostly these hills are nothing but soil—deep and rich. This soil is so rich and the climate so stable that the area, Whitman County particularly, is known as the best wheat-growing area in the world.

The Palouse Country begins just south of Spokane and runs all the way south to the Snake River and the Blue Mountains. It is bounded on the east by the Selkirk Mountains in western Idaho, and on the west by the Channel Scablands. The soil in this area is all loess, meaning it was blown in over the centuries by the steady southwest wind. It is more than 100 feet deep in many places, and as you drive through this part of the state you will notice that the wind has piled the soil up against the southern ends of buttes, especially in the Channel Scabland area, while the northern ends are barren and blunt.

The Palouse Country (locals simply call it "the Palouse") is also set apart from the rest of eastern and central Washington by rainfall. The amount of rainfall increases as you travel east in Washington because of the gradual elevation gain.

Wheat isn't the only crop in the region. Peas, soybeans, lawn-grass seed, rape, and a variety of other crops can be seen as you drive south toward Pullman and Clarkson.

Tourism is not a major factor in most of the small towns here, so expect lower prices for straightforward food and motels that are plain, clean, and cheap.

PULLMAN

Pullman was founded by Bolin Farr, who came from Missouri to settle at the confluence of Dry Fork Creek, Missouri Flat Creek, and the south fork of the Palouse in 1876. Thus, the town was first called Three Forks. By 1881, it had grown—to a population of three. The citizens decided to call their "city" Pullman, after Chicago industrialist George Pullman, who funded their $50 Fourth of July celebration. A railroad branch extended to the town, the "crossroads of the Palouse," in 1883; by then Pullman was two stores, a hotel, the post office, and the blacksmith shop.

The dark, rich land of the Palouse is one of the most productive agricultural soils in the country.

ARCHIE SATTERFIELD

Following the common pattern of the West, two fires devastated the wooden downtown district in 1887 and again in 1890; structures were rebuilt in brick, and many of these buildings are still standing.

Pullman looks like a typical small college town, with an abundance of we-deliver pizza and submarine-sandwich shops and beer by the keg.

Washington State University

The Washington Agriculture College and School of Engineering opened in January 1892 with 26 students. Today, Washington State University has nearly 2,000 faculty members and a student body of more than 16,000 distributed throughout one graduate school and eight undergraduate colleges.

The WSU Cougars field teams in football, basketball, baseball, gymnastics, and track and field; for a schedule of athletic events, phone 335-9626. The 12,000-seat **Beasley Performing Arts Coliseum** stages events from rock concerts to opera; for a schedule phone 335-1514. The new **Pullman Summer Palace Theater** in Daggy Hall performs in June and July; tel. 335-7236. Other places to visit on campus include the **Connors Museum of Zoology** (in the Science Building) with the largest public collection of animals and birds in the Pacific Northwest, the Museum of Fine Art (in the Fine Arts Center), and the Museum of Anthropology (in College Hall).

Ferdinand's Bar in Troy Hall is a soda fountain run by the university's agricultural school and the campus's most popular tourist attraction; have some university-made ice cream or pick up a tin of WSU's Cougar Gold Cheese to take home. A nine-hole golf course and 2,000-square-foot putting green on the west edge of the campus are open to the public. For a campus map or other information, stop by the visitor information center in the Safety Building on Wilson Rd., or phone 335-3564 for general information.

Parks

On the west side of town, **Sunnyside Park** has hiking trails, picnic areas, tennis and basketball courts, and playgrounds; this is

the site of Pullman's annual Fourth of July picnic and fireworks.

Follow the signs from Hwy. 195 and drive to the top of **Steptoe Butte,** about 25 miles north of Pullman, for panoramic views of the Palouse River farmland and Idaho's mountains to the east. The state park has picnic areas, but no water or overnight facilities. Three-hundred-acre **Kamiak Butte County Park,** about 15 miles northeast of Pullman on

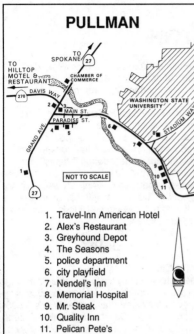

PULLMAN

TO SPOKANE 27

TO HILLTOP MOTEL & RESTAURANT

CHAMBER OF COMMERCE

DAVIS WAY

270

WASHINGTON STATE UNIVERSITY

MAIN ST.

PARADISE ST.

STADIUM WAY

GRAND AVE.

27

NOT TO SCALE

1. Travel-Inn American Hotel
2. Alex's Restaurant
3. Greyhound Depot
4. The Seasons
5. police department
6. city playfield
7. Nendel's Inn
8. Memorial Hospital
9. Mr. Steak
10. Quality Inn
11. Pelican Pete's

©MOON PUBLICATIONS, INC.

Hwy. 27 near Palouse, has camping, picnicking, a one-mile hiking trail to the top of the 3,360-foot butte, and views of the Palouse Hills to compete with Steptoe Butte.

Hot-air Balloon Rides
For an exciting way to view the scenery, try a hot-air balloon ride with **Fantasy Flights.** Departing year-round from Pullman, a 1½-hour ride costs $75 pp, and a half-hour flight is just $45, including complimentary champagne. For reservations or more information write them at N.W. 1250 State Hwy. #4, Pullman, WA 99163, or phone 332-7676.

Accommodations
The lodging in Pullman is modest. By far the best in town is the **Quality Inn Motel,** S.E. 1050 Johnson Rd., tel. 332-0500, with 66 rooms from $36-60 s, $50-67 d, plus a pool,

hot tub, sauna, and an adjoining dressed-up Mr. Steak restaurant. **Nendel's Inn,** S.E. 915 Main St., tel. 332-2646, has 60 rooms near the entrance to WSU and adjacent to the railroad tracks—still used by thundering locomotives at odd hours of the night. Rates are $29-37 s, $34-40 d (higher during college events), plus a pool. The **Travel-Inn American Motel,** S. 515 Grand Ave., tel. 334-3500, has 34 rooms from $30 s, $32-40 d, with a pool. The **Hilltop Motel,** on top of the hill on Colfax Hwy., tel. 334-2555, has budget rooms that look it for $21 s, $26 d. Take a short drive to Moscow, Idaho, for more lodging options.

Campers can stay at **Pullman RV Park** at the city playing field, corner of South and Riverview Streets, for $8 a night from April through Nov.; for reservations call the Parks and Recreation Dept., tel. 334-4555, ext. 227.

Food
Enjoy authentic Mexican cuisine at **Alex's Restaurante,** N. 139 Grand Ave., tel. 332-4061. The **Hilltop Restaurant,** Colfax Hwy., tel. 334-2555, serves steak and seafood, plus Sunday brunch, with a panoramic city view but not much atmosphere. **Pelican Pete's,** next to the Quality Inn at S.E. 1100 Johnson Ave., tel. 334-4200, serves burgers, steaks, and salads for lunch and dinner daily with a lounge open till 2 a.m. **The Seasons,** S.E. 215 Paradise St., tel. 334-1410, serves a broad variety of moderately priced dinners, including seafood, chicken, and lasagna, accompanied by Washington wines. Open daily for dinner, weekdays for lunch, and Sunday brunch. **Rusty's Tavern,** N.E. 1515 Merman Dr., is popular with WSU students for its beer, wine, and burgers.

Getting Around
Pullman is about 75 miles of wheatfields south of Spokane via Hwy. 195. By bus, connect to virtually any point in the country from the **Greyhound** stations in Colfax, at N. 804 Main St., tel. 397-4524, or Pullman, at E. 115 Olsen, tel. 334-1412. **Pullman Transit,** N.W. 725 Guy, tel. 332-6535, provides scheduled bus service throughout town.

CLARKSTON

Clarkston is Washington's most inland seaport, more than 450 miles east of the Pacific via the Columbia River and its chief branch, the Snake. The region's first settlers were cattle ranchers, taking advantage of the nearly endless grazing lands. The Asotin Creek irrigation project of 1895 brought much-needed water to the parched region; the wagon bridge built in 1896 between Clarkston and Lewiston provided access to Lewiston's railroad. These projects, as well as the dams that turned the wild lower Snake into a navigable waterway, paved the way for agriculture, industry, and population growth.

Clarkston's first containerized shipment departed for Japan in 1975; today's primary exports are peas to Europe and paper products to Japan. However, agriculture and forest products, not international shipping, are the mainstay of the city's economy.

Clarkston is in the portion of eastern Washington often referred to as "The Banana Belt," because it has, as early Indians put it, "no wind, no snow." Some may take exception to the "no snow" part, but the climate is generally milder than that of other areas east of the Cascades. When driving to Clarkston

BOB RACE

pygmy rabbit

or Pullman from the north or west, you can't help but notice the wheatfields, covering the land with intriguing patterns of gold and brown as far as the eye can see.

Early French fur traders called this area of green grassland pelouse ("lawn"). The name was soon given to the land, the Indians who lived here, and the river that runs through it. The Indians rode spotted horses that the white settlers dubbed palouse or palousey horses; "a palousey" eventually became "appaloosa." Today, the national headquarters of the Appaloosa Horse Club is a few miles east of Pullman.

SIGHTS

Hell's Canyon

The highlight of any trip to southeast Washington is a jet-boat ride through the deepest river gorge in the world, the Snake River's 5,500-foot-deep Hell's Canyon, separating Oregon and Idaho. Along the way you'll see mysterious petroglyphs, an ancient lava flow, abundant wildlife, and rugged canyon scenery.

Beamer's Landing Jet Boat Tours offers one- to five-day excursions to Dug Bar, Hells Canyon National Recreation Area, or Copper Creek Lodge, plus a whitewater boat-and-float combination. Rates start at $55, including lunch, for a one-day excursion from Hellsgate State Park Marina to Dug Bar, where Chief Joseph and his band of Nez Percé crossed the Snake as they fled the Cavalry. A one-day Hell's Canyon scenic excursion goes for $75. Enjoy the two-day mail run, with an overnight stop at Copper Creek Lodge, for $185. Other trips include a three-day, two-night Copper Creek getaway ($325) and a five-day jet-boat tour with whitewater rafting on Hell's Canyon rapids ($695). A special Saturday-night cruise from Hellsgate Marina to Heller Bar Lodge, 30 miles upriver, includes a prime-rib dinner and winetasting on the deck for $35 pp. For more information write Box 1223, Lewiston, ID 83501, or phone (800) 522-6966.

Snake River Adventures, 717 Third St., Lewiston, ID 83501, tel. (208) 746-6276 or (800) 248-1045, offers three one-day Hell's Canyon jet-boat tours, starting at $75 pp for a 184-mile roundtrip to $120 for a 216-mile roundtrip to Hell's Canyon Dam. Lunch and soft drinks are provided. They also offer overnight excursions to rustic Sheep Creek Ranch from $160 pp, and overnight hunting and fishing excursions for $220 pp.

Snake Dancer Excursions, 614 Lapwai Rd., Lewiston, ID, tel. (800) 234-1941 or (208) 743-0890, offers a one-day, 182-mile roundtrip jet-boat tour into Hell's Canyon, beginning at Swallows Nest Park boat launch in Clarkston. They follow the traditional mail route, without delivering the mail. The $75 pp fare ($40 kids under 12) includes lunch and snacks (bring your own pop or beer) and swimming as weather permits.

For an even more exciting trip, take a three- to six-day, 34- to 85-mile camping and float trip through Hell's Canyon with **Row River Odysseys West,** Box 579, Coeur d'Alene, ID 83814, tel. (208) 765-0841. Meals, tents, and equipment are provided for $360 pp for the three-day trip, $695 for the six-day trip.

Parks

Five miles south of Clarkston, **Chief Looking Glass Park** provides boat access to the Snake River with launch ramps, docks, and moorage, plus picnic tables and a playground. The 16-mile wheelchair-accessible **Clearwater and Snake River National Recreation Trail** connects parks, historic sites, and attractions from Chief Looking Glass Park north to Hellsgate State Park, Swallows Nest Rock, and up to West Pond. Hiking, biking, fishing, swimming, and picnicking are permitted along portions of the trail.

Eight miles west of town on Hwy. 12, **Chief Timothy State Park** sits on Silcott Island in the middle of the Snake River. The park was named for a Nez Percé Indian chief who befriended the early white settlers. The area's history is depicted in the park's Al-

powai Interpretive Center in exhibits and audiovisual programs. Enjoy the limited shade and cool breeze off the river, and camp at one of 33 standard ($8) sites or 33 full-hookup ($9.50) sites. Other facilities include a boat launch, playground, swimming beach, and concession stand in summer.

Head south on Hwy. 129 for 4½ miles past Anatone to **Fields Spring State Park** for a panoramic view of three states, the Snake River basin, and the Wallowa Mountains from the summit of 4,500-foot Puffer Butte, reached by a one-mile hike. Along the way you'll see numerous birds and 150 varieties of wildflowers, at their best in late spring. Camp in one of 20 standard ($7) sites; winter visitors will enjoy the miles of cross-country skiing.

Museum And Artifacts

Visit the **Asotin County Historical Museum,** Third and Filmore in Asotin, tel. 243-4659, to see early Asotin artifacts and buildings such as the 1882 Forgey log cabin and a pole barn housing carriages and a collection of branding irons. Open Tues. through Sat. afternoons.

Stop by the Clarkston Chamber of Commerce, 731 Fifth St., for directions to several Indian petroglyphs that can be seen from the road or from Hell's Canyon tour boats. These carvings are over 5,000 years old (and difficult to find).

Events

The small **Asotin County Fair,** held the last weekend in April, features a rodeo, parade, cowboy breakfast, and stock show and sale; late April through mid-May, the **Dogwood Festival** celebrates spring's flowering dogwoods with concerts, Art in the Park, historical walking tours, and the Bing Band Ball. June's **I Made The Grade** 13-mile bicycle ride starts at Chief Timothy State Park, crosses the Snake River, and heads up the old Lewiston grade for a total ascent of 1,000 feet. Mid-December's **Reflections on the Confluence** is a lighted boat parade on the Snake River, from Swallows Nest Park. Phone the **Clarkston Chamber of Commerce,** tel. 758-7712, for further information on these events.

The **Valley Art Center,** 842 Sixth St., features rotating exhibits and sales, including a Valentine's Day art show in which all works sell for $100 or less, and offers workshops and classes in all media.

ACCOMMODATIONS AND FOOD

The **Golden Key,** 1376 Bridge St., tel. 758-5566, has 17 budget rooms for $21 s, $25 d, and a pool. **Nendel's Valu Inn,** 222 Bridge St., tel. 758-1631 or (800) 547-0106, has 83 rooms from $34 s, $40 d, plus pool, restaurant, and bar. The **Best Western Rivertree Inn,** 1257 Bridge St., tel. 758-9551 or (800) 528-1234, has 47 rooms for $44 s, $48 d (higher rates apply during football season), with a heated pool, hot tub, sauna, and free airport and bus station shuttle.

Henry's, just over the bridge at 200 Bridge St., tel. 758-9613, serves sandwiches, steak, pasta, seafood, and chicken for $7-14; open seven days for lunch and dinner. **Fazzari's,** 1281 Bridge St., tel. 758-3386, features pizza, spaghetti, and sandwiches; open daily for lunch and dinner. Peking Restaurant, 907 Sixth St., tel. 758-5555, serves Chinese food and an all-you-can-eat lunch buffet. Cross the state line into Lewiston for more food and lodging options.

SERVICES AND INFORMATION

The Clarkston area code is 509. For maps or other current information contact the **Clarkston Chamber of Commerce,** 731 Fifth St., Clarkston, WA 99403, tel. 758-7712, or for Pullman information, the **Pullman Chamber of Commerce,** N. 415 Grand Ave., Pullman, WA 99163, tel. 334-3565.

All of Asotin County has 911 service for fire, police, and medical emergencies. Phone (800) 626-6780 for the State Patrol. Medical assistance is available at **Tri-State Memorial Hospital,** 1221 Highland Ave. in Clarkston, tel. 758-5511, or **Memorial Hospital,** Washington Ave. in Pullman, tel. 332-2541.

TRANSPORTATION

By Air
The Lewiston Airport is served by three regional airlines with connections and joint fares with five national airlines. Call AAA, tel. (208) 746-0407, or AIA Travel, tel. (800) 635-1519, for reservations or information.

By Car
Clarkston is about 100 miles south of Spokane; take Hwy. 195 past Pullman and across the Idaho border, then follow the signs for Hwy. 12 and Clarkston. The Idaho stretch follows the top of a ridge, providing spectacular views of Lewiston, Clarkston, and the Snake and Clearwater rivers as you descend; stop at one of the scenic viewpoints for a better look.

By Bus
Greyhound serves the Palouse region from the station at 1002 Idaho St. in Lewiston; phone (208) 746-8108 for schedule and fares.

WEST OF CLARKSTON

The Snake River offers a variety of parks and boat launches for year-round recreation. **Wawawai County Park,** about 25 miles from Clarkston on Whitman County Rd. #9000, has camping (no hookups) for $4 per night, picnic areas, playground, and hiking trails. Just south of the park, **Wawawai Landing** has a launch ramp and dock on Lower Granite Lake, created by the Snake River's **Lower Granite Dam,** 25 miles north of Pomeroy. The dam has a visitor center and restrooms. On Lake Bryan, just west of Lower Granite Dam, **Boyer Park and Marina** has launch ramps, moorage, docks, swimming area and bathhouse, picnic area, and camping. **Central Ferry State Park,** on Hwy. 127 about 12 miles north of Dodge, features a swimming area with lifeguards, boat launches and docks, picnic area, snack bar, and camping in 60 hookup sites ($9.50).

Little Goose Dam, the cause of Lake Bryan, is about a mile west of Starbuck on Hwy. 261. Facilities here include a boat dock, fish-cleaning room, and visitor center. In Lake Herbert G. West, created by the Lower Monumental Dam, **Lyons Ferry State Park** has good fishing, swimming, and boating at the confluence of the Snake and Palouse rivers, eight miles northwest of Starbuck on Hwy. 261. Enjoy a picnic here by Palouse Falls, or stay overnight in one of 50 standard campsites ($7); no hookups. **Lyons Ferry Marina,** across the river from the state park,

also has a boat launch, dock, boat fuel and service, plus picnic areas and camping from $7 (hookups extra).

Palouse Falls State Park, about six miles north of Lyons Ferry, offers picnicking and a scenic view of 190-foot Palouse Falls, plus 10 primitive campsites ($3-4.50). The **Lower Monumental Dam,** about six miles from Kahlotus on Devils Canyon Rd., has a visitor center, picnic area, and boat dock.

For information on Ice Harbor Dam and Lake Sacajawea at the west end of the Snake River, see "Tri-Cities," p. 410.

WALLA WALLA

Walla Walla is in a class apart from most of its eastern Washington neighbors. Whereas many cities on the dry side of the mountains are hot, dry, and without character, Walla Walla is a refreshing change. Here, trees have been cultivated for decades and offer much-needed shade and visual relief from the sameness of the eastern Washington landscape; parks are cool and well cared for; old homes and commercial buildings add to the city's elegance, Whitman College supplies the youthful influence, and the famous Walla Walla sweet onion gives the town of 25,600 a unique identity. The restaurants may not be first class, but some of the motels are as accommodating as any in Seattle or Spokane.

Walla Walla has four distinct seasons, with an average of four days over 100° in summer and two winter days below zero and about 20 inches of snow. The Walla Walla Valley also enjoys a variation in height that much of eastern Washington lacks; the western end of town lies at 300 feet above sea level, while the Blue Mountain foothills to the east rise to 3,000 feet. The weather, trees, and historic buildings combine to give the city a distinctive New England flavor. The valley enjoys a long growing season, with wheat, potatoes, barley, asparagus, alfalfa, and the Walla Walla sweet onion the big money crops; live-

stock and dairy products are also significant parts of the Walla Walla economy.

HISTORY

In 1805, Lewis and Clark passed through the Indian hunting ground at the confluence of the Columbia and Walla Walla rivers, and in 1818, Fort Walla Walla (originally named Fort Nez Percé for the Native Americans in the area) was established by the North West Company as a fur-trading post. Dr. Marcus Whitman, a medical missionary, built the first white man's home in the Northwest in 1836, in a spot called Waiilatpu (wy-EE-la-poo), "Place of the Rye Grass." His attempts to teach Christian principles to the Cayuse Indians met with little success, as they had no real interest in religion or books. Whitman's daughter was the first white girl born west of the Rockies and north of California; the Whitmans also adopted the seven Sager children whose parents had died on the trail.

As noted earlier, the whole family was massacred by Cayuse Indians in 1847, partly in response to Whitman's cruel treatment of them and because they had grown suspicious of the white man's intentions. There was no further white settlement in Walla Walla until after the Indians and white men

1. Veteran's Memorial Golf Course
2. Comfort Inn
3. Greyhound Station
4. Imperial Inn
5. Tapadera Budget Inn
6. Whitman Hotel
7. Walla Walla Symphony
8. Kirkman House
9. chamber of commerce
10. Red Apple
11. Liberty Theater
12. Best Western Pony Soldier
13. TraveLodge
14. Mill Creek Art Gallery
15. Carnegie Center

agreed to the terms of the treaties laid out by Isaac Stevens's Great Council.

In 1856, Colonel Edward Steptoe built an army barracks at Mill Creek to keep the peace; "Steptoeville" rose up around it and was later named Walla Walla, or "Many Waters." In 1859, the city was named county seat; no small honor, since the county included half of Washington, all of Idaho, and parts of Montana. When gold was discovered in Idaho in the 1860s, prospectors came to Walla Walla for supplies, and the town prospered. Like a number of other Northwest cities, Walla Walla suffered a substantial loss

when a series of fires swept through the wooden downtown area in the 1880s. Most of the oldest buildings still standing date back to the late 1880s, when the town was rebuilt in brick. Walla Walla was the site of the Northwest's first railroad and the state's first bank and college.

SIGHTS

Whitman Mission
You can get the whole story of Marcus and Narcissa Whitman's pioneer mission on the Oregon Trail at the Whitman Mission, a na-

tional historic site seven miles west of Walla Walla on Hwy. 12. None of the original buildings remain, but you can walk the self-guiding trails to the mission site, grave, monument, and sites of the first house, blacksmith shop, and grist mill. The visitor center is open daily except major holidays; admission $1.

Museums
Step back in time with a visit to the **Fort Walla Walla Museum Complex** at Fort Walla Walla Park on Myra Rd., tel. 525-7703. The museum features 14 original and re-created pioneer buildings, including the 1880 Babcock Railway Station and the cabin built by Ransom Clark just south of Walla Walla in 1859. A large horse-era agricultural display, including a 33 mule-team combine, fills five buildings. Open 1-5 p.m., weekends only in May and Oct., daily except Mon. in June through Sept.; admission is $2 adults, $1 kids.

Visit the **Kirkman House,** a mansion built in 1880 by entrepreneur William Kirkman and the town's only period house museum, at Main and Colville. The ornate structure features a beautiful widow's walk and figurehead keystones; open Thurs. and by appointment, tel. 529-4373.

Walking Tour
Pick up a brochure from the chamber of commerce, 29 E. Sumach, for a walking tour of the historic downtown area. Some of the sites you'll pass are the 1917 **Liberty Theatre,** built on the site of Steptoe's fort at W. Main and Colville, and the **Dacres Hotel,** built in 1899 at W. Main and Fourth to replace the burned-down Stine House built in 1873; historians speculate that the brickwork on the Fourth St. facade is part of the original structure, while the W. Main pressed-metal columns were added in the reconstruction. The **Sheriff's Office,** built in 1906, is a classic building with ornate rooftop balustrade. It's hard to miss the 10-story **Marcus Whitman Hotel,** built in 1928 at Second and W. Rose.

Parks And Camping
Fort Walla Walla Park, Dalles Military Rd., has camping with hookup sites, showers,

and fireplaces, plus the Fort Walla Walla Museum, described above; tel. 525-3700. Other city parks include the well-kept, 47-acre **Pioneer Park,** with aviary, duck pond, play equipment, picnic tables, and gardens, and **Veterans Memorial Park,** Sumach St. E, with a jogging and exercise trail. Outside of town, **Lewis and Clark Trail State Park** has 30 standard campsites on treed land—a rarity in these parts—four miles east of Waitsburg on Hwy. 12; fish in the river and enjoy historical campfire programs in summer.

Wineries
Visit **Woodward Canyon Winery,** tel. 525-4129, about 10 miles west of town of Hwy. 12 in Lowden, for a taste of top-quality chardonnay and cabernet. These wines are higher priced than some of the mass-producers', but they're worth it; open weekends May through New Year's.

ACCOMMODATIONS

Motels
For inexpensive lodging, try the **Tapadera Budget Inn,** 211 N. Second Ave., tel. 529-2580 or (800) 722-8277, with 29 rooms from $18 s, $42 d, or the **Imperial Inn,** 305 N. Second Ave., tel. 529-4410 or (800) 368-4400, with 35 rooms for $27 s, $30-34 d, plus a pool. Also inexpensive, the **Capri Motel,** 2003 Melrose, tel. 525-1130, has 40 rooms and a heated pool; rates are $30 s $40 d. One of Walla Walla's newer motels, the **Comfort Inn,** 520 N. Second, tel. 525-2522 or (800) 228-5150, has a pool, sauna, and hot tub, plus rooms from $42 s, $57 d. The **TraveLodge,** 421 E. Main St., tel. 529-4940 or (800) 255-3050, has 38 rooms for $39 s, $50 d, plus a pool and hot tub.

The historic **Whitman Motor Inn,** 107 N. Second Ave., tel. 525-2200, has a pool, one of the town's best restaurants, valet service, and some refrigerators, with 71 rooms starting at $43 s, $46-49 d. The **Best Western Pony Soldier,** 325 E. Main St., tel. 529-4360 or (800) 634-7669, offers the best lodging in town. Freebies include continental breakfast, pool, hot tub, exercise room, laundry, and some refrigerators and balconies; the 85 rooms are well worth the $52 s, $72 d.

FOOD

The **Modern Restaurant,** 2200 Melrose Ave. at the Eastgate Plaza, tel. 525-8662, specializes in Cantonese cuisine plus steak and sandwiches; open for lunch and dinner daily and Sunday brunch. The **Red Apple,** 57 E. Main, tel. 525-5113, serves moderately priced steak and seafood in a casual atmosphere with a piano bar on weekends; open 24 hours daily.**The Whitman,** 107 N. Second, tel. 529-6000, is a little fancier, serving steak, seafood, and chicken in the $7-13 range, although it looks like you're eating in the lobby; entertainment and dancing in the lounge. The **Homestead Restaurant,** 1528 Isaacs, tel. 522-0345, serves three meals daily from a varied menu including steaks, seafood, sautés, and vegetarian selections, with dinners in the $7-14 range. The fast-food chains are all concentrated around Wilber and Isaacs. For a pizza delivery, call **Pepe's Pizza,** 1533 Isaacs, tel. 529-2550.

ENTERTAINMENT AND EVENTS

Festivals
One of the events most popular with photographers is the **Hot Air Balloon Stampede,** held at Walla Walla High School in mid-May; after the balloons go up, enjoy the arts and crafts displays and demonstrations. Labor Day weekend brings the **Southeastern Washington Fair** to the fairgrounds on Orchard St., with horse racing, an evening rodeo, concerts, and educational exhibits.

The Arts
Little Theatre, 1130 E. Sumach, tel. 529-3683, is a community theater founded in 1944 that produces four plays each season. **Harper Joy Theatre** at Whitman College, 345 Boyer, tel. 527-5180, stages 10 productions each year. The **Walla Walla Sym-**phony Orchestra,** 3 W. Alder, tel. 529-8020, has been performing since 1907 with 80-100 amateur and professional musicians.

Art buffs will want to visit the **Clyde and Mary Harris Gallery** at Walla Walla College, off College Avenue. Other galleries include the **Sheehan Gallery** at Whitman College, tel. 527-5111, **Carnegie Center,** 109 S. Palouse, tel. 525-4270, and **Mill Creek Art Gallery,** upstairs at 39 E. Main, tel. 525-7722.

SPORTS AND RECREATION

Enjoy the **bike path** from Cambridge Dr. to Rooks Park or from Ninth and Dalles Military Rd. to Myra Road. **Veterans Memorial Golf Course,** off Hwy. 12, is an 18-hole course open to the public; tel. 527-4507. For information on hiking and camping in the Blue Mountains of Umatilla National Forest (most of which is in Oregon), visit the **Walla Walla Ranger Station** on W. Rose St. for detailed maps and information.

Skiing
Ski Bluewood, 21½ miles southeast of Dayton and 52 miles from Walla Walla, offers Alpine skiing on 1,125 vertical feet in the Umatilla National Forest. Because Ski Bluewood is over 300 miles from the coast, conditions here are generally dryer than on most Washington ski slopes. In operation since 1979, the ski area has two chair lifts and one platterpull serving beginner through expert terrain. All-day lift tickets are $15 adult, $12 kids; phone 529-9685 from Walla Walla or 545-6651 from Tri-Cities for conditions and more information.

SHOPPING

Walla Walla and Umatilla counties (the latter county is in Oregon) are the world's only producers of genuine **Walla Walla sweet onions,** guaranteed not to bring tears to your eyes when you slice them. These onions are so mild you can bite into one like an apple, and so soft they have to be harvested by hand. Write or visit one of these packers to get a bag sent home: Bossini Packing, Rt. 1, Pranger Rd., tel. 525-2122; Walla Walla Gardeners Assoc., 205 N. 11th, tel. 525-7070; or Amerfresh, 1137 N. 13th, tel. 525-5922. All addresses are in Walla Walla, 99362.

The **Blue Mountain Mall,** 1600 W. Rose St., hosts JCPenney, Sears, and Fred Meyer plus upwards of 40 other shops. For groceries and other supplies, shop at the **Albertson's** and **Pay Less Drug Store** at the corner of Wilbur and Isaacs.

SERVICES AND INFORMATION

The Walla Walla area code is 509. For further information, contact the **Walla Walla Chamber of Commerce,** 29 E. Sumach, Walla Walla, WA 99362, tel. 525-0850.

Dial 911 for fire, medical, and police emergencies in Walla Walla. In College Place, 911 won't work; phone 525-3242 for fire or medical help, 525-7773 for police. For other medical problems, phone **St. Mary Hospital,** 401 W. Poplar St., 525-3320, or **Walla Walla General Hospital,** 1025 S. Second Ave., tel. 525-0480.

TRANSPORTATION

Walla Walla is 260 miles from Seattle, 160 miles from Spokane. From Seattle, take I-90 eastbound to Ellensburg, then head south on I-82 to Tri-Cities; from there, take Hwy. 12 southeast to Walla Walla. The highways aren't as wide coming from Spokane; the most direct route is to take Hwy. 195 south from Spokane to Colfax, then head west on Hwy. 26, south on Hwy. 127, then south on Hwy. 12 to Walla Walla. There's a lot of nothing out here, so stock up on soft drinks before leaving Spokane.

Fly into **Walla Walla Regional Airport,** Airport Way, on **Horizon Air,** tel. (800) 547-9308, from most major West Coast cities.

Get around town on **Valley Transit,** 1401 W. Rose, tel. 525-9140, with five routes serving the Walla Walla/College Place area Mon. through Sat. from 6 a.m.-7 p.m. Take **Greyhound,** 315 N. Second, tel. 525-9313, for nationwide connections.

TRI-CITIES

Kennewick, at 42,000 residents, is the largest and fastest growing of the Tri-Cities. Richland is the second-most populous with 32,000, while Pasco has 27,000. These three cities comprise the fourth-largest metropolitan area in the state. The nearby Hanford Site was in business since 1944 employing thousands in the production of defense-related nuclear materials. Its shutdown in the late 1980s not only didn't hurt the local economy; it actually spawned economic *growth*. The environmental cleanup has proven to be far bigger than the reactor ever was—there are more Ph.D's per capita in Kennewick than any other town in the western U.S.

Besides the reactor, the Tri-Cities are famous for their hydroplane race—held annually in July—and their wineries, at the southeast end of the fruitful Yakima Valley. The Tri-Cities area is also heavily involved in farming, with 1,800 farms covering 1,300,000 acres—400,000 of them irrigated—in Benton and Franklin counties; potatoes, wheat, apples, grapes, alfalfa, field corn, and hops are the big money producers here.

The Tri-Cities suffer weather extremes that western Washingtonians never see. Plenty of below-zero days have been recorded here, as well as summer temperatures soaring over 100 bone-dry degrees; fortunately, a fairly constant breeze keeps the air clean and the heat almost tolerable. The area receives an average annual precipitation of just 6.25 inches, scattered between 225 sunny days; 44% of the total occurs from Nov. through Jan., generally in the form of snow, though accumulations of more than six inches are uncommon.

HISTORY

The Lewis and Clark expedition arrived at the confluence of the Columbia and Snake rivers in 1805. The first permanent settlers arrived in 1861 to raise cattle on these wide-open plains. Railroad workers established the town of Ainsworth, now Ainsworth Junction, in 1871 at the terminus of the Northern Pacific Railway. Ainsworth grew rapidly until the workers completed the Snake River railroad bridge; then the railroaders packed their bags, and Ainsworth faded into history.

Pasco had been growing quietly alongside Ainsworth, and in 1885 claimed the county seat. Incorporated in 1891, Pasco has always been the transportation hub of southeast Washington: the first airport west of the Mississippi was built here in 1910; the first U.S. airmail service operated out of Tri-Cities Regional Airport by what would later become United Airlines; and Pasco is a significant upriver terminal for Columbia River barge traffic.

Franklin County irrigation projects began in the 1890s, when schemes were developed to pump water from the Snake River into the dry fields. Planners had little luck until the government got involved in the Columbia Basin Irrigation Project; now over 500,000 acres are irrigated by the Grand Coulee Dam and Columbia Basin irrigation projects, with projections of up to one million irrigated acres.

SIGHTS

Parks And Dams

Nine miles east of Pasco on the Snake River, **Ice Harbor Lock and Dam** is the first of four dams on the Lower Snake, with one of the highest single-lift locks in the world, rising 103 feet. Take a self-guided tour, watch the fish climb the ladders, or stop by the visitor center, open daily April through October. The Ice Harbor Dam creates **Lake Sacajawea**, accessible for fishing, waterskiing, or swimming via four developed parks: the dam itself, **Levey Park** on the Pasco-Kahlotus Rd. on the lake's west side, **Charbonneau Park**, and **Fishhook Park** off Hwy. 124 on the east side. **Big Flat,** on the west side just northeast of Levey Park, is a wildlife-development area and open to foot traffic only; you can camp here April through Oct., tel. 547-7781.

The Columbia River's **McNary Lock and Dam**, 30 miles south of Pasco in Umatilla, Oregon, creates 61-mile-long Lake Wallula, which reaches up past the Tri-Cities to Ice Harbor Dam. The McNary Dam is open daily for self-guided tours, with guided tours given in summer; tel. 922-3211. One of 12 parks on Lake Wallula is **Columbia Park,** two miles west of Kennewick on Hwy. 12. This 609-acre park has four boat ramps for fishing and waterskiing, an 18-hole golf course, tennis courts, picnic area, 6.2-mile paved bike path, nature trails, and standard camping and hookup sites ($6 for tent sites, $7-9 for hookups). Open year-round; tel. 783-3711 or 783-3118. The **McNary National Wildlife Refuge,** next to McNary Dam, has a mile-long hiking trail popular with birdwatchers. Area species include hawks, golden and bald eagles, and prairie falcons.

Five miles east of Kennewick off Finley Rd., **Two Rivers Park** is open daily for boating, swimming, and picnicking.

Two miles east of Pasco off Hwy. 12, **Sacajawea State Park** sits at the junction of the Snake and Columbia rivers, at the site where Lewis and Clark camped in 1805. You can fish, waterski, or picnic here, or visit the interpretive center with displays about the famed expedition as well as local Indian history, open Wed. through Sun., mid-April to mid-September.

Horn Rapids Off-Road Vehicle Park, off Hwy. 240 in Richland, has two motocross tracks, four-by-four obstacle course, sand drag strip, and go-cart track, plus camping for $5 a night. Open all year; tel. 967-5814.

Wineries

The bulk of the wineries in southeast Washington are covered in "Yakima," p. 357. But the Tri-Cities area has a handful of its own, including **Preston Wine Cellars**, tel. 545-1990, one of the area's biggest, off Hwy. 395 in Pasco. Established in the early 1970s, Preston produces a full range of wines from cabernet sauvignon and merlot to rieslings

and fumé blanc. The tasting room and gift shop are open daily 10 a.m.-5:30 p.m.; take a self-guided tour or enjoy a picnic on the parklike grounds.

Bookwalter Winery, just north of Pasco near the junction of Hwys. 395 and 12, opened in 1984 with a 1983 chenin blanc and johannesburg riesling, followed by a chardonnay a year later and a cabernet sauvignon in 1987. The winery is open daily, 10 a.m.-5 p.m.; tel. 547-8571.

Started in 1985, **Gordon Brothers Cellars,** overlooking the Snake River at 531 Levey Rd. in Pasco, has won medals in Northwest wine competitions for all of its first releases. Open weekends and holidays May through Sept., 10 a.m.-5 p.m.; tel. 547-6224.

Quarry Lake Vintners has opened a temporary facility at 2505 Commercial Ave. C in Pasco, tel. 547-7307, where you can taste their johannesburg riesling, chenin blanc, semillon, chardonnay, and sauvignon blanc; open Mon. through Fri. noon to 5 p.m.

Two other small wineries in the area are covered under "Walla Walla," p. 407. For wineries to the east, see "Vicinity of Yakima," p. 356.

Museums

Kennewick's **East Benton County Historical Museum,** 205 Keewaydin Dr., has exhibits from pioneer days in the Tri-Cities area; free, tel. 582-7704. At 305 N. Fourth St. in Pasco, the **Franklin County Historical Museum,** tel. 547-3714, has exhibits depicting early Indian culture, railroad and aviation history, pioneer life, and agriculture. It's open Wed. through Sun. afternoons; free.

ACCOMMODATIONS

See the chart on p. 414 for hotel and motel accommodations

Camping

At 611 Columbia Dr. SE in Richland, **Desert Gold Motel and Travel Trailer Park,** tel. 627-1000, has RV hookup spaces for $9 per

TRI-CITIES

© MOON PUBLICATIONS, INC

TRI-CITIES

Richland
1. Kadlec Medical Center
2. Tri-Cities Gallery of Fine Arts
3. Richland Chamber of Commerce
4. Greyhound
5. Allied Arts Gallery
6. Arts Council of the Mid-Columbia
7. Sha-Na-Pum Golf Course

Kennewick
8. Columbia Center Dunes
9. Tri-Cities Chamber of Commerce
10. vista field
11. Water Slide Park
12. Shaniko Inn and Clearwater Cinema
13. Flamingo Beach Club
14. Chapter 11
15. Columbia Park Golf course
16. Tapadera Inn
17. Beaux Art Gallery, Appleseed Gallery and Shops, C.D.'s Texas Barbecue, and Bruce's Steak & Lobster House
18. East Benton County Museum
19. Kennewick General Hospital
20. Benton-Franklin Fairgrounds and Racetrack
21. Clover Island Inn

Pasco
22. Apple Inn
23. Our Lady of Lourdes Hospital
24. Pasco Chamber of Commerce and Greyhound
25. Amtrak
26. Red Lion
27. Municipal Golf Course

night or $63 per week; see chart above for motel rates and features. For camping in area parks, see "Parks and Dams" above.

FOOD

The **Blue Moon,** 21 W. Canal Dr., Kennewick, tel. 582-6598, is one of the best in the region. The prix-fixe menu ($28) features seafood, pork, chicken, and more, and the wines are all local; open weekends for dinner only.

Kennewick's **Chapter Eleven,** 3311 W. Clearwater, tel. 783-7433, specializes in prime rib and seafood at moderate prices. Open weekdays for lunch, daily for dinner. At the Hanford House Thunderbird Motel at 802 George Washington Way, the **Hanford House** restaurant overlooks the Columbia River, specializing in moderately priced steak, veal, and seafood. Open for three meals daily, including Sunday brunch; tel. 946-7611. **Baron's Beef 'N' Brew,** 1034 Lee Blvd. in Richland, has a good selection of Washington wines and microbrewery beers, plus what they claim is the largest bottled beer selection in the Northwest; tel. 946-5500.

The **Flamingo Beach Club,** next to the water park on W. Canal Dr., tel. 735-3434, serves a moderately priced American menu, outdoors in summer. **Bruce's Steak and Lobster House,** 131 Vista Way in Kennewick, tel. 783-8213, serves lunch and dinner daily with entertainment in the lounge. For a gourmet burger, salad, or sandwich, visit the **Red Robin** at 924 George Washington Way in Richland. **Henry's,** next door to the Holiday Inn on George Washington Way, serves moderately priced steak and seafood. Try **C.D.'s Texas Style Barbecue,** 101 B Vista Way in Kennewick, tel. 582-4269, for authentic pit-cooked barbecue. Clearwater and Kennewick avenues comprise fast-food city.

ENTERTAINMENT

Festivals And Events
Heat up the cold Pasco winter with a visit to the **Winter Wine Fair and Mardi Gras** in late February. Late May or early June means the start of Richland's **Sunfest,** a summer-long series of weekend events that feature international food, music, and dancing; one of these is **Jazzin' Up The Park,** a jazz festival with arts and crafts, held annually in June or July. Mid-July brings the **Tri-Cities Northwest Wine Festival** to Kennewick, featuring

TRI-CITIES ACCOMMODATIONS

Name	Address	Phone	Rates	Comments
RICHLAND				
Bali Hai Motel	1201 G. Washington	943-3101	$31-35 s $35-42 d	pool
Columbia Center Dunes	1751 Fowler SE	783-8181	$23-25 s $28-30 d	pool, sauna, laundry
Hanford House Thunderbird	802 G. Washington	946-7611	$65-75 s $75-85 d	pool, poolside service, cafe, bar, dock
Holiday Inn	1515 G. Washington	946-4121	$60-75 s $70-75 d	pool, sauna, hot tub, room and poolside service, cafe, bar, sun deck
Imperial Inn	515 G. Washington	946-6117	$30 s $30-34 d	heated pool
Nendel's	615 Jadwin Ave.	943-4611	$30 s 35 d	pool, shuttle
Shilo Inn Rivershore	50 Comstock	946-4661	$52 s, 58 d	pool, cafe, bar, laundry, golf, boats, tennis
KENNEWICK				
Cavanaugh's	1101 N. Columbia Center Blvd.	783-0611	$58-66 s $68-78 d	pool, hot tub, lounge, cafe
Clover Island Inn	Clover Island	586-0541	$44-48 s $48-57 d	pool, hot tub, sauna, cafe, piano bar
Nendel's	2811 W. Second	735-9511	$41 s $45 d	pool, some kitchenettes
Shaniko Inn	321 N. Johnson	735-6385	$34 s $38 d	pool, laundry
Tapadera Inn	300 N. Ely	783-6191	$29-35 s $34-38 d	pool, laundry
PASCO				
Hallmark Motel	720 W. Lewis St.	547-7766	$24 s, $29-37 d	pool
Motel 6	1520 N. Oregon St.	546-2010	$27 s 32 d	pool
Red Lion	2525 N. 20th Ave.	547-0701	$66-76 s $76-86 d	pool, poolside service, cafe, lounge, golf
Valu-Inn	1800 W. Lewis	547-0791	$34-43 s $40-45 d	indoor pool, hot tub, sauna, laundry

180 wines represented by 60 wineries. Also in mid-July, Pasco hosts the **Tri-Cities Air Show** featuring high-flying acrobatics, and Richland sponsors **Free Day in the Country,** a picnic with country music. One of Tri-Cities' biggest events is the annual unlimited hydroplane races on the Columbia River, the highlight of the late-July **Tri-Cities Water Follies and Columbia Cup.**

Also in late July is southeast Washington's largest arts and crafts show, the **Allied Arts Sidewalk Show** in Richland. Kennewick hosts the **County Fair and Rodeo** every Aug., with top entertainers performing at the fairgrounds at 1500 S. Oak St., off 10th Avenue. Not to be outdone by the wine festival, nine area micro-breweries come together for the late summer **Brew Ha-Ha** in Richland, featuring food, good beer, and entertainment. Summer winds down with the late Oct. **Rotary Chili Blast-Off** in Pasco, a chili cook-off with entertainment. December's big event is the **Christmas Lights Boat Parade,** when decorated boats cruise down the Columbia.

Horse Racing
At Kennewick's Benton-Franklin Fairgrounds on E. 10th Ave., **Sun Downs Horse Racing Track** has quarter-horse racing in spring and fall; tel. 586-9211.

Art Galleries And Shows
In the Tri-Cities area, Richland comes out way ahead in art galleries. Visit the **Allied Arts Gallery,** 89 Lee Blvd., tel. 943-9815, and see paintings, pottery, and weavings by local artists. **The Arts Council of the Mid-Columbia,** 650 George Washington Way, sponsors the arts and crafts displays at the June International Folk Festival; tel. 943-0524. The **Tri-Cities Gallery of Fine Arts,** 802 George Washington Way A, tel. 943-ARTS, displays works by Southwest and Northwest artists in various media.

In Kennewick, **The Appleseed Gallery and Shops,** 108 Vista Way, tel. 735-2874, has 11 shops filled with local arts and crafts, oil and watercolor paintings, toys, cards, and more. Across the street at 135 Vista Way, **Beaux Art Gallery,** tel. 783-4549, has stained glass, pottery, paintings, and crafts.

The Arts
For those of classical taste, phone for scheduled events staged by the **Mid-Columbia Symphony Society,** Box 65, Richland, WA 99352, tel. 735-7356, the **Mid-Columbia Regional Ballet,** 1405 Goethals, Richland, tel. 946-1531, and the **Tri-City Repertory Theater,** 2212 Benton, Richland, tel. 375-0673 or 627-3802.

Movies
Escape the heat and reality *with* a movie at Kennewick's **Clearwater Cinema,** 325 N. Johnson, tel. 735-7511; Richland's **Uptown Cinema,** 1300 Jadwin, tel. 943-6671; near the mall at **Columbia Center,** 900 Columbia Center Blvd., tel. 783-1354; or **Metro 4 Cinemas,** 1390 Columbia Center Blvd., tel. 735-0414. Save your quarters by phoning the **Theater Movie Line,** tel. 582-5058, to see what's playing at all Tri-Cities and Walla Walla theaters.

SPORTS AND RECREATION

Golf
The Tri-Cities' public courses include Pasco's **Municipal Golf Course,** 2335 N. 20th, tel. 545-3440; Kennewick's **Columbia Park Golf Course** at Columbia Park, tel. 586-4069; **Canyon Lakes,** 3700 Canyon Lakes Dr., tel. 582-3736; **Tri-Cities Country Club,** 314 N. Underwood, tel. 783-6014 (nonmembers are allowed to play); Richland's **Sham-Na-Pum Golf Course,** 72 George Washington Way, tel. 946-1914; and West Richland's **Tapteal Community Golf Course,** 4000 Fallon Dr., tel. 967-2165. These are all 18-hole courses, open daily.

Work Out
The **Tri-City Court Club,** 1350 N. Gran St. in Kennewick, tel. 783-5465, has facilities for racquetball, tennis, weightlifting, swimming, an indoor track, aerobics classes, and a sauna, and offers one-day passes for $7.

Waterslide

With all this heat and unrelenting sunshine, you'll need a place to cool off. Take your suit to **Oasis Waterworks**, 6321 W. Canal Dr. in Kennewick, tel. 735-8442, and try their 10 waterslides, 5,000-square-foot swimming pool, shaded picnic area, AstroTurf sunbathing area, hot tub, basketball and volleyball courts, and more. All-day admission is $8.45.

SHOPPING

Columbia Center is the Tri-Cities' largest shopping mall, with 70 stores including The Bon and JCPenney; take the Columbia Center Blvd. exit off Hwy. 12. There are smaller shopping centers across the street. For the Tri-Cities' best selection of Northwest and imported wines, stop by **Le Cave du Vin Wine Merchants**, 1341B George Washington Way, Richland, tel. 946-8300. For a different shopping experience, visit the **Pasco Farmers Market**, Fourth and Lewis streets, for local produce, arts, and crafts, from early May through Nov.; tel. 545-0738.

SERVICES AND INFORMATION

The Tri-Cities area code is 509. You can get all the current maps and information you need from the **Tri-Cities Visitor and Convention Bureau**, housed in the Vista Airport building at the end of Grandridge Blvd. in Kennewick, tel. 735-8486 or (800) 835-0248. Or, more specifically, try the **Richland Chamber of Commerce**, 700 George Washington Way, Richland, WA 99352, tel. 946-1651, or the **Pasco Chamber of Commerce**, 129 N. Third, Pasco, WA 99301, tel. 547-9755.

Dial 911 in the Tri-Cities area for all emergencies. For medical attention, contact **Our Lady of Lourdes Hospital**, 520 N. Fourth, Pasco, tel. 547-0009; **Kadlec Medical Center**, open 24 hours at 888 Swift Blvd. in Rich-

land, tel. 946-4611; or **Kennewick General**, W. 10th Ave. and Dayton, tel. 586-6111.

TRANSPORTATION

By Car

The Tri-Cities are an easy 200-mile drive from Seattle on I-90 to Ellensburg, then south on I-82 to Yakima and east on Hwy. 12.

By Train

The Tri-Cities are served by **Amtrak's** *Empire Builder,* providing daily service between Chicago and Seattle/Portland. The station is at W. Clark and N. Tacoma in Pasco, tel. 545-1554 or (800) 872-7245.

By Bus

Greyhound serves the Tri-Cities from stations at 1325 Lee Blvd. in Richland, tel. 946-4504, and 115 N. Second in Pasco, tel. 547-3151. Hop aboard **Ben Franklin Transit**, tel. 735-5100, to get around town, cheap: $.30 adults, 159 kids, with free transfers, with service to Tri-Cities Airport, downtown Kennewick, Richland, and Pasco, and out to West Richland.

By Air

Departing from the Tri-Cities Airport in Pasco, **Horizon Air**, tel. (800) 547-9308, connects the Tri-Cities with Seattle, Spokane, Boise, Portland, and San Francisco. Other airlines serving the area are **Alaska**, tel. 547-4242, and **USAir**, tel. 545-1204.

By Balloon

Get an entirely different perspective on the Tri-Cities and the Columbia River—from sagebrush level to 3,000 feet up—by taking a hot-air balloon ride with **Over Land Ballooning**, Game Farm Rd., Kennewick, tel. 586-9265. Flights last one to two hours, departing from a number of Tri-Cities locations, and cost $100 per person with a four-person maximum, including a champagne celebration upon landing.

BOOKLIST

DESCRIPTION AND TRAVEL

Begoun, Paula. *Best Places To Kiss In The Northwest*. Seattle: Beginning Press, 1989. A silly title, sure, but a fun guide to romantic hideaways, intimate restaurants, viewpoints, gardens, and more in Oregon, Washington, and British Columbia.

Brewster, David. *Seattle Best Places*. Seattle: Sasquatch, 1988. The most complete guide on the market to restaurants, hotels, shopping, sights, and things to do in and around Seattle.

Brewster, David. *Northwest Best Places*. Seattle: Sasquatch, 1989. A thorough guide to restaurants and lodging, with a smattering of things to do, in Washington, Oregon, and British Columbia.

Burke, Clifford. *Exploring Washington's Smaller Cities*. Seattle: Quartzite Books, 1984. Informative and readable guide to 11 of Washington's smaller cities along the lines of Pullman, Port Angeles, Yakima, and Vancouver.

Canniff, Kiki. *Washington Free*. Portland: Ki2 Enterprises, 1984. Listing of parks, dams, and other free attractions.

Green, Lewis. *Bed and Breakfast Washington*. Seattle: New Horizons Publishers, 1984. Photos, addresses, rates, and descriptions of bed and breakfasts throughout the state.

Holden, Ronald, and Glenda Holden. *Touring the Wine Country of Washington*. Holden Pacific, Inc., 1983. Detailed information on Washington wineries.

Keith, Gordon. *The Ferryboat Islands: A Practical Guide To Washington State's San Juan Islands*. A detailed guide to beaches, sights,

and points of interest by a 20-year island resident. Plenty of maps and photos.

Krenmayr, Janice. *Exploring Puget Sound by Car*. Seattle: The Writing Works, 1984. Tours, sights, parks, shops, and more around Puget Sound.

McFarlane, Marilyn. *Best Places To Stay In The Pacific Northwest*. Boston: The Harvard Common Press, 1988. There is more than one "best places" guide, and this one from the east coast does a fine job. Easy-to-use breakdowns by type of facility—destination resorts, island getaways, ski lodges—make vacation planning a breeze.

Meredith, Ted. *Northwest Wine*. Kirkland, WA: Nexus Press, 1983. Guide to wineries in Washington, Oregon, and Idaho.

Satterfield, Archie. *The Seattle Guidebook*. Seattle: Pacific Search Press, 1986. A guide to Seattle walking tours, sights, sports, parks, outdoor activities, and more.

Schmeltzer, Michael; photographs by Phil Schofield. *Spokane: The City and The People*. Helena, Montana: American Geographic Publishing, 1988. History, sights, lifestyle, economy, and people of Spokane highlighted by superb photography.

Shanks, Ralph, and Lisa Shanks. *North American Indian Travel Guide*. Petaluma, California: Costano Books, 1987. A complete guide to North American Indian and Eskimo cultural centers, museums, pow-wows, reservations, historical sites, and more throughout the U.S. and Canada, with ample photos, background material, and specific information for visitors.

Speidel, Bill. *The Wet Side of the Mountains*. Seattle: Nettle Creek Publishing Co., 1981.

Tours and highlights of western Washington, peppered with little-known historical facts.

Sunset Washington Travel Guide. Menlo Park, CA: Lane Publishing Co., 1987. Washington's highlights, beautifully photographed.

Welke, Elton. *Places To Go With Children Around Puget Sound*. San Francisco: Chronicle Books, 1986. State parks, fish hatcheries, museums, and attractions that appeal to all ages.

HIKING AND CLIMBING

Adkison, Ron. *The Hiker's Guide To Washington*. Helena, Montana: Falcon Press Pubishing Co., 1988. Seventy-five of Washington's most popular hikes, from Hurricane Ridge to Mt. Spokane, along with lesser-known trails in wilderness areas; maps included.

Beckey, Fred. *Cascade Alpine Guide: Climbing And High Routes*. Seattle: The Mountaineers, 1987. Three volumes of very detailed Cascade climbing routes, plus historical information and photos.

Burton, Joan. *Best Hikes With Children In Western Washington & The Cascades*. Having kids doesn't have to mean the end of your days on the trail! Ninety hikes from 1½ to 6½ miles RT, all featuring lakes, waterfalls, views, or other points of interest that will motivate kids of all ages.

Darvill, Fred T. *Hiking the North Cascades*. San Francisco: Sierra Club Books, 1982. Pocket-size guide to North Cascade trails.

Landers, Rich, and Ida Rowe Dolphin. *100 Hikes in the Inland Northwest*. Seattle: The Mountaineers, 1987. Descriptions, photos, and maps of hikes in eastern Washington plus parts of Idaho, Montana, and Oregon.

Manning, Harvey. *Backpacking One Step At A Time*. New York: Vintage Books, 1980. A beginner's guide to backcountry travel covering equipment, route finding, winter camping, bugs, food, and more.

Manning, Harvey. *Footsore 1, 2, 3, 4: Walks And Hikes Around Puget Sound*. Seattle: The Mountaineers. Descriptions and photos of hikes from Bellingham around the sound to the Olympic Peninsula.

Manning, Harvey. *Guide to Trails of Cougar Mountain and Squak Mountain*. Issaquah, WA: Issaquah Alps Trail Club, 1982. Maps and trail descriptions.

Perreault, Norm, and Diane Perreault. *Photographers Guide To Mt. Baker*. Glacier, WA: Norm and Diane Perreault. Excellent guide to Mt. Baker's charms for hikers, photographers, and sightseers, written in a friendly, conversant style and loaded with valuable tips and quality photos.

Peters, Ed. *Mountaineering: The Freedom of the Hills*. Seattle: The Mountaineers, 1982. The backcountry traveler's bible, filled with tips and techniques on snow travel, navigation, rock climbing, first aid, equipment, and alpine cuisine.

Spring, Ira, and Harvey Manning. *50 Hikes in Mount Rainier National Park*. Seattle: The Mountaineers, 1978. Maps, descriptions, and photos of 50 Mt. Rainier hikes.

Spring, Ira, and Harvey Manning. *100 Hikes in the Alpine Lakes, South Cascades, and Olympics*. Seattle: The Mountaineers, 1978.

Spring, Ira, and Harvey Manning. *100 Hikes in the Glacier Peak Region*. Seattle: The Mountaineers, 1988. Lesser-known areas of Glacier Peak Wilderness from Darrington to Wenatchee and Lake Chelan; maps, photos, trail descriptions.

Spring, Ira, and Harvey Manning. *101 Hikes in the North Cascades*. Seattle: The Mountaineers, 1979.

Spring, Ira, and Harvey Manning. *100 Hikes in the South Cascades and Olympics*. Seattle: The Mountaineers, 1985.

Sutliff, Mary. *Teanaway County: A Hiking and Scrambling Guide to Washington's Central Cascades*. Seattle: Signpost Books, 1980. Descriptions and photos of hikes from Lake Kachess to Blewett Pass.

Whitney, Stephen R. *Nature Walks In & Around Seattle*. Seattle: The Mountaineers, 1987. Short nature walks at 25 parks and natural areas between Redmond and Federal Way. Great for families, nature photographers, or a quick escape to the outdoors.

Wood, Robert L. *Olympic Mountains Trail Guide*. Seattle: The Mountaineers, 1984. Detailed trail descriptions, maps, and photos of national park and national forest trails on the Olympic Peninsula.

HISTORY

Bennett, Robert A. *Walla Walla: Portrait of a Western Town 1804-1899*. Walla Walla: Pioneer Press Books, 1980. Indians, treaties, trails, and Walla Walla's beginnings in Washington Territory days. The three-book series features excellent historical photos and drawings and informative, interesting text.

Bennett, Robert A. *Walla Walla: A Town Built To Be A City 1900-1919*. Walla Walla: Pioneer Press Books, 1982. Early automobiles, aviation, Chinese community, street cars, and over 400 photos celebrating Walla Walla's turn-of-the-century growth spurt.

Bennett, Robert A. *Walla Walla: A Nice Place to Raise a Family 1920-1949*. Walla Walla: Pioneer Press Books, 1988. WW II, a new airport, the rise of the canning industry, and Walla Walla's emergence as a modern city.

Brewster, David, and David M. Buerge. *Washingtonians: A Biographical Portrait of the State*. Seattle: Sasquatch Books, 1988. This ambitious Centennial project presents Washington's history in a series of insightful biographies. Enjoyable reading.

Dodds, Gordon B. *The American Northwest: A History of Oregon and Washington*. Arling-

ton Heights, Illinois: The Forum Press, Inc., 1986. A comprehensive history of the Northwest from 15,000 B.C. to the present, with emphasis on the people and their politics.

Dryden, Cecil. *Dryden's History of Washington*. Portland: Binfords and Mort, 1968. A very readable history of Washington.

Fiege, Bennye. *The Story of Soap Lake*. Soap Lake, WA: Soap Lake Chamber of Commerce, 1976. Photos and text describing Soap Lake's heyday.

Lambert, Dale A. *The Pacific Northwest: Past, Present, and Future*. Wenatchee, WA: Directed Media, Inc., 1986. A very readable, well-illustrated textbook on Pacific Northwest history.

Lampman, Ben Hur. *Centralia: Tragedy and Trial*. Seattle: reproduced by The Shorey Book Store, originally published by the American Legion, 1920. The American Legion's story of the Centralia Massacre.

LeWarne, Charles P. *Washington State*. Seattle: University of Washington Press, 1986. A detailed Washington history textbook covering pre-history through modern times.

McCoy, Keith. *The Mount Adams Country: Forgotten Corner of the Columbia River Gorge*. White Salmon, Washington: Pahto Publications, 1987. History of the Mt. Adams area from pre-Indians, Lewis and Clark, and early pioneers to modern-day climbers, the CCC, and Bigfoot. Interesting reading and numerous photographs, assembled by a lifetime Mt. Adams area resident.

Martinson, Arthur D. *Wilderness Above The Sound: The Story Of Mount Rainier National Park*. Flagstaff, Arizona: Northland Press, 1986. An enjoyable history covering the mountain's discovery, early ascents, and development of the national park, illustrated with lots of historical photos.

Olmsted, Gerald. *Fielding's Lewis & Clark Trail*. New York, New York: William Morrow & Co., Inc., 1986. A delightful blend of historical chronicle and travel guide. Relive Lewis and Clark's journey from Missouri to Oregon through excerpts from their journal while appreciating the sights, parks, and attractions of today.

Olson, Joan, and Gene Olson. *Washington Times and Trails.* Grants Pass, Oregon: Windyridge Press, 1970. A very enjoyable and readable history covering Washington's earliest explorers to modern times, illustrated with top-quality full-page photographs.

Ross, Alexander. *Adventures of the First Settlers on the Oregon or Columbia River, 1810-1813.* Lincoln: University of Nebraska Press, 1986. A reprint of Ross's original eyewitness account of John Jacob Astor's 1810 expedition from New York to the Columbia River aboard the Tonquin. Fascinating and lively, the book describes the fur-trade existence as it happened, based on Ross' original journal entries.

Ruby, Robert H., and John A. Brown. *A Guide to the Indian Tribes of the Pacific Northwest.* Norman, Oklahoma: University of Oklahoma Press, 1986. History, location, numbers, culture, and contemporary life of over 150 Indian tribes of the Pacific Northwest. An excellent reference tool.

Ruby, Robert H., and John A. Brown. *The Chinook Indians: Traders of the Lower Columbia River.* Norman, Oklahoma: University of Oklahoma Press, 1976. Comprehensive history of the relationship between whites and the Indians of the lower Columbia Valley, from fur trading to modern-day legal battles.

Schwantes, Carlos, et al. *Washington: Images of a State's Heritage.* Spokane: Melior Publications, 1988. A comprehensive pictorial history of the state, covering early Native American life through the eruption of Mt. St. Helens and Bill Gates' Microsoft. Rarely seen photos and historic drawings highlight the easily digestible text.

Scofield, W.M. *Washington's Historical Markers.* Portland: The Touchstone Press, 1967. A handy reference book consisting of photographs of 49 roadside markers posted at notable historical sites throughout the state.

Shorey Book Store, The. *The Pacific Northwest: Oregon and Washington Territory.* Seattle: The Shorey Book Store, 1971. Reprint of an 1883 text describing the railroads, land, and settlement of Oregon State and Washington Territory.

Speidel, William C. *Sons of the Profits.* Seattle: Nettle Creek Publishing Co., 1967. Irreverent history of Seattle's growth between 1851-1901.

Spranger, Michael S. *The Columbia Gorge: A Unique American Treasure.* Pullman: Washington State University, 1985. History, geology, sights, development, maps, and photos of the Gorge. Interesting reading for visitors and researchers alike.

The Great Seattle Fire. Seattle: reproduced by The Shorey Book Store, 1965. A fascinating collection of original documents and news clippings describing the Seattle fire of 1889.

Wing, Robert C., with Gordon Newell. *Peter Puget.* Seattle: Gray Beard Publishers, 1979. Coffee-table-quality history of Peter Puget's meanderings around the Northwest.

NATURAL SCIENCES

Angell, Tony, and Kenneth C. Balcomb III. *Marine Birds and Mammals of Puget Sound.* Seattle: University of Washington Press, 1984. Habits and habitats of western Washington birds and marine mammals.

Grzimek's Animal Life Encyclopedia. New York: Van Nostrand Reinhold Company, 1974. Thirteen volumes of facts on everything from slugs to killer whales.

Hanners, Al. *Northwest Beginning Birding.* Bellingham, WA: North Cascades Audubon Society, 1984. Where to find which birds in western Washington.

Hora, Bayard. *The Oxford Encyclopedia of Trees of the World*. Oxford: The Oxford University Press, 1981.

Kirk, Ruth. *The Olympic Seashore*. Port Angeles, WA: The Olympic Natural History Association, 1962. Detailed information on where to go and what you'll find on Washington's most scenic coastline.

Smith, Lynwood. *Common Seashore Life of the Pacific Northwest*. Healdsburg, CA: Naturegraph Company, 1962. Everything you need to know about clams, starfish, crabs, and other sea creatures.

Sweeney, James B. *A Pictorial History of Sea Monsters and Other Dangerous Marine Life*. New York: Crown Publishers, 1972. What to look out for in the deep blue sea.

OUTDOOR RECREATION

Furrer, Werner. *Water Trails of Washington*. Edmonds, WA: Signpost Books, 1979. Maps and descriptions of Washington rivers for kayaks and canoes.

Kaysing, Bill. *Great Hot Springs Of The West*. Santa Barbara, California: Capra Press, 1984. A complete guide to well-known and obscure hot springs from Washington to Colorado, complete with maps, facilities, and clothing requirements; plenty of photos.

Kirkendall, Tom, and Vicky Spring. *Cross-Country Ski Trails of Washington's Cascades and Olympics*. Seattle: The Mountaineers, 1983. Descriptions and photos of more than 80 ski trails.

Mueller, Marge, and Ted Mueller. *North Puget Sound: Afoot & Afloat*. Seattle: The Mountaineers, 1988. Painstakingly detailed guide to North Puget Sound, from Point Roberts to Whidbey Island and west to Neah Bay, helpful to both boaters and landlubbers. Boat launches, parks, points of interest, plus photos and maps.

Mueller, Marge, and Ted Mueller. *The San Juan Islands: Afoot & Afloat*. Seattle: The Mountaineers, 1988. Thorough guide to "the big four" and numerous lesser islands in the San Juan chain. Boating, biking, sightseeing, and more, with maps and photos.

Nelson, Sharlene P., and Joan LeMieux. *Cruising the Columbia and Snake Rivers*. Seattle: Pacific Search Press. Eleven cruises in the inland waterway.

North, Douglass A. *Washington Whitewater I*. Seattle: The Mountaineers, 1988. Seventeen white-water trips on the Cascades' most popular rivers for paddlers and rafters; every detail is covered, from put-ins and take-outs to camping, scenery, and special hazards.

North, Douglass A. *Washington Whitewater II*. Seattle: The Mountaineers, 1987. Seventeen lesser-known white-water trips from the Olympic Peninsula to Spokane and Washington's southeast corner.

Perry, John, and Jane Greverus Perry. *The Sierra Club Guide to the National Areas of Oregon and Washington*. San Francisco: Sierra Club Books, 1983. Features, activities, camping, boating, and more in national forests, parks, and beaches.

Schwartz, Susan. *Wildlife Areas of Washington*. Seattle: Superior Publishing Co., 1976. Flora and fauna (especially birds) of the national recreation areas, refuges, islands, and national parks.

Sheely, Terry W. *The Northwest Sportsman Almanac*. Edmonds: Alaska Northwest Books, 1988. A beautiful and thorough book, loaded with superb color photographs and artwork as well as exhaustive coverage of hunting, fishing, camp cooking, shellfishing, woodlore, and more in the northwest U.S. and Canada.

Sterling, E.M. *Trips And Trails 2*. Seattle: The Mountaineers, 1972. Short hikes, view roads, and family campgrounds in the South Cascades and Mt. Rainier.

Stienstra, Tom. *Pacific Northwest Camping.* San Francisco: Foghorn Press, 1988. No better guide to Washington's campgrounds! Over 1,400 campgrounds, from boat-in island sites to RV parks, state parks to wilderness areas.

Washburne, Randel. *Kayak Trips in Puget Sound and the San Juan Islands.* Seattle: Pacific Search Press, 1986. Destinations, routes, ratings, and launching info.

Williams, Chuck. *Mount St. Helens National Volcanic Monument.* Seattle: The Mountaineers, 1988. Great pocket guide for post-eruption hikers, sightseers, and skiers; photos, history, and detailed trail descriptions.

Woods, Erin, and Bill Woods. *Bicycling The Backroads.* Seattle: The Mountaineers. Three volumes—*Around Puget Sound, Of Northwest Washington,* and *Of Southwest Washington*—provide in-depth information on bike routes, terrain, elevation gain, and points of interest, plus explicit directions and plenty of maps.

MISCELLANEOUS

Climates Of The States. Port Washington, New York: Water Information Center, Inc., 1974. Two volumes with more than you ever wanted to know about weather.

Herold, Stephen. *Tulipmania: The Skagit Valley Tulip Festival.* Berkeley, California: Celestial Arts, 1989. This official tulip festival guidebook features area history plus background on Skagit bulb growing and the festival itself, color photos, and listings of festival events and places to stay and eat.

Robbins, William G., et al. *Regionalism in the Pacific Northwest.* Corvallis, Oregon: University of Oregon Press, 1983. Ten essays examine the concept of regionalism and discuss the Pacific Northwest as a geographic, economic, political, and cultural entity.

Saling, Ann. *Our Superlative Pacific Northwest.* Edmonds, WA: Ansal Press, 1984. Pacific Northwest trivia and fun facts.

Scott, James W., and Ronald L. DeLorme. *Historical Atlas of Washington.* Norman, Oklahoma: University of Oklahoma Press, 1988. Very informative atlas depicting the many faces of Washington in map form, from the earliest explorers to the present day.

Washington's Almanac. Seattle: Evergreen Publishing, 1988. Unusual facts, recipes, and folklore from the editors of *Washington* magazine.

INDEX

Page numbers in **boldface** indicate the primary reference;
numbers in *italics* indicate information in captions, illustrations, charts, or maps

ABOUT THE AUTHORS

Born to a Missouri farm family, Archie Satterfield came to Washington while a student at the University of Missouri after four years in the U.S. Navy. Satterfield immediately fell in love with the Pacific Northwest; he finished his degree at the University of Washington and landed his first newspaper job with the *Seaside Signal*. After dozens of books on the Emerald State and hundreds of articles to his credit, Archie Satterfield still wouldn't live anywhere else.

Dianne J. Boulerice Lyons

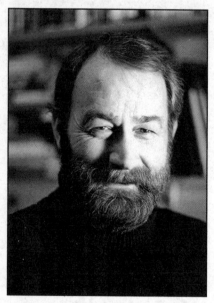

Archie Satterfield

Born in Connecticut, Dianne Boulerice caught the travel bug early in life; on various trips she's been through Colorado, Florida, Montreal, San Francisco, Washington, and along the East Coast. She returned home with a love of the Pacific Northwest's breathtaking scenery.

After majoring in psychology and working in computer programing, Dianne's latent writing talents surfaced with her first article sold in June, 1984. Dianne later moved to Washington with her husband, Bob Lyons, and eventually combined her love of the state—and writing—in *Washington Handbook*. Dianne currently lives with her husband and children in Naperville, Illinois.

Moon Handbooks—The Ideal Traveling Companions

Open a Moon Handbook and you're opening your eyes and heart to the world. Thoughtful, sensitive, and provocative, Moon Handbooks encourage an intimate understanding of a region, from its culture and history to essential practicalities. Fun to read and packed with valuable information on accommodations, dining, recreation, plus indispensable travel tips, detailed maps, charts, illustrations, photos, glossaries, and indexes, Moon Handbooks are ideal traveling companions: informative, entertaining, and highly practical.

To locate the bookstore nearest you that carries Moon Travel Handbooks or to order directly from Moon Publications, call: (800) 345-5473, Monday-Friday, 9 a.m.-5 p.m. PST

The Pacific/Asia Series

BALI HANDBOOK by Bill Dalton
Detailed travel information on the most famous island in the world. 12 color pages, 29 b/w photos, 68 illustrations, 42 maps, 7 charts, glossary, booklist, index. 428 pages. **$12.95**

INDONESIA HANDBOOK by Bill Dalton
This one-volume encyclopedia explores island by island the many facets of this sprawling, kaleidoscopic island nation. 30 b/w photos, 143 illustrations, 250 maps, 17 charts, booklist, extensive Indonesian vocabulary, index. 1,000 pages. **$19.95**

SOUTH KOREA HANDBOOK by Robert Nilsen
Whether you're visiting on business or searching for adventure, *South Korea Handbook* is an invaluable companion. 8 color pages, 78 b/w photos, 93 illustrations, 109 maps, 10 charts, Korean glossary with useful notes on speaking and reading the language, booklist, index. 548 pages. **$14.95**

SOUTHEAST ASIA HANDBOOK by Carl Parkes
Helps the enlightened traveler discover the real Southeast Asia. 16 color pages, 75 b/w photos, 11 illustrations, 169 maps, 140 charts, vocabulary and suggested reading, index. 873 pages. **$16.95**

BANGKOK HANDBOOK by Michael Buckley
Your tour guide through this exotic and dynamic city reveals the affordable and accessible possibilities. Thai phrasebook, 16 color pages, 55 b/w photos, 30 maps, 19 illustrations, 9 charts, booklist, index. 214 pages. **$10.95**

PHILIPPINES HANDBOOK by Peter Harper and Evelyn Peplow
Crammed with detailed information, *Philippines Handbook* equips the escapist, hedonist, or business traveler with thorough coverage of the Philippines's colorful history, landscapes, and culture. 8 color pages, 2 b/w photos, 60 illustrations, 93 maps, 30 charts, index. 587 pages. **$12.95**

HAWAII HANDBOOK by J.D. Bisignani
Winner of the 1989 Hawaii Visitors Bureau's Best Guide Book Award and the Grand Award for Excellence in Travel Journalism, this guide takes you beyond the glitz and high-priced hype and leads you to a genuine Hawaiian experience. 12 color pages, 86 b/w photos, 132 illustrations, 86 maps, 44 graphs and charts, Hawaiian and pidgin glossaries, appendix, booklist, index. 879 pages. **$15.95**

KAUAI HANDBOOK by J.D. Bisignani
Kauai Handbook is the perfect antidote to the workaday world. 8 color pages, 36 b/w photos, 48 illustrations, 19 maps, 10 tables and charts, Hawaiian and pidgin glossaries, booklist, index. 236 pages. **$9.95**

MAUI HANDBOOK: Including Molokai and Lanai by J.D. Bisignani
"No fool-'round" advice on accommodations, eateries, and recreation, plus a comprehensive introduction to island ways, geography, and history. 8 color pages, 60 b/w photos, 72 illustrations, 34 maps, 19 charts, booklist, glossary, index. 350 pages. **$11.95**

OAHU HANDBOOK by J.D. Bisignani
A handy guide to Honolulu, renowned surfing beaches, and Oahu's countless other diversions. 12 color pages, 93 b/w photos, 67 illustrations, 18 maps, 8 charts, booklist, glossary, index. 354 pages. **$11.95**

BIG ISLAND OF HAWAII HANDBOOK by J.D. Bisignani
An entertaining yet informative text packed with insider tips on accommodations, dining, sports and outdoor activities, natural attractions, and must-see sights. 12 color pages, 72 b/w photos, 73 illustrations, 22 maps, 5 charts, booklist, glossary, index. 347 pages. **$11.95**

SOUTH PACIFIC HANDBOOK by David Stanley
The original comprehensive guide to the 16 territories in the South Pacific. 20 color pages, 195 b/w photos, 121 illustrations, 35 charts, 138 maps, booklist, glossary, index. 740 pages. **$15.95**

MICRONESIA HANDBOOK:
Guide to the Caroline, Gilbert, Mariana, and Marshall Islands by David Stanley
Micronesia Handbook guides you on a real Pacific adventure all your own. 8 color pages, 77 b/w photos, 68 illustrations, 69 maps, 18 tables and charts, index. 287 pages. **$9.95**

FIJI ISLANDS HANDBOOK by David Stanley
The first and still the best source of information on travel around this 322-island archipelago. 8 color pages, 35 b/w photos, 78 illustrations, 26 maps, 3 charts, Fijian glossary, booklist, index. 198 pages. **$8.95**

TAHITI-POLYNESIA HANDBOOK by David Stanley
All five French-Polynesian archipelagoes are covered in this comprehensive guide by Oceania's best-known travel writer. 12 color pages, 45 b/w photos, 64 illustrations, 33 maps, 7 charts, booklist, glossary, index. 225 pages. **$9.95**

NEW ZEALAND HANDBOOK by Jane King
Introduces you to the people, places, history, and culture of this extraordinary land. 8 color pages, 99 b/w photos, 146 illustrations, 82 maps, booklist, index. 546 pages. **$14.95**

OUTBACK AUSTRALIA HANDBOOK by Marael Johnson
Australia is an endlessly fascinating, vast land, and *Outback Australia Handbook* explores the cities and towns, sheep stations and wilderness areas of the Northern Territory, Western, and South Australia. Full of travel tips and cultural information for adventuring, relaxing, or just getting away from it all. 8 color pages, 39 b/w photos, 63 illustrations, 51 maps, booklist, index. 355 pages. **$15.95**

BLUEPRINT FOR PARADISE: How to Live on a Tropic Island by Ross Norgrove
This one-of-a-kind guide has everything you need to know about moving to and living comfortably on a tropical island. 8 color pages, 40 b/w photos, 3 maps, 14 charts, appendices, index. 212 pages. **$14.95**

The Americas Series

NORTHERN CALIFORNIA HANDBOOK by Kim Weir
An outstanding companion for imaginative travel in the territory north of the Tehachapis. 12 color pages, 200 b/w photos, 54 maps, 36 illustrations, booklist, index. 759 pages. **$16.95**

NEVADA HANDBOOK by Deke Castleman
Nevada Handbook puts the Silver State into perspective and makes it manageable and affordable. 34 b/w photos, 43 illustrations, 37 maps, 17 charts, booklist, index. 400 pages. **$12.95**

NEW MEXICO HANDBOOK by Stephen Metzger
A close-up and complete look at every aspect of this wondrous state. 8 color pages, 85 b/w photos, 63 illustrations, 50 maps, 10 charts, booklist, index. 375 pages. **$13.95**

TEXAS HANDBOOK by Joe Cummings
Seasoned travel writer Joe Cummings brings an insider's perspective to his home state. 8 color pages, 79 b/w photos, 60 maps, 45 illustrations, 18 charts, booklist, index. 483 pages. **$11.95**

ARIZONA TRAVELER'S HANDBOOK   by Bill Weir
This meticulously researched guide contains everything necessary to make Arizona accessible and enjoyable. 8 color pages, 194 b/w photos, 74 illustrations, 53 maps, 6 charts, booklist, index. 505 pages.   **$13.95**

UTAH HANDBOOK   by Bill Weir
Weir gives you all the carefully researched facts and background to make your visit a success. 8 color pages, 102 b/w photos, 61 illustrations, 30 maps, 9 charts, booklist, index. 452 pages. **$12.95**

ALASKA-YUKON HANDBOOK   by Deke Castleman and Don Pitcher
Get the inside story, with plenty of well-seasoned advice to help you cover more miles on less money. 8 color pages, 26 b/w photos, 95 illustrations, 92 maps, 10 charts, booklist, glossary, index. 384 pages.   **$13.95**

WASHINGTON HANDBOOK   by Dianne J. Boulerice Lyons and Archie Satterfield
Covers sights, shopping, services, transportation, and outdoor recreation, with complete listings for restaurants and accommodations. 8 color pages, 92 b/w photos, 24 illustrations, 81 maps, 8 charts, booklist, index. 400 pages.   **$13.95**

OREGON HANDBOOK   by Stuart Warren and Ted Long Ishikawa
Brimming with travel practicalities and insider views on Oregon's history, culture, arts, and activities. 8 color pages, 113 b/w photos, 26 illustrations, 28 maps, 20 charts, booklist, index. 422 pages.   **$12.95**

IDAHO HANDBOOK   by Bill Loftus
A year-round guide to everything in this outdoor wonderland, from whitewater adventures to rural hideaways. 8 color pages, 35 b/w photos, 21 illustrations, 42 maps, 1 chart, booklist, index. 275 pages.   **$12.95**

WYOMING HANDBOOK   by Don Pitcher
All you need to know to open the doors to this wide and wild state. 16 color pages, 30 b/w photos, 42 illustrations, 64 maps, 19 charts, booklist, index. 427 pages.   **$12.95**

MONTANA HANDBOOK   by W.C. McRae and Judy Jewell
The wild West is yours with this extensive guide to the Treasure State, complete with travel practicalities, history, and lively essays on Montana life. 8 color pages, 62 b/w photos, 43 illustrations, 49 maps, 10 charts, booklist, index. 393 pages.   **$13.95**

COLORADO HANDBOOK   by Stephen Metzger
Essential details to the all-season possibilities in Colorado fill this guide. Practical travel tips combine with recreation—skiing, nightlife, and wilderness exploration—plus entertaining essays. 8 color pages, 92 b/w photos, 15 illustrations, 57 maps, 10 charts, booklist, index. 422 pages.   **$15.95**

BRITISH COLUMBIA HANDBOOK   by Jane King
With an emphasis on outdoor adventures, this guide covers mainland British Columbia, Vancouver Island, the Queen Charlotte Islands, and the Canadian Rockies. 8 color pages, 56 b/w photos, 45 illustrations, 66 maps, 4 charts, booklist, index. 381 pages.   **$11.95**

CATALINA ISLAND HANDBOOK: A Guide to California's Channel Islands
by Chicki Mallan
A complete guide to these remarkable islands, from the windy solitude of the Channel Islands National Marine Sanctuary to bustling Avalon. 8 color pages, 105 b/w photos, 65 illustrations, 40 maps, 32 charts, booklist, index. 245 pages.   **$10.95**

BAJA HANDBOOK   by Joe Cummings
A comprehensive guide with all the travel information and background on the land, history, and culture of this untamed thousand-mile-long peninsula. 8 color pages, 40 b/w photos, 28 illustrations, 41 maps, 29 charts, booklist, index. 356 pages.   **$13.95**

YUCATAN HANDBOOK   by Chicki Mallan
All the information you'll need to guide you into every corner of this exotic land. 8 color pages, 154 b/w photos, 55 illustrations, 57 maps, 70 charts, appendix, booklist, Mayan and Spanish glossaries, index. 391 pages.   **$12.95**

CANCUN HANDBOOK and Mexico's Caribbean Coast   by Chicki Mallan
Covers the city's luxury scene as well as more modest attractions, plus many side trips to unspoiled beaches and Mayan ruins. 12 color pages, 76 b/w photos, 25 illustrations, 24 maps, 12 charts, Spanish glossary, booklist, index. 257 pages.   **$10.95**

BELIZE HANDBOOK   by Chicki Mallan
Complete with detailed maps, practical information, and an overview of the area's flamboyant history, culture, and geographical features, *Belize Handbook* is the only comprehensive guide of its kind to this spectacular region. 8 color pages, 65 b/w photos, 43 illustrations, 25 maps, 30 charts, booklist, index. 212 pages.   **$11.95**

JAMAICA HANDBOOK   by Karl Luntta
From the sun and surf of Montego Bay and Ocho Rios to the cool slopes of the Blue Mountains, author Karl Luntta offers island-seekers a perceptive, personal view of Jamaica. 8 color pages, 21 b/w photos, 35 illustrations, 16 maps, 7 charts, booklist, glossary, index. 213 pages.   **$12.95**

The International Series

EGYPT HANDBOOK   by Kathy Hansen
An invaluable resource for intelligent travel in Egypt. 8 color pages, 20 b/w photos, 150 illustrations, 80 detailed maps and plans to museums and archaeological sites, Arabic glossary, booklist, index. 510 pages.   **$14.95**

PAKISTAN HANDBOOK   by Isobel Shaw
For armchair travelers and trekkers alike, the most detailed and authoritative guide to Pakistan ever published. 28 color pages, 86 maps, appendices, Urdu glossary, booklist, index. 478 pages.   **$15.95**

MOSCOW-LENINGRAD HANDBOOK   by Masha Nordbye
Provides the visitor with an extensive introduction to the history, culture, and people of these two great cities, as well as practical information on where to stay, eat, and shop. 8 color pages, 36 b/w photos, 20 illustrations, 16 maps, 9 charts, booklist, index. 205 pages.   **$12.95**

NEPAL HANDBOOK   by Kerry Moran
Whether you're planning a week in Kathmandu or months out on the trail, *Nepal Handbook* will take you into the heart of this Himalayan jewel. 16 color pages, 76 b/w photos, 45 illustrations, 46 maps, 9 charts, booklist, glossary, index. 378 pages.   **$12.95**

NEPALI AAMA   by Broughton Coburn
A delightful photo-journey into the life of a Gurung tribeswoman of Central Nepal. Having lived with Aama (translated, "mother") for two years, first as an outsider and later as an adopted member of the family, Coburn presents an intimate glimpse into a culture alive with humor, folklore, religion, and ancient rituals. B/w photos. 165 pages.   **$13.95**

Moonbelts

Made of heavy-duty Cordura nylon, the Moonbelt offers maximum protection for your money and important papers. This all-weather pouch slips under your shirt or waistband, rendering it virtually undetectable and inaccessible to pickpockets. One-inch-wide nylon webbing, heavy-duty zipper, one-inch quick release buckle. Accommodates traveler's checks, passport, cash, photos. Size 5 x 9 inches. Black.   **$8.95**

**New travel handbooks may be available that are not on this list.
To find out more about current or upcoming titles,
call us toll-free at (800) 345-5473.**

IMPORTANT ORDERING INFORMATION

FOR FASTER SERVICE: Call to locate the bookstore nearest you that carries Moon Travel Handbooks or order directly from Moon Publications:
 (800) 345-5473 · Monday-Friday · 9 a.m.-5 p.m. PST · fax (916) 345-6751

PRICES: All prices are subject to change. We always ship the most current edition. We will let you know if there is a price increase on the book you ordered.

SHIPPING & HANDLING OPTIONS:
 1) Domestic UPS or USPS first class (allow 10 working days for delivery):
   $3.50 for the first item, 50 cents for each additional item.

Exceptions:
 · **Moonbelt** shipping is $1.50 for one, 50 cents for each additional belt.
 · Add $2.00 for same-day handling.
 2) UPS 2nd Day Air or Printed Airmail requires a special quote.
 3) International Surface Bookrate (8-12 weeks delivery):
   $3.00 for the first item, $1.00 for each additional item. Note: Moon Publications cannot guarantee international surface bookrate shipping.

FOREIGN ORDERS: All orders which originate outside the U.S.A. must be paid for with either an International Money Order or a check in U.S. currency drawn on a major U.S. bank based in the U.S.A.

TELEPHONE ORDERS: We accept Visa or MasterCard payments. Minimum order is US $15.00. Call in your order: 1 (800) 345-5473. 9 a.m.-5 p.m. Pacific Standard Time.

ORDER FORM

Be sure to call (800) 345-5473 for current prices and editions or for the name of the bookstore nearest you that carries Moon Travel Handbooks · 9 a.m.-5 p.m. PST
(See important ordering information on preceding page)

Name:_____Date:_____

Street:_____

City:_____Daytime Phone:_____

State or Country:_____Zip Code:_____

Quantity	Title	Price

Taxable Total	
Sales Tax (7.25%) for California Residents	
Shipping & Handling	
TOTAL	

Ship: ☐ 1st class   ☐ UPS (no P.O. Boxes)   ☐ International Surface

Ship to: ☐ address above   ☐ other_____

_____

_____

Make checks payable to:
Moon Publications Inc., 722 Wall Street, Chico, California 95928 U.S.A.
We Accept Visa and MasterCard
To Order: Call in your Visa or MasterCard number, or send a written order with your Visa or MasterCard number and expiration date clearly written.

Card Number: ☐ **Visa** ☐ **MasterCard**

☐ ☐ ☐ ☐   ☐ ☐ ☐ ☐   ☐ ☐ ☐ ☐   ☐ ☐ ☐ ☐

Exact Name on Card: ☐ same as above   expiration date:_____

☐ other_____

signature_____